Mary-Ann Gallagher, Matthew Gardner,
Sadakat Kadri and James Stewart

GW00492914

flying visi
CENTRAL &
EASTERN EUROPE

CADOGANguides

Contents

About the authors

Mary-Ann Gallagher (*Austria, Poland*) has written, and contributed to, more than a dozen Cadogan guides, including *Dublin, Flying Visits Ireland* and, most recently, *Flying Visits Mediterranean* and *Flying Visits Central and Eastern Europe*. Her travels have taken her everywhere from Japanese hill villages to glossy European capitals. Born in the UK, she is constantly on the move, but recently settled under the blue skies of Barcelona. *Mary-Ann would like to offer grateful thanks to all at Vienna Apartments, and to the taxi drivers, museum curators and coffee shop staff for their wonderful stories and insights.*

Matthew Gardner (*Hungary, Slovakia, Bulgaria, Serbia*) is an unrepentant hedonist who loves travel almost as much as football, jazz, food and Shiraz. Though raised in outer London, he lives in a remote valley in Western Canada with his wife Alison, their rumbustious two-year-old son Theo, Lola and Frankie the dogs, Aspen the cat, occasional itinerant packrats, and baby no.2, a formidable kicker whose arrival is imminent. *Matthew would like to thank Viera Norisová, Jozsef, and Dr Oz Furth in Bratislava; Judit Mihalcsik in Budapest; Mladen Milenković, Goran Pilipović at Five Star, and Dejin Veselinov and all the ladies at TOB in Belgrade; everyone at Magelan in Novi Sad; Roomie, Marin, and Anelia Genova in Sofia.*

Sadakat Kadri (*Czech Republic*) was born in Fulham in 1964 of a Pakistani father and a Finnish mother. He studied history and law at Trinity College, Cambridge, and took a Masters degree at Harvard Law School. He is a qualified New York attorney and a practising London barrister.

James Stewart (*Croatia, Slovenia*) was born in London, and after studying music at City University and journalism as a postgraduate he took to editing, travel and writing in a big way. He is also the author of *Flying Visits Germany* and co-author of *Flying Visits Croatia and the Adriatic*; when not shackled to a computer in his London home, he flees to the coast.

Cadogan Guides
Network House, 1 Ariel Way
London W12 7SL
info@cadoganguides.co.uk
www.cadoganguides.com

The Globe Pequot Press
246 Goose Lane, PO Box 480, Guilford,
Connecticut 06437–0480

Copyright © Mary-Ann Gallagher, Matthew
  Gardner, James Stewart and Cadogan Guides
  2005

Cover design by Sarah Gardner
Book design by Andrew Barker
Cover photographs: © Alison Bigg, Medioimages/
  Alamy, Chris Warham/Alamy, DIOMEDIA/Alamy,
  Celestial Panoramas Ltd/Alamy, FAN & MROSS
  Travelstock/Alamy, allOver photography/Alamy,
  Art Kowalsky/Alamy, Adam Tiernan Thomas/Alamy.
Maps © Cadogan Guides, drawn by Maidenhead
  Cartographic Services Ltd
Managing Editor: Natalie Pomier
Flying Visits Series Editor: Linda McQueen
Editors: Linda McQueen, Dominique Shead, Alison
  Copland, Nicola Jessop
Proofreading: Catherine Bradley
Indexing: Isobel McLean

Printed in Italy by Legoprint
A catalogue record for this book is available
  from the British Library
ISBN 1-86011-191-2

Introduction

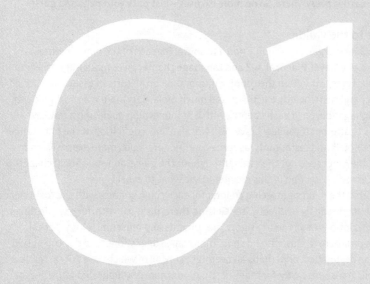

The part of the world covered by this guide has changed beyond recognition in the last few decades. The region from Poland in the north to Bulgaria in the south, with a central area once dominated by the mighty Hapsburg empire, has for centuries been ravaged by war, endlessly subject to changing borders, and more recently swallowed by and then freed from Communism; the Cold War was mainly fought here, and even 25 years ago life was grim in some of the cities that now are a delight. But today the map has changed – small republics have broken free from the larger countries (e.g. Yugoslavia, Czechoslovakia) of the 19th and early 20th centuries – and with it has come a new spirit of openness and a desire to be part of modern Europe, independent but not isolated, integrated yet free.

At the same time, for the visitor there are many attractions, such as glorious undisturbed Austro-Hungarian architecture, surprisingly reaching as far south as Zagreb; a low cost of living that makes your money go a long way; and a conviviality and urban beauty packaged, human-scale, into small, walkable historic kernels filled with amiable squares, impressive boulevards, grand glittering palaces, chandelier-lit 19th-century cafés and coffee houses, excellent restaurants, and enough 'difference' from the more familiar countries of western Europe to make every trip still an adventure.

As if this were not enough reason to visit, just outside the cities suggested as your starting point in this guide is incredible natural beauty: Alpine peaks and the wide, flowing Danube in Austria; spa towns where you can be treated like royalty in Hungary or outside Prague; magical caves near Salzburg or Ljubljana or Kraków; national parks; quiet lakes around Ljubljana or Vienna; and, near Dubrovnik, one of Europe's most outstanding coastlines, with unspoilt islands and some of the cleanest seas on the planet. You can visit original Roman settlements, often a few miles only from today's cities, or take wine tours from Graz, Vienna and even Belgrade. And castles, castles everywhere. So no more excuses – just pack your bags and go!

Guide to the Guide

This guide is organized roughly north to south. For each of the nine countries included, the **Travel, Practical A–Z and Language** chapter gives reassuring background on public transport within the country, information on all sorts of essentials such as currency and costs, health, electricity and much more; plus there is a short guide to the language spoken in each country, with a pronunciation guide and a few key phrases to attempt if you feel brave. You will also find a definition of the price ranges used for hotels and restaurants; as some countries are much more expensive than others, the ranges are not the same throughout the guide, and you should check the 'Price Categories' section in this chapter to see what to expect.

After this, the main sightseeing chapter for each country starts with the main city or cities that you can fly to directly (*see* **Getting There**, pp.3–10), with, for each destination, descriptions of all the top sights, monuments and museums, plus practical listings on where to stay, eat and shop. Then come suggestions for a day trip or two from the destination, or perhaps an overnight stay, all of which are easily accessible by public transport. Lastly, for many destinations there is a suggested four-, five- or six-day touring itinerary for those who'd like to hire a car and explore the area further.

Getting There

By Air

In the last few years the airline industry has undergone a revolution. Inspired by the success of Stelios Haji-Ioannou's easyJet company, other airlines flocked to join him in breaking all the conventions of air travel to offer fares at rock-bottom prices. After September 11th 2001, while long-haul carriers hit the ropes in a big way, these budget airlines experienced unprecedented sales, and responded by expanding their list of destinations throughout Europe.

Whereas in their first years no-frills airlines had an undoubted 'backpackerish' feel, this has become an increasingly mainstream way to travel. Most importantly, larger national airlines have got in on the act, copying some of the more attractive aspects of budget travel, such as Internet booking with discounts, and one-way fares.

No Frills, No Thrills

The ways in which low prices are achieved can sometimes have a negative effect on the experience of travellers, but can sometimes be a bonus too. First, these airlines often use **smaller regional airports**, where landing fees and tarmac-time charges are at a minimum. In the UK this means you may be able to find a flight from nearer your home town.

The **planes** tend to be all one-class and with the maximum seating configuration.

Fares are one-way – so there is no need to stay over on a Saturday night to qualify for the lowest fares – and can vary enormously on the same route, according to when you travel and how far in advance you book: the most widely advertised, rock-bottom deals are generally for seats on very early-morning, early-in-the-week flights. Because of this constantly changing price system it is important to note that **no-frills airlines are not always the cheapest**, above all on the very popular routes at peak times. One of the benefits of the no-frills revolution that is not always appreciated is not so much their own prices as the concessions they have forced on the mainstream carriers. It is **always** worth comparing no-frills prices with those of the main airlines, and checking out what special offers are going. For flights and price comparisons on the Internet,

Who Goes Where?

	Page	Adria Airways	Aer Lingus	Air Berlin	Air Slovakia	Austrian Airlines	BMIbaby	British Airways	British Midland (BMI)	Bulgaria Air	Centralwings	Croatia Airlines	ČSA Czech Airlines	easyJet	EUjet	FlyBE	JAT Yugoslavian Airlines	Jet2	LOT Polish Airlines	Malév Hungarian Airlines	Ryanair	SkyEurope	Thomsonfly	Wizz Air
		●	★	●	★	●	★	●	★	●	★	●	★	●	★	●	★	●	★	●	★	●	★	●
Belgrade	296							●									★							
Bratislava	96			★										●								●		
Budapest	198	★	●					●						●						●		●		●
Dubrovnik	273		★					●				●										●		★
Graz	164					●															★			
Klagenfurt	178																				★			
Krakow	36						★	●			★								★					
Ljubljana	230	●												●										
Prague	66					★	●					★	●	★						●		★		
Salzburg	140					●												★	●			★	★	
Sofia	320							●		●										●				
Vienna	120			●		●	★	●														●		
Warsaw	18		★				★	●			★			●					★			●		●
Zagreb	254											●												

Airlines

UK and Ireland

Adria Airways, *www.adria-airways.com*. From Gatwick and Manchester.

Aer Lingus, t (01) 886 8844, *www.flyaerlingus.com*. From Dublin.

Air Berlin, t 08707 388 880 (8p/min), *www.airberlin.com*. From Stansted and Manchester.

Air Slovakia, t 0121 515 2000, *www.airslovakia.sk*. From Birmingham.

Austrian Airlines, t 020 (020) 7766 0300, *www.aua.com*. From Heathrow and Gatwick.

Bmibaby, t 08702 642 229, *www.bmibaby.com*. From many UK airports.

British Airways (BA), t 0870 850 9850, *www.ba.com*. From Heathrow, Gatwick and Manchester.

British Midland (BMI), t 08706 070 555, *www.flybmi.com*. From Heathrow, Gatwick and many UK airports.

Bulgaria Air, t (020) 7637 7637, *www.balkanair.co.uk*. From Gatwick.

Centralwings, t (0048) 801 45 45 45 (in Poland), *www.centralwings.pl*. From Gatwick.

Croatia Airlines, t (020) 8563 0022, *www.croatiaairlines.hr*. From Gatwick, Heathrow, Manchester and Nottingham.

ČSA Czech Airlines, t 0870 444 3747, *www.czechairlines.com*. From many UK airports.

easyJet, t 0905 821 0905 (bookings/changes; 65p/min) or t 0871 244 2366 (customer services; 10p/min), *www.easyjet.com*. From Luton, Gatwick, Stansted, Bristol, Newcastle and Nottingham East Midlands.

EUjet, t 0870 414 1414, *www.eujet.com*. From Kent International.

FlyBE, t 0871 700 0123, *www.flybe.com*. From Birmingham and Southampton.

JAT Yugoslavian Airlines, t (020) 7629 2007, *www.jatlondon.com*. From Heathrow.

Jet 2, t 0870 737 8282, *www.jet2.com*. From Manchester.

LOT Polish Airlines, t 0870 414 0088, *www.lot.com*. From Gatwick, Heathrow and Manchester.

Malév Hungarian Airlines, t 0870 909 0577, *www.malev.com*. From Heathrow, Gatwick, Stansted, Dublin, Edinburgh, Birmingham, Glasgow and Manchester.

Ryanair, t 0871 246 0000, *www.ryanair.com*. From Stansted.

SkyEurope, t (020) 7365 0365, *www.skyeurope.com*. From Stansted and Manchester.

Thomsonfly, t 0870 1900 737, *www.thomsonfly.com*. From Gatwick, Manchester, Doncaster and Coventry.

Wizz Air, t (0036) 1470 9499, *www.wizzair.com*. From Luton and Liverpool.

USA and Canada

American Airlines, t 800 433 7300, t 800 543 1586 (TDD), *www.aa.com*. To Prague, Vienna, Warsaw and Budapest via London Heathrow.

Austrian Airlines, USA t 800 843 0002, Canada t 888 817 4444, *www.aua.com*. Directly to Vienna from New York (JFK) and Toronto.

British Airways, t 800 AIRWAYS, *www.ba.com*. To Belgrade, Budapest, Dubrovnik, Krakow, Prague, Salzburg, Sofia, Vienna and Warsaw via London Gatwick, London Heathrow, Birmingham, Manchester.

Air Canada, t 1 888 567 4160 (Canada), t 800 268 0024 (USA), *www.aircanada.ca*. To Vienna from Toronto, Prague and London Heathrow. To Warsaw from Toronto, Vienna, Prague and Salzburg.

Continental, USA and Canada t 800 231 0856, *www.continental.com*. To Budapest, Prague, Vienna and Warsaw via Amsterdam.

CSA Czech Airlines, t 800 223 2365, *www.czechairlines.com*. To Prague direct from New York (JFK and Newark) and Toronto.

Delta, USA and Canada t 800 241 4141, t 800 831 4488 (TDD), *www.delta.com*. To Prague direct from New York.

LOT Polish Airlines, t 800 223 0593, *www.lot.com*. To Warsaw direct from New York (JFK and Newark), Chicago and Toronto. To Kraków direct from New York and Chicago.

Malév Hungarian Airlines, t (212) 566 9944, *www.malev.com*. To Budapest direct from New York (JFK) and Toronto.

Northwest Airlines, t 800 447 4747 (24hr), *www.nwa.com*. To Budapest, Prague, Vienna and Warsaw via Amsterdam.

Trans-Meridian Airlines, t 1 866 I FLY TMA, *www.transmeridian-airlines.com*. Summer only, Zagreb from Chicago and New York.

United Airlines, t 800 538 2929, t 800 323 0170 (TDD), *www.united.com*. To Vienna from New York (JFK) and Washington DC. To Warsaw from Chicago and New York. To Kraków from Chicago. To Budapest and Graz via Frankfurt.

Getting to Europe by Air from North America

You can fly directly to a few of the bigger cities in this guide from North America. But it is also possible for North Americans to take advantage of the explosion of cheap inter-European flights, by taking a charter flight to London, and booking a UK–Europe budget flight in advance on a low-cost airline's website (see p.5). This will need careful planning: you're looking at an 8–14hr flight followed by a 3hr journey across London and another 2hr hop to Europe.

Direct to Europe

The main airports in this guide receiving transatlantic flights are the cities of **Budapest**, **Prague**, **Vienna**, **Warsaw** and **Zagreb** (in summer). The main carriers flying direct to these cities are **American Airlines**, **ČSA**, **Delta**, **LOT Polish Airlines**, **United**, **Air Canada** and **Trans Meridian**; see boxes on pp.4 and 5.

Since **prices** are constantly changing and there are numerous kinds of deals on offer, the first thing to do is find yourself a travel agent who is capable of laying the current options before you. The time of year can make a great difference to the price and availability; prices can range from around $350 for the best bargain deals to well over $1,000.

A number of companies offer cheaper **charter flights** to Europe – look in the Sunday travel sections of the *New York Times*, *Los Angeles Times*, *Chicago Tribune*, *Toronto Star* or other big-city papers. For fares, schedules and price comparisons on the **Internet**, see *www.traveljungle.us*, *www.lastminute.com*, *www.expedia.com*, *www.orbitz.com*, *www.travelocity.com* and *www.flyaow.com* (discounted fares and schedules on 500 worldwide airlines, also car hire and hotels).

Via London

Start by finding a charter or discounted scheduled flight to London. When you have the availability and arrival times for London flights, match up a convenient flight time on the website of the budget airline that flies to your chosen European city. *If you are flying to London, be careful to choose only flights from the airports near London: Luton, Gatwick, Heathrow, London City and Stansted.*

You will most likely be arriving at Heathrow terminals 3 or 4 (or possibly Gatwick), and may be flying out from Stansted, Luton, London City or Gatwick, all of which are in different directions and will mean travelling through central London, so leaving enough time is essential. Add together the journey times and prices for Heathrow into central London and back out again to your departure airport. You could mix and match – the Tube to Victoria and the Gatwick Express, or a taxi from Heathrow to St Pancras and a train to Luton – but don't even think of using a bus or taxi at rush hours (7–10am and 4–7pm); train and/or Underground (Tube) are the only sensible choices. Always add on waiting times and delays in London's notoriously creaky transport system; and finally, although the cheapest airline fares are early morning and late at night, make sure your chosen transport is still operating at that time (see below).

For travel information within London, call **t** (020) 7222 1234, *www.tfl.gov.uk*.

Airport to Airport Taxis

A taxi directly between airports might avoid central London, but is an expensive option: Heathrow–Gatwick: 1hr 30mins, £110–120. Heathrow–Stansted: 2hrs 15mins, £150–170. Heathrow–Luton: 1hr 15mins, £100–130.

For booking taxis in advance, try **Dial-A-Cab**, **t** (020) 7253 5000, **Taxi One-Number**, **t** 0871 871 8710 and **Data Cab**, **t** (020) 7432 1540, or see *www.londonblackcabs.co.uk* or *www.londontaxicabs.net*.

Heathrow

Heathrow is about 15 miles west of the centre. **Airport information**: **t** 0870 0000 123, *www.baa.co.uk*.

By train: The Heathrow Express (**t** 0845 600 1515) is the fastest option: trains every 15mins between 5.07am and midnight to Paddington station, which is on the Tube's Bakerloo, Circle and District Lines, taking 15mins, or 7–8mins more to Terminal 4. £14 single, £26 return.

By Tube to Terminals 1, 2 and 3: Heathrow is on the Piccadilly Line. Tube trains from central London to Heathrow depart every 10mins from 6.32am (or 7.51am Sun) to 00.32am (or 11.38pm Sun) and the journey takes 55mins. Tube trains from Heathrow to central

London depart every 10mins from 5.13am (or 5.57am Sun) until 11.49pm (or 11.30pm Sun). Single fare to the centre: £3.80.

By Tube to Terminal 4: Owing to construction works on Terminal 5, the Tube service to Terminal 4 has been suspended until September 2006. Until then passengers can take a frequent bus shuttle from Hatton Cross Tube station on the Piccadilly Line; the journey takes an additional 5–10 minutes.

By coach: National Express 403 from Heathrow's Central Bus Station (CBS) terminates at Victoria Station and takes 30mins–1hr London–Heathrow or 45mins–1hr 25mins Heathrow–London, depending on traffic. £10 single, £15 return. You can book National Express tickets in advance, t 08705 808080, *www.nationalexpress.com*.

By bus: A vast network of local buses operates from Heathrow's Central Bus Station; some services also stop at Terminal 4. A single bus fare to anywhere in London costs £1.20.

By taxi: Black cab from or to central London: £45–60.

Gatwick

Gatwick is about 20 miles south of London. There are two terminals, North and South, linked by a fast shuttle service. **Airport information**: t 0870 000 2468.

By train: The fastest service is the Gatwick Express (t 0845 850 1530 or t 08457 48 49 50, *www.gatwickexpress.com*), which runs from Victoria Station to South Terminal every 15mins and takes about 30mins or 35mins on Sundays. £12 single, £23.50 return.

By taxi: Black cab from/to central London: £85.

Luton

30 miles north of London. **Airport information**: t (01582) 405 100, *www.london-luton.co.uk*.

By bus/coach: easyBus runs an express bus service from Luton Bus Station bay 4 to Baker Street/Gloucester Place, every 45mins–1hr from as little as £1 single; book at *www.easybus.co.uk*, or pay the driver. Alternatively, Green Line 757 (t 0870 608 7261) runs roughly every half-hour between Luton Airport and Buckingham Palace Road, Victoria, via Finchley Rd, Baker St and Marble Arch. £12.50 return, £9.00 single. 1hr 15mins.

By train: Between 8am and 10pm, Thameslink (t 08457 48 49 50, *www.thameslink.co.uk*) runs frequent trains from St Pancras station to Luton Airport Parkway. Tickets cost from £10 if you buy online. At Luton Airport Parkway a free shuttle bus (10 mins) takes you on to the airport; in total the journey takes around 45–55mins.

By taxi: Black cab from/to central London: £80.

Stansted

Stansted is the furthest from London, about 35 miles to the northeast. **Airport information**: t 0870 000 0303.

By bus: Terravision Express Shuttle, t (01279) 662931, *www.lowcostcoach.com*, to London Victoria departs Stansted coach bay 26 every hour 7.15am–00.40am, and departs London Victoria every hour 3am–10.30pm; the journey takes around 75mins; £8.50 single or £14 return. The National Express A6 Victoria–Stansted and A7 Stansted–Victoria run 24hrs every 15–30mins from Victoria Station via Marble Arch, Hyde Park Corner, Baker Street, St John's Wood, Finchley Rd and Golders Green, taking 1hr 25mins–1hr 45mins in traffic; see *www.nationalexpress.com*, t 0870 5 747 777. £10 single or £15 return.

By train: The Stansted Express (*www.stanstedexpress.com*) runs every 15–30mins 5am–11pm Liverpool Street station–Stansted and 6am–11.45pm Stansted–Liverpool St station, taking 45mins. £14.50 single, £24 return.

By taxi: Black cab from/to central London: £85.

Sample Journeys

Heathrow–Luton: get to Heathrow Express from terminal 15mins; wait for train 10mins; journey 15mins; go from Paddington Station down into Tube 10mins; Tube to Farringdon 15mins; go up and buy Thameslink ticket 10mins including queueing; train and shuttle to Luton 55mins. **Total journey time** 2hrs 10mins, plus 45mins for delays and hitches, so 3hrs would be safest.

Heathrow–Stansted: get to Tube station from terminal 10mins, wait for Tube 5mins, Piccadilly Line to King's Cross 1hr 10mins, change to Circle Line and continue to Liverpool Street Tube station 15mins, up into main line station and buy Stansted Express ticket 10mins, wait for train 20mins, train journey 45mins. **Total journey time** 2hrs 55mins, plus 45mins for delays and hitches, so 3hrs 40mins would be safest.

Making it Work for You: 10 Tips to Remember

1 Whichever airline you travel with, the earlier you book, the cheaper seats will be.

2 Book on-line for the best prices, as there are often discounts of £2.50 to £5 per journey for on-line sales. Always compare the no-frills lines' prices with those of main carriers

3 Be ready to travel at less convenient times. But be sure to check there is a means of getting from your destination airport if you arrive at night, allowing for at least an hour's delay – if you have to fork out for a taxi rather than a shuttle bus or local bus service, this could eat up the saving.

4 Think hard whether you want to book by credit card. You will have the consumer protection that that offers, but there is likely to be a supplement of anything up to £5. Consider using a debit card instead.

5 If you intend to travel often and can go at short notice, sign up for airlines' e-mail mailing lists to hear news of special offers.

6 Check whether airport taxes are included in the quoted price; they are usually extra.

7 Check the baggage allowance and don't take any excess. If you can travel light, take hand baggage only to avoid a long wait.

8 Take your own food and drink, to avoid paying for airport or on-board snacks.

9 Make sure you take your booking reference and confirmation with you to check in (this will have been e-mailed or posted to you).

10 Never ignore the advised check-in times, which are generally two hours. Don't be tempted to cut it fine, as check-in takes longer with budget airlines than with traditional carriers. If you are tall and want an aisle seat, or are travelling in a group, check in even earlier or get to the departure gate as early as possible.

see www.skyscanner.net, www.whichbudget. com (claims to include all routes flown by budget UK airlines on a single site), www. traveljungle.co.uk, www.opodo.co.uk, www. travelocity.co.uk, www.expedia.co.uk or www. aboutflights.co.uk. Make sure also that you read the small print to see what **airport taxes** are charged.

No-frills airline tickets are only sold direct. To get the lowest prices you must book **online**, not by phone. You may not be issued with an actual **ticket** when you book, but given a reference number to show with your ID at check-in. With some airlines you are not issued with an **assigned seat** at check-in either, but will board on a first-come, first-served basis. There are no 'air miles' schemes, and no **meal** will be included. There are no **refunds** if you miss your flight for any reason, although some of the airlines will allow you to **change** your destination, date of travel or the named traveller for a fee of around £15. There are also charges for any **excess baggage**.

Another way in which prices are kept down is by keeping **staffing levels** very low, especially on the ground. This means that check-in can take longer than for main-carrier flights.

With no-frills flights, you're supposed to get what you pay for. If you pay a really low fare

and get to your destination without a hitch, you think, hey, this is great. It's when a problem does arise, though, that you start to notice the downside of no-frills operations. All the budget operators accept far fewer obligations towards customers in the event of lost bags, delays and so on than main carriers traditionally have.

For travel to central and eastern Europe, you should always check out the national airline of the country you want to visit and those of neighbouring countries, as these can offer extremely good deals if you are flexible and book early.

By Train

If you hate flying, or relish the romance of rail, you can take the train all the way from the UK, via the Eurostar from London Waterloo to Paris or Brussels, though the journeys are long (e.g. 23hrs London–Prague), and onnections are complicated. It's a good idea to book ahead (reservations can only be made a maximum of two months in advance).

Rail passes would mean you could see more than one of the cities in this guide for the same cost, for example Budapest–Bratislava–

Vienna, Graz–Klagenfurt–Ljubljana–Zagreb, or Sofia–Belgrade–Zagreb.

Train Operators, Booking Agencies and Other Useful Websites

Eurostar, t 08705 186 186, *www.eurostar.com*.

Deutsche Bahn UK, t 0870 243 5363, *www. deutsche-bahn.co.uk*; trains to Austria via Brussels and Germany; website features timetables for all journeys within Europe.

Rail Europe, UK: 178 Piccadilly, London W1, **t** 08705 848 848, *www.raileurope.co.uk*; USA and Canada: *www.raileurope.com*.

Ffestiniog Travel, t (01766) 512400, *www.fest travel.co.uk*. Can book Eurostars, intercity trains throughout Europe, rail-sea-rail journeys and every kind of rail pass.

Trains Europe, *www.trainseurope.co.uk*.

The Man in Seat Sixty-One, *www.seat61.com*. Excellent website featuring lyrical descriptions and meticulously researched details on every conceivable aspect of train travel.

Rail Passes

If you are planning to make journeys within or between countries, it might be worth investing in a rail pass.

The excellent-value **Eurodomino** or **'Freedom' Pass** entitles European citizens of at least 6 months' duration to unlimited rail travel within one country for one month. Passes are available for 3–8-day periods; prices vary slightly according to the agency you use, but for 8-day passes expect to pay around £185 (Austria), £84 (Bulgaria), £123 (Croatia), £118 (Czech Republic), £131 (Hungary), £109 Poland or £94 (Slovakia).

Alternatively you might consider a one-month **All Zone Inter-Rail Pass**, offering one month's unlimited travel through Zone E (France, Belgium, the Netherlands and Luxembourg) , Zone C (Austria, Germany, Switzerland and Denmark) and Zone D (Czech and Slovak Republics, Hungary, Croatia and Poland), available from £295 (under-26s) or £415 (26 or over).

Passes include discounted fares on some ferries plus reduced fares on Eurostars.

The equivalent North American **Eurail Pass** takes in first class travel through 17 countries including France, Germany, Austria and Hungary, but not Bulgaria, the Czech Republic, Croatia, Poland, Slovakia, Slovenia or Serbia.

Eurail passes are valid for 15, 21, 30, 60 or 90 days; prices range from $588–$1,654 for adults travelling 1st class or from $382–$1,075 for under 26s travelling 2nd class. Cards are also not valid for travel on trains in the UK; however, all include discounts on Eurostar, plus free or discounted travel on selected ferries, lake steamers, boats and buses.

Rail Passes for UK and Europe Residents

www.raileurope.co.uk/railpasses. Rail pass enquiry line, **t** 08707 30 44 95.

www.railchoice.co.uk.

www.seat61.com/Railpass.htm.

Rail Passes for US/Canadian Residents

www.raileurope.com, USA **t** 877 257 2887; Canada *www.raileurope.com/canada*, **t** 800 361 RAIL.

www.europeonrail.com, **t** (201) 255 2898: rail passes, rail and drive, car hire, timetables.

www.railconnection.com, **t** 888 RAILPASS.

www.railpass.com, **t** 800 722 7151.

www.eurorailways.com, **t** 866 768 8927: rail passes, rail 'n' drive passes, senior and youth passes, car rental, air tickets.

www.europrail.net, **t** 888 667 9734.

By Coach

Travelling by coach is tiring but cheap. For example, it takes 25hrs on Eurolines to Vienna, and return tickets booked 30 days in advance cost £66. It takes 31–35hrs to Zagreb, £179 return; 23hrs to Prague, £59 return; 45–48hrs to Sofia, £212 return; 28hrs to Budapest, £69 return; 26–27hrs to Kraków, £89 return.

An excellent cost-cutting option for travelling between countries is a **Busabout pass**, allowing flexible travel on coaches used exclusively by independent travellers. Unlimited passes span from 2 weeks (£259 or £229 for under 26s) to 6 months; flexipasses start at £299 or £259 for under 26s and are valid for 8, 12, 16 or 20 days, with each extra day costing £35. There is no service to Bulgaria, Croatia, Poland, Slovenia or Slovakia. Eurolines also offer a pass ranging from 15, 30 to 60 days.

Busabout, 258 Vauxhall Bridge Rd, London SW1V 1B7, **t** (020) 7950 1661, *www.busabout.com*.

Eurolines, t 08705 808080, *www.eurolines.com*.

By Car

Driving to even the nearer cities of central and eastern Europe is no picnic: it takes almost two days of solid driving via Belgium and Germany to reach Vienna or Prague, for example. Drivers will need to ensure that they have proof of ownership of the car, or a letter from the owner giving permission to drive the car (smuggling of stolen cars is a common crime). All vehicles must be roadworthy, registered and insured, at least third party; you'll need a 'green card' international insurance form. UK and the Republic of Ireland driving licences are accepted, so long as they carry a photograph. If yours doesn't, either trade your old one in for a new-style photocard, or get an International Driving Permit (IDP). Canadian and American drivers also need an IDP.

Crossing the channel is cheapest by ferry from Dover, quickest via the Channel Tunnel. For ferries, check out *www.ferrybooker.com*.
Eurotunnel, t 08705 35 35 35, *www.eurotunnel. com*. Operates the shuttle through the Channel Tunnel, Folkestone to Calais.
Hoverspeed, t 0870 240 8070, *www.hover speed.co.uk*. Dover to Calais.

Car Hire

For an online price comparison, log on to *www.autosabroad.com,* **t** 08700 66 77 88.

UK
Avis, t 08700 100287, *www.avis.co.uk*.
Budget, t 08701 539170, *www.budget.com*.
easyCar, t 09063 33 33 33 (60p/min), *www.easycar.com*.
Europcar, t 08706 075000, *www.europcar.com*.
Hertz, t 08708 448844, *www.hertz.co.uk*.
Thrifty, t (01494) 751600, *www.thrifty.co.uk*.

USA and Canada
Auto Europe, t 888 223 5555, *www.autoeurope.com*.
Avis Rent a Car, USA **t** 800 230 4898, Canada **t** 00 272 5871, *www.avis.com*.
Europe by Car, t 800 223 1516, *www.europebycar.com*.
Europcar, t 877 940 6900, *www.europcar.com*.
Hertz, USA **t** 800 654 3131, **t** 800 854 3001 (international toll free), *www.hertz.com*.

P&O Ferries, t 08705 20 2020, *www.poferries. com*. Dover to Calais and Zeebrugge.
Seafrance, t 08705 711 711, *www.seafrance. co.uk*. Dover to Calais.

Belgian and German motorways are free but you must buy a **pass** for motorways in many of the destination countries, usually available at border crossings, post offices and petrol stations.

Motoring organizations can provide more information on routes and petrol prices.
AAA (USA), **t** (407) 444 4000.
AA (UK), **t** 08706 000 371, *www.theaa.com*.
RAC (UK), **t** 08705 722 722, *www.rac.co.uk*.
Moto Europa, (Europe), *www.ideamerge.com/ motoeuropa*. Driving-abroad website.

Hiring a Car

All the day trips we propose in this guide are chosen specifically to be readily accessible by public transport, but for the touring itineraries a car is essential. You could therefore also consider hiring a car when you get there.

Car hire is an expensive business. Although quotes of international players fluctuate between firms and by season, you can expect to pay €45 per day for a modest runaround and €90 or more for a top-end motor. Shopping around will turn up discount weekend deals, and local outlets are usually cheaper if you're not overly concerned with cosmetics. The minimum age for hiring a car is always 21 and often 25. Specific local rules and regulations are outlined in the Travel chapters for each of the countries in this guide, and local addresses and phone numbers for car hire are given in each city, for spur-of-the-moment decisions. However, if you want to book in advance with one of the larger chains, details are given in the box, left. To save money, look into flight plus car deals.

Entry Formalities

Many but not all of the countries in this guide are EU member states, which greatly simplifies access and customs issues for UK and Irish citizens. Specific details are given for each country in the **Travel, Practical A–Z and Language** chapter that precedes the sightseeing chapters.

Poland:
Travel, Practical A–Z and Language

Travel

Entry Formalities

Passports and Visas

Poland joined the EU in May 2004. A **visa** is not required for EU nationals, nor for citizens of the USA, Canada, South Africa, Australia and New Zealand, who may enter Poland for up to 90 days (up to 180 days for UK citizens) with a valid **passport**. Other nationals should check with the Polish embassy in their country.

Customs

Allowances for **EU nationals** are: 3,200 cigarettes/400 cigarillos/200 cigars/3kg of tobacco; plus 10 litres of spirits, 90 litres of wine and 110 litres of beer; 10 litres of spirits, 90 litres of wine (60 litres maximum sparkling wine) and 110 litres of beer.

For **non-EU travellers**, tobacco and alcohol allowances are: 200 cigarettes/100 cigarillos/50 cigars/250g of tobacco; 1 litre of liquor over 22% alcohol, 2 litres under 22% alcohol, 2 litres of sparkling wine, 2 litres of wine, 50g perfume or 0.25 litres *eau de toilette*. US citizens should contact US Customs (**t** (202) 354 1000, *www.customs. gov*) or read its pamphlet *Know Before You Go*.

Getting Around

Getting around can be an adventure in Poland: the public transport system is comprehensive and very cheap by Western European standards, but often achingly slow and usually overcrowded. In general, trains are faster and more useful, while buses come into their own in rural areas which are not on the train network. The tourist offices can provide timetables.

By Bus

Poland's comprehensive bus network, run by PKS, is most useful for exploring rural areas which are not on the rail network. **Tickets** can be bought at bus stations (usually next to the train station in larger towns), or on board the bus for a small supplement. Ordinary or local buses (*zwykłe*) are still creaky and old-fashioned survivors from the Communist years, and very slow, but fast buses (*pospieszne*) on longer routes are usually more modern and comfortable. Increasingly, private coach operators such as **Polski Express** (*www.polski express.pl*) are offering more luxurious services between the major cities. More information from *www.pekaesbus.com.pl*.

By Car

Travelling by car is the fastest and most relaxed way of exploring Poland, although traffic is heavy, signing poor, and the Poles have one of the worst accident rates in Europe. Poland's secondary roads can be a delightful way of exploring.

Speed limits are as follows: 130kph on motorways, 110kph on dual carriageways, 90kph on country roads and 60kph in built-up areas. The word for **petrol** is *benzyna*. Note that few petrol stations accept credit cards. There are strict penalties for drink-driving, generally ignored by locals, but foreign visitors should be careful or face heavy fines. You will need your **driving licence**, and an international insurance **green card**, although not compulsory, is highly recommended.

All the major **car hire** firms are represented in Poland, along with several local firms, and prices are comparable to those in Western Europe. Shop around on the Internet for the best deals. The average cost of a standard car for one week is around €400.

By Train

Polish trains are run by **Polish State Railways (PKP)**, and are usually the quickest means of getting around the country. There are three kinds of train. Intercity or express services (*ekspresowy*) link major cities, such as Warsaw and Kraków; fast trains (*pospieszny*) have considerably more stops; normal (*normalny* or *osobowy*) are the slowest and only worth taking if there is no other option.

Reservations are compulsory on express trains, and **tickets** can be bought at stations, at agencies such as Orbis, or from the guard for a small supplement. First-class tickets are about 50% more expensive, but very reasonable and worth considering as the compartments are considerably less crammed. Note that train stations, particularly Warsaw's Centralna (central) train station, are infamous hunting grounds for thieves. More information from *www.pkp.pl*, **t** (022) 9436 or **t** (042) 9436.

Practical A–Z

Crime and the Police

Police, t 997, but there is a special number for foreigners, t 0800 200 300. From mobile phones, call the pan-European general emergency number t 112.

Poland is generally a safe country to travel around. However, petty crime is a serious problem on the public transport system and you should take particular care around the main bus and train stations of the major cities. Some areas of the larger cities are still no-go areas, at least after dark: this is particularly true of the Praga district in Warsaw. Park in a guarded car park if possible and don't keep valuables in the car. Leave the glove box open to show that there is nothing to steal.

Report any thefts to the police (*policja*), who will give you a copy of the statement for insurance purposes, though stolen belongings are rarely recovered.

Disabled Travellers

Facilities for disabled travellers are generally poor in Poland, although things are gradually improving. There are lifts available at the larger train stations and on the metro line in Warsaw, but buses are rarely wheelchair accessible. The new luxury chain hotels that are mushrooming across the country usually have reasonable facilities for disabled travellers.

The Warsaw tourist office has a *Guide For Disabled Travellers* available in English; unfortunately Kraków only produces a pamphlet in Polish.

For more information, contact Integracja, ul. Dzielna 1, Warsaw, t (022) 831 8582, *www.integracja.org* (Polish only).

Electricity

The electrical current in Poland is 220 volts, 50Hz. The standard two-round-pin European-style plugs are used.

Embassies and Consulates

Polish Embassies Abroad

UK: 47 Portland Place, London W1B 1JH, t 0870 774 2700, *www.polishembassy.org.uk*.
USA: 2640 16th St NW, Washington DC, t (202) 234 3800, *www.polandembassy.org*.
Canada: No embassy; contact USA embassy.

Foreign Embassies in Warsaw

UK: al. Róż 1, t (022) 311 0000, *www.britishembassy.pl*.
USA: al. Ujazdowskie 29–31, t (022) 504 2000, *http://warsaw.usembassy.gov/*.
Canada: al. Jerozolimskie 123, t (022) 584 3100, *http://www.dfait-maeci.gc.ca/canadaeuropa/poland/menu-en.asp*.

Festivals and Events

Easter: A huge event in Catholic Poland. The week begins with the Palm Sunday processions; on Holy Saturday the churches are full with people bringing baskets of food, including the traditional painted eggs, to be blessed; on Easter Sunday mass is often followed by processions; and on Easter Monday girls are traditionally doused with water (or pelted with water bombs) in an ancient fertility rite.

15 Aug: Assumption: Another important Catholic festival, with pilgrims setting off from all over Poland to the Black Madonna in Częstochowa.

1 Nov: All Saints' Day: Families visit cemeteries which are filled with flowers and candles.

Christmas: Every Polish town has its Christmas markets, and a big family dinner usually takes place on Christmas Eve before midnight Mass (services are always packed).

New Year's Eve: There are balls and parties in all the major towns: in Warsaw, everyone congregates on the square in front of the Royal Castle to hear the clock chime midnight.

Health and Emergencies

Ambulance, t 999 but note that you are unlikely to find an English-speaker.

Most minor ailments can be easily dealt with at the pharmacy (*apteka*), but for more serious illnesses you should go directly to the nearest **outpatient clinic** (*przychodnia*) of any **hospital** (*szpital*). In theory, reciprocal agreements with most European countries, including the UK, mean that basic and emergency healthcare is free if you carry a stamped E111 form (available from UK post offices, soon to be replaced by a card), but Poland's public health service is very poor and you are highly recommended to take out private insurance.

Internet

Internet cafés have mushroomed in Warsaw, Kraków and all the major cities, and you'll find it very easy to keep in touch electronically. In rural areas and provincial towns, Internet access is still difficult to find.

Money

The Polish national currency is the **złoty** (abbreviated as zł, or PLN), which is broken broken down into 100 **groszy** (gr). Prices, particularly for hotels and the smarter restaurants, often appear in euros.

Cash is still king in Poland: **credit cards** and, less commonly, **traveller's cheques** are increasingly accepted in the major cities only. **ATMs**, called *Bankomats*, are easily available in larger towns, but rare in provincial areas. You can change money in banks, exchange offices (*kantors*, note that these almost never change traveller's cheques), tourist offices and many hotels, and the best deals are usually to be had at the ubiquitous *kantors* which charge between 1 and 2% commission.

Banks are usually open Mon–Fri 8–5, with larger branches also opening on Saturday mornings from 9–1.

At the time of writing, **exchange rates** were as follows: €1 euro = 3.92 zł, $1 = 2.98 zł, £1 = 5.67 zł; this works out for quick calculations at roughly 60 zł = £10, 100 zł = €25.

National Holidays

1 Jan New Year's Day
Easter Monday
1 May Labour Day
3 May Constitution Day

Corpus Christi (May or June)
15 Aug Assumption Day
1 Nov Feast of All Saints
11 Nov Independence Day
25 Dec Christmas Day
26 Dec Boxing Day

Opening Hours

Most **shops** are usually open Mon–Fri 10–6, until 2pm on Sat, although delicatessens and grocery stores open earlier. Supermarkets and department stores often open until 8 or 9pm, but almost all shops are closed on Sundays. The major cities have 24-hour supermarkets.

Churches are usually open all day, particularly in the big cities, but will probably only be open for Mass on Sundays in rural areas.

Museum opening hours vary greatly, although most close on Mondays. Ticket offices often shut up to an hour before closing time.

Post

Red post boxes are for post outside the city and for international destinations, while **green post boxes** are for post within the city. The major cities have several **post offices** (*Poczta*) and in Warsaw the main post office (*Poczta Główna*) is open 24 hours a day.

Stamps can also be bought at tobacconists. The postal system is slow but reasonably reliable. Prices for airmail (*lotnicza*) letters are comparable with the rest of Europe: a postcard or letter sent to Europe costs 2.50 zł, or 3.20 zł to the USA and Canada.

Price Categories

Hotels

The price you should expect to pay, for a double room with bath in high season, is as follows (prices are often quoted in euros):

luxury over 500 zł / €125
expensive 350–500 zł / €85–125
moderate 200–350 zł / €50–85
inexpensive under 200 zł / €50

Restaurants

You should expect to pay roughly the following for a three-course dinner, including wine or beer, for one person:

luxury over 150 zł / €35
expensive 100–150 zł / €25–35
moderate 50–100 zł / €12–25
inexpensive under 50 zł / €12

Shopping

Poland is well known for its traditional arts and crafts, including embroidered fabrics and local costumes, leather goods, glassware and ceramics. The naïve and colourful folk art is very charming.

Other good buys include amber jewellery, which is very reasonably priced, and the traditional Polish firewater, vodka.

Sports

Poland is an excellent destination for sports enthusiasts: beautiful, wild national parks will appeal to hikers and wildlife-lovers, the lakes and rivers boast a variety of watersports facilities, and Zakopane (*see* p.58) in the magnificent Tatra mountains has expanded into a lively and important ski resort.

All the major cities have gyms, pools (both indoor and outdoor), tennis courts, etc.

Telephones

The Polish national telephone network has developed rapidly since the end of the Communist regime, but remains unreliable. Perhaps as a result of this, the mobile phone market has exploded and coverage is excellent throughout the country.

When **calling Poland from abroad**, dial the country code **t** (00) 48 and drop the first zero in the area code.

When **calling abroad from Poland**, dial 00 plus the country code: UK 44, Ireland 353, USA and Canada 1, Australia 61, New Zealand 64.

When **calling within the city**, you don't need to dial the **area code** (e.g. Warsaw **t** 022, Kraków **t** 012).

Public telephone boxes which actually work are thin on the ground, although you can usually find functioning phones at post offices. All are now operated with **phone cards** (available from newsagents or post offices for in denominations of 25, 50, or 100 units and costing between 10 and 40 zł).

Time

Poland is one hour ahead of GMT, and the clocks go forward one hour on the last Sunday in March, and back one hour on the last Sunday in October.

Tipping

Locals rarely tip, but waiters, taxi drivers and other service staff have come to expect a little something from tourists. Tip between 5 and 10% depending on the service.

Toilets

There are few public toilets in Poland, and even fewer that you would actually want to use, but you can always use those in a bar or restaurant. These regularly charge a small fee, usually 1 zł, even for customers: keep a pile of coins handy. Toilets (*toaleta*) are marked with symbols: circles or upward-pointing triangles for the ladies' and downward-pointing triangles for the men's.

Tourist Information

UK: Polish National Tourist Office, Level 3, Westec House, West Gate, London W5 1YY, **t** 08700 675 010, **f** 08700 675 011, *www.visitpoland.org*.

USA: Polish National Tourist Office, 5 Marine View Plaza, Hoboken, NJ 07030–5722, **t** (201) 420 9910, **f** (201) 584 9153, *www.polandtour.org*.

Canada: There is no official Polish national tourist office in Canada. Visitors can request information from the New York office.

Language

Polish is a Slavic (or Slavonic) language. It uses a Latin-based alphabet which includes letters with the addition of daunting little dots and hooks (called diagraphs and diacritics) which change the pronunciation of the letter. Away from major cities, English is not widely spoken.

Pronunciation

Where the letters differ substantially from English:

ą	a nasal 'awn' sound
ę	nasal 'en' sound, like ten
ó and u	short 'o', as in foot, or 'u' as in put
i	'ee', as in feet
ie	'ye', e.g. *wiem* = vy-em'
c	'ts', as in bats
ć	'ch', as in church
ch	'ch', as in Scottish loch
dz	'dz', except when followed by i or e, when it is pronounced as a j
cz	'ch'
sz	'sh'
szcz	'sh-ch' as in pushchair
j	'y', as in yellow
ł	'w', as in willow
ń	like Spanish ñ, or the 'ni' in onion
y	'i', as in it
ź and ż	'zh', as in Zhivago

Useful Words and Phrases

yes/no *Tak/Nie*
please *Proszę*
thank you *Dziękuję*
good morning *Dzień dobry*
good evening *Dobry wieczór*
goodnight *Dobranoc*
goodbye *Do widzenia*
hi/bye (inf.) *Cześć*
see you later *Do zobaczenia*
excuse me/I'm sorry *Przepraszam*
Do you speak English? *Czy Pan mówi po angielsku?* (to a man)/*Czy Pani mówi po angielsku?* (to a woman)
I don't understand *Nie rozumiem*
I don't speak Polish *Nie mówę po polsku*
How much?/How many? *Ile?*
where? *Gdzie?*

what? *Co?*
how? *Jak?*
when? *Kiedy?*
open/closed *otwarte/ zamknięte*
I'm lost *Zgubłem sę*
Can I have a ticket? *Proszę bilet?*
bank *bank*
post office *poczta*
letterbox *skrzynka poztowa*
stamp *znaczek*
telephone card *karta telefoniczna*
police *policja*
Help! *Pomocy!*

Where is the toilet? *Gdzie jest toaleta?*
Men *Panowie*
Women *Panie*

hotel *hotel*
Do you have any rooms available? *Czy są wolne pokoje?*
I'd like a double/single room *Poproszę pokój dwuosobowy/jednoosobowy*
restaurant *restauracja*
I'm a vegetarian *Jestem jaroszem*
Cheers! *Na zdrowie!*
I would like to order *Chciałbym zamówić*
Bill, please *Proszę rachunek*

Days and Months

Monday *poniedziałek*
Tuesday *wtorek*
Wednesday *środa*
Thursday *czwartek*
Friday *piątek*
Saturday *sobota*
Sunday *niedziela*

January *styczeń*
February *luty*
March *marzec*
April *kwiecień*
May *maj*
June *czerwiec*
July *lipiec*
August *sierpień*
September *wrzesień*
October *październik*
November *listopad*
December *grudzień*

Poland: Warsaw and Kraków

04

Warsaw

Just a decade and a half after the collapse of the Communist regime, Warsaw has transformed itself into the hottest city on the ex-Soviet bloc: boutique hotels, chi-chi restaurants, designer shops and slick new clubs are opening every day, the skyline is a sea of cranes as developers cash in on Warsaw's startling rise in the fashion stakes, and even the Soviet Realist monoliths which dominate the centre of the city have acquired a cool, retro cachet. While its true that the suburbs and much of the city centre retain their gloomy Soviet-era aspect, with monotonous ranks of dour apartment buildings and bombastic monuments to Communist ideals, Warsaw still manages to confound the old stereotypes. Few first-time visitors expect to discover the jewel of an Old Town, a perfect ensemble of Gothic and Renaissance mansions clustered around a magnficent central square; to stroll along elegant boulevards lined with opulent palaces and flamboyant churches; or to wander through vast shady gardens scattered with lakes and charming follies. Most extraordinary of all is the fact that Warsaw's splendid architectural heritage has been preserved in the face of utter devastation: singled out with particular malevolence during the Second World War, Hitler declared his aim of wiping the city off the map. He almost succeeded: its emergence from the ashes seems little short of miraculous, and the face of Warsaw stands testament to the courage and perseverance of its citizens.

The city's history remains a poignant undercurrent beneath its increasingly glitzy exterior. For centuries, Poland has been fought over, annexed, and subsumed by its powerful neighbours – but never without a fight. It may have lost its nationhood, but never its nationalism, and its capital is replete with monuments and museums to the countless uprisings which have marked its stormy history. Among the most symbolic of these is the Warsaw Uprising of 1944, an episode which is deeply etched in the Polish pysche, which is finally being properly addressed with a vast new museum. The infamous Warsaw ghetto, into which the Nazis crammed almost half a million Jews before herding them off to the death camps, was the scene of a terrible uprising in 1943. Of the city's once-flourishing Jewish community, only around 300 Jews survived, and the area occupied by the ghetto is now an eerily silent Soviet-style suburb. Another new museum, expected to open in 2008, marks a hopeful shift in Poland's historically poor Jewish relations.

Change is in the air in Warsaw: the transformation from dour Soviet-bloc citadel to increasingly stylish, cosmopolitan capital of a new EU member country has suffused the city with a heady excitement reminiscent of Prague or Berlin a decade or so ago.

History

Contemnit procellas (It defies the storms).
Warsaw´s motto

A sizeable settlement already existed on the banks of the Vistula river (Wisła in Polish) river by the 10th century. In 1413, the bustling and affluent town became the official residence of the Duke of Mazovia, Janusz the Elder. When the last Mazovian

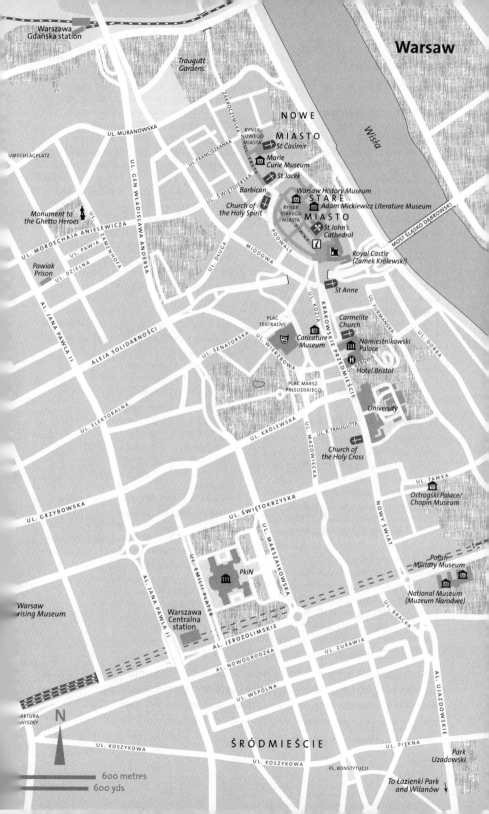

Getting There

See **Getting There**, pp.4–10.

Getting from the Airport

Warsaw's Frédéric Chopin Airport is 10km southwest of the city centre and contains all the expected amenities, from shops and cafés to banks and ATMs. Note that the Etiuda terminal, used by most budget airlines, has no services – eat, drink and shop before you check in. More info from *www.lotnisko-chopin.pl*.

Bus nos.175 and 188 (*daily 4.44am–23.10pm, single 2.40 zł if purchased from news kiosks, or 2.90 zł if bought from driver*) run every 8–15 minutes from outside the Arrivals hall. A **night bus** (no.611) runs all night between the airport and the main train station. The airport also has express bus links to several other Polish towns (*see* airport website for details).

Official licensed **taxis** depart from the taxi rank outside the arrivals hall. Don't use the touts (nicknamed the 'taxi mafia') inside the hall. Fares into the city should be around 30–40 zł. Always ask for a receipt.

Getting Around

The best way to explore the city centre is on foot, as much of the old city is pedestrianized and it's an attractive walk straight down the Royal Way to the Łazienki Park.

Warsaw has a single **metro line** which connects the city centre with the southern suburbs and is being expanded to the north. There is only one platform: the terminus is on the front of the train (those going towards the city centre are signed 'Centrum'). You must date stamp your ticket before boarding, and hang on to it in case of inspections (ensure inspectors are carrying valid ID). Be on your guard for pickpockets on all forms of public transport in Warsaw. Warsaw's boxy white **trams** are often faster and more convenient than buses. Tram stops have timetables and routes. There is also an extensive **bus** network, most useful for reaching outlying suburbs as routes through the city centre can be slow. Timetables can be found at bus stops.

Tickets are valid on buses, trams and the metro line and are available from news stands and kiosks. Single tickets can be bought from the driver with a 0.50 zł surcharge. Tickets are available for a single journey (2.40 zł), 60 mins (3.60 zł), 90mins (4.50 zł), 2hrs (6 zł), 24hrs (7.20 zł), and one week (24 zł). Stamp your ticket in the machine next to the doors on buses and trams, or behind the platform on the metro. Standard single tickets and passes are not valid on night buses.

Don't hail a **taxi** on the street, or you will almost certainly be ripped off. They can be picked up at numerous taxi ranks, but it can be hard to work out which are licensed and which are not: the largest and best-known official taxi company is **MPT**. Fares are up to a third cheaper if you order one by phone. Reliable taxi numbers include **MPT**, t 919, **Sawa-taxi**, t 96 61, **Tele-taxi**, t 9627.

By Car

The public transport system will efficiently, if not necessarily speedily, ferry you around the city centre. A car is only useful for the suburbs and exploring further afield.

Car Hire
Avis, t (022) 572 6565 (airport), *www.avis.pl*.
Europcar, t (022) 853 6677 (city), t (022) 650 2564 (airport), *www.europcar.com.pl*.
Hertz, t (022) 621 1360 (city), t (022) 650 2896 (airport), *www.hertz.com.pl*.
Budget, t (022) 630 7280 (city), t (022) 650 4062 (airport), *www.budget.com*.
Sixt, t (022) 616 3536 (city), t (022) 650 2031 (airport), *www.sixt.pl*.
Trust Rent a Car, t (022) 339 0256 (city), *www.trustrentacar.pl*.

duke died without an heir in 1526, the duchy was incorporated into Poland. In 1572 the Republic of Nobles was declared after the death of King Stanisław August, which gave the Polish aristocracy the right to elect their rulers. In order to accommodate the new political order, Warsaw replaced Kraków as Polish capital in 1596, thanks largely to its geographical location at the centre of a huge empire which by now stretched from

Tourist Information

Warsaw: The main tourist office is in front of the castle at ul. Krakowskie Przedmieście, Plac Zamkowy, **t** (022) 9431, *www.warsaw tour.pl*, with branches at the airport, Central train station and Western coach station. They can reserve hotels and guided tours and are all open daily.

The **Warsaw Tourist Card** is valid for 24hrs (35 zł) or 3 days (65 zł). It offers unlimited use of public transport, reductions or free admission for many museums and monuments, and discounts in some restaurants, shops, sports facilities, etc.

Guided Tours

Tourist tram, train and horse-drawn carriage: The historic **tourist tram** (*daily in July and August and at weekends during the rest of the year*) makes a circular route from Plac Narutowicza southwest of the city centre. Buy tickets (2 zł) on board. A cheesy **tourist train** tours the Old City daily from 9am–4pm (14 zł), and departs from in front of the Royal Castle. You can also hire **horse-drawn carriages** from here: prices are around 60 zł for 30 minutes but bargaining is *de rigueur*.

Boat excursions: White Fleet (Biała Flota) run boat trips along the Wisła river daily from May–Sept; departures from near the Śląsko-Dąbrowski Bridge just below the Royal Castle. Fares 14 zł.

Bus tours: Mazurkas Travel, ul. Długa 8/14, **t** (022) 635 66 33, *www.mtravelp.pl*, offer bus excursions to sights in and around Warsaw, including the palaces of Wilanów and Nieborów, and Chopin's birthplace.

Festivals

Contact the tourist information offices (*see above*) or visit the official website for more information on Warsaw's numerous festivals.

Mar/April: Easter (*Wielkanoc*) is the most important religious festival in Catholic Poland, and is solemnly celebrated in Warsaw with traditional parades and the blessing of food in the churches.

April: Polish Contemporary Opera Festival.

June: Outdoor **Chopin concerts** in the Łazienki Park on Sundays from June to September, *www.chopin.pl*; **Garden Theatre Festival**, a festival of street theatre in Warsaw's squares and gardens, held throughout the summer. **Midsummer's Eve** (*Noc Świętojańska*) is celebrated with girls tossing wreaths of flowers into the Wisła, and concerts and firework shows across the city.

July: Warsaw Summer Jazz Days. Three-day jazz festival held in venues across the city.

Aug: The religious festival of the Assumption is a public holiday and marked by a major pilgrimage to the Black Madonna at Częstochowa.

Sept–Oct: Warsaw Autumn Festival. Major contemporary music festival featuring international performers.

Oct: International Film Festival. One of the biggest in Europe, *www.wff.pl/en*.

Nov: Piano Festival, with world class recitals held at the Royal Castle.

Dec: Christmas fairs held across the city: the best are in the Royal Castle and in PKiN.

Shopping

Empik, ul. Marszałkowska 104–22, **t** (022) 551 4442. Huge megastore with books in several languages, cds, ticket service, a good choice of international press and a coffee shop.

Salon Muzyczny Z. Hołdysa, ul. Wspólna 41, **t** (022) 628 5182. Legendary music shop, with CDs.

Galeria Centrum, ul. Marszałkowska 104–22, **t** (022) 561 4141. Newly revamped department store, with local and international fashions, perfume and cosmetics.

the Baltic to the Black Sea. The city blossomed: aristocratic palaces and elaborate churches sprang up, and the Mazovian fortress was remodelled as an opulent royal residence. Despite the Swedish incursions in the 1650s which wreaked havoc on much of Poland and reduced its capital to rubble, by the end of the 17th century the city was flourishing once more. The 18th century was a Golden Age, particularly

Galeria Mokotów, ul. Wołoska 12, t (022) 541 4141, *www.galeriamokotow.pl*. Huge new shopping centre with international chain stores and a good supermarket with an excellent deli.

Folk Art and Crafts Gallery, Plac Konstytucji 2, t (022) 621 6669. Hand-made Polish folk crafts, including embroidered fabrics, ceramics and glassware.

Cepelia, ul. Marszałkowska 99–101, t (022) 621 9694. There are several branches of Cepelia dotted around the city, and it's a reliable place to find attractive folk art and souvenirs.

Markets

Bazar na Kole, ul. Obozowa 99. Huge flea market where you can turn up all kinds of weird and wonderful treasures if you're prepared to rummage. *Open 8am–2pm*.

Russian Market, Stadion Dziesięciolecia, Praga. This vast, run-down stadium has become one of the biggest and most extraordinary markets in Europe, with more than 12,000 stalls selling everything up to and including the kitchen sink. Catch it while you can, as its days are numbered. *Open 6am–afternoon*.

Sports and Activities

Football

Legia Warszawa (*www.legia.pl*) is Warsaw's most successful football team, locked in perpetual rivalry with **Wisła Kraków**. You can see a match at their stadium in ul. Łazienkowska.

Swimming

Wodny Park, ul. Merliniego 4, t (022) 646 1361. Olympic-sized swimming pool and water chutes.

Kompleks Basenów, ul. Inflancka 8, t (022) 831 9229. Outdoor pool in summer.

Horse-racing

Służewiec Racetrack, Puławska 266, t (022) 843 14 41. Popular Sunday horse racing meetings – and it's free too.

Where to Stay

Note: Hotel star ratings are not official and are given here as guidelines only.

Warsaw t (022) –

★★★★★**InterContinental**, ul. Emilii Plater 49, t 328 8888, *www.warsaw.intercontinental. com* (*luxury*). This plush modern hotel is right next to the Palace of Culture and Science, with chic rooms and luxurious extras including gym, pool and solarium.

★★★★★**Royal Méridien Bristol**, ul. Krakowskie Przedmieście 42–4, t 551 1000, *www. lemeridien-bristol.com* (*luxury*). The city's most opulent, atmospheric hotel, restored to its former splendour on the Royal Way.

★★★★★**Le Régina**, Kościelna 12, t 531 6000, *www. leregina.com* (*luxury*). This gorgeous boutique hotel has newly opened in a sump-tuous (rebuilt) 18th-century mansion, and is located in a tranquil street in the New Town. Extras include a swimming pool.

★★★★**Rialto**, ul. Wilcza 73, t 628 4622, *www.hotel rialto.com.pl* (*luxury*). A delightful boutique hotel with charming rooms in Art Deco style. The attention to detail makes the difference here, and the service has rightly won the hotel numerous accolades.

★★★★**Sheraton**, ul. Prusa 2, t 657 6100, *www. sheraton.com/warsaw* (*luxury*). Smart and with plenty of facilities, south of the centre near the National Museum.

★★★★**Marriott**, al. Jerozolimskie 65–79, t 630 6306, *www.marriott.com/wawpl* (*expensive*). A modern skyscraper in the heart of the city, with stunning views from the crisply deco-rated rooms, excellent service, a pool, and good business facilities.

during the reign of the last Polish King, Stanisław August Poniatowski, when Warsaw became one of the most elegant and cultured capitals in Europe.

But Poland's powerful neighbours had designs on the kingdom: Russia, Prussia and Austria divided it up between themselves with three partitions. In the Third Partition of 1795, Poland lost its independence and Warsaw was absorbed into Prussia. The

****Maria**, al Jana Pawła II 71, **t** 838 4062 (*expensive*). This is a small, family-run hotel at the bottom of this price bracket, some way northwest of the New Town, with chintzy but well-equipped rooms. It also offers good-value apartments.

***Europejski Hotel Orbis**, ul. Krakowskie Przedmieście 13, **t** 826 5051, *www.orbis.pl* (*moderate*). Once the *grande dame* of Warsaw hotels, this may have lost some of its shine but none of its appeal. With its perfect location, spacious newly refurbished rooms, welcoming staff and glorious retro décor, it's the best value hotel in the city.

***Ibis Stare Miasto**, ul. Muranowska 2, **t** 310 1000, *www.orbis.pl* (*moderate*). A bland but reliable chain hotel, worth considering for its reasonable prices and excellent location on the fringes of the Old Town.

***Reytan**, ul. T. Rejtana 6, **t** 646 2989, *www.reytan.pl* (*moderate*). A modest hotel, down a quiet side street, with bright, newly refurbished rooms, 2km south of the centre.

Old Town Apartments, ul. Rynek Starego Miasta 12, **t** 887 9800, *www.warsawshotel.com* (*moderate*). There are few decent hotels in the Old Town, but this friendly, helpful company have a good range of apartments to suit all pockets. Highly recommended.

****Mazowiecki**, ul. Mazowiecka 10, **t** 827 2365, *www.mazowiecki.com.pl* (*inexpensive*). This plain, central little hotel may have little in the way of charm, but its functional rooms are spotless and the price can't be beaten. It offers a 20% discounts on weekend stays.

***Premiere Classe**, ul. Towarowa 2, **t** 624 0800, *www.premiereclasse.com.pl* (*inexpensive*). A simple hotel which may well be the best bargain in the city: rooms are spartan, but all have en suite facilities and TVs.

Nathan's Villa Hostel, ul, Piękna, **t** 622 2496, *www.nathansvilla.com* (*inexpensive*). Warsaw's best backpacker's hostel, with bright and immaculately kept rooms. No curfews or lockouts.

Eating Out

Warsaw **t** (022) –

Outstanding hotel restaurants include the Malinowa at the Royal Méridien Bristol, and Kurt Scheller's Restaurant in the Rialto. Lalka at the Sheraton and Lila Weneda at the Marriott are popular for Sunday brunch.

Belvedere, ul. Agrykoli 1, **t** 841 4806, *www.belvedere.com.pl* (*expensive*). Dine on sophisticated European fare in this elegant restaurant, set in the Orangerie in the heart of the beautiful Łazienki Park.

Absynt, ul. Wspolna 35, **t** 621 1881, *www.siesta.com.pl* (*expensive*). A chic, sleek restaurant catering to an equally chic and sleek crowd, serving elegant and creative French cuisine.

Dom Polski, ul. Francuska 11, **t** 616 2432 (*expensive*). A classic in Warsaw, this traditional and elegant restaurant serves some of the finest Polish cuisine in the country. It's located in a pretty villa close to the Wisła river, and you can dine in the garden in summer.

Karczma Gessler, Rynek Starego Miasta 21, **t** 831 4427 (*expensive*). Cellar restaurant serving Polish dishes and Jewish specialities.

Rybak, Rynek Starego Miasta 3–9, **t** 635 3769 (*expensive–moderate*). The best place for fish and seafood in the Old Town.

Café Kredens, ul. Przemysłowa 36, **t** 625 1578, *www.kredens.com.pl* (*moderate*). Watching the staff negotiate the bric-a-brac which fills this bustling restaurant alone makes it worth a visit – but add to that huge portions of Greek, Italian and Polish food and it's easy to see why it's always packed.

Delicja Polska, ul. Koszykowa 54, **t** 630 8850, *www.delicjapolska.pl* (*moderate*). A romantic restaurant with two elegant dining areas which deliberately recall a pre-war country mansion. Refined Polish dishes are on the menu, and the roast duck is recommended.

Senator, ul. Szeroki Dunaj 1–3, **t** 831 7968, *www.restauracja–senator.pl* (*moderate*).

Poles looked to Napoleon for help in 1806, but his defeat by the Russians shattered their hopes, and Warsaw was put under Russian control by the Congress of Vienna in 1814. The Poles refused to submit quietly: the people of Warsaw rose in 1830 and again in 1864, but the forbidding Citadel, a former Tsarist prison, still stands testament to the vast numbers of political prisoners executed or exiled to Siberia.

In the heart of the Old Town, this serves sturdy Polish cuisine in a formal setting.

Sense, ul. Nowy Świat 19, **t** 826 6570, *www.sensecafe.com.pl* (*moderate*). One of Warsaw's new breed of restaurant, lounge bar and club rolled into one, Sense stands out for the exceptional fusion cuisine. It's a favourite with celebs and the fashion pack.

Orchidea, ul. Szpitalna 3, **t** 827 3436 (*inexpensive*). This trendy new fusion restaurant has a great budget menu featuring tasty Thai-style curries and the like.

Pod Samsonem, ul. Freta 3–5, **t** 831 1788 (*inexpensive*). An old-fashioned Jewish restaurant in the New Town, with a frightening fleet of old-school waitresses with bouffant platinum hair and grim expressions. It's an experience, and the food is plentiful.

Podwale Piwna Kompania, ul. Podwale 25, **t** 635 6314 (*inexpensive*). A big atmospheric barn of a place, serving enormous platters of traditional Jewish and Polish food. The staff are in traditional costume, and don't be surprised if the punters stand on the tables and start singing national songs after a few beers.

Cafés and Coffee Houses

Antrankt, Pl. Piłsudskiego 9, **t** 827 6211. An atmospheric café full of flea market finds, where you can sink into a leopard print sofa and enjoy an intimate chat.

Coffee Karma, pl. Zbawiciela 3–5, **t** 875 8709. Trim modern café with deckchair-style wooden furnishings, vast windows for people-watching and a very decent cup of java.

Café Nowy Świat, ul. Nowy Świat 63, **t** 826 5803. This grand old café first opened in 1883 and after a crisp modern makeover, it still remains the preferred gathering point for politicians, celebs and fur-clad ladies who lunch.

Entertainment and Nightlife

Music, Theatre, Ballet

Teatr Narodowy (National Theatre), plac Teatralny 3, **t** 692 0770. Poland's most prestigious theatre.

Opera Narodowa (National Opera House), plac Teatralny 1, **t** 692 0200. The splendid neoclassical Opera House was completely rebuilt after the Second World War and is Poland's finest opera venue.

Filharmonia, ul Jasna 5, **t** 828 7479, *www.filharmonia.pl*. Another neoclassical venue raised from the ashes.

Jazz

Jazz Bistro Gwiazdeczka, ul. Piwna 40, **t** 887 8764. A popular and immaculate venue which sadly falls short on ambience.

Tygmont, ul. Mazowiecka 6–8, **t** 828 3409. Satisfyingly louche cellar bar which showcases emerging musicians.

Jazz Café Helicon, ul. Freta 45–7, **t** 635 9505. Friendly, laid-back jazz café and shop with regular live gigs.

Bars and Clubs

Pierkarnia, ul. Młocińska 11, **t** 636 4979, *www.piekarnia.org.pl*. A hip club with a buzzing crowd and top DJs where you are guaranteed a good night out.

NoBo, ul. Wilcza 58a, **t** 622 4007. Sleek, red, ultra-cool bar, restaurant and club with mellow music (the Parisian Buddha Bar DJs are regular fixtures) and excellent cocktails.

Lucid, al. Jerozolimskie 179. Warsaw's hottest new club: dress to impress or you won't get past the door.

The Living Room, ul. Foksal 18, **t** 826 3928. Chic, minimalist bar full of slinky young things in designer gear.

Zakątek, ul. Chmielna 5. A laid-back, arty bar with battered furniture and an enjoyably mellow vibe.

After the First World War, Poland briefly regained its independence, only to lose it once more in 1939 when German troops marched across the border. The Jews of Warsaw were crammed into a walled ghetto, then herded to the death camps: more than 300,000 were to perish, despite the courageous but doomed Ghetto Uprising in 1943 (*see* p.31). The Warsaw Uprising of 1944 was similarly fated: the lives of more than

20,000 Polish troops and 150,000 civilians were lost and, at the culmination of the battle, Hitler ordered that Warsaw's surviving buildings be numbered in order of their importance to Polish culture and systematically dynamited. At the end of the war, the city lay in smoking ruins and more than three-quarters of its 1939 population were dead or missing. The Herculean task of rebuilding the city began as Poland was once again thrust under foreign control. As the Old City was being painstakingly reconstructed, the new Communist regime was busy changing the face of Warsaw in an entirely different way: grey, Soviet-style apartment buildings unfurled throughout the suburbs and a parade of monolithic towers in bombastic Soviet Realist style mushroomed in the city centre. By the early 1980s, the Solidarność (Solidarity) movement

Food and Drink

Polish food is traditionally hearty and filling, with a strong emphasis on **meat**, particularly beef (*wołowina*) and pork (*wieprzowina*). Lamb (*baranina*) is popular in mountain areas, and the rivers and lakes provide carp (*karp*) and trout (*pstrąg*) which appear on local menus. Chicken (*kurczak*) and roast duck (*kaczka*, often stuffed with apples, *kaczka z jabłkami*) are also common, and smarter restaurants will often serve game in season. The classic **staple Polish dish** is *bigos*, a stew of sauerkraut, cabbage and a variety of meats, which is slowly simmered over a low heat – sometimes over several days. *Flaczki*, a spicy tripe dish, is a local speciality which is much tastier than it sounds. Other standards include the delicious filled dumplings, *pierogi*, and *barszcz*, a spiced beetroot soup. **Soup** (*zupa*) is a feature of every restaurant, and ranges from substantial broths which can be a filling meal in themselves to clear *consommés*.

Although the Poles are prodigious meat-eaters, **vegetarians** are increasingly catered for, particularly in the big cities. Most menus now feature a vegetarian section, which will often include scrumptious potato pancakes (*placki ziemniaczane*) served with sour cream, *kopytka* (the Polish version of gnocchi) and *pierogi*. Wild mushrooms (*grzyby*) are very popular, and are usually served sautéed, and tasty salads include *mizeria*, grated dill cucumber in sour cream, or *ćwikła z chrzanem*, grated beetroot with horseradish. The Poles don't excel at **desserts**, and many restaurants will offer only ice-cream (*lody*), sometimes served with fruit compôte, or pancakes (*naleśniki*).

Poland doesn´t produce its own **wine** (*wino*), and most restaurants serve inexpensive wines from Hungary and Bulgaria: French, Italian and other wines are usually very pricey. **Beer** (*piwo*), usually sold on draught, is widely consumed, and there are several excellent local producers of which the biggest and best-known is Żwiec. The national drink *par excellence* however, is **vodka** (*wódka*), which Poland claims to have invented: drunk neat and cold, you should down it in one gulp, Polish-style. (Just don't get into a drinking competition with a Pole.) There are dozens of varieties, flavoured with fruit or spices, and one of the best is Żubrowka or 'bison vodka', made with grass from the Białowieża forest where the bison can be found. In the fancy new cafés, cappuccinos and espressos are now common, but traditionally Polish **coffee** (*kawa parzona*) is a thick, pungent brew. The Poles also love **tea** (*herbata*), which is usually served in a glass with a slice of lemon.

was gaining ground as dissatisfaction with the Soviets reached fever pitch. In 1989, the Communist regime collapsed and a year later Lech Wałęsa became the first popularly elected president of Poland. In 1999, the country joined Nato, and in 2004 became part of the EU.

Old Town (Stare Miasto)

The beautiful **Old Town Square** (Rynek Starego Miasta) is Warsaw's most evocative symbol of the city's rise from the ashes after the Second World War. The exquisite ensemble of 15th-century houses has been meticulously recreated, complete with the graceful Renaissance and Baroque façades added by affluent burghers in the 17th and 18th centuries. In summer, a sea of tables unfurls across the square, and street musicians and human statues regale the crowds.

The townhouses along the northern flank of the square now contain the **Warsaw History Museum** (Muzeum Historyczne m.st. Warszawy; *open Tues–Thurs 11–6, Wed and Fri 10–3, Sat–Sun 10–4; adm*). Like most Polish museums, there is a frustrating lack of English signs and the fleets of dour, unsmiling guards can be off-putting; nonetheless it offers a fascinating glimpse into the city's past. It's worth investing in the English-language guide in the bookshop. On the ground floor, photographs show how the Old Town Square looked before and after the devastation of the Second World War, and chart its painstaking restoration from charred ruins. Rebuilding should have begun in 1945, but didn't begin until 1948: this is brushed over as a mere 'difference of opinion' and there is no mention of the fact that many of Poland's smaller towns, particularly Szczecin, were forced to sacrifice their historic buildings and monuments to rebuild the capital.

Few of Warsaw's ancient treasures survived the terrible fires, but there are some medieval charters and seals, Renaissance statuary and early woodcuts illustrating Warsaw's development from small market town to opulent capital from the 15th–17th centuries. Look out for a copy of an 18th-century allegory which shows Josef II of Germany and Frederic III of Prussia arguing over a map of Poland, as Catherine the Great pulls off a chunk for herself and King Stanisław August tries in vain to keep his crown from slipping. Poland may have been divided summarily between its powerful neighbours, but it continually revolted against its oppressors and there are portraits of famous heroes, including the leader of the 1794 Insurrection Tadeusz Kościuszko (*see* Kraków), and exhibits describing the November Rising in 1830. The top floor is dedicated to the city during the Second World War, with stark exhibits (none, sadly, signposted in English) describing the work of the Resistance, the Ghetto Uprising (*see* p.31), and a wealth of photographs (including some depicting executions) and documents showing the horrors that the citizens of Warsaw endured during the Nazi occupation.

Across the square, two delightful merchant houses now contain the interesting **Adam Mickiewicz Literature Museum** (Muzeum Literatury im. Adama Mickiewicza; *open Mon–Tues and Fri 10–3, Wed–Thurs 11–6, Sun 11–5; closed Sat; adm*), dedicated to Poland's finest Romantic poet, with original manuscripts, first editions, curios and memorabilia gathered in elegant period salons outlining his life and work. In 1823,

Mickiewicz (1798–1855) was arrested for joining an anti-Russian clandestine organisation, jailed and sent into exile. He would never see his homeland again. After his release he finally settled in France where his nationalism intensified, and his idealistic poetry and drama, particularly the epic poem *Pan Tadeusz*, became anthems for the oppressed Poles. He died during a cholera epidemic in Turkey, where he was trying to raise forces to overturn the Russians.

Ul. Świętojańska leads down from the Old Market Square to Plac Zamkowy and Warsaw Castle (*see* p.28), past the imposing red-brick stepped gable of **St John's Cathedral** (Katedra św. Jana; *open Mon–Sat 10–6, Sun 2–6; adm to crypt*), the oldest church in Warsaw and, like the rest of the old city, rebuilt from ruins after the war. It was begun in 1339, and only finally raised to the status of a cathedral in 1798, but it retains a deeply symbolic place in the hearts of all Poles: it was here that the last Polish king, Stanisław August Poniatowski, was crowned in 1764 and where the Polish Parliament (Sejm) was sworn in after the constitution of 1791, and the crypt contains the remains of Poland's first president, Gabriel Narutowicz, assassinated only two days after taking the presidential oath in 1922. The cathedral is filled with sumptuous tombs, including those of the dukes of Mozavia, and the faithful still pray to the 16th-century *Baryczka Crucifix* which has been credited with several miracles. At the rear of the cathedral, the covered passage that links it to the Royal Castle was added after a failed assassination attempt on King Zygmunt III in 1620. According to local legend, Michał Piekarski, would-be assassin of the king, was punished by being skinned alive, stretched between four horses, having his hands chopped off and finally being dispatched with a blunt axe. Unsurprisingly, he babbled incoherently during his torture, leading to the local saying 'to mutter like Piekarski'.

New Town (Nowe Miasto)

Follow ul. Nowomiejska north from the Old Town Square to the city walls, passing through the sturdy **Barbican** (Barbakan), a 16th-century bastion with a passage that now doubles as a small craft market. The elegant, tranquil New Town began to develop outside the old city's defensive walls from the 14th century, and was granted its own charter in 1408. When the New Town was incorporated into Warsaw in 1791, a slew of handsome Baroque mansions sprang up and its churches were elegantly remodelled. After the Second World War, New Town was rebuilt to look much as it would have in the early 19th century when it was regarded as one of the city's most fashionable neighbourhoods.

Heading up ul. Freta, the twin-spired **Church of the Holy Spirit** (Kościół św. Ducha) is the traditional starting point for an important pilgrimage to the Polish Holy-of-Holies, the Black Madonna at Częstochowa, and almost faces the even more extravagant Baroque church of **St Jacek** (Kościół św. Jacka). At No.16, you can visit the former home of Nobel-prize winning scientist Marie Curie, now a **museum** (Muzeum Marii Skłodowskiej-Curie; *open Tues–Sat 10–4, Sun 10–2; adm*) dedicated to her life and Nobel Prize-winning work in physics and chemistry.

The serene, tree-lined **New Town Square** (Rynek Nowego Miasta) is dominated by the sleek neoclassical church of **St Casimir** (Kościół św. Kazmierza) with a lofty dome.

The palace-lined street of Ul. Zakroczymska leads smoothly north to the leafy **Traugutt Gardens** which spread languidly around the **Citadel**, a vast pentagon-shaped fortress enclosed by massive walls studded with forbidding gateways. The fortress was built by the Russians in the wake of the Insurrection of 1830, and became a terrifying symbol of their determination to crush the Poles. Insult was added to injury when the Poles were forced to bankroll the massive construction costs. The infamous Tenth Pavilion was used to hold Polish political prisoners, many of whom were executed on the slopes of the Citadel, while thousands more were sent to Siberian labour camps. It's now an outpost of the **Museum of Independence** (Muzeum Niepodległości; *open Wed–Sun 9–4; adm*), and you can explore the network of tunnels and dingy cells, and see the photographs, weaponry and other exhibits dedicated to the 40,000 prisoners who passed through the Citadel's gates.

The Royal Castle and the Royal Way

Plac Zamkowy, on the edge of the Old Town, is dominated by the impressive complex of Warsaw's **Royal Castle** (Zamek Królewski; *www.zamek-krolewski.art.pl; open Tues–Sun 10–4, Sun 11–4; adm, free on Sun*), meticulously restored at dizzying expense during the 1970s and 80s, although patches of blackened stone are chilling reminders of the destruction wrought by the Nazis who blew it up in 1944. Dating back to the 14th century, the palace was expanded and remodelled in lavish Renaissance style under King Zygmunt III when the Polish capital was transferred from Kraków to Warsaw in the late 16th century. It is now filled with a magnificent collection of period furniture, paintings and *objets d'art*, although, in time-honoured Polish tradition, some galleries are sure to be closed.

There are two colour-coded routes (*separate adm for each*) for the castle interiors: the Blue takes in the sumptuous Jagiellonian Rooms, and includes admission to the **Parliamentary chambers** where the Polish constitution (the second in the world after that of the USA) was passed in 1791; while the Yellow takes in the even more opulent **Baroque apartments** commissioned by Stanisław August Poniatowski, the **Royal Chapel** (where Tadeusz Kościuszko's heart is kept in a silver urn) and the glittering **ballroom**. On Sundays (*free*), a single tour takes in the highlights of both routes.

The second floor contains a series of permanent exhibitions dedicated to the decorative arts, including the **Lanckoroński Gallery**, which features some outstanding paintings including a pair of works by Rembrandt, and the **Gallery of Decorative Arts** which brings together almost 200 *objets d'art* from ancient Oriental porcelain to vast tapestries, many of which originally belonged to the castle and were spirited away before the Nazi invasion.

Sweeping grandly from the Royal Castle towards the beautiful Łazienki Park (*see* p.32), the **Krakowskie Przedmieście** and its continuation, **Nowy Świat**, has been Warsaw's most aristocratic boulevard for centuries, known as the **Royal Way** (Trakt Królewski). It is still flanked with an eye-popping array of splendid churches, opulent palaces and flamboyant monuments – increasingly interspersed with the city's chicest boutiques, restaurants and shops.

The elegant neoclassical façade of **St Anne's Church** (Kościół św. Anny) was tacked on to the original Gothic construction, while the interior is Baroque at its most fanciful, with plenty of giddy stucco and gilt. This is the university church, and tradition has it that all marriages celebrated here will be happy, making it a popular choice with students. The early 19th-century **belltower** (*open May–Oct daily 11–8; adm*) can be climbed for splendid views. Just beyond the pretty, globe-topped **Carmelite Church**, the grand **Namiestnikowski Palace** (Pałac Namiestnikowski; *not open to visitors*) has been the official residence of Polish presidents since 1994, and is where the Warsaw Pact was formally ratified in 1955.

It's worth a detour down the charming cobbled alley of **ul. Kozia**, one of the most atmospheric of the city centre's old-fashioned streets. It runs parallel to Krakowskie Przedmieście and is also home to the excellent little **Caricature Museum** (Muzeum Karykatury; *open Tues–Sun 11pm–5pm; adm*), the only one in Europe.

Back on the Royal Way, the historic **Hotel Bristol** (*see* p.22) has been restored to its former splendour and remains the most atmospheric of the city's luxury hotels. Beyond it lies the vast and impressive complex of **Warsaw University** (Uniwersytet Warszawski), spread behind ornamental wrought-iron gates. The pair of fine aristocratic mansions on either side are also part of the university: the **Tyszkiewicz Palace** (Pałac Tyszkiewiczow) at No.32 and the **Uruski Palace** (Pałac Uruskich) at No.30. The elegant **Czapski Palace** (Pałac Czapskich) opposite is now part of the Warsaw Fine Arts Academy. Close by, the church of **St Joseph the Guardian** (Kościół Opieki św. Józefa) is one of the only churches in Warsaw to have survived the Second World War relatively unharmed, and its interior retains the original 18th-century fittings.

The handsome twin spires of the **Church of the Holy Cross** (Kościół św. Krzyża) dominate the southern end of Krakowskie Przedmieście, and an urn just off the left aisle famously contains the heart of Frédéric Chopin (1810–1849). Chopin fans can make the short stroll east to the elegant 18th-century **Ostrogski Palace** (Pałac Gnińskich-Ostrogskich; *ul. Okólnik 1, www.chopin.pl; open summer Mon, Wed and Fri 10–5, Thurs 12–6, Sat–Sun 10–2; winter Mon, Wed and Fri–Sat 10–2, Thurs 12–6; closed Tues; adm*) which contains a small museum dedicated to Frédéric Chopin (1810–1849), with manuscripts, letters and a grand piano on which he composed some of his best-known works. It also regularly hosts concerts.

Around PKiN

Leave behind the Baroque splendour of the Krakowskie Przedmieście and head west down al. Świętokrzyska to the heart of the modern city, where bombastic monuments to the Soviet age are clustered amid grey, boxy residential blocks. This may not be the most attractive part of the city, but it's certainly the most vibrant, and the monolithic Soviet Realist structures have an oddly exotic appeal.

The intersection with al. Marszałkowska is the best place to spot these strange beasts, of which the tallest and most bizarre is the enormous **PKiN** (Pałac Kultury i Nauki, Palace of Culture and Science) at Plac Defilad 1. Built by the Russians between 1952–5, it was the second-highest building in Europe when completed, and still dominates the entire city. It was originally intended to house the Communist Party HQ, but now contains a complex of restaurants, museums and a vast Congress Hall where the Rolling Stones played to an ecstatic audience in 1967. For incredible panoramic views, take the elevator to the blustery **viewing platform** on the 30th floor (*open June–Aug 9–8; Sept–May 9–6; adm*).

For a reminder of pre-war Warsaw, head to the wonderful **Bracia Jabłkowscy** department store nearby at ul. Bracka 25, with early 20th-century stained glass and marble, which has been recently revamped to contain a host of chichi boutiques. You could also stop for a hot chocolate at the **Wedel Pâtisserie** on ul. Szpitalna: Emil Wedel is Poland's best-known chocolatier, and this turn-of-the-20th-century café still retains its glittering chandeliers and gleaming wooden counters. If, however, you want another dose of Socialist Realism, continue down al. Marsałkowska to **Plac Konstytucji**, laid out in the early 1950s as a focal point for state parades, and the heart of the MDM housing development.

Poland's newest and most talked-about museum is located a 10-minute walk west of PKiN: the **Warsaw Uprising Museum** (Muzeum Powstania Warszawskiego; *ul. Przyokopowa, www.1944.pl; check website for opening hours*) is located in a massive former tramway power station, and partially opened on 1st August 2004, the sixtieth anniversary of the Uprising (*see* 'History') in an emotional ceremony attended by more than 3,000 veterans. The museum has yet to be completed, but the high-tech exhibits and installations promise to attract huge numbers of visitors. One of the highlights of the museum is an extraordinary collection of photographs taken by ex-Olympic athlete and platoon commander Eugeniusz Lokajski which provided incontrovertible proof of the slaughter of the people of Warsaw – despite the efforts of the Communist regime to expunge the Uprising from history for forty years after the war had ended, partly because of tensions over why the Soviets didn't help.

The Jewish Ghetto

Almost nothing remains of Warsaw's Jewish quarter: razed to the ground during the Second World War, it's now a bleak neighbourhood just to the east of the Old Town with ranks of stark, standard Soviet blocks. The area remains a place of pilgrimage, and a **Path of Remembrance** links the central Umschlagplatz with the Monument to the Ghetto Heroes on the corner of Zamenhofa and Anielewicza streets. Along the route, 16 black granite blocks with inscriptions in Polish and Hebrew commemorate all the Jews who died and each single out a particular hero, including Adam Czerniakow and Mordecai Anielewicz.

More than 300,000 Jews were transported to their deaths from the **Umschlagplatz**, and they are commemorated in a boxy white marble monument that recalls the cattle wagons in which they were transported. Among the names inscribed on the monument is that of Janusz Korczak, the director of a Jewish orphanage who insisted on accompanying his young charges to the death camp at Treblinka. The powerful **Monument to the Ghetto Heroes** (Pomnik Bohaterów Getta) overlooks a grassy expanse which was once the centre of the Ghetto, and depicts the Jews being pushed towards their deaths by the Nazis. Ironically, the stone cladding used on the monument was ordered by Hitler and was originally intended to be used for a victory arch.

The Ghetto Uprising

In August 1940, Warsaw was split into three zones: German, Polish and Jewish. Around 450,000 Jews were crammed into a tiny area which was then walled off. By August 1942, the Jews were being herded on to cattle wagons bound for the death camp at Treblinka. Adam Czerniakow (1880–1942), who had refused to escape and abandon his fellow Jews, was leader of the Judenrat (the Jewish council established by the Nazis), but committed suicide after he was pressured to hand over Jewish children to be deported and sent to their deaths. In 1943, after the second wave of deportations had begun, the desperate Jews led by Mordecai Anielewicz (1919–43) rose against the Nazis, only to be viciously put down with tanks, flame-throwers and aerial bombardments. The Jewish Ghetto was razed to the ground, and barely 300 of Warsaw's Jews survived the war.

The Polish authorities have recently announced that a new Museum of Jewish History commemorating eight centuries of Jewish presence in Poland will be built close to the Monument to the Ghetto Heroes, and should be completed by 2008.

West of the Umschlagplatz, the **Jewish History Institute** (Żydowski Insytut Historyczny; *ul. Tłomackie 1–5; museum open Mon–Wed and Fri 9–4, Thurs 11–6; adm*) contains a research library and extensive archives, along with a small museum containing relics of the ghetto and the death camps. To the south of Umschlagplatz, the grim **Pawiak Prison** (Więzienie Pawiak; *ul. Dzielna 24; open Wed 9–5, Thurs and Sat 9–4, Fri 10–5, Sun 10–4; closed Mon and Tues; under 14s not admitted*) was erected by the Tsarist Russians, but became a feared Gestapo prison during the Second World War. Dynamited as the Nazis fled, it has been restored as a harrowing memorial to the 100,000 Jewish and Polish prisoners who passed through its gates, most of whom were executed or sent to the death camps. At the entrance, a charred and twisted tree is still thickly hung with obituary notices dating back to 1994.

The National Museum, and around Łazienki Park

The beautiful park of Łazienki is one of the loveliest and most romantic of any European city, a graceful, tree-filled expanse scattered with lakes, statues, pavilions and palaces. Clustered around the fringes of the park are some of the city's most important museums and cultural institutions, along with the Parliament building and a clutch of embassies housed in opulent 19th-century villas along the graceful Ujazdowskie avenue.

Poland's most important museum, the **National Museum** (Muzeum Narodowe; *al. Jerozolimskie 4, www.mnw.art.pl; open Tues–Sun 10–7; adm, free on Sat*), is located in a vast, dour Modernist building to the north of the Embassy district. Although many of its treasures were lost or stolen during the Second World War, it still contains an extraordinary collection of painting, sculpture, decorative arts, antiquities and coins, spanning several millennia. Among the highlights is a fine collection of Greek vases from between the 10th and 3rd centuries BC, a stunning array of medieval religious frescoes rescued from the Nubian town of Faras (in present-day Sudan), exquisite medieval Polish altarpieces and a vast collection of paintings by some of Poland's most celebrated artists. This includes Jan Matejko's heroic historical paintings, such as the celebrated *Battle of Grunwald*, and emotionally wrought self-portraits by Stanisław Wyspiański. The museum's greatest treasure is Botticelli's luminous *Virgin and Child*, in the galleries dedicated to 14th–18th-century Italian and French painting; there is also a spectacular array of Polish decorative arts, with beautifully crafted furniture, glassware, porcelain and gold.

Next door, the **Polish Military Museum** (Muzeum Wojska Polskiego; *al. Jerozolimskie 3, Wed–Sun 11–5; adm*) is almost as vast, and contains ranks of armour, weaponry, tattered banners, uniforms and sumptuous silk tents and carpets taken from the Turks as booty after the Battle of Vienna in 1683. The park contains tanks and aircraft from the Second World War.

Stroll south along the elegant al. Ujazdowskie, flanked on one side by the handsome 19th-century palaces now largely occupied by embassies and on the other by the serene and leafy **Park Ujazdowski**. Overlooking a tranquil lake, the handsome Baroque Ujazdowski Palace now contains the city's excellent **Centre for Contemporary Art** (Centrum Sztuki Współczesnej; *al. Ujazdowskie 6, www.csw.art.pl; open Tues–Thurs and Sat–Sun 11–5, Fri 11–9; closed Mon; adm*), one of Warsaw's most exciting and innovative art centres which hosts temporary art exhibitions as well as organising theatre, dance and film events. There's an excellent café boasting beautiful views. A corner of the park contains the immaculate **Botanical Gardens** (Ogród Botaniczny; *al. Ujazdowskie 4; open April–Oct Mon–Fri 9–8, Sat–Sun 10–8; adm*) with a charming medicinal garden and a host of exotic plants and trees.

Spreading languidly south of here is the lovely **Łazienki Park** (Park Łazienkowski), laid out in the 18th-century, with manicured gardens, tree-fringed lakes and a smattering of sumptuous palaces. On Sundays, half of Warsaw seems to congregate here, strolling along the peaceful paths and picnicking on the elegant lawns. Regular concerts are held on Sundays in summer by the Secessionist **Chopin monument** close to the entrance, and sinuous paths snake gently through oak groves towards the magnificent **Łazienki Palace**, commonly known as the Palace on the Water for its breathtaking location straddling the river. The original 17th-century bathing pavilion which gave the park its name (Łazienki means 'bath') was completely remodelled in splendid neoclassical style to serve as a royal residence during the late 18th century for the last Polish king, Stanisław August Poniatowski. The fleeing Nazis intended to blow it up, but ran out of time and set fire to it instead, leaving the palace substantially intact. Now beautifully restored, it has become a hugely popular **museum** (*open Tues–Sun 9.30–4; closed Mon; adm, free on Sat*), and the opulent interiors offer a spellbinding glimpse into the magnificence of the Polish royal court at the end of the 18th century. Numerous smaller palaces, pavilions and follies are strewn around the elegant gardens, and the charming amphitheatre poised on an island in front of the palace is still occasionally used for summer performances. The graceful **Orangerie** contains one of the few surviving 18th-century theatres in Europe, with an immaculately preserved interior of swirling stucco and elaborately carved woodwork.

Outside the Centre

Warsaw's most extravagant royal residence, the **Wilanów Palace and Park**
(*ul. St Potockiego 1, www.wilanow-palac.art.pl, bus 116, 130 164, 180, 410 or 522 from the
city centre; open winter Mon and Wed–Sun 9–4; summer Mon and Thurs–Sat 9–4, Wed
9–6, Sun 9–7; closed Tues; visitors admitted until one hour before closing; adm, park and
Orangerie free on Thurs*) lies in extensive parklands on the west of the city and has
been nicknamed the 'Versailles of Poland'. This vast, exuberantly Baroque palace was
constructed as a summer residence for King Jan III Sobieski, who was tinkering with
its design right up until his death in 1696. It remained popular with subsequent
monarchs, each of whom had it extended and remodelled to suit the fashions of the
age, but what survives still largely reflects Sobieski's original vision. The sumptuous
interior can be visited as part of a guided tour, and includes the glorious Baroque
chambers at the centre of the palace, the equally opulent 18th-century South Wing,
and the stiffly formal 19th-century wing added by the Potockis, all filled with lavish
furniture, wall hangings and exquisite *objets d'art*. The second floor contains the celebrated portrait galleries, with paintings from the 16th to the 19th centuries, and
includes Jacques-Louis David's masterly portrait of Stanisław Kostka Potocki astride a
prancing horse. The palace is surrounded by stunning **formal gardens**: an elaborate
Baroque ornamental garden descends in steps to the lake, and charming English- and
Chinese-style gardens were added during the 18th century. The **Orangerie** now
contains a collection of Polish folk art.

Northwest of the city centre, on the fringes of the former Jewish Ghetto (*see*
pp.30–31), Warsaw's oldest cemeteries are nudged up against each other at **Powązki**
(*ul. Powązkowska; open daily dawn till dusk*). The vast, tree-filled Catholic section is
filled with opulent tombs and mausoleums, many belonging to famous writers,
musicians and politicians. The adjoining Jewish Cemetery is ill-kept and overgrown,
yet even more atmospheric: among the tombs is a poignant monument to Janusz
Korczak, the orphanage director who accompanied his wards to the death camps.

Day Trips from Warsaw

Żelazowa Wola (Frédéric Chopin Birthplace)

The tiny village of Żelazowa Wola sits prettily on the fringes of the extensive forests
of the Kampinos National Park. On March 1 1810, Frédéric Chopin (christened Fryderyk
Szopen) was born in a charming whitewashed villa, and, although his parents left
when he was only a year old, he regularly returned to this simple Mazovian village.
Bought by public subscription in 1929, the house was restored to its early 19th-
century aspect and opened as a museum in 1931. After a few brief years in existence,
the Nazis plundered it and banned the public performance of Chopin's music. It was
restored once again after the Second World War and has become a shrine to Poland's
de facto national composer.

Getting There

It is possible, but slightly awkward, to reach Żelazowa Wola, 50km west of Warsaw, by public transport. If you don't have your own transport, consider taking a tour, which is more expensive but less inconvenient (ask at the tourist office in Warsaw, or at Mazurkas Travel, *see* p.21). Otherwise, you can take a train from Warsaw's Zachodnia station for Sochaczew, and then take local bus no.6 to Żelazowa Wola. There are also infrequent direct buses, which depart from Warsaw's main bus terminal.

Tourist Information

Available from the main tourist information office in Warsaw (*see* above); they can also book excursions to Żelazowa Wola. The Chopin Society, *www.chopin.pl*, can provide information on concert schedules.

Eating Out

Pod Wierzbami, a typical local inn, is one of the few places to eat in little Żelazowa Wola, but is convenient and inexpensive.

The house is a typical Mazovian country residence, and has preserved many charming details such as the painted ceiling in the kitchen. For music fans, the bedroom in which baby Frédéric was born, and the cases full of musical manuscripts, will be of more interest. In summer, **concerts** are held on Sundays at 11am and 3pm, with extra performances at 11am on Saturdays in July and August. Many of the tour operators from Warsaw include a concert with the price of the excursion, and also take groups to the little church in **Brochów**, 11km northwest, where Chopin's parents were married and their son baptised.

Pułtusk

The appealing little market town of Pułtusk has a thousand-year-old history, and its historic core is perched daintily on an island in the Narew river. The town reached the peak of its fortunes during the 15th and 16th centuries, when it was the seat of the bishops of Płock, who liberally endowed the town with churches and palaces. Unfortunately, it was virtually destroyed during a vicious battle between the Russians and the Napoleonic armies in 1806 and left in ruins once more at the end of the Second World War. However, after an extensive renovation programme Pułtusk has reconstructed its harmonious old centre, which centres on an expansive cobbled **market square** (Rynek), one of the largest in Europe. The town's finest monuments are clustered here, including the solid 15th-century town hall in the centre of the square, which once formed part of the city's defences and which is now a **regional museum** (Muzeum Regionalne; *Rynek 1; open summer Tues–Sat 10–4; winter Sat–Sun 10–4;*

Getting There

Pułtusk is served by frequent **buses** (roughly every 30mins) from Warsaw.

Tourist Information

Available from the main tourist information office in Warsaw (*see* p.21).

Eating Out

Dom Polonii, ul. Szkolna 11, **t** (023) 692 9000. The Dom Polonii contains a clutch of restaurants, serving everything from top-notch Polish cuisine to down-to-earth local favourites for a modest price. It also has a good café serving delicious cakes (try the 'Apple in a Gown').

adm). It contains all kinds of odds and ends gathered during the archaeological digs that preceded the town's reconstruction, from tiles to wooden boats. Climb the lofty tower for fabulous views. Dominating the square is the handsome Gothic-Renaissance **Collegiate Church of the Virgin Mary**, which contains an exquisite Renaissance chapel, and to the south is the remarkable circular **castle** which formerly belonged to the Bishops of Płock, now a luxurious hotel and conference centre (Dom Polonii) specifically created for Polish emigrés but open to all. The castle gardens, laid out after the moat was filled in during the 16th century, lead gently down to the riverside, where paths continue along the riverbanks and there are plenty of opportunities to mess about in boats. You can hire one of the traditional wooden Pułtusk 'gondolas', skippered by staff in local costume.

A Mini-tour from Warsaw

You can make an overnight trip that takes in the birthplace of Frédéric Chopin, a Baroque palace, a romantic garden and a modest little Polish town which is famous for its arts and crafts. It's designed for those with their own car, but all of the places mentioned are accessible by public transport (the Warsaw tourist information office can provide bus and train timetables).

Day 1: Chopin and Shoppin'

Morning: Head west of Warsaw on the 580 for 50km through the rolling Mazovian plain, and visit Chopin's birthplace at **Żelazowa Wola**. Time your visit, if possible, to coincide with the summer weekend piano recitals at 11am.

Lunch: Tuck into Polish specialities at the Pod Wierzbami (*see* box, top left opposite).

Afternoon: Take the 2/E30 another 30km west to the ancient Mazovian town of **Łowicz**, seat of the archbishops of Gniezno for more than six centuries and now famously a centre for local crafts. You can stroll around the clutch of splendid churches which are the legacy of the archbishops, explore the fascinating regional museum on the market square (Rynek), or pick up some local embroidered fabrics, glassware or pretty, naïve folk paintings to be found in the many craft shops. The town has a smattering of reasonable hotels and restaurants which make it a good place for an overnight stay.

Dinner and Sleeping: Zajazd Łowicki, ul. Blich 36, **t** (046) 837 4164 (*inexpensive*) is a simple but charming hotel, with a friendly, family atmosphere and spacious if rather basic rooms. There's also a good restaurant (*inexpensive*). Zacisze, ul. Kaliska 5, **t** (046) 837 3326 (*inexpensive*) is another modest but central option, with comfortable rooms and a decent restaurant.

Day 2: A Garden and a Palace

Morning: Drive 10km southeast of Łowicz (on the 70) towards the village of **Nieborów**, and stop for a stroll through the deeply romantic gardens of **Arkadia** (*open May–Sept Tues–Sun 10–6; Oct–April Tues–Sun 10–4; adm*), established at the end of the 18th century by Princess Helena Radziwiłł, whose family owned the sumptuous Baroque Palace at Nieborów (*see* below). Strewn with classical temples and Gothic ruins, the gardens are made yet more atmospheric by the long neglect which has allowed them to run wild. Five kilometres further south, the immaculate Baroque **Nieborów Palace** was erected in the late 17th century and surrounded by elegant gardens. In the late 18th century, the palace was acquired by the wealthy Radziwiłł family. They lavishly remodelled it and filled it with exquisite furnishing and artworks, including a celebrated classical bust of Niobe. Now an outpost of the National Museum in Warsaw, it has become a spectacular **museum** (*open May–Sept Tues–Sun 10–6; Oct–April Tues–Sun 10–4; adm*).

Lunch: The palace contains a good restaurant and café for lunch, or you could try one of the old-fashioned inns in the village.

Afternoon: Return to Warsaw along the same route.

Kraków

Kraków, the ancient capital and spiritual heart of Poland, is a miraculously beautiful city: invaded by Tatars and Turks, Russians and Prussians, annexed and deprived of its independence, it has emerged astonishingly unscathed from a thousand years of often tragic history. Its serene medieval core spreads in an elegant grid from one of the largest and most beautiful squares in Europe, and has a place on UNESCO's list as one of the twelve most important historical sites in the world. With the fall of the Iron Curtain, and Poland's new membership of the EU, Kraków is enjoying a boom: the new affluence shows in the recently cleaned façades of its historic buildings, the proliferation of smart restaurants and boutique hotels, the chic little cafés and drinking dens, and the sheer numbers of visitors who congregate in this most congenial of cities.

But it isn't just foreign tourists who are flooding to Kraków: the city has long held a deeply symbolic place in the hearts of all Poles. The castle at Wawel was the glittering residence of Polish kings for more than five hundred years, and all but four of the Polish monarchs are buried in the cathedral. Here, too, lie the coffins of Polish saints and martyrs, military heroes and national poets. It was in Kraków's main square that Tadeusz Kościuszko, hero of the Insurrection of 1794, swore to regain Poland's freedom. He is buried in the Cathedral, and commemorated in a huge mound on the edge of the city. Kraków is the city of the great historical painter Jan Matejko, who celebrated momentous events in Polish history, and cradle of the Young Poland movement at the end of the 19th century which took Art Nouveau and made it uniquely Polish at a time when the nation had no official existence. The workers at the Soviet-built steel works of Nowa Huta on the outskirts of Kraków were instrumental in the downfall of the Communist government, rioting during the period of Martial Law in the 1980s and remaining staunchly faithful to the Catholic Church. Ironically, it is the Nowa Huta steelworks that have given the city its current biggest headache: the acid rain caused by the pollution has corroded the ancient stone of many of the inner city's historic edifices, and, although toxic emissions have now been reduced, they remain a serious problem.

The last ghosts of the Communist era have virtually been laid to rest. It's sometimes hard to get a smile from the older generation, who usually speak no English and gaze balefully at the crowds of foreign tourists milling around the Market Square. But Kraków is a university city, with students making up about 10 per cent of the population: with their confident English, logo-emblazoned clothes and mobile phones, they have become the face of the new, westernized Poland. Cafés, once the haunt of Solidarity-supporters and intellectuals, have proliferated, and become the trendy meeting places of boho-chic hipsters in designer clothes. Many of these are concentrated in Kazimierz, formerly home to the city's vast Jewish community, obliterated in the death camps during the Second World War. Kazimierz is beginning to reclaim its roots, with new museums, cultural centres and the renovation of its ancient monuments, helped in part by the success of the film *Schindler's List* (1993).

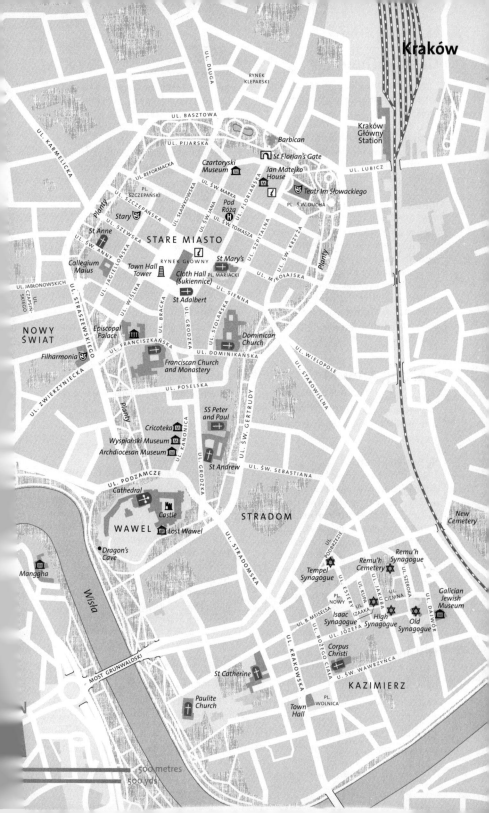

Getting There

See **Getting There**, pp.4–10. You can also take a train from Warsaw, which takes just under three hours.

Getting from the Airport

John Paul II International Airport at Kraków is in Balice, 11km west of the city centre. Facilities include a bank, *bureau de change*, ATM, shops, cafés and several car rental offices (*see* below). More information from *www. lotnisko-balice.pl*, **t** (012) 285 51 20.

Bus nos.192 and 208 (single fare 2.70 zł) link the airport with the city centre and depart regularly from outside the terminal. Timetables are available at *www.mpk. krakow.pl* and *www.komunikacja.krakow.pl*.

There is a **taxi** rank outside the terminal. Fares into the city centre cost around 40 zł, although note that fares rise after 11pm. Always ask for a receipt.

Getting Around

The best way to see Kraków is on foot: the tiny, egg-shaped core of the Old City is packed with most of the major sights, and much of it is pedestrianized.

By Bus and Tram

Beautifully battered old **trams** (and an ever-growing number of smart new ones) clatter over the cobbles in the old city, and out to the suburbs. Timetables and tram route numbers are posted at all stops. **Bus** services complement the tram system, and the older versions have a shabby retro charm all of their own. Again, timetables and route numbers are posted at stops. Standard single tickets and passes are not valid on **night buses**.

Tickets are valid on buses and trams and are available from news stands, kiosks, and shops

with the MPK symbol. Single tickets can be bought from the driver with a 0.50 zł surcharge. Tickets are available for a single journey (2.80 zł), one hour (3 zł), one day (9 zł), 24hrs (10 zł), and 48hrs (18 zł).

One-day family tickets, weekly and monthly **passes** are also available. Stamp your ticket in the machine next to the doors, and hang on to it as there are frequent ticket inspections.

The Kraków Card (*see* below) offers free public transport.

By Taxi

Taxis can be picked up at numerous taxi ranks, but fares are up to a third cheaper if you order one by phone. Taxi numbers include **t** (012) 9621, **t** (012) 9622, **t** (012) 9623 and **t** (012) 9625.

By Car

The old city has strict parking rules: parking spaces are few and far between, car parks fill up quickly and most of the city centre is closed to traffic anyway. If you're hiring a car to follow the tour (see pp.57–8), leave your car in a car park and forget about it while you are in the city.

Car Hire

Avis, **t** (012) 629 6108 (city), **t** 0601 200 702 (airport), *www.avis.pl*.
Europcar, **t** (012) 633 7773 (city), **t** (012) 285 5045 (airport), *www.europcar.com.pl*.
Hertz, **t** (012) 429 6262 (city), **t** (012) 285 5084 (airport), *www.hertz.com.pl*.
Budget, **t** (012) 637 0089 (city), **t** (012) 285 5025 (airport), *www.budget.com*.
Joka, **t** (012) 429 6630 (city), *www.joka.com.pl*.

By Bike

Rent a bike and give yourself your own guided tour – particularly around outlying areas such as the woods of Las Wolski.

History

Wawel Hill has been settled since prehistoric times, but little is known of Kraków's early history. By the 10th century the settlement, located at the nexus of major east–west trading routes, had grown into an affluent city and bishopric. In the first half of the 11th century, Kraków became capital of the emerging Polish kingdom under **Kazimierz Odnowiciel** (Kasimir the Restorer) of the Piast dynasty. A century later, Boleslaus the Wrymouth divided the Polish kingdom into three duchies, of which the

Jordan Travel Agency, ul. Długa 9, t (012) 421 2125.
Renting Bicycles, ul. Józefa 5, t (012) 421 5785.

Festivals

The following are just some of the vast number of festivals and events that take place every year in Kraków. The tourist office have a comprehensive calendar of events: *see www.krakow.pl.*

Mar: **International Festival of Alternative Theatre**: a prestigious and long-running contemporary theatre festival.

May: **Constitution Day**: Poland's national holiday is celebrated with parades and fairs; **Juvenalia**: for a week in May (dates vary), Kraków's students take to the streets in crazy costumes and party hard in the city's clubs and bars; **Corpus Christi**: solemn procession from Wawel Cathedral to the Rynek Główny.

June: **Kraków Summer**: a huge number of festivals, special cultural events, concerts and performances are held between June and August; information from *www.krakow2000.pl*; **Jewish Cultural Festival**: a major celebration of Jewish history and culture in Kazimierz, *www.jewishfestival.pl*; **Lajkonik Pageant**: parade of the Kraków Hobby Horse through the city streets in commemoration of Kraków's victory over the Tatars in 1287, takes place a week after Corpus Christi, *www.mhk.pl*; **Wianki**: on Midsummer's Eve, wreaths of flowers and herbs set with candles are traditionally sent floating down the river, and there are concerts and a spectacular firework show from the castle

June–Aug: **Organ concerts** in Tyniec, *see* p.53.

Aug: '**Music in Old Kraków' International Festival**: classical music in historic venues

around the city, *www.capellacracoviensis. art.pl.*

Oct: **Organ Music Festival**: recitals in the Philharmonic Hall and in churches around the city, *www.filharmonica.krakow.pl.*

Nov–Dec: **Christmas markets** on the Rynek Główny and other squares around the city; children present their *szopki* (nativity scenes) and a prize for the best one is awarded; **New Year's Eve** is celebrated with much carousing on the Rynek Główny.

Tourist Information

Kraków: City tourist information office, ul. Szpitalna 25, t (012) 432 0060, *www. krakow.pl.*

Małoposka tourist information office, Rynek Główny 1 (in Sukiennice Cloth Hall), t (012) 421 7706. Information on the whole Małoposka (Little Poland) region as well as Kraków.

The **Kraków Card**, *www.krakowcard.com*, is valid for two (45 zł) or three (60 zł) days, and offers free admission to most of the city's main museums, free public transport and discounts for tours, restaurants and shops. It is also valid on bus 192 out to the airport. Note that Wawel Castle is not included in the card.

Guided Tours and Excursions

Walking tours: **Guide Kraków**, *www.guide-cracow.pl*, offer a range of tours with multilingual guides: information on tours and the guides is available on the website. Walking tours of the old city and Kazimierz are organized by **Kraków Tours**, *www.krakow-tours.com*, led by young, enthusiastic guides.

Jewish tours: The **Jarden** bookshop and café, ul. Szeroka 2, t (012) 421 7166, *www.jarden.pl*, runs guided tours of the city and outside, focusing on Jewish heritage, including tours

---

Duchy of Kraków remained the most important. In 1241, Kraków was destroyed by the Tatars, but was rebuilt a few years later to the elegant grid plan centred around a vast central square which still survives. The city flourished under **King Kazimierz the Great** (1333–70) who established Europe's third-oldest university and founded Kazmierz. On his death, the crown passed briefly to Ludwig I Węgierski, the king of Hungary, but the Poles chose Ludwig's daughter, **Jadwiga** (1384–99), to succeed him. Jadwiga married Lithuanian Grand Duke Władysław Jagiełło (a pagan who was forced to be

of Kazimierz, Auschwitz and the death camps. The charismatic owner is full of fascinating information and wonderful stories. Highly recommended.

Boat excursions: Boat services operate from May to September. Żegluga Krakowska, t (012) 422 0855, run hour-long trips along the river past Wawel Castle, departures every 90mins Mon–Fri 9.30–7.30, Sat–Sun 9.30–4. They also have weekend cruises to Tyniec (see p.53). River trips are also offered by **River Tram, t** (mobile) 0503 900 218, and **Piotruś Pan Pleasure Boats, t** (012) 626 8140.

Bus tours: There are no bus tours of the tiny city centre but dozens of tour operators run visits to outlying attractions. The tourist information office has a full list, and most hotels can arrange trips.

Horse-drawn cabs: These depart, summer and winter, from next to the Cloth Hall in the Rynek Główny. An hour's trip costs around 120 zł, and a 30min trip is 60 zł. Haggling is expected, and you should agree the fare before setting off.

Shopping

The main shopping streets in Kraków are around the **Rynek Główny**, where international chains have mushroomed in recent years. International fashion labels are often considerably less expensive here and there is plenty of home-grown fashion to choose from.

For local crafts, wander past the ranks of little stalls in the **Cloth Hall**, which sell everything from hand-painted toys to traditional clothing. One of the most popular gift items is amber jewellery, which is very reasonable and often beautiful.

Polish glassware is also world-renowned, both old and new.

Books and Music
Empik, Rynek Główny 5, t (012) 422 0538. A huge, well-equipped store with books in several languages, CDs, maps and interffnational press, along with a good Internet café and coffee-shop.
High Fidelity, ul Podbrzeże 6, no tel. A cool little spot in Kazimierz, with plenty of second-hand vinyl, CDs and books to rummage through.
Massolit, ul. Felicjanek 4, t (012) 432 4150, www.massolit.com. The best English-language bookshop in the city, with a huge range of titles (new and second-hand).

Fashion and Accessories
Batycki, Rynek Główny, t (012) 617 0232. Fabulous range of fashionable bags and accessories by a well-known Polish designer.
Bielak Gallery, ul. Sławkowska 4, t (012) 422 8386. A stunning array of contemporary Polish jewellery by the country's top designers next to the Cloth Hall.

Gifts and Souvenirs
Mikołajczyki Amber, ul. Kanonicza 22, t (012) 422 3696. Gifts made from amber, including jewellery, chess sets and Art Nouveau-style lamps.
Glass and Ceramics Gallery, ul. Grodzka 29, t (012) 421 4419. A good range of contemporary glassware and ceramics by Polish designers.

Markets
Plac Nowy, Kazimierz. This market sells fresh produce market every day (7am–dusk) except Sunday, when a fabulous flea market takes over (Sun 7am–1pm).
Stary Kleparz, Rynek Kleparski. Located just to the north of the old town, this is one of the oldest fresh produce markets in Poland (daily 7am–dusk).

baptised before acceding to the throne), linking their territories in a vast empire which stretched from the Baltic to the Black Sea.

Under the Jagiellonian dynasty, Kraków experienced a Golden Age: the city was embellished in the Renaissance style, and under Jadwiga's patronage the university flourished, attracting students from Poland and across Europe, including astronomer Nicolaus Copernicus. When King Sigismund (Zygmunt) August (1520–72) died without heir, the **Republic of Nobles** was declared, by which the Polish aristocracy elected their

Sports and Activities

Football

Kraków's main football team, **Wisła Kraków** (*www.wisla.krakow.pl*), have been Polish champions since 1998. They play at the Wisła Stadium, ul. Reymonta, on the outskirts of town. Meanwhile, **Cracovia**, the oldest-established team in Poland, languish in the third division but can be seen at their stadium on ul. Józefa Kałuży.

Skiing

Zakopane (*see* p.58) is the nearest ski resort to Kraków, with spectacular skiing in the Tatra mountains.

Swimming

Park Wodny Swimming Pool, ul. Dobrego Pasterza 126, (012) 616 3190, *www.parkwodny.pl*. This is a glitzy, modern water park, 5km north of the centre, with wave pools, slides, a sauna and gym.

Where to Stay

Kraków t (012) –

★★★★**Hotel Copernicus**, ul. Kanonicza 16, t 424 3400, *www.hotel.com.pl* (*luxury*). George Bush stayed at this luxurious new hotel, in a beautifully renovated Gothic mansion at the foot of the Wawel Hill. The antique-furnished rooms with wooden-beamed ceilings are very atmospheric, but unfriendly service lets it down.

★★★★**Grand Hotel**, ul. Sławkowska 5–7, t (12) 421 7255, *www.grand.pl* (*luxury*). A palace is the setting for this swish hotel, which exudes *fin-de-siècle* charm, with antiques, chandeliers and beautifully restored original details including fireplaces and frescoes. There's a smart restaurant and café.

★★★★**Hotel Amadeus**, ul. Mikołajska 20, t 429 6070, *www.hotel-amadeus.pl* (*expensive*). A pretty, whitewashed charmer just a stone's throw from the Rynek Główny, the Amadeus has bright rooms, suites and an apartment, traditionally decorated with creamy floral prints. There's an excellent restaurant and café.

★★★★**Hotel Pugetów**, ul. Starowiślna 13-15, t 432 4950, *www.donimirski.com* (*expensive*). An intimate boutique-style hotel with individually decorated rooms full of antiques and period details. It's on a smart avenue, just outside the Planty gardens.

★★★**Hotel Pód Różą**, ul. Floriańska 14, t 424 3300, *www.hotel.com.pl* (*expensive*). One of the most enchanting hotels in the city, this Renaissance mansion on an elegant street just off the Rynek Główny has been lovingly refurbished. Most of the antique-filled rooms boast high ceilings and wooden beams, and there's a romantic restaurant.

★★★★**Hotel Wentzl**, Rynek Główny, t 430 2664, *www.wentzl.pl* (*expensive*). You can't get more central than this, located in an impeccably restored 15th-century mansion right on the Market Square. The ground floor contains the historic Wentzl restaurant.

★★★**Hotel Batory**, ul. Sołtyka 19, t 294 3030, *www.hotel-batory.pl* (*moderate*). A 10-minute walk from the old centre, this friendly, family-run hotel offers a mix of rooms and apartments, suitable for groups of 2–6. It offers free parking and has a decent restaurant. All rooms are no-smoking.

★★★**Hotel Eden**, ul. Ciemna 15, t 430 6767, *www.hoteleden.pl* (*moderate*). A delightful Jewish hotel in Kazimierz, set in a much-renovated 15th-century building. The restaurant serves kosher food, there's a mikveh (the only ritual Jewish bath in the city), plus a tiny sauna.

rulers. In order to facilitate this, the capital was moved to Warsaw in 1596, closer to the centre of the sprawling empire. Although Kraków remained the ceremonial centre of Poland, this removal spelt disaster for the city, which began a slow decline. This was compounded by repeated attacks by the Swedes in the 1650s, and throughout the 18th century Poland was caught up in aggressive territorial struggles between Sweden, Russia, Prussia and Austria. Under the **Third Partition** of 1795, Poland ceased to exist as an independent state, and Kraków was annexed by Austria.

★★★**Hotel Fortuna**, ul. Czapskich 5, **t** 422 3143, *www.hotel-fortuna.com.pl* (*moderate*). A good mid-priced choice, just outside the old centre on a 19th-century avenue. It has been recently refurbished and offers light, modern rooms and a traditional restaurant serving classic Polish cuisine.

★★★**Karmel**, ul, Kupa 15, **t** (12) 430 6697, *www.karmel.com.pl* (*moderate*). This sweet newly opened guesthouse is in the heart of boho-chic Kazimierz, with classically decorated, high-ceilinged rooms in a charming 19th-century building.

Wielopole, ul. Wielopole, **t** 422 1475, *www.wielopole.com* (*moderate*). A spotless, charming guest house with sunny, well-equipped rooms and a couple of apartments, all with free Internet access and modern bathrooms, just around the corner from the Rynek Główny.

Cybulskiego Guest Rooms, ul. Cybulskiego 6, **t** 423 0532, *www.freerooms.pl* (*inexpensive*). You won't find prices much lower than this in the city centre: rooms are spartan, but all have bathrooms and most have basic kitchen facilities.

Globtroter, Plac Szczepański 7, **t** 422 4123, *www.cracow-life.com/globtroter* (*inexpensive*). A very popular guesthouse tucked away in a peaceful courtyard close to the Rynek Główny. The staff couldn't be friendlier or more helpful, and the rooms are simple but prettily decorated in warm colours. It also has three apartments.

University Guest House, ul. Floriańska 49, **t** 421 1125 (*inexpensive*). Priority is given to guests of the Jagiellonian University, but if rooms are available, they are offered to visitors. The dated and rather worn furnishings are made up for the low, low prices in one of the loveliest streets of the old centre.

Further Afield

Pod Kopcem, Al. Waszyngtona 1, **t** (12) 427 0355, *www.hotel.fm.pl* (*expensive–moderate*). For a completely different experience, stay at this fortress right on top of the Kościuszko Mound (*see p.52*), which has been recently renovated by a local radio station (which is next door).

Eating Out

Kraków **t** (012) –

Cyrano de Bergarac, Sławkowska 26, **t** (12) 411 72 88, *www.cyranodebergerac.pl* (*luxury*). Beautifully located in a spectacular medieval mead cellar, this serves some of the finest French cuisine in Poland, perfectly accompanied by fine wines and an extraordinary range of cheeses. In summer, you can dine out in the pretty, plant-filled garden.

Pod Aniołami, ul. Grodzka St, **t** (12) 421 3999, *www.podaniolami.pl* (*expensive*). More medieval cellars are the setting for 'Under the Cherubs', an elegant formal restaurant serving delicious Polish specialities along with a good range of wines. It's a Kraków classic, and the succulent grilled meats are especially recommended. In summer (April–Oct), you can dine aboard the *Pod Aniolami Galleon*, zakole Wisły (off ul. Powisle), moored just below the castle.

Restaurant Wierzynek, Rynek Główny 15, **t** 424 9600 (*expensive*). A legend on the Market Square, this splendid restaurant is set in a handsome 14th-century building and has been going since 1364. Dine in magnificent Renaissance interiors on refined Polish cuisine, and the service (you'll be greeted by princesses) is excellent. There's a less expensive cellar restaurant serving a wide range of fondues, and a traditional coffee house.

However, it remained the focus of Polish nationalism, and Polish culture continued to flourish. The **Congress of Vienna** in 1814 established Kraków briefly as an independent city-state, but it was absorbed once again into Austria in 1846. It wasn't until the end of the **First World War** that Poland eventually regained its independence, but this was short-lived: in 1939, the **Second World War** was declared when German troops invaded Poland. Kraków, as residence of the Nazi governor of Poland, was spared the violence that destroyed other Polish cities. Kraków's buildings may have survived, but its

Restaurant Panorama Klub, ul. Zwierzyniecka 50, **t** 422 2814 (*expensive*). For the best views in town, try this striking restaurant with pared-down minimalist décor at the very top of the Jubilat building. There's nothing minimalist about the big plates of Polish food on offer, and the views encompass the curving river and the castle.

Alef, ul. Szeroka 17, **t** 421 3870, *www.alef.pl* (*moderate*). Take a trip back in time at this old world Jewish (but non-kosher) restaurant, where antiques, oil paintings and a battered piano eloquently evoke pre-war Kazimierz. It also has some equally charming guest rooms and apartments (*moderate*).

Cherubino, ul. Św. Tomasza 15, **t** 429 4007 (*moderate*). Cherubs ooze from every inch and tasty grilled meats are prepared over an open fire. There's a good range of Polish food, along with a few Tuscan dishes, and you can even eat in a 19th-century carriage.

Chimera, ul. Św. Anny 3, **t** 423 2178 (*moderate*). This welcoming, arty restaurant is popular with artists, and diners are entertained with live music from local musicians. It also has an adjoining (cheaper) salad and juice bar.

Chłopskie Jadło, ul. Św Jana 3, **t** 429 5157 (*moderate*). The 'Peasant Kitchen' is a classic in Kraków: pull up a long bench (or a sleigh) and choose from all kinds of traditional favourites, including wild boar and great filling soups. There are several branches around town.

Szabla i Szklanka, ul. Poselska 22, **t** 426 5440 (*moderate*). A delightful Hungarian restaurant, with crisp modern decoration: you can eat at one of the red booths under white-washed vaults, or in the adjoining dining room decorated with colourful naïve prints.

Balaton, ul. Grodzka 37, **t** 422 0469 (*inexpensive*). For heaped platefuls of simple Polish-Hungarian fare, you won't find better

than Balaton, a long-established, battered old favourite on the Royal Way.

Bar Vega, ul. Gertrudy 7, **t** 422 3494 (*inexpensive*). This sweet little veggie spot with its lace tablecloths and bunches of dried flowers was one of the first vegetarian restaurants in the city, and is popular with a studenty, arty crowd.

Pierogarnia, ul. Sławkowska 32, **t** 422 7495 (*inexpensive*). *Pierogi* are Polish dumplings, stuffed with all kinds of delicious fillings, and this tiny place offers eight varieties.

Cafés and Coffee Houses

Kraków **t** (012) –

Café Camelot, ul. Św. Tomasza 17, **t** 421 0123. It's hard to get a seat at this hugely popular little café: wooden tables are crammed into three adjoining salons, all with lacy mats and candles. There are changing art exhibitions on the walls and a good selection of newspapers.

Jama Michalika Café, ul. Floriańska 45, **t** 422 1561. A glorious Art Nouveau café which has been an institution since it was founded in 1895. It's one of the few smoke-free places in town – smoking has been banned in order to preserve the historic interior.

Klubokawarnia, ul. Beera Meiselsa 20, **t** 421 8532. Perhaps the loveliest café in the city: it's a dim, eccentric little spot, crammed with ancient radios and antiques, and candles flicker on wooden tables. A favourite with a Kazimierz boho-chic crowd, it has delicious sandwiches and cakes.

Les Couleurs, ul. Estery 10, **t** 429 4270. For an authentic taste of France, try this arty café with great coffee and croissants. It's decorated with French film posters, and there are French newspapers and mags to flick through.

people did not: as well as tens of thousands of Poles, the once flourishing Jewish community of Kazimierz was virtually wiped out in the death camps of Auschwitz and Birkenau. In the postwar era, Poland came under **Soviet** Communist control and the Nowa Huta steelworks were built just outside Kraków in order to dilute its perceived overly intellectual and bourgeois character. The plan backfired when the area became a hotbed of resistance to Communist rule, underpinned by a fierce adherence to the Catholic Church that was intensified by the appointment of Karol

Loża, Rynek Główny 41, t (12) 429 2962. A fancy, upmarket café right on market square with a smart restaurant and bar boasting sleek designer décor and an equally sleek crowd. There's a popular summer terrace, too.

the best jazz acts around. Slick, smooth and very laid-back.

Indigo, ul. Floriańska 26, t 421 4865. Another atmospheric cellar bar, the legendary Indigo offers some of the best jazz around (but avoid the food).

Entertainment and Nightlife

Kraków t (012) –

Classical Music, Theatre And Ballet

Teatr Stary, ul. Jagiellońska 1, t 422 4040. The oldest theatre in Poland, tucked behind an elegant Secessionist façade. It remains one of the most prestigious theatres of central Europe.

Teatr im Słowackiego, pl. Ducha 1, t 423 1700. Kraków's main opera venue, in a splendid 19th-century building with a dazzling *fin-de-siècle* interior.

Philharmonic Hall, ul. Zwierzyniecka 1, t 422 9477. Home to celebrated Kraków Philharmonic Orchestra, this is the city's finest classical music venue. Nigel Kennedy is an honorary Artistic Director.

Jazz

Art Club Cieplarnia, ul. Bracka 15, t 429 2898. This delightful spot has a little bit of everything – poetry readings, art exhibitions, dramatic sketches. And there's also live Jazz at weekends.

Harris Piano Jazz Bar, Rynek Główny 28, t 421 5741. A classic on the Polish jazz scene, with live gigs featuring classic jazz on Tuesdays, jam sessions on Thursdays, blues on Friday, and concerts by well-known local and international jazz musicians on Saturday.

Piec'Art, ul. Szewska 12, t 429 6425. A groovy cellar space with live concerts by some of

Cinemas

ARS Cinema, ul. Jana 6, t 421 4199. An opulent cinema in a pair of historic mansions just off the Market Square: the largest screen is in the former ballrooms. Foreign films, as in all Kraków cinemas, are shown in their original language with Polish subtitles.

Pasaż, Rynek Główny 9, t 422 7713. A tiny arthouse cinema which has seen better days, but is nonetheless a Kraków institution.

Bars and Clubs

Bodega Marqués, ul. Sławkowska 12, t 425 4980. A fancy wine bar with slick modern interior and huge wine list which includes wines from around the world. It also has great tapas.

Club Fusion, ul. Floriańska 15, t 422 4460. Currently the coolest club in town, with a funky mix of ultra-contemporary décor, brick lined vaults and pumping music.

Faust, Rynek Główny, t 423 8300. Big, popular club in vaulted cellars under the Market Square. A wild time is guaranteed.

Club Pod Jaszczurami, Rynek Główny 8, t 429 4538. One of the oldest and most famous student bars in Kraków, with regular live music, cheap prices, vaulted ceilings and battered wooden tables. It also runs exhibitions and shows cult films.

CK Browar, ul. Podwale 6–7, t 429 2505. The Royal Emperor's Brewery is a classic: enjoy flagons of their own Polish ales at long wooden tables in a huge cellar. It also shows sporting events on a big screen.

Wojtyła, former Archbishop of Kraków, to the Holy See in 1978. In 1989, Poland became the first country to leave the Soviet Bloc, and it joined the EU in 2004.

Old City (Stare Miasto)

The heart and soul of the old city for the last thousand years has been the splendid **Rynek Główny** (Market Square), the largest medieval square anywhere in Europe, hemmed in with a splendid parade of newly restored Gothic and Renaissance

The Brave Bugler

Every hour, an oddly truncated bugle call erupts from the crown-topped northern tower of St Mary's Basilica. According to legend, a medieval bugler was sounding the alarm to warn Kraków's citizens of impending attack when an arrow struck him in the throat. But the locals managed to fight off the enemy, and, ever since then, the tune is stopped at exactly the same point in commemoration of the bugler's bravery.

mansions. Tables spill out from terrace cafés, street musicians serenade the endless ebb and flow of crowds, and stalls are bursting with flowers and souvenirs.

The most extravagant building is the 700-year-old **Cloth Hall** (Sukiennice), right in the very centre, with creamy balustrades and cupolas added in a 19th-century remodelling. The arcades now contain a string of pretty stalls selling souvenirs, from amber jewellery to traditional embroidered fabrics. Inside, a **Gallery of Polish Painting** (open Tues and Fri–Sat 10–7, Wed–Thurs 10–4, Sun 10–3; adm, free on Thurs) – the first public museum for the Polish people, even though the country at that time was divided between Prussia, Russia and Austria – contains paintings from the late 18th to the early 20th century, a patchy collection which nonetheless contains some fine pieces by Jan Matejko, Jósef Chełmońskí and Władysław Podkowiński.

The **Town Hall Tower** (Wieża Ratuszowa; open 10–4.30; adm) is marooned on the southern side of the square under a frothy Baroque cap, and is all that survives of the original 14th-century town hall. Formerly a prison, it now contains an historical museum, with a model of the medieval town hall, fascinating black and white photographs of Kraków and bird's-eye-views of the square.

Behind the Sukiennice, the twin spires of **St Mary's Basilica** (Kościół Mariacki; open Mon–Sat 11.30–6, Sun 2–6; adm) loom magnificently. This extravagant Gothic church was built on the ruins of an earlier church, destroyed by the Tatars in the 13th century, and contains a dazzling Gothic interior, with cobalt-blue vaults scattered with glimmering stars and ranks of multicoloured columns. There are two entrances, one for worshippers (free) at the front, and another, on the side, for visitors. The visitors' fee allows you to get a close-up view of Veit Stoss' beautiful Gothic High Altar, the largest in Europe. The vivid murals which adorn the walls and vault of the presbytery are the work of Jan Matejko. Numerous flamboyant Baroque altars and tombs are scattered around the church, and another masterpiece by sculptor Viet Stoss, a deeply expressive Crucifix, hangs above an altar on the southern aisle.

From the Rynek Główny, the palace-lined **ulica Floriańska** sweeps grandly northwards, although nowadays the splendid Renaissance mansions jostle awkwardly with mushrooming kebab shops and souvenir outlets. Jan Matejko (1838–1893), Poland's outstanding historical painter, was born at No.41, and later returned to live here with his family. After his death, the house was opened as a museum, **Jan Matejko House** (Dom Jana Matejki; open Tues–Thurs and Sat–Sun 10am–3pm, Fri 10am–5.30pm, closed every third Sun; adm), with a pair of salons kept as they would have looked during his lifetime and an odd collection of the eccentric paraphernalia that he gathered to ensure the historical accuracy of his works featuring everything from coins to torture instruments. Ulica Floriańska culminates at **St Florian's Gate** (Brama Floriańska), set into the only surviving stretch of the medieval defensive walls which once completely encircled the city, now colourfully hung with tacky souvenirs.

Just east, the **Czartoryski Museum** (Muzeum Czartoryskich; *www.muzeum-czartoryskich.krakow.pl; open Tues, Thurs, Sat and Sun 10–3.30, Wed and Fri 10–6; adm, free on Sun*) is the city's finest art museum. The collection, which encompasses painting, sculpture and the decorative arts, was founded in 1796 by Princess Izabela Czartoryska, and expanded by the family during the succeeding centuries. During the Second World War it was confiscated by the Nazis and taken to Dresden, and several pieces have yet to be recovered, including a self-portrait by Raphael. The pride of the collection, Leonardo da Vinci's *Lady with an Ermine* (1496), barely escaped the same fate: it was appropriated by Dr Hans Frank, the notorious Nazi governor of Poland who lived at the Wawel, and only returned after his arrest. The luminous portrait, one of only three Leonardo paintings in the world, depicts Cecilia Gallerini, mistress of da Vinci's patron Ludovico Sforza, with an ermine cradled in her arms. The ermine played on both her name (*galle* means ermine in Greek) and Ludovico Sforza's emblem, L'Ermellino. The other great highlight of the picture gallery (on the second floor) is Rembrandt's haunting *Landscape with the Good Samaritan*. The first floor contains exhibits tracing the history of Poland from the 14th to the 19th centuries.

Pass through St Florian's Gate, which was once linked by a covered passage to the fairytale **Barbican** (Barbakan; *open daily 10.30–6; adm*) just beyond. This romantically turreted bastion was the starting point for the Royal Way, the ceremonial coronation and funeral route of Polish kings which was used even after the capital moved to Warsaw in 1596. The **Planty gardens** that spread from here in both directions were laid out in the early 19th century after the city's medieval defences were razed. Scattered with benches and lit with elegant gas lamps, these elegant gardens entirely ring the old city and are perfect for a romantic stroll. Head left (west) around the Planty until you reach an elegant square, plac Szczepański, dominated by a pair of impressive Viennese Secessionist-style buildings: the **Palace of Arts** (Pałac Sztuki; *open daily 8–8; adm*), used for major temporary art exhibitions, and the opulent **Old Theatre** (Stary Teatr), which is Poland's oldest theatre, built in 1798 and lavishly remodelled at the turn of the 20th century. Just beyond the square, the Brutalist **Bunker of Art** (Bunkier Sztuki; *open Tues–Sun 11–6; adm*) may be spectacularly ugly, but hosts usually excellent temporary exhibitions of contemporary art.

The Planty continues towards the frothy **Church of St Anne** (Kościół św. Anny; *open during services only*), one of the most extravagant Baroque churches in the city, which was built to house the remains of St John of Kęty (Jan Kanty), a 15th-century professor at the nearby university, buried here in a sumptuous sarcophagus. Beyond the church, backed by lush gardens, is the mellow, red-brick **Collegium Maius** of Kraków's cele-brated university (*entrance on ul. Jagiełłońska*). Founded in 1364 as the Academy of Kraków by King Kazimierz the Great, it is the third oldest university in Europe, and famously the *alma mater* of astronomer Nicholas Copernicus (1473–1543). At the centre of the college is a breathtaking lovely Gothic courtyard, with a fountain, elegant arcades and a sweeping staircase. You can take tours of the interior (*demand is high so book in advance, **t** (012) 422 0549, tours depart every 20mins Mon–Fri 11–3, Sat*

11–2; adm), which include visits to the sumptuous Great Hall, the vaulted 16th-century Library and the 14th-century Common Room.

Return to the Rynek Główny along ul. Św Anny and take up the Royal Way once more by turning down **ul. Grodzka**, near the humble little church of **St Adalbert** (Kraków's oldest) in the southern corner of the square. The first section of this long, grand thoroughfare is a busy, commercial street crammed with shops, restaurants and cafés, which soon give way to a series of extravagant churches. The first of these is the imposing red-brick **Dominican Church** (Kościół św Trójcy (Dominikanów); *entrance on ul. Stolarska; open daily 10–5*), which dates back to 1250, although it was largely rebuilt in the late 19th century after a devastating fire which incinerated much of the area. It still contains a miraculous image of the Virgin in the Rosary Chapel, popularly believed to heal the sick. On the other side of ul. Grodzka, the hulking **Franciscan Church and Monastery** (Kościół św Franciszka z Asyżu i zespół oo Franciszkanów; *open daily 10–5*) was the first brick building in the city when it was erected in the 13th century. It witnessed the baptism of the pagan Grand Duke of Lithuania, Prince Jagiełło, in 1385 (*see* 'History'), but it too has been destroyed by fire several times. The glowing Art Nouveau stained glass and swirling murals were added by Stanisław Wyspiański in 1900. Opposite the church, a statue of the late Pope John Paul II, arms raised in blessing, stands outside the **Episcopal Palace** (Pałac Arcybiskupi) where he resided from 1963 until his appointment to the Apostolic See in 1978.

The grandest church of all down ul. Grodzka is the flamboyant Baroque **Church of SS Peter and Paul** (Kościół św. Piotra i Pawła; *open Mon–Fri 9–5; adm to crypt*), unmistakably the work of the Jesuits, who were invited to Kraków to spearhead the Counter-Reformation in the mid-16th century. The inflammatory 16th-century Jesuit preacher Piotr Skarga (commemorated with a much-derided contemporary statue outside the church) is buried beneath the altar.

After all the heady Baroque flummery of the Church of SS Peter and Paul, it would be easy to miss the quiet little **Church of St Andrew** (Kośkiół św. Andrzeja; *open daily 8–5*) standing inconspicuously at its side. This 11th-century church is Kraków's finest Romanesque church, and withstood the first Tatar attack on the city earning it a sentimental place in the heart of every Krakovian. Sadly, the interior is uninspiring.

Running parallel to ul. Grodska, the gentle curve of **ul. Kanonicza** is a tranquil, cobbled street which survived the fires that decimated much of the old quarter in the 19th century. The string of small museums clustered here begins with the most modern, although the setting is an elegant Gothic palace: the **Cricoteka** at No.5 (*open Sept–June Mon–Fri 10–4, July–Aug daily 10–4; adm*), which recounts the history of Kraków's most celebrated avant garde theatre, Cricot 2, and its charismatic director Tadeusz Kantor (1915–90). Close by, at No.15, the **Wyspiański Museum** (Muzeum Wyspiańskiego; *open Tues–Thurs 10–6, Wed and Fri–Sun 10–3.30; adm, free on Sun*) is dedicated to Kraków's foremost exponent of Art Nouveau, Stanisław Wyspiański. Among the exhibits are designs for his lush, swirling stained glass windows, models for theatre sets, paintings, sketches and photographs. At No.19, the **Archdiocesan Museum** (Muzeum Archidiecezjalne; *open Tues–Fri 10–4, Sat–Sun 10–3; adm*) faithfully preserves a room which formerly belonged to Karol Wojtyła, better known as the late

Pope John Paul II, who lived at the adjoining deanery for sixteen years. The remaining galleries are given over to temporary exhibitions of religious art.

Wawel Hill

*Only limited tickets are sold, so it's best to get here early, particularly in summer. The ticket booth is at the top of the ramp leading up to the castle. Each section of the castle is visited with a separate ticket, and visits are timed. For admission to the **cathedral** (which includes access to the crypt, cathedral museum and the Zygmunt Bell), buy tickets from the nuns in the shop opposite the cathedral entrance; open Mon–Sat 9–3, Sun 12.15–3. **State Rooms**, **Private Apartments**, **Crown Treasury** and **Armoury** and **Oriental Art exhibition** open Tues–Sat 9.30–3; adm. State Rooms also open Sun 9.30–12; free. **Lost Wawel exhibition** open Mon and Wed–Sat 9.30–3; adm; plus Sun 10–3, free. **English-speaking guides** bookable at Royal Castle Tour Agency, Wawel 5, t (012) 422 0904 (office next to the ticket booth). Information: www.wawel.krakow.pl.*

The residence and burial place of Polish kings for more than five hundred years, Wawel remains the spiritual heart of Poland and a place of pilgrimage for many Poles. The complex, high on a crag above the river, began with a sprinkling of early Christian churches in the 8th century, and the first royal residence was built here in the 10th century, although its current aspect is the result of a spectacular Renaissance remodelling during the 16th century.

The 14th-century **cathedral** (Katedra Krakowska), the third to have been built on this site, is the Polish holy-of-holies, and a resonant symbol of Polish nationhood: monarchs have been baptised, crowned and interred here, along with poets, saints and bishops. Just beyond the **entrance gate** are some dusty bones, once believed to have belonged to the dragon slain by King Kazimierz (*see* p.50), and legend has it that the cathedral will stand as long as they remain. The interior is solemn, the aisles cluttered with splendid chapels containing royal tombs; among the finest is the 16th-century Renaissance **Sigismund Chapel** with an exquisite silver altar under a magnificent dome – you can admire its glittering gold cap outside in the courtyard. The central **nave** is dominated by an enormous silver sarcophagus containing the relics of St Stanisław, the murdered 11th-century bishop and patron saint of Poland. Behind the gilded **High Altar**, the much-venerated 14th-century 'Black Christ's Crucifix' belonging to Queen Jadwiga (1384–99), whose remains are kept beneath it, is still a place of pilgrimage.

All but four of Poland's 45 monarchs are buried in the cathedral: the medieval rulers were buried beneath the floor of the cathedral but, from the mid-16th century, monarchs were laid to rest in the **Royal Crypt** (Groby Królewskie). Steps lead down to the shadowy, vaulted crypt, where the tombs of ten Polish monarchs, their wives and children are laid out. National heroes including Tadeusz Kościuszko are also honoured with burial here, and a Romanesque chapel contains the tombs of Poland's finest poets, Adam Mickiewicz and Juliusz Słowacki. You can make the stiff climb up the **belltower** to touch the huge 8-ton **Zygmunt Bell**, cast in Kraków in 1520 and one of the largest in the world; allegedly if you touch its clapper, your wishes will come true. The views across the city are spellbinding.

Wawel and Chakra

According to Chakra doctrine, the world, like the body, has seven energy points. One of these is to be found in the northwestern corner of the courtyard of the Wawel, and streams of New Age travellers have been gathering to the spot to press themselves against the wall and soak up the energy. This is frowned on by the castle authorities, who have dismissed it as mumbo jumbo, and have forbidden guides to mention it.

An archway leads through to the vast, elegantly tiered courtyard at the heart of the **castle**, designed by a Florentine architect in the mid-16th century. Tours of the **State Apartments** (Komnaty Królewskie) depart from the southeastern corner of the courtyard. The apartments where court officials lived and worked are decorated with period furniture, but are relatively sombre and unadorned. Things pick up upstairs, with a series of lavishly decorated *salons* and grand halls, many hung with the castle's unparalleled collection of Flemish **tapestries** commissioned by King Sigismund August in the 16th century. Ornate coffered polychrome ceilings studded with gilded roses adorn many of the rooms, but the most extravagant ceiling of all is in the extraordinary **Deputies Hall** (also called the Hall under the Heads). Thrusting out from the ceiling is a sea of carved heads, each with a different expression: of the 30 surviving heads, you can pick out one with tiny horns, another bearing a crown and one of a woman with a gag across her mouth. Strangely, no one has any idea what these figures signify or why they are here. The apartments in the north wing, refurbished at the turn of the 17th century, are gloomy and rather oppressive, hung with heavy wallpaper, dark oil paintings and solid Baroque furniture. They begin with the **Bird Room**, with a remarkable gilded coffered ceiling from which wooden birds were once suspended. The tour culminates with the huge **Senator's Hall**, the former ballroom, with tapestries depicting biblical stories (there's a bloody scene of Cain killing Abel) and another splendid ceiling.

The **Royal Private Apartments** (Prywatne Apartamenty Królewskie) can only be visited as part of a tour (*English tours 12pm*). Largely Baroque in style, they still bear traces of the original Gothic structure, including the fine wooden ceilings and some fresco fragments. Two rooms have been filled with elaborate 18th-century porcelain and *objets d'art*, and another has been preserved much as it would have looked in the first decades of the 20th century under President Ignacy Mościcki. The opulent Colonnaded Hall is filled with gilded furniture and lined with formal portraits.

Back out in the courtyard, the entrance to the **Royal Treasury and Armoury** (Skarbiec i Zbrojownia) is in the northeastern corner of the square. After occupying powers had picked over the Polish treasures, and poverty-stricken monarchs had been forced to sell off many more, relatively little survives. Nonetheless, the collection contains some extraordinary objects, including a crown found in the tomb of Sigismund the Old, the coronation sword of the Polish kings, royal insignias, beautiful 16th- and 17th-century jewellery and opulent Baroque liturgical plate and vestments. The adjoining Armoury is crammed with beautifully crafted weaponry, and ranks of vicious halberds, lances and other hacking instruments. Downstairs are elaborate cannon, with handles in the form of frolicking dolphins, and splendid suits of armour.

Across the courtyard is the entrance to the **Orient of the Wawel** (Sztuka Wschodu) exhibition, filled with booty taken from the Turks. The highlight is undoubtedly a glorious carpet depicting the Garden of Paradise, captured during the Battle of Vienna in 1683. There are silk tents, beautifully inlaid scimitars, prayer mats and an exquisite silver horseshoe, and another gallery contains a collection of fine Chinese porcelain, including ritual vessels which date back to more than a thousand years BC. To find out more about the origins of the Wawel, visit the **Lost Wawel** (Wawel Zaginiony) exhibition in the remnants of the Rotunda of the Virgin Mary, which was Kraków's first church – an audiovisual presentation describing the early history of the Wawel.

Out on the western wall, you can clamber down steep steps to the **Dragon's Cave** (Smocza Jama; *open May–Sept daily 10–5; adm*), which extends for 270 metres into the rock at the base of the cliff. Outside, a rearing dragon installed in 1972 sporadically emits bellows and puffs of smoke. According to popular myth, legendary ruler Krak who lived on Wawel Hill ordered his sons to get rid of the dragon which had been terrorising locals by devouring their livestock and stealing virgins. They enticed it out of its lair with a sheep stuffed with tar and sulphur. The dragon gobbled it down and immediately lunged for water, which caused the sulphur to explode.

Manggha

Across the river from the Wawel you can see the sleek forms of one of Kraków's newest museums. The Centre of Japanese Art and Culture, known as Manggha, contains the National Museum's excellent collection of Japanese artefacts, donated by local collector Feliks Jasieński (1861–1929). The museum café has excellent views over the river to the castle. To get there, head south from Wawel along the riverbank until you get to the Grunwaldzki bridge.

Kazimierz

Kazimierz was once an independent town on the southeastern fringe of Kraków. Under the patronage of King Kazimir, it grew to rival its grand neighbour: its Market Square was only slightly smaller from that of Kraków and it was liberally endowed with magnificent churches. The area's Jewish community swelled after 1495, when the Jews were expelled from Kraków. By the end of the 19th century, the neighbourhood was almost completely Jewish – a vibrant, flourishing community which made up a quarter of Kraków's total population. Those who could afford it moved out to smart suburbs like Podgórze, but Kazimierz continued to be the heart of the community's religious and commercial life. There were about 70,000 Jews in Kraków when the Nazis arrived in 1939: fewer than 5,000 would survive the horrors of the Holocaust. For decades, the historic Jewish community of Kazimierz was just a memory, but in recent years an important cultural revival has taken place. The synagogues and cemeteries have been restored, Jewish shops, restaurants and cultural centres are opening, and the film *Schindler's List*, based on events which took place here during the Second World War, has brought international interest in the area. Simultaneously, Kazimierz has been growing into Kraków's funkiest neighbourhood, with boho-chic cafés, trendy bars and funky record shops mushrooming along its ancient streets.

For centuries, **ul. Szeroka** was the heart of the religious community. It's dominated by the handsome **Old Synagogue** (Stara Synagoga; *open Wed–Thurs 9–3.30, Fri–Sun 11–6; adm, free first Sat and Sun of month*), built at the turn of the 16th century and the oldest surviving example of Jewish religious architecture in Poland. Destroyed by the Nazis, it has been painstakingly restored and contains a fascinating museum dedicated to Jewish life, along with a beautiful Prayer Hall, completely unadorned but for the elegant bimah (the platform used for readings for the Torah). At the other end of the square, a small archway leads to the tiny **Remu'h Synagogue** (Bożnica Remuh; *open Mon–Fri and Sun 9–5; adm, includes entry to cemetery*), still used by Orthodox Jews. The passage outside the synagogue is lined with sobering memorials to the Jews exterminated by the Nazis. Behind the synagogue is the haunting **Remu'h Cemetery** (Cmentarz Remu'h), established in 1552 and filled with beautifully worn gravestones, including that of Moses Isserlus, the Rabbi Remu'h after whom the synagogue was named. It is the only gravestone to survive intact: according to legend, when the Nazis attempted to shatter it, they were struck by a bolt of lightning. The cemetery was closed down by the Austrians in 1801, and most of the graves were covered by layers of earth. Ironically, this neglect saved them from Nazi destruction, and the graveyard was restored after the war. Fragments of broken tombs discovered during the renovations were hung mosaic-style against the wall, which has become known as the Wailing Wall of Kraków.

Kazimierz's newest and most striking museum is the **Galician Jewish Museum** (Galicja Muzeum; *open daily 9–8; adm*), in a converted factory at ul. Dajwor 18. As well as an excellent bookshop and café, it contains a beautiful exhibition of photographs taken by Chris Schwarz, a British photo-journalist who spent 12 years documenting the physical remains of Jewish culture and civilisation in Polish Galicia.

On nearby ul. Jakuba, the **Isaac Synagogue** (Synagoga Ajzyka) is an imposing white 17th-century building which has managed to retain an exquisite stucco ceiling and now houses the Jewish Education Centre. Two black and white films are permanently on show: one from 1936 which eloquently evokes Kazimierz's lost past, and another, taken by the Germans in 1941, showing stricken Jews being herded away to the Płaszów work camp a few kilometres south of Kazimierz. On **ul. Józefa**, one of the main thoroughfares of Kazimierz, still lined with cafés and shops, the **High Synagogue** (Synagoga Wysoka) was built in the 16th century, but is still awaiting restoration. The grandest surviving synagogue is the Reform Synagogue, also known as the **Tempel Synagogue** (Synagoga Tempel; *ul. Miodawa, open by appointment only, t (012) 429 5735*), erected in the late 19th century.

Across the train tracks on the eastern edge of Kazimierz, the vast **New Cemetery** (Nowy Cmentarz) was established in the early 19th century; it was destroyed by the Nazis who ripped out the gravestones to use as building materials, but subseqently has been restored. It contains the graves of numerous influential leaders and rabbis, but the catastrophe of the Holocaust is remembered with weed-strewn tombstones recalling entire families wiped out during the Second World War.

The western side of Kazimierz contains its most important Christian monuments, including the **Church of Corpus Christi** (Kościół Bożego Ciała; *ul. Bożego Ciała 25, open*

Mon–Sat 9–12 and 1.30–7) and the **Church of St Catherine** (Kościół św. Katarzyny; *ul. Augustiańska, open for services only*), both established by King Kazimierz the Great in the 14th century. Overlooking the river is the serene, Baroque **Paulite Church 'On the Rock'** (Kościół Paulinów Na Skałce; *open Mon–Sat 9–12 and 1.30–3*), where the crypt was transformed into a national pantheon for those who had made an extraordinary contribution to Polish culture. Among the tombs are those of artist Stanisław Wyspiański (1869–1907) and poet Adam Asnyk (1838–97).

The most outstanding secular monument in Kazimierz is the Renaissance **Town Hall** (Ratusz Kazimierski) on Plac Wolnica, which was begun in the early 15th century and remodelled substantially in the 17th and 19th centuries. It now contains an ethnographical museum, with folk art, traditional costumes and musical instruments from the Little Poland region.

Outside the Centre

Kościuszko Mound

Take bus 100 to the foot of the mound.

This grassy mound is on top of a hill that rises for 326m above the tranquil, village-like suburb of Zwierzyniec in the west of the city and offers a breathtaking panorama of the old city and the curve of the Vistula river. It was raised between 1820 and 1823 to honour Tadeusz Kościuszko (1752–1817), military hero and leader of the 1794 insurrection. The mound is a focus for Polish national pride and a place of pilgrimage.

Nowa Huta

Tram 4, 9, 15 or 22 to plac Centralny.

For a fascinating glimpse behind the Iron Curtain, head for the 'ideal city' of Nowa Huta. In the late 1940s, the Russians decided that the bourgeois and cultivated Krakovians needed an injection of solid proletarianism. They decided to raise a model city filled with Socialist Realist architecture centred around a vast steelwork complex on the site of an ancient village 7km west of the city centre. The plan backfired: the steel-workers became some of the most vociferous opponents of the Communist regime, and riots regularly rocked the neighbourhood, particularly during the period of Martial Law in 1981–3. The steelworks, formerly known as the **Lenin Steelworks** but renamed the Senzimir Works after the fall of the Iron Curtain, produces more than half of Poland's steel and employs around 200,000 workers. But it is one of the worst polluters in Europe; the acid rain caused by its belching chimneys has caused untold damage to the ancient stone of the city centre. Although pollution levels have dropped dramatically in recent years, the steelworks remain a serious environmental concern. The grey suburb, with its endless monotonous streets, could hardly provide a greater contrast with the beautiful, historic cityscape of the centre. Although religious buildings were not included in the original plans for the model city, permission was finally granted after years of battling to build the extraordinary **Ark of God** church (Arka), one of the finest examples of contemporary ecclesiastical architecture.

Wolski Forest (Las Wolski) and the Piłsudski Mound

Take bus 134 from the city centre to the zoo.

The languid woodlands and gardens of Las Wolski, just beyond Zwierzyniec to the west of the city, are perfect for a picnic or a bike ride. Spread languidly around Kraków's **Zoological Garden** (Ogród Zoologiczny; *open daily 9am–dusk; adm*), they make a refreshing break from the city's hustle and bustle. Appearing magically atop Silver Hill in the southern end of the park, the **Church and Hermitage of the Camaldolese Monks** (Kościół I Erem Kamedułow; *open summer daily 8–11 and 3–5, winter daily 8–11 and 3–4*) is home to an ascetic order of monks. Only men may enter, although women are allowed on major feast days.

About half a kilometre north of the zoo, the **Piłsudski Mound** is dedicated to Józef Piłsudski (1867–1935), leader of Poland during the inter-war years. The mound was deliberately neglected by the Communist authorities during the post-war era, and the original granite plaque was bulldozed by a tank in 1953. The mound has been completely restored and offers beautiful views across the city.

Tyniec Abbey

There are summer cruises from Kraków, see p.40; or bus 112 from the city centre.

The magnificent Benedictine abbey at Tyniec, 10km east of the city centre, long guarded the approach to Kraków from its isolated cliff above the Vistula River. It was heavily fortified, but over the centuries the Mongols, Swedes and Russians breached its defences and destroyed the abbey. Only fragments of the original medieval construction survive, but there are traces of Gothic frescoes in the current imposing Baroque church, built in the 17th century. The complex is still surrounded by defensive walls, and only the **church** is open to visitors (*daily 7.30am–6.30pm*). It regularly hosts concerts, including a season of organ recitals in the summer (*see* 'Festivals', p.39).

Day Trips from Kraków

Wieliczka Salt Mines

www.kopalnia-wieliczka.pl; open April–Oct daily 7.30–7.30; Nov–Mar 8–5; adm.

The extraordinary salt mines at Wieliczka are among the oldest in the world, and have been designated a World Heritage Site by UNESCO. Salt has been mined here since the 11th century, when it was a source of great wealth to the Polish monarchs who ensured the mines remained royal property. The vast underground labyrinth grew to encompass almost 300km of tunnels, reaching to a depth of 327m. The visit (about two hours, with lots of walking) takes in three of the upper levels (there are nine in all), with a series of weird and wonderful **chambers** and **chapels** – even, bizarrely, a basketball court – hewn by hand by the mine-workers. The highlight is the magnificent **Chapel of the Blessed Kings**, entirely made of salt, including the carved reliefs of biblical scenes adorning the walls, and even the elaborate chandeliers. It

Getting There

There are infrequent **trains** from Kraków to Wieliczka, 15km southeast, but the easiest option is to take a private **Luxbus minibus** from the train station (*departures every 10mins*). All tour operators run day trips to Wieliczka, which often include lunch.

Eating Out

The mine has its own underground **restaurant** (*inexpensive*) serving simple snacks along with more substantial fare.

Or you can try the **Halit** (*moderate*), across the street from the mine entrance, which offers sophisticated Polish cuisine.

took the mine-workers thirty years to complete, and its amazing acoustics have made it a popular venue for concerts. There's a fascinating **museum** on the third level which outlines the history of the mine.

Auschwitz (Oświęcim)

*The Auschwitz-Birkenau Memorial and Museum is open daily mid-Dec–Feb 8–3; Mar and Nov–mid-Dec 8–4; April and Oct 8–5; May and Sept 8–6; June–Aug 8–7. Admission is free. There is a **visitors' centre** located at the entrance to Auschwitz I. Auschwitz I and Auschwitz II-Birkenau are located 3km apart. **Shuttle buses** link the camps hourly between mid-April and October, or **taxis** are available outside the visitors' centre. Between mid-April and October, there are **guided visits in English** at 11am (40 zł, includes shuttle between the sites). Private **English-speaking guides** can be requested at least two weeks in advance: more information at the official website, www.auschwitz.org.pl.*

In 1940, the Nazis established a concentration camp in an outlying suburb of the grey, industrial town of Oświęcim (pronounced *Osh-VYEN-chim*) west of Kraków. Originally built to house Polish political prisoners, under its German name of Auschwitz it has become synonymous with the Holocaust. In 1941, the Nazis had agreed on the 'Final Solution' to the Jewish question – the complete annihilation of all Jews in areas controlled by the Third Reich – and another camp, three kilometres away at Birkenau, was added. In 1942, vast numbers of Jews began to arrive from all parts of Europe. Crammed for days into cattle trucks and goods wagons, they emerged dazed on to ramps where they were immediately lined up for selection by SS physicians: men in one line, women and children in another. Those classified as fit for work were sent to the camp. Those who weren't – between 70 and 75 per cent – were sent to their deaths in the gas chambers. The first experimental gassings with the pesticide Zyklon B took place in September 1941, and it was used routinely from 1942. In 1944, the killing machine was made even more efficient: the railway tracks were extended to the gates of the gas chambers and electric lifts were installed to lift the bodies to the cremation ovens. Two thousand people could be gassed at a time. Death took 15–20 minutes. By 1945, at least one-and-a-half million people – overwhelmingly Jewish along with vast numbers of disabled people, homosexuals, Soviet POWs, Poles, Romanies and more than 15 other nationalities – had been killed in the Auschwitz death camps. When the Nazis fled in January 1945, just before Auschwitz was liberated by the Soviets, they attempted to destroy the evidence of their crimes, burning documents and razing the infamous gas chambers. What remains has become a harrowing museum, a horrifying reminder of man's infinite capacity for cruelty.

The **visitor's centre** at the entrance to the camp contains a small **cinema** (*adm*), where a short and deeply disturbing film shows the Soviet liberation of the camp. Barbed wire twists around the **entrance gate**, topped by the cynical German slogan *Arbeit Macht Frei* ('Work Makes You Free'), and beyond it stretch the **prison blocks**. **Block 4** contains a model of the camp and a description of how it functioned, along with a terrible mound of hair, shorn from the victims before their deaths. **Block 5** is a storehouse for an overwhelming array of personal belongings which survived the Nazi attempt to destroy evidence, and includes suitcases hopefully labelled with the names and addresses of their owners, glasses, false limbs, dentures, clothes and shoes. **Blocks 6 and 7** describe life in the camp, the inhuman living conditions, the summary executions, the hard labour – most who were not gassed were quite literally worked to death – and the chilling experiments carried out by Dr Josef Mengele after his arrival at the camp in 1942, particularly on twins. There are photographs of the painfully thin survivors, children among them, discovered by the Soviets in January 1945. The **courtyard** between Blocks 10 and 11 was used for shooting prisoners before the mass gassings began, and it was in Block 11 that the first gassings with Zyklon B were carried out on 600 Soviet POWs and 250 sick camp inmates. Many of the prison blocks have been converted into national memorials, filled with photographs and moving testimonies to the millions who died. **Block 27** has been dedicated to the 'suffering and struggle of the Jews', a belated recognition of the enormous sacrifice of Jewish life. When the museum was under Communist control, it was described as an 'International Monument to Victims of Fascism' and there were no references to the fact that most of the prisoners killed in the death camps were Jewish. Since the fall of the Iron Curtain, the museum has attempted to redress the balance, but many Jewish groups feel that there is still a long way to go.

Beyond the prison blocks are the crematoria and gas chambers. Rudolf Höss, the camp commandant, was executed in the courtyard here in 1947 after being found guilty of war crimes. These buildings were used between 1940 and 1943, before the much larger and more efficient chambers at Birkenau were erected.

Birkenau, called Auschwitz II when it was established in 1941, is located 3km from Auschwitz I. Shuttle buses and taxis link the camps (*see* above), but many choose to walk between them, through the so-called 'Interest Zone', where German factories

Getting There

There are regular **trains** to Oświęcim from the main train station in Kraków, but the bus is more convenient as it drops visitors off by the gates. If you take the train, numerous local buses make the journey out to the camp. Several **tour operators** in Kraków offer guided visits of Auschwitz-Birkenau. Those run by Jarden (*see* p.39) are highly recommended.

Tourist Information

From the Małopolska tourist information office in Kraków (*see* p.39). See the official website *www.auschwitz.org.pl*.

Eating Out

There's a small snack bar by the entrance to the Auschwitz I camp.

and administrative buildings were located. There are few exhibits or descriptions in Birkenau: it has been left as it was found in January 1945 and the camp's installations, some still partly coated in human ash, speak for themselves. The camp was huge: climb the tower by the entrance gate to see its vast extent. About half of the buildings have survived, including the train tracks which were extended into the camp in May 1944 in order to speed up the extermination process. The immense gas chambers and crematoria were blown up by the SS shortly before the arrival of the Soviets in 1944, but even the remnants are a horrifying sight. Behind **Gas Chamber and Crematorium IV** is a murky pond, still grey with human ashes. Upon arrival, prisoners were sent to the red-brick building near the crematoria which became known with black survivor's humour as the 'Sauna'. Here, they were stripped of their clothes and personal belongings, shaved and disinfected, and assigned the numbers that were tattooed on their arms – Auschwitz was the only camp which tattooed its inmates in this way. The final room contains a moving exhibit of personal photographs and possessions found among the ruins.

Ojców National Park

This is Poland's smallest national park, a beautiful stretch of forested hills, cave-pocked cliffs, gorges and romantic castles. It's a popular destination with walkers and birdwatchers, and a scenic road winds through the spine of the park along the banks of the Prądnik river. The village of **Ojców**, 25km northwest of Kraków, a delightful straggle of traditional wooden houses, is the main hub of the park, with a pair of museums, one housing the **Museum of the National Park** (*open April–Oct daily 9–4.30; Nov–Mar Tues–Fri 8–3; adm*), a dramatic ruined **castle**, and the park information office. The castle is the most southerly of a ring of fortifications known as 'Eagles' Nests' built by Kazimierz the Great to guard the western border of his kingdom in the early 14th century. Only a tower survives, but you can climb it (*open Mon–Sat May–Sept 9–4; Oct–April 10–4; adm*) for spectacular views.

A gentle 8km hike north of Ojców or directly accessible by bus, another of the 'Eagles' Nests' has been beautifully preserved high on a rock at **Pieskowa Skała**. The original 14th-century castle was remodelled by Italian architect Nicolo da Castiglione during the 16th century, when the Renaissance courtyard was added. During the 18th century, it belonged to the Wielopolski family who added the layers of frilly Baroque decoration and used it as a hunting lodge. Badly neglected for decades, it has been handsomely restored and filled with period furniture, paintings and *objets d'art*.

The limestone gorges and cliffs of the Ojców valley are riddled with caves, many accessible from Ojców. The largest and most impressive is the **Wierzchowska Górna Cave** (*open daily May–Aug 9–5; Sept–Oct 9–4; adm*), close to the village of Wierzchowska, which extends for more than a kilometre into the rock.

Getting There

There are infrequent daily **bus** services between Kraków and Ojców, which continue to the castle of Pieskowa Skała.

Tourist Information

Ojców: park information , **t** (012) 389 2036.

Touring from Kraków: South to the Tatra Mountains

Day 1: Salt Mines and Castles

Morning: Take the 4/E40 to **Wieliczka**, 15km southeast of Kraków, and explore the ancient salt mines (*see* 'Day Trips', pp.53–4).

Lunch: *See* 'Day Trips', p.54.

Afternoon: Continue east along the 4/40, and head south from Bochnia to the tiny, castle-topped town of **Nowy Wiśnicz**. Begun in the 14th century, this Gothic castle (*open May–Oct daily 10–4; Nov–April Mon–Fri 9–2; adm*) with Renaissance and Baroque elements was neglected for more than a century. Restoration only began after the Second World War and is still under way, but you can tour the elegant apartments filled with period furniture and historical exhibits.

Dinner and Sleeping: Adjoining the castle, **Hotel Kmita, t** (014) 612 8825 (*moderate*) offers the most comfortable rooms in town, along with a good restaurant serving Polish cuisine. **Hotel Atlas**, Stary Wiśnicz, **t** (014) 685 5930 (*inexpensive*) is a whitewashed country hotel on the outskirts of town, with simple rooms, friendly English-speaking owners, and a decent little restaurant.

Day 2: Nowy and Stary Sącz

Morning: Head south from Nowy Wiśnicz towards **Nowy Sącz**: take the 965 to Muchówka, turn left on to the 966, and then right on to the 75 at Czchów. Nowy Sącz is a prosperous little town with a mountain backdrop which was a royal residence from the 14th to the 17th centuries. The castle is now in ruins, but the delightful medieval centre spreads out from the vast main square (Rynek), and its narrow streets are dotted with churches. The Regional Museum (*ul. Lwowska 3, open Tues–Thurs 10–3, Fri 10–5.30, Sat–Sun 9–2.30; adm*) contains interesting folk art and burnished icons.

Lunch: Try **Ratuszowa**, Rynek 11, **t** (018) 443 6515 (*inexpensive*), an atmospheric, traditional restaurant in vaulted dining rooms underneath the Town Hall. Or **Kupiecka**, Rynek 10, **t** (018) 442 0831 (*inexpensive*), an elegant cellar restaurant with slightly more adventurous Polish and international cuisine.

Afternoon: On the outskirts of Nowy Sącz, if it's summer, you can explore a collection of typical rural buildings from the region in the **Sącz Ethnographic Park** (*open May–Sept Tues–Sun 10–5; Oct–April Mon–Fri 10–2; adm*). Just 8km southeast of Nowy Sącz, its smaller, older cousin **Stary Sącz** boasts one of Poland's few surviving cobbled main squares. It's an enchanting little town, with tranquil tree-lined streets and a pair of Gothic churches half-hidden under over-the-top Baroque decoration. Duck into the courtyard at Rynek 21, a former folk art gallery, to see the vaulted ceiling with charming local paintings.

Dinner and Sleeping: Tucked away in the old town of Nowy Sącz, ★★★**Hotel Panorama**, ul. Romanowskiego 4a, **t** (018) 443 7110 (*inexpensive*) is a comfortable little hotel with a good restaurant serving tasty traditional local fare. The best-equipped hotel in Nowy Sącz is ★★★**Beskid Hotel**, ul. Limanowskiego 1, **t** (018) 443 5770 (*moderate*), but it's in an ugly modern block near the train station.

Day 3: A Sporty Day...

Morning: Head west from Stary Sącz to Zabrzeż, and turn south to **Szczawnica**. This pretty spa resort is sprawled along the Dunajec river in a steep valley backed by the Pieniny mountains (a National Park), and is a popular base for hikers and canoeists. The upper part of town is filled with traditional wooden houses, and you can take the waters, hike or bike off on one of several easy trails which begin by the river banks, or head up in the chairlift for splendid views from the 772m-high Góra Palenica peak.

Lunch: In Szczawnica, **Halka**, ul. Główna 2, **t** (018) 262 2254 (*inexpensive*) is one of dozens of modest eateries which line this busy strip, with basic regional fare. **Vena Café**, ul. Park Górny 2, is a delightful café, with delicious coffee, snacks and cakes.

Afternoon: Szczawnica is well known for the **raft trips through the Dunajec Gorge**. These log-built rafts, guided by locals in traditional costume, are a wonderful and surprisingly gentle way of enjoying the magnificent gorge. Trips (which take around 2 hours) depart from Kąty and finish at Szczawnica, but the tourist office in Szczawnica (ul. Główna 1, **t** (018) 262 1479) runs tours which include transport to Kąty. Trips take place between April and October: more info from the Pieniny Raftsmen Association, *www.flisacy.com.pl*.

Dinner and Sleeping: In Szczawnica, **Willa Hamernik**, ul. Kowalczyk 3b, **t** (018) 262 1301, *www.hammernik.com.pl* (*inexpensive*), a whitewashed chalet-style villa, has balconies bursting with flowers. **Hotel Batory**, Park Górny 13, **t** (018) 262 0271 (*inexpensive*) is the plusher option, in a modern hotel built in traditional mountain style with a good central location. Eat outside at chalet-style **Zakopianka**, al. Parkowa 8, **t** (018) 262 2464 (*inexpensive*).

Day 4: The Heart of the Spisz

Morning: The 969 leads west of Szczawnica towards Dębno, but you should turn off just before Kluszkowce and follow signs for **Niedzica**. This is the start of a tiny, little-travelled (and unnumbered) road through a beautiful, rural region called the **Spisz**, where time seems to have stood still. Niedzica is a delightful village, with an impossibly picturesque castle perched beautifully above the river. It contains a small museum (*adm*), and if you find it hard to leave, it also has guest rooms (*moderate*).

Lunch: In Niedzica, the elegant **Restaurant Manor House**, **t** (018) 262 9403 (*moderate*) now contains a fine restaurant serving typical Polish and Hungarian fare, prepared in stone ovens fired with beech wood.

Afternoon: Continue westwards, through the heart of the Spisz, and the tiny villages of Łapsze-Niżne, Łapsze-Wyżne and Trybsz. Stop off at the wooden church in **Trybsz**, with its colourful 17th-century reliefs. At Białka, turn south on to the 49, then take the 961 from Bukowina Tatrzańska for Poronin, where it's just 4km along the 47 to the main resort of the region, **Zakopane**.

Dinner and Sleeping: In Zakopane, **Hotel Belvedere**, ul Droga do Białego 3, **t** (012) 421 4865, *www.belvederehotel.pl* (*luxury*) is the fanciest choice in town, in a charming traditionally styled modern building. The endless amenities include a spa, pool and saunas. It also houses the best restaurant in town, the **Ziemiańska** (*expensive*). Welcoming **Pensjonat Tuberoza**, ul. Pilsudskiego 31, **t** (018 20) 13719 (*moderate*)offers elegant

rooms oozing old world charm, along with a sauna, Jacuzzi and restaurant. **Karczma Bacówka**, ul. Krupówki 61, **t** (018 20) 6433 (*inexpensive*), one of dozens of restaurants which line this lively street, has local dishes served by staff in traditional costume.

Day 5: Zakopane

Morning: Zakopane is the biggest resort of the magnificent Tatra mountains (a national park), and one of the most popular holiday centres in Poland. There's plenty to do here all year round, including skiing, hiking, mountain-biking and para-gliding, and the sprawling mountain town retains much of its charming, traditional wooden architecture and a clutch of cultural attractions. The tourist office at ul. Kościuszki 17, **t** (018) 201 2211, *www.zakopane.pl*, and the National Park information office, ul. Chałubińskiego 44, **t** (018) 206 3799, are both excellent resources for information.

Lunch: **Pod Aniołem**, ul Droga do Białego 3, **t** (012) 421 4865 (*moderate*), on the top floor of the upmarket Hotel Belvedere, boasts some of the best views in town. **Sabała**, ul. Krupówki 11, **t** (018 20) 15092 (*moderate*), located in one of Zakopane's most historical hotels, is a wonderful, traditional restaurant decorated in typical Highlander style and offering hearty local cuisine. There's an enormous terrace in summer.

Afternoon: The 47 heads north, past the dusty market town of Nowy Targ to **Rabka Zdrój**, a quiet, traditional old spa town, famous for its crisp air and mild climate, which is surrounded by the forested Gorce mountains. These mountains are another national park, and have a host of well-marked gentle trails which don't attract the crowds of the Tatras. In the morning, return to Kraków along the 7/E77.

Dinner and Sleeping: Simple **U Wujaszka**, ul. Tarczkowka 111a, **t** (018) 268 5010 (*inexpensive*), an unassuming little *pension* in Rabka Zdrój, has basic rooms, all with TV and en suite facilities, in a steep-roofed traditional house. **Hotel Cegielski**, ul. Na Banię 42, **t** (018) 267 7260 (*inexpensive*) is a large, 70s-style spa hotel which has seen better days, but boats a big outdoor pool, all kinds of treatments, and plenty of facilities for kids, including bike rental and ping-pong.

Czech Republic:
Travel, Practical A–Z and Language

Travel

Entry Formalities

Passports and Visas

The Czech Republic is a member of the European Union. Citizens of all EU countries can visit the Czech Republic for up to 90 days without a visa, while UK visitors can stay for 180 days. US citizens can stay for 30 days; Canadians need a visa to make the trip.

Customs

On arrival, you're allowed to import unlimited personal effects and up to two litres of wine, a litre of spirits, 50ml of perfume and 200 cigarettes. When you leave, EU nationals can now import a limitless amount of goods, the proviso that they are for personal use ensures a common sense cap: limits are 3,200 cigarettes; plus 10 litres of spirits, 90 litres of wine and 110 litres of beer; 10 litres of spirits, 90 litres of wine (60 litres maximum sparkling wine) and 110 litres of beer.. Anything over the value of 7,500kčs, including gifts, must be declared. There is a 20,000kčs limit on the import and export of Czech currency.

Getting Around

By Car

Czech roads leave a lot to be desired: check your suspension. **Seatbelts** are compulsory, unless you are under 1.5m tall, in which case you must sit in the back seat.

If you have an **accident**, you must report the news to the police. If you've moved your car a centimetre, or if you test positive for alcohol, it is curtains for your insurance claim.

Speed limits are as follows: built-up areas 60kph, main roads 90kph, motorways 110kph. Driving with alcohol in your bloodstream is punishable by an on-the-spot fine of just under 20,000kčs.

Leaded petrol is *special*, diesel is *nafta*, and unleaded is *natural* or *bleifrei*.

Car hire is not a problem in the Czech Republic; all the major firms are represented: check websites for details.

Avis: *www.avis.com*.
Budget: *www.budget.com*.

Europcar: *www.europcar.com*.
Hertz: *www.hertz.com*.

By Coach and Bus

Prague's central Florenc bus station is huge, ugly and confusing, but it is right by the Florenc metro stop (lines B and C). There are smaller termini at Želivského (line A), Smíchovské nádraží (line B) and nádraží Holešovice (line C). Arrive with time in hand to board a bus; queues build up well before departure. As a visitor, you will be more likely to find coaches useful for local day trips.

By Train

For day trips, trains northwards depart from Prague's Hlavní nádraží or nádraží Holešovice; trains southwards go from Smíchovské nádraží; trains head in all directions from Masarykovo nádraží. Buy your ticket in advance, or pay a small supplement to the conductor. There are timetables on rollers in the stations: look up your route on the map, and then refer to the corresponding table. The word for 'arrival' is *příjezd*; 'departure' is *odjezd*.

Rail fares are cheap, although marginally more than buses (around 65kčs per 100km), with a fast-train supplement. The difference between 1st- and 2nd-class is negligible on short journeys, but on longer trips extra legroom can be worth the 50 per cent premium. Couchettes and sleepers are a bargain.

Prague may be only one stop on your grand tour. Prague's once-legendary travel bargains (Moscow for £2/$3, for example) have joined the Communist bloc in the dustbin of history, but travelling east remains cheap and there are reductions for students and under-26s.

Practical A–Z

Crime and the Police

Municipal police, t 156; **national police, t** 158

Municipal police (*městská policie*) wear black and deal with minor crime and traffic. National police wear navy and deal with everything else. Watch out for the third kind of policeman – the fake ones. A popular scam is for a fake policeman to ask to see your currency and passport in order to check for counterfeits.

Though petty crime (theft from cars and hotel rooms, pickpocketing) is commonplace, rates of crime are still relatively low compared with elsewhere in Europe and North America. As a precaution, take a photocopy of your passport and note travellers cheque and credit card numbers. Use the hotel safe, if there is one.

Travel insurance policies require you to file a report with the police within 24 hours of a theft. You can also contact your embassy for help; the British Embassy is sympathetic.

Disabled Travellers

Even the most powerful wheelchair is likely to whine to a halt on Prague's hills, and its crowded public transport system can be inaccessible to the most able-bodied, but the city is addressing the problems of people with limited mobility. Olga Havel, the wife of Václav, worked tirelessly for disabled people until her death in 1996, and the foundation that she created, Výbor dobré vůle (*see* below), is the most useful information source for visual, auditory or dietary problems, and for wheel-chair users.

The capital is starting to provide for blind people. Metro entrances bleep; train and tram stops are announced, and opening and closing of doors signalled; traffic lights click or squeak when it is safe to cross.

The Czech Republic's thermal springs and spas are said to alleviate scores of medical conditions, from cerebral palsy to psoriasis.

Czech Organizations

Czech Association of Disabled People (Sdruženi zdravotné postižených), Karlinské nám. 12, **t** 224 816 997. Helpful advice.

PIS (Prague Information Service), Old Town Hall, Staroměstské náměsti., Prague 1, **t** 224 482 202 or 12444 (general info), *www.pis.cz*. Information on accessibility.

Prague Wheelchair Users Association (Pražská organizace vozíčkářů), Benediktská 6, **t** 224 827 210, **f** 224 826 079, *www.pov.cz*. Offers assistance for disabled visitors, but its 'Accessible Prague' guide is more useful.

Výbor dobré vůle (Committee of Good Will), Senovážné nám. 2, **t** 800 110 010, *www.rdv.cz*. Foundation set up by Olga Havel, *see* above.

Electricity

The Czech Republic's voltage is 220v, but you'll need a plug with two round prongs before anything will fire up. Get a universal adaptor before leaving that can deal with the earthing prong that sticks out of some sockets. The voltage in older parts of town may be 110v, although this is now rare. It is fine for US equipment, but UK hairdriers will work at half speed, while your laptop and fax will not work at all. If in doubt, pack a transformer.

Embassies and Consulates

Czech Embassies Abroad

UK: 26 Kensington Palace Gardens, London W8 4QY, **t** (020) 7243 1115, **f** (020) 7727 9654, *london@embassy.mzv.cz*, *www. czechembassy.org.uk*.

USA: 3900 Spring of Freedom Street NW, Washington DC, **t** (202) 274 9100, **f** (202) 966 8540, *washington@embassy.mzv.cz*, *www.mzv.cz/washington*.

Foreign Embassies in Prague

Canada: Mickiewiczova 6, **t** 272 101 800, **f** 272 101 890, *www.dfait-maeci.gc.ca*.

UK: Thunovská 14, **t** 257 402 111, **f** 257 402 296, *www.britain.cz*.

USA: Tržiště 15, **t** 257 530 663, **f** 257 530 583, *www.usembassy.cz*.

Health and Emergencies

Ambulance, t 155; **fire, t** 150

If you hold a British or Irish passport, you're entitled to the same free emergency medical treatment as Czech citizens. You may have to pay for it upfront and get reimbursed later. E111 forms (soon to be replaced by a card, Dec 2005) are available free from post offices in the UK and Ireland. You can fill in the form on the spot and a cashier will then stamp it to validate it. You will need your national insurance number and your passport. Take the form/card with you when you travel.

British and Irish citizens may consider taking out health insurance. US and Canadian travellers have no alternative. Check if your credit card covers you – many do. Some clinics do not, however, accept health insurance, or else only accept Czech health insurance policies. Take out a policy with one of the insurance providers who have clinics in the city (*see* below), or be sure to ask for a list of hospitals and clinics that will accept your insurance.

Aetna Global Healthcare, 29 Kingstone Rd, Bristol BS3 1DS, UK, **t** (0117) 966 3724, **f** (0117) 966 1186, *info@integraglobal.com*, *www.integraglobal.com/integrahealth*.

AXA PPP HealthCare, Phillips House, Crescent Rd, Tunbridge Wells, Kent TN1 2PL, UK, **t** 0870 608 0850, *www.axappphealthcare.com*.

BUPA, Perlová 1, **t** 221 667 359, **f** 221 667 387, *info@health-insurance.cz*, *www.health-insurance.cz*.

Internet

Terminals are plentiful in cafés and bars but there are not many specialist outlets. As you would expect, access becomes scarcer in more rural areas.

Money

The Czech currency is the **crown** (*koruna česká*, abbreviated to kč), which is made up of 100 **heller** (*haléř*).

In Prague, the plastic revolution is well under way, but cash is still ubiquitous. The easiest way to access your cash is to use a credit or debit card in an **ATM machine**. MasterCard and Visa cards attract a 1.5% commission, Maestro or Cirrus about 2% but the rates will be better than at a bank or bureau de change. Cash advances can be obtained from banks and *bureaux de change* with your card, and major cards can now be used in all the swankier restaurants, shops and hotels, but are not accepted everywhere. Few shops accept travellers' cheques in payment, but they are the safest way to carry around large sums in Prague. *Bureaux de change* exist all over town, though commission is high; try to change your money at a bank, for a 1–2% charge.

Banking hours are Mon–Fri 9–5.

Current **exchange rates** (March 2005) are: £1 = 46kčs, $1 = 25kčs and €1 = 31kčs.

National Holidays

1 Jan New Year's Day
Easter Monday
1 May Labour Day
8 May VE Day
5 July Introduction of Christianity
6 July Death of Jan Hus
28 Oct Foundation of the Republic
17 Nov Struggle for Freedom and Democracy Day
24 Dec Christmas Eve
25 Dec Christmas Day
26 Dec St Stephen's Day

Opening Hours

Standard **shop** hours are 9–6 on weekdays and 9–1 on Saturdays.

Churches are usually locked due to a spate of art thefts in recent years. Early morning (7 or 8) or evening (6 or 7), before or after services is the best time. Otherwise, times may be posted outside the main doors.

Museum opening hours are usually 9 or 10–4, without lunctime closing. Most are open all year (Tues–Sun in summer and Mon–Fri during winter).

Post

Correspondence can take anything from five days to two weeks to reach home. There is an **Express Service** that does not cost much and can halve that time.

Stamps (*známka*) can be bought from tobacconists and card shops, as well as post-office counters. Don't expect post offices to sell basics such as envelopes or brown paper; look instead for a shop marked *papír* or *papírnictví*.

Price Categories

Hotels

The price for a double room with bath in high season, is as follows:

luxury over 7,500kčs
expensive 4,500–7,500kčs
moderate 3,000–4,500kčs
inexpensive 1,500–3,000kčs
cheap under 1,500kčs

Rates are 20–50 per cent lower off-season (November to March, except Christmas and New Year). Most expensive and moderate hotels include breakfast in the price and take credit cards, but few cheap hotels accept them.

Restaurants

Restaurant selections are divided into three categories: expensive, moderate and cheap. You should expect to pay roughly the following for a three-course dinner for one person, including wine or beer:

expensive over 800kčs
moderate 500–800kčs
cheap under 500kčs

Most foreign visitors will still find eating out to be good value in all but the most exclusive restaurants, but remember that for many Czechs a meal even in the moderate category is something of a luxury. All places listed take credit cards unless otherwise stated.

Sports

With active participants in football, American football, rugby, horse-racing, horse riding, squash, swimming and tennis as well as countless other acytivities, the Czech Republic will certainly keep sports enthusiasts amused. Czechs are also fierce puckers, having reached the ice-hockey world championships on several occasions. The official Czech ice-hockey website is *www.hokej.cz*.

For information on Czech football, visit *www.fotbal.cz* (the official site of the Czech Football Association).

Telephones

Directory enquiries, **t** 120; **international, directory enquiries, t** 0149; **operator, t** 0102 **international operator, t** 0131.

All Czech numbers now have 9 digits and there is no area code.

To **call abroad from Prague**, dial the following codes: to Canada, **t** 00 1; to Ireland, **t** 00 353; to the UK, **t** 00 44; to the USA, **t** 00 1.

To **call Prague from abroad**, dial +420 and then the number.

Most UK **mobiles** can be used throughout the Czech Republic, assuming that you've asked your company to activate roaming. Very few of Prague's public phones take cash; to use them, invest in a phone card, available from newsagents and tobacconists, post offices, hotels, etc.

Time

The Czech Republic is on Central European Time (CET) which is one hour ahead of GMT, going forward one hour in synchronization with British Summer Time (BST).

Tipping

Praguers will round up a bill in a restaurant or a pub by a few crowns, but there is no hard and fast rule. In restaurants, leave 5–10 per cent if the service was good, and about the same to your taxi driver in the unlikely situation that you were not ripped off anyway. Tour guides in castles and at monuments outside Prague rely almost entirely on tips, so be sure to give them a few coins.

Toilets

There are toilets in every metro station, and in strategic locations across town. If you're desperate, it is acceptable to rush into the nearest café or wine bar and ask for the *záchod*, a.k.a. WC (pronounced *ve tse*). 'Men' is *muži*; 'women' is *ženy*.

Tourist Information

UK: Czech Tourist Centre, Morley House, 320 Regent Street, London W1B 3BG, **t** (020) 7631 0427, **f** (020) 7631 0419, info@visit czechia.org.uk, *www.visitczechia.org.uk*.
USA: Czech Tourist Centre, 1109 Madison Avenue, New York, NY 10028, **t** (212) 288 0830, **f** (212) 288 0971, *travelczech@pop.net*.
Canada: Czech Tourist Centre, 401 Bay Street, Suite 1510, M5H2Y4 Toronto, Ontario, **t** (416) 363 9928, **f** (416) 363 0239, *ctacanada@ iprimus.ca*.

Language

It is difficult to imagine how Czech could be more alien to English-speakers. The language is Slavonic, with Latin influences, and in its modern form it dates from the 19th century, when, after 200 years of Germanization, it was re-established by scholars, with the help of peasants, a few old texts and Polish, Serbo-Croat, Bulgarian and Russian dictionaries.

Pronunciation

Czech is a phonetic language (pronounced consistently according to its spelling) with no silent letters. That's simple enough – the problem is learning how to pronounce the letters. If the language of the English southern middle class is used as a benchmark, the main differences are that **c** is spoken as 'ts', **j** is a vowel sound like the English 'y', and **r** is rolled at the front of the mouth. **Ch** is a consonant in itself – it's pronounced as in the Scottish 'loch', and you'll find it after 'h' in the dictionary.

A haček (˘) above a consonant softens it: thus **č** is pronounced 'ch' as in 'chill', **š** is 'sh', and **ž** is the 'zh' sound in 'pleasure'. With **ř**, even Czech children have to be taught how to say it; try rolling an 'r' behind your teeth and then expelling a rapid 'zh'.

Vowels are less complicated – **a** is the 'u' in 'up', **e** is as in 'met', **i** and **y** are both as in 'sip', **o** as in 'hot', and **u** as in 'pull'. The sounds are lengthened if the vowel is topped with an accent (´) (or in the case of 'u', also the symbol °) – they're pronounced like the vowels in, respectively, 'bar', 'bear', 'feed', 'poor', and 'oooh!'. The letter **ě** is pronounced as though it were 'ye' as in 'yet' and softens the consonant that comes before it. Accents affect only the sound of a vowel; and when pronouncing a word, it's the first syllable that's stressed.

Useful Words and Phrases

yes/no *ano/ne*
Please/thank you *prosím/děkuji*
My name is... *jmenuji se...*
I don't understand *nerozumím*
I don't know *nevím*
Do you speak English? *mluvíte anglicky?*
How are you? *jak se máte?*

where is...? *kde je...?*
help! *pomoc!*
are there any rooms available? *máte volné pokoje?*
Do you have a table for two? *máte volný stůl pro dva?*
Do you have vegetarian dishes? *máte bezmasé jídlo?*

Days and Months

Monday *pondělí*
Tuesday *úterý*
Wednesday *středa*
Thursday *čtvrtek*
Friday *pátek*
Saturday *sobota*
Sunday *neděle*

Czech uses the Slav system, using descriptive words to denote the months.

January *leden (ice)*
February *únor (renewal)*
March *březen (birch)*
April *duben (oak)*
May *květen (blossom)*
June *červen (red)*
July *červenec (redder)*
August *srpen (sickle)*
September *zaří (blazing)*
October *říjen (rutting)*
November *listopad (leaves falling)*
December *prosinec (slaughter of the pig)*

Numbers

1 *jedna*
2 *dva*
3 *tři*
4 *čtyři*
5 *pět*
6 *šest*
7 *sedm*
8 *osm*
9 *devět*
10 *deset*
100 *sto*
1,000 *tisíc*

Czech Republic: Prague

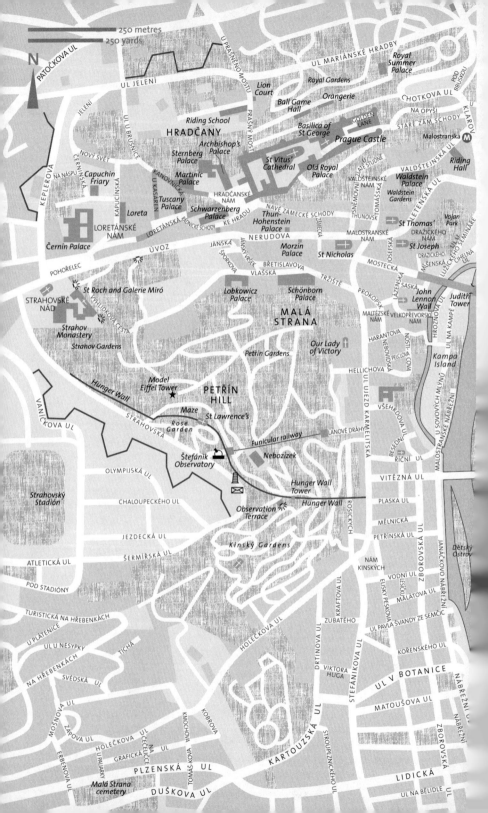

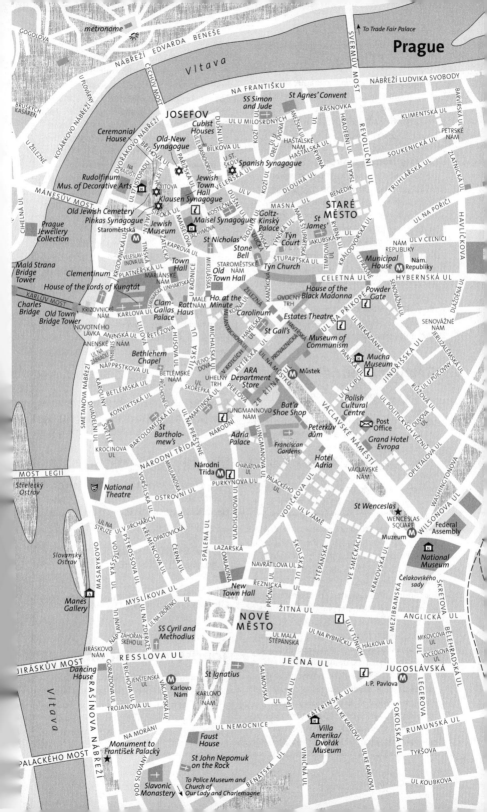

Getting There

Many airlines fly direct to Prague from London and other UK airports (see **Getting There**, pp.4–5), and from the USA and Canada (pp.6–7). You can also travel by train via the Channel Tunnel, see pp.8–9.

Getting from the Airport

The **minibus** is the most convenient and reliable method of transport into the city. The drivers are helpful and will drop you at or very near your precise destination for approximately 300kčs per person. For a mere 90kčs, you can be dropped at Náměstí Republiky, a central square. Buses depart every 30 minutes after 6am from outside the arrivals hall; the last bus leaves at 9pm. Journey time is 20–40 minutes. Alternatively, a regular **city bus** (no.119) leaves the airport every 10 minutes for the Dejvická metro station. **Taxi** fares to the city centre should be around 400–500kčs.

Getting Around

Public Transport Information, t 296 191 111, www.dp-praha.cz (offices at Ruzyně Airport, train and bus stations and major metro interchanges) provide leaflets in English. The PIS has a free transport map.

You can buy **tickets** (jízdenka) for buses, trams and metro from yellow machines in metro stations and on street corners, or at newsagents, tobacconists (look for the 'trafika' sign) and cafés. You cannot buy them on trams or buses, so get a few at a time. Validate your ticket by punching it in the machines on board the tram or bus, and in the ticket hall of metro stations. Tickets are valid for metro, tram and bus. A single ticket costs 8kčs (valid for 15 mins once validated), or 12kčs if you want to make a transfer (valid for 60 mins).

A 24hr pass costs 70kčs; a 72hr pass costs 200kčs; a 168hr (one week) pass costs 250kčs. **Day passes** (celodenní jízdenka) covering all three services can be bought from the red machines in most stations, and you can get passes of up to a week from almost any tabák. Remember to validate passes as you do individual tickets when you start your journey.

By metro: this is the easiest and most efficient way to get around town. It has three lines and three intersections. Trains run from 5am to midnight, every few minutes at peak hours. Stops are scattered all over the centre. The junctions are at Muzeum (lines A and C), Můstek (lines A and B) and Florenc (lines B and C). Lines are colour coded. You need to know the station at the end of the line to go in the right direction. The metro symbol is a white 'M' in a white triangle on a green square.

By tram: these quaint beasts run from 4.30am to midnight, every 5–10mins. You can rely on them to arrive almost to the minute at the time advertised on the stop. Night trams take over all major routes after midnight.

By taxi: always ask the price before setting off. Hailing taxis at a hotel, airport or station will double the fare. The least stressful option is to dial a cab. The following are safe, cheap and reliable: **Profi Taxi**, t 800 118 294, and **AAA Radio Taxi**, t 14014. Tipping is optional. Main taxi ranks are in Wenceslas Square; on the corner of Národní and Spálená; in Malostranské náměstí, on the Staré Město side of Charles Bridge; in Staroměstské náměstí, and next to the Powder Tower.

Car Hire

Avis, Klimentská 46, t 221 851 225, (airport) t 235 362 420, www.avis.cz (open Mon–Fri 8–4.30, Sat–Sun 8–2).
Budget, Čistovická 100, t 224 88 99 95, www.budget.cz (open daily 8–5).
Europcar, Pařížská 28, t 224 81 05 15, www.europcar.cz (open daily 8–8).
Hertz, Karlovo nám. 28, t 222 231 010, t (airport) 220 114 270, www.hertz.cz (open Mon–Fri 8–8, Sat–Sun 8–10).
National, t (airport) 220 114 554.
Sixt, t (airport) 220 115 346.

Bike Hire

City Bike, Králod-vorská 5, t (0776) 180 284 (open daily 9–7).

Tourist Information

The **Prague Information Service (PIS)** has branches around the city (see below). Helpful bilingual staff can help you to find a hotel room, sell you a museum pass, fill you in on events and tell you about places to see in and around Prague. They also stock leaflets on walking tours. The website is very useful.

Prague Information Service (PIS), infoline **t** 12444 (*Mon–Fri 8am–7pm*), **t** 187 for general information (Czech and English), *www.pis.cz*; **Na příkopě 20** (*open April–Oct Mon–Fri 9–7, Sat–Sun 9–5; Nov–Mar Mon–Fri 9–6, Sat–Sun 9–3*); **Old Town Hall** (*open April–Oct Mon–Fri 9–7, Sat–Sun 9–6; Nov–Mar Mon–Fri 9–6, Sat–Sun 9–5*); **Hlavní nádraží** (*open April–Oct Mon–Fri 9–7, Sat–Sun 9–4; Nov–Mar Mon–Fri 9–6, Sat–Sun 9–3*); **Malá Strana Bridge Tower** (*open April–Sept daily 10–6*).

The **Prague Card** is a three-day pass which allows unlimited use of the public transport system and gives free entrance to the city museums and state-run galleries. It costs 790kčs for adults and 610kčs for students and is available from **Čedok**, Na příkopě 18, Staré Město, **t** 224 197 111, and other travel agencies.

Post office (main): Jindřišská 14, **t** 221 131 111; main hall *open Mon–Fri 7am–8pm*; fax, telegram, post and telephone services available 24 hours. Other branches at Kaprova 12, Third Courtyard of Prague Castle, and Hybernská 15.

Emergencies: ambulance **t** 155; fire **t** 150; municipal police **t** 156.

Hospitals: American Medical Center, Kladenská 68, **t** 221 433 130, *www.amcenters. com*; **Nemocnice na Homolce**, Roentgenova 2, **t** 257 271 111, *www.homolka.cz* – the best Czech hospital, used to foreigners.

24-hour pharmacies (*lékárna*): Palackého 5, **t** 224 94 69 82; Belgická 37, **t** 222 519 731; Štefanikova 6, **t** 257 320 194.

Festivals

Prague Spring Music Festival (May/June), the biggest event in Prague's musical calendar.
Dance Prague (*Tanec Praha*; June), featuring contemporary dance.
Prague Autumn (September), classical music.
International Jazz Festival (September).
Musica Judaica (November).

Shopping

The free market has hit Prague big-time. Its department stores, once palaces of command-economy kitsch, have in recent years become showcases for imported Western goods. Shopping malls seem to spring up daily; there's a monster mall in Smíchov and at least half a dozen along **Na příkopě**. *Standard shopping hours are 9–6 weekdays and 9–1 Sat.*

The Globe Bookstore and Coffeehouse, Pštrossova 6. Good collection of English-language novels and non-fiction works (secondhand and new), and a buzzing café attached. *Open till midnight.*

Originál Moda, Jungmannova 13. Czech-designed fashion, jewellery, cards, hand-painted scarves and knick-knacks. A good place to pick up a present or two.

Bohemia Crystal, Na příkopě 17. Sparkling selection of pricey crystal goods (Bohemian crystal is said to be among the finest in the world). *Open daily.*

Moser, Na příkopě 12 (first floor). A glittering treasure trove of crystal. Silverware and porcelain too.

Where to Stay

Casa Marcello, Řásnovka 783, Staré Město, **t** 222 310 260, **f** 222 313 323, *www.casa-marcello.cz* (*luxury*). Plush and intimate, in a former nuns' dormitory on a cobbled street near St Agnes' Convent.

The Iron Gate, Michalská 19, Staré Město, **t** 225 777 777, **f** 225 777 778, *www.irongate.cz* (*luxury*). A fine historic conversion, with two wings from the 14th and 16th centuries; painted ceiling beams and original 14th-century frescoes. Kitchenettes are hidden away inside antique wardrobes.

The Charles, Josefská 1, Malá Strana, **t** 257 532 913, **f** 257 532 910, *www.hotels-of-prague.com* (*luxury*). Extremely friendly hotel in a converted Baroque townhouse close to Charles Bridge. Velvet curtains, engraved furniture, wood and terracotta floors and Persian rugs beneath ceilings with painted beams.

Hotel Metamorphis, Malá Štupartská 5, Staré Město, **t** 221 771 011, *www.metamorphis.cz* (*expensive*). Overlooking busy, touristy Týn Court. The elegant rooms have superb views of the old town. Restaurant, café and bar.

Hotel U Prince, Staroměstské nám., Staré Město, **t/f** 224 213 807, *www.hoteluprince.cz* (*expensive*). In front of the Astronomical

Clock on Staroměstské náměstí, this 12th-century building offers five-star comforts, including two vaulted restaurants, a rooftop terrace, rooms and apartments stuffed full of antiques and slick service.

Hotel Josef, Rybná 20, Josefov, t 221 700 111, f 221 700 999, *www.hoteljosef.com* (*expensive*). Frosted glass, curves of chrome and white walls – the rooms are chic but plain. Superiors have glass-walled bathrooms, DVD-CD players, mini-bars and Internet access. Book a room with a terrace on the 7th or 8th floor.

Romantik Hotel U raka, Černínská 10, Hradčany, t 220 511 100, f 220 510 511, *www.romantikhotels.com/ prag* (*expensive*). A quiet stay in one of Prague's most beautiful streets. The log cabin extension is warmer and more comfortable than the mess of cottages around it. No meals, but the owner can book dinner reservations.

The Golden Wheel, Nerudova 28, Malá Strana, t 257 535 490, f 257 535 491, *www.thegolden-wheel.com* (*expensive*). This 14th-century building has been converted into Nerudova's latest and most stylish hotel, with 17 individually designed rooms. Old photos and contemporary art adorn the walls.

U páva (The Peacock), U Lužického semináře 32, Malá Strana, t 257 533 360, f 257 530 919, *www.romantichotels.cz* (*expensive*). A charming hotel, perfectly located, with courteous staff. Prices vary according to the view; pay the premium to get one of the third-floor rooms looking up to the castle.

U tří pštrosů (The Three Ostriches), Dražického nám. 12, Malá Strana, t 257 532 410, f 257 533 217, *www. utripstrosu.cz* (*expensive*). Perhaps the most picturesque hotel in Prague, set in a 16th-century townhouse all but built into the Charles Bridge. Rooms with views are more expensive.

Hotel Liberty, 28. října 11, Nové Město, t 224 239 598, f 224 237 694, *www.hotelliberty.cz* (*expensive*). New, plush hotel in a refurbished Art Nouveau mansion just off Václavské náměstí. Extras include a gym, sauna and jacuzzi plus a beauty salon.

Cloister Inn, Konviktská 14, Staré Město, t 224 211 020, f 224 210 800, *www.cloister-inn.cz* (*moderate*). The upmarket cousin of the infamous Penzion Unitas (*see* below), which sits

below it, while the nuns who own it live next door. Good value; book ahead.

U Krále Jiřího (King George's House), Liliová 10, Staré Město, t 221 46 61 00, f 221 46 61 66, *www.kinggeorge.cz* (*moderate*). Cosy, stylish, Baroque pension in the middle of the old town and a stroll away from Charles Bridge. Excellent value; book at least two months ahead. Eight rooms and four apartments.

U Krále Karla (King Charles), Úvoz 4, Hradčany, t 257 53 35 94, f 257 53 09 19, *www.thecharles hotel prague.com* (*moderate*). A Baroque house with modernized, stylish interior. Painted beamed ceilings and fireplaces in each of the three suites. Set on the tranquil hill leading up to Strahov Monastery.

Dům U velké boty (House at the Big Shoe), Vlaška 30, Malá Strana, t 257 533 234, f 257 531 360, *www.bigboot.cz* (*moderate*). Friendly, family-run pension in a converted 17th-century townhouse, surrounded by cobbled alleyways. Only 12 rooms, so book ahead. In-house laundry; no breakfast.

Hotel Dientzenhofer, Nosticova 2, Malá Strana, t/f 267 914 576, *www.vol.cz/rfk/dientzen. html* (*moderate*). Charming pension, in the 16th-century birthplace of Prague's greatest Baroque architect. Tucked away on a silent street and backing on to the Čertovka stream. Very popular – book months ahead.

Grand Hotel Evropa, Václavské nám. 25, Nové Město, t 224 228 117, f 224 224 541, *www. hotelevropa.cz* (*moderate*). Prague's legendary Art Nouveau hotel. The rooms are stark but the common areas are sumptuous indeed, filled with dusty *chaises longues*, mirrors, lanterns and the fronds of plants.

Penzion U medvídků (The Little Bear), Na Perštýně 7, Staré Město, t 224 211 916, f 224 220 931, *www.umedvidku.cz* (*inexpensive*). A former brewery; the old-fashioned beer hall is one of Prague's best. Garden and restaurant too. Simple rooms, but some have Gothic rafters and painted Renaissance ceilings.

Penzion Unitas, Bartolomějská 9, Staré Město, t 224 221 802, f 224 217 555, *www.unitas.cz* (*inexpensive*). Cheap boarding house in a former monastery, opposite a police station that used to be the central interrogation centre of Prague's secret police. Interviewees were often held here; Václav Havel spent several nights in room P6.

Eating Out

All restaurants are open daily for lunch and dinner unless otherwise stated.

Bellevue, Smetanovo nábř. 18, Staré Město, **t** 222 221 443, **f** 222 220 453, *www.zatisigroup.cz* (*expensive*). Elegant furnishings, attentive service and excellent food in this riverside restaurant. Fabulous views up to the castle. Live jazz brunch on Sun.

U modré růže (The Blue Rose), Rytířská 16, Staré Město, **t** 224 225 873, **t/f** 224 222 623, *www.umodreruze.cz* (*expensive*). The 14th-century vaults and tinkling piano make this far more suitable for a lingering evening meal than lunch. One of Prague's most exceptional restaurants.

Zelezná Brata, Michalská 19, Staré Město, **t** 225 777 334, *www.irongate.cz* (*expensive*). Set in the 14th-century vaults of the Iron Gate Hotel, just south of the old town square, this restaurant is a good place to sample Bohemian cuisine. The menu features pastoral favourites such as *halusky*, a form of *gnocchi* served in a sheep's cheese sauce. The highlight, though, is the live gypsy music.

Pravda, Pařížská 17, Josefov, **t** 222 326 203 (*expensive*). Next to the Old-New Synagogue, serving a pricey but delicious range of dishes from across the world. Outdoor seating.

Peklo (Hell), Strahovské nádvoří 1, Hradčany, **t** 220 516 652 (*expensive*). An extraordinary dining experience, in the 12th-century beer cellars of the Strahov Monastery; the dishes are sparse, expensive and delicious. The décor is unexpected: fairy lights line the steps that sweep down from the entrance, and one chamber has been made into a disco.

U zlaté hrušky (The Golden Pear), Nový Svět 3, Hradčany, **t** 220 514 778, **t/f** 220 515 356, *www.zlatahruska.cz* (*expensive*). Wonderful Czech and French food in a cottage on the most romantic alleyway in Prague. Outdoor dining in summer; cosy, wood-panelled dining rooms in winter. Unctuous service.

Circle Line, Malostranské nám. 12, Malá Strana, **t** 257 530 021, *www.praguefinedining.cz* (*expensive*). French cuisine and seafood in undoubtedly one of Prague's best restaurants.

U modré kachničky (The Blue Duckling), Nebovidská 6, Malá Strana, **t** 257 320 308, *www.umodrekachnicky.cz* (*expensive*). The first post-revolutionary restaurant to take Czech food seriously; game is a speciality. Extremely popular; a quiet walk away from Charles Bridge.

La Perle de Prague Dancing House (Tančící Dům), Rašínovo nabřeží 80, Nové Město, **t** 221 984 160, *www.laperle.cz* (*expensive*). French gourmet restaurant at the top of Frank Gehry's 'Fred and Ginger' building.

Reykjavík, Karlova 20, Staré Město, **t** 222 221 218 (*moderate*). The prefabricated steakhouse décor of this place conceals one of Prague's better fish restaurants, serving a daily range of scaly creatures flown in fresh from Iceland. Try the legendary fish soup.

7 Angels, Jilská 20, Staré Město, **t** 224 226 955 (*moderate*). A cosy Czech restaurant serving pork, goulash and dumplings to jolly accordion music (Wed–Sun).

King Solomon, Široká 8, Josefov, **t** 224 818 752 (*moderate*). Welcoming, low-key kosher restaurant in the heart of the Jewish quarter. The friendly staff will help you order if you are unused to kosher food. *Reserve for Fri dinner and Sat lunch* .

Bazaar, Nerudova 40, Malá Strana, **t** 257 535 050 (*moderate*). A hotchpotch of a menu, from Mediterranean to Thai, in a glittering restaurant which assaults your senses from the moment you enter its candle-lit vestibule. Transvestite shows and fortune-telling nights add to the bizarre mix.

Country Life, Melantrichova 15, Staré Město, **t** 224 213 366 (*cheap*). Vegetarian café with great views of the old town, serving delicious sandwiches, soups, casseroles and juices. *Closed Fri eve and w/e; cash only.*

Klub Architektů, Betlémské nám. 5a, Staré Město, **t** 224 401 214 (*cheap*). Set in Gothic cellars, this serves satisfying portions of tasty Czech food at reasonable prices. Popular among Czech students and resident foreigners. Outdoor terrace in summer.

Chez Marcel, Haštalská 12, Josefov, **t** 222 315 676 (*cheap*). Large, laid-back French café with big windows perfect for idling away an afternoon. Downstairs there's a basement bistro, serving good mussels and *steak-frites*.

U Čerta (At the Devil), Nerudova 4, Malá Strana, **t** 257 531 526 (*cheap*). A homely little restaurant serving simple Czech dishes.

Cafés and Coffee Houses

The following cafés are open every day from morning to evening.

Café Milena, Staroměstské nám. 22, Staré Město, t 221 632 602. One of the more civilized cafés on the square, with a menu of sandwiches, pancakes and ice-cream.

Obecní Dům Kavárna, Nám. Republiky 5, Staré Město, t 220 002 763. One of the most glamorous Art Nouveau cafés in town.

Bakeshop Praha, Kozi 1, Josefov, t 222 316 823. Excellent bakery with a small café.

Malostranská Kavárna, Malostranské náměstí 5, Malá Strana, t 257 532 110. This legendary café is one of the best places in the city for cream cakes and coffee.

Entertainment and Nightlife

To find out what's going on, scour the *Prague Post* (the weekly 'Night and Day' supplement provides listings); *Prague Guide* (monthly English-language freebie, available in hotel lobbies); *Culture & Guide* (another English-language freebie in tourist offices); Prague Information Service (PIS).

Opera and Classical Music

There are two opera companies: the **National Opera** (Národní opera; Národní 2, Nové Město, t 224 901 448, *www.narodni-divadlo.cz*) and the **State Opera** (Státní opera; Wilsonova 4, Nové Město, t 224 227 266, *www.opera.cz*). Or you can take in a Mozart opera at the **Estates Theatre** (Stavovské divadlo; Ovocný trh 1, Staré Město, t 224 215 001, *www.narodni-divadlo.cz*). The **Smetana Hall of the Municipal House** (Smetanova síň Obecního domu; Nám. Republiky 5, Nové Město, t 222 002 100, *www.obecnidum.cz*) houses the Prague Symphony Orchestra, and the Czech Philharmonic Orchestra is based at the **Rudolfinum** (Alšovo nábřeží 12, Staré Město, t 227 059 309). *See also* 'Festivals'.

Theatre

The largest theatres are the **National Theatre** (Národni 2, t 224 90 14 48, *www.narodni-divadlo.cz*) and the neighbouring **Lanterna Magika Theatre** (Národní Třída 4, Nové Město, t 224 931 482, *www.laterna.cz*).

Dance

The National Theatre is the home of the **Czech National Ballet** (*www.balet.cz*) and most performances are held here or at the Estates Theatre. *See also* 'Festivals'.

Bars

Château, Jakubská 2, Staré Město, t 222 316 328. This maelstrom of the city's social scene is a good place to begin the night. *Open daily 4pm–5am; 4am in winter.*

U supa (The Vulture), Celetná 22, Staré Město, t 224 212 004. A spacious beer hall, serving a rich dark brew called Purkmistr 12°. It also serves steak, duck and tasty game dishes. *Open daily noon–midnight.*

U zlatého tygra (The Golden Tiger), Husova 17, Staré Město, t 222 221 111. Dank but lively beer hall. Václav Havel brought ex-President Clinton here for a beer. *Open daily 3–11pm.*

Alcohol Bar, Dusni 6, Josefov, t 224 811 744. Posey bar in a neighbourhood packed with them; this one does cigars and cocktails for the jet set. *Open daily 7pm–2am.*

U sv. Tomáše (St Thomas'), Letenská 12, Malá Strana, t 257 533 466. One of Prague's best-known and oldest beer halls, with crooners, bassoonists, dumplings aplenty and droves of homesick Germans. *Open 11.30am–midnight; music from 8.*

Clubs

Karlovy Lázné (Charles Baths), Karlův Most, Staré Město, t 222 220 502. Four heaving dancefloors in the erstwhile municipal public baths of Prague. *Open 9pm–5am.*

Lávka, Novotného lávka 1, Staré Město, t 222 222 156. On an island under Charles Bridge, with a view of river, bridge and castle that can be hallucinogenic during a hard night's outdoor dancing. *Open daily 10pm–4am.*

Roxy, Dlouhá 33, Staré Město, t 224 826 296. A former cinema, stripped down to its concrete essentials; recent names have included Asian Dub Foundation, Royksopp and Faithless. *Open club nights 8pm–5am.*

Jo's Garáž, Malostranské nám. 7, Malá Strana, t 257 53 14 22. Funk and house in two cavernous chambers. *Open daily 9pm–5am.*

Prague

Years of smears and smokescreens have added to the mystery that now surrounds Prague. It is the capital of Bohemia, which has been a byword for outlandishness for centuries. The city's golden age began with Emperor Charles IV in the 1300s. He encouraged the Czech language and the country's traditions and built a new bridge, cathedral and the first university in central Europe. In 1556, the Catholic Habsburgs introduced the Jesuit Order to counteract the spread of Lutheranism, and Emperor Rudolf II came to the throne. The religious fratricide of the Thirty Years' War culminated in the Battle of the White Mountain in 1620, with the Protestant armies scattering in defeat. By the mid-1800s the Habsburg empire was dying and Czech nationalism was growing; independence was declared in 1918. In 1939, Hitler invaded Czechoslovakia. At the end of the war the Soviet army entered Prague to a rapturous reception, and Prague – farther west than Vienna, and considerably closer to Dublin than to Moscow – became lost in 'Eastern Europe'. The city of dreams began a 41-year nightmare. And then in 1989 came the Velvet Revolution: a few million people pinched themselves, the tinpot emperors of Communism shivered, and the city returned to where it belongs: the heart of Europe.

Prague is now the capital of the Czech Republic – made up of Bohemia, Moravia and a slice of Silesia – and comprises some 1,213,800 inhabitants; 503 spires, towers and sundry aerial protrusions; 495 square kilometres; 10 districts; eight islands; seven hills (like most legendary cities); and an agglomeration of what were historically five separate towns. Since 1989 it has barely stopped echoing to the rhythm of pile-drivers and, under the glare of oxyacetylene torches, the magical metropolis is being transformed into a city fit for the 21st century. It is still scarred by the barbed-wire wounds of the Cold War but, as it busks, dances, works and kisses its way back to the light, the old divisions are being healed on its streets. Prague doesn't *always* feel so dreamy – particularly as you wade through the tourists, chew through its accursed dumplings or cross swords with a hobgoblin of the bureaucracy – but, if you pack your senses of humour, adventure and romance, a visit is an unforgettable jaunt into a city where history is in the making, and where a thousand years has already been made.

Old Town (Staré Město)

Charles Bridge (Karlův Most)

For centuries the city's energy has squeezed through the narrow channel of Charles Bridge, and it remains Prague's jugular vein. There was a wooden way across the river more than 1,000 years ago; nothing is left of that structure, but remnants of the Judith Bridge, built in 1158 and Europe's second stone bridge after Regensburg, survive in the piers of the present work. The Judith Bridge was destroyed by floods in 1342, but construction of the present structure was completed in the early 1400s by Charles IV's architect, 27-year-old Peter Parléř. The titanic **Old Town Bridge Tower** (Staroměstská mostecká věž; *open daily from 10am; adm*) is part of the city's fortification walls.

The stark structure of the bridge is perfectly complemented by the 30 **sculptures** that now line it. In the 1600s an entire avenue of Baroque saints was added, but many

Food and Drink

There are several types of eating and drinking establishments in Prague: beer joints (*pivnice, hostinec* or *hospoda*), wine bars (*vinárny*), cafés (*kavárny*) and restaurants (*restaurace*). The most distinctive delicacy of the Czech kitchen is the *knedlík*, or **dumpling**. Praguers treat it as the highest culinary expression of the country: if you say that you recently ate an unexciting one, you are almost certain to be told that you just have to know where to go. The main distinction is between floury *houskový knedlík* and *bramborový knedlík*, made of mushy potato. Both are usually served with a lump of meat in a thick gravy, and are staple fare in beer halls. *Špekové knedlíky* are marginally more interesting, mixed with bacon, while *kynuté knedlíky* are downright wild in comparison, centred on lumps of stewed fruit.

You're on tastier ground when it comes to **cold meats**. Prague ham (*yunka*) is of high quality, but it's generally agreed that the best salamis are the harder Hungarian varieties, particularly the flat *lovecký salám*, and both *Uherský salám* and *salám alékum*. Sausages are much loved, and you can pick up a *párek* (two long porkers) in stands across the city. The frankfurter-like *Liberecký párek* and the paprika-flavoured *čabajka* are the best varieties. If you avoid pork, you can eat *hovězí párky* and *drubeží párky*, made of beef and chicken respectively.

Freshwater **fish** are a healthy alternative: carp and trout are bred in the lakes of southern Bohemia and, along with the pike and eel that are occasionally found with them, are widely available in Prague. **Soups** (*polévky*) are often delicious, and in cheaper beer halls and cafés they are often the most likely winners on the menu. *Dršt'ková* is one of the most popular soups and comprises floating pieces of a cow's stomach, while *zabijačková polévka* is a pungent concoction made largely of pigs' blood. The name, roughly translated, means 'slaughter soup'.

There are a few other **snacks** that you'll probably encounter. *Vafle* (waffles) are everywhere, and to find one you generally need do no more than follow your nose. There are also stalls across the city selling *bramborák*, a garlicky potato pancake that is delicious if not too greasy. *Dábelský toust* is a fiercely tasty mixture of meat (usually beef) on toast. *Smažený sýr* is fried cheese, which is more appetizing but no less unhealthy than it sounds.

Czech **beer** needs little introduction: Plzěn is the home of Pilsner Urquell, the first lager and the father of a thousand German imitators, while the brewing town of Budweis (České Budějovice) has become part of the American dream. In fact, US company Busch borrowed little more than the name, and the potent concoction produced in the Czech Republic puts the US slop to shame. (Perhaps realizing that, Busch has kept Czech Budweis off the US market for decades.) Both Czech beers are chock-full of alcohol and sugar, all created naturally during the brewing process, unlike that in additive-laden Western rivals. You may already like sweet beers, and if not you should acquire the taste: look out for beer halls and bottles marked Plzěnský prazdroj and Budvar. Prague also produces beers of its own – Staropramen, Braník and Smíchov – which are slightly more bitter. Czech **wine** might yet become a force to be reckoned with, but at present is more suitable mulled; ask for *svařené víno*.

of the works have now been replaced by copies. The oldest work is the bronze *Crucifixion* (1657), third on your right going east to west. The fifth statue on your left shows **St Francis Xavier** being borne aloft by grateful bearers. About halfway across on the right there is said to be a small bronze **Lorraine Cross** embedded in the wall. According to rumour, the Dalai Lama recognized this point as the centre of the universe during his visit to Prague in 1990. It also marks the spot where **St John Nepomuk** was hurled into the river. John was a vicar-general of Prague who was put in a sack and dropped into the Vltava in 1383 by Wenceslas IV. Further along, **SS Vincent Ferrer and Procopius** deserve a mention: among the feats noted on their statute are the salvation of 100,000 souls, the conversion of 2,500 Jews, 70 exorcisms and 40 resurrections. Of the petrified melodramas that remain, take a look at Matthias Braun's **St Luitgard**. Generally agreed to be the best-crafted sculpture on the bridge, it shows Christ letting the blind saint nuzzle His wounds. Two statues along is F.M. Brokof's pantomime-like tribute to the **Trinitarian Order**, established for the age-old purpose of ransoming Christian hostages from infidel clutches.

The western end of the bridge is punctuated by the **Malá Strana Bridge Tower**, which was built in the early 1400s, and the stumpy **Judith Tower** (*open April–Oct daily 10–6; adm*), which despite its Renaissance decoration belonged to the 12th-century predecessor of the Charles Bridge.

Mariánské Square (Mariánské Náměstí)

Despite the magnificence of the buildings which border it, Mariánské Square is now sadly little more than an overgrown passage with a car park in the middle. On the eastern side is Prague's modern town hall. The western side is dominated by the **Clementinum** (*Library and Astronomical Tower open Tues–Sun 10–7, Mon 2–7*), formerly a Jesuit college and now housing the **Czech State Library**. On display for visitors are some of the oldest illuminated manuscripts in the library's collection and a selection of Baroque astronomical instruments. A step away is the **Great Library**, designed by Kaňker in 1727; its cherub-topped rococo bookshelves are overlooked by an enormous fresco in three parts. In the centre is a spectacular collection of Baroque globes. The **Astronomical Tower** is at the very centre of the complex; creak up the original wooden staircase to see the measuring device for establishing noon.

Old Town Square (Staroměstské Náměstí)

The Old Town Square is the Brothers Grimm in stone: Gothic towers, a sparkling white church and a pastel wave of pink and blue Baroque rooftops. The best place for an overview is from the steps of the **Monument to Jan Hus**, a Protestant heretic and symbol of Czech nationalism whom the Pope had burned alive in 1415. The triangular junction known as the **Malé Náměstí** (Small Square) is dominated by Aleš-inspired paintings on the 1890 neo-Renaissance **Rott Haus**, house of connoisseur, patriot and ironmonger Mr Rott (it is now a huge shop devoted to Bohemian glass).

Construction of the **Old Town Hall** (*Staroměstská Radnice; open April–Oct Tues–Sun 9–6, Mon 11–6; Nov–Mar Tues–Sun 9–5, Mon 11–5; adm; guided tours available*) started in 1338, but the maroon and white façades – encrusted with Gothic and Renaissance survivals from earlier days – are 18th-century. The Old Town Hall's pride and joy is its **astronomical clock** (Orloj; *clock chimes daily on the hour 9–9*). As well as telling the time, its astronomical symbols, pointers and interlocking circles also register the phases of the moon, the length of the day, the equinoxes, Babylonian time and the dates of innumerable mobile feasts. Every hour two cuckoo-clock windows open and statues of the 12 Apostles mince past while bony Death tinkles his bell.

The small **Gothic chapel** on the first floor of the Town Hall dates from 1381. Its main attraction is up on your right as you face the oriel: through a glass door, the figures of the 12 Apostles wait on the spokes of two wheels for their moment of glory. From the chapel, you can climb to the top of the **tower**. The guided tour of the **Town Hall's rooms** passes a memorial cross made from two charred wooden beams. At least 14 men died in the building during a Nazi assault; it was the headquarters of the committee that led the Prague Uprising. The **Old Council Chamber** dates from about 1470. In 1483, the councillors found themselves at the receiving end of some rough justice, when a Hussite mob threw the Catholic mayor and several cronies out of the window, in the second of Prague's four 'defenestrations'.

The striking cream and brown façade of the **House at the Minute** (Dům u Minuty), adjacent to the Old Town Hall, fronts one of Franz Kafka's many childhood homes in Prague (1889–96). The *sgraffito* scenes that cover the building date from around 1610. The **Goltz-Kinschych Palace** (*open Tues–Sun 10–6; adm*) dates from 1755–65, and is one of the best examples of rococo architecture in the city, with its frilly stucco garlands and pink and white façade. The creamy façade of the **Stone Bell House** (Dům u Kamenného Zvonu; *open Tues–Sun 10–6; adm*) belongs to the oldest intact Gothic house in Prague, built in the mid-13th century and named after the stone bell set into the corner. Thorough remodellings after the late 1600s left it concealed until restorers in the 1960s realized what lay behind its unremarkable neo-Baroque façade.

Týn Church (Kostel Panny Marrie před Týnem; *access in Celetná; open for Mass only, Mon–Fri 5.30pm, Sat 1pm, Sun 11.30am and 9pm*), with its multi-steepled towers bristling like Gothic missile batteries and dominating the square, was founded in 1385; it was a hub of Hussitism right up to the 1620 rout, when it was commandeered by the Jesuits. The central vault, altars and decorations are largely Baroque, but they are swamped by the cavernous Gothic structure of the triple-naved church. Walk across the high altar and on the pillar to your left is the **tomb of Tycho Brahe** (1546–1601), Emperor Rudolf II's imperial mathematician for two years during the period when astrology, alchemy and sciences held great sway over the city's imagination.

The buildings lining the south side of the square are constructed over older subterranean houses; almost all of them bear a painted or carved house sign.

East of Old Town Square

In 1786, the **Estates Theatre** (Stavovské Divadlo) saw a performance of Mozart's *The Marriage of Figaro*, which had been panned by the snooty Viennese. But Prague's critics could not praise too highly, and Wolfgang came to town and was fêted. The theatre management commissioned him to write another opera; he returned with the score of *Don Giovanni*, which he conducted here for the first time in October 1787.

Celetná is one of the oldest streets in Prague. Behind the Baroque and rococo façades are remnants of earlier Gothic buildings. Just north of it is **Týn Court**, a handsome, arcaded courtyard dating from the 11th century, which was the enclave of the eastern traders. It had everything: church, inn and even a hospice. Now it has emerged from an expensive renovation with a stack of chichi shops, terrace cafés and restaurants. The nearby **St James' Church** (Kostel sv. Jakub; *open Mon–Sat 9.30–12.15 and 2–4, Sun 9.30–12 and 2–6*), founded in 1374, escaped the overkill that turned some of Prague's churches into grotesqueries during the Counter-Reformation. Its interior is now one of the most elegant in the city. Although the Gothic proportions of the hall-church keep the 21 Baroque altars firmly under control, the splendid tableau of the **Tomb of Count Jan Václav Vratislav of Mitrovice** (1714–16), built by the daunting late Baroque duo of Vienna's J.B. Fischer von Erlach and Prague's F.M. Brokof, tries its hardest to break free.

In Náměsty Republiky the **Municipal House** (Obecní Dům; *open daily 10–6; guided tours in English daily every 2hrs in summer, weekends only in winter; adm*) is an Art Nouveau masterpiece, a forest of crystal and mirrors, whiplash curves, organic excrescences and sensual homages to Czechdom and civic virtue. A wander round the staircase between the ground-floor restaurant, café and bars is free, but you'll need to join the guided tour to see most of the interior, recently restored to its original lustre. Originally one of the gates into the Staré Město, the adjacent **Powder Gate** (Prašná Brána; *open April–Oct daily 10–6; adm*) was begun in 1475, but not finished until the late 19th century.

Josefov

This area was originally the site of Prague's Jewish ghetto, built in the 13th century. In 1784, under Emperor Josef II, the ghetto gates were thrown open, and in 1850 it was formally incorporated into Prague and renamed Josefov, as it is still known. Integration proceeded apace, but by the end of the 19th century the district was a set of 288 stinking slums, brothels and bars. The authorities chose to destroy the buildings, and broad streets, crowded with turn-of-the-century mansions, now stand over winding medieval alleys. Of the old ghetto, only six synagogues, the town hall and the cemetery were spared. Of the Jews themselves, some 80,000 of the 90,000 who remained in Bohemia and Moravia in March 1939 were killed.

One of the oldest functioning synagogues to survive in Europe, the **Old-New Synagogue** (Staronová Synagoga; *open Sun–Thurs 9.30–5, Fri 9.30–2*) is still used today by Prague's Orthodox community. Jewish legend gives one explanation for the synagogue's name: *alt-neu* ('old-new' in German) is actually a corruption of *al-tenai*, or 'with reservation' in Hebrew. Angels and/or outriders of the Diaspora are said to have built the synagogue from the rubble of the last Temple in Jerusalem, which they carried over in about AD 135. The name stands as a reminder that when the Messiah finally arrives, Prague's Jews have to take it back. Unless the legend is true, the synagogue appeared around 1270. The splayed chinks of light, and the pillar supports, show how much the synagogue owed to Romanesque building techniques; but the vaulted naves, and the slenderness of the octagonal pillars themselves, represent the beginnings of Gothic architecture in Prague. In the centre is the *almemar* (pulpit), surrounded by a 15th-century wrought-iron grille. Rabbi Loew (*see* below) apparently fought his final and most heroic battle here when, alerted by a dream, he hurried to the darkened synagogue and found an apparition waving swords, dripping with gore and ticking off a list of all Prague's Jews. Ninety-six-year-old Loew realized that this was Pogrom personified, and lunged for the beast. He ripped the scroll from Death's bloody grip, saved the ghetto from extinction and missed only a scrap containing his own name.

Jewish Museum (Židovské Muzeum)

Open Sun–Fri except Jewish holidays, April–Oct 9–6; Nov–Mar 9–4.30; adm.

The Jewish Museum comprises six major sights in the former Jewish Ghetto: the Maisel Synagogue, the Spanish Synagogue, the Pinkas Synagogue, the old Jewish Cemetery, the Klausen Synagogue, and the Ceremonial Hall.

The **Maisel Synagogue** (Maiselova Synagoga) was a gift from Mayor Maisel to the ghetto. The hall contains an exhibition devoted to the history of Jews in Bohemia from the 10th to the 18th century, including a spectacular silver collection. The arabesques and keyhole-shaped windows of the **Spanish Synagogue** (Španělská Synagoga) are the last reminder of the Sephardic Jews who settled in this part of the Staré Město after their mass expulsion from Spain at the end of the 15th century. This neo-Moorish structure dates from the end of the last century. It contains a permanent exhibition devoted to the history of Czech Jews from the late 18th century to 1945. The present building of the **Pinkas Synagogue** stands over the 11th-century foundations of what may have been the first synagogue in Prague. After the Second World War it was chosen to house the Czech monument to the victims of the Holocaust.

The **Old Jewish Cemetery** (Starý židovský hřbitov; *entrance through Pinkas Synagogue*) is the second oldest in Europe and is an astonishing sight. For more than three centuries until 1787 it was the only burial ground the Jews were permitted. As space ran out, it was covered with earth, older gravestones were raised, and a new layer of burials was begun. As you walk through, there are thought to be some 20,000 people under your feet, buried in up to 12 subterranean storeys. The oldest known plot is that of poet **Avigdor Kara**, dating from 1439. In 1389, Kara lived through and lamented the most vicious pogrom in Prague's history, in which 3,000 were massacred: more than half the ghetto's inhabitants. Along the western wall of the cemetery, near the Pinkas Synagogue, is the grave of **Rabbi David Oppenheim** (1664–1736), whose 5,000-volume library went on a tour across Europe, making it to Oxford's Bodleian in 1829 as the Oppenheimer Collection. Just as you emerge from the Pinkas Synagogue courtyard into the cemetery, you can find the grand tomb of **Mordechai Maisel** (1528–1601), the mayor of the ghetto during the reign of Rudolf II. The best-known of all the cemetery's occupants is **Rabbi Loew ben Bezalel** (1512–1609). His tomb is along the western wall, opposite the entrance gate. Loew was one of the leading scholars of 16th-century Jewry. Most of his life was spent in Prague and, in 1597, he took over as chief rabbi of the ghetto. The legend now inextricably linked to him is that of the *golem*, or artificial man. After communing with the cosmos, he was warned of imminent danger and told to make a *golem*. He built a man out of Vltava mud, walked around it several times, and then placed the unknown names of God (the *shem*) in its mouth. 'Joseph Golem' was born and embarked on various adventures, eventually being laid to rest in the Old-New Synagogue's roof.

The crooked little neo-Romanesque **Ceremonial House** (Obřadní síň; *entrance at exit of Old Jewish Cemetery*) was built in the early 1900s for the Prague Burial Society Hevrah Kaddishah. The late 17th-century **Klausen Synagogue** (Klausová Synagoga) (*entrance by the exit gates for the Old Jewish Cemetery*), remodelled in 1884, was built on the site of a mess of schools and prayer halls. Rabbi Loew taught in an older building. Both this synagogue and the Ceremonial House house exhibits devoted to Jewish customs and traditions in daily life.

St Agnes' Convent (Klášter sv. Anežky)

The oldest remaining Gothic building in Prague, the convent (*open Tues–Sun 10–6; adm*) now houses the National Gallery's collection of **Bohemian and Central European Gothic Art**. The earliest Gothic art in Bohemia dates from the beginning of the 14th century. The slender and elegant *Madonnas* in the opening gallery show how Bohemian art was beginning to escape the rigid formality of its Byzantine progenitors. In the next room is the *Vyšši Brod (Hohenfurth) Altarpiece*. The most notable feature of the nine paintings is their use of contrasting colours to create an illusion of depth. As you gaze at the six paintings on display by **Master Theodoric**, the first of Bohemia's painters to emerge from misty anonymity, you'll understand the reasons for his fame. Bohemian artists' experiments with colour values and facial modelling reach their culmination in these panels. The work in the final galleries represents the final period of Bohemian Gothic art, already showing characteristic Mannerist signs.

Prague Castle (Pražská Hrad)

Grounds open summer 5am–midnight, winter 6am– 11pm; Monuments open April–Oct daily 9–5, Nov–Mar daily 9–4; adm for St Vitus' Cathedral, Old Royal Palace, Basilica of St George and Powder Tower; other museums within the castle grounds charge separately; guided tours in English Tues–Sun 9–3.

From its beginnings as a pagan mound to the day when Václav Havel was sworn in as president, Prague Castle has been the backdrop for Prague's history. Its neoclassical veneer now stretches half a lazy mile over the capital, the cathedral's onion domes and demented prongs rising from its core. It is almost certainly the oldest continuously inhabited part of the city and is still the seat of the president.

Enter the castle from Hradčanské Náměstí through the main gateway under the Art Nouveau **Battling Giants**. Between the pine flagpoles of the **First Courtyard** is the **Matthias Gate** (1614). The north wing is approached by way of the **Hall of Columns** (Sloupová sín), built between 1924 and 1926 and the work of Jože Plečnik. A stone staircase leads up to the **Spanish Hall** (Španělský Sál), accessible to the public only occasionally and the former venue for Communist Party Central Committee meetings. Opposite the Hall of Columns a doorway leads to the **presidential rooms**.

The most notable feature of the **Second Courtyard** is the **Chapel of the Holy Cross** (Sv. Kříz), which is now used for exhibitions. Part of the former stables houses the **Castle Picture Gallery** (Obrazárna; *open Tues–Sun 10–5; adm*), containing works of art kept in the castle since the reign of Emperor Rudolf II. The gallery was pillaged by occupying Protestant forces in the Thirty Years' War; what's left includes works by Massari, Guido Reni, Gentileschi, Tintoretto, Titian and Rubens.

An arched tunnel leads from the Second Courtyard into the **Third Courtyard**, bringing you up short before the looming St Vitus' Cathedral. On the southern façade of the church is the **central tower**, which is almost 100 metres high, although a fair chunk of that is made up of the multi-storey Baroque dome. Four bells hang in the tower, of which the largest is **Sigismund**, an 18-ton monster on the first floor, dating from 1549. Bells caused no end of trouble in the 16th century. They couldn't be touched by anyone impure (a category that included all women), and pubescent boys dressed in white had to be engaged to transport them from foundry to belfry. To the right of the tower is the **Golden Portal**, once the cathedral's main entrance. Above the gate is a **mosaic** of *The Last Judgment* dating from 1370–71, featuring Charles and his fourth wife, Elizabeth of Pomerania. Directly opposite the mosaic façade is the **Bull Staircase**, another ingenious Plečnik construction, which leads to the Garden on the Ramparts.

St Vitus' Cathedral (Katedrála sv. Víta)

It was under Charles IV that the cathedral, one of the finest 14th-century churches in Europe, began to take shape; building commenced in 1344. Charles hoped to make Prague into a great imperial metropolis and the cathedral its centrepiece. Brought up in Paris, he turned first to a French architect, summoning Matthew of Arras from the papal court at Avignon. Matthew built the east end of the chancel on standard French lines but, luckily for Prague's Gothic architecture, he died in 1352. His replacement, called to the court from Swabia, was Peter Parléř, the scion of a distinguished family of German masons. His new plan for the nave inaugurated a half-century during which Prague became the most significant centre of Gothic architecture in Europe. However, the entire western part of the church, including its grand façade, was only completed between 1871 and 1929, the neo-Gothic architects giving Prague's skyline a focus it had lacked for 500 years. The cathedral was dedicated to St Vitus because in pagan times a four-headed war and fertility god of that name was worshipped here.

Mammoth pillars line the noble arch of the **nave**. The stained glass is a modern addition dating from the 1930s. The original Gothic church is thought to have had only one coloured window, and its bold use of clear light was one way in which architect Parléř broke from the church's French origins. The window in the third chapel was paid for by an insurance company, and celebrates prudent risk-assessment with the psalm, 'Those Who Sow in Tears Shall Reap in Joy'. The original part of the building contains the **tower** of the old cathedral, the highest vantage point in Prague (*adm*).

To the right of the choir is Peter Parléř's shining goldmine, **St Wenceslas' Chapel**, built between 1362 and 1367. The interior is an inviting mosaic of gilt plaster and semi-precious stones, unevenly framing and crowding over the painted Passion scenes below. The number of stones (about 1,370) corresponds to the date of its construction.

The emperor also gave the chapel tremendous secular significance by establishing a new coronation ceremony linked closely to the cult of Wenceslas. The forged door in the southwest corner leads to a small room containing the old crown jewels of Bohemia. You'll have a job getting to see them, though: the door is closed with seven different locks. In any case, any plebeian who puts them on signs his own death warrant. The legend was last fulfilled in 1942, when Reichsprotektor Reinhard Heydrich is said to have sneered with Teutonic arrogance when the grizzled guardian of the jewels warned him of the curse; shortly after trying on the crown, he was assassinated. Down the stairs you can see the 11th-century **crypt** of the basilica, the cathedral's foundations and those of its original choir, 20th-century masonry and the northern apse of Wenceslas' rotunda.

Back in the nave, you're now entering the oldest part of the church, but to go any further you have to get round the incandescent Baroque **tomb of St John Nepomuk**. St John's not-so-humble abode was fashioned from 3,700 pounds of solid silver, after a design by Fischer von Erlach the Younger.

East of the Cathedral

Since the castle was first fortified, the **Old Royal Palace** (Starý královský Palác) has been the site of the royal residence, and inside are three layers of palace. The topmost palace is the **Vladislav Hall** (Vladislavský Sál), built between 1486 and 1502 by Benedict Ried. In its magnificent vault, ribs shoot up like monstrous tendrils from its wall shafts, intertwining across five gently articulated bays and somehow meandering into star-like flower petals in the centre. Ried used anything that seemed to fit the opulence required: the broad rectangular windows are pure Renaissance. Since 1918, the president of the Republic has been sworn in here. At the lowest level is the Romanesque gloom of the 12th-century **Soběslav Palace**.

The interior of the **Basilica of St George** (Bazilika sv. Jiří) dates back to 1142, and it has two asymmetrical towers: medieval rules said that a fat male tower had to protect a slim female tower from the midday sun. The façade is early Baroque. The chapel on the right of the entrance is the **Chapel of St Ludmilla**. The saint was Prince Wenceslas' grandmother and spiritual adviser, strangled at prayer with her veil by his pagan mother Drahomirá, who hoped to coax her son back into the cock-worshipping fold. The adjoining Benedictine **St George's Convent** (Jiřský Klášter; *open Tues–Sun 10–5; adm*) holds the **National Gallery of Czech Baroque Art**.

The huddled cottages along **Golden Lane** (Zlatá ulička) date from the later 16th century and look like a Matisse painting come alive: tiny blocks of colour stretching higgledy-piggledy down the street. The cottages originally housed 24 of Rudolf II's marksmen. **No.22** was where Franz Kafka lived and wrote between December 1916 and March 1917.

The **White Tower** (Bílá Věž) and the **Dalibor Tower** (Daliborka) were built in the 15th century as part of Vladislav II's fortifications of the castle, and served as prisons. The White Tower's torture chamber still contains a rack, stocks, branding irons and so on. The **Lobkovicz Palace Museum** (*adm*) contains copies of the coronation jewels.

The **Royal Gardens** (*open April–Oct daily 10–6*) stretch to the northeast of the castle, and are best reached across the **Powder Bridge** (Prašný Most) in the Second Courtyard. Ferdinand I built the bridge and, in his weird Habsburg way, included a not-very-secret tunnel underneath, so that he could sneak off to his newly built Royal Summer Palace. Far below is the **Stag Moat** (Jelení příkop). Over the bridge to the left is the **Riding School of Prague Castle** (Jízdárna Pražského hradu) and, opposite, the **Lion Court** (Lví dvůr) – once the Habsburg zoo. Beyond the house is the *sgraffito*-covered **Ball Game Hall** (Míčovna), dating from 1567–9. The one-time **Orangerie** stretches along the slope below the garden.

Also known as the **Belvedere**, the **Royal Summer Palace** (Královský letohrádek; *no public access*) was built between 1538 and 1564 by Ferdinand I for his wife. It's the purest example of Italian Renaissance architecture in Prague.

Hradčany

The shadow of the castle has always fallen between Hradčany and the city below. The district was founded in 1320 as a set of hovels in which the royal serfs could sleep and breed – and although it slipped out of the castellan's personal control in 1598, it never grew into a normal town. Locked into a slowly turning backwater, monks and nobles indulged their peccadilloes here for centuries; today, its cobbles and courtyards are a silent suburb of the castle which many visitors never see.

The **National Gallery of Pre-modern European Art** in the **Sternberg Palace** (*Hradčanské Náměstí 15; open Tues–Sun 10–6; adm*), which used to be the finest in Prague, was decimated by a double-whammy in 2000: its superb modern collection was hived off to the new Trade Fair Palace (*see* p.85), while many of its older works were returned to the monasteries and nobles from whom they were confiscated by the Communists. It still contains a few excellent pieces from the 14th–18th centuries.

The original Loreto in Italy was one of the most visited shrines in Europe: it was the house where Archangel Gabriel told Mary the good news, rescued from pagan hands and flown over from Nazareth by a flock of angels in 1291. The Prague **Loreta** (*Loretaánské naměstí; open Tues–Sun 9–12.15 and 1–4.30; adm*) was begun in 1626, and is an outlandish piece of Baroque fantasy designed to reconvert the masses to Catholicism after the Thirty Years' War. The **Santa Casa**, halfway round the cloister, is a replica of the Nazarene hovel itself, complete with rich Baroque stucco reliefs. Walking around the shrine, you may hear the appealing but cacophonous chimes of Loreta's 27 mechanical bells.

Behind is the **Church of the Nativity** (Kostel Narození Páně). On the far right is a painting of the tortured martyr St Agatha – the patron saint of women with breast complaints – handing her own severed breasts like poached eggs on a dish to an angel. In the chapel on the corner, the figure with the beard, on the cross to your left, is not Christ but the Portuguese **St Wilgefortis**. She prayed on the eve of her wedding to be saved from her heathen suitor; God gave her facial hair and the prospective groom withdrew. She is the patron saint of unhappily married women.

Up the stairs just before the entrance is the **Loreta Treasury**, a priceless collection of glittering monstrances and reliquaries. The most impressive bauble is a diamond monstrance, more than 6,200 of the stones sprayed out like the quills of a horror-struck hedgehog. It was designed by Fischer von Erlach in 1699.

Strahov Monastery (Strahovský Klášter)

Strahovská; open daily 9–noon and 1–5; adm.

The Premonstratensian canons were an austere order who assembled a library in the monastery that became the finest in Bohemia. The books came in useful in 1782, when Josef II announced the dissolution of almost all the monasteries and convents of the empire; the wily abbot of Strahov saved the day by turning the monastery into a research institute for scholars. As you enter, the crooked little church of St Roch, now the **Galerie Miró** (*open daily 10–5; adm*), features work by contemporary Czech artists and paintings by Picasso, Miró and Braque.

The **Philosophical Hall** (Filosofický Sál; *access with Strahov Monastery ticket*) **library** was built in a frenzy between 1780 and 1782, after Abbot Mayer got wind of the new Emperor Joseph's monastery-razing plans. After climbing the staircase, you'll find yourself in the anteroom, which leads into the opulence of the hall beyond. Walnut bookcases, strung with overripe gilt Rococo decoration, rise two levels. Any sensible library would stop at the gallery, but here the tomes march on, climbing 15 metres in all to the ceiling. The ceiling fresco dates from 1794. There are more than 40,000 books, comprising works that Strahov had picked up from benefactors and monasteries less fortunate than itself. Displayed in cabinets outside the hall are monstrous creatures of the deep: a sad crocodile and cases of shining beetles and butterflies.

The **Theological Hall** (Teologický Sál) **library** was built in 1671, during the restoration of the monastery after the Thirty Years' War. It does not have the solemn majesty of the Philosophical Hall, but its stucco-laden barrel vault is even more sumptuous.

Most of the works in the **Strahov Art Gallery** (*open Tues–Sun 9–noon and 12.30–5; adm*), acquired over the centuries by the monastery, were confiscated by the Communists after 1950. It features paintings from the 14th to the 17th centuries.

Malá Strana

The name Malá Strana translates roughly as 'Lesser Quarter' or 'Little Side'. Sloping from the castle to the left bank of the Vltava, its swirling canopy of orange tiles and chalky-green domes covers one of the finest Baroque preserves in Europe. The quarter was founded way back in the 13th century but a fire and the Thirty Years' War cleared out the rotundas and Gothic clutter in time for the Counter-Reformation. This area demonstrates their schemes and dreams.

Church of St Nicholas (Kostel sv. Mikuláš)

The Baroque mass of St Nicholas' Church (*open daily 9–4*) and adjoining one-time Jesuit College towers over Malostranské náměstí. The **façade** was the work of Munich-born Kristof Dienzenhofer, and the church exudes the confidence and ideology of Prague Jesuitry at its height. The nave's piers jut out at a diagonal, dragging your attention upwards, while the balconies sway forwards from pier to pier, over vast saints urging you onwards to the high altar. The vault adds to the intoxicating confusion, flowing almost imperceptibly from the pillars into three central bays, while the *trompe l'œil* extravaganza of the 1,500-square-metre **fresco** (1760) makes it almost impossible to say where construction ends and illusion begins. The fresco was the work of Johann Lukas Kracker, and opens the vault into the dark drama of the life of St Nicholas (better known to pagans as Father Christmas). The size of the **dome** caused terror; no one would enter the church until a commission of experts certified in 1750 that it would not collapse.

Waldstein Palace Gardens (Valdštejnská Zahrada)

Gardens open daily 9–6; palace closed to visitors.

The majestic maze of beech hedges, gravel paths and gurgling fountains make the Waldstein Gardens an idyllic summer retreat, as well as a monument to General Albrecht Waldstein (1581–1634), successful commander of the Catholic armies in the Thirty Years' War and Prague's most epic megalomaniac. At the end of the magnificent terrace, or *sala terrena*, is a café. At the opposite end is a grotto containing a door leading to what was once Waldstein's observatory.

Nerudova and Further South

This street is named after Jan Neruda (1834–91), a 19th-century Czech poet and journalist who lived here. His name was later filched by the Chilean writer, 1971 Nobel Laureate and inspiration for *Il Postino*, Pablo Neruda. More a chasm than a street, its Baroque and Renaissance façades cling on to the incline. Nerudova has more **painted house signs** than any other street in Prague: multicoloured beasts, birds and apparently random objects which sometimes date back 600 years. The **Morzin Palace** and **Thun-Hohenstein Palace** were built in the 1700s and are now embassies. Each palace features atlantes, fashionable in the 18th century.

To the south, the **Church of Our Lady of Victory** (Kostel Panny Marie vítězně; *open April–Oct daily 8–6*) has a famous exhibit: the **Bambino di Praga**, venerated throughout the Hispanic world. The Bambino's rise to stardom began when Polyxena of Lobkowicz, one of many Spanish brides taken by Czech Catholics at this time, gave the figure to the friars in 1628. After numerous miracles, enough money was made to buy the doll its silver altar; it has also been given scores of costumes.

New Town (Nové Město)

The New Town is actually not very new, having got its name way back in 1348. Over the last century, it has become the commercial and administrative centre of the city.

Wenceslas Square (Václavské Náměstí) and the Charles Bridge were founded almost simultaneously in the mid-14th century by Emperor Charles IV. The equestrian figure of **St Wenceslas** is one of the motifs of Bohemian nationalism, and was designed by J.V. Myslbek. Although a familiar name to English carol singers since the 1850s, Good King Wenceslas ruled as a prince rather than a king, until murdered by his brother, Boleslav the Cruel, in 935. The saint's reputation arose from his Christianity, but over the years Wenceslas has metamorphosed from religious to national hero.

At the southern end of the square stands the **National Museum** (Národní Muzeum; *open May–Sept daily 10–6; Oct–April daily 9–5; adm*), a museum of Bohemian history. Around the square is an undulating skyline of Art Nouveau mansions, offices and hotels, of which the most famous is undoubtedly the **Grand Hotel Evropa**. Revolving doors spin you from the glorious Art Nouveau façade (1903–6) into a shabby and beautiful room of mirrors, mahogany, crystal chandeliers and carriage lamps. Moving north, the rest of the square is a hotchpotch of 20th-century architecture, but wedged between the functionalist Alfa and Tatra buildings is the **Hotel Adria**, one of the last Baroque façades on the square. Further down, at No.8, is the **Peterkův Dům**, perhaps Prague's most elegant Art Nouveau façade. The north end of the square opens into the **Golden Cross**, a popular meeting point.

Outside the Centre

Trade Fair Palace (Veletržní Palác)

The **National Gallery of Modern Art** (*Dukelských hrdinů 47, Holešovice, open Tues–Wed and Fri–Sun 10–6, Thurs 10–9; adm*) is housed in the spectacular functionalist interior of the Trade Fair Palace, built in the 1920s.

Fourth floor (1800–1900): the 19th-century collection opens with the work of J.V. Myslbek, the country's most influential 19th-century sculptor. Further galleries are piled high with the work of the 'National Theatre generation'. These heroes were firm believers in the unity of art and architecture, and many worked on the Municipal House. There are a couple of smouldering paintings by Sarah Bernhardt's favourite poster artist, Alfons Mucha, and a few feisty, bittersweet portraits by Karen Spiller. The prolific Mikoláš Aleš (1852–1913) defaced almost every public edifice of the era in Prague. Mainstream Czech Art Nouveau sculpture is represented by Ladislav Šaloun, and a series of gentle copper and bronze reliefs by Stanislav Sucharda. The belated influence of Rodin, who exhibited in Prague in 1902, is reflected in the early works of Josef Mařatka and Bohumil Kafka. There are several notable works by Germanic artists, including Gustav Klimt and Egon Schiele. Edvard Munch is also represented.

Third floor (1900–30): Prague's artists discovered Impressionism, post-Impressionism and Cubism within a few years of each other in the first decade of the 20th century, and the collection shows the profound effect of this ferment. The most Czech work of this period is the social realist work of the 1920s and '30s, which was inspired by a genuine regard for the real lives of 'ordinary' people. There is also a distinctive collection of non-Czech art, including several works by Rodin. The gallery's collection of early Cubist works is the best in central Europe – the director of the National Gallery in the 1920s, Vincenc Kramář, had lived in Paris during the early years of the century and appreciated the emerging style. Works by Picasso form the core of the collection. As well as pieces of hazy Impressionism, there are a handful of works by the romantic heroes of post-Impressionism: Gauguin, Van Gogh and Matisse.

Second floor (1930–present): this floor opens with a bang with Surrealist work by Frantisek Janonšek, Zdeněk Pešánek and Josef Šima. A small gallery is devoted to Josef Sudek's early photography. Look out, too, for exceptional paintings by Oskar

Kokoschka. After decades of restrictions, Czech artists were liberated to some degree by the death of Stalin. The collection ends with a mixed bag of post-1989 work.

Petřín Hill

The funicular railway runs between 5am and midnight.

Petřín Hill is the green and wooded hump on the left as you cross the Charles Bridge from Staré Město. The forest that used to stretch for miles to the south has disappeared, and vineyards no longer clamber up the hill, but its patchwork of gardens still makes for a perfect retreat. You can stroll as far as the gardens of the Strahov Monastery. One of the loveliest walks in Prague is down from Nebozízek on the path which turns from asphalt to forest as it sinks into Malá Strana's sea of olive domes.

Nebozízek, the first stop on the funicular, is marked by an eponymous terrace restaurant, on the site of a vintner's cottage. In the woods is a monument to the Romantic poet Karel Mácha, where generations of Praguers necked for the first time.

At the **summit** is a rose garden. On the left is the **Štefaník Observatory** (*open Tues–Sun, hours vary*) and the Baroque Church of St Laurence. To the right is a **model of the Eiffel Tower** (*open April–Oct daily 9.30am–7pm; Nov–Mar Sat and Sun only 10am–5pm; adm*), built in 1891 (two years after the original) by the Club of Czech Tourists. The Tourists also contributed the nearby **Magic Maze** (Bludiště; *adm*), with a diorama depicting the Swedish attack on the Charles Bridge in 1648.

Troja Château (Trojský Zámek)

www.citygalleryprague.cz; metro Holešovice Nádraží, then bus 112.
Open April–Oct Tues–Sun 10–6; Nov–Mar Sat–Sun 10–5; adm.

The château houses an extensive collection of 19th-century Czech art. But it is the gaudy, illusionistic decoration of Baroque Troja itself that is worth the trip. It was built in the 1600s by an ambitious Czech nobleman so anxious to please Bohemia's masters that he covered his main hall with an apotheosis of the Habsburgs. Painted by the Flemish-born and Roman-trained Abraham Godyn between 1691 and 1697, it is the capital's richest *trompe l'œil*. Austrian triumphalism is the order of the day. The gaudy masterpiece heaps scorn on the Turks, who had been defeated at Vienna in 1683.

Vyšehrad

www.praha-vysehrad.cz; metro Vyšehrad; tram 3, 17 or 21.

This ancient crag over the Vltava has spun a web of nationalistic lore. Praguers still reel off the myths, but its romantic heyday was a century ago, when it was infested with poets and painters in search of patriotic inspiration. It is now a pleasant retreat on a lazy afternoon, with grassy parks covering the remnants of ancient walls.

Before leaving the area, be sure to see the **Cubist houses** designed by Josef Chochol between 1911 and 1913. There is a trio on the embankment below Vyšehrad, at Podolské nábř. 6–10, one at Libušina 3, and, most impressively, the prismatic apartment block jutting outwards and upwards from the corner of Přemyslova and Neklanova.

Day Trips from Prague

Karlovy Vary

Carlsbad, as the Germans called it, was long one of central Europe's most elegant watering holes; its casino and promenades were the playground of Russian aristocrats and European monarchs. Lovers of bygone charm will find few better spots in Bohemia. The town's famous springs are forced up from subterranean hot rocks 2 kilometres down, and reach the surface at temperatures of 30 to 72°C. Now 12 of the 60 springs have established medicinal benefits. Beware the hypochondriacal regulations that apply along the promenades – no dogs, smoking or loud noises – and in the colonnades, where 'long objects' are forbidden, too.

Up the Teplá from the landmark **Thermal Hotel**, you pass **Dvořák Park** (Dvořákovy sady). Further upriver is the neoclassical splendour of the **Mill Colonnade** (Mlýnská kolonáda), where five springs hiss and gurgle to the surface. In the centre of town is the wooden **Market Colonnade**. Here you will find the **Vřídlo** ('Spring'), the fountain responsible for Karlovy Vary's rise to glory, housed in a glass Communist-era temple. When Charles IV chanced upon a spring while deer-hunting he was advised by his physician that it was suitable only for bathing – an understandable opinion when you taste the foul potion; but in 1522, its oral advantages were publicized by early spa maniac Václav Payer, who recommended a daily dosage of 60 cups and 12-hour baths.

Salvation of the soul always took second place to sins of the flesh in Karlovy Vary. The town was blessed with just one Counter-Reformation masterpiece, the oval **Church of St Mary Magdalene** (Kostel sv. Marie Magdalena) by Kilian Dienzenhofer in 1732–6, on the hill across the river. An enjoyable approach is by **funicular** (*lanovka*).

Getting There

Karlovy Vary is 132km west of Prague. By car join the E48 on Milady Horákové running north by Letná Park. Coaches leave Florenc bus station more or less hourly and take 1½–2hrs; a one-way ticket costs around 100kčs. Trains leave from Masarykovo nádraži train station three times a day and take 3hrs; tickets cost around 140kčs one way.

Tourist Information

Karlovy Vary: Infocentrum, Lázenská 1, t 353 236 377, f 353 232 858, *www.karlovyvary.cz*.

Eating Out

Embassy, Nova louka 21, t 353 22 11 61 (*expensive*). To dine in style, make a reservation at the dark and discreet Embassy, and gorge yourself on smoked eels and asparagus tips.
Promenáda, Tržište 31, t 353 225 648 (*moderate*). Huge, Baroque vinotheque for fine dining.
Zámecký Vrch, Zámecký Vrch 14, t 353 221 321 (*cheap*). Sprawling old mansion with a garden near the river; wooden beams, vaults and classic Czech dishes.

Spa Treatments

The town's clinics handle conditions from indigestion to quadriplegia. Infocentrum (next to the Vřídlo) can tell you if Karlovy Vary can treat your ailment. Of the municipal baths, Baths III and V, luxurious Bath I and the new Bath VI are open to foreigners. They offer watery services from massage to low-voltage electric shock. If you just want a dip, there's an outdoor pool on the hill behind the Thermal Hotel, filled with water from a cool spring. With a breathtaking view over the town, there are few more satisfying swims in Bohemia.

The 500-bed **Grand Hotel Pupp**, the core of which is 300 years old, marks the end of the town. The twilight splendour of the neo-Renaissance **Bath 1** (Lázně 1), opposite the hotel, offers the chance to munch water biscuits in Emperor Franz Josef's imperial bathtub, before heading upstairs for the roulette tables.

Karlštejn

Open 2 weeks Christmas and April and Oct Tues–Sun 9–4; May, June and Sept Tues–Sun 9–5; July–Aug Tues–Sun 9–6; adm by guided tour only. The chapel tour is for groups of 12 or fewer and must be booked in advance.

Bohemia is full of Gothic castles. Karlštejn is one of the closest to Prague and most popular; its slate roofs and towers, perched on their limestone peak, are almost too perfect to believe. Karlštejn was begun in 1348 by Charles IV, and by 1367 it had been turned into a vast symbol of the strange universe that the emperor inhabited. Its three components were designed to mark a mystical ascent from the mundane level of temporal power (the emperor's quarters) up 260 metres to the pinnacle of the castle, the Chapel of the Holy Rood.

The tour of the lowest level takes you into a richly panelled **Audience Hall**, past an altarpiece by Tomaso da Modena (1325–79) and into the **Luxembourg Hall**. A minuscule model shows how the original room looked. Spiritual concerns begin to take over in the **Church of the Virgin**. Its lively *Relic Scenes* (c.1357) are among the earliest European portraits. They show the emperor receiving oddments of the Passion from Charles V of France (left), and placing them in his Reliquary Cross. *Scenes of the Apocalypse* cover the other walls. Next to the church is **St Catherine's Chapel**, consecrated to one of Charles' patron saints, adopted by the emperor after she saved his life on an Italian battlefield. The oratory is studded with chalcedonies, amethysts and jaspers set in gilt stucco. Paintings of the seven Bohemian patron saints line the side of the chapel. On the altar is a votive scene of the emperor kneeling under the Virgin.

In the third and last stage of Karlštejn the fervent religious chiliasm of the emperor and his age reaches an unparalleled climax in the **Chapel of the Holy Rood**. Accessible only via a corkscrew staircase and fortified with walls up to 5½ metres thick, the chapel was designed by Charles to house his crown jewels and Reliquary Cross. It also represented the promised Heavenly City, where he could contemplate the bliss of salvation after the tribulation of revelation in the church below. Under its gilt vaults, studded with hundreds of glass stars, a moon and a sun, he would pray in the light of 1,300 candles. The emperor's painter, Master Theodoric, painted over 120 saints, prophets and angels to guard Charles and his jewels – Gothic gems.

Getting There and Around

Karlštejn is 28km southwest of Prague. To get there by car follow signs on Strakonická (southbound), the western embankment of the Vltava. Trains to Karlštejn leave from Smíchovské nádraží hourly, taking 35 mins, for 55kčs. The castle is a stiffish (2km) walk from the railway station. Or you could book an organized trip and go by coach.

Eating Out

The road up to Karlštejn is lined with cafés. Eat in Prague before leaving, take potluck on a free table, or picnic in the woods.

Slovakia:
Travel, Practical A–Z and Language

Travel

Entry Formalities

Passports and Visas

Slovakia joined the European Union in 2004. EU citizens do not require a visa to enter the country, and can stay for 90 days. US and Canadian citizens do not need a visa either. All passports must be valid for a minimum of six months after the return date.

Customs

Those arriving from another EU country do not have to declare goods imported into Slovakia for personal use if they have paid duty on them in the country of origin. In theory, you can buy as much as you like, provided you can prove the purchase is for your own use. In practice, Customs will be more likely to ask questions if you buy in bulk. Travellers from the USA are allowed to bring home, duty-free, goods to the value of $800, including 250 cigarettes or 50 cigars, plus one litre of alcohol.

Getting Around

By Train

Slovakia's train system, run by **Železnice Slovenskej Republiky (ŽSR)**, t (02) 5058 7582, *www.zsr.sk*, is generally fast, cheap, clean, punctual and efficient, linking Bratislava with almost all major destinations within Slovakia on a daily basis. Service to smaller towns and villages is less frequent and in many cases seasonal. Most stations have a left-luggage office. Express trains also leave Bratislava for Vienna (1½hrs); Budapest (3hrs); Prague (4½hrs); and Brno (1½hrs).

By Domestic Ferry

Hydrofoils from Bratislava to Vienna leave daily Wed–Sun (twice daily Thurs–Sat in peak season) and take 1¾hrs. They also sail to Budapest daily mid-April–Oct (twice daily in Aug), taking 4hrs. Ferries cross the river between Devin Castle and Hainburg in Austria.

By Local Bus

Various branches of **Slovenská Autobusová Doprava (SAD)** link Bratislava with all destinations, but the service tends to be slower and less comfortable than the train, and barely any cheaper.

By Car

Slovakian drivers are maniacs, given to insane overtaking almost anywhere. Those in brand new Mercedes and BMWs are the worst, driving so fast that they will suddenly appear in your rear view mirror, then disappear in a cloud of dust, calling for constant vigilance. Just when you think anything goes, you'll find yourself to be the only one caught by a cunning speed trap.

The maximum **speed limit** within city boundaries is 60kph; on expressways it is 130kph and on country roads 90kph. Driving while under the influence of alcohol is absolutely prohibited. **Seat belts** are compulsory, and children under 12 cannot sit in the front seat. The word for **petrol** is *benzin* (unleaded is *natural* or *bezolovnatý*; diesel is *nafta*).

Hiring a car in Bratislava can be a tricky business, as almost every car hire place in town is prone mysteriously to run out of cars altogether. The bigger companies will let you book ahead by e-mail. You must be over 21 and in possession of a valid **driver's licence** (your UK one is fine). All cars are fully insured, and hire companies take credit cards. *See* p98 for car hire companies in Bratislava.

Practical A–Z

Crime and the Police

Police, t 158.

The state police (*polícia*) wear khaki-green uniforms, whilst the local municipal police (*mestská polícia*) wear a variety of different uniforms. You should carry your passport with you at all times, though you're highly unlikely to get stopped.

Theft from cars and hotel rooms is not uncommon, pick-pocketing is always possible in cities, and robberies have been reported on international trains. All this aside, crime in Slovakia is still low compared to western countries. Dangerous driving is the most obvious threat to visitors.

If caught breaking a law, such as speeding, police may well be intimidating in the attempt to impose an outrageous 'fine'. If this seems excessive, negotiate, and ask for a receipt. As always, if you're doubtful as to the identity or behaviour of a policeman, ask to be taken to the police station.

Disabled Travellers

Slovakia has few facilities for the disabled. Bratislava's extensively pedestrianized Old Town, however, makes it much more wheelchair-friendly than most cities, and travel by public transport there is barely necessary.

For more information, contact the **Alliance of Organisations of Disabled People in Slovakia**, Žabotova 2, Bratislava, t 5244 4119, *www.zutom.sk/aozpo*.

Electricity

220 volts/50 Hz, using the standard continental European plug with two round pins.

Embassies and Consulates

Slovakian Embassies Abroad

UK: 25 Kensington Palace Gardens, London W8 4QY, t (020) 7313 6490.
USA: 3523 International Court NW, Washington, DC 20008, t (202) 237 1054.
Canada: 50 Rideau Terrace, Ottawa, Ontario K1M 2A1, t (613) 749 4442.

Foreign Embassies in Bratislava

UK: Panská 16, t (02) 5441 9632.
USA: Hviezdoslavovo nám. 4, t (02) 5443 0861.
Canada: Mišikova 28d, Palisady, t (02) 5244 2175.

Festivals and Events

Few national festivals seem to unite the Slovakian people, but there are plenty of more localized events to keep you amused, a selection of which are listed below. Ask at local tourist offices for more details if festivals are your thing.

February: During **Carnival** season, there are events at various locations.
April: **Wine festivals** take place in various locations, including Prievdza and Bojnice.
May: **Musical Spring** festivals in Prešov, Humenné and Trnava.
June: **Ceramic Fair**, Pezinok; **Folk Festivals** at Banská Bystrica, Prievidza and Trenčanske Teplice.
June–Aug: **Fest Piešt'any** (classical music).
Late July: **Novohrad Folk Fest**, Lučenec.
Aug: **Jánošík Days** contemporary music festival, Terchová; **Classical Music**, Bojnice; **Trnava Gate Folk Fest**.
September: **International Film Fest**, Piešt'any.
October: **International Jazz Fest**, Košice.

Health and Emergencies

Ambulance, t 155; **fire**, t 150; **Slovak Rescue System**, t 154;

No vaccinations are required to enter Slovakia. Medicines can be obtained with prescriptions written abroad, and most common over-the-counter drugs are available. Pharmacies (*lekáreň*) are the first place to go for minor ailments. If they cannot help, you will be sent to a hospital (*nemocnica*). Foreign citizens are entitled to first-aid and emergency ambulance treatment free of charge if injured, though medicines must be paid for.

Now that Slovakia has joined the European Union, EU citizens from other countries are entitled to full hospital treatment there for free; UK nationals should take with them an E111 form, available from post offices (to be replaced by a card in Dec 2005). The service in hospitals, however, is not likely to be as gentle as in most western countries, so you are strongly advised to take out insurance.

In Bratislava there are 24hr pharmacies at Nám. SNP 20, t 5443 2952, and Palackého 10, t 5441 9665.

Internet

Slovakia's larger towns contain as many Internet cafés as anywhere else. Expect to pay in the region of 70–150Sk/hr.

Rural villages are less likely to have a machine. If they do, it will be in the library, where useage is usually free. E-mails sent abroad may not always make it.

Money

Slovak **crowns** (*Slovenská koruna*; Sk) are divided into 100 **hellers** (*halier*). There are coins of 10, 20 and 50 hellers, and 1, 2, 5 and 10 crowns; and notes of 20, 50, 100, 200, 500, 1,000 and 5,000 crowns.

The best way to travel in Slovakia is with a bank card using **ATMs**, which are incredibly frequent in all but the smallest villages, and give a better exchange rate. Exchange offices tend to give better rates for changing cash than banks, though be sure to double check that the commission and exchange rates displayed are what apply to you. There are many possible catches. **Traveller's cheques** are not recommended, as few places will touch them. Those banks that will, charge an inflated commission rate. *Slovenska Sporitel'Àa* is currently the least unreasonable. Never change money on the street.

Most **banks** are open from 8 or 9am to 4 or 5pm, while exchange offices tend to keep much longer hours.

The **rate of exchange** at the time of writing is: US$1 = 29.83 crowns; €1 = 38.67 crowns; £1 = 55.86 crowns.

National Holidays

1 Jan New Year's and Slovak National Day
5 Jan St Cyril and St Method Day
Mar/April Good Friday and Easter Monday
1 May May Day
5 July Introduction of Christianity
29 Aug Slovak National Uprising Anniversary
1 Sept Constitution Day
15 Sept Our Lady of Sorrows Day
1 Nov All Saints' Day
24–26 Dec Christmas

Opening Hours

Shops stay open from roughly 8 or 9am until 5 or 6pm on weekdays. Almost everything but the bigger department stores is closed on Saturday afternoon and all day Sunday.

Churches tend to stay open at least during hours of daylight.

Most **museums and castles** are open roughly 9–5 and closed on Monday and the day after a national holiday. Many tourist attractions outside the capital close down between November and April.

Post

Most **post offices** (*pošta*) are open weedays from 7 or 8am to 5 or 8pm, and to noon at weekends. It is also possible to buy stamps (*známky*) from some tobacconists (*tabák*) and street kiosks.

Airmail from Slovakia is reliable up to a point. Parcels over 2kg need to be sent from a customs office: ask post workers where the nearest one is.

Price Categories

Prices are mostly quoted in euros.

Hotels

The approximate price you should expect to pay, for a double room with bath in high season, is as follows:

luxury over €180
expensive €125–180
moderate €65–125
inexpensive under €65

Restaurants

For a three-course meal with wine:

luxury over €20
expensive €15–20
moderate €10–15
inexpensive under €10

Shopping

As in much of the region, ceramics are probably the most noteworthy local product. Glass and crystal can also be very fine. Hand-made folk crafts such as textiles, embroidery and toys are a perennial favourite. Bratislava has a lot of great art and antiques, but be warned that customs will scrutinize anything that looks too valuable. Lovers of semi-precious stones will find garnets at favourable prices. Wines and dried meats are always worth taking home.

Sports

Slovakia is a top destination for hiking, rock-climbing, mountaineering and cycling, and has some of the cheapest ski resorts in Europe. Unfortunately, the best locations for all of these activities are too far east from Bratislava to consider as an excursion from the capital. The prime region is the High Tatras, with Poprad as the obvious base, and Kraków the closest international destination.

Some more gentle hiking is possible in the Little Carpathian Mountains. Take trolleybus No. 203 northeast from Hodžovo nám. to its terminus at Koliba, then walk 20mins to the TV tower on Kamzík Hill, where maps outline the many trails.

Major rivers such as the Váh and Nitra offer good canoeing and kayaking possibilities. White-water rafting is possible just 20km from Bratislava, **t** (02) 6353 1064.

Telephones

Operator, t 149; **international operator, t** 0123

To **dial abroad from Slovakia**, dial 00 plus the country code (UK 44, Ireland 353, USA and Canada 1, Australia 61, New Zealand 64), then the local area code minus the first 0.

To **call Slovakia from abroad**, use the country code **t** 421 (e.g. from UK and Europe **t** 00 421; from USA and Canada **t** 011 421) and drop the first zero in the area code. Bratislava area code is **t** 02. Directory enquiries: **t** 120 or 121.

When calling Brno in the Czech Republic (*see* pp.107–8), the country code is **t** 420.

It is possible to make cheap local calls from any phone, but for international calls it's best to use a card phone. Some coin phones exist in Slovakia, but most take cards (*telefonná karta*), a variety of which can be bought from post offices and tobacconists.

With international cards, ask for the booklet listing international toll-free access numbers. These cards can also be used to make local calls. Post offices also have phone booths with extended hours.

Time

Slovakia is within the Central European Time zone: one hour ahead of GMT (+2hrs Mar–Oct), six hours ahead of Eastern Standard Time and nine hours ahead of Western Standard Time.

Tipping

Tipping in Slovakia is optional, and should reflect your satisfaction with the service provided. Waiters are certainly happy with 10%, though it is more customary to simply round up the bill. The latter is also the norm with taxis.

Toilets

Public toilets, as elsewhere, are a rarity. Those that do exist, even in public places such as railway stations, tend to charge a small fee. Toilets in restaurants maintain a good level of cleanliness. Those of the squatting variety exist in smaller towns, but are very rare in Bratislava.

Tourist Information

The only Slovak Tourist Board office abroad is in Prague, though embassies (*see* p.91) are generally prepared to offer information.

The Slovak Tourist Board's site is *www.slovakiatourism.sk*.

Other general info sites are: *www.sacr.sk*; *www.slovakia.org*; *www.travelguide.sk*.

If all else fails, then most towns have some kind of **tourist office**, generally with English speakers on hand. In summer **opening hours** are: Mon–Fri 9–6, Sat–Sun 9–2; in winter they tend to close an hour earlier and all day Sun.

The **map** of Slovakia (1:500,000) produced by Austrian publisher Freytag and Berndt is widely available throughout the country and abroad. It shows relief, and has a decent multi-lingual key, with a useful town index on the back. It also covers the southern part of Moravia, including all locations mentioned in the touring sections.

Language

Slovak is a West Slavic language, very closely related to Czech. Most people who have dealings with tourists in the larger towns speak at least some English, and you can certainly get by without trying your hand at Slovak. In rural areas very few people have any English, though some may have a smattering of German.

Pronunciation

Most letters are pronounced like the English, with the exception of those below, and words are pronounced as written. An accent lengthens a vowel, and the emphasis is always on the first syllable.

Vowels: **a** as *a* in 'art'; **e** as *e* in 'end'; **i** as *ee* in 'feet'; **o** as *o* in 'dog'; **u** as *u* in 'flu'. **ia** as *yo* in 'yonder'; **ie** as *ye* in 'yes'; **iu** as *you*; **ô** as *wo* in 'won't'; **ou** as *ow* in 'know'; **y** as *i* in 'machine'.

Consonants: **c** as *ts* in 'cats'; **č** as *ch* in 'much'; **ć** is similar but softer; **dz** as *ds* in beds; **dž** as *j* in 'jug'; **j** as *y* in 'yes'; **š** as *sh* in 'shell'; **ž** as *si* in 'vision'.

Useful Words and Phrases

hello/goodbye *ahoj/dovidenia*
yes/no *áno/nie*
please *prosim*
thank you *D'akujem*
excuse me *Prepáčte mi*
I'm sorry *Ospravedlnujem sa*
how are you? *ako sa máte?*

I don't understand *Nerozumiem*
What is it called? *Ako sa do volá?*
How much is it? *Kol'ko to stoji?*

What time does the *Kedy odchádza/*
  bus/train/boat *prichádza*
  leave/arrive? *autobus/vlak/loç?*
arrival/ departure *príchod/ odchod*
Where is the...? *Kde je...?*
bus stop *autobusová zastávka*
station *stanica*
entrance/exit *vchod/ východ*
open/closed *otvorené/ zatvorené*
help! *pomoc!*
I'm lost *Nevyznám sa tu*

Do you have rooms? *Máte vol'né izby?*
I am vegetarian *som vegeteriám/ vegeteriánka (fem.)*
toilets *záchod*

What time is it? *Kol'ko je hodín?*
today *dnes*
tonight *dnes večer*
tomorrow *zajtra*
yesterday *včera*
day *deň*
week *tý ždeň*
month *mesiac*
year *rok*

Days and Months

Monday *pondelok*
Tuesday *utorok*
Wednesday *streda*
Thursday *štvrtok*
Friday *piatok*
Saturday *sobota*
Sunday *nedel'a*

January *január*
February *február*
March *marec*
April *apríl*
May *máj*
June *jún*
July *júl*
August *august*
September *september*
October *október*
November *november*
December *december*

Numbers

1 *jeden*
2 *dva*
3 *tri*
4 *štyri*
5 *pät'*
6 *šest'*
7 *sedem*
8 *osem*
9 *devät'*
10 *desat'*
100 *sto*
1,000 *tisíc*

Slovakia: Bratislava

08

Bratislava

Sitting at the crossroads of the Danubian and Amber trading routes that connected the known medieval world, Bratislava's strategic clifftops have held fortified settlements since *c.* 3000 BC. Using the Danube as their northern border, the Romans occupied the fortress of Posonium during the first four centuries AD. Six centuries later, the Hungarians built their own border fortress, around which a Romanesque medieval town blossomed in the 12th century. By the time the Turks occupied Buda in 1536, Bratislava had acquired enough commercial clout to act as Hungary's surrogate capital, which it remained from 1563 until 1830. Much of today's Old Town was constructed at this time, especially during the 1740–80 reign of Habsburg Empress Maria Theresia, who was crowned in St Martin's and often held court here. The city was put under siege by Napoleon in 1809, and both its castles burned down within a few years. Despite the constant buffeting of large neighbouring empires, however, Bratislava has come off relatively unscathed. Its small Old Town is undeniably picturesque, with lots to appreciate in a very compact area. It also receives a fraction of the tourist hordes that blight Prague, Budapest and Vienna, and is close enough to use as a calm, central base for exploring all three.

Food and Drink

A typical Slovakian menu is mostly meat: predominantly pork and chicken, but also beef, lamb and turkey, and sometimes goose or game such as rabbit, venison and wild boar. These are fried, roasted, grilled, prepared as *Schnitzel*, sausages or a stew, or stuffed with the likes of cheese and fruits – key ingredients also in the delicious sauces so important in traditional Slovak cooking. Fish (*ryby*) tends to be carp (*kapor*) or trout (*pstruh*). Side dishes such as potatoes and vegetables (*zelenina*) are ordered separately. Slovaks favour dumplings (*knedle*), even though they're essentially just steamed bread. Vegetarians usually have little choice beyond salads (*šaláty*) and deep-fried cheese (*vysmážaný syr*). Sauerkraut is ubiquitous (try it with crispy goose), as is goulash (*segedín* or *koložárska kapusta*). Two traditional dishes well worth trying are *bryndzové halušky*, dumplings baked with sheep's cheese and bits of bacon; and *cesnaková polievka*: garlic soup, often served in a hollowed out loaf of bread. Starters (*predjedlá*) usually consist of soups, dried or smoked meat or fish, paté, etc. Desserts (*zákusok*) are limited: fruit, ice cream or fruit dumplings (*ovocné knedle* or *gul'ky*), which come with cottage cheese or crushed poppy seeds, and melted butter. Most locals would rather go to a café (*kaviáren* or *cukráren*) for pastries, cakes, great ice-creams and good strong coffee. The pastries are rarely as good as they look.

Slovakians will tell you that their wine is as good as the Hungarians', their beer as good as the Czechs'. The latter is almost true. The beer (*pivo*) is excellent (try the *Zlatý Bažant*), and darker brews are readily available. The wine (*víno*) is disappointing, though reds such as *Kláštorné* from the Modra region can be decent, especially the more expensive bottles.

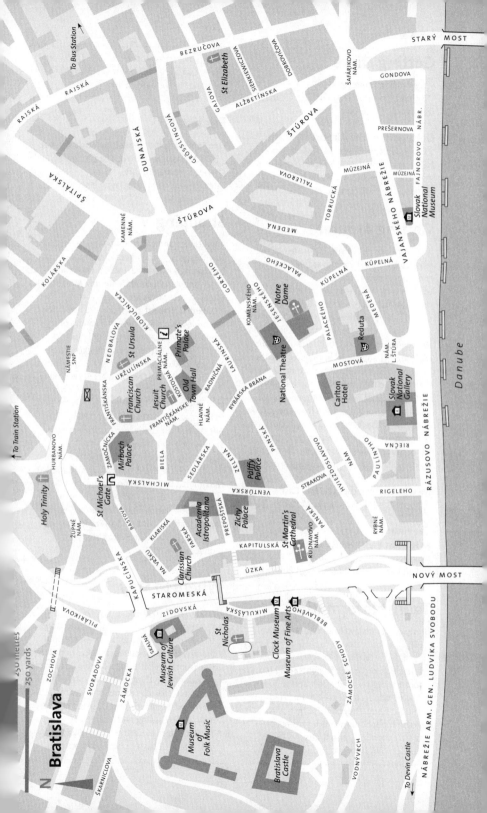

Getting There

See **Getting There**, pp.4–10.
By road, Prague is 321km on E65, Vienna is 65km on E75, Budapest is 200km on E75.

Getting from the Airport

Bratislava's airport, Letisko MR Štefánika, **t** 4857 3353, *www.letiskobratislava.sk*, is 7km from the centre. **Bus 61** runs to the train station. A **taxi** will cost around €20.

Getting Around

All sights except Devin Castle are best reached on foot. There's an extensive, confusing network of buses, trolleybuses and trams run by **DPB**, **t** (02) 5950 1111, *www.imhd. sk*. **Tickets** valid for 10, 30 and 60 minutes, or 1,2 and 3 days, can be bought from DPB offices at bus and train stations, in the passage below Hodžovo nám. and on Obchodná ul., or from machines (change only) at major stops. They must be validated (punched by machines) when you board. Large bags also require a half-fare ticket. Fines are frequent.

Long-distance buses leave from the station at Mlynské Nivy (**t** 0984 222 222), 800m east of the centre (bus 70 from waterfront). The main **train station** (Hlavná Stanica, **t** (02) 5058 7565) is 1km north of the centre (bus 34, 83 or 84 from Hodžovo nám.). **LOD**, **t** (02) 5296 3518, *www.lod.sk*, run **ferries** to Devin Castle from opposite the Slovak National Museum.

Car Hire

Auto Rotos, **t** 4487 2666, *www.autorotos.sk*.
Avis, Hotel Danube, **t** 534 1611.
Favorit Car, Pri vinohradoch 275, **t** 4488 4152.

Tourist Information

Bratislava: Bratislava Information Service (BKIS), Klobučnícka 2, **t** (02) 5443 3715, **f** 5443 2708, *bkis@ bratislava.sk*, *www.slovakia-tourism.sk*, organize 2hr sightseeing tours on foot, various themed walks, and, in June–Aug only, tours by historic tram (Wed 4pm and Sat 6pm). They can also help with accommodation, and have pictures of private rooms. Try also **Bratislava Tourist Service**, Ventúrska 9, **t** 0900 211 221, *www.*

bratislava-info.sk (open daily 10–8, Nov–Mar 10–4), who organize 2hr tours in English leaving Hlavné nám. at 2pm.

Festivals

Late Sept–early Oct: **Bratislava Music Festival**. Mostly classical, with rock bands playing in Hviezdoslavovo Square.
Late Oct: **Bratislava Jazz Days** weekend.

Shopping

Boutiques and galleries abound in the Old Town, especially on Panská/Laurinská, or tucked away in many a discreet courtyard. Locals shop on **Obchodná**, literally 'Market Street', where prices are lower.

Galéria Donner at 4 Klobučnícka has much desirable **art**, old and new, in a variety of media. **In Vivo**, at Panská 13, is the place for beautiful, original ceramics and glass, while **Nie Jesklo Ako Sklo**, at Laurinská 6, specializes in glass. Michalský **Dvor** and **Art Shop Gallery**, both at 3 Michalská, are full of more funky, contemporary art. For all kinds of folk art, head to **Úľuv**, at Michalská 4 or Nám. SNP 12. The gift store at the castle also carries a range of surprisingly non-tacky local crafts.

Speciality food, like smoked meats, salami and sheep's cheese, is beautifully displayed at **Maximilian Delikatéso** on Hlavné nám. A wide range of local wines can be bought or drunk in comfortable surroundings accompanied by a cheese plate at **Vinotéka San Francesco**, Panská 14, or **Vinotéka Sveta Urbana**, Klobučnícka 4.

Where to Stay

Bratislava **t** (02) –
*******Hotel Hradné Brána**, Slovanské nábrežie 15, **t** 6010 2511, **f** 6010 2512, *www.hotelhb.sk* (*luxury*). Sumptuous new hotel 20mins bus-ride from the centre, below Devin Castle and superior to anything in town. Tastefully luxurious, spacious rooms, many with castle views. Extras include feng-shui furnishings, sauna, baby-sitting and disabled access.
******Radisson SAS Carlton Hotel**, Hviezdoslavovo nám. 3, **t** 5939 0000, **f** 5939 0010,

www.radissonsas.com (*luxury*). A handsome, historic building, perfectly located, with a plush lobby, highly regarded restaurant and tip-top facilities. Sadly the rooms, in 'classic' and 'modern' styles, are small and unimpressive, but those on higher floors have views.

★★★★Hotel Marrol's, Tobrucká ul. 4, **t** 5778 4600, *www.hotelmarrols.sk* (*expensive*). Hands down the best in town, this exquisitely furnished hotel (and its Restaurant Messina) has the kind of genuine class others fail to emulate. Rooms, suites and service are impeccable, and the location, close to Hviezdoslavovo nám., is ideal.

★★★★Hotel Perugia, Zelená ul. 5, **t** 5443 1818, **f** 5443 1821, *www.perugia.sk* (*expensive*). Smart, modern, stylish and angular little hotel in the heart of the Old Town. Rooms are much bigger than usual, and only let down by the ugly bedspreads. The terrace restaurant is surprisingly reasonable.

★★★Hotel Tatra, Námestie 1 mája 5, **t** 5927 2111, **f** 5927 2135, *www.hoteltatra.sk* (*moderate*). Within an ugly, functional exterior lurks a surprisingly stylish, modern hotel. The decent-sized rooms have hardwood floors, big windows and tasteful art. The Old Town is a short walk away.

Hotel No.16, Partizánska ul. 16a, **t** 5441 1672, **f** 5441 1298, *www.internet.sk/hotelno16* (*moderate*). Situated in a quiet residential street 10mins from the Old Town, this upmarket *pension* offers cosy, somewhat rustic, rooms, attentive service and a lovely garden.

Chez David Penzion, Zámocká ul. 13, **t** 5441 3824, **f** 5441 2642, *recepcia@chezdavid.sk* (*moderate*). Simple but bright and pleasant rooms with shower, fridge and TV, close to the Old Town and castle. Breakfast is €5 extra in the highly regarded kosher restaurant (*moderate*).

Castle Club B&B, Zámocké schody 4, **t** 903 264 357, **f** 5464 1472, *castleclub2003@yahoo.co.uk* (*inexpensive*). Two attractive rooms with shared bath, and one large suite (*moderate*). Friendly, knowledgeable staff, and a great, quiet location just below the castle. They also have some gorgeous private rooms in town (*inexpensive*).

Old City Hotel, in a courtyard at Michalská ul. 2, **t** 5443 0258, **f** 5464 8304 (*inexpensive*). Rather small but modestly plush rooms with a historic theme and sloping roofs in an aged timber-frame building at the heart of the Old Town. Shower only, and cheaper rooms have shared bathrooms. Newly opened and great value. No breakfast.

Gremium Hostel, Gorkého 11, **t** 5413 1026, **f** 5443 0653, *cherrytour@mail.pvt.sk* (*inexpensive*). The best hostel, with dormitories and double small but pleasant rooms, usually fully booked. Its café and restaurant are good places to meet other travellers and ex-pats.

Private Apartments

Private rooms and apartments (*inexpensive*), usually with shared kitchen, offer the best value in town. Contact the Bratislava Information Service (*see* left), which has pictures, or try *www.bratislava-apt.com*.

Eating Out

Bratislava **t** (02) –

Slovenska Restauricia, Hviezdoslavovo nám. 20, **t** 544 34883 (*luxury*). Considered the best restaurant in the country for traditional Slovak specialities, immaculately prepared and served in sumptuous surroundings.

Le Monde, 1 Ventúrska, **t** 5922 7518 (*luxury*). Le Monde's interior, decorated with varnished newspaper, is self-consciously, almost off-puttingly chic. And empty. Its small but sophisticated and very international menu, however, is one of the town's best, and the terrace is nicely placed. Also a long wine list.

Woch, Františkánska nám. 7, **t** 5443 2927, *www.woch.sk* (*expensive*). Named after Bratislava's oldest known citizen, Woch's mandate is to resurrect ancient Slovakian cuisine, whose rich sauces, stews and seasonal game specialities have a real edge over today's obsession with *Schnitzels* and grills. The tasteful historic interior comprises two bright and breezy rooms, and a vaulted brick cellar. Frequent live folk or jazz.

Caribic, Žižkova 1/a, **t** 5441 8334 (*expensive*). The Caribic's location on a litter-strewn highway south of the castle might leave much to be desired, but its seafood is the best in town.

Café Roland, Hlavné nám. 5, **t** 5443 2398 (*moderate*). Given its location on the Main Square, and the attractive, busy terrace, it's surprising how good, and reasonably priced, the Roland's food turns out to be.

Steam Café, at the Carlton, Hviezdoslavovo nám. 3, t 5939 0000 (*moderate*). A recommended place for typical but upbeat Slovakian food, in lovely classic surroundings.

Leberfinger, Viedenská cesta u. 257, South bank of Danube, t 6231 7590 (*moderate*). Fancy Slovakian food at surprisingly moderate prices. Choose between the comfortable dining room with its murals of Old Bratislava, downstairs in a cellar pub, or outside on a moored boat.

Modra hviezdá (Blue Star), 229 Beblavého, t 5443 2747 (*moderate*). Tasty Slovak specialities, including game, fish and veggie dishes, served in a historic and atmospheric warren of small vaulted rooms (one of them non-smoking) just below the fortress. Great service and a decent choice of wines.

U Vodnika, Lovinskeho 11, t 5477 4277 (*moderate/inexpensive*). Far from the centre, and almost impossible to get to on your own except by taxi (all the drivers know it), this is the place for massive portions of delicious, home-cooked, traditional Slovak cuisine. Situated on a lake, its terrace is also a wonderful spot to while away a sunny afternoon. The sort of place businessmen use to impress their contacts.

Prasna Basta, 11 Zámočnícka, t 5443 4957 (*inexpensive*). Extremely popular with locals. Choose between the sophisticated but unpretentious white domed cellar and the pleasant private courtyard. Predictable Slovak dishes are well-prepared and reasonably priced, plus there's a decent wine list.

Crêpería Francuska Palacinky, 11 Laurinska (*inexpensive*). Tasty French-style crêpes, savoury and sweet, served in a nice little courtyard.

Slovak Pub, Obchodná 62, www.slovakpub.sk (*inexpensive*). The ultimate venue (apart from U Vodnika) for down-to-earth and very tasty Slovak food. A maze of rooms, all with a medieval theme and rustic wood furnishings. Very popular, especially with students. Great service, and a fine choice of ales.

Cafés and Coffee Houses

Bratislava's cafés possess far more variety and class than its restaurants or bars, though the line between the three can be very slim. The following is the cream only:

Antik Café, Hlavné nám./Rybárska. Small, old-style coffee house with a well-placed terrace that's sheltered in inclement weather. Not ruined by its popularity.

Café Apponyi, courtyard behind Primate's Palace, or reached from Radničná. A prime but quiet location.

Café De Zwaan, 7 Panská. Stylish Belgian brasserie boasting a wide variety of superb beers, plus a small menu of favourites like steak and mussels (*moderate–inexpensive*).

Café Exit, courtyard at 11 Laurinská. An enticing, trendy little space.

Café Galéria, 12 Panská. Unpretentious little French-style café-cum-art gallery.

Café Kút, 11 Zámočnícka. Deliciously louche, with red walls and intimate spaces.

Caffé Divan, 9 Panská. Unabashedly sophisticated, with comfy armchairs, burgundy walls and exposed brickwork.

Caffé Zik Zak, Rybárska/Laurinská. Tiny terracotta vaulted room, very stylish. Pavement seating for people-watching.

Coffee and Co, Obchodná. Probably the best coffee in town, in spacious surroundings.

Espresso U Ruzo, Zámočnícka. A pretty little spot on a quiet street serving great coffee.

Entertainment and Nightlife

The Slovak National Theatre on Hviezdoslavovo nám., t 5443 3083, www.sud.sk, is the main venue for opera and ballet, which can be outstanding. The Reduta Palace across the road is home of the Slovenská Filharmonia and the main classical music hall. Nová Scéna, Kollárovo nám. 20, hosts operettas, musicals and Slovak drama. Státne Bábkové Divadlo at Dunajska 36 puts on children's puppet shows.

17's Bar at Hviezdoslavovo nám. 17 has frequent live jazz; Cafe Club Studio at Laurinská /Nedbalova has varied live music nightly.

For drinks, Slovak Pub on Obchodná is the best traditional choice, while Paparazzi at 1 Laurinská, t 5464 7971, is certainly Bratislava's most successfully stylish locale, uncluttered and elegant. Technically an Italian restaurant (*moderate*), it's more fitting for cocktails. Budha Bar on Medena is an atmospheric and smoky little vaulted cellar serving up booze, chilled electronica till late, and lots of teas.

The Old Town

Less than a square kilometre in size, Bratislava's Old Town has a near monopoly on sights. Completely renovated in 2002, and almost entirely pedestrianized, it is a delight to explore. Former site of the town market, atmospheric **Hlavné námestie** (literally Main Square) is surrounded by boastful burghers' houses, plus the fascinating 1912 Art Nouveau **Kooperativa** building. The focal **Roland Fountain**, named after the Breton knight, was actually built in 1572 to honour Maximilian II of Habsburg. Brave-hearted natives of Bratislava, for whom kissing by the fountain will bring long happiness together, can see the statue come to life twice a year: on New Year's Day and Good Friday. Ask them! And look out for the bronze Napoleon leaning over a conspicuously eroded park bench nearby.

The **Old Town Hall** (Staromestská radnica) is a renovated Gothic structure from 1421, with a picturesque Renaissance inner courtyard that hosts concerts in summer, and a neo-Gothic annexe. A cannon-ball lodged in the tower's side, supposedly a stray shot from Napoleon's army, is now painted gold with a black cartoon face. The interior, which boasts some highly decorated vaulted ceilings, contains the **Historical Museum and Museum of Feudal Justice** (*open Tues–Fri 10–5, Sat–Sun 11–6; adm*). Artefacts and commentaries (in English) trace the town's history from prehistoric times, with special emphasis on the craft guilds that played so vital a role in driving a wedge into the feudal system. After a variable collection of 20th-century paintings of Bratislava, you're ushered to the dungeon, where a grisly collection of favourite torture instruments is accompanied by medieval wood-block prints showing the tools at work on glum-faced victims. Finally, climb to the top of the tower for arguably the best views in (and of) town.

Behind the Town Hall is the **Primate's Palace**, aka City Hall (Primaciálny palác; *open Tues–Sun 10–5; adm*), a gem of Viennese classical architecture, built in 1778–81 for the Bishops of Esztergom in Hungary. The tectonic façade, with its pompously symmetrical pillars and pilasters, is topped with a 150kg cast-iron bishop's hat, while the attic gable is covered with rich allegorical sculptures. The highlight of the antique- and chandelier-heavy interior is the Picture Gallery, which contains Bratislava's most vaunted possession: a collection of six rare English tapestries from the 1630s, depicting the Greek myth of Leander's love for Hero, found hidden in the walls during renovations in 1903. The Mirrored Hall is famous as the location where the treaty was signed between the Austrian Emperor and Napoleon after the Battle of Austerlitz in 1805. On Saturdays the palace is crowded with couples getting married. To the north is the 17th-century **St Ursula's Church**, whose Baroque interior contains a copy of the Virgin Mary of Loreto.

To its north, Hlavné námestie runs into a square named after the **Franciscan Church** (Františkánsky kostol), Bratislava's oldest. Originally a Gothic structure from 1297, based on Paris' Sainte-Chapelle, it was rebuilt in Renaissance style (1613–16), then thoroughly 'Baroqued' in 1746, from which time the interior primarily dates. Look out for a valuable early 15th-century statue of the *Pietà* on the side altar. On the church's north flank is a separate two-floor Gothic **Chapel of St John** from the 14th century, containing the skeleton of a saint enclosed in glass. Opposite is **Mirbach Palace** (Mirbachov palác), a 1770 classical structure whose façade and interior feature some wonderful rococo ornamentation. It houses two temporary art exhibitions, and a permanent collection of Baroque paintings (*open Tues– Sun 11–6; adm*).

St Michael's Gate (Michalská brána) to the west is the only surviving gate and watchtower from the town's medieval fortifications. While its base dates from the 14th century, much is from two centuries later, while the gate and onion-shaped steeple (topped with a copper figure of Archangel Michael fighting a dragon) are the result of Baroque alterations around 1758. The tower contains the **Museum of Arms and City Fortification** (Múzeu historických zbraní; *open May–Sept Tues–Fri 10–5, Sat–Sun 11–6; Oct–April Tues–Sun 9.30–4.30; closed Mon; adm*).

Just north, outside the Old Town walls, **Holy Trinity** is the finest Baroque church in town, with a splendid *trompe l'œil* domed ceiling painted by Italian master Antonio Galli Bibiena in 1740.

In 1997, the town resurrected the **Old Promenade** or Korso, which leads from Michael's Gate down Michalská and Sedlárska to Hlavné nám., then down Rybárska to Hviezdoslavovo nám. (the gold crowns on the paving stones mark a different route: the coronation path of ancient Hungarian kings). A series of bronze statues added in commemoration includes Napoleon, a smiling gent waving his top hat on Rybárska, Cumil popping out of his manhole at the junction with Laurinská, and a paparazzi outside the eponymous restaurant. At Michalská 1 is the **Palace of the Royal Chamber** (Král'ovská mad'arská komora; 1756). Now the university library, it once housed the Hungarian Parliament, where serfdom was abolished in 1848. Don't miss **Ventúrska**, which has some impressive buildings, such as **Zichy Palace** at No. 9, Leopold Palace at No. 11, the Baroque **Pálffy Palace** (now the Austrian Embassy) and the newly renovated **Academia Istropolitana**, Slovakia's first university, founded by Hungarian King Matthias Corvinus in 1465.

West of Michael's Gate is the **Clarissian Church**, built *c.* 1400 and possessing an unusual buttressed neo-Gothic pentagonal tower from 1360. **Kapitulská**, Bratislava's most authentic and atmospheric street, runs south from here to **St Martin's Cathedral** (Dóm sv. Martina). The 300kg Hungarian royal crown set on a gilded pillow atop its tower commemorates the eleven kings and eight queens who were crowned here from 1563 to 1830, but the edifice itself retains little dignity. Repeated bouts of recon- struction have resulted in an ugly, grey hotchpotch, cowering beneath the relentless traffic that thunders across the adjacent Nový Most (New Bridge). The oldest sections are the tower and parts of the outer walls, which are 14th-century Romanesque, built by the architects responsible for St Stephen's in Vienna. In the 18th century, Austrian master G.R. Donner provided the church's finest features: the altar, the Baroque Chapel of St John the Almoner, and the bronze statue of St Martin cutting off the corner of his cape for a beggar. None of this can be seen, however – except on Sundays during mass – as the church is closed for archaeological research. Much more appealing, anyway, is the Art Nouveau building, **Salvator Apotheke**, behind the church on Panská.

Panská is Bratislava's most appealing street, lined with chic bars and boutiques. The purely classical façade of the (other) **Pálffy Palace** (Pálffyho palác) hides a building from the 1840s whose historical origins date back to the 13th century when it was a Gothic palace. Mozart gave a recital here in 1762 at the age of six. Inside is a gallery (*open Tues–Sun, 10–5; adm*) hosting varied exhibitions of modern art, and a permanent collection of 19th-century Central European works.

Hviezdoslavovo Námestie and the Danube

Named after the bard of Slovak poetry, Pavol Orsagh, **Hviezdoslavovo nám.** is the town's second key square, an elongated space whose long bridged fountain recalls the filled-in moat whose course the square follows. It's a favourite wandering and meeting place, dominated to the east by the impressive 1886 neo-Baroque **National Theatre** (Slovenské národné divadlo), whose façade features busts of Goethe, Liszt and Shakespeare. The marble and bronze **Ganymede's Fountain** (Ganymedova fontána) in front was inspired by the ancient myth in which Ganymede is kidnapped and taken to Mount Olympus. Just south is the appealingly humble **Notre Dame Church**, its front broken up by columns of exposed masonry, its steeple covered in wood shingles. West is the splendid **Carlton Hotel**, while towards the river on Mostová is the curvaceous neo-Baroque **Reduta**, built in 1914 as a dance hall, now home to a casino, bookshop and the Slovakian Philharmonic.

Sadly, Bratislava's **waterfront** is devoid of interest and views, dominated by a busy road and three ugly bridges. The **Slovak National Gallery** (Slovenské národné galéria; *open Tues–Sun 10–5.30; adm*), however, is well worth a visit. Its extensive foreign collection includes works by Caravaggio, Rubens, Hogarth, Rodin, Gauguin, Monet and Picasso. The best Slovak pieces are from the 19th century, including the vast, very dark *Night Pilgrims at the Crucifix* by Mednyánszky. Don't miss a collection of 69 busts entitled *Character Heads* by eccentric local artist Messerschmidt. Executed between 1777 and 1783, and re-cast in the 1980s, these bizarre sculptures portray the most extreme facial expressions, with titles like *Hypocrite and Slanderer* and *The Extreme Smell*. The nearby **Slovak National Museum** (Slovenské narodné múzeum; *open Tues–Sun 9–5; adm*) contains anthropology, archaeology, natural history and geology exhibitions. It's worth making a loop from here back to Hviezdoslavovo nám. via **Štúrova**, the whole western side of which, as far as Jesenského, is lined with a jamboree bag of superb Art Nouveau buildings, in various glorious stages of decay. To the east, at Bezručova 2, is the lovely Art Nouveau church of **St Elizabeth** (kostol sv. Alžabety), aka the Blue Church.

Bratislava Castle and Around

Sadly, nothing remains of the fortresses built by the Celts and Romans on the steep hill which is the southernmost spur of the Little Carpathian Mountains. Today's **Bratislava Castle** (Hrad), a graceless box surrounded by an intact system of sturdy walls, was first built for King Sigismund of Luxembourg in the 1430s, incorporating a 13th-century tower in the southwest corner. It was rebuilt as a four-wing Renaissance palace for King Maximilian's coronation in 1563, then Nicholas Pálffy added more details from 1635 to 1649, including the turreted towers and the third floor. Maria Theresia made her own adjustments, such as widening the stairs: too heavy to climb them herself, she had taken to riding her horse around the palace. Gutted by fire in 1811, and bombed during the First World War, it was rebuilt in 1953–62 by the Communists, who no doubt appreciated its lack of ornamentation and elegance. The building's highlight is its **well**, reached via a brick-lined tunnel from the northwest corner of the inner courtyard. Otherwise, the grassy grounds are good for strolling and for the views. South of the Danube, hidden at ground level by a thin strip of forest, a nightmare vision unfolds: row upon endless row of hideous tower blocks, flanked by a jungle of smoke-stacks. Leading there, and importunately separating castle from Old Town, is the horribly busy **Nový Most** (New Bridge), for whose construction (1967–72) over two-thirds of the original Old Town was bulldozed. It's known locally as the UFO Bridge, owing to the giant saucer that caps its 85m-high central pylon, soon to contain a panoramic restaurant.

Much of the castle's interior is given over to the uninteresting **Historical Museum** (Historické múzeum; *open Tues–Sun 9–5; adm*). On the second floor, look out for two bizarrely stylized woodcarvings, both from the Spiš area *c.* 1520: *The Two Thieves* and *Altar of the Three Magi*. Less missable is the *Treasures of the Far Past* exhibition on the ground floor (*same hours; extra adm*), if only for the headless fertility goddess known as the Moravany Venus. Carved from a mammoth bone, she's estimated to be almost 23,000 years old. Also in the grounds, north of the castle, is the interesting **Museum of Folk Music** (Hudobné múzeum; *open Tues–Sun 9–5; adm*).

The winding cobblestoned streets below the castle are worth lingering over. At the bottom are three minor museums. The **Museum of Fine Arts** (Umeleckých remesiel; *open Tues–Sun 9.30–6; adm*) contains a humble collection, mostly ceramics, metal-work and furniture. Opposite, the charming wedge-shaped building named 'Good Shepherd' House after its façade statue contains the **Clock Museum** (Múzeum hodín; *open Tues–Sun 9.30–4.30; adm on same ticket as above*), a delightful little collection with several notable pieces. Further north, the **Museum of Jewish Culture** (Múzeum zidovskej kultúry; *open 10–5, closed Sat; adm exp*) is important chiefly for the underground mausoleum opened in 2002 to house the remains of respected scholar and rabbi Chatam Sofer, as well as 64 tombs of other important Jewish figures, following the near-complete destruction of the whole Jewish quarter during bridge-building.

Devin Castle

Just 25 minutes' bus ride from town (no.29 from beneath Nový Most), or reached by ferry from opposite the Natural History Museum, the site of **Devin Castle** (Hrad Devín; *open April–Nov Tues–Sun 10–5; adm*) was probably the first to be settled in Slovakia, and remains a symbol of national independence. First mentioned in manuscripts from AD 864, when it was a major stronghold of the Great Moravian Empire, it burned down in 1811 and, despite recent renovations, has mercifully been left as substantial, evocative ruins. There's still plenty to see, and the scale of the place won't fail to make an impression. A large collection of artefacts tells the story of the Celts, who occupied the area around 400 BC; a second exhibition extensively documents the castle's many other periods of construction and occupation. Expansive views take in the highly cultivated Slovak countryside, and the blending of colours where the grey-green Danube meets the mud-brown Moravian river. Look out for the highly photogenic but disappointingly small turret balanced atop a gnarly column of rock.

Devin itself is a pretty enough village, worth exploring if time allows. Ferries sail from near the bus stop to **Hainburg** in Austria, a good idea for a day trip.

Day Trips and Overnighters from Bratislava

Trnava

Just 45km northeast of Bratislava, Trnava was Slovakia's first free town, granted royal privileges by Hungarian King Béla IV in 1238 that enabled its rapid development. Extensive fortifications built at this time to enclose a 60-hectare area rendered Trnava almost impregnable, so when Central Hungary fell to the Turks, thousands sought sanctuary here, and the town's significance grew. When the archbishop of Esztergom moved his chapter here in 1543, Trnava become the cultural and religious centre of the whole country, and remained so for almost 300 years. Hungary's first university was founded here in 1635, the builders and artists remaining to construct and decorate scores of handsome burgher houses. All this was to change: the university moved to Buda in 1777, and the archbishopric returned to Esztergom; but by this time Trnava's architectural prowess, embracing 11 major churches, had gained it the epithet 'The Slovak Rome'. Today this may seem overblown, but the historic core, cobblestoned, substantially pedestrianized, tastefully illuminated at night and surrounded by almost entirely intact Gothic town walls, is a delight to explore, and entirely unspoilt by tourism.

Trnava's picturesque central square, **Trojičné námestie**, surrounded by fine buildings like the **Town Theatre** (Trnavské divadlo), is focused on and named after a striking Holy Trinity statue. A clutch of key buildings are nearby: the handsome **Town Tower** and the **Church of the Holy Trinity** on Štefánikova; and the church of **St Jacob** on parallel Františkánska. Divadelná leads east through the most intact medieval gate to a particularly well-preserved section of the town wall, which is flanked by the only remaining stinky moat. At its north corner is **Koppel's Castle** and the **Galéria J. Koniarka**. Pedestrianized **Hlavná**, literally Main Street, leads south from Trojičné nám. past the impressive **town hall** to the 14th-century church of **St Helen** and the easily overlooked **Námestie SNP**, a gorgeous little square surrounded by some lovely buildings, including the distinctive, circular **Evangelists' Church**.

Trnava's set-piece is the road leading east from Trojičné nám. to the unmissable **Cathedral of St Nicholas** (Dóm sv. Mikuláš), constructed in the second half of the 14th century and arguably the finest church here. On the way you pass several more worthwhile sights: the church of **St Anne**; the **House of Music** (Dom hudby; *t (033) 551*

Getting There

Regular **trains** from Bratislava to Trnava take 30 mins. The **bus** takes 45 mins.

Tourist Information

Trnava: Trnavsky Informacny Servis (TINS), Trojičné námestie 1, t/f (033) 551 1022, tins@nextra.sk, www.trnava.sk.

Festivals

Trnava hosts spring and autumn music festivals, with concerts held in its many churches throughout the summer.

In May is the **Lumen International Gospel Festival**.

The international music and dance festival **Dobrofest** takes place in the last week of August, and the international **Trnava choir days** is held in October.

The **Traditional Trnava market** in September includes demonstrations of traditional folk handicrafts, and various cultural events.

Where to Stay

Trnava t (033) –
★★★**Hotel Barbakan**, Štefánikova 11, t/f 551 4022, www.barbakan-trnava.sk (moderate). Attractive hotel in the centre with a good restaurant, café, beer house and brewery on the premises.

★★★**Hotel Dream**, Kapitulská 12, t 592 4111, f 592 4115, www.hoteldream.sk (inexpensive). A comfortable, modern hotel on Trnava's most atmospheric but quiet street. Decent, varied restaurant. Parking.

Penzión U Mami, Jeruzalemská 3, t/f 535 4216, www.penzionumami.sk (inexpensive). Perfectly located on a quiet street right next to St Nicholas' Cathedral. Rooms are small and plain. Buffet breakfast included. Friendly, laidback and great value. Parking.

Eating Out

Trnava t (033) –
Symphony Restaurant, Hlavna 13, t 535 4060 (moderate). Set way back in a quiet courtyard, this is Trnava's most upmarket eatery with pleasant in- or outdoor seating. Its lengthy menu includes a good number of salads and seafood dishes.

Láry Fáry Taverna, Halenárska 15/1, t 553 3050, www.laryfary.sk (moderate). Greek, Italian and international food served in a classic brick vaulted cellar.

Vináren U Josefa, Hlavna 18, t 551 1294 (moderate/inexpensive). A decent if predictable menu, and an attractive cellar setting.

Santa Lucia, Hlavna 2, t 551 6651 (moderate/inexpensive). Set back in a narrow courtyard with a busy terrace, this pub-style favourite offers big portions, and specializes in steak.

2556; open daily 9–4.30; adm), with an exhibition of resonator instruments in honour of the Slovak immigrant Dopyera Brothers who invented the Dobro guitar; and **Olah's Seminary**. Dotted along or near Jána Hollého are the **Adalbertínum**, **Marianeum** and **Stephaneum**; the grandiose **synagogue**; and the church of **St Joseph**. At its north end is the **University Church of St John the Baptist** (Univerzitný kostol sv. Jána Krstitl'a), surrounded by stately old faculty buildings. Next to St Nicholas' Cathedral stands a statue of St Joseph, and the excellent **Archbishop's Palace** (Archibiskupský palác).

Heading south is Trnava's most atmospheric historic street, **Katipulska**, a step back in time that appropriately leads to the **Church of the Ascension of Virgin Mary**, and the 14th century Clarissan convent that now houses the **Western-Slovakia Museum** (Západoslovenské múzeum), one of the biggest and most important in the country (Múzejné nám. 3, t (033) 551 2913; open Tues–Fri 8–6, Sat–Sun 11–5; closed Mon).

Brno (Czech Republic)

Situated halfway between Bratislava and Prague, Brno feels at least as large, sophisticated and historically significant as the latter, with almost no tourists at all to taint the atmosphere. The capital of Moravia since 1641, it is packed with impressive historic buildings. The Old Town centre is fairly compact and largely pedestrianized, hemmed in by the significant remains of hefty fortified walls. Lacking Bratislava's manicured quaintness, it is a city for city-lovers, bustling with culture and life.

Brno's best landmark is the central **Old Town Hall** at Radnická 8 (Staroměstská radnice; *open daily 9–5; adm*). Originally built in the 13th century, it combines Gothic, Baroque and Renaissance structures, with an excellent late-Gothic pinnacled portico, behind which are the municipal symbols: a stuffed crocodile, equated with the dragon that once terrorized the city, and a bewitched wheel that was made with the aid of the devil. Highlights of the interior are the Crystal Hall, Fresco Hall, Treasury and Galleries, and you can climb up the tower for views.

To the south is Zelný trh, site of the colourful **Old Marketplace**, with an exuberant 17th-century Parnas Fountain at its centre, and impressive Baroque façades all around. Among them is the Reduta Theatre, and the former Dietrichstein Palace, now the **Moravian Museum** (Moravské muzeum; *open Tues–Sun 9–5; closed Mon; adm*), which contains a mock medieval village. Just southeast on Kapučinské tér is the 1651 **Capuchin Church and Monastery** (Kapucínský kostel sv. Kříže; *open Mon–Sat 9–12 and 2–4.30, Sun 11–11.45 and 2–4.30; Feb–Dec closed Mon*), whose crypt stores mummified monks and local aristocrats from pre-1784. Southwest of Zelný on Petrov Hill, occupying the site of Brno's first castle, is the **Cathedral of SS Peter and Paul** (Katedrála sv. Petra). Several bouts of renovation have resulted in a neo-Gothic building containing remnants of the original 12th-century Romanesque church. Inside is a stone statue of *Madonna with Child* from c. 1300.

Northwest of the Old Town Hall on Dominikánské tér is the **New Town Hall** (Nová radnice), built during the Renaissance, adapted in Baroque times, and housing part of a medieval Dominican monastery. Its picturesque courtyard features the 17th-century Fountain of Twelve Months. Nearby at 18 Husova is the **Moravian Gallery of Applied Art** (Moravská galerie, **t** (542) 169 111; *open daily 10–6; adm*), an extensive collection that includes exhibitions of modern Czech art in the Pražákův Palace. On the hilltop to the west is the notorious **Špilberk Castle** (Hrad Špilberk). Built in Gothic style in the 13th century, it was later converted into a Baroque fortress with military barracks and a notorious underground prison that held opponents of the Habsburgs in the 19th century and prisoners of the Nazis during the Second World War. Today it houses the **Municipal Brno Museum** (Múzeum Města Brna, **t** (542) 123 611; *open Tues–Sun 9–6, closed Mon; adm*), whose three exhibitions cover art, history and architecture.

Brno's broad main square, **nám. Svobody**, contains the 16th-century Renaissance Schwarz House at No. 17, the neo-Renaissance Klein Palace at No.15, and centres on a splendid **Plague Column** from 1690. Rašinova leads north to **St James's Parish Church** (Kostol sv. Jakuba), built in 1220 and probably Brno's most significant Gothic structure. Further north on Moravské nám. is **St Thomas' Church** (Kostol sv. Tomáše; 1350) and

Getting There

There are three direct **trains** daily from Bratislava to Brno: at 6.16, 8.40 and 12.40, taking 1½hrs. The station is just south of the old city walls, within easy walking distance of the centre.

Tourist Information

Brno: The very helpful tourist office is conveniently placed in the Old Town Hall at Radnická 8, **t** (542) 211 090, **f** 210 758, *www. kultura-brno.cz*, *www.brno.cz* (*open Mon–Fri 8–6, Sat–Sun 9–5*). The free fortnightly leaflet *Do města* – Downtown – contains a useful entertainment listing.

The Czech Republic telephone country code is **t** 420, if calling from Slovakia.

Festivals

End Aug: Brno Motorcycle Grand Prix.

Where to Stay

Brno t (542) –
★★★★**Grandhotel Brno**, Benesova 18–20, **t** 518 111, **f** 210 345 (*luxury*). Living up to its name, the best in town in terms of service and appearance.
★★★★**Hotel Slavia**, Solnicni 15/17, **t** 321 249, **f** 211 769 (*expensive*). Tends to get a lot of the business and tour-bus traffic, but a good option nonetheless, in a handy location, though the rooms are nothing special.
★★★★**Hotel Royal Ricc**, Starobrnenska 10, **t** 219 262, **f** 219 265, *hotelroyalricc@brn.inecnet.cz* (*moderate*). A handsome Baroque building close to Zelný trh, with very comfortable, quite modern, if rather small, historic rooms.

★★★**Hotel Pegas**, Jakubská 4, **t** 210 104, **f** 214 314 (*inexpensive*). Well-located on a central but quiet street, with simple but bright and attractive rooms. Breakfast included.
★★**Hotel Avion**, Česka 20, **t** 215 016, **f** 214 055 (*inexpensive*). Situated in an architecturally important functionalist building from 1928, this very central hotel has charmingly dated rooms with padded doors and a bittersweet sense of faded grandeur.

Eating Out

Brno t (542) –
Café Restaurant Hlídka, Hlídka 2, **t** 216 642 (*moderate*). Located in a former guard house in a park setting below Špilberk Castle, this popular spot offers Czech specialities on arguably the most attractive terrace in town. Dominated by a central bar, the interior is also extremely elegant.
Restaurace U Minoritů, Orlí 17, **t** 215 614 (*moderate*). Stylish restaurant in the ancient interior of the Minorite monastery, founded in 1230 and decorated with Baroque sculptures. Moravian wines and cuisine. Recommended.
Vinárna a restaurace Tramín, nám. Svobody 21, **t** 129 577 (*moderate/inexpensive*). Stylish, well-located restaurant with a medieval theme, and a wide selection of Czech dishes and wine.
Restaurace Pod radničnim kole, Mečová 5 (*inexpensive*). Tasty Moravian specialities served in a romantic red-brick cellar.
Stopkova Pivnice, Česka 5, **t** 211 094 (*inexpensive*). Renowned beer house and restaurant in the centre of town in a historical building protected by the Czech National Trust. Good beer and Moravian food.
Restaurace špaliček, 21 Zelný trh, **t** 211 556 (*inexpensive*). Traditional but tasteful restaurant favoured by locals.

the former Augustinian Monastery where G.J. Mendel grew peas and devised his theory of heredity. It's now home to the **Moravian Gallery** (*open daily 10–6; adm*). Church fans might be tempted out of the Old Quarter by the **Basilica of the Assumption of Virgin Mary** (Bazilika Nanebevzetí panny Marie; 1323) on Mendlovo

Touring from Bratislava

Day 1: Castles in the Area

Morning: Follow Hwy 502 north – maybe stopping to tour a porcelain factory (*www.majolika.sk*) or taste local wines in **Modra** – to the outstanding 13th-century castle of **Červený Kameň**, one-time residence of the Hungarian royal family.

Lunch: Have a traditional lunch by the castle gates at **Taverna Pod Baston**, *www. tavernapodbaston.sk* (*moderate– inexpensive*).

Afternoon: Check out the romantic 19th-century **Smolenice Castle** (Smolenický zámok) with its distinctive bulky tower, and maybe also the famous 'pagoda-like' stalagmites of nearby **Driny Cave** (*summer only*, **t** *0805 92200*). Then head south on Hwy 51 to **Trnava**, Slovakia's oldest free royal town (*see* pp.105–106), and for a while the country's main centre of religious and artistic life. Roam the cobble-stoned, largely pedestrianized streets, admiring the 11 churches, Archbishop's Palace, and extensive 13th-century town walls.

Dinner and Sleeping: Romantically illuminated at night, Trnava – the 'Slovak Rome' – is a fine place for a night-time stroll. Dine in the quiet courtyard of the upmarket **Symphony Restaurant**, Hlavna 13, **t** 535 4060 (*moderate*). Or for international food in a classic brick vaulted cellar head to **Láry Fáry Taverna**, Halenárska 15/1, **t** 553 3050 (*moderate*). The two best hotels in town also have good restaurants. **Hotel Barbakan**, Štefánikova 11, **t/f** 551 4022 (*moderate*), is a historic building with an on-site brewery. **Hotel Dream**, Kapitulská 12, **t** (033) 592 4111 (*inexpensive*), is a comfortable, modern hotel on Trnava's most romantic street.

Day 2: Spas and More Castles

Morning: Follow Hwy 61 north to the pretty spa town of **Piešt'any**. The scenic, traffic-free Spa Island (Kúpel'ný ostrov) is a beautiful place to wander, with thermal tarns, paths snaking through some giant trees, and many fine buildings. You can take the waters at the Napoleon Baths (Napoleónske kúpele).

Lunch: For top-notch traditional Slovakian cooking in a wonderful setting, sometimes with live folk music, locals head across the car bridge to **Koliba**, on Cervená Veža, **t** 762 3428 (*inexpensive*). To be where the action is, take an outdoor table at the **Art Jazz Gallery**, Winterova 29, **t** (0331) 762 5559 (*inexpensive*), or enjoy their handsome old-style European interior. **City Hotel Restaurant** at 35 Winterova (*inexpensive*) has a slightly more exciting menu, with dishes such as Chateaubriand and stroganoff.

Afternoon: Head west, then bear north on an unnumbered secondary road, following signs to the early 13th-century **Čachtice Castle**. Now largely in ruins, but still impressive, this site was home to the semilegendary 'Blood Countess' who bathed in virgins' blood to retain her youth. Head north, west under the motorway, then north again to the 13th- to 15th-century **Beckov Castle**, another splendidly ruined building, that's flanked by a Baroque church and an 18th-century Renaissance monastery. Take any road north to **Trenčin**, whose late 13th-century castle is pick of the bunch, though the town itself is unremarkable.

Dinner and Sleeping: Trenčin's culinary options are limited. For home-cooked Slovakian food, try the **Restaurant Lanius**, Mierové nám. 22, **t** 744 1978, or **Reštaurácia U sveta Urbana**, nám. sveta Anny 34, **t** 640 0988. But the town's best restaurant is in its best hotel, the luxurious and nicely located **Hotel Tatra**, M.R. Štefánika 2, **t** 650 6111, *www.hotel-tatra.sk* (*moderate*). Or you can get a very comfortable room with breakfast included just out of the centre at the friendly **Penzión Tiberia**, Kukučínová 13, **t** 744 1584, *www. tiberia.sk* (*inexpensive*).

nám., a jewel of Moravian Gothic architecture, which also contains some precious artefacts, such as an Italian-Byzantine type icon, a Baroque gold-plated tabernacle, and a monumental late-Gothic seven-arm candlestick.

Day 3: Hello, Brno

Morning: Follow Hwy 50 northwest into the Czech Republic, where the scenery starts to get more interesting. Don't miss the turn-off to **Buchlov Castle**. You can rent a bike or horse from the hotel below to tour the charming surroundings, maybe riding as far as the Italian-style Baroque **Buchlovice Château**, a sumptuous structure surrounded by palace gardens.

Lunch: Hotel Buchlov Park, t (572) 577 924, *www.buchlovpark.cz* (*moderate*) is the only choice, but it's a fine one, offering Belgian and Czech cuisine in a beautiful setting, and some good beers on tap.

Afternoon: If you're not castled out, the 16th-century Italian Renaissance **Nesovice Castle** some 20km further on is smaller and much prettier than most, with ornate battlements. A little further, the 16th-century **Bucovice Chateau** is a highly ornate structure known as the 'Pearl of Moravia'. Otherwise head straight to the capital of Moravia, **Brno** (*see above*). This bustling, sophisticated city overflows with culture and historical sights, including many churches and galleries, the absorbing Old Town Hall, and the notorious **Špilberk Castle**, a former underground prison. You may decide to stay here for an extra day.

Dinner and Sleeping: Café Restaurant Hlídka, Hlídka 2, t 216 642 (*moderate*), occupies a former guard house below Špilberk Castle, with a gorgeous terrace and an elegant interior. **Restaurace U Minoritů**, Orlí 17, t 215 614 (*moderate*), is housed in the ancient interior of a Minorite monastery, kitted out with Baroque sculptures. Both offer Moravian cuisine and a good selection of wines. The best place to stay is the **Grandhotel Brno**, Benesova 18–20, t 518 111 (*luxury*), which certainly lives up to its name. **Hotel Royal Ricc**, Starobrnenska 10, t 219 262 (*moderate*), is a handsome and central Baroque building with comfortable historical rooms.

Day 4: More of Moravia

Morning: Take Hwy 52/E461 south to **Mikulov**, a heavily pedestrianized town with lots to see, including a castle built right into the surrounding rock, a fine synagogue and church, caves, a crypt and a hilltop church whose path winds past a geographical enactment of the stations of the cross. Tanzberg Mikulov winery, t (519) 500 040, in nearby **Bavery** offers informal tours and tastings.

Lunch: In Mikulov's main square, the very popular local choice for classic Moravian cuisine in nicely authentic surroundings is **Restaurace Alfa**, Námestie 27, t 4337 7785 (*moderate/inexpensive*). **Petit Café** next door serves up tasty crêpes in a pretty courtyard.

Afternoon: A well-signed minor road leads east to **Lednice Chateau Park**. Created by the phenomenally wealthy Liechtenstein family, this vast castle complex surrounded by acres of intense, highly groomed gardens is comparable to Europe's very finest estates. As well as exploring miles of scenic paths on foot, you can take a boat to the fanciful minaret at the far end of a large island-dotted lake. There's also a giant hothouse with botanical gardens, a hedge maze, a giant aquarium, an art gallery, a Romantic copy of a medieval castle and a horticultural museum. You may want to spend an extra day here, too. If so, the nearby Baroque **Valtice Château** is also worth a look.

Dinner and Sleeping: In Lednice, eat at **Onyx Restaurant**, Malinovskeho namestie 25, t (519) 340 988 (*moderate/inexpensive*), or **Myslivna Restaurant** on Nadrazni, t (604) 564 111 (*moderate/inexpensive*). The best place to stay is the attractive **My Hotel**, 21. dubna 657, t (519) 340 135 (*moderate*). More intimate and economical is **Penzion Lednice**, Mikulovská 120, t (519) 340 986 (*inexpensive*).

Austria:
Travel, Practical A–Z and Language

Travel

Entry Formalities

Passports and Visas

Austria is an EU member state. UK and Irish citizens need a passport valid for at least 6 months; visas are not required and visitors may stay for an unlimited period provided their passports remain in date. US and Canadian citizens need a passport valid for at least 6 months: visas are not required for US and Canadian citizens staying less than 90 days; visas are required for a stay exceeding 90 days.

Customs

Duty-free customs allowances depend on whether you arrive from an EU country or a non-EU country. While EU nationals can now import a limitless amount of goods, the proviso that they are for personal use ensures a cap: limits are 800 cigarettes/400 cigarillos/200 cigars/1kg of tobacco; 10 litres of spirits, 90 litres of wine (60 litres maximum sparkling wine) and 110 litres of beer.

For non-EU travellers, tobacco and alcohol allowances are: 200 cigarettes/100 cigarillos/50 cigars/250g of tobacco; 1 litre of liquor over 22% alcohol, 2 litres under 22% alcohol, 2 litres of sparkling wine, 2 litres of wine, 50g perfume or 0.25 litres *eau de toilette*. US citizens should contact US Customs (**t** (202) 354 1000, *www.customs.gov*) or read its pamphlet *Know Before You Go*.

Getting Around

Austria's public transport system is clean, efficient and useful. Almost everywhere you go will be well served by train or bus, and even the most remote villages have local bus services. Efficiency comes at a price, though, and fares are generally high. Train journeys are faster and more comfortable, while buses are marginally cheaper and best used for reaching small villages not on the rail network.

By Bus

Bundesbus services link the main towns and villages around Austria. In most cities, the main bus station is located next to the main train station. Single and 24-hour bus tickets can be bought from drivers, but weekly or monthly passes must be bought from information offices.

By Car

Motorway breakdown, t 120

Travelling by car around Austria allows greater flexibility, and driving conditions are good. The speed limits are as follows: 50kph in built-up areas, 100kph on main roads and 130kph on motorways. The word for petrol is *benzin* (unleaded is *bleifrei*).

You must buy a special pass ('*vignette*') to drive on Austrian motorways and failure to do so will result in a fine. These are available at post offices or larger petrol stations and are valid for 10 days, two months or one year. A 10-day pass costs around 8 euros. More information (German only) at *www.vignette.at*. Car hire addresses are given in the listings by city.

By Train

Tickets can be bought in train stations, or on trains in rural areas where the stations are unstaffed. Austrian rail passes are valid for a year and are therefore not useful for travellers but some areas, such as Carinthia (*see* 'Klagenfurt'), have special visitor passes which offer discounts on transport.

International rail passes can be useful if you are travelling extensively in Central Europe (*see* p.9). Train schedules and information are available at *www.oebb.at*.

Practical A–Z

Crime and the Police

Police, t 113

Austria is uniformly safe for tourists, though it makes sense to exercise a few basic precautions: be vigilant in seedier areas and beware of pickpocketing in crowds. Keep your valuables in the hotel safe, if there is one.

Disabled Travellers

For Vienna, go to *www.vienna.info* and click on Specials and 'Vienna for visitors with disabilities', where you will find 120 pages for downloading, with information on hotels, transport, restaurants, cinemas and theatres and sightseeing, regularly updated.Salzburg also has a useful leaflet for disabled travellers called *Exploring Salzburg*, which you can order from the tourist office: go to *www.salzburg. info* (click on 'Sights', and then on 'Exploring Salzburg'). On the Graz city website, *www.graz tourismus.at*, you can look for accommodation.

The UK charity **Holiday Care** offers a wealth of information for disabled travellers. They provide fact sheets on many destinations, including Austria (available online at *www. holidaycare.org.uk/datasheets/Austria.html*).

Electricity

The current used in Austria is 220v, which is fine for British applicances (240v). Visitors from North America, with 110v appliances, will need to use a transformer. Plugs have two pins in Austria, but adaptors are easily available in department stores or electrical shops.

Embassies and Consulates

Austrian Embassies Abroad

UK: 18 Belgrave Mews West, London SW1X 9HU, **t** (020) 7235 3731, *www.austria. org.uk*.
USA: 3524 International Court NW, Washington DC, **t** (202) 895 6700/6767, *www.austria.org*.
Canada: 445 Wilbrod St, Ottowa, K1N 6M7, **t** 613 789 1444, *www.austro.org*.

Foreign Embassies in Vienna

UK: Jaurèsgasse 12, **t** (01) 716130, *www.britishembassy.at*.
USA: Boltzmanngasse 16, **t** (01) 31339, *www.usembassy.at*.
Canada: Laurenzerberg 2, **t** (01) 531 383 000, *www.dfait-maeci.gc.ca*.
Australia: Winterthur House, Mattiellistrasse 2, **t** (01) 50674, *www.australian-embassy.at*.

Festivals and Events

Jan–Feb: The carnival season (*Fasching*), building since early November, reaches its climax on Shrove Tuesday; during this time and is celebrated by balls in major cities and towns. **Ash Wednesday** (and the start of Lent) is marked by the eating of pickled or salted fish.
Mar/April: At **Easter** (*Oster*) families celebrated the extended weekend with outings and by visiting colourful Easter markets. Food is central to the festival and hand-painted eggs are given.
May: Whitsun (*Pfingsten*): 6th Sunday after Easter. **Corpus Christi** (*Fronleichnam*): 2nd Thursday after Whitsun. The day is marked by religious processions in some regions.
November: All Saints' Day (1st) is taken seriously all over Austria with people visiting cemeteries to remember the dead.
Dec: In addition to the huge Christmas markets (*Christkindlmarkt*) that take place all over Austria at the beginning of the month, there are a few other festivals and events that are worth noting. **St Nicholas' Day** (5th) is marked with processions in some regions; in the evening, St Nicholas (and the devil, or *Krampus*) hand out sweets to children; meanwhile the **Krampuslaufen**, which represents evil spirits being chased away by St Nicholas, is a popular event in many regions. **Christmas** (*Weihnacht*) is a great family celebration with the baby Jesus (*Christkindl*) handing out presents on Christmas Eve.

Health and Emergencies

All services, t 112 ; **fire, t** 122; **ambulance, t** 144
EU-citizens are entitled to emergency health care though reciprocal health-care agreements, but you'll need to bring a stamped form E111 with you (available from post offices in the UK, to be replaced by a card in December 2005). In practice, this is a time-consuming bureaucratic process and visitors (both from the EU and other countries) are advised to take out travel insurance which covers health emergencies.

Local **pharmacies** are well-equipped to deal with minor ailments, and are usually open Mon–Fri 8am–noon and 2–6pm, Sat 8am–noon. Lists of pharmacies and 24-hour pharmacies are posted outside all pharmacies. In an emergency head for the nearest *Ambulanz* (emergency room) at any hospital.

The helpful **Vienna Medical Association Service for Foreign Patients**, 1 Weighburgasse 10/12, **t** (01) 5150 1213, 24hr hotline **t** (01) 513 95 95 (U1, U3 to Stephansplatz), is open Mon–Wed 8–4, Thurs–Fri 8–6. Information on English-speaking doctors and local hospitals.

Money

Austria's unit of currency is the **euro**, available in coins (1, 2, 5, 10, 20 and 50 cents, 1 and 2 euros) and notes (5, 10, 20, 50, 100, 200, 500).

ATMs (*bankomats*) are found on virtually every street corner, and almost all accept foreign credit cards and have instructions in English. Some central banks also have automatic money-changing machines which accept foreign banknotes. Banks usually offer a better rate of exchange than the various *bureaux de change* clustered in the city centre, although it is often cheaper to withdraw money using your credit card from an ATM. Major **travellers' cheques** are accepted, and those issued by AmEx, Thomas Cook and Visa are instantly replaced in case of loss of theft.

Banks are usually open Mon-Fri 8–12.30 and 1.30–3, and until 5.30 on Thurs, although some city centre banks don't close at lunchtimes.

National Holidays

1 Jan New Year's Day
6 Jan Epiphany
Easter Sunday
Easter Monday
1 May Labour Day
Whit Monday (6th Mon after Easter Sun)
Ascension Day (6th Thurs after Easter Sun)
2 June Corpus Christi
15 Aug Maria Himmelfahrt
26 Oct National Holiday
1 Nov Allerheiligen
8 Dec Maria Empfängnis
25 Dec Christmas Day
26 Dec Stefanitag

Opening Hours

Most **shops** are usually open Mon–Fri 8–6, until noon on Sat. Most shops are closed on Sundays.

Churches are usually open all day, particularly in the big cities, but will probably only be open for Mass on Sundays in rural areas.

Museum opening hours are usually 10–4 (though may close up to 7pm); once a week many stay open until 9pm and most close one day a week, usually Monday.

Post and Post Offices (*Post- und Telegrafen*)

Post offices have yellow signs, and the post-boxes are also yellow. Those with an orange strip have weekend post collections. Postcards sent to destinations within Europe will take 3–4 days, and cost 52 cents; those sent outside Europe take around 5 days and stamps are 1.10 cents.

More information can be found at *www.post.at* (some information in English).

Stamps can also be bought from newsagents, and most post offices also have stamp-vending machines.

Price Categories

Hotels

Average price for a double room with bath/shower and WC in high season.

luxury over €200
expensive €150–200
moderate €100–150
inexpensive under €100

Restaurants

Three-course meal for one person with wine.

luxury €60 to astronomical
expensive €40–60
moderate €25–40
inexpensive under €25

Shopping

Tyrolean costumes and walking sticks are popular souvenirs to take home from the Innsbruck area. The wine of Lower Austria is also a good buy, as is the glassware of Styria. It is possible to buy enormous cow bells if you're looking for something to amuse the folks back home.

Sports

Austria is a fantastic destination for a huge variety of outdoor activities – there is plenty to do away from the slopes. If you want to try your hand at canoeing, rafting, golf, hang-liding, ballooning, horseriding, mountain climbing or simply take a bicycle tour, Austria is the place to do it. Contact local tourist offices for details. That said, it is blessed with hundreds of miles of piste and facilities abound for tobogganing, bobsledding, cross-country skiing, snowboarding and curling. Contact the National Tourist Office in Vienna, **t** (01) 587 2000, for the latest snow reports; in addition, *www.tirol.at* has avalanche report information.

Telephones

Phone numbers vary in length, and some of them include direct dial extensions, which are tacked on to the end of the main number, sometimes with a dash, sometimes not.

To **call Austria from abroad**, dial 00 43, then drop the first 0 of the city code.

To **call abroad from Austria**, dial 00 plus the country code (USA and Canada 1, UK 44, Ireland 353, Australia 61, New Zealand 64).

For **directory enquiries** relating to Austria or the EU call 118877, or **international directory enquiries** on 0900 118877 (both usually have English-speaking operators).

There are plenty of public telephones scattered around, most of which have instructions in English. They accept coins or phonecards (available from post offices or newsagents). Post offices have phone booths, which are usually cheaper for long-distance calls. Rates are high, but are cheaper after 6pm on weekdays and all day at weekends.

Time

Austria is on Central European Time, which is one hour ahead of GMT. Clocks go forward one hour on the last Sunday of March, and go back on the last Sunday of October.

Tipping

In restaurants, add about 10% to the bill, or round it up to the nearest euro in cheaper places. Taxis usually expect around 10%. Hotel porters usually expect a euro for each piece of baggage, plus hotel cleaning staff (in the smarter hotels at least) and anyone else who provides a service.

Toilets

There are public toilets scattered around the city centre, many of which are open 24 hours. Those with attendants usually charge 50 cents. Underground (U-Bahn) stations also have toilets, in varying states of cleanliness.

Tourist Information

UK: Austrian National Tourist Office, P.O. Box 2363, London W1A 2QB, **t** 020 7629 0461, **f** 020 7499 6038.

USA: Austrian National Tourist Office, P.O. Box 1142, New York NY 10110-1142 **t** (112) 944 6880, **f** (112) 730 4568.

Canada: 2 Bloor Street East, Suite 3330, Toronto M4W 1A8 **t** (416) 967 3381.

Language

German is a complex language. There are three, not two, genders; nouns and adjectives decline; it is full of irregular verbs and deceptive conjugations; the syntax itself is ornate. The verb often comes only at the end. But there are some advantages. Nouns are capitalized and easy to spot and spelling is phonetic.

Austrians speak German with a softer accent and many of their own colloquialisms; most importantly, *Grüss Gott* is the usual greeting – not *Guten Tag* – which you should use whenever you meet someone, to be polite.

Pronunciation

Consonants

Most are the same as in English. There are no silent letters. **G**s are hard, as in English 'good', but **ch** is a guttural sound, as in the

Scottish 'loch'—though **sch** is said as 'sh'. **S** is also pronounced 'sh', when it appears before a consonant (especially at the beginning of a word), as in *stein*, pronounced 'shtine'. Otherwise the sound is closer to 'z'. **Z** is pronounced 'ts' and **d** at the end of the word becomes 't'. **R**s are rolled at the back of the throat, as in French. **V** is pronounced somewhere between the English 'f' and 'v', and **w** is said as the English 'v'.

Vowels

A can be long (as in 'father') or short, like the 'u' in 'hut'. Similarly **u** can be short, as in 'put', or long, as in 'boot'. **E** is pronounced at the end of words, and is slightly longer than in English. Say **er** as in 'hair' and **ee** as in 'hay'. Say **ai** as in 'pie'; **au** as in 'house'; **ie** as in 'glee'; **ei** as in 'eye' and **eu** as in 'oil'.

An **umlaut** (¨) changes the pronunciation of a word. Say **ä** like the 'e' in 'bet', or like the 'a' in 'label'. Say **ö** like the vowel sound in 'fur'. **ü** is a very short version of the vowel sound in 'true'. Sometimes an umlaut is replaced by an e after the vowel. The printed symbol **ß** is sometimes seen instead of **ss**, though this guide uses 'ss'.

Useful Words and Phrases

yes/no *ja/nein*
please/thank you *bitte/danke (schön)*
hello *guten Tag; hallo; Grüss Gott (in Austria)*
goodbye; bye *auf Wiedersehen; tschüss*
I am sorry *es tut mir leid*
how are you?(formal/informal) *wie geht es Ihnen?/wie geht es Dir? or wie geht's?*
I'm very well *mir geht's gut*
do you speak English? *sprechen Sie Englisch?*
and/but *und/aber*
I would like... *ich möchte...*
where is/are...? *wo ist/sind...?*
I am lost *ich weiss nicht wo ich bin*

open/closed *geöffnet/geschlossen*
toilet *Toilette*
Ladies/Gents *Damen/Herren*
police *Polizei*
railway station *Bahnhof*

do you have a single/double room? *Haben Sie ein Einzelzimmer/Doppelzimmer?*
do you have a table? *Haben Sie einen Tisch?*

I am vegetarian *ich bin vegetarier*
breakfast *Frühstuck; Brotzeit*
lunch *Mittagessen*
dinner *Abendessen*

morning *Morgen; Vormittag*
afternoon *Nachmittag*
evening *Abend*
week *Woche*
month *Monat*
year *Jahr*
today/yesterday/tomorrow *heute/gestern/morgen*

Days and Months

Monday *Montag*
Tuesday *Dienstag*
Wednesday *Mittwoch*
Thursday *Donnerstag*
Friday *Freitag*
Saturday *Samstag*
Sunday *Sonntag*

January *Januar; Jännar (Austria)*
February *Februar; Feber (Austria)*
March *März*
April *April*
May *Mai*
June *Juni*
July *Juli*
August *August*
September *September*
October *Oktober*
November *November*
December *Dezember*

Numbers

1 *eins*
2 *zwei*
3 *drei*
4 *vier*
5 *fünf*
6 *sechs*
7 *sieben*
8 *acht*
9 *neun*
10 *zehn*
100 *hundert*
1,000 *tausend*

Austria: Vienna, Salzburg, Graz and Klagenfurt

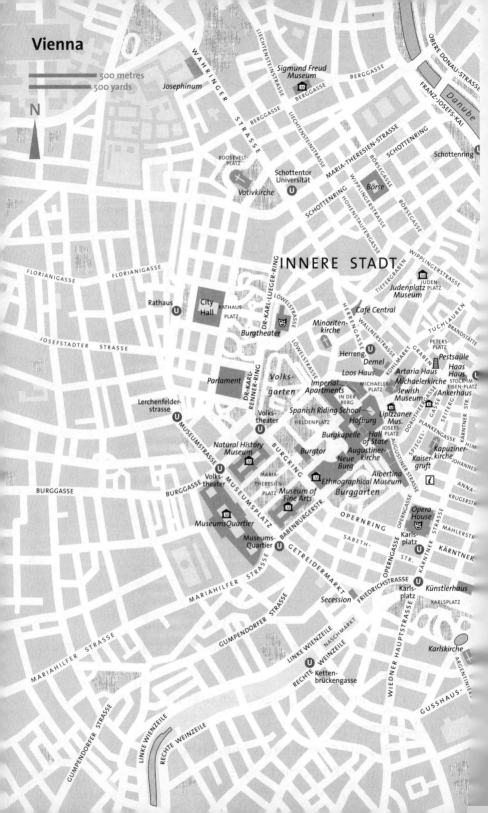

Vienna

500 metres
500 yards

N

Josephinum

WÄHRINGER STRASSE

Sigmund Freud Museum

BERGGASSE

Berggasse

LIECHTENSTEINSTRASSE

LIECHTENSTEINSTRASSE

OBERE DONAU-STRASSE

FRANZ-JOSEFS-KAI

Danube

MARIA-THERESIEN-STRASSE

Schottenring

BÖRSEGASSE

SCHOTTENRING

WIPPLINGERSTRASSE

Schottenring

ROOSEVELT-PLATZ

Schottentor Universität

Votivkirche

SCHOTTENRING

HOHENSTAUFENGASSE

Börse

BÖRSEGASSE

WIPPLINGERSTRASSE

INNERE STADT

TIEFERGRABEN

Judenplatz Museum

JUDEN-PLATZ

FLORIANIGASSE

FLORIANIGASSE

Rathaus

City Hall

RATHAUS-PLATZ

DR-KARL-LUEGER-RING

LÖWELSTRASSE

HERRENGASSE

WALLNERSTRASSE

Café Central

Minoriten-kirche

TUCHLAUBEN

BRANDSTÄTTE

PETERS-PLATZ

Pestsäule

Burgtheater

Herreng.

KOHLMARKT

GRABEN

JOSEFSTÄDTER STRASSE

Parlament

DR-KARL-RENNER-RING

LÖWELSTRASSE

Volks-garten

Imperial Apartments

Demel

Loos Haus

MICHAELER-PLATZ

IN DER BERG

Artaria Haus

Michaelerkirche

Jewish Museum

Haas Haus

STOCK-IM-EISEN-PLATZ

Ankerhaus

Lerchenfelder-strasse

Volks-theater

HELDENPLATZ

Spanish Riding School

Hofburg

Lipizzaner Mus.

JOSEFS-PLATZ

DOROTHEER-GASSE

SEILERG.

KÄRNTNER STR.

PLANKENGASSE

SPIEGEL-GASSE

Natural History Museum

BURGRING

Burgtor

Burgkapelle

Hall of State

Augustiner-kirche

Kapuziner-kirche

Kaiser-gruft

JOHANNES

Neue Burg

Albertina

ANNA-

KRUGERSTR.

Volks-theater

MUSEUMSTRASSE

MARIA-THERESIEN-PLATZ

Museum of Fine Arts

Ethnographical Museum

Burggarten

Opera House

OPERNGASSE

KÄRNTNER STR.

MAHLERSTR.

KÄRNTNER

BURGGASSE

BURGGASSE

MuseumsQuartier

Museums-Quartier

BABENBERGERSTR.

OPERNRING

SABETH-

Karls-platz

KARLSPLATZ

MARIAHILFER STRASSE

GETREIDEMARKT

Secession

FRIEDRICHSTRASSE

Karls-platz

Künstlerhaus

KARLSPLATZ

WIENER HAUPTSTRASSE

GUMPENDORFER STRASSE

LINKE WIENZEILE

RECHTE WIENZEILE

NASCHMARKT

Ketten-brückengasse

Karlskirche

ARGENTINIERSTR.

GUSSHAUS-

MARIAHILFER STRASSE

GUMPENDORFER STRASSE

LINKE WIENZEILE

RECHTE WEINZEILE

Vienna

Vienna, long the glittering capital of a vast empire, oozes Imperial magnificence: from its opulent palaces and glorious gardens to the equestrian ballets at the Spanish Riding School, the city gorgeously evokes the splendour of the Habsburg court during the Baroque age. The Hapsburgs enjoyed six centuries of rule, an empire on which the 'sun never set'; under Empress Maria Theresia (1717–80), Vienna enjoyed unparalleled peace and prosperity, and Haydn, Mozart and Beethoven were just three of the musical giants who made their homes in the capital. The Habsburgs have been gone for almost a century, but they left behind their splendid art collections and priceless jewels in extraordinary, world-class museums – as well as their hearts and entrails in the city's macabre catacombs and burial crypts.

1848 was the year of revolution across Europe, and Vienna was no exception. In the new post-Revolution Habsburg order, Ferdinand I was forced to abdicate in favour of Franz Josef (1830–1916), who would rule for 68 years. As Habsburg influence began to wane, the increasingly powerful burghers of Vienna were flaunting their wealth by erecting the showcase monuments which still line the Ringstrasse, the circle of streets that replaced the old city walls. In the lavish new Opera House, they whirled to the strains of Strauss waltzes as far-flung territories were shorn from the Empire.

Fin-de-siècle Vienna was explosive: its coffee houses were brimming with writers, artists and philosophers; Mahler was presiding over the Staatsoper; the Secessionists, led by Gustav Klimt, had electrified the art world; Jugendstil architecture was blooming across the city, replacing the graceful but plainer domestic Biedermeier style, and Freud published *On the Interpretation of Dreams*. The decadent atmosphere of turn-of-the-20th-century Vienna has long vanished, but its memory is still evoked in the city's coffee houses, or when a street musician breaks into a poignant waltz.

The 20th century was a whole different story: two world wars and their aftermath put an end to the party. The last Habsburg emperor abdicated in 1918, when the Republic of Austria was declared, and the Reds took over the capital. Red Vienna erected the vast public housing projects which still stand on the fringes of the city, but Austria was on its knees. Rich, neighbouring Germany seemed to provide the only solution, and in 1938 Hitler declared the incorporation of Austria into the German Reich from a balcony of the former Imperial palace. The once-thriving Jewish community was virtually wiped out, and the city was destroyed by bombs. Finally, the Soviets reached the city in spring 1945. After a decade of Allied Occupation, Vienna began to repair its monuments and its relationship with the rest of Europe, formally joining the EU in 1995. But the country has found it difficult to shake off its reputation for xenophobia and anti-Semitism, and the recent antics of Jörg Haider, the extremist right-wing populist, have brought sanctions and unwelcome international attention. However, with the awarding of the 2004 Nobel prize for literature to Elfriede Jelinek, whose works bitterly condemn her homeland, the spotlight is now on those who oppose the ugly prejudice which has long blighted the country.

For decades, Vienna has clung to the splendour and romance of its Imperial heritage. The first major sign that things were changing was the erection of Hans

Addresses

Vienna is divided into 23 numbered districts or *Bezirke*. Addresses are commonly prefixed with a number indicating the district, and the street number follows the street name (for example, 1 Dorotheergasse 11 means No.11 Dorotheergasse, in the First District). The Innere Stadt (Inner City) is the 1st district.

Getting There

Many airlines fly direct to Vienna; *see* Getting There, pp.4–10.

Getting from the Airport

Flughafen Wien-Schwechat, **t** (01) 7007 222 33, *www. viennaairport.com*, is 20km southeast of the city. There are three **bus** services to the city centre, leaving every 30mins 5am–11.30pm and costing €6. A faster option is the **city–airport train**, which departs at least every half-hour between 5.05am and 11.35pm and costs €15 (return); *www.cityairporttrain.at*. There is also an **S-bahn** (commuter train), line S7, to Wien Nord, Mitte and Rennweg stations, which costs €3 (single).

There is a **taxi** rank outside the arrivals hall. Journeys to the city centre cost €25–35.

Getting Around

You can get information, plans and tickets for the U-Bahn, tram and bus systems at the **transport information offices** at U-Bahn stations across the city, *www.wienerlinien.at*.

Tickets, available from ticket machines at tram and bus stops and in U-Bahn stations, or at newsagents, are valid for all forms of public transport. A **single ticket** costs €1.50; a **24hr Rover ticket** costs €5; a **72hr Rover ticket** is €12; and an 8-day **strip ticket** or *Streifenkarte* (which can be shared – just date-stamp a strip for each person) costs €24. The **Vienna Card** (*see* opposite) offers concessions.

By U-Bahn

There are five colour-coded and numbered underground lines (U1, U2, U3, U4, and U6), and plans are available in all U-Bahn ticket offices. Date-stamp your ticket in the small orange machines at the entrance.

By Tram (Strassenbahn)

Vienna's trams don't penetrate the old city, but trams 1 and 2, which circle the Ringstrasse, are the most useful for visitors. Date-stamp your ticket in the machines by the doors.

By Bus

Bus stops have useful bus maps and you should date-stamp your ticket in the machines by the doors. **Night buses** run every 30mins from around 12.30am to 5am, and the standard public transport tickets are valid.

By Taxi

Vienna's taxis have a 'taxi' sign on the roof, illuminated when they are free. They can be found at taxi ranks (but not hailed on the street), or call **t** 40100 or **t** 60160.

By Car

Don't try to negotiate Vienna's city centre in a car, though your own transport can be useful for visiting sights outside the centre. **Avis**, **t** (01) 7007 32700 (airport), **t** (01) 587 6241 (city centre), *www.avis.com*.
Europcar, **t** (01) 7007 32699 (airport), **t** (01) 512 8677 (city centre), *www.europcar.com*.
Hertz, **t** (01) 7007 32661 (airport), **t** (01) 714 6565 (city centre), *www.hertz.com*.
Budget, **t** (01) 7007 32711, **t** (01) 714 6717 (city centre), *www.budget.com*.

On Foot

The old heart of Vienna is perfect for strolling, with most of the main sights within easy walking distance of each other.

Tourist Information

Vienna: 1 Albertinaplatz, **t** (01) 211 14, hotel booking **t** (01) 24 555, *www.vienna.info*. Open daily 9–7, U1, U2, U4 to Karlsplatz. There are smaller branches at the airport and at the Westbahnhof train station.
Rest of Austria: Austrian tourist information office, 4 Margaretenstrasse 1, **t** (01) 587 2000, *www.austria.info*.

The **Vienna Card** offers discounts of between 10% and 35% at museums and attractions, shops and restaurants, plus 72hrs' unlimited use of public transport. It costs

€16.90 and can be bought at the tourist office, main train stations, some hotels, or by credit card on t (01) 798 44 00-148. Each card allows you to take a child under 15 along free.

Guided Tours

The tourist office has a booklet listing the various **walking tours** offered by official guides in Vienna. Visit *www.wienguide.at* for more information, or call t (01) 774 8901.

Pedal Power, 2 Ausstellungssrasse 3, t (01) 729 72 34, *www.pedal power.at*, offer **cycling tours** of the city, which begin from the Prater.

During the summer, **boat excursions** along the Danube and the Danube Canal are offered by **DDSG Shipping Co.**, Handelskai 265, t (01) 726 8123/588 80-0, *www.ddsg.blue-danube.at*, and **Pyringer-Zopper Danube Shipping,** t (01) 715 1525-20, *www.donauschiffahrtwien.at*.

The **Vienna Sightseeing Bus** runs a 'Hop-on Hop-off' tour from the Staatsoper, with multilingual audioguides. Tickets are available for 1, 2 or 24hrs, and prices start at €12. Info from **Vienna Sightseeing**, t (01) 712 46 830, *www.viennasightseeing.at*.

Horse-drawn carriages (*fiaker*) clatter around the cobbled streets and are available from outside Stephansdom and the Hofburg. It costs around €50 for a 30min tour of the city, but agree the terms before you get in.

Internet Access

The easiest option is to head for one of the three branches of **Bignet**: 6 Mariahilfer Strasse 27, *open daily 10am–2am*; 1 Kärntner Strasse 61, *open daily 10am–midnight*; 1 Hoher Markt 8, *open daily 10am–midnight*.

Skiing

Many Vienna-based travel agencies offer one-day ski packages, including transport and lift-pass. These usually head for the slopes at Semmering (about 60 miles/90km from the city). For more information, contact the Semmering tourist information office, p.141.

Festivals

31 Dec and 1 Jan: New Year's Eve concerts, Musikverein and, Konzerthaus.
6 Jan–Ash Wed: *Fasching* (Carnival). All kinds of events, including lavish balls.

Jan (usually 2nd and 3rd weeks): *Resonanzen*, a festival of medieval music, Konzerthaus.
Late Feb–mid-Mar: Dance Festival, classic and modern dance; *Haydn Tage*, Konzerthaus.
Mar: Easter Market at the Freytung.
April–May: *Frühlingsfestival*, a festival of classical music, hosted in alternate years by either the Musikverein or the Konzerthaus.
1 May: *Tag der Arbeit*, Labour Day; *Maifest*, concerts and funfairs in the Prater.
Mid-May–mid-June: Vienna *Festwochen*, festival of the performing arts, info at t (01) 589 2222, *www.festwochen.at*.
June–July: *Jazzfest Wien*, *www.viennajazz.org*.
Oct: *Viennale*, international film festival, *www.viennale.at*.
Nov: *Wien Modern*, festival of contemporary music, Konzerthaus, *www.konzerthaus.at*.
Dec: Christmas markets (*Christkindlmärkte*).

Shopping

Traditional Viennese and Austrian specialities include cut glass, embroidered lace, typical Austrian clothes like dirndls and *lederhosen*, the ubiquitous chocolate 'Mozart Balls' from Salzburg and a wonderful range of cakes including the celebrated *Sachertorte* (which can be expensively packed up and even posted by the Hotel Sacher shop, *see* opposite).

The main shopping streets are **Kärntner Strasse** and **Mariahilfer Strasse**, with department stores, all the major fashion chains, and a couple of shopping malls. Along **Graben** and **Kohlmarkt**, you'll find *chi chi* designer fashion, and the fancy *pâtisserie*-cum-café **Demel** (*see* 'Cafés'). **Dorotheergasse** and **Josefstädter Strasse** are lined with smart antique dealers. The narrow streets and passages of the **old town** have tiny shops selling everything from religious objects to designer household goods.

Many of the museum shops are excellent, especially the **MAK shop** (*see* p.136) and the **MuseumsQuartier shop** (*see* p.135).

Shops are usually **open** from Monday to Saturday from 9 or 10am to 6 or 7pm, although many close earlier (around 5pm) on Saturdays. Few shops are open late, and even fewer are open on Sundays.

Dorotheum, 1 Dorotheergasse 14, t (01) 5156 0280, *www.dorotheum.com*. Set up as a pawn shop more than 200 years ago, this is now the oldest and most prestigious auction house in Central Europe. You can pick up cheaper items in the Glashof.

Gasometer, 11 Guglgasse, *www.g-town.at*. A stunning architectural *tour de force*, this shopping centre (and apartment complex) is housed in four former gas containers. Unfortunately the shopping doesn't live up to the dramatic setting. *U-Bahn Gasometer*.

Ringstrassen Gallerien, 1 Kärntner Ring 11–13. A big, upmarket shopping centre spread over two adjoining buildings. *Open Mon–Sat 7.30am–10pm*.

Steffl, 1 Kärntner Strasse 19, t 514310. This convenient department store has several floors of fashion, an electrical goods department and a panoramic bar.

Loden-Plankl, 1 Michaelerplatz 6, t (01) 533 8032, *www.loden-plankl.at*. One of the oldest and most famous stores dedicated to traditional Austrian clothing.

Meinl am Graben, 1 Graben 19, t (01) 532 3334. Vienna's premier gourmet supermarket, also with an excellent restaurant upstairs. *Open Mon–Fri 8–8, Sat 8.30–8*.

J&L Lobmeyr, 1 Kärntner Strasse 26, t (01) 512 0508. If you've admired the cut-glass chandeliers at the Vienna Opera House, you can pick some up at this world-famous store. There's also a small museum.

Markets

Naschmarkt, 4 Naschmarkt. The city's famous open-air food market is a riot of colour and smells *Mon–Fri 6am–6.30pm, Sat 6am–2pm*.

Kunst und Antikmarkt, Donaukanal-Promenade. Art, antiques, bric-a-brac and plain old junk by the Danube Canal. *Open May–Sept Sat 2–8, Sun 10–8. U-Bahn to Schwedenplatz*.

Where to Stay

Vienna t (01) –

The tourist office has a booking service, and can provide lists of rooms in private houses. Prices include breakfast at most hotels.

Innere Stadt

★★★★★Hotel Sacher, 1 Philharmonikerstrasse 4, t 514 560, f 514 56 810, *www.sacher.com* (*luxury*). The *grande dame* of the Viennese

hotel scene boasts splendid rooms filled with extraordinary art and antiques, a fabulous restaurant and a legendary café.

★★★★Astoria, 1 Kärntnergasse 32–4, t 515770, f 515 7782, *www.austria-trend.at* (*luxury*). A classic old-fashioned hotel, which still oozes turn-of-the-20th-century opulence although its facilities are bang up-to-date.

★★★★Mailberger Hof, 1 Annagasse 7, t 5120 6410, f 5120 64 110, *www.mailbergerhof.at* (*luxury*). One of the prettiest hotels in central Vienna, in a an elegant former palace overlooking a graceful stone courtyard.

★★★★Kaiserin Elisabeth, 1 Weihburgasse 3, t 51526, f 515267, *info@kaiserinelisabeth.at* (*expensive*). This delightful hotel retains much of its grandiose 19th-century opulence, and guests are greeted with a swirl of velvet and crystal in the lobby.

★★★★Pension Pertschy, 1 Habsburgergasse 5, t 534 4949, f 534490, *www.pertschy.com* (*moderate*). The building has seen better days, but it overlooks a stone courtyard off Graben and most of the comfortable rooms have been newly renovated.

★★★König von Ungarn, 1 Schulerstrasse 10, t 515840, f 515848, *www.kvu.at* (*expensive*). The framed signatures of famous guests line the walls at this charming, good-value hotel which shares the same 16th-century building as the Figarohaus. Passages lead to the bedrooms. Book well in advance.

★★★Nossek, 1 Graben 17, t 5337 0410, f 535 3646, *www.pension-nossek.at* (*moderate*). This modest, family-run hotel offers attractive rooms, with basic bathrooms, but otherwise tastefully furnished with Persian rugs.

★★★Wandl, 1 Petersplatz 9, t 534550, f 534 5577, *www.hotel-wandl.com* (*moderate*). This slightly ramshackle, family-run hotel has been going for almost two centuries. Rooms vary widely; some boast original fittings while others are much plainer.

★★★Zur Wiener Staatsoper, 1 Krugerstrasse 11, t 513 1274, f 513 127 415, *office@zurweiner staastoper.at* (*moderate*). Tucked down a pedestrian street off Kärntner Strasse, this welcoming hotel is squeezed into a tall, narrow 19th-century townhouse.

★★★Pension Suzanne, 1 Walfischgasse 4, t 513 2507, f 513 2500, *www.pension-suzanne.at* (*inexpensive*). Possibly the best central budget option, with old-fashioned rooms, some with kitchenettes, and friendly service.

***Schweizer Pension Solderer**, 1 Heinrichgasse 2, **t** 533 8156, **f** 533 6469, *schweizer.pension@ cello.at* (*inexpensive*). A pristine little pension. Rooms have cable TV.

Around the Ringstrasse

*****Bristol**, 1 Kärntner Ring 1, **t** 515 160, *www. westin.com/bristol* (*luxury*). Possibly the most luxurious hotel in the city.

*****Das Triest**, 4 Wiedner Hauptsrasse 12, **t** 89180, **f** 589 1818, *www.dastriest.at* (*luxury*). This sleek modern hotel is slotted behind an elegant old façade. Pared down minimalism and light-filled public spaces.

*****Im Palais Schwarzenberg**, 3 Schwarzenbergplatz 9, **t** 798 4515, **f** 798 4714, *www.palais- schwarzenberg.com* (*luxury*). Beautiful Baroque palace surrounded by ornamental gardens, elegantly converted into a chic and wonderfully intimate hotel.

*****Le Meridien**, 1 Opernring 13, **t** 588900, **f** 588 90 90 90, *http://vienna.lemeridien.com* (*luxury*). Near the Opera House, with a historic façade hiding minimalist modern 'design' style, all glass and cool colours.

****Hotel Regina**, 9 Rooseveltplatz 15, **t** 404 460, **f** 408 8392, *www.kremlehnerhotels.at* (*expensive*). This grand old pile next to the Votivkirche has been going for more than a century, and is awash with velvet drapes.

****Hotel am Schubertring**, 1 Schubertring 11, **t** 717020, **f** 713 9966, *hotel.amschubertring@ chello.at* (*moderate*). Housed in a graceful Jugendstil building, a charming hotel filled with Art Nouveau-style lamps, murals and furniture. Much cheaper in winter.

***Hotel Baltic**, 9 Skodagasse 15, **t** 4056 2660 (*inexpensive*). A faded, but still charming, *pension* located in a battered Jugendstil building. Most of the rooms are spacious, all are crammed with a rickety mix of antique and 70s furniture. Cash only.

***Pension Wild**, 8 Langegasse 10, **t** 406 5174, **f** 402 2168, *www.pension-wild.com* (*inexpensive*). Rooms are basic, but pristine, and the owners are utterly charming.

Vienna Apartments, **t** 493 3257, *http://vienna. apartments.at*. Friendly, family-run business offering delightful self-catering apartments outside the centre, but close to transport.

Eating Out

Vienna **t** (01) –

Innere Stadt

Do & Co, 6th floor, Haas-Haus, 1 Stephansplatz 12, **t** 535 3969, *www.doco.com* (*luxury*). Elaborate, award-winning international cuisine served to a well-heeled crowd.

Meinl am Graben, 1 Graben 19, **t** 532 3334 (*luxury*). This relaxed restaurant above the excellent Meinl gourmet supermarket serves some of the finest cuisine in the city.

Cantinetta Antinori, 1 Jasormigottstrasse 3–5, **t** 533 7722, *www.antinori.it* (*expensive*). One of the chicest Italian restaurants in the city; delicious, ultra-fresh cuisine in a flamboyant red setting lit with chandeliers.

fabios, 1 Tuchlauben 6, **t** 532 2222, *www. fabios.at* (*expensive*). Currently one of the hottest ultra-stylish restaurants in town, with imaginative Italian cuisine.

Zum Schwarzen Kameel, 1 Bognergasse 5, **t** 533 8125, *www.kameel.at* (*expensive*). A stunning Jugendstil restaurant, 'The Black Camel' is a Viennese institution. There's a formal dining room, and an easygoing bar next to the fabulous deli. *Closed Sun.*

Aioli, 3rd floor, Haas-Haus, 1 Stephansplatz 12, **t** 535 3969, *www.doco.com* (*moderate*). In the emblematic Haas-Haus building, this brasserie-cum-*tapas* bar offers exquisitely prepared Catalan dishes in a cool chrome setting. *Open till 2am; closed Sun.*

Kiang, 1 Rotgasse 8, **t** 533 0856 (*moderate*). One of the pioneers of Asian fusion cuisine in Vienna. *Closed Sun.*

Palmenhaus, 1 Burggarten, **t** 533 1033 (*moderate*). Dine on Mediterranean fare amid the foliage in this glorious Jugendstil palmhouse. In summer, there's an outdoor barbecue and the terrace is packed.

Hoher Markt sausage stand, 1 Hoher Markt (*inexpensive*). *Open daily 7am–5am.*

Kern's Beisl, 1 Kleeblatgasse 4, **t** 533 9188 (*inexpensive*). This delightful, crowded and atmospheric *Beisl* serves up stews and other Austrian dishes to a mixed crowd. Cash only.

Wrenkh, 1 Bauernmarkt 10, **t** 533 1526, *www.wrenkh.at* (*inexpensive*). Christian Wrenkh's flagship restaurant is glassy and modern, and the (mostly) vegetarian cuisine is inspired and delicious.

Zum Finsteren Stern 2, 1 Schulhof 8, **t** 535 2100 (*inexpensive*). The original Zum Finistern Stern (Sterngasse 2) is a fabulous wine bar selling delicious snacks, but owner Ella de Silva's newest venture is more of a bistro.

Around the Ringstrasse

Steirereck, Meierei im Stadtpark, **t** 713 3168, *www.steirereck.at* (*luxury*). One of the most lauded restaurants, beautifully set in the Stadtpark. Reinvents classic Austrian dishes with spectacular success. *Closed Sat and Sun.*

Indochine 21, 1 Stubenring 18, **t** 513 7660, *www.indochine.at* (*expensive*). Lazy paddle fans, potted palms and dazzling yellow walls provide a sleek backdrop for the superb French-Vietnamese cuisine.

Café Florianihof, 8 Florianigasse 45, **t** 402 4842, *www.florianhof.at* (*moderate*). The beautiful original Jugendstil décor has been preserved. It serves delicious breakfasts, and you can linger over newspapers.

Gasthaus Wild, 3 Radetzkyplatz 1, **t** 920 9477 (*moderate*). One of the best of the new breed of neo-*Beisln*; authentic Austrian recipes prepared with the finest local ingredients. *Restaurant closed Mon.*

Ra'mien, 6 Gumpendorfer Strasse 9, **t** 585 4798 (*moderate–inexpensive*). With perfectly spiced Asian food upstairs, and DJs and cocktails in the cool-but-kitsch bar downstairs. *Open Tues–Sun 11am–midnight, bar open till 2am, until 4am Thurs–Sat; closed Mon.*

Das Moebel, 7 Burgasse 10, **t** 524 9497, *www.dasmoebel.at* (*inexpensive*). This bright, funky café does reasonable breakfasts, cakes and snacks – and the café functions as a gallery for young furniture designers. A good place to come for a drink in the evenings.

Una, 7 Museumsplatz 1, **t** 523 6566 (*inexpensive*). A stunning blue and gold mosaic ceiling, and assured bistro cuisine at reasonable prices. *Closed Sun eve.*

Further Afield

Altwienerhof, Herklotzgasse 6, **t** 892 6000 (*luxury*). This splendid restaurant is a wonderful place for a splurge, with stunning French and modern European cuisine served in a pretty cobbled Beidermeier courtyard.

Steirer Stub'n, 5 Wiedner Hauptstrasse 111, **t** 544 4349 (*expensive*). A firm favourite.

Stadtwirt, 3 Untere Viaduktgasse, **t** 713 3828 (*moderate*). Great Austrian food, prepared without fuss and served up in hearty portions; it's usually packed out.

Ubl, 4 Pressgasse 26, **t** 587 6437 (*inexpensive*). A classic Viennese *Beisl*, with authentic 1920s décor and wood panelling.

Heurigen

The wine-growing areas which ring Vienna are famous for their *Heurigen*, traditional taverns selling local wines. According to custom, *Heurigen* serve the new vintage, or *Heuriger*, wines from their own wineries, usually accompanied by a buffet of hot and cold snacks. Call in advance to check opening times, or contact the tourist office.

Heuriger Göbel, 21 Stammersdorger Kellergasse 151, **t** 294 8420. This elegant, glassy *Heuriger* was designed by architect Hans-Peter Göbel, whose wines are among the best produced in Vienna.

Hirt, 19 Eiserhandgasse 16, **t** 318 9641. A delightful rustic little *Heuriger* which serves simple snacks on two panoramic terraces.

Sirbu, 19 Kahlenberger Strasse 210, **t** 320 5928. This traditional spot offers fabulous views over the Danube.

Wiengut Heuriger Wieninger, 21 Stammersdorfer Strasse 78, **t** 292 4106. Franz Wieninger produces some of the top Viennese wines.

Cafés and Coffee Houses

Innere Stadt

Aida, 1 Stock-im-Eisen-Platz 2, **t** 512 2977, *www.aida.at*. Much-loved chain, famous for kitsch 1950s styling and low prices.

Café Bräunerhof, 1 Stallburggasse 2, **t** 512 3893. One of the loveliest, if least flamboyant, and most authentic.

Café Central, 1 Herengasse 1, **t** 533 3764-26. Linked with giants of the literary and artistic world at the turn-of-the-20th-century.

Demel, 1 Kohlmarkt 14, **t** 535171, *www.demel.at*. Perhaps the grandest *Konditorei* in the city, with prices to match. *Open daily 10am–7pm.*

Café de l'Europe, 1 Graben 31, **t** 532 1469. Has suffered unsympathetic remodelling in recent years, but it remains a classic on the chic Graben. *Open till midnight.*

Café Frauenhuber, 1 Himmelpfortgasse 6, **t** 512 8383. This is the oldest café in Vienna, with an opulent interior. *Closed Sun.*

Café Hawelka, 1 Dorotheergasse 6, **t** 512 8230, *www.hawelka.at.* This famous old place remains a much-loved institution, partly thanks to the presence of the Hawelkas themselves. *Closed Sun lunch and Tues.*

Café Sacher, 1 Philharmonikerstrasse 4, **t** 514 56661, *www.sacher.com.* A bastion of tradition, elegant origin of *Sachertorte.*

Around the Ringstrasse

Café Prückel, 1 Stubenring 24, **t** 512 6115. Huge, light-filled café right opposite MAK.

Café Landtmann, 1 Dr Karl-Lueger-Ring 4, **t** 241000, *www.landtmann.at.* Once a favourite haunt of Freud.

Café Sperl, 6 Gumpendorfer Strasse 11, **t** 586 4158, *www.cafesperl.at.* This coffee house has appeared in countless films, thanks to its beautifully untouched, if now rather threadbare, original décor.

Entertainment

The weekly *Falter* magazine (in German) has the most comprehensive listings section. The monthly *Wien Magazin*, free from the tourist office, has listings with some information in English. The **Wien-Ticket Pavilion**, by the Staatsoper (*open daily 10–7*), has tickets for all venues and its commissions are reasonable.

Theatre and Dance

Burgtheater, 1 Dr. Karl-Lueger-Ring 2, **t** 514 444140, *www.burg theater.at.* This magnificent 19th-century theatre is Austria's most prestigious. Also manages the **Akademietheater**, 3 Lisztstrasse 1, *www.akademie theater.at*, and the **Kasino am Schwarzenburgplatz**, 3 Schwarzenburgplatz 1, which showcases up-and-coming talent.

Tanzquartier Wien, **t** 581 359160, *www.tqw.at.* Vienna's only dedicated dance-space.

Volkstheater, 7 Neustiftgasse 1, **t** 524 7263, *www.volkstheater.at.* Another grand institution in Vienna; classical drama.

Opera, Ballet and Classical Music

Konzerthaus, Lothringerstrasse 20, **t** 242 0200, *www.konzerthaus.at.*

Musikverein, Karlsplatz 6, **t** 505 8190, *www.musikverein.at.*

Staatsoper, 1 Opernring 2, **t** 514 442250, *www. wiener-staatsoper.at.* Vienna's legendary opera and ballet house.

Cinemas

Burg, 1 Opernring 19, **t** 587 8406, *www. burgkino.at.* Famously screens *The Third Man* (in English) most Fri, Sat and Sun nights.

Österreiches Filmmuseum, 1 Augustinerstrasse 1, **t** 533 7054, *www.filmmuseum.at.* In the Albertina, films in the original language.

Nightlife

American Bar, 1 Kärntner Strasse 10, **t** 512 3283. Adolf Loos designed this sleek modernist bar in 1908. *Open daily 12pm–4am.*

Flex Halle, 1 Donaukanal/Augartenbrücke, **t** 533 7525. Still one of the hottest clubs in town. *Open from 11pm.*

Krah Krah, 1 Rabensteig 8, **t** 533 8193, *www. krah-krah.at.* Big and noisy. *Open Mon–Sat 11am–2am, Sun and hols 11am–1am.*

Vis à Vis, Wollzeille 5, **t** 512 9350, *www.weibel. at.* A must for all wine-enthusiasts – a great place to try a wide range of Austrian wines with snacks. *Open daily 3pm–10.30pm.*

Zwölf-Apostelkeller, Sonnenfelsgasse 3, **t** 512 6777. A raucous but fun brick cellar, with wooden tables, sturdy wines and traditional grub. *Open daily 4.30pm–midnight.*

Aux Gazelles, 6 Rahlgasse 5, **t** 585 6645. A sumptuous North African-themed restaurant-bar-club. *Open Mon–Thurs 10am–2am, Fri–Sat 10am–4am, Sun 10am–9pm.*

Volksgarten, Volksgarten/Burgring, **t** 533 0518. One of the most popular and over-the-top clubs in Vienna, with a huge dance floor which opens up on summer nights. *Open Wed–Sat from 11pm.*

Titanic Bar, 6 Theobaldgasse 11, **t** 587 4758, *www.titanic.at.* Tucked behind the MuseumsQuartier complex, the Titanic Bar is an achingly cool spot for a cocktail and some elegant snacks. *Open Tues–Thurs 7pm–2am, Fri–Sat 7pm–4am.*

U4, 12 Schonbrünner Strasse 222, **t** 815 8307, *www.u4club.at.* An institution, U4 has been going for years and still packs in a young, studenty crowd.

Hollein's glass and steel Haas Haus right opposite the Viennese holy-of-holies, the
Stephansdom. Baroque riding stables have been glamorously converted into one of
the world's largest cultural complexes. The Albertina has had a futuristic makeover
and the city's culinary scene has never been so creative. The palaces, cafés and opera
houses still provide Vienna with its alluring old world charm, but the recent injection
of 21st-century confidence and optimism have given the city a welcome dynamism.

Inner City (Innere Stadt)

The historic core of Vienna is a maze of narrow passages and cobbled squares,
where ancient churches, Baroque mansions and modern shopping streets jostle
cheek-by-jowl. It's dominated by the glittering tiled roof and jagged spires of
Stephansdom, and the sprawling Hofburg palace. Horse-drawn carriages clatter
romantically across the cobbles, and coffee houses beckon cosily from every corner.

Stephansplatz and Around

The spiky towers and steeple of **Stephansdom** (*1 Stephansplatz, t 5155 23526; open
daily 6am–10pm; guided tours*) soar theatrically above the huddled streets of the
Inner City, much as they have for almost 800 years. The original church was begun in
the 12th century, and was later expanded to become one of the largest and most
magnificent Gothic cathedrals in Europe. The vast, dim interior, with its vaulted
ceiling and ranks of slender columns, is crammed with masterpieces of Gothic craftsmanship. The most celebrated is the beautiful **Pilgram's Pulpit** (1515), carved with such
delicacy that the stone appears as insubstantial as foam. The **North Tower** (*open
daily; adm*), left unfinished, according to legend, after a lovelorn young architect
threw himself off the top. It houses the huge *Pummerin* ('Boomer') bell, originally
made from melted-down cannons taken from the Turks after they were defeated in
1683. The original plummeted through the roof in 1945, and the present bell – even
larger than the first – was made from its remains. The **South Tower** (*open daily; adm*),
fondly known as 'Steffl', can also be climbed for spectacular views. The **Catacombs**
(*open by guided visit every 15–30 mins, Mon–Sat 10–11.30 and 1.30–4, Sun and hols
1.30–4.30; adm*) contain the remains of the principal members of the Habsburg
family. The earlier rulers were left intact, but by the 17th century Habsburg burial
customs had been formalised in macabre fashion: their hearts were presented to the
Augustinerkirche, and their entrails were given to Stephansdom. What was left was
entombed in the Kaisergruft (*see p.129*). The cathedral treasures are kept in the
Cathedral and Diocesan Museum (Erzbischöfliches Dom- und Diözesanmuseum;
1 Stephansplatz 6; open Tues–Sat 10am–5pm; adm). Opposite the Stephansdom, the
curving steel and glass **Haas Haus** (*Stephansplatz 12; open daily 6am–2am*) by
celebrated architect Hans Hollein, was erected in 1990 amid huge controversy.

The narrow, medieval lanes to the east of Stephansplatz are perfect for an aimless
stroll, each corner throwing up a cobbled courtyard or elaborate Renaissance
doorway. **Blutgasse**, **Singerstrasse** and **Domgasse** are some of the prettiest. The
Figarohaus (*1 Domgasse 5; open daily Tues–Sun 9–6; adm*) is where Mozart spent some
of his happiest and most productive years, creating some of his greatest works,

Food and Drink

Vienna, like most major capitals, has a wide range of restaurants serving everything from sturdy local dishes to chic fusion cuisine (although the latter is a relative newcomer to Vienna's culinary scene). The traditional *Beisln* – simple inn-like places – have been going upmarket in recent years, and, in the best, classic Austrian recipes have been given a new lease of life. This reflects what's happening to Viennese palates: food, a long ignored facet of Austrian culture, is now sexy, and the city's gourmets have an ever-growing number of excellent restaurants.

Traditional Austrian cooking is simple and hearty, and always good for keeping out the cold: meat features heavily, particularly pork and veal, along with game, goose and duck in winter. The classic dish is *Wiener Schnitzel*, a breaded veal escalope, and delicious soups, like *Leberknödelsuppe* (a herby beef broth with dumplings) are also common. An excellent local dish which appears on menus in winter is *Martinigansl*, roast goose served with red cabbage and potato dumplings, Another favourite is Hungarian goulash, well seasoned with paprika, or local variations made with potatoes or frankfurters. For a quick snack, the city is liberally sprinkled with *Würstelstands*, simple outdoor booths selling hot sausages (best eaten doused in mustard). In late spring, try the delicious fresh asparagus, and in summer juicy fruits like local strawberries and apricots are piled high at market stands. In autumn, the Viennese collect pungent wild mushrooms, particularly chanterelle and porcini mushrooms, which are delicious simply sautéed.

Vienna's fabulous **cafés** are legendary, many oozing *fin-de-siècle* grandeur, and all serving a dazzling array of cakes and pastries. The most famous is the *Sachertorte*, a moist chocolate cake with an apricot filling hidden beneath a thick chocolate topping: the Hotel Sacher and the fancy pâtisserie Demel both claim the original recipe (although when these claims led to the courts, it was the Hotel Sacher that was finally granted rights to the term 'the original *Sachertorte*').

The pause for afternoon coffee and cake is called the *Jause*. Don't miss sweet delights like the delectable *Topfenknödel*, dumplings made of curd cheese with a crispy, nutty coating which come served with a fruit compote, the delicately spiced apple strudel or the rich, chocolatey *Mohr im Hemd*, a steamed pudding with a thick chocolate sauce and vanilla-scented cream.

Viennese coffee is taken very, very seriously: the most common is the *melange*, a coffee with milk, but if you want it black, ask for a *Schwarzer*. With whipped cream and rum, it's a *Fiaker*, and with an egg yolk and brandy, it's a *Kaisermelange*. Strong, syrupy Turkish coffee, made in a special long-handled copper pot, is also common.

Vienna is almost completely circled by **vineyards**, many with restaurants to sample the new vintages along with simple (and, in some cases, more elaborate) Austrian specialities. A visit to a local *Heurigen* is a pleasure that shouldn't be missed (see below). The most famous local grape is the *grüner veltliner*, which produces a fruity white wine, but there are also some excellent rieslings and pinot blancs. Red wines are generally soft and fruity, but there are some robust reds made with the blaufränkisch grape.

including *The Marriage of Figaro* after which the building is named. Unfortunately, as Mozart died impoverished, there's almost nothing to see inside.

South of the Figarohaus, the **House of Music** (Haus der Musik; 1 *Sielerstätte 30, www.hdm.at; open daily 10–10*) is one of Vienna's newest and most high-tech museums, housed in an elegant former palace. Most of the excellent exhibits are interactive – you can compose your own waltz, or conduct the Vienna Philharmonic. The top-floor café has fabulous views over the rooftops to Stephansdom.

Just east of the big shopping boulevard of **Kärntnerstrasse**, **Neuer Markt** contains one of Vienna's most popular sights: the **Imperial Burial Vault** (Kaisergruft; 1 *Neuer Markt/Tegetthoffstrasse, www.kaisergruft.at; open daily 9.30–4*) inside the Kapuzinerkirche. In 1618, the church of the Capuchins was selected as the last burial place of the Habsburg rulers –at least, what was left of them after their hearts were taken to Augustinerkirche (*see* p.132) and their entrails to Stephansdom (*see* p.127). The most opulent coffin is the famous double-tomb of the redoubtable Maria Theresia (1717–1780) and Franz Stephan (1708–65).

West of Stephansplatz

The **Graben** is one of the most chi-chi streets in Vienna, lined with expensive boutiques. It's dominated by the elaborate Baroque **Plague Column**, commissioned by Emperor Leopold I after the city was delivered from the plague in 1679.

Leading off Graben, smart **Dorotheergasse** reeks of old money, with its elegant antique shops and legendary auction house, the Dorotheum (*see* 'Shopping'). The fascinating **Jewish Museum** (Jüdisches Museum der Stadt Wien; 1 *Dorotheergasse 11, www.jmw.at; open Sun–Wed and Fri 10–6, Thurs 10–8; closed Mon; adm, combined ticket with Judenplatz Museum and Synagogue available*), outlines the history of the Jewish community in the city through imaginative exhibitions.

Even snootier than the Graben, adjoining **Kohlmarkt** is lined with designer shops, but it's most famous for the legendary *Konditorei* **Demel**. In opulent 19th-century surroundings, ladies-who-lunch and tourists gather over sublime cakes. It opens on to **Michaelerplatz**, dominated by a pompous neo-Baroque gateway to the Hofburg palace. In stark contrast, the **Loos Haus** facing it across the square is resolutely unadorned, and caused a furore while still in the planning stages. The Imperial family despised the 'house without eyebrows', a reflection of Adolf Loos' decision not to add the customary Viennese window boxes, and planning permission was only finally given once he promised to add some. The **Michaelerkirche** (*open daily 6.30–6; adm*), originally built in the 13th century, was once the Imperial church. The interior is over-whelmingly Baroque, and a small fee grants admission to the macabre crypt, where the desiccated remnants of former parishioners can be glimpsed in their open coffins.

Heading back down Kohlmarkt, the street name changes to Tuchlauben. At No. 19, the **Neidhart Frescoes** (*www.wienmuseum.at; open Tues–Sun 9–12; adm*) are the oldest secular frescoes in Vienna, which were discovered by chance during building work in 1979. Schultergasse winds from Tuchlauben to the **Judenplatz**, dominated by Rachel Whiteread's lovely *Memorial to Austrian Holocaust Victims*, dedicated to the 65,000 Austrian Jews killed by the Nazis. The **Judenplatz Museum** (Museum Judenplatz

Wien; *1 Judenplatz 8, www.jmw.at; open Sun–Fri 10–6, Thurs 10–8; adm; combined ticket with Jüdisches Museum and Beidermeier Synagogue at Seitengasse 4 available*) outlines the history of medieval Jewish Vienna, linked by an underground passage to the sparse remains of the city's oldest **synagogue**.

On the other side of Tuchlauben, **Hoher Markt**, Vienna's oldest square, is now an unappealing car park, with a Baroque fountain serving as the sole reminder of the square's former glory. The extravagant Jugendstil **Anker Clock** draws a crowd each day at noon, when twelve little figures from Viennese history shuffle across the clock-face to the accompaniment of tinny organ music. Beneath the Hoher Markt, scanty **remains of Roman Vindobona** (*open Mon 1–4.30, Tues–Sun 9–12.15; adm*), dating from around AD 1, have been discovered.

Imperial Palace (Hofburg)

*There are various **combination tickets** available for some of the attractions of the Hofburg Palace and the Kunsthistoriches Museum: **Gold Pass** (€23): Kunsthistoriches Museum, Lipizzaner Museum, Neue Burg (Collection of Ancient Musical Instruments, Collection of Arms and Armour and the Ephesus Museum), Austrian Theatre Museum, Schatzkammer (Imperial Treasury) and the Wagenburg (Carriage Museum, at Schönbrunn). **Silver Pass** (€21): Kunsthistoriches Museum, Neue Burg, Austrian Theatre Museum, Schatzkammer (Imperial Treasury). **Bronze Pass** (€19): Kunsthistoriches Museum, Neue Burg, Treasury. **Sisi Pass** (€19): offers a Grand Tour of Schönbrunn Palace, plus admission to the Sisi Museum and Kaiserappartements, and entrance to the Imperial Furniture collection.*

The spectacular Imperial Palace is a sprawling, confusing maze, built over more than six centuries in a dizzying array of architectural styles. The earliest fortress was built here in 1275 by Ottokar II of Bohemia, and became the official residence of the Habsburg rulers under Ferdinand I (1503–64). He remodelled the **Old Castle** (Alte Burg), beginning a trend which was continued with increasing relish under succeeding rulers. Most chose to build new apartments in the latest fashions, rather than take over those of their predecessors, with the result that the Palace grew in all directions – a wing added here, a courtyard there – with a complete disregard for uniformity. Now one wing contains the apartments of the Austrian President, and the rest has been converted into a string of museums dedicated to everything from weaponry to Esperanto.

The oldest surviving part of the palace complex is the **Schweizerhof**, dominated by a Renaissance archway (Swiss Gate). The **Gothic Imperial Chapel** (Burgkapelle; *1 Schweizerhof, t 533 9927; open for guided tours only Mon–Thurs 11–3, Fri 11–1; adm*) is where the world-famous Vienna Boys' Choir sing Sunday mass (*Sun at 9.15am Jan–June and mid-Sept–end Dec; reservations hmk@aon.at, or t (+42) 1 533 9927-75*). It's an unforgettable experience, but tickets should be booked months in advance.

The dimly lit chambers of the **Secular and Ecclesiastical Treasuries** (Weltliche und Geistliche Schatzkammer; *entrance below the Burgkapelle; open Wed– Mon 10–6; adm, English audioguide*) contain a dazzling array of jewel-studded crowns, Imperial robes and regalia, and magnificent religious objects, attesting to the extraordinary wealth and power of the Habsburg dynasty over 800 years.

Walk through the Swiss Gate to the grand **In der Burg** courtyard, where you'll see the entrance to the **Imperial Apartments** (Kaiserappartements; *www. hofburg-wien. at; open Wed–Mon 10–6; closed Tues; adm*) The Imperial Apartments are rather dull, but they have been pepped up for visitors with the addition of the new **Sisi Museum**, dedicated to the Empress Sisi, whose tragic life and death (often compared to that of Princess Diana) fascinate millions. Elisabeth of Bavaria, better known as Sisi, was never meant to be Empress of Austria. Franz Josef's mother had chosen her elder sister, Hélène, and arranged for the pair to meet in the spa town of Bad Ischl. But the young prince was instantly smitten with 16-year-old Sisi, and the pair were engaged within three days. Their whirlwind romance captured the hearts of everyone in the empire. But, while Franz Josef adored Sisi, his new wife was quickly disillusioned with court life and escaped whenever she could. She was obsessed with her appearance, particularly the luxuriant ankle-length hair which had so captivated her husband, and refused to be photographed or painted after the age of 40. Tragedy struck in 1890, when Crown Prince Rupert committed suicide in mysterious circumstances in Mayerling (*see* p.139) and Sisi withdrew completely. She wore black until her untimely death in 1898, when she was assassinated by an Italian anarchist on Lake Geneva.

Beyond the Sisi Museum, the Imperial Apartments where the Empress and her uxorious husband Franz Josef I lived have been preserved virtually intact. The rooms are frankly dull, with the exception of those which retain some personal touches, like Franz Josef's study which contains family photographs and a famous portrait of 'Angel Sisi'. In Sisi's apartments, gym equipment and a lavish bathroom reveal her obsessive concern for her appearance. The visit culminates with the Dining Room, where the table has been set for a family dinner. For grand occasions, the Habsburgs dug out the best china, in this case a spectacular collection of porcelain and silverware (the *Silberkammer*) displayed on the ground floor.

The next swath of the Hofburg's attractions are off **Josefsplatz**, home to the Hofburg's most celebrated attraction, the **Spanish Riding School** (Spanische Hofreitschule; *1 Josefsplatz 1, www.srs.at; performances and morning work Feb–June and end Aug–beginning of Nov; detailed programme on website; adm exp*). Entering the Baroque **Winter Riding School** is like stepping inside a wedding cake. The origins of the legendary Spanish Riding School date back to the end of the 16th century, when the elegant horses were first bred from Spanish, Italian and North African stallions at the Imperial Stud in Lipizzaner, near Trieste. It was Emperor Karl VI (1685–1740), born and brought up in Spain, who gave it its current form and commissioned the lavish Winter Riding School from Josef Emanuel Fisher von Erlach. The graceful manoeuvres performed today date back to this period, although they are based on steps developed during the Renaissance by cavalrymen who needed nimble mounts in battle. Lucky visitors who booked their tickets well in advance can see the beautiful Lipizzaner horses perform their intricate ballets under massive chandeliers and creamy stucco. Tickets to performances are expensive, but it's possible to see the horses rehearsing their moves during morning training sessions for a reasonable fee, and just watching the horses being led across from their stables to the Winter Riding School each morning is a romantic sight.

Opposite the Winter Riding School is the **Lipizzaner Museum** (*1 Reitschulgasse 2, open daily 9–6; adm*), set in the stables, where once, but sadly no longer, you could peek at the stars of the show in their stalls. The museum contains few exhibits, mainly old prints and riders' uniforms, plus videos detailing the intricate moves.

Back on Josefsplatz proper, the **Austrian National Library** (Nationalbibliothek) contains the dazzling **Hall of State** (Prunksaal; 1 Josefsplatz 1; *www.onb.ac.at; open Jan–April and Nov–Dec Fri–Wed 10–2, Thurs 10–7; May–Oct Fri–Wed 10–4, Thurs 10–7; adm*), the largest Baroque library in Europe, a giddy whirl of columns, gilt, statuary and heavily allegorical frescoes. The work of Johann Bernhard Fischer von Erlach, who also designed the Karlskirche (*see* below), it's one of the masterpieces of the late 18th century. The handful of ancient globes are just a harbinger of what's to come in the **Globe Museum** (*www.onb.ac.at/sammlungen/globen; open Mon–Wed and Fri 11–12, Thurs 2–3; adm*) on the third floor. There are two other museums, one dedicated to **Esperanto** (*open Oct–June Mon–Wed 9–4; July–Sept Fri 9–1; adm*) and the other containing the collection of **papyrus** (*www.onb,ac,at/sammlungen/papyrus; open Mon–Wed and Fri 10–4; adm*). In late 2005 the Globe and Esperanto Museums are to move to a new home in the Palais Mollard-Clary, 1 Herrengasse 9.

Overlooking Josefsplatz, the 14th-century **Augustinerkirke** (*1 Augustinerstrasse 3; open daily 8am–5pm*) is one of the oldest surviving churches in Vienna. It's dominated by Antonio Canova's sentimental memorial to Maria Theresia's favourite daughter, Maria Christina (who is actually buried in the Imperial burial vault in the Kapuzinergraft). But dead Habsburgs are still the main draw in this church: their hearts are arranged in silver caskets in the tiny Loreto Chapel.

Augustinerstrasse leads to the **Albertina** (*1 Augustinerstrasse 3; open daily 8–5; free, adm to Loreto Chapel*), which contains one of the finest collections of graphic art in the world, with almost 70,000 drawings and over a million graphic prints. There are works by Raphael, Leonardo da Vinci, Michelangelo, Rembrandt, Picasso, Matisse, Schiele and Klimt among others, but the star of the Albertina is undoubtedly the enormous number of works by Albrecht Dürer. The building emerged from a glossy and daring €100million expansion in 2003, which repaired the war damage to the Imperial Apartments and installed brand-new exhibition spaces. Those with a penchant for Imperial interior design can visit the Imperial Apartments, which have been painstakingly restored to look as they would have in 1822.

Wriggle back through the palace courtyards to emerge on **Heldenplatz** (Heroes' Square), where the splendid curve of the **New Castle** (Neue Burg) was built between 1881–1913. Adolf Hitler infamously proclaimed the incorporation of Austria into the Third Reich (the *Anschluss*) from one of its balconies. Now the castle houses several **museums,** all accessible with a single ticket (*t 525240, www.khm.at; all museums open Wed–Mon 10–6; adm*).

The interior of the Neue Burg is every bit as florid as the exterior, with monumental staircases and elaborate stucco ceilings providing a splendid backdrop to the museums' collections. The **Collection of Arms and Armour** (Hofjagd-und Rüstkammer) is vast and surprisingly engrossing, with prancing horses decked out in full jousting gear and fanciful costume armour. The **Collection of Ancient Musical Instruments** (Sammlung alter Musik-instrumente) is altogether more soothing – literally, as the audioguide provides a gentle musical background to the exhibits. It's another enormous collection, with one of the most remarkable collections of Renaissance instruments in the world. The lower galleries contain the archaeological fragments discovered at **Ephesus**, site of the Temple of Artemis, one of the Seven Wonders of the World. Make sure you see the massive *Parthermonument* (Parthian Monument), a series of exquisitely wrought relief panels which may have been part of an altar.

The Ethnographical Museum (Völkerkundermuseum; *open Wed–Mon 10–6; adm*) has a separate admission fee. It is housed in what was originally intended to be the Imperial guest house, and has a separate entrance on the Heldenplatz. It has an enjoyably diverse collection spanning every continent: there is a striking series of bronze sculptures from Benin, and a magnificent 16th-century feathered head-dress which belonged to the Aztec king Montezuma, stoned to death by his own people for submitting to the Spanish conquistadors.

Around the Ringstrasse

When the city walls were finally demolished in 1857, work began on this spectacular circular boulevard, designed to outshine anything which Paris or London had to offer. It was lined with some of Vienna's most emblematic buildings.

Museum of Fine Arts (Kunsthistoriches Museum)

1 Maria-Theresien-Platz, t 525240, www.khm.at. Hauptgebäude (Main Building). Open Tues, Wed and Fri–Sun 10–6, Thurs 10–9; closed Mon; Coin Cabinet Tues–Sun 10–6.

The vast, grandiose Kunsthistoriches Museum across the Ringstrasse from the Hofburg contains one of the finest and largest art collections in Europe. The overwhelming setting and the sheer size of the collection may leave you breathless. The collection is divided into several parts: the first floor houses the Picture Gallery (Gemäldegalerie), which is what everyone mainly comes to see. A connecting series of inner galleries in both wings are numbered with Roman numerals, while a second, outer ring of smaller rooms are given standard numbers. A floor plan is essential.

Gemäldegalerie East Wing: German, Dutch and Flemish collection: Room X is easily the most popular gallery in the entire museum, with a spectacular and virtually unrivalled collection of the works of Pieter Brueghel the Elder, including a sublime series of paintings depicting the seasons which mark the apotheosis of 16th-century landscape composition. Other highlights include monumental Baroque canvases by Jordaens and Snyders, delicate portraits by Van Dyck, and a big collection of the works of Rubens and Rembrandt. There is also a mesmerising collection of German paintings from the Danube School, including Dürer's tender *Virgin and Child with a Pear*. Look out too for Vermeer's magnificent *The Artist's Studio* (Room 24).

Gemäldegalerie West Wing: Italian, Spanish and French collection: This collection begins with a bang – a whole room full of the works of Titian, court painter to Karl V.

There are more Italian Mannerists in Rooms II and III, with a vivid *Judith with the Head of Holofernes* by Veronese, and Tintoretto's exquisite, light-drenched *Susannah Bathing*. Room 4 contains Raphael's serene *Madonna im Grünen*, and Pietro Perugino's moving painting of the Virgin surrounded by children, which has just emerged from restoration and glows. There are fabulous Habsburg portraits by Velázquez in Room 10, including one of Charles III, who was spectacularly ugly.

Collection of Sculpture and Decorative Art (*undergoing major restoration until at least 2006; in the meantime, many of the works are displayed around the Picture Gallery*): The collection is quirkier than its name suggests, and includes all kinds of curiosities acquired by Rudolf II and Archduke Ferdinand, for their Kunskammern, or Chambers of Art and Marvels.

Collection of Greek and Roman Antiquities (*closed for restoration, due to open spring 2005*): They are stuffed full of ancient treasures, from Etruscan art and vases to ancient Greek and Cypriot sculpture.

Egyptian and Near Eastern Collection (*partially closed for restoration*): This contains ancient sarcophagi, mummified animals and canopic jars (for the entrails removed during the mummification process). The reconstructed tomb chapel of Ka-ni-nisut dates back five millennia, and there is a whole menagerie of fantastical votive figures and amulets, and a beautiful, lapis-lazuli-blue ceramic hippopotamus.

Natural History Museum (Naturhistoriches Museum)

1 Maria-Theresien-Platz, t 52177, www.nhm-wien.acc.at; open Thurs–Mon 10–6, Wed 10–9; adm; roof tours Wed at 5 and 6.30, Sun 2 and 4; adm.

Erected at the same time as the Kunsthistoriches Museum across the square, Vienna's Natural History Museum is equally sumptuous; little has changed since it opened in 1889. Elegant wooden cabinets are crammed with every imaginable stuffed creature from around the world, many displayed in delightfully old-fashioned dioramas. The dinosaur skeletons in Rooms IV and V on the Upper Ground Floor are the big draw; there is also a spectacular 17-million-year-old tusked mammoth-like creature excavated in the Czech Republic, and the well-preserved skeleton of the Austrian rhino. In the last room on this floor, you can see Honzo, the beer-swilling, cigarette-smoking, fight-picking chimpanzee who lived in Vienna zoo in the 1950s.

The Staatsoper to Karlsplatz

Vienna's extravagant **Opera House** (Staatsoper; *1 Opernring 2, t 514 442606, www. wiener-staatsoper.at; guided visits available; adm; but check times posted under the arcades on the Kärntnerstrasse side of the Opera House; for booking information, see 'Entertainment', p.126*) opened with a performance of Mozart's *Don Giovanni* in 1869. It suffered extensive damage during the Second World War but has been restored with all the latest technological equipment, losing much of its original flamboyance in the process. Still, there are enough grand staircases and opulent salons to flounce around for a visit to the Opera to remain a heady and romantic experience.

Kärtnerstrasse leads to **Karlsplatz**, overlooked by **Karlskirche** or Church of St Charles Borromeo (*Karslplatz, www.karlskirche.at; open Mon–Sat 9–12.30 and 1–6, Sun 1–6; last* *lift up to the dome 5.30; adm to dome*), commissioned by Emperor Karl VI in thanks for Vienna's delivery from the plague in 1713 and one of the most extravagant expressions of European Baroque. Johann Bernhard Fischer von Erlach designed and began work on the church, which was completed by his son around 1739. The two minaret-like towers were inspired by Trajan's Column in Rome, and are decorated with a spiralling series of reliefs describing the life of St Charles Borromeo. A lift up to the ethereal dome allows close-up views of Rottmayer's vast fresco depicting the *Apotheosis of St Charles*.

Opposite the church the **Vienna History Museum** (Wien Museum; *4 Karlsplatz, www.wienmuseum. at; open Tues–Sun 9–6; adm*) which documents the city's history from prehistoric times until the 20th century. The top floor is the most rewarding, and contains a small but excellent collection of early 20th-century art, including several pieces by Klimt and some bleak portraits by Egon Schiele.

At the other end of Karlsplatz, stranded between major roads, you can't miss the glistening golden dome of the beautiful **Secession Building** (*1 Friedriechstrasse 12, www.secession.at; open Tues, Wed and Fri–Sun 10–6, Thurs 10–8; adm*). In 1897, a group of young artists, including Gustav Klimt, Josef Hofmann, Josef Maria Olfbrich and Kolo Moser, withdrew from the conservative Society of Artists at the Künstlerhaus and formed the Association of Visual Artists Secession. This sparkling white building (completed in 1898) was a physical embodiment of the new movement's fundamental tenets, and is emblazoned with their motto: *Der Zeit ihre Kunst, der Kunst ihre Freiheit* ('To the Age its Art, to Art its Freedom'). The spaces are deliberately divided into the ornamental entrance area, and the purely functional galleries – sleek, white and unadorned. Bizarrely, the only permanent exhibit was intended to be temporary: Klimt's haunting *Beethoven Frieze*, painted for the 9th exhibition of the Viennese Secessionists in 1902.

MuseumsQuartier

U-Bahn to MuseumsQuartier.

The former Imperial riding stables, designed by the indefatigable Johann Fischer von Erlach at the end of the 18th century, have been expensively converted into the MuseumsQuartier, one of the world's largest cultural complexes. Bold contemporary buildings have been slotted into the spacious central courtyard, now called the **Museumsplatz**, which is full of terrace cafés. There's an information office-cum-shop (*www.mqw.at; open daily 10–7*), a good first port-of-call to find out what's on when – the complex hosts several one-off events.

The pale, gleaming cube inserted into the main square of the MuseumsQuartier houses the **Leopold Museum** (*www.leopoldmuseum.org; open Wed, Thurs and Sat–Mon 10–7, Fri 10–9; closed Tues; adm*), with a superb collection of the works of Austrian expressionist Egon Schiele. The second floor is dedicated to Schiele, but there is plenty of art by other late 19th-century and 20th-century artists, including Klimt, Gerstl and Kokoschka.

Jutting out at an awkward angle on the other side of Museumsplatz is the unrelentingly contemporary **Museum of Modern Art** (Museum moderner Kunst) known as

MUMOK (*www. mumok.at; open Tues, Wed and Fri–Sun 10–6, Thurs 10–9; closed Mon; adm*). The collection spans most of the major 20th-century art movements, which can usually be seen as part of changing exhibitions, though some highlights are on permanent view. The basement is devoted to Viennese Actionism, a provocative performance art movement whose proponents outdid each other with a succession of shocking public displays which regularly incorporated blood, offal and faeces.

The former Winter Riding School of the Imperial stables has been converted into a vast, contemporary exhibition space and performance hall, the **Kunsthalle Wien** (*www.kunsthallewien.at; open Fri–Wed 10–7, Thurs 10–10; adm*), which is deservedly one of the most popular art institutions in the city.

The **Zoom Children's Museum** (ZOOM Kindermuseum; *t 524 7908, www.kinder museum.at; open Mon–Fri 8.30–5, Sat–Sun 10–5.30; adm; sessions must be pre-booked in advance, particularly for weekends*) is a must for kids, who will be having too much fun to mind the language barrier. Vienna's dedicated children's museum runs hugely popular workshops for kids of all ages.

Belvedere Palaces and MAK

The glorious Baroque Belvedere Palace was built by Johann Lukas von Hildebrandt for Prince Eugene of Savoy. The elegant Lower Belvedere, a summer palace, was built in 1714–16, but the prince required something even grander and commissioned the magnificent Upper Belvedere in 1721 – which functioned essentially as an extravagant party pavilion. The palaces are linked by graceful formal **gardens** (*open daily 6am–dusk*) and have been restored to house the Austrian Gallery collection of art.

The **Upper Belvedere** (Oberes Belvedere; *3 Prinz-Eugen-Strasse 27, www.belvedere.at; open Tues–Sun 10–6; closed Mon; adm; combined ticket to all the Belvedere collections available*) contains the 19th- and 20th-century collections, beginning with several fine views of Vienna and a throng of sentimentalized portraits. It then picks up steam with paintings by Renoir, Van Gogh, and Munch. There's an early portrait by Klimt, of a sour-faced miss in a pink, frilly dress, but the following gallery contains the real star of the Belvedere: Klimt's famous *Kiss*. Several galleries are devoted to the Viennese Expressionists, and feature a whole room full of works by Egon Schiele, including a pearly autumnal scene. The Baroque collection is housed in the main building of the **Lower Belvedere** (Unteres Belvedere; *3 Rennweg 6*), perfectly at home in the lavish marble and gilt halls. Look out for a series of grimacing, laughing, crying busts – unintentionally hilarious character studies by Franz Xaver Messerschmidt. Take the path outside to the medieval collection, housed in the former **Orangerie**, which contains beautiful religious paintings and altarpieces. The palace gardens link with Vienna's extensive **Botanical Gardens** (*Rennweg 14; open daily 9–dusk, closed in bad weather*).

The Austrian **Museum of Applied Arts and Contemporary Art**, better known simply as **MAK** (*1 Stubenring 5, www.mak.at; open Wed–Sun 10–6, Tues 10am–midnight; closed Mon*), may be housed in a monumental, 19th-century Ringstrasse building, but its displays are anything but stuffy. In 1993, the curators invited celebrated artists to redesign the exhibition halls and the results (while sometimes annoyingly pretentious) have been a huge success. The ground floor exhibits begin with embroidered

liturgical vestments in the Romanesque and Gothic collection and culminates with
the chair collection in the Historismus, Jugendstil, Art Deco room (arranged by
Barbara Bloom) which is back-lit and visible in silhouette through white screens, the
forms emerging like shadow-puppets. Upstairs, a gallery is dedicated to the Wiener
Werkstätte (Vienna Workshops), which considered everything worthy of design, from
ashtrays and postage stamps to furniture and ceramics. The main highlight of the
Art Nouveau and Art Deco gallery is a series of drawings by Klimt for a panelled frieze.

Around the Edge

Sigmund Freud Museum

*9 Berggasse 19, t 319 1596, www.freud-museum.at; tram D to Schlickgasse,
tram 37, 38, 40, 41 to Schwarzspanierstrasse, or bus 40 A to Berggasse. Open
daily July–Sept 9–6; Oct–June 9–5; adm. Audioguide; guided tours by appt.*

Freud lived and practised here from 1891 until the Nazis forced him to emigrate in
1938. The waiting room is the only room which has been restored to look just as it did
in Freud's time, and the rest of the apartment is now a temporary exhibition space
and study centre. One small room contains multilingual video screens showing black
and white films of the Freud family, narrated by his daughter Anna.

Schönbrunn

*13 Schönbrunner Schloss Strasse 47, t 811 3239, www.schoenbrunn.at;
U-Bahn to Schönbrunn, tram 10, 58, bus 10a to Schloss Schönbrunn.
See below for opening times of attractions within palace complex.*

*Admission tickets: **Imperial Tour**: 22 rooms in the palace, €8 with audioguide.
Grand Tour: 40 rooms, including the ornate 18th-century audience rooms,
€10.50 with audioguide, guided tour €13. **Classic Pass**: Grand Tour, plus
admission to Privy Garden, Gloriette, Maze and Labyrinth, and Schönbrunn
Bakery, €14.90. **Gold Pass**: Classic Pass plus admission to Schönbrunn Zoo,
Palm House, Desert Experience House, Carriage Museum, €36. See also
Sisi Pass (under Hofburg, p.130).*

The Habsburgs commissioned Johann Bernhard Fischer von Erlach to build them a
new summer lodge in 1695. He planned a gigantic palace to outshine Versailles, but
the Imperial family were forced to make do with a mere 1,441 rooms in the final
design by Nikolaus Pacassi. It's possible to escape the hordes in the beautiful gardens,
which contain a maze, a 19th-century palm house, the Imperial carriage museum, and
the oldest zoo in the world.

The tour of the palace's **Imperial Apartments** (*open Nov–Mar daily 8.30–4.30;
April–June and Sept–Oct daily 8.30–5; July–Aug daily 8.30–6; tickets are marked with an
entrance time; adm exp*) begins with the humdrum apartments belonging to Franz
Josef and Sissi, but Baroque magnficence kicks in when you reach Maria Theresia's
apartments. The Mirror Room was used for family concerts, including one given by
the 6-year-old Mozart and his sister (when the young prodigy apparently smothered

the Empress with kisses). The magnificent Great Gallery was used for balls, including during the Congress of Vienna in 1815 ('the congress danced but didn't advance'), and also for a celebrated meeting between Kennedy and Khrushchev in 1961. The Carousel Room and the Ceremonial Hall follow, and mark the culmination of the Grand Tour. If you've opted for the Imperial Tour, the best is yet to come: the following salons are the most opulent of all. The Blue Chinese Salon, with delicate hand-painted wallpaper, is where negotiations were held leading to Karl I's abdication in 1918. The Millions Room is covered in rare rosewood panelling inset with Indo-Persian etchings. In the bedroom, the only surviving State Bed, built for the marriage of Maria Theresia and Franz Stephan, is barely discernible under the weight of cherubs and drapes.

The former stables now house the **Imperial Coach Museum** (Wagenburg; *www.khm. at; open April–Oct daily 9–6; Nov–Mar 10–4; adm*), where glittering Baroque carriages and sleighs, monumental funerary carriages, and sleek early automobiles eloquently convey the dazzling opulence of the Habsburg court.

Schönbrunn's gorgeous **gardens** (Schlösspark; *open daily 10am–dusk*) stretch for miles, formally laid out in the French style in the 18th century and scattered with statuary and fountains. For fabulous views over the whole park, make for the **Gloriette** (*access above the café, open April–June and Sept daily 9–6; July and Aug 9–7; Oct 9–5; adm*), a huge victory arch erected in 1775. Kids will enjoy the **maze** and **labyrinth** (*same opening times as Gloriette; adm*) and the **Vienna Zoo** (Tiergarten; *www.zoovienna.at; open daily Nov–Jan 9–4.30; Feb 9–5; Mar and Oct 9–5.30; April 9–6; May–Sept 9–6.30; adm*), successor to Franz Stephan's Imperial Menagerie, which still contains some of the original Baroque cages and is the oldest zoo in the world. The 19th-century **Palmenhaus** (*open May–Sept daily 9.30–5.30; Oct–April daily 9.30–4.30; adm*) is a graceful wrought iron-and-glass pavilion based on the greenhouses of Kew.

Hundertwasserhaus and KunstHausWien

On the corner of Löwengasse with Kegelgasse. Closed to the public. U-bahn, tram to Landstrasse or Hetzgasse.

Slap bang in the middle of an otherwise unremarkable residential street, architect Friedensreich Hundertwasser's playful, multi-coloured curvy **apartment building** (1985) appears to have been transported from another planet. Committed fans can head around the corner to the fairytale **KunstHausWien** (*3 Untere Weissgerberstrasse 13, www.kunsthauswien.at; open daily 10–7, guided tours Sun and hols 12 and 3; adm*), an exhibition space boasting another wacky blend of styles and bold colours.

The Prater

U-Bahn, tram 5, 21, O to Praterstern.

This fabulous stretch of parkland has been the city's most celebrated playground since Josef II opened it to the public in 1766. The **Volksprater funfair** (*open daily 10am–11pm*), at the northwest end, is the most popular section, dominated by the giant **Reisenrad** or ferris wheel (*open daily May–Sept 9am–midnight, Mar–April and Oct 10–10; Nov–Feb 10–8; adm*), immortalized in *The Third Man*.

Day Trips from Vienna

The Wienerwald (Vienna Woods)

Vienna is blessed with the leafy Wienerwald right on its doorstep, a gently undulating region of forests and hills which almost completely encircles the city and extends for more than 400 square miles. Much of it is protected forest, criss-crossed with excellent walking and cycling trails, but it's also peppered with elegant spa towns and unassuming wine villages full of excellent *Heurigen*.

Mödling, 10 miles from Vienna, has a tiny but appealing old quarter, with 16th- and 17th-century houses clustered around cobbled squares, and a miniature Rathaus with a graceful loggia. Beethoven spent the summer of 1819 in Mödling, and rented rooms at Hauptstrasse 79, which have been converted into a **museum** (*open Tues–Sun 9–12*). You can take a dip in the town's Jugendstil swimming pool, or walk in the forest.

West of Mödling, the unassuming hamlet of **Mayerling** is set in one of the most beautiful valleys in the Vienna Woods, with craggy hills, swift-flowing rivers and dense forests. The village has become inextricably linked with the tragic double suicide of Prince Rupert and his 17-year-old lover Maria Vetsera in 1889. The Imperial hunting lodge in which the pair shot themselves was torn down and replaced by a Carmelite convent, which now contains a few sticks of furniture and photographs of the tragic pair. Maria Vetsera was buried at **Stift Heiligenkreuz**, a beautiful Cistercian abbey lost in a peaceful expanse of woods, a few miles from Mayerling. The original abbey was built during the Middle Ages as a burial chapel for the Babenburg dukes and, although it was substantially rebuilt after Turkish attacks in the 1690s, it still contains some lovely Romanesque and Gothic elements. Come for mass if you can.

Southwest of Mayerling, the delightful spa town of **Baden** has a slightly battered turn-of-the-20th-century charm. The Romans discovered the curative effects of its natural springs, and the town reached the height of its fame in the 19th century

Getting There

There are frequent **trains** (every half-hour) to Mödling, Baden and Gumpoldskirchen from Vienna Südbahnhof. An infrequent **bus** service links Baden with Mayerling, but, to explore the woods properly, it is best to have your own transport. You can download **cycling** maps from *www.mtbwienerwald.at*.

Tourist Information

Mödling: K Elizabetherstrasse 2, **t** (02236) 26727, *www.moedling.at. Open Mon–Fri 9–5.*
Baden: Brusattiplatz 3, **t** (02252) 22600-600, *www.baden.at. Open summer Mon–Sat 9–5, Sun 10–12; winter Mon–Fri 9–5.*
Gumpoldskirchen: Schrannenplatz 5, **t** (02252) 63536, *www.gumpoldskirchen.at.*

Eating Out

Babenbergerhof, Babenbergergasse 6, Mödling, **t** (02236) 2224 6405 (*moderate*). Smart hotel-restaurant.
Buchner, Hauptstrasse 54, Mayerling, **t** (02236) 41415 (*inexpensive*). A traditional *Heuriger* with tasty Austrian specialities to accompany the local wine.
Badner Stübel, Gutenbrunnerstrasse 19, Baden, **t** (02252) 41232 (*moderate*). An old-fashioned, family-run restaurant serving good local dishes.
Heuriger Bruckberger, Wienerstrasse, Gumpoldskirhcen, **t** (02252) 62230 (*inexpensive*). One of several traditional *Heurigen* clustered along Wienerstrasse and Neustiftsgasse, this one is particularly friendly and serves great food.

when celebrated artists, musicians and even the Imperial family would summer here and take the waters. The old centre is a higgledy-piggledy maze of 16th-and 17th-century mansions spiralling out from the Hauptplatz, dominated by a Baroque plague column. You can still take the waters at one of the spas or investigate the *Heurigen*.

Gumpoldskirchen, with its redolent fairy-tale name, is the most celebrated wine village in these parts. The town erupts twice a year with a fabulous wine festival (in June and August), and the countless excellent *Heurigen* produce the world-famous Gumpoldskirchner wines. Local tourist offices publish lists of all the *Heurigen*.

Around the Neusiedler See

The northern tip of Austria's easternmost province, **Burgenland**, is dominated by the vast, reed-fringed lake of the **Neusiedler See**. Thanks to its unusual microclimate, the lake attracts a wealth of bird and animal life and is now a National Park. The baking heat of summer has made it a popular excursion for the beach-starved Viennese, who come to sunbathe and swim, while in winter it freezes to become one huge ice-rink.

Eisenstadt, the charming, tiny capital of Burgenland, has long been linked with Haydn, who lived here for much of his life under the patronage of the powerful Hungarian Esterházy family. Their castle still dominates the town, an immense medieval fortress which is now primarily Baroque and neoclassical. The otherwise dull guided tours of the **castle** (still owned by the wealthy Esterházy family), include a visit to the lavishly frescoed Haydnsaal, where the composer once conducted his own works and where concerts still regularly take place. Close by, Eisenstadt's medieval Jewish quarter, the **Unterberg**, remains astonishingly intact, although its small community were sent to the death camps by the Nazis during the Second World War. The history of the Jews in Eisenstadt is recounted in the small **Jewish Museum** at Unterbergasse 6, which contains one of the only synagogues in the area to have survived the horrors of *Kristallnacht*. Most of Eisenstadt's other attractions are linked to Haydn, and include his home, the Haydnhaus, on Josef-Haydn-Gasse (only for die-hard fans), and his mausoleum, in the frilly Baroque **Bergkirche**.

Getting There

There are direct **trains** to Neusiedl am See from Vienna Südbahnhof at least every hour, with **bus** links to villages and towns around the lake. There is one daily direct train to Eisenstadt from Vienna, but otherwise change at Neusiedl. There are scores of **bicycle** rental outlets in every town and hamlet.

Tourist Information

Eisentadt: Schloss Esterházy, t (00800) 2837, *www.tiscover.at/eisenstadt*.
Neusiedl am See: Obere Haupstrasse 24, t (02167) 8600, *www.neusiedlersee.com*.

Eating Out

Im Esterházy, Schloss Esterházy, Eisenstadt, t (02682) 62819 (*moderate–inexpensive*). This is a handsome restaurant in the castle itself, where you can linger over the papers in the café, or dine substantially on excellent modern Austrian cuisine.
Inamera, Oggauerstrasse 29, Rust, t (02685) 6473 (*moderate*). A stylish whitewashed place serving sophisticated local cuisine.
Am Nyikokspark, Landgasthaus,, Neusiedl am See, t (02167) 40222 (*moderate*). An elegant restaurant in the magnificent surroundings of the former Langasthaus, with creative Austrian cuisine.

Close to the shores of the Neusiedler See, **Rust**, the smallest town in the country, is crammed with 16th- and 17th-century houses, many sporting an untidy fringe of storks' nests. Nesting storks bring luck according to local superstition, but, if they fail to return, an unpleasant surprise is in store. The reeds from the nearby lake are used in local crafts, but Rust is best known for its wines.

To the north, brash and unappealing **Neusiedl am See** is the main transport hub of the region, with train and bus connections to Vienna, but it's not worth lingering here. South of Rust, the tiny village of **Mörbisch**, a straggle of brilliantly whitewashed houses with brightly painted doors, sits on the Hungarian border and feels distinctly un-Austrian. At the end of July, the village hosts an excellent operetta festival (more information at *www.seefestpiele-morbisch.at*), with performances on a floating stage.

The Southern Alps

Less than 80 miles from Vienna, the Alps make their last thrust before levelling out into the Hungarian steppes. The dramatic scenery and famously clean air drew wealthy 19th-century excursionists, and a spectacular railway was constructed through the Semmering Pass in 1854. This, along with a delightfully old-fashioned cog-wheel steam engine at Puchberg-am-Schneeberg, is still much-loved.

Semmering, an elegant mountain town sprinkled with Jugenstil villas, is the largest of the Southern Alpine resorts. It sprawls across a hillside overlooking the Semmering Pass, and is liberally strewn with upmarket hotels (including the Imperial family's favourite, the Grand Hotel Panhans) and restaurants. In winter it's a popular skiing centre, with plenty of facilities (travel agents in Vienna sell special packages for a day or a weekend trip). The extraordinary mountain railway, built in the mid-19th century, is one of the most dramatic and beautiful train journeys in Europe, particularly the last section between Payerbach and Semmering. To the north of the resort, the **Höllental** (Valley of Hell) is a staggeringly beautiful, narrow gorge.

Scheeberg, at 2,076m, is the highest mountain range close to Vienna and another hugely popular destination for winter sports. In 1897, a cog-wheel steam engine was completed, which still makes a dramatic ascent up the mountain from Puchberg-am-Schneeberg to the small station at Hochschneeberg (with a restaurant). From here, you can strike out into the peaks: the highest, **Klosterwappen**, is about an hour's hike.

Getting There

The most spectacular route is on the **train** from Vienna Südbahnhof (hourly trains).

By **car**, it's an easy journey straight down the S6 motorway from Vienna.

Tourist Information

Semmering: Passhöhe 248, **t** (02664) 20025, *www.semmering.at*.

Puchberg: Sticklergasse 3, **t** (02636) 2256, *www.tiscover.at/puchberg-am-schneeberg*.

Eating Out

Semmering

Restaurant Wintergarten, Hotel Panhans, Hochstrasse 32, **t** (02664) 8181 (*expensive*). Dine in style in the sumptuous restaurant of the beautiful Jugendstil Hotel Panhans.

Zum Stoasteirer, Zaubergasse 2, **t** (02664) 2498 (*moderate*). This chalet-style restaurant offers excellent Austrian cuisine, which changes with the season, along with a good list of regional wines. There are welcoming staff and fabulous views.

Touring from Vienna: Up the Danube

The slow-moving river meanders gently through the verdant Danube Valley, past medieval villages, orchard-covered hills that blaze with blossom in spring, and snaking vines. The massive fortresses and monasteries which glower from the hills attest to the valley's strategic location at the crossroads of East and West, a reminder of hotly contested territorial battles. The most beautiful section of the Danube Valley is called the **Wachau**, the stretch of river between Krem and Melks. It is a paradise for gourmets, and for cyclists, who potter along the riverside cycling paths.

Day 1: Castles and Churches

Morning: From Vienna, take the B14 north to **Klosterneuburg** (8 miles), a pretty market town surrounded by a sea of vines and dominated by the impressive **Stift Klosterneuberg** (*open daily 10–noon and 1.30–4.30; adm*). This 12th-century fortified abbey was built to house the last remains of St Leopold, and was dramatically expanded under Karl VI in the 18th century. It contains the celebrated 12th-century *Verduner Altar*, one of the most extraordinary examples of medieval craftsmanship, and you can try the abbey's own wines in the vaulted cellars.

Lunch: In Klosterneuberg, try the **Stiftscafé**, Rathausplatz 20, t (02243) 411611 (*moderate*). There's an informal café for snacks, a smart restaurant upstairs, and a pretty courtyard terrace for summer. Or have a simple pasta and salad at **Café Epicur**, Rathausplatz 8 (*inexpensive*), in a pretty Baroque building.

Afternoon: The B14 continues 23km towards the ancient town of **Tulln**, founded by the Romans and Austria's first capital under the Babenburgs. Now a sleepy provincial town, it is scattered with ancient churches like the magnificent Minoritenkirche, but is best known as the birthplace of Egon Schiele, whose life and work are outlined in a small museum (*open Tues–Sun 1–6; adm*).

Dinner: **Der Floh**, Tullnerstrasse 1, Langenlebarn (6km from Tulln), t (02272) 62809 (*expensive–moderate*) is a welcoming, stylish wood-panelled restaurant and guesthouse serving gourmet Austrian cuisine from an award-winning young chef. **Sodoma**, Bahnhofstrasse 38, t (02272) 64616 (*expensive–moderate*) is the best restaurant in Tulln, with two cosy dining areas full of oil paintings and knick-knacks.

Sleeping: **Gasthof Buchinger**, Weinerstrasse 5, Langlebarn, t (02272) 62527 (*moderate*) is a pretty, riverside inn with basic rooms, a shady garden and a simple restaurant. Simple little pension **Zum Springbrunnen**, Hauptplatz 14a, t (02272) 63115 (*inexpensive*). is in the heart of Tulln old city, and offers double rooms and an apartment.

Day 2: Wine and Monks

Morning: From Tulln, take the S5 to **Krems an der Donau**, a picture-postcard town at the start of the Wachau proper, enchantingly set in a sea of vines. Medieval Krems and Renaissance Stein, once separate settlements, have merged over the years, and the cobbled streets are lined with pretty ice-cream-coloured houses and a smattering of ancient mansions. Most visitors confine their wanderings to Krems, but it's worth strolling over to Stein, particularly its atmospheric main street sprinkled with squares opening out on to the river. Krems has been producing excellent wines for centuries and there are *Heurigen* in the area: the tourist office, in a former Capuchin monastery, has full details and a wine museum.

Lunch: Wonderful traditional *Konditorei* **Hagmann**, Untere Landstrasse 8, t (02732) 83167 (*inexpensive*) has coffee, cakes and award-winning chocolates. For something more substantial, **Klosterstüberl**, Steiner Landstrasse 24, t (02732) 75780 (*moderate*) is a delightful, old-fashioned 250-year-old restaurant serving hearty Austrian dishes along with local wines and delicious cakes.

Afternoon: From the top of Krems, you can see the romantic onion-domed spires of **Stift Göttweig** (*open Mar–Nov daily 10–5; adm*), an 11th-century Benedictine abbey which was destroyed by fire in the 18th century and rebuilt to designs by Johann Lukas von Hildebrandt, architect of the Belvedere palace in Vienna. It's still home to a community of monks, but you can visit the flamboyant Baroque interior as part of a guided tour (German only). The highlight is

Hildebrandt's frothy marble staircase, topped with an elaborate allegorical fresco.

Dinner: **Landhaus Bacher**, Südtiroler Platz 2, Mautern an der Donau, t (02732) 82937 (*expensive*) is an extraordinary restaurant (5km from Krems) run by Liesl Wagner-Bacher, one of the finest chefs in Austria, and her husband, Klaus Wagner, whose knowledge of wine is legendary. This is easily one of the finest restaurants in the country, with two Michelin stars. If your budget won't stretch, try **Zum Kaiser von Österreich**, Körnermarkt 9, t (02732) 86001 (*moderate*), an elegant wood-panelled restaurant serving refined Austrian and Italian cuisine, accompanied by wonderful local wines and a delicious Italian *prosecco*.

Sleeping: Pretty **Hotel Restaurant am Förthof**, Donaulände 8, t (02732) 83345 (*expensive*) is set in gardens on the banks of the Danube, and facilities include a pool, sauna and excellent restaurant. Little **Hotel Alte Post**, Obere Landstrasse 32, t (02732) 82276 (*inexpensive*) is housed in a 500-year-old building with a delightful courtyard. The restaurant serves tasty local specialities.

Day 3: More Castles and More Wine

Morning: About five miles upstream of Krems, medieval **Dürnstein** is piled winsomely on the riverbank, dominated by the stony ruins of a battered castle. Richard the Lionheart was kept prisoner here in the 12th century: according to legend, Lionheart was discovered by his faithful minstrel, Blondel, who searched the countryside looking for his master and finally found him by playing a song known only to the two of them beneath his window. The castle is now in ruins, but it's worth the climb for the staggering views over the countryside.

Lunch: At **Schloss Durnstein**, t (02711) 212 (*inexpensive*), a café unforgettably set in Dürnstein's extraordinary castle, offering staggering views over the vine-clad hills and winding river. You can also dine at the upmarket restaurant (*expensive*) or stay in the luxurious hotel (*luxury–expensive*). Welcoming guesthouse **Gasthof Sänger Blondel**, t (02711) 253 (*moderate*), set in an 18th-century family home covered in wisteria and surrounded by gardens, has an

excellent traditional restaurant (*closed 15 Nov–15 Mar*).

Afternoon: All the Wachau is filled with wineries and *Heurigen*; here's an idea for a tour of some of the best **vineyards** in the Dürnstein area, but there are hundreds more throughout the region. Always call or visit the tourist information offices to check opening times in advance, or, even better, arrange visits in advance through the Austrian Wine Marketing Board (*www. winesfromaustria.com*). The following award-winning vineyards are all concentrated in **Unterloiben**, just to the east of Dürnstein: the Leo Alzinger winery, t (02732) 77900, *www.alzinger.at*; Dinstlgut Loiben, t (02732) 85516, *www.dinstlgut.at*; Knoll, t (02732) 79355, *weingut@knoll.at*; F.X. Pichler, t (02732) 85375, *www.fx-pichler.at*.

Dinner: **Richard Löwenherz**, Dürnstein 8, t (02711) 222 (*moderate*), a beautiful guesthouse (*expensive*), boasts one of the finest restaurants in the region, where you can dine sumptuously on delicious regional dishes and choose from a fine wine list. There's a panoramic terrace. *Closed Nov–mid-April*. In Weissenkirchen, **Florianihof**, Wösendorf 74, t (02715) 2212 (*moderate*), a handsome townhouse with an elegant vaulted dining room, is also one of the best restaurants in the region, offering exquisite contemporary Austrian cuisine.

Sleeping: **Burg Oberanna**, Mühldorf, 5km from Spitz, t (02713) 8221 (*moderate*), a stunning 12th-century walled castle, is surrounded by forest, and has been handsomely converted into a friendly family-run hotel, offering rooms as well as self-catering apartments. **Raffelsbergerhof**, Weissenkirchen, t (02715) 2201 (*moderate*) is a deeply romantic hotel, housed in a pair of elegant French-style 16th-century townhouses.

Day 4: Medievalism along the Danube

Morning: The river continues to wind sinuously past medieval villages like delightful **Weissenkirchen**, with its charming cobbled streets, sturdy Gothic church, and terraced vineyards, and **Spitz an der Donau**, an atmospheric huddle of Renaissance and Baroque town houses, which is a popular starting point for some fantastic hiking with more than 50km of marked trails in the vicinity. Just beyond **Aggstein**, the fairytale castle of **Aggsbachdorf** is perched vertiginously on a rocky outcrop.

Lunch: At **Zum Schwarzen Bären**, Marktplatz 7, Emmersdorf, t (02752) 71249 (*moderate*); this elegant hotel has been run by the same family for almost a century, and the restaurant serves tasty local dishes using organic produce where possible. Or try **Jamek**, Joching, t (02715) 2235 (*moderate*), an award-winning winery with an elegant restaurant and a rose-filled garden terrace in summer.

Afternoon: The little Renaissance town of **Melk** huddles in the shadow of **Stift Melk** (*open daily 9–5, guided visits at 11 and 2, German only; adm to abbey, church free*), a magnificent Baroque monastery. Once the site of a Babenburg fortress, the building was given to the Benedictines in 1089, and became a renowned centre of scholarship during the Middle Ages (described in Umberto Eco's *The Name of the Rose*, which is partly set here). The highlights of the abbey museum are only sporadically on view, but include medieval reliquaries studded with precious stones.

Dinner: **Tom's**, Hotel Stadt Melk, Hauptplatz 1, t (02752) 52475 (*expensive*) is the best restaurant in the town, serving creative interpretations of traditional Austrian recipes. **Zum Alten Brauhof**, Linzer Strasse 25, t (02752) 52296 (*inexpensive*) is a cheerful, vaulted *Heuriger* serving old-fashioned local dishes, and wines from the Wachau.

Sleeping: **Hotel Stadt Melk**, Hauptplatz 1, t (02752) 52475 (*moderate*) is a cosy hotel slap bang in the heart of the town with modest but comfortable rooms, some of which have views of the abbey. **Gasthof Goldener Hirsch**, Rathausplatz 13, t (02752) 52257 (*inexpensive*), a small, family-run guesthouse in a 16th-century house in the old town, has small but adequate rooms and a reasonably priced restaurant.

Day 5: A Little Bit More Modern

Morning: The B1 leaves Melk and heads west towards pretty little **Pöchlarn**, birthplace of Austrian Expressionist Oskar Kokoshka who is commemorated in a small museum. This stretch of the Danube is known as the **Nibelungenlau**, after the great 12th-century German epic poem the *Nibelungenlied*. Cross the river to **Morbach**, and head for the celebrated pilgrimage church of **Maria Taferl** (*open Mon–Fri 8–12 and 1–4*), built to commemorate the discovery of a miraculous crucifix attached to an oak tree in 1633. The flamboyant Baroque church is set in spectacular countryside, with excellent hiking.

Lunch: Modern hotel **Krone Shachner**, Maria Taferl 24, t (07413) 6355 (*expensive–moderate*) boasts the best restaurant in the area, with delicious Austrian and Mediterranean specialities served on an expansive terrace with beautiful river views. **Gasthof zum Goldenen Löwen**, Maria Taferl 6, t (07413) 340 (*inexpensive*) serves simple old-fashioned Austrian fare.

Afternoon: Return to Melk on the B1 and head to **St Pölten** on the B3. St Pölten is a lively, provincial capital which is usually overlooked by tourists but contains a smattering of handsome Baroque buildings, particularly the lavish cathedral. On the outskirts of the city, you can visit the exquisite 16th-century **Schloss Pottenbrunn** (6km northeast), still surrounded by a moat, and the impressive monastery of **Herzogenburg** (4km north) which was given a lavish Baroque face lift by Fischer von Erlach in the 18th century.

Dinner: **Gaststätte Figl**, Hauptplatz 4, Ratzersdorf an der Traisen, t (02742) 257402 (*inexpensive*), a rustic guesthouse and restaurant close to the Pottenbrunn monastery, has a pretty courtyard terrace. For tasty regional specialities, including particularly good roast meats, elegant **Galerie**, Fuhrmansgasse 1, t (0272) 351305 (*moderate*), is the place to go.

Sleeping: The prettiest hotel in St Pölten, **Hauser Eck**, Schulgasse 2, t (02742) 73336 (*moderate*) is set in a whitewashed Jugendstil mansion. The family welcome and individual rooms make it a charming city centre choice. **Austria Trend Hotel Metropol**, t (02742) 70700 (*moderate*) is the only four-star option, a large modern hotel in the city centre location, very reasonably priced for the amenities (which include a sauna). In the morning, fly back to the capital on the A1 *autobahn* (make sure you have a pass, *see* p.112, or else stick to B roads).

Salzburg

Caught magically in a circle of wooded hills, with Alpine peaks shimmering hazily in the distance, Salzburg sits serenely on the banks of the Salzach river. Graceful Baroque churches and palaces adorn elegant squares, narrow passages and ancient streets are hung with twirling guild signs, tables spill out from opulent 19th-century cafés, and a vast fortress looms from the clifftop. If its pristine, picture-book perfection isn't enough, the city's heady musical heritage brings thousands of visitors every year for the Salzburg Festival alone. It may sound as sickly-sweet as a *Salzburger Nockerl*, the sugar-dusted meringue dessert served in every local restaurant, and yet the city has managed to avoid becoming a mummified museum piece and remains a vibrant and enjoyable provincial capital.

Wolfgang Amadeus Mozart, born here in 1756, has been the cornerstone of the city's tourist industry since his statue was erected on the Mozartplatz in 1842. It may have taken the Salzburgers almost a century to fully appreciate the composer's importance, but they learned their lesson well. Festivals featuring Mozart's compositions, musical dinners and even chocolates (the famous *Mozartkugel*, or 'Mozart Balls', invented by a local dessert chef in 1890) abound, and celebrations for Mozart Year 2006, which commemorates the 250th anniversary of his birth, have already kicked off. None the less, for every tourist tavern advertising 'Mozart's Favourite Dish' there are a dozen lively, upbeat bars and restaurants, and for every over-visited site on the well-trodden Mozart trail there is a quiet corner for contemplation in a secret square or hidden courtyard. Salzburg's genteel citizens are less happy, however, with the other musical legend associated with their city: very few Austrians have even seen *The Sound of Music*, but it's one of the most popular musical films of all time. Tours of the various film locations in and around the city cater to the thousands of fans who descend in their droves every year.

History

Salzburg, as its name (which means 'Fortress of Salt') suggests, has long derived its wealth from the 'white gold' mined here since around 1000 BC. The early miners were Celts, who built settlements in the surrounding hills (recreated in a pair of major tourist attractions; *see* 'Bad Dürnberg Salt Mines', p.159), followed by the Romans, who established the trading centre of Juvavum. After the Romans abandoned the region, the town fell into ruins until St Rupert, a Frankish missionary, arrived here around AD 700 and built St Peter's Abbey and the Nonnberg Abbey. In 739, Salzburg was raised to a bishopric and in 798 to an archdiocese, when it was granted extensive lands. By the end of the 13th century, the archbishops had become Princes of the Holy Roman Empire and would rule as absolute royal sovereigns for 500 years.

One of the most influential archbishops was Wolf Dietrich von Raitenau (1559–1617), who brought in Vicenzo Scamozzi and a team of Italian craftsmen to remodel the city and establish it as 'the Rome of the North'. Palaces, squares and broad avenues were erected, dramatically changing the face of the formerly cramped medieval city. After a quarrel over salt revenues with the neighbouring Duke of Bavaria, Wolf Dietrich was

Getting There

In the UK, there are direct flights from Birmingham and Southampton with **Flybe**, from Kent International with **EUjet**, from Coventry with **Thomsonfly**, and from Stansted with **Ryanair**; *see pp.4–10*.

There are no direct flights from the USA and Canada.

Getting from the Airport

Salzburg's Wolfgang Amadeus Mozart airport, **t** (0662) 85800, *www.salzburg-airport.com*, is 4km from the city centre.

Buses leave every 15mins (30mins on Sun and public hols) for the Central train station (Hauptbahnhof), with further bus links to the city centre (*see* below) between 5.32am and 11.12pm on Mon–Fri, 6.12am–11.12pm on Sat, and 6.20am–11.12pm on Sun. Tickets cost €1.80 (€0.90 for children) and are available from the driver.

Taxis are available from the rank outside the terminal building. A journey to the city centre (15–20mins) costs around €10–15.

Getting Around

By Bus

The most useful bus lines for visitors are nos. 1, 2, 5, 6, 51 and 55, which run from the city centre to the Central train station. **Stadt Bus** covers central and suburban routes, and **Post Bus** will take you further afield. For more information, visit *www.stadtbus.at*.

Tickets can be bought from *Tabaks* (tobacconists) or from machines next to major stops. Single tickets (which are also available from drivers) cost €1.80, a better-value 24hr pass costs €3.60 and a week-long pass costs €11. Passes should be date-stamped in machines behind the driver.

By Taxi

Taxis are not usually hailed on the street in Salzburg. There are taxi ranks outside the train station, and on Makartplatz and Mozartplatz. Fares are relatively high.

To order a taxi, call **t** (0662) 8111.

By Car

If you bring your car to the city, leave it in a garage and forget about it until you leave – the tiny streets are crammed, parking is hard to find, and the city centre is easy to get around on foot. A car is, however, very useful for sights outside the centre.

Avis, **t** (0662) 877278 (airport), **t** (0662) 877278 (city centre), *www.avis.com*.

Budget, **t** (0662) 855038 (airport), *www.budget.com*.

Europcar, **t** (0662) 850208 (airport), **t** (0662) 871616 (city centre), *www.europcar.com*.

Denzeldrive, **t** (0662) 852949 (airport), *www.denzeldrive.at*.

Sixt, **t** (0662) 856051 (airport), *www.sixt.com*.

On Foot

The narrow streets and hidden courtyards of old Salzburg are best seen on foot. It's a small, compact city, with all the main sights clustered together and plenty of beautiful cafés to enjoy whenever you need a break.

Tourist Information

Salzburg: Mozartplatz 5, **t** (0662) 8898 7330, *www.salzburg.info. Open daily in summer and Dec; closed Sun in winter*. There is also an office at the Central train station, **t** (0662) 88987340 (*open daily*).

The **Salzburg Card** offers free admission to all city attractions, free use of all public transport including the fortress funicular and panorama boat, and discounts on some cultural events, tours and excursions. It costs €21 for 24hrs, €28 for 48hrs and €34 for 72hrs (half-price for children 6–15), and is available from tourist offices and most hotels. The card chip can be transferred to a special Swatch access watch, which you buy separately.

Guided Tours

The **Salzburg Guide Service**, Pfiefergasse 3, **t** (0662) 840406, *www.salzburg-guide.at*, runs **walking tours** with themes ranging from Mozart to celebrated women from the city.

If you like **cycling**, **Fraulein Maria's Bicycle Tour**, **t** (0676) 372 6297, *www.marias-bicycle-tour.com*, is a *Sound of Music*-themed bike ride around the main film locations (runs May–Oct). **Helmut's Culture-Biking, t** (0662) 884839, does bike tours of the city centre, along with themed excursions.

The *Amadeus* **panorama boat, t** (0662) 825858, *www.salzburgschifffahrt.at*, offers hour-long **cruises** down the Salzach river daily (*May and Sept 10–5; June 9.30–6; July and Aug 9.30–7;* €10 *for adults,* €6 *for children*). There are also daily (*twice daily June–Aug*) trips to Schloss Hellbrunn (€13/7), as well as dinner cruises and music cruises.

For **bus trips, Salzburg Sightseeing Tours,** Mirabellplatz 2, **t** (0662) 881616, *www. salzburg-sightseeingtours.at,* **Panorama,** Schrannengasse 2/2, **t** (0662) 883 2110, *www.panoramatours.com,* and **Bob's Special Tours,** Rudolfskai 38, **t** (0662) 849 5110, *www.bobstours.com,* are among dozens of tour operators offering bus tours of the city, as well as excursions further afield to the salt mines, *Sound of Music* locations, etc.

You can pick up a **horse-drawn carriage** (*fiaker*) at the Residenzplatz, to clop around the city in style. Rates are around €35 for 25mins, but confirm prices before you set off.

Festivals

Check dates in advance with the tourist office, or online at *www.salzburg.info.*

Jan: Mozart Week, a week of concerts and festivities to celebrate Salzburg's favourite son, *www.mozarteum.at.*

Feb: Aspeckte Festival, a month-long festival of contemporary music, with performers from across the globe.

Mar: Easter Festival – an opera at the Grosses Festspielhaus, which is Salzburg's largest opera venue, is the popular highlight of this music festival, *www.osterfestspiele-salzburg.at/en/.*

April: St George's Country Fair, including a market, procession and blessing of the horses in the fortress.

May: Whitsun Baroque Festival of Baroque music, with international performers, *www.salzburgfestival.at.*

June: Linzergasse Festival, a traditional street festival in the Linzergasse neighbourhood on the right bank of the river.

June–July: *SommerSzene,* an excellent festival of contemporary dance and performance, *www.sommerszene.net.*

July–Aug: Salzburg Festival – this is the world-famous performing arts festival, with opera, classical music concerts and theatre performances held in venues across the city, *www.salzburgfestival.at.*

Sept: Stiegl Swing Festival – classic jazz bands take over the Stiegl brewery for a fortnight in September, *www.jazz.or.at;* **St Rupert's Day Fair,** *www.salzburg-alstadt.at.*

Oct: Juvavum Brass Festival – international soloists and ensembles make the annual pilgrimage here for the weekend-long festival of brass instruments, *www. juvavumbrass.com;* **Culture Days** – the last fortnight of October is dedicated to opera, ballet and classical music performances in major venues across the city, *www. salzburg.com/kulturvereinigung.*

Nov: Jazz Festival – for a week every autumn (*usually late Oct–early Nov*), the city is taken over by celebrated international jazz performers, *www.viennaentertainment.com.*

Dec: *Christkindlmärkte* (Christmas market) around the old city, in the fortress, and on Mirabellplatz, *www.christkindlmarkt.co.at;* **Winter Festival,** a performing-arts festival with the emphasis on experimental theatre and dance, *www.winterfest.at;* **Krampus Runs** – while good children are rewarded with gifts from St Nicholas on 6 Dec, naughty children are punished by the Krampus, when every year (dates vary) these horned wild spirits run through the old city streets, in a terrifying spectacle.

Shopping

Salzburg, with its long and prestigious musical tradition, boasts plenty of music shops selling CDs, instruments and sheet music, and you can pick up all kinds of kitsch *Sound of Music* tat in every souvenir shop. The Advent **markets** are celebrated across Europe, and are great for wooden toys and cosy sheepskin clothes. Best of all are the tiny hot-water bottles: tuck them inside gloves to keep your hands warm. Every cake-shop window in Salzburg is piled high with the chocolate

'Mozart Balls', made from nougat and marzipan (cheaper in the supermarkets). For scrumptious cakes and chocolates, see 'Cafés and Coffee Houses', p.151.

Sports and Activities

Skiing

The main ski resorts around Salzburg are in the south of the province (see www.salzburgerland.com). Closer to the city, the area around **Wolfgang See** is a popular local skiing area. The **Salzburg Snow Shuttle**, t (0662) 8898 7300, www.salzburg.info, operates late Dec to end Mar, and offers day trips to surrounding ski resorts and the services of a multilingual guide.

Swimming and Fitness

There are three **outdoor swimming pools** in the city: you'll find them at Alpenstrasse, t (0662) 620832; Leopoldskronstrasse 50, t (0662) 829265; and Volksgarten, Hermann-Bahr-Promenade 2, t (0662) 623183. **Paracelsus Hallenbad**, Auerspergstrasse 5, t (0662) 883544, has an indoor swimming pool, gym, classes and an adjoining beauty centre, with a range of health and beauty treatments. Day passes are available.

Where to Stay

Salzburg t (0662) –

The tourist information office has a booking service, t 8898 7314, hotels@salzburg.info, www.salzburg.info. It regularly offers special packages which might include a free Salzburg Card (see p.147) or entrance to one of the regular cultural events along with the accommodation. It's also the place to contact if you want to book a private room, which is often a cheap option, but it's likely that your hosts will live some way out of the centre.

City Centre

★★★★★Altstadt Radisson SAS, Rudolfskai 28/Judengasse 15, t 848 5710, f 848 5716, www.austria-trend.at/ass (luxury). An exquisitely restored 14th-century townhouse with individually decorated rooms, some with ancient beams, and a plush restaurant (expensive). The attention to detail sets it apart from other hotels – rooms are even kitted out with umbrellas.

★★★★★Goldener Hirsch, Getreidegasse 37, t 80840, f 843349, www.goldenerhirsch.com (luxury). The classic luxury option, in an elegantly restored mansion which has been an inn since 1563. On the prettiest shopping street in the city, it has opulent, antique-furnished rooms, and a fabulous vaulted restaurant (expensive).

★★★★★Bristol, Makartplatz 4, t 873 5570, f 873 5576, www.bristol-salzburg.at (luxury). For plush, old-world grandeur, the Bristol can't be beaten: drapes and chandeliers adorn the sumptuous rooms, and the list of celebrated guests includes Emperor Franz Josef I and Sigmund Freud.

★★★★★Hotel Sacher, Schwarzstrasse 5–7, t 889770, f 8897 7551, www.sacher.com (luxury). The Salzburg branch of the celebrated Hotel Sacher in Vienna (see p.123), in a perfect riverside location; the best rooms look out over the old city. In the café, you can try the original Sachertorte.

★★★★Arthotel Blaue Gans, Getreidegasse 41–42, t 842 4910, f 842 4919, www.blauegans.at (expensive). The oldest inn on the ancient Getreidegasse, but it boasts sleek, ultra-contemporary decoration, an excellent modern art collection and a sculpture gallery. The award-winning restaurant (expensive) is set under vaults still bearing medieval murals.

★★★Kasererbräu, Kaigasse 33, t 842 4450, f 842 44551, www.kasererbraeu.at (expensive–moderate). A wonderful old mansion in the heart of the old town, with charming rooms decorated with a mixture of antiques and modern amenities. There's an over-the-top gilded spa, with sauna and steam bath. Note that rooms vary considerably in size, and larger rooms are in the expensive price category.

★★★Hotel Wolf, Kaigasse 7, t 843 4530, f 842 4234, www.hotelwolf.com (moderate). In a perfect location just off the Mozartplatz is this friendly little hotel, with immaculate whitewashed rooms, a terrace café offering splendid views, and helpful staff.

**Chiemsee, Chiemseegasse 5, t 844208, f 8442 0870, *hotel-chiemsee@aon.at* (*inexpensive*). An intimate little hotel, with just six simple but prettily decorated rooms, the Chiemsee is one of few budget choices in the city centre and fills up quickly.

Gasthaus Hinterbrühl, Schanzlgasse 12, t 846798, f 841859, *www.downtownhotel.at* (*inexpensive*). A cosy inn close to the heart of the old city, with a traditional tavern downstairs and trim, traditional rooms at a very reasonable price. As the best bargain in town, it books up early.

Further Afield

Schloss Mönchstein, Mönchstein Park 26, t 848 5550, f 848 559, *www.monchstein.com* (*luxury*). For a real treat, you could book a suite in this miniature fairytale castle, set in its own extensive gardens and perched on the hillside high above the city (a lift or short taxi ride will take you down to the town centre). The **Paris Lodron** restaurant is exquisite (*see below right*).

Vitahotel Kobenzl, Gaisberg 11, t 641510, f 642238, *www.kobenzl.at* (*luxury–expensive*). Owned by an eccentric and utterly charming Austrian baroness, this chalet-style hotel has a breathtaking setting with views of the Austrian Alps. There are excellent spa facilities, and an Ecopark offers New Age relaxation.

Pension Elisabeth, Vogelweiderstrasse 52, t/f 871664, *www.pension-elisabeth.at* (*inexpensive*). A simple little pension tucked away in a residential district near the train station. Rooms are crisp and modern, and the staff very friendly.

Eating Out

Salzburg t (0662) –

Some of the city's finest restaurants can be found in its best hotels, including the **Bristol**, the **Goldener Hirsch** and the **Altstadt Radisson SAS** (*see* p.149).

City Centre

Esszimmer, Müllner Haupstrasse 33, t 870899, *www.esszimmer.com* (*expensive*). Ultra-hip Michelin-starred restaurant recently opened

by celebrated chef Andreas Kaiblinger. It's light and spacious with splashes of bright colour, serving perfect French cuisine with an Austrian twist.

Alt Salzburg, Bürgerspitalgasse 2, t 841476 (*expensive–moderate*). A classic, this tourist favourite restaurant is still one of the finest places to eat in the area, with a cosy wood-panelled dining room and sophisticated versions of classic Austrian recipes. *Booking essential. Closed Sun, and Mon lunch.*

Bei Bruno im Ratsherrnkeller, Sigmund-Haffner-Gasse 4, t 877414 (*expensive–moderate*). Stylish restaurant in a vaulted cellar (part of the Hotel Elefant), with sunny peach-coloured walls, and highly creative Mediterranean cuisine. *Closed Sun.*

Culinarium, Saint-Julien-Strasse 2, t 878885 (*moderate*). A small, chic, light-filled restaurant by the river, serving delicate international dishes with a creative twist. Everything is made with the freshest local ingredients, the wine list is perfectly chosen, and prices are incredibly reasonable. *Closed Sun.*

Andreas Hofer, Steingasse 65, t 872769 (*moderate–inexpensive*). A pretty, popular, traditional restaurant, with candlelit dining areas, and a good menu of Austrian and Tyrolean specialities. *Closed Sun.*

Alter Fuchs, Linzergasse 47, t 882200 (*inexpensive*). Friendly, down-to-earth pub serving tasty traditional Austrian dishes. There's also an attractive beer garden at the back.

Gasthaus Wilderman, Getreidegasse 20, t 874213 (*inexpensive*). An authentic, old-fashioned cellar restaurant, with sturdy wooden tables and equally sturdy Austrian fare, including legendary roast pork.

Cappu Vino, Sigmund-Haffner-Gasse 18 (*inexpensive*). A tiny, stylish Italian bar with excellent coffee, fresh panini and simple snacks, along with a very good range of wines.

Further Afield

Paris Lodron, Schloss Mönchstein, t 8485550 (*luxury*). Elegant, romantic restaurant in a fairytale castle (now a hotel, *see* above left), with sophisticated French cuisine and formal service.

Mönchsberg 32, t 841000, *www.m32.at*
(*moderate–inexpensive*). Part of the glossy,
ultra-modern **Museum of Modern Art**, this
spectacular restaurant and café offers good
international dishes in the restaurant
(which also does a good set-price lunch
menu for €12) and lighter fare in the café. It's
a favourite with the fashion crowd and there
are stunning views from the terrace.

Cafés and Coffee Houses

Salzburg t (0662) –

Café Tomaselli, Alter Markt 9, t 844 4880. This
is the most famous coffee house in the city,
established in 1703 and still going strong.
Aproned staff will offer you a trolley full of
delectable goodies, and you can linger over
a huge range of international papers. In
summer, the sought-after terrace is an ideal
place for people-watching.

Café Bazar, Schwarzstrasse 3, t 874278. The
Bazar is almost as old as the Tomaselli, and
cultivates grand 19th-century theatricality
(traditionally, the Tomaselli was the haunt of
musicians, while the Bazar attracted actors
from the nearby Landestheater). Its leafy
summer terrace with river views is fabulous.

Café Fürst, Brodgasse 13, Alter Markt, t 843759.
The very first Salzburger *Mozartkugel* (the
ubiquitous chocolate 'Mozart Balls' were
invented here in 1890). It's one of the finest
examples of a cake shop (*Konditorei*) in the
city, with a café attached.

Konditorei Fingerlos, Franz-Josef-Strasse 9,
t 874213. Sleek, minimalist and ultra-
modern, providing excellent, beautifully
packaged designer chocolates and
wonderful cakes which you can demolish
at palm-shaded tables.

Entertainment and Nightlife

Salzburg t (0662) –

Music, Theatre, Opera and Ballet

Landestheater, Schwarzstrasse, t 871512-222,
www.theater.co.at. Salzburg's premier venue
for drama, opera, musicals and ballet.

Grosses Festspielhaus/Kleines Festspielhaus,
Hofstallgasse, t 849097. The adjoining Large
and Small Festival Halls are the main venues
for the celebrated Salzburg Festival (*see*
'Festivals ').

Marionettentheater, Schwarzstrasse, t 872
4060, *www.marionetten.at*. A world-
renowned puppet theatre, where exquisitely
crafted marionettes enact famous operas.

Schloss Mirabell, info and tickets,
Theatergasse 2, t 848586, *www.salzburger.
schlosskonzerte.at*. Classical music concerts
in the spectacular Marble Hall and in the
gardens from May to August.

Salzburg Fortress (Festung Hohensalzburg),
t 825858, *www.mozartfestival.at*. The city's
lofty fortress provides an atmospheric
setting for regular classical music concerts.

Bars and Clubs

Most of the old city's nightlife is clustered
along the streets **Rudolfskai**, **Giselakai** and
Gstättengasse (situated at the bottom of
Mönschberg). If you want something a bit
more traditional and relaxed (most of the
time), head for a traditional tavern.

Augustinerbräu, Augustinergasse 5, t 31246.
This former monastery has long been a
tavern, where the beer is poured straight
from the barrel. Enjoy it out on the terrace.

Havana, Priesterhausgasse 14, t 220 1005. Here
you can sink into a plush leather sofa and
linger over an expertly made cocktail.

Jexx, Gstättengasse 7, t 844181. Café by day
and chic lounge bar and club by night,
Jexx is simply a classic on Salzburg's
nightlife scene.

Pepe Gonzales, Steingasse 3, t 873662.
Small, buzzy and perennially popular, Pepe
Gonzales brings sultry Latino rhythms and
Spanish *tapas* to Salzburg.

Stieglbräu, Rainerstrasse 14, t 77692. Tavern in
the Hotel Stiegl, serving draught beers from
the local Stiegl brewery.

Stiegkeller, Festungsgasse 10, t 842681.
Traditional Austrian tavern, with a lovely
garden that is pleasantly shaded by
chestnut trees and commands fabulous
views across the old city.

Zweistein, Giselakai 9, t 877179. Mellow,
gay-run bar and café with a mixed,
boho-chic crowd.

deposed and replaced by his nephew Markus Sitticus von Honehems, who commissioned the cathedral and the palace at Hellbrunn. The transformation of the city was continued by the wily statesman Archbishop Paris Lodron, who managed to keep Salzburg out of the Thirty Years' War, expanded the Residenz and commissioned outstanding Baroque architect Johann Bernhard Fischer von Erlach to create a pair of flamboyant Baroque churches. But, by 1756, when Mozart was born in the creaking townhouse on Getreidegasse, Salzburg had lost much of its political influence. It wavered on until 1803 when the religious principality was secularized, and the region was shunted from Bavaria, Austria and France before finally being incorporated into Austria, once and for all, in 1816. Salzburg, now relegated to a minor role, sank into a decline briefly reversed by the encouragement of tourism from the 1840s (based, then as now, on the reputation of Mozart).

The First World War, in which more than 6,000 Salzburgers died, and the collapse of the Habsburg Empire in 1916 were followed by the establishment of the Republic of Austria in November 1918. The Republic lasted two decades, until Hitler announced the incorporation of Austria into the Third Reich in 1938. During the Second World War the city was bombed, causing severe damage to more than 40 per cent of its buildings and monuments. After a decade of Allied Occupation, the Austrian State Treaty was finally ratified in 1955 and the country joined the United Nations. Salzburg began rebuilding and tourism was once again encouraged. In the 1960s, another musical legend joined that of Mozart after the film *The Sound of Music* was shot in the city, bringing a deluge of fans ever since. In 1997, the city was granted World Heritage Status by UNESCO, and recently made history once again by electing its first female head of government, Gabi Burgstaller, in 2004.

The Left Bank (Linkes Salzachufer)

The best place to begin a tour of the **old city** (Altstadt) is the elegant **Mozartplatz**, dominated by a statue of the man himself, leg thrust forward in a pert catwalk pose. It's hemmed in by ancient townhouses with delicate Baroque façades, and a plaque at No.8 commemorates Mozart's wife Constanze, who died here in March 1842.

The Mozartplatz leads into the splendid **Residenzplatz**, lined with palaces and sporting a frilly, triple-decker Baroque fountain, the largest outside Italy. The square is flanked by a pair of magnificent palaces belonging to the prince-archbishops: the **New Residence** (Neue Residenz), built under Wolf Dietrich as a lavish guesthouse, has a lofty **carillon** with 32 bells which chime melodies at 7am, 11am and 6pm. The New Residence has recently been revamped to house the **Salzburger Carolino Augusteum Museum** with an eclectic collection spanning everything from Roman mosaics and Gothic altarpieces to less interesting 19th-century landscape paintings.

Across the square, the **Old Residence** (Alte Residenz; *Residenzplatz 1, t 8042 2690, www.salzburg-burgen.at; open daily 10–5; adm*), is a medieval complex built for the prince-archbishops, which has been added to and modernized over the centuries, most notably by Wolf Dietrich in the early 17th century. The tour of the apartments begins with the oldest section, the enormous Carbinieri Hall, which contains a

Tourist Trapp

A recent survey found that eight out of ten Brits get their holiday destination ideas from films. Tourists from all over the world make the pilgrimage to Salzburg to see where *The Sound of Music* was shot in 1964. Not all Salzburgers are thrilled with what they feel is an overly cutesy representation of their city, but tour operators and souvenir shops make big bucks from what has become a major industry.

If you want to make your own musical tour of the city, you can follow in Julie Andrews' footsteps and belt out 'Maria' in front of **Nonnberg Abbey** (*see* p.156), 'I have confidence in me' as you stride across the **Residenzplatz** (*see* p.152), 'Do Re Mi' in the **Mirabell Gardens** (*see* p.156) and 'You are 16, going on 17' in the *Sound of Music* gazebo which is now in the gardens surrounding **Schloss Hellbrunn** (*see* p.157).

curious balustrade that doubles as a glockenspiel. Mozart's first court performance, at the age of six, took place in the Council Chamber, with lavish High Baroque decoration and Bohemian crystal chandeliers. The most opulent hall of all is the Audience Chamber, designed to impress visitors with its gorgeous flurries of gilded stucco and handsome inlaid parquet floor. More exquisite apartments follow, including the Gallery, a sumptuous setting for the Archbishops' art collection with *trompe l'œil* frescoes, and the magnificent guest bedroom with a tiny chapel containing a gold reliquary with a fragment of the True Cross.

The Old Residence also contains a **gallery** (*www.residenzgalerie.at; open daily 10–5; adm*), with a collection of paintings from the 16th–19th centuries. There are some fine Flemish paintings, including a tiny landscape by Jan Brueghel the Elder and Rembrandt's impressive *Allegory of Charles V as Master of the World* and a touching portrait of an old woman praying. In the Italian collection, a portrait by Tiepolo and Luca Giordano's *Resurrection* stand out, and the best of the Austrian works include an emotionally charged *Last Supper* by Franz Anton Maulpertsch and Waldmüller's jolly scene of *Children at the Window*.

From Residenzplatz, arches lead through to the expansive **Domplatz**, dominated by the enormous **cathedral** (Domkirche; *open daily 9–6; donation requested*), begun in 1614. It was designed by Italian architect Santino Solari and is considered one of the finest early Baroque buildings north of the Alps. A pair of cupola-capped towers flank a marble façade, with a restrained collection of sculpted saints, including the city's founder and patron saint St Rupert, characteristically depicted with a salt box. Inside, the cathedral is drenched with light, flooding in from windows in the dome and illuminating ranks of elaborately gilded pillars and a sea of frescoes. To the left of the entrance is the 14th-century baptismal font used to christen baby Mozart.

From the cathedral porch, stairs lead to the **Cathedral Museum** (Dommuseum; *open Mon–Sat 10–5, Sun and hols 11–6; adm*) with a fine collection of religious objects, art and sculpture, including the *Rupertuskreuz* (St Rupert's Cross), an 8th-century reliquary, and the spectacular 14th-century Grillinger Altar. Don't miss the Cabinet of Curiosities on the first floor – this is an eccentric jumble of odds and ends from shells and hour-glasses to nautical instruments and macabre reliquaries displayed in magnificent ebony-and-gold cabinets. You can see the musty remnants of the previous Romanesque cathedral, along with the vestiges of a Roman villa, in the **Cathedral Excavation Museum** (Domgrabungsmuseum; *entrance on Residentplatz; open July–Aug daily 9–5; adm*).

Another archway in the Domplatz leads into Franziskanergasse, which culminates with the 13th-century **Franciscan Church** (Franziskanerkirche; *open daily 6.30am– 7.30pm; closed to visitors during mass*), notable for its elegant octagonal choir. Imperial favourite Fischer von Erlach was responsible for the fussy Baroque remodelling, which jars awkwardly with the soaring Gothic lines of this sober and contemplative space. His effusive pink and gold high altar retains a lovely late-Gothic *Madonna* by Michael Pacher, all that remains of Pacher's original high altar.

Returning along Franziskanergasse, a narrow passage leads to **St Peter's Abbey** (Peterskirche), a beautiful Romanesque building overlooking a tranquil little square. Founded around AD 700 by St Rupert (*see* 'History'), the original church suffered the same fate as most of Salzburg's churches and was destroyed by fire, but much of what survives dates back to the early 12th century. The Romanesque vestibule is enchanting, with worn stone and a delicate, wrought-iron grille separating it from the main church. This underwent a lavish rococo transformation in the 18th century, but the gentle curves of the original medieval edifice are still visible beneath the whirls of gilt and stucco. St Rupert is buried off the right aisle, where a permanently burning light has kept away evil since the 12th century. Behind the church, the atmospheric **cemetery** huddled under the cliff face contains the graves of prosperous 18th- and 19th-century Salzburgers, and a worn stone staircase inside the cliff leads to ghostly **catacombs**, hollowed out by 3rd-century Christians from Roman Juvavum (*open May–Sept Tues–Sun 10.30–5; Oct–April Wed–Thurs 10.30–3.30, Fri–Sun 10.30–4; adm*).

Heading directly across the square, follow the narrow passage, cross another pretty square with a fountain, and wiggle right until you emerge at Maz-Reinhardt-Platz, which leads into Hofstallgasse. Here, the **Large Festival Hall** (Grosses Festspielhaus) and adjoining **Small Festival Hall** (Kleines Festspielhaus) are wedged tightly against the cliff-face, and are the main venues for the celebrated Salzburg Festival. A tunnel, built in the 18th century, burrows right through the Mönchsberg mountain, and, further down, the **Mönchsberg Lift** (Mönchsberg Aufzug; *open daily 9–9; adm*) will swoop you up to the top of the hill for breathtaking views, an alternative route to the Salzburg Fortress (Festung Hohensalzburg; *see* right) and the glistening new **Museum of Modern Art** (Museum der Moderne; *open Tues and Thurs–Sun 10–6, Wed until 9; adm*). The latter occupies a stunning contemporary building and offers magnificent views and a great café-restaurant, Mönchsberg 32 (*see* p.151). The collection spans the last century, with paintings by Gustav Klimt and Richard Gerstl, along with contemporary installations, photographs and digital art.

Back down in the old city, continue down almost to the river bank for Salzburg's **Natural History Museum** (Haus der Natur; *open daily 9–5; reptile zoo open 10–5; adm*), a hugely enjoyable display of dinosaur skeletons, an excellent reptile zoo full of live creepy-crawlies and poisonous snakes, old-fashioned dioramas and slick interactive exhibits on everything from astronomy to the human body.

Leading off to the right of Hofstallgasse is **Getreidegasse**, an impossibly picturesque medieval street, with elegant boutiques and cafés sprouting elaborate overhanging wrought-iron signs. The main commercial street of old Salzburg, it's no longer quite the exclusive address it once was, and chain stores have mushroomed over the last few years. By day, it's always a little too crammed for comfort but, when night falls and the crowds melt away, it can feel utterly magical.

In January 1756, Mozart was born in the primrose-yellow townhouse at No.9, now the much-visited museum **Mozart's Birthplace** (Mozarts Geburtshaus; *open daily 9–6, July and Aug until 7; adm, combined adm with Mozart Residence available*). It's an endearingly rickety old house, originally built in the 12th century, with leaning walls and wobbly floors, but the endless torrent of strident tour groups strip it of atmosphere. Exhibits are thin, although aficionados will appreciate the miniature violin used by the child prodigy, along with a full-size concert violin, viola and clavichord. There's a model apartment decked out in period furniture, and some entertaining information panels on life in 18th-century Salzburg (describing, among other things, the old city's stench that eventually drove richer citizens, like the Mozarts, across the river).

Behind the Getreidegasse, Fischer von Erlach's enormous **Collegiate Church** (Kollegienkirche) dominates the **Universitätplatz**, built in 1696 as a place of worship for Salzburg's university. Huge and overblown, it's had a patchy history, having served as a hay barn for the Napoleonic armies shortly before being closed, along with the university, when Salzburg became part of Bavaria in 1810. It only regained its original purpose when the university was re-established in 1964. From the Universitätplatz, Ritzer-Bogen-Strasse leads to the **Alter Markt**, with another pretty fountain ringed with a 16th-century railing, and a fringe of smart boutiques and canopied cafés with delightful terraces to stop for cake and coffee. The classic is the Tomaselli, established in 1703, and the longest-running café in Austria (*see* p.151).

Salzburg Fortress (Festung Hohensalzburg)

Open daily Oct–April 9–5.30; May and Sept 9–7; June–Aug 9–7.30; adm.

A watchtower existed on this lofty hill high above the Salzach river long before the Romans established their settlement, but the Salzburg Fortress, which dominates the city, was built in the 11th century to repel marauding German princes (and later to keep out angry locals resentful of high tithes). It was enlarged by succeeding archbishops, notably Leonhard von Keutschach who had to hole himself up here for safety during the Peasants' War and added the opulent apartments which are liberally strewn with depictions of his unlikely personal device – the turnip.

From **Festungsgasse** (lined with cheerful, if touristy, taverns with beer gardens), a **funicular** (*open same hours as fortress; adm, combined adm to fortress apartments available*) makes the rapid ascent to the fortress. Or you can make the gentle stroll (about 15mins) up the hill and enjoy the fabulous views unfolding along the way. The complex is set around a string of charming courtyards, with sturdy bastions and battlements offering magnificent views over the old city in one direction and patchwork fields and snow-capped mountains in the other. Audioguides are available for the exterior of the fortress (there's a kiosk near the funicular exit), and you can also visit the **Fortress Apartments** (Fürstenzimmer; *open mid-Mar–mid-June daily 9.30–5.30; mid-June–mid-Sept daily 9–6; mid-Sept–mid-Mar daily 9.30–5; adm, inc audioguide, last adm 30mins before closing*). The guided tour sweeps through the extravagant 16th-century apartments: the Golden Room and Golden Hall are particularly splendid, with burnished wood panelling, impressive coffered ceilings and opulent marble doorways, and both are used for nightly concerts (*see* p.151). The admission ticket includes the **Military Museum** (Rainer Museum), crammed with uniforms and ancient weaponry, and an outpost of the Salzburger Carolino Augusteum Museum (*see* p.152), with a fascinating collection of original furniture, ceramics, toys, weaponry and musical instruments which evocatively recreate life in 16th- and 17th-century Salzburg. There's separate admission to the little **Marionette Museum** (*www.mozartfestival.at; open April–June daily 10–5; July–Aug daily 9.30–6; Sept–Oct, 25 Dec–5 Jan and Advent Sat and Sun 10–5; adm*), which is fun for kids.

Just below the fortress, the red onion dome of **Nonnberg Abbey** (Stift Nonnberg; *open daily 7–dusk; closed during mass*) appears to float above the old city. The convent was established by St Rupert around the year 700 (*see* p.145) and is still home to a community of nuns, making it one of the oldest continuously running convents in Europe. (The nuns are no longer necessarily blue-blooded, as the ban on allowing non-aristocrats to enter was lifted in 1848.) The tranquil Gothic church commemorates its first abbess, a niece of St Rupert called Erentrudis, who is buried in the crypt, but the abbey is best known as Maria's convent from *The Sound of Music* (see 'Tourist Trapp', p.153).

The Right Bank (Rechtes Salzachufer)

The **Makartplatz**, a neat, flower-filled square on the right bank of the Salzach river, is overlooked by Fischer von Erlach's monumental **Church of the Holy Trinity** (Dreifaltigkeitskirche; *open daily 10–5*) which contains a remarkable fresco of the *Coronation of the Virgin* by Johann Michael Rottmayr under its lofty dome. Mozart's family lived in a spacious apartment overlooking the square at No.8 from 1773 to 1780, which was destroyed during the Second World War but has since been carefully reconstructed. It's now an interesting museum, the **Mozart Residence** (Mozart-Wohnhaus; *t 87422740, www.mozarteum.at; open Sept–June daily 9–6, July and Aug daily 9–7; adm, includes audioguide*), with some period furniture (all the original furnishings belonging to the family were sold at auction), letters and other mementos, along with films and recordings in the downstairs **Mozart Audio and Film Museum** (*open Mon, Tues and Fri 9–1, Wed and Thurs 1–5*).

The exquisitely manicured **Mirabell Gardens** (Mirabellgarten; *always open*) spread northwest of Makartplatz, with elegant paths, flower gardens and extravagant fountains. At the centre is the splendid **Schloss Mirabell** (Mirabellplatz, *t 8072 2338; open Mon, Wed and Thurs 8–4, Tues and Fri 1–4; adm*), built in 1606 by Archbishop Wolf Dietrich for his mistress, Salome Alt, who bore him 15 children. Extended and

Paracelsus

Paracelsus (1493–1541) is now regarded as one of the most original and advanced medical thinkers of the Renaissance. During his lifetime, however, he managed to rile the medical establishment with his arrogance and vanity. Born Theophrastus Bombastus von Hohenstein, he gave himself the name Paracelsus (meaning 'the equal of Celsus', the Roman author of influential medical encyclopedias) and condemned his contemporaries as 'useless rabble [who] befoul the art of medicine with their bungling'. He quickly lost his appointment at Basel University by publicly burning the works of the 3rd-century Greek physician Galen whose teachings were still the main authority for 16th-century medical practice.

His contemporaries may have held him in contempt, but Paracelsus made enormous contributions to medical knowledge: he rejected conventional beliefs that the body was controlled by the four humours, and sought to cure disease with chemicals, thereby laying the foundations of modern pharmacology. He died in Salzburg and is buried in the cemetery of St Sebastian.

remodelled over the centuries, the palace is now the official residence of Salzburg's mayor, but it's possible to visit the lavish Baroque chambers, including the dazzling Marble Hall, where Mozart and his sister Nannerl performed for the court, and the sumptuous 'angel staircase' designed by Lukas von Hildebrandt, with its clouds of plump marble cherubs. The former Orangerie is a charming setting for the **Baroque Museum** (Barock Museum; *t 877432, www.barockmuseum.at; open Tues–Sat 9–12 and 2–5, Sun 10–1; adm, guided tours Sat 2pm*), with a collection of effusive 18th-century paintings and drawings.

Linzergasse is the Right Bank's down-to-earth answer to the chichi Getreidegasse, a narrow, bustling medieval street which skirts the lower flanks of **Kapuzinerberg**. This hill gets its name from the **Capuchin Church** (Kapuzinerkloster), which is a stiff 15-minute climb through a florid archway and up a flight of steps. While the church itself is dull, the views over the old city and up to the hill top fortress on the other side of the river are breathtaking. Linzergasse leads eventually to the **Church of St Sebastian** (Sebastianskirche), a dour 19th-century recreation of the original Baroque edifice, with a wonderful, rambling **cemetery** (*open daily summer 9–7; winter 9–4*). Archbishop Wolf Dietrich's opulent mausoleum takes centre stage, but other famous graves include that of Mozart's wife, Constanze, buried near the composer's father (who in life couldn't stand her). The grave of Paracelsus (*see* box, above) can be found in the southwest corner.

Further Afield

The **Schloss Hellbrunn** (take bus no.25; *t 820 3720, www.hellbrunn.at; fountains open daily for guided tours every 30mins April and Oct 9–4.30; May, June and Sept 9–5.30; July and Aug 9–6 plus evening tours at 7, 8, 9 and 10pm; adm*), a dreamy summer villa built by the Italian architect Santino Solari for the Archbishop Wolf

Dietrich, is located 5km from the city centre. The archbishop's resplendent **apartments**, with their extraordinary *trompe l'œil* frescoes, can be visited but the fame of Hellbrunn rests still on the playful and not-to-be-missed **trick fountains**, accessible only by guided tour. Be warned: Wolf Dietrich had a wicked sense of humour, and the guides ensure that no one escapes a soaking. The magnificent gardens and extensive parkland contain a smattering of other attractions including a small **zoo** (*www.salzburg.at; open winter daily 8.30–4.30, summer daily 8.30–5.30; adm*) with lions, rhinoceroses and other exotic creatures, and a delightful little **museum of folklore** (*open April–Oct daily 10–5.30; adm*) in a fairytale villa set in woodland overlooking the park.

Another 5km further down the road, the bus will deposit you in the small hamlet of St Leonhard, where the **Untersburg cable car** (*open Mar–June and Oct daily 9–5; July–Sept daily 8.30–5.30; mid-Dec–Feb daily 9–4; closed Nov and early Dec; adm*) makes its dizzying ascent – a nerve-jangling climb of almost 6,500ft. From the top, several hiking paths strike out into the surrounding peaks, or you can just be content with the astounding views.

Day Trips from Salzburg

When the busy city gets overwhelming, mountains and lakes beckon. To the east is the beautiful lake district of Salzerkammergut, with its aristocratic spa towns, ancient villages and endless possibilities for watersports, skiing and hiking. Closer at hand, the Salzach valley boasts storybook castles and ancient salt mines which make enjoyable excursions. There are countless tour operators (the tourist office has a full list) offering trips to the wealth of attractions in the Salzburg area, but most are reasonably accessible using public transport.

Salzburgerland Open-Air Museum (Salzburger Freilichtmuseum)

www.frielichtmuseum.com; open April–Oct Tues–Sun 9–6; adm.

The Open-Air Museum for the Salzburgerland region is located 18km southwest of the city near the rather nondescript village of Grossgmain on the German border. Set in the Untersberg Nature Preserve, it contains more than 60 historic buildings – including rural farmhouses, blacksmiths' forges, churches and inns – and evokes rural life in Salzburgerland over the last four centuries with exhibitions of various tools and crafts; there are also some interesting demonstrations of traditional crafts (*Sun and hols only*).

Getting There

There are hourly **buses** to Grossgmain leaving from outside Salzburg's Central train station (Hauptbahnhof), which will drop you off at the gates of the museum.

Eating Out

There are no good eating options in Grossgmain, so you'll either have to make do with the snacks available in the museum or take a picnic with you.

Getting There

For visiting the **salt mines**, the best option is to get the special combined ticket (available from Salzburg Central train station) which includes the return train journey, connecting bus from Hallein to Bad Dürnberg and entrance to the mines. This works out considerably cheaper than tour-operator fees.

Tourist Information

Bad Dürnberg: Unterer Markt, **t** (06245) 85394, *www.hallein.com*.

Eating Out

There are several convenient, if rather unexceptional, options within the salt mine complex, but try the following if you can:
Braun, Unterer Markt 8, Hallein, **t** (06245) 80486 (*inexpensive*). A stylish coffee house, with wonderful cakes and chocolates.
Gasthof Halleiner Stadtkrug, Bayrhamplatz 10, Hallein, **t** (06245) 83085 (*inexpensive*). A cheerful tavern situated right in the heart of the town, serving sturdy Austrian specialities with a popular and good-value lunchtime buffet.

Bad Dürnberg Salt Mines

www.salzweten.at; open daily 11–3; adm exp.

You can find out all about the 'white gold' that made Salzburg rich at the Bad Dürnberg Salt Mines, a big, family-friendly attraction which features a miniature train ride through the salt mine and a raft tour across the salt lake. There's also a reconstructed **Celtic Village** on site (*adm included in entrance ticket*), with costumed attendants offering a glimpse into Celtic culture and daily life 2,500 years ago, along with displays of archaeological finds discovered here. It's very touristy (there's even a McDonald's) but it's hugely popular with kids. The mines are about 5km from the attractive town of **Hallein**, with handsome 17th-century townhouses and charming squares built by the wealthy merchants who controlled the salt trade.

The Salzkammergut: Hallstatt

East of Salzburg, the lovely lake district of **Salzkammergut** was described by Emperor Franz Josef I (who summered here every year) as 'an earthly paradise'. On the prettiest of its glittering lakes, enchanting **Hallstatt** is one of the region's biggest draws. Dramatically caught between a cleft in the mountains on the shore of the Hallstätter See, this ancient town is a delightful huddle of narrow streets clustered

Getting There

Take the **train** from Salzburg Central station to Bad Ischl and change for a local train to Hallstatt (there are about 10 daily). There are also regular **buses**, but the train is the most romantic option, as you arrive on the other side of the lake and then take the **ferry** across.

Tourist Information

Hallstatt: Seestrasse 169, **t** (06134) 8208, *www.hallstatt.net*.

For information on the whole region, see *www.salzkammergut.at*.

Eating Out

Bräugasthof, Seestrasse 120–121, Hallstatt, **t** (06134) 20012 (*moderate–inexpensive*). Traditional 15th-century guesthouse standing right on the lakeside, with antique-furnished rooms (*moderate*) and a good range of regional favourites in the patio restaurant.

around a Gothic church. You can find out all about its long history, which dates back to a substantial Celtic settlement, at the **Cultural Heritage Museum** (*open Nov–Mar Tues–Sun 11–3; April and Oct Tues–Sun 10–4; May–Sept daily 9–6; adm*).

Above the town, the **Salzweten Hallstatt** (*open end-April–Oct daily 11–3; adm, available with or without funicular adm*) is a family attraction centred around the ancient salt-mining tradition. The mine is accessible by funicular and offers a mixture of fun exhibits (including a mine train, raft ride across a salt lake and a long wooden chute), along with weightier cultural attractions including an extraordinary prehistoric necropolis, with more than 4,000 ancient graves.

The other tourist attraction in these parts is the magnificent **Dachstein Ice Caves** (*open May–Oct daily 9.30–4; adm*), near the village of **Obertraun** and accessible from the first stage of the panoramic Dachstein cable car. If you want to swim or sunbathe, Obertraun has the best beaches, and it's a skiing area in winter.

Werfen: Adventure Castles and Ice Caves

The tiny village of Werfen (40km from Salzburg) is dominated by the picture-book **Hohenwerfen** (*open April Tues–Sun 9.30–4.30; May–Sept daily 9–5, July and Aug daily 9–6; Oct–Nov daily 9.30–4.30; closed Dec–Mar; adm*), a medieval fortress built by the prince-archbishops with a breathtaking mountainous backdrop. The grand apartments can be visited, but the real highlight is the daily flight demonstrations from the **Salzburg Falconry Centre**, which is based here. From Werfen, you can also visit one of the most extraordinary natural wonders in Austria: the vast **Ice Caves** (Eisriesenwelt; *open May–Oct daily 9–3.30, July and Aug until 4.30; adm, available with or without cable-car ride*). A shuttle bus from the station will deposit you at the start of the cable-car journey up the mountain – it's not for the faint-hearted, as this is the steepest cable-car ride in Austria. The giant ice caves stretch back for several kilometres (only a small section is accessible) and have a hallucinatory beauty with their cresting waves of ice, monumental frozen cascades, and delicate sculptural pinnacles reaching an impossible height. The views of endless snow-capped peaks framed by the cave openings are spellbinding.

Getting There

Regular southbound **trains** from Salzburg Hauptbahnhof stop at Werfen; to see the castle and the caves in a day, set off early.

Tourist Information

Werfen: Markt 24, t (06468) 5388, www.werfen.at.

Eating Out

There is just one street in Werfen, which is lined with guesthouses and restaurants offering everything from pizza to *Schnitzel*. For a treat, try the following:

Gasthof Obauer, Markt 46, t (06468) 52120, www.obauer.com (*expensive*). This very smart hotel contains one of the finest restaurants in the whole of Austria: you can expect elegant, contemporary Austrian cuisine from two award-winning young chefs. All the dishes are prepared with the freshest local ingredients.

Zur Steige, Markt 10, t (06468) 5256 (*expensive–moderate*). More delicious regional cuisine served up in traditional wood-panelled surroundings.

Touring from Salzburg: Mountains, Lakes and Waterfalls

This tour will take you to the spectacular south of **Salzburgerland**, a region crammed with superlatives: Austria's highest mountain range, tallest waterfall and most famous mountain drive can all be found here. This tour requires a fair amount of driving. If you prefer a more leisurely version, base yourself in the charming lakeside resort of **Zell am See** and visit the main highlights from there; the Krimml waterfalls and Grossglockner High Alpine Road are popular and easy day trips.

Day 1: Taking the Waters

Morning: From Salzburg, you can shoot down the A10 motorway (*toll*) or meander along the B159 to **Werfen** (*see* left) and see one of the extraordinary falconry displays at the storybook castle perched above the village.

Lunch: In Werfen (*see* left).

Afternoon: Head down the B311 and B167 to **Bad Gastein** (55km south), a smart 19th-century spa town surrounding a magnificent waterfall. You can 'take the waters' in time-honoured tradition, strike out into the surrounding mountains for some exhilarating walks (there are two cable-car routes up the closest peaks in summer) or simply enjoy a stroll through the elegant streets which offer breathtaking views at every twist and turn.

Dinner and Sleeping: In Bad Gastein, there's the **Cordialsanotel**, Conrad-Srochner-Strasse 2, t (06434) 25010, *www.cordial.co.at* (*luxury–expensive*), in a gorgeous location right next to the waterfall. It has all imaginable facilities, including pools, a Roman spa, health and beauty treatments, and restaurants and bars to suit all pockets. Or try **Grüner Baum**, Kötschachtal 25, t (06430) 25160, *www.gruenerbaum.info* (*expensive–moderate*), a traditionally built hotel complex set in its own beautiful valley, a mile or so outside Bad Gastein. It offers modern, well-equipped rooms along with spa, tennis and pool facilities at the adjacent **Lindhaus Lindy** (*www.hauslindy.at*), which has good-value apartments available by the

night. Another option is **Zum Toni**, Eisenstein 1, t (06432) 6629 (*moderate–inexpensive*), a friendly, family-run hotel on the edge of town, with pristine, rustic-decorated rooms, a sauna and spa. There's a good restaurant (*moderate*) as well as an informal tavern (*inexpensive*) serving local fare.

Day 2: Lakeside Luxury

Morning: Return along the B167 and turn left on to the B311 which is signposted for **Zell am See** (50km from Bad Gastein). This picture-postcard resort is prettily poised on the shores of a lake, with a charming promenade along the front that is perfect for a lazy stroll. In summer you can hire boats, and in winter, if it freezes sufficiently, join the locals for a spot of ice-skating.

Lunch: In Zell am See, 500-year-old inn **Gasthof Steinerwirt**, Dreifaltigkeitsgasse 2, t (06542) 72502 (*moderate*), is the best bet for good Austrian specialities at a good price. For something different, try **Antonio**, Kitzsteinhornstrasse 27, t (06542) 53650 (*moderate–inexpensive*), a sunny Italian restaurant with tasty pastas, seafood and other specialities from across the border.

Afternoon: Take a break from driving and explore the town of Zell am See: the little municipal **museum** has exhibits on the Krampus, a horned evil spirit who appears on the night of 5 Dec to punish the naughty children (the good ones get presents from St Nicholas). There are several cable cars up the surrounding peaks, but the most accessible is the **Zellerbergbahn** which swoops up to the top of Hirschkogel for mesmerizing views over the valley, across glaciers, and endless snow-capped peaks.

Dinner and Sleeping: The smartest option on the lake is **Salzburgerhof**, Auerspergstrasse 11, Zell am See, t (06452) 765, *www. salzburghof.at* (*luxury*), a spectacular hotel in glorious gardens, with every imaginable luxury, including a lavishly appointed spa and an excellent restaurant (*expensive*). The **Grand Hotel**, Esplanade 4, Zell am See, t (06452) 788, *www.grandhotel-zellamsee.at* (*luxury–expensive*) is a gleaming white wedding cake of a hotel, built a century ago and with its own private stretch of lake front. It has been thoroughly modernized, and there are several dining options to suit all pockets. Then there's **Schloss Prielau**, Hofmannthalastrasse 12, Zell am See, t (06542) 729110, *www.schloss-prielau.at* (*luxury–expensive*). This romantic castle has heavenly rooms and suites, many with four-poster beds, and boasts the award-winning restaurant **Mayer's**, the finest in the region, which serves memorable contemporary Austrian cuisine. The **Landhotel Erlhof**, Erlhofweg 11, Thumersbach, t (06452) 56637 (*moderate*) is a lovely traditional hotel, with flower-filled balconies offering beautiful views. Its award-winning restaurant (*moderate*) offers tasty regional dishes prepared with imagination and flair. If you prefer a cheaper option, try **Gasthof Schmittental**, Schmittenstrasse 60, Zell am See, t (06542) 72332 (*inexpensive*), a friendly, family-run (and family-friendly) guesthouse in a rural setting on the fringes of Zell am See, with a down-to-earth restaurant serving pizzas and steaks along with local dishes (*inexpensive*). Alternatively, **Gasthof Steinerwirt**, Dreifaltigkeitsgasse2, Zell am See, t (06542) 72502 (*inexpensive*), with its great traditional restaurant (*see* lunch), also has great-value, simple rooms.

Day 3: Scaling the Heights

Morning: The **Grossglockner High Alpine Road** (Grossglockner Hochalpenstrasse; *www. grossglockner.at; open May–Nov; toll*), the B107, is justifiably considered one of the most astonishing drives in Europe. It begins south of Zell am See, and weaves through lush Alpine pasture before the toll road proper begins. Then the road begins to hairpin alarmingly, climbing the highest mountain range in Austria. It's part of the **Hohe Tauern National Park**, with snow-covered peaks unfolding spectacularly in all directions. Just beyond the tunnel, a right fork will take you to **Franz-Josefs-Höhe**, a viewing point facing the highest peak in Austria, the 12,460ft high **Grossglockner**. There's a hotel and a smattering of restaurants for lunch, or you could continue another 8km for **Heiligenblut**, one of the most beautiful mountain villages in Austria.

Lunch: The pair of tourist-trap restaurants on the Franz-Josefs-Höhe will provide

sustenance, if nothing more, but the views can't be beaten. In Heiligenblut, try **Hotel-Chalet Haus Senger**, Hof 23, t (04824) 2215, a wonderful, 400-year-old chalet-style hotel (*expensive–moderate*) that offers amazing views of the Grossglockner peak; you can tuck into traditional dishes by a roaring fire in the restaurant (*moderate*). Or there's **Landhotel Post**, t (04824) 2245 (*inexpensive*), a central wooden chalet-style guesthouse with a cosy, old-fashioned restaurant serving filling schnitzel and other simple fare.

Afternoon: Return leisurely to Zell am See.

Dinner and Sleeping: In Zell am See; *see* 'Day 2'.

Day 4: Wondrous Waterfalls

Morning: Pick up goodies for a picnic in Zell am See before heading west on the B168 and B165 (55km) to **Krimml**. On the fringes of the Hohe Tauern National Park, the village of Krimml boasts a beautiful setting but is most famous for the extraordinary **waterfalls (Krimmler Wasserfälle)**, the highest in the Austrian Alps, which thunder in three stepped cascades down the cliff face. The falls are one of Austria's top attractions, with more than 700,000 visitors a year. The **Wasser Wunder Welt** (*www.wawuwe.at; open May–Oct daily 10–5; adm*) is a new theme park at the entrance, which is good for kids; it has an Aqua Park and plenty of interactive exhibits relating to the falls.

Lunch: Unpack your picnic next to the falls, or eat in Krimml: **Krimmler Kirchenwirt**, Unterkrimml 75, t (06564) 7269 (*inexpensive*) is a charming, family-run guest house with simple rooms and a decent restaurant (*inexpensive*) serving home-cooked specialities – out in the garden in summer, or next to the cosy fireplace in winter. **Gasthof Schönangerl**, t (06564) 7555 (*inexpensive*), has a fabulous location next to the middle section of the falls, and the restaurant offers traditional Austrian fare.

Afternoon: A 4km hiking path leads up alongside the falls: try to make it at least to the upper level, where the most impressive section drops for 46oft, creating rainbow-filled clouds of spume. After 4km, the path culminates in an Alpine meadow with more breathtaking views. If you can't make the climb, there's a minibus service between the middle and upper levels (contact the Gasthof Schönangerl; *see* lunch).

Dinner and Sleeping: Around Krimml, **Kaltenhauser**, Hollersbach 17, **t** (06562) 81170, *www.kaltenhauser.com* (*moderate*), is a 14th-century country hotel with old wooden beams and plenty of rustic charm, along with modern amenities including a spa, a feng shui garden and good restaurant (*expensive–moderate*). The four-star **Hotel Krimmlerfälle**, Wasserfallstrasse 42, **t** (06564) 7203, *www.krimmlerfaelle.at* (*moderate*) is conveniently located right at the entrance to the falls. Large and well equipped, many of its rooms boast beautiful views of the famous waterfall. It also offers less expensive B&B accommodation and rents apartments (*moderate–inexpensive*).

Day 5: Glitz and Glamour

Morning: Return east on the B165 to **Mittersill**, a cheerful little resort which is a ski centre in winter and a paradise for mountain-bikers and walkers who want to explore the Hohe Tauern National Park in summer.

Lunch: In Mittersill, **Bräurup**, Kirchgasse 9, **t** (06562) 6216, *www.braurup.at*, is a beautiful 18th-century guesthouse (*moderate*), and its lovely wood-panelled restaurant (*expensive*) is probably the best in town (*closed Nov*). Or try the pretty ochre-painted **Meilinger Taverne**, Marktplatz 10, **t** (06562) 4226 (*moderate–inexpensive*), in the centre of Mittersill, which provides excellent Austrian specialities and a sunny outdoor terrace on the square in summer.

Afternoon: Take the B161 north of Mittersill to the glitzy resort of **Kitzbühel**, which has long been a favourite haunt of the jet set who descend in droves every winter to plummet down the surrounding ski slopes in their designer gear. Although plenty of modern development has been tacked on to this ancient mining town, its medieval core, with its colourful gabled houses and spiky Gothic church, remains utterly delightful.

Dinner and Sleeping: In Kitzbühel, **Adler Kitz**, Florianigasse 15, **t** (05356) 6922, *www.adlerkitz.at* (*luxury–expensive*), is a very elegant hotel, which stylishly combines tradition and contemporary design. There's a wonderful, ultra-modern spa and an

excellent restaurant (*expensive–moderate*) serving authentic Austrian cuisine prepared with the freshest local ingredients. **Hotel Schloss Lebenberg**, Lebenbergstrasse 17, **t** (05356) 6901, *www.austria-trend.at* (*expensive*), is a much-restored medieval castle overlooking Kitzbühel from a sunny mountain slope (it provides a shuttle bus to make the short hop into the town centre) and offers luxurious rooms and suites and several dining options. For a friendly little guesthouse, try **Gasthof Eggerwirt**, Goensbachgasse 12, **t** (05356) 62455 (*expensive–inexpensive*), built in the 17th century, with simple rooms and a good restaurant serving traditional Tirolean fare. Prices soar in the height of the skiing season, but the rest of the year it's a good bargain. **Zum Rehkitz**, Am Rehbühel 30, **t** (05356) 66122 (*moderate*), is a traditional wooden mountain inn housing an elegant restaurant serving sophisticated international cuisine. **Haselsburger**, Maurachfeld 4, **t** (05356) 62866, *www.haselsburger.com* (*moderate–inexpensive*), is a simple chalet next to the slopes. Rooms are basic but pleasing, and there are great views. Book early as it fills up quickly.

Day 6: Return to Gentility

Morning: From Kitzbühel, begin the drive back to Salzburg (80km northeast; take the B178 which joins the B312 at Lofer for the German border). Follow signs for the handsome and genteel Bavarian spa town of **Bad Reichenhall**, with lots of shops and restaurants, beautifully kept expansive parks and a long musical tradition.

Lunch: In Bad Reichenhall, **Restaurant die Holzstube**, Ludwigstrasse 33, **t** (08651) 6040 (*moderate*), is a charming restaurant with a pretty garden, which serves inventive international cuisine and has an excellent set gourmet lunch for around €30. Or try **Brauerei–Gasthog Bürgerbräu**, Waaggasse 2, **t** (08651) 6089 (*inexpensive*), a cavernous traditional tavern with excellent draught beer, a beer garden and a menu of sturdy Bavarian specialities.

Afternoon: Bad Reichenhall is close to the Salzburg–Munich motorway (*toll*), and you can get back to Salzburg very quickly.

Graz

Austria's second-largest city, Graz is one of its most vibrant and engaging. The enchanting old city (Altstadt) is a harmonious ensemble of Renaissance and Baroque mansions huddled under red-tiled roofs, and was declared a World Heritage Site in 1999. Old Graz oozes picture-book prettiness, but to this it adds an exciting 21st-century buzz, epitomized in the startling new architecture erected to celebrated its appointment as European Cultural Capital of 2003. The traditionally working-class area across the river from its glorious ancient core has been revitalized by the construction of an exciting new museum of modern and contemporary art (the Kunsthaus), housed in one of the most striking new buildings in Europe. Its bluish, blobby form has given it the nickname the 'Friendly Alien', and it is complemented by the Murinsel, a futuristic, glassy 'island' in the middle of the Mur river, which has become one of the hottest nightspots in the city.

If the Kunsthaus and the Murinsel are the most talked-about monuments in Graz, the grassy hill of Schlossberg which floats beautifully above the fairytale rooftops remains its most emblematic sight. Graz grew up around a fortress called the *gradec* ('little castle') by the Slav-speaking population which eventually gave the city its name. Once the area came under the control of the Habsburgs, it began to flourish: briefly the residence of Emperor Freidrich III, who built the castle and the florid Imperial mausoleum, it became the most impregnable city on the front line against the Turks after the heavy fortification of the Schlossberg castle in 1543. Italian stonemasons drafted in to help the building works also left their signature on the exquisite Renaissance mansions sprinkled throughout the old city. By now the city was capital of Inner Austria, and an important Imperial seat under the governorship of Archduke Karl II. His successor, Archduke Ferdinand, was a zealous supporter of the Counter Reformation, which led to the exodus of liberal intellectuals (including astronomer Johann Kepler) who had given the city a glittering reputation for learning and culture. When Archduke Ferdinand became emperor and moved his court to Vienna, Graz drifted into decline. The removal of the Turkish threat after 1683 meant that the city lost its strategic importance. Sidelined, it drifted along for the next couple of centuries, withstanding a Napoleonic siege in 1809, but otherwise failing to make much of a stir. At the end of the 19th century, Graz began to acquire a reputation for quiet gentility and a flood of elderly aristocrats made the city their home (earning it the nickname 'Pensionopolis'). This reputation proved hard to shake off: it stuck around even after the devastation of two World Wars, and it wasn't until as late as the last decades of the 20th century that the city began its energetic transformation.

All eyes turned eastwards once the Balkan states and eastern Europe began to open up, and Graz found itself once more centre stage. The city's designation as a World Heritage Site followed by its appointment as European Cultural Capital breathed new life into Graz, which chose to celebrate its historic status by ensuring it entered the 21st century in style. The beautiful old city remains one of the loveliest in central Europe, but the glittering new architecture and high-tech museums have added a

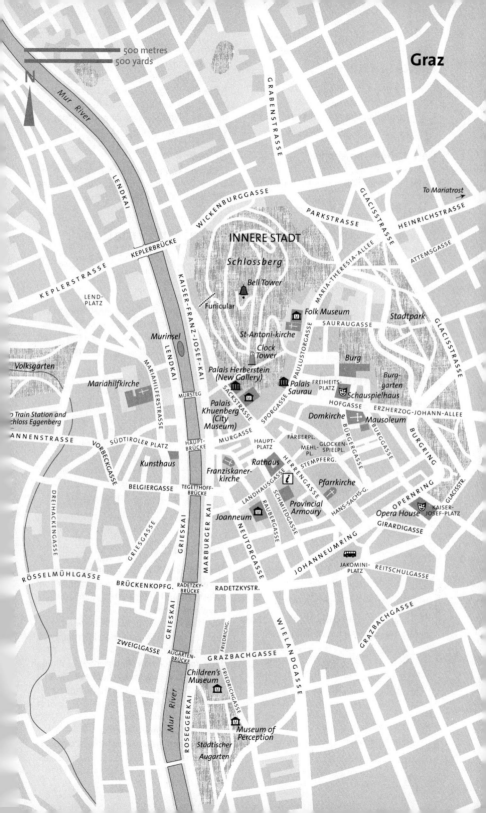

Getting There

The only direct flight from the UK is with **Ryanair** from London Stansted; *see* pp.4–10. There are no direct flights from the USA and Canada.

Getting from the Airport

Graz's airport, **t** (0316) 29020, *www. flughafen-graz.at*, is 7km south of the city centre in Feldkirchen.

Buses 630 and 631 (journey time approx 30mins) depart from outside the terminal for the city centre (Jakominiplatz) from 6.13am to 23.33pm. Times vary: check the airport website.

There are hourly **trains** (6am–11pm, journey time approx 8mins) from the airport to the main train station (Graz Hauptbahnhof). Timetables are posted on the airport website.

Taxis are available from just outside the terminal and cost €15–20 to the city centre (journey time approx 30mins).

Getting Around

By Bus and Tram

It's unlikely that you will need to use the integrated bus and tram system in Graz, as most sights are close together. Most useful for visitors are trams 3 and 6 which go from the train station to the city centre. Tram no.1, which links Schloss Eggenberg in the west with the pilgrimage church of Mariaklost in the east, is a famously easy way to catch many of the city's sights in comfort. Single (€1.70) and 24hr tickets (€3.40) are available from drivers and from newsagents, who also sell good-value tickets valid for 10 rides (€13). The tourist office also sells the 24hr pass.

Taxis

There are taxi ranks across the city, including at the train station and Jakominiplatz. Prices are fairly high.

To book a taxi, call any of the following numbers: **t** (0316) 878, **t** (0316) 889, **t** (0316) 1718, **t** (0316) 2204.

Car Hire

Avis, t (0316) 812290 (airport), **t** (0316) 812920 (city), *www.avis.com*.

Europcar, t (0316) 290 2340 (airport), **t** (0316) 821364 (city), *www.europcar.com*.

Hertz, t (0316) 234432 (airport), **t** (0316) 825007 (city), *www.hertz.com*.

Budget, t (0316) 290 2342 (airport), **t** (0316) 722074 (city), *www.budget.com*.

On Foot

The best way to explore Graz is on foot: the centre is small and charming, and most sights are conveniently clustered together.

Tourist Information

Graz: Herrengasse 16, **t** (0316) 80750, *www.graztourism.at*.

Guided Tours

Walking tours of the city depart from the tourist office April–Oct daily at 2.30 (in both German and English) and Jan–Mar on Fri–Sun at 2.30. The cost is €8.50 for adults and €4.25 for children.

The tourist office runs guided **bus tours** (departing from the tourist office) April–Oct on Sat at 2.30 (book in advance). Tickets cost €12.50 for adults and €6.25 for children. In May and June there's an additional tour, which takes in the contemporary architecture, on Wed at 5 (in German and English) at the same prices. The tourist office also offers a range of **one-day excursions** to sights around the city, including the Lipizzaner stud farm and the Styrian wine route (*see* pp.176–7).

Festivals

Mar: Easter Festival, classical music concerts, *www.grazkonzertagentur.at*; Diagonale Film Festival, prestigious Austrian film festival, *www.diagonale.at*.

May: Tales of Graz, the world's largest story-telling festival (in English and German), *www.graz.tales.org*.

June: *Tour de Charme*, vintage car rally through the old city, *www.tourdecharme.at*; *Styriarte*, a prestigious festival of performing arts taking place from mid-June until the end of July, *www.styriarte.com*.

July: Dance Summer Graz, ballet and contemporary dance, *www.tanzsommer.at*.

July–Aug: Serenata, evening concerts in the Landhaushof courtyard; **Jazz Sommer** – jazz legends converge on the city for a huge jazz festival, *www.jazzsommergraz.at*.

Aug: La Strada, international puppet and street theatre festival, *www.lastrada.at*.

Sept: Styrian folk festival, a one-day traditional folk festival, *www.aufsteirern.at*.

Oct: *Steirischer Herbst*, excellent festival of contemporary performing arts, featuring music, dance, theatre, art and multimedia, *www.steiricherbst.at*.

Dec: Christmas markets (*Christkindlmärkte*) across the city.

Shopping

Central Graz has plenty of chic boutiques selling international fashions, along with traditional Styrian costumes. The city is a paradise for shoe fetishists – every second store front seems to be devoted to shoes in every shape and colour. **Steirisches Heimatwerk**, Paulustorgasse 4, is good for gifts: everything is made in Austria, and the range includes clothing, glassware, ceramics, books and hand-made souvenirs.

There are plenty of enticing pâtisseries where you can either pick up delicious cakes to eat on the hoof or stop for a well-earned break. **Sackstrasse** is known for its galleries and antique shops, and there are morning farmers' **markets** on **Lendplatz** and **Kaiser-Josef-Platz** (*Mon–Sat 7–12*).

Sports and Activities

Skiing

Styria's top skiing area is **Schladming**, 150km from Graz. Local tour operators offer weekend packages. More information can be found at *www.schladming-rohrmoos.com*, which also offers an online accommodation booking service.

Hiking

There are endless possibilities for hiking in the rolling hills around Graz. The tourist office publishes a number of useful leaflets listing local hiking routes.

Where to Stay

Graz t (0316) –

Graz offers a reasonable range of upmarket accommodation, and plenty of attractive little *pensions* for visitors on a budget. Sadly, there is little in the moderate price bracket that stands out: a smattering of chain hotels offer reasonably priced accommodation and a central location, but little in the way of charm. These include Ibis, Mercure and Comfort Hotel. The tourist office has a list of private rooms, which offer B&B-style accommodation but are usually some way out of the city centre. Look out for excellent deals on hotel websites which have discounts on 'rack' prices.

★★★★★Grand Hotel Wiesler, Grieskai 4–8, t 70660, *www.hotelwiesler.com* (*luxury*). Easily the grandest hotel in the city, this gorgeous Jugendstil building oozes *fin-de-siècle* charm. Rooms and suites are light and prettily furnished, and most offer fabulous views over the Baroque spires and rooftops of the old city. The amenities include sauna and jacuzzi, and the restaurant is one of the finest in Austria.

★★★★Erzherhog Johann, Sackstrasse 3–5, t 811616, *www.erzherzog-johann.com* (*luxury*). An elegant hotel on a splendid, palace-lined street, set in a gorgeous 16th-century building. Traditional rooms are decorated with a tasteful mixture of antiques and modern fittings, some have four-posters and there's a lovely glassed-over courtyard with a fabulous restaurant.

★★★★Romantik Parkhotel, Leonhardstrasse 8, t 36300, *www.romantik-parkhotel.at* (*luxury–expensive*). A primrose-yellow 16th-century mansion on the edge of the city park (Stadtpark). There's a good restaurant, and a spa with pool, gym and sauna.

★★★★Schlossberg Hotel, Kaiser-Franz Josef-Kai 30, t 80700, *www.schlossberg-hotel.at* (*luxury–expensive*). This pretty, pastel-blue charmer sits at the foot of the Schlossberg, and has traditional rooms furnished with bold contemporary art and antiques and large marble bathrooms. There's a rooftop pool with wonderful views out over the red-tiled roofs of the old city.

★★★★Das Weitzer, Grieskai 12–14, t 7030, *www.weitzer.com* (*expensive*). This large, imposing hotel has been going since 1910, and has elegant rooms, many with river views. There's a fine restaurant and a spa with sauna and steam baths, and a rooftop terrace. It's a favourite with business travellers – which means good deals at weekends.

★★★★**Zum Dom**, Bürgergasse 14, t 824800, *www.domhotel.co.at* (*expensive*). Perhaps the loveliest place to stay in Graz, this beautiful Baroque palace has been stylishly renovated to contain an elegant boutique-style hotel. Many of the individually decorated rooms have original wooden beams or vaulted ceilings. The award-winning restaurant, **Mod**, serves superb contemporary Austrian and international cuisine (*www.modgraz.at*).

★★★**Stoffbauer**, Oberer Plattenweg 21, t 685300, *www.soffbauer.com* (*moderate*). Out in the green outskirts of Graz, this is a charming, typical Styrian country house with wood-panelled guest rooms, a delightful garden, and a simple restaurant serving regional specialities.

★★★**Mariahilf**, Mariahilferstrasse 9, t 713 1630, *www.hotelmariahilf.at* (*moderate–inexpensive*). A good, central budget choice, this is close to the Kunsthaus in Graz's pedestrianized old centre. It's a handsome old building, with pleasant rooms and a decent restaurant.

★★★**Das Wirtshaus Greiner**, Grabenstrasse 64, t 685090, *http://wirtshaus-greiner.at* (*moderate–inexpensive*). A 10min tram-ride from the city centre, this cosy guesthouse is set in a 400-year old building and is attached to one of the city's best traditional restaurants, also called Das Wirtshaus Greiner (*moderate*).

★★★**Gasthof Schlaraffenland**, Keplerstrasse 33, t 72400 (*inexpensive*). A simple, old-fashioned inn with a cheerful tavern-style restaurant in a good central location close to the Lendplatz. There's a garden, and it also has simple apartments (no kitchens).

★★★**Gasthof Zum Sternwirt**, Waltendorfer Hauptstrasse 45, t 475245, *www.sternwirt.at* (*inexpensive*). A 10min bus-ride from the city centre will take you to this spotless guesthouse offering crisp, newly renovated rooms and apartments, plus free parking.

★★★**Gasthof-Pension Zur Stiererstub'n**, Lendplatz 8, t 716855, *www.pension-graz.at* (*inexpensive*). A wonderful little *pension* in the centre of the city: the 13 simple rooms are spotlessly whitewashed and many offer views of the Schlossberg. There's also a good little restaurant.

Eating Out

Graz t (0316) –

Outstanding hotel-restaurants are mentioned in the 'Where to Stay' section.

Landhauskeller, Schmiedgasse 9, t 830276, *www.landhaus-keller.at* (*expensive*). Romantic and elegant restaurant with outdoor dining in the magnificent Landhaus courtyard. It serves refined Austrian cuisine, with an emphasis on local beef, which is accompanied by a lengthy wine list.

Iohan, Landhausgasse 1, t 821312, *www.vogue-johan.at* (*expensive*). One of the slickest restaurants in town, you can dine on delicious contemporary cuisine under creamy vaults in the sleek minimalist interior, or out in the beautiful courtyard in summer. *Closed Sun.*

Ohnime di Gallo, Purbergstrasse 56, t 391143, *www.ohnime.at* (*moderate*). This elegant restaurant with charming blue and white décor has a beautiful setting on the hillside overlooking the Baroque Mariatrost church. It serves delicious, exquisitely presented international cuisine. If you can't stagger back into town, it also has simple, modestly furnished guest rooms (*inexpensive*). *Closed Sat eve and Sun.*

Maroni, Mehlplatz 1, t 828702, *www.maroni.at* (*moderate*). A buzzy and fashionable restaurant on two floors, with slick creamy décor and pop art. It serves sophisticated Mediterranean dishes, and there's a summer terrace on a lively square.

Gasthaus zur Goldenen Pastete, Sporgasse 28, t 823416 (*moderate*). One of the best-known restaurants in the city, this upmarket, traditional inn serves Austrian and Styrian specialities on a splendid terrace in summer.

Eckstein, Mehlplatz 3, t 828710, *www.eckstein.co.at* (*moderate*). For Styrian cuisine at its most refined, you need look no further than this chic brick-vaulted restaurant. The wine list is particularly good, and they have a garden for summer wining and dining.

Les Vipères, Lendkai 1, t 8017 9292, *www. lesviperes.at* (*moderate–inexpensive*). Inside the Kunsthaus, this visually striking restaurant has glass and steel walls and gleaming white tables and chairs. It serves fancy French cuisine, good snacks and breakfasts, but the bar takes over late.

Glöckl Bräu, Glockenspielplatz 2–3, t 814781, *www.gloecklbraeu.at* (*inexpensive*). Traditional brewery and tavern, serving sturdy Styrian standards and home-brewed beer. It has a terrace out on a pretty square.

Stoffbauer, Oberer Plattenweg 21, t 685300, *www.stoffbauer.com* (*inexpensive*). This old-fashioned charmer sits on a green hill on the edge of the city, with fabulous views from the beer garden. It serves hearty, home-cooked local specialities, and is well known for its tasty fried chicken (*Backhendl*).

Mangolds, Griesgasse 11, t 718002 (*inexpensive*). Popular veggie spot, serving a cheap and tasty buffet of salads and hot dishes, along with fresh juices and smoothies. *Closed Sun and eves.*

Cafés and Coffee Houses

Graz **t** (0316) –

Frankowitsch, Stempfergasse 2–4, t 822 2120. This pretty café is an institution in the Old City, serving exquisite open sandwiches with a range of toppings, traditionally served with a miniature glass of beer (a *pfiff*). It's also a delicatessen selling delicious local goodies. *Closed Sun.*

Café Fotter, Attemsgasse 6, t 322146. A traditional and delightful *Konditorei* and café, complete with antique furnishings. In summer, linger over your cakes and coffee in the magical, secluded garden.

Café Sacher, Herrengasse 6, t 8005. An outpost of the famous hotel and café in Vienna, this is the place to try authentic *Sachertorte*.

Operncafé Temmel, Opernring 22, t 830436. Bustling, traditional café near the Opera House with a fabulous array of cakes.

Edegger-Tax, Hofgasse 8, t 8302 3051. Perhaps the most famous in the city, this Imperial

bakery has an elaborate Renaissance doorway and handsome wooden façade. The cakes are as wonderful as the location.

Entertainment and Nightlife

Graz **t** (0316) –

Music, Theatre, Opera, Ballet

Graz Opera House, Kaiser-Josef-Platz 1, t 8008, *www.theater-graz.com*. This ornate 19th-century building is the main opera and ballet venue in Graz.

Schauspielhaus, Freiheitsplatz, t 8000, *www.theater-graz.com*. Another imposing 19th-century institution devoted to drama and dance.

Landhaushof, Herrengasse 16, info from Graz tourist office. The sublime Renaissance courtyard hosts classical music concerts in summer, and many other cultural events.

Bars and Clubs

The **Bermuda Triangle** (Bermuda Dreieck) – the area between Sporgasse and Hans-Sachs-Gasse – is full of bars and clubs, mostly catering to Graz's student population.

Aiola Island, Mur 1, t 890335, *www.aiola.at*. This slick contemporary café-bar in the spectacular Murinsel is open all day for snacks and coffee. At night, drinks and DJs take over, with weekend clubbing nights. There are two more outposts, one a terrace at the top of the Schlossberg, t 818797, and another at Mehlplatz 1, t 815998.

Barcelona, Reitschulgasse 20, t 0676 6129537. Popular gay café-bar.

Brot & Spiele, Mariahilferstrasse 17, t 715081. A cheerful, down-to-earth Austrian pub, with billiards, darts, a big screen for sports events, and filling snacks.

M1, Färberplatz 1, t 8112330. You'll have to fight for a place on the rooftop terrace in this modern café-bar, a classic in the Bermuda Triangle. Great during the day, too.

Miles, Mariahilferstrasse 24, t 0699 1076 9662. A classic jazz club, with regular live concerts and a relaxed atmosphere.

Postgarage, Dreihackengasse 42, t 722937. Cool club playing hot electro-dance music.

glossy, 21st-century appeal. Concentrating on the future while preserving the past has proved a canny move: Graz has shaken off its old stick-in-the-mud image to become one of Austria's most dynamic cities.

The Old City (Altstadt)

Hauptplatz, with crooked streets splintering off in all directions, is the buzzy little heart of the old city. Trams clank past, the square is often awash with the striped awnings of market stalls, and it exudes a constant buzz and bustle. The grandest building on the square is the **town hall** (Rathaus), a white cream puff built in the late 19th century, when the pompous fountain dedicated to Archduke Johann at the centre of the square was also erected.

Herrengasse leads southwest: it was a dead end in the Middle Ages, but now it's the grandest street in town, lined with chichi boutiques and opulent mansions. Most extraordinary of all is the **Gemalte Haus**, with a lavishly painted façade depicting stories from Greek and Roman mythology. The **Landhaus** at No.16 (which also contains the helpful tourist office; *see* p.166) is a superb Renaissance building, begun in 1557 to designs by Italian architect Domenico dell'Aglio, with sumptuous Baroque additions in the 18th century. It still houses the Styrian provincial government, and there are guided tours of its opulent interior when the politicians are not in session (*book well in advance through the tourist office; adm*). But the highlight of the complex is the enchanting Renaissance courtyard – three layers of rosy arcades liberally scattered with statues and grinning gargoyles, which make a magnificent backdrop for regular outdoor concerts.

You can enjoy a bird's-eye view of the courtyard from the **Provincial Armoury** (Landeszeughaus; *open April–Nov daily 10–6, Thurs until 8; Dec–Mar Tues–Sun 10–3; adm*), in a 17th-century building adjoining the Landhaus. Head through a doorway surmounted by the Styrian panther and marvel at the extraordinary collection of 17th-century weaponry – four dizzying floors crammed with endless ranks of helmets, spears, armour, blunderbusses, muskets, shields and cannon. There's an ancient smell of must and metal: this armoury has remained virtually untouched for centuries and is unique in the world. The ground floor offers an insight into Styrian and Austrian history during the 17th century with absorbing audiovisual displays.

Behind the Landhaus, the flamboyant neoclassical **Joanneum Museum** (Landesmuseum Joanneum; *Raubergasse 10, www.museum-joanneum.at; open Tues–Sun 9–4; adm*) contains a clutch of worthy but rather dull museums devoted to geology and palaeontology, mineralogy, zoology and botany. More interesting are the usually excellent temporary exhibitions of contemporary art in the nearby branch of the museum at Neutorgasse 45.

Return to Hauptplatz and head up the elegant curve of **Sporgasse**, a steep narrow street overlooked by impressive Renaissance and Baroque mansions, which skirts the base of the Schlossberg (*see* p.172). The **Luegg Haus**, on the corner, is covered with pretty twirls of stucco like piped icing, and, at No.25, the curious little figure of a mustachioed Turkish warrior sprouts from beneath the eaves of the **Saurau Palace** (Palais Saurau).

Turn right up **Hofgasse**, and stop off for delicious cakes at the Imperial bakery Edegger-Tax (*see* p.169), with an extravagant Renaissance portal topped with a huge golden eagle. The **Freiheitsplatz** on the left is dominated by the showy **Schauspielhaus**, a venerable 19th-century theatre which remains one of the city's main venues. Beyond it is the **Burg**, a palace built for Freidrich III in the 15th century and expanded and remodelled ever since. Now home to the local governor, it's closed to the public, but you can stroll around the impressive Renaissance gateways, courtyards and bastions. In a tower which connects the first and second courtyards, don't miss the sinuous Gothic **double staircase**, built in 1499. During the summer, the elegant, formal **Burg gardens** (Burggarten) are open (*weekdays only*), or you can stroll through an archway into the grassy, green expanse of the delightful **city park** (Stadtpark), which curls around the old heart of Graz for about 1km and has a good smattering of cafés.

On the other side of Hofgasse loom the splendid domes of the **Mausoleum** (*entrance on Burggasse; open Mon–Thurs and Sat 11–12 and 2–3; adm*), built under Emperor Ferdinand II and expanded by Fischer von Erlach for Friedrich III in the 1680s. (Fischer von Erlach – *see also* 'Vienna', pp.132 and 137, and 'Salzburg', pp.152 and 154 – was to become the most important Austrian architect of the 18th century, but this is his only building in his home town of Graz.) The florid Baroque church is thickly covered with elaborate frescoes idealizing the Habsburg emperors (notably Leopold I, who had himself depicted valiantly subduing the Turks). Stairs lead down to a musty crypt, where slanted mirrors reflect the sumptuous marble tomb of Emperor Ferdinand II and his wife Maria Anna, and an opening covered with a wrought-iron grille looks up to the oval cupola.

The adjoining **cathedral** (Domkirche; *open daily 10–6; adm*) is a late-Gothic construction half-hidden beneath a frilly, Baroque coating added by the Jesuits, who were given the church in 1573. Above the altar, note Emperor Friedrich III's curious acronym 'AEIOU', shorthand for his private motto, which was emblazoned across everything from castles to cutlery during his lifetime. He only revealed its meaning

Graz for Kids

The funicular railway and miniature train ride inside the caves of the Schlossberg (*see* p.172) can be counted on to appeal to children. There are a couple of transport museums which can be fun too: the **Johann Puch Museum** (*Puchstrasse 85, www.johann-puch-museum-graz.com; open weekends 11–4; adm*) with vintage cars; and the **Tramway Museum** (*Mariatrosterstrasse 202; open mid–July to mid–Sept Sat 4–7; adm*), where you can clamber aboard an antique tram or even go for a ride through the old city. Kids of all ages will enjoy the glossy new **Museum of Perception** (Museum der Wahrnehmung; *Friedrichgasse 41, www.muwa.at; open Wed–Mon 2–6.30; adm*) which uses hi-tech tricks to show how we can't always trust our senses. The nearby **Children's Museum** (Kindermuseum FRida & freD; *Friedrichgasse 34, www.fridaundfred.at; open Mon, Wed and Thurs 9–5, Fri 9–7, Sat–Sun and hols 10–5; adm*) is a brand new museum with interesting exhibitions, art workshops and drama performances (although these are currently in German only).

on his deathbed: Alles Erdreich Ist Österreich Untertan ('The whole world is subject to Austria'). Outside, on the southern wall of the cathedral, the grim 15th-century *Landplagenbild* ('Plague Painting') gruesomely depicts the plague of locusts, the arrival of the Turks and the plague epidemic which all struck the city in 1480.

The web of narrow lanes and tiny passages between Burggasse and Herrengasse are among the most atmospheric in the city: wiggle down to **Enge Gasse** (as narrow as its name suggests) and turn right into **Glockenspielplatz**. This square, along with nearby **Mehlplatz** and **Färberplatz**, is the heart of Graz's '**Bermuda Triangle**' (Bermuda Dreieck), packed with bars and taverns, many with outdoor terraces. Daily, at 11am, 3pm and 6pm, a pair of wooden figures dressed in traditional Styrian costume dance for the gawking crowds in the bell tower at No.4. This house formerly belonged to a 'seller of spirits' who had the figures installed as a pre-neon advertisement. Tiny **Stempfergasse**, which leads down from the square, is known for its collection of chic international fashion boutiques.

Schlossberg

Schlossberg, the diminutive wooded hill which rises above the city, is everyone's favourite playground: the medieval castle which once stood here was blown to smithereens in 1809 (Napoleon's armies failed to take it from the feisty Styrians and destroyed it in revenge). The hill was converted into gardens in the early 19th century, with romantic stony ruins and shaded walkways. Peaceful and romantic, it's celebrated for the magnificent views of the huddled red-tiled rooftops below.

To get there, stroll down **Sackstrasse** from the Hauptplatz, perhaps stopping to browse awhile in the countless galleries and antique shops, or in Graz's fine department store, Kastner & Öhler. There are several more graceful Renaissance and Baroque mansions here, including the **Khuenberg Palace** (Palais Khuenberg) at No.18, where the ill-starred Archduke Franz Ferdinand (assassinated in Sarajevo in 1914) was born. The palace is now home to the **City Museum** (Stadtmuseum; *www.stadtmuseum-graz.at; open Tues 10–9, Wed–Sat 10–6, Sun and hols 10–1; adm*), where a collection of archaeological fragments, paintings, furniture, maps and reconstructions of, among other things, a Beidermeier pharmacy outline the history of the city. They are complemented by a multimedia presentation, and the sumptuous halls and galleries are worth a visit in their own right. The **New Gallery** (Neue Galerie), in the **Herberstein Palace** (Palais Herberstein) at No.16, contains the provincial modern and contemporary art collection, with usually interesting temporary exhibitions (*open Tues–Sun 10–6, Thurs until 8; adm*).

There are a number of ways to reach the top of the hill: the fit might want to tackle the **balustraded steps** (Schlossbergsteig) which zigzag elegantly to the top; those in a hurry could shoot up in the **glass lift** (*open daily 9–1.30; adm, public transport tickets valid*) which burrows through the centre of the rock (kids will want a go on the mini-train inside the grotto at the entrance to the lift); but, for old-fashioned romance, take the **funicular railway** (Schlossbergbahn; *open May–Sept daily 9am–11pm; Oct–April daily 10–10; adm, public transport tickets valid*), which was built in 1894 and has been making the steep climb in style ever since.

The funicular culminates at a balustraded viewing point, where a pretty **bell tower** (Glockenturm) has stood since the 16th century. It, along with the clock tower (*see* below), were saved from the French after the people of Graz paid a ransom. Guided tours of the Schlossberg depart from here daily on the hour in summer (*9–6; adm*). The bell tower is affectionately known as 'Liesl' after its bell, made, according to legend, from 101 captured Turkish cannonballs (it strikes 101 times at 7am, 1pm and 7pm). The tower contains a tiny museum, with an intricate wooden model of the fortress made just before it was torn down in 1809.

The most distinctive feature of the Schlossberg is its pretty, whitewashed **clock tower** (Uhrturm) which has become Graz's best-loved symbol and is visible from all around the city. The tower was built in the 16th century, incorporating the remnants of a medieval watchtower. Curiously, the hands of the clock are back-to-front: the hour hand is the longer of the two. For many years, it was the only hand on the clock, deliberately built to be seen from across the city. Another viewing point offers lovely views over the fairytale rooftops of the old town, and across the river to the huge amorphous blob which is the city's spanking new Kunsthaus (*see* below). Near the tower, the fashionable terrace café Aiola is a good place to stop for a break or enjoy lunch with panoramic views.

The extensive gardens and elegant paths lit with gas-lamps are perfect for a stroll. A tree-lined path leads down the hill back towards Sporgasse, where the **Folk Museum** (Volkskundemuseum; *Paulustorgasse 11, www.volkskundemuseum-graz.at*; *open Tues–Sun 10–6, Thurs until 8; adm*), in a much-modernized former Capuchin monastery, offers an insight into rural Styrian life.

Across the Mur River

The city of Graz celebrated its appointment as European Cultural Capital of 2003 by commissioning two striking contemporary buildings: the Murinsel, and the Kunsthaus. The **Murinsel** ('island in the Mur') is a stunningly beautiful steel and glass construction poised between two glass walkways in the centre of the Mur river. The curving, shell-shaped building was designed by New York-based architect Vito Acconci, and it contains a small outdoor theatre as well as an excellent café-bar, Aiola Island.

It's impossible to miss the huge, amorphous **Kunsthaus** which looks like a cross between a giant spacehopper and an aircraft hangar. Designed by British architects Peter Cook and Colin Fournier, it's known as the 'Friendly Alien', and its bluish, bulbous form has taken over from the clock tower as the city's hottest symbol. Inside, there's a museum of contemporary art, with excellent temporary exhibitions, along with a great, hyper-fashionable café-restaurant called Les Vipères (*see* p.169).

Further Afield

The no.1 tram must be one of the most scenic tram routes anywhere in Europe: it connects two of the finest outlying attractions in Graz, and passes through the heart of the charming old city. At the western end, about 4km from the city centre, is the

The Terminator

Arnold Schwarzenegger was born in the little village of Thal, 10km from Graz, in 1947. He went on to become the youngest athlete to gain the title of Mr Universe and left Europe for Hollywood, where he had a string of blockbuster roles in films including *Conan the Barbarian* and *The Terminator*. The citizens of Graz were so proud of their famous son that they named their stadium after him, and installed a small museum about his life. The ex-Mr Universe was elected Governor of California in 2003, to the giddy delight of many Austrians, who issued commemorative 'Arnie' stamps and urged the USA to change the constitution to allow foreign-born politicians to run for president. Then, in January 2005, Schwarzenegger approved the execution by lethal injection of Donald Beardslee – the first execution in California for three years. Some angry Austrians have been calling for Schwarzenegger to be stripped of his Austrian passport (he holds dual nationality), and there is a campaign in Graz to rename the stadium once again.

Schloss Eggenberg, a magnificent 17th-century castle known as the 'Styrian Escorial' after the Habsburg palace near Madrid. The castle is surrounded by a glorious **park** (*open daily summer 8–7, winter until 5; adm €1*), where peacocks stalk the gardens and tree-lined paths lead to romantic bowers and pergolas. The Italianate palace was built for Hans Ulrich von Eggenberg, favourite of Emperor Ferdinand II and governor of Inner Austria, according to precise astronomical and mathematical calculations: each façade represents one of the seasons; the 365 windows provide a different view for every day of the year; and each floor contains 31 rooms – one for each day of the month. Extravagant Baroque and rococo decoration gilds every room, some of which you can see on the hourly guided tours of the **State Rooms** (*open Oct–April Tues–Sun 10–5; adm*). The lower floors house museums (*all open May–Nov Tues–Sun 9–4; adm*) dedicated to Prehistory and Early History, an extensive Coin Collection and a gathering of Roman and ancient sculpture in the Lapidarium in the palace grounds. After a recent reshuffle, the city's **Old Gallery** (Alte Galerie) has also been transferred here (*open from summer 2005*) and includes haunting Gothic sculpture and altar-pieces, some fine works by Brueghel and Cranach, and grandiose Baroque paintings.

At the other end of the no.1 tram line, about 3km east of the city centre, is the lavish Baroque **Mariatrost Basilica** (*open daily 9–6*), built in 1709 to house a supposedly miracle-performing 15th-century image of the Virgin. A steep flight of steps (215 in all) leads up to the primrose-yellow church, which has a lofty, light interior and frescoes of battling Habsburgs. The Virgin sits resplendent above the altar, and Graz's most aristocratic families are represented in the surrounding marble chapels. It remains a popular pilgrimage destination.

Seven kilometres south of the city, the new **Austrian Sculpture Park** (*www.skulpturenpark.at; open daily June–Aug 10–8.30; April–May and Sept–Oct 10–6; adm*) has more than 40 sculptures and installations by both Austrian and international artists including Eve&Adele, Nancy Rubins and Markus Wilfling. It's laid out in award-winning modern gardens designed by Deiter Kienast.

Day Trips and Overnighters from Graz

Close to Graz, you can visit the Lipizzaner stud farm where horses are raised for the famous Spanish Riding School, or pop into Bärnbach where Friedensreich Hundertwasser has transformed the parish church. For an insight into rural life throughout Austria, check out the national open-air museum. To the south of Graz, wine-lovers will appreciate an overnight trip to the Styrian wine region, where the vine-covered hills and the trim rows of poplars and cypress trees recall Tuscany.

West of Graz: Horses and Hundertwasser

The town of **Piber**, 45km west of Graz, is home to the most important **stud farm** (Bundesgestüt Piber) in Austria (*t (03144) 3323; open Easter–Oct, tours daily at 9.30 and 1.30, you must book the 75-minute guided tours in advance; adm*). The world-famous Lipizzaner horses for the **Spanish Riding School** in Vienna (*see* p.131) have been bred and raised here since 1920. The tour begins with an introductory video, but visitors can then visit the stables and see the beautiful white horses and their dark foals (they lighten as they grow up) out in the fields.

Bärnbach, 2km from Piber, contains the playful, multicoloured church of St Barbara (*t (01342) 62581; adm*), unmistakably the work of Hundertwasser. He redesigned the post-war parish church, adding his characteristic golden onion domes, plenty of undulating lines and a blazing stained-glass window depicting the 'circle of life'.

Austrian Open-Air Museum (Österreichisches Freilichtmuseum)

www.stuebing.at; open late Mar–Oct Tues–Sun 9–5, last adm 4pm; adm.

The Austrian Open-Air Museum is just outside **Stübing**, a small market town set in wooded hills 15km north of Graz. Each Austrian province has its own open-air museum with rural architecture from the region, but this one covers the entire country, with more than 70 typical buildings attractively scattered over extensive grounds which spread greenly for more than 2km. These include traditional farmsteads, a grocery store, a smithy, a bakery, impressive smoke-houses (Rauchstubenhäuser) and delightful herb gardens. There are regular, but not daily,

Getting There

The easiest way to get to the **stud farm** is to book the convenient **trip** (*every Sat*) with the Graz tourist office. Otherwise, you will need your own **car** as the nearest train station (Köflach) is 3km away, and linking buses are infrequent.

Tourist Information

Deutschlandberg: Hauptplatz 34, **t** (03462) 43152, *www.sws.st*. Or ask in Graz.

Eating Out

Caballero, Piber stud farm, **t** (01334) 3323170 (*expensive–moderate*). The best place to dine in the area is this elegant restaurant housed within the stud farm complex, which offers sophisticated Spanish and Austrian fare.

Gasthof Decelak, Voitsbergerstrasse 38, Bärnbach, **t** (03142) 62285 (*inexpensive*). Cheap and cheerful home-cooked food is available in this modest guest house.

Getting There

There are regular **trains** from Graz to Stübing, but it's a good 15–20min walk from the station. Direct **buses** leave from Lendplatz in Graz at 9am and 12.30pm and will drop you at the museum. The Graz tourist office has plenty of information.

Eating Out

There are a few options to be found within the museum, including an old-fashioned **bakery and grocery** where you can pick up picnic goods for an alfresco meal, and a traditional *Gasthof* by the entrance if you feel the need for something more substantial.

exhibitions of rural crafts from thatching to cheese-making, but it's worth checking in advance to see what's on. Come, if you can, on the last Sunday in September when the traditional **festival** (Erlebnistag) is held, with folk music, handicraft exhibitions and all kinds of events.

Styrian Wine Country

The rugged, vine-covered hills and dreamy villages of southern Styria make for a blissful break from the hurly-burly of the city and are an easy drive from Graz. Make this trip in autumn if you can, when the villages celebrate the wine harvest with festivals and events. Almost all the wine produced around Leibnitz and Ehrenhausen is white: once you hit western Styria and Deutschlandberg, you are in **Schilcher** country, a light, aromatic rosé which has become hugely popular. To find out more about Austrian wines and wineries, visit *www.winefromaustria.com*.

The multi-named *autobahn* (A9/E57/E59) shoots south from Graz through wooded hills and seas of vines to unassuming **Leibnitz**, which, despite appearances, has had a long, long history. An ancient Celtic settlement (one of the oldest in Austria) on the hill of Frauenberg just south of the city centre was taken over by the Romans, who erected a cult temple complex for the citizens of Flavia Solva, 3km southeast. A few atmospheric stones are all that survive, but there are wonderful views of rolling hills. You can explore the excavated ruins of **Flavia Solva**, along with a small museum containing a collection of Roman fragments (*open Tues–Sun 10–12 and 1–6; adm*). Perched on another hilltop overlooking the city, the impressive **Schloss Seggau** was built by the archbishops of Salzburg in the 13th century; guided tours are offered of the opulent interior (*t (03452) 824350, www.seggau.com; tours May–Oct Sat 3pm, Sun 11am, book in advance; adm*) or you could content yourself with a stroll around the handsome Renaissance courtyard.

If you have time, head 10km west of Leibnitz to find tiny **Kitzeck**, a lofty wine village (Europe's highest at 1,850ft above sea level) with a small museum of wine and a host of traditional wine-producers (the Leibnitz tourist office have a list of those which can be visited). Another 10km south of Kitzeck, **Grossklein** was the site of extensive 8th-century BC burial grounds, and archaeologists have unearthed some extraordinary ancient treasures which can be found in a small history museum (*open May–Oct Tues–Sun 10–12 and 2–4.30; adm*).

South of Leibnitz (10km), delightful **Ehrenhausen** is huddled in the shadow of an impressive fortress, built by the Eggenbergs (*see* Schloss Eggenberg, p.174) in the 16th century. The castle is closed to the public, but on an adjacent hilltop you can visit the mausoleum of Ruprecht von Eggenberg, a 17th-century temple which was later given a frothy Baroque facelift by the most important Austrian architect of the 18th century, J.B. Fischer von Erlach. There are commanding views across the valley from the top of the hill, particularly lovely early in the morning when the mist is rising off the vines. This trim, appealing little town is the perfect place to stop for the night.

In the morning, head west along the B69 to **Gamlitz**, a storybook village in a vine-covered hollow. This is the largest wine-producer in Styria, and the village's 300-year-old castle now contains an interesting wine museum (*open mid-May–mid-Nov daily 9–6; adm*). The B69 continues through rolling vineyards dotted with picturesque villages like **Leutschhach** and **Arnfels**, until reaching the modest market town of **Eibiswald**, where you should turn north onto the B76 for **Deutschlandsberg**. A quiet, genial little town, splayed neatly around a handsome central square, this is the centre of Styria's Schilcher-producing region. Make the steep climb up to the ancient, but much renovated, **Schloss Landsberg** for wonderful views and a small city museum (*open April–Nov daily 9.30–5; adm*). Heading north, stop off at the appealing market town of **Stainz**, with another imposing castle (which now contains a folklore museum), before returning to Graz.

Getting There

This trip is best for those with their own transport, but there are **trains** running at least once an hour from Graz to Stainz and Deutschlandberg, and, on a separate line, to Leibnitz and Ehrenhausen. Local **buses** ply between these towns and the smaller villages, but they are infrequent.

Tourist Information

Deutschlandberg: Hauptplatz 34, **t** (03462) 43152, *www.sws.st*. The main regional office.
Leibnitz: Sparkassenplatz 4a, **t** 00800 8472 6837.

Where to Stay

Zum Goldenen Löwen, Marktplatz 28, Ehrenhausen, **t** (03453) 20415 (*moderate*). Delightful, traditional inn in the heart of the pretty town, this is an excellent choice to spend the night. The restaurant serves good country fare, along with local wines.
Sattlerhof, Sernau 2a, Gamlitz, **t** (03453) 44540. This winery has won several top awards for its excellent wines. There are stylish guest rooms and suites (*expensive–moderate*) and an excellent restaurant (*expensive–moderate*), where you can dine out in the garden with beautiful views.

Eating Out

You'll find plenty of simple *Buschenschänken* ('bushel taverns') scattered all over the region, where you can try local wines and tuck into local specialities.
Gasthof Sailler, Hauptplatz 5, Leibnitz, **t** (03452) 82263 (*inexpensive*). Right in the centre of the city, a traditional tavern with a beer garden.
Kirchenwirt, Stienriegel 52, Kitzeck, **t** (03456) 2225 (*moderate*). One of the best restaurants in the region, with creative Styrian and international fare. It's very popular, so book in advance. *Closed Sun–Tues.*
Gasthof Goldener Krowne, Marktplatz 24, Ehrenhausen, **t** (03453) 2640 (*inexpensive*). Old-style guest house with a reasonable restaurant on a charming square.
Stainzerhof, Grazerstrassse 2–4, Stainz, **t** (03463) 2115 (*inexpensive*). Pretty, family-run 18th-century hotel with charming vaulted restaurant where you can choose from a menu of local dishes.

Klagenfurt

Klagenfurt is the miniature provincial capital of Carinthia, Austria's southernmost province. A laid-back little city with a distinctly Mediterranean feel (the Italian border is just 60km away), it sits pretty on the banks of the lovely Wörther See. This beautiful lake is backed by dizzying mountain peaks, and its smart resorts have been a popular summer retreat since the 19th century. Carinthia contains no fewer than 1,270 lakes, many of which are easily accessible from Klagenfurt, and the astonishing landscape, balmy temperatures and relaxed way of life have long made it a favourite with Austrian and Italian tourists. During the baking heat of summer, the lakes provide a refreshing retreat and hiking trails extend magnificently across the cool mountain peaks. In winter, these peaks become ski runs, with several resorts within easy reach of Klagenfurt.

This region sits squarely at the crossroads of Europe, the nexus of ancient trading routes: Magdalensburg, just outside Klagenfurt, was the capital of a Celtic kingdom before being annexed by the Roman Empire. The Romans built a substantial

Getting There

The only direct flight from the UK is with Ryanair from London Stansted; *see* p.4. There are no direct flights from the USA and Canada.

Getting from the Airport

Klagenfurt's Alpe-Adria airport, t (0463) 41500, *www.klagenfurt-airport.at*, is 3km north of the city centre. It's a small airport, but it has all the usual facilities, including ATMs, shops, cafés and several car-hire agencies (*see* right).

An express airport **bus** service departs from outside the terminal every 30mins (*Mon–Sat 6am–6pm and every hour on Sun*) for the bus station at Heiligengeistplatz (the most central stop) and the main train station (Hauptbahnhof). The fare is €1.80. The nearest **train** station to the airport is Klagenfurt-Annibichl, a 5min walk from the terminal building. There are hourly services, journey time is 5mins and the fare is €2.70.

There is a **taxi** rank outside the terminal. Fares to the city centre are around €10–12.

Getting Around

By Bus

Most city buses depart from **Heiligengeist-platz**, which is just west of the Neuer Platz. They are useful for getting to Europapark and Wörther See (served by buses 10, 11 and 20, among others). Bus tickets cost €1.60 for a single ticket, €4 for a 24hr ticket and €6.80 for a 24hr family ticket, and these can be purchased from the driver or from *Tabaks*. Weekly (€13) and monthly (€33) tickets are also available. There is more information at *www.stw.inhalt/317.htm*.

By Taxi

There are taxi ranks around the city: the most central include Neuer Platz and Heiligengeistplatz. Fares are fairly high. You can order taxis by calling t (0463) 31111, t (0463) 1715, or t (0463) 2711.

By Car

You won't need a car to explore the old city, but it's very useful for touring the nearby lakes and mountains. The following all have offices at Klagenfurt airport.

Avis, t (0463) 55938, *www.avis.com*.
Europcar, t (0463) 21525, *www.europcar.com*.
Hertz, t (0463) 41500321, *www.hertz.com*.
Budget, t (0463) 9159175, *www.budget.com*.

On Foot

The centre of Klagenfurt is tiny and best explored on foot, and there are good public transport links to Europapark and Wörther See.

Tourist Information

Klagenfurt: Rathaus, Neuer Platz 1, t (0463) 537 2223, *www.info.klagenfurt.at*.

There are no special passes specifically for Klagenfurt. However, the **Kärnten Card**, valid throughout Carinthia, offers substantial (up to 50%) discounts on public transport, museums and attractions, *www.kaerntencard.co.at* (German only). It costs €32 for adults and €13 for children, and is valid for 2 weeks.

Guided Tours

The tourist office offers free guided **walking tours** of the old city centre daily in summer, and you can do a self-guided tour by following the green markers painted through the old town. The tourist office also has useful pamphlets with three themed tours which you can do yourself.

No organized **cycling tours** are available but cycling is very popular in Klagenfurt and there are several bike-rental outlets, including at the train stations. The tourist office has a leaflet called *Cycling Tours* which lists routes both in the centre and around town.

One of the loveliest ways to explore the Wörther See is by **boat**. All the resorts are served by steamers run by STW (*see also* p.186), *www.stw.at/inhalt/schifffahrt.htm* (German only). They also run themed cruises offering dinner and dancing, etc.

Festivals

There's a full list of exhibitions and other forthcoming events at the tourist information website, *www.info.klagenfurt.at*.

Feb: Carnival, street parades and processions.

Mar: Easter Market – stalls are set up throughout the old town with crafts, souvenirs and traditional foods.

May: International Balloon Cup, a competitive balloon festival held in Europapark; **Festival of the Valleys**, traditional food, drink and dancing from across the Carinthian region.

June: Wörther See Classics Festival, a week-long festival of classical music held at the Wörther See Hall at the exhibition centre, *www.woertherseeclassics.com*; **Klagenfurt Sports Festival** – the streets are taken over with sports from street soccer to roller-skating, *www.info.klagenfurt.at*; *Ingeborg Bachmann Preis* (Festival of German-speaking literature), a prestigious literary festival, *www.bachmannpreis.at*.

July: Carinthian Ironman Austria – triathlon athletes from around the world compete in this extremely demanding event, *www.ironmanaustria.at*; **Music Forum Viktring**, jazz and contemporary music festival held in Viktring, *www.musikforum.at*.

Aug: Smart Meeting – Smart car fans gather for a celebratory drive around the lake, *www.whitehouse.at*; **Old Town Magic Festival** – magicians, jugglers, acrobats and stilt-walkers take over the old city on the last weekend of the month.

Oct: Ursula Market, a 4-day-long market of traditional and hand-made local goods held at the end of the month; **Festival of Carinthian Horse-lovers**, a riding tournament and exhibition.

Nov–Dec: Christmas Markets, held across the region from late Nov; **New Year's Eve Carnival**.

Shopping

Klagenfurt is a tiny provincial capital and not a major shopping destination. However, browsing through the elegant boutiques tucked away in the beautiful courtyards is always a pleasure. You'll find plenty of typical Austrian souvenirs including cut glass, embroidered lace and traditional clothing, along with several outdoor shops selling clothes and mountain gear.

For traditional Carinthian goods, visit the **Kärntner Heimatwerk**, Herrengasse 2, t (0463) 55575, which has a range of glassware, ceramics and embroidered fabrics.

Sports and Activities

Skiing

The closest skiing to Klagenfurt is to be found at the resorts north of Villach, such as **Bad Kleinkirchheim**, but the best skiing in Carinthia is to be had in its northwestern corner, on the southern slopes of the spectacular **Hohe Tauern** range. For more information on ski resorts and packages, visit the regional website, *www.carinthia.at*, or *www.skiaustria.com*. For kids, the **Schleppe Alm City Park**, *www.schleppalm.at*, is a small slope, floodlit at night, just 5mins from the centre of Klagenfurt.

Golf

Golf is immensely popular in Carinthia, particularly around the Wörther See. The closest golf course to Klagenfurt is **Golfanlage Klagenfurt-Seltenheim**, Seltenheimer Strasse 137, Klagenfurt, t (0463) 40223, *www.gcseltenheim.at*, but the tourist office can provide details of the many others in the region. The regional website, *www.carinthia.at*, has details of courses, special golf passes and all-inclusive packages.

Swimming and Watersports

All the resorts around the Wörther See have municipal beaches. All kinds of watersports are available.

Where to Stay

Klagenfurt t (0463) –

★★★★**Hotel Garni Schloss St Georgen**, Sandhofweg 8, t 46849 (*luxury–expensive*). A beautiful castle hotel set in extensive parkland on the edge of the city. While it has all the amenities you would expect of a luxury hotel, it's family-run and charmingly intimate. All kinds of outdoor activities, from tennis to horse-riding, can be arranged.

★★★★**Hotel Palais Porcia**, Neuer Platz 13, Pörtschach, **t** 511590, *www.hotel-palais-porcia.at* (*expensive–moderate*).
A splendid hotel in a magnificently refurbished townhouse, this is filled with antiques and *objets d'art* from the 18th and 19th centuries. It's located to the west of Klagenfurt, in the most stylish resort on the Wörther See.

★★★**Schlosshotel Wörthersee**, Villacher Strasse 338, **t** 211580, *www.schloss-hotel.at* (*expensive–moderate*). A classic in the area, this is an atmospheric hotel in a 19th-century fake castle, which is right on the shores of the Wörther See. It has definitely seen better days, but still manages to exude a creaky charm. Unfortunately, nearby road and rail lines can make it noisy.

★★★★**Fuchs Palast**, Prof. Ernst Fuchs Platz 1, St Veit an der Glan 1, **t** (04212) 46600, *www.rogner.com* (*moderate*). This extraordinary multicoloured hotel is located 25km from Klagenfurt in the charming historic town of St Veit (*see* pp.189–90). It was designed by the artist Ernst Fuchs, and is covered with dazzling stained glass, rainbow-coloured pillars and huge murals. It boasts individually decorated rooms based, rather oddly, on astrological signs, and the amenities include indoor and outdoor pools.

★★★★**Goldener Brunnen**, Am Domplatz, Karfreitstrasse 14, **t** 57380, *www.goldener-brunnen.at* (*moderate*). This is a friendly hotel in the city centre, with bright modern rooms set around a handsome courtyard. It has a good beauty centre, and the eager-to-please staff are happy to offer advice on what to see and do.

★★★**Hotel Garni Blumenstökl**, 10 Oktober Strasse 11, **t** 57793 (*moderate*). Perhaps the best city-centre address, this is a modest but welcoming family-run hotel in a 16th-century building set around a lovely courtyard. Rooms have been thoroughly modernized and are very comfortable. Book early as it's popular with returning guests.

★★★**Hotel Geyer**, Priesterhausgasse 5, **t** 57886 (*moderate–inexpensive*). A simple little hotel in a good central location, with a pretty, flower-filled patio in summer and plain but comfortable rooms. The nicest are set in the wood-panelled attic.

★★★**Gasthof Jerolitsch**, Jerolitschstrasse 43–44, Krumpendorf-Klagenfurt, **t** (04229) 2379, *www.jerolitsch.at* (*inexpensive*). A delightful, traditional guest house with a pool and its own stretch of private beach on the Wörther See. It's very family-friendly, and it's also popular with walkers who enjoy the proximity of Kreuzbergl.

★★★**Pension Waldwirt**, Josefiwaldweg 2, **t** 42642, *www.waldwirt.at.tf/* (*inexpensive*). A cheerful little inn on the outskirts of the city, this has a wonderful traditional restaurant and tastefully furnished simple rooms. It's also well located, next to the lovely wooded slopes of Kreuzbergl.

★★**City Hotel zum Domplatz**, Karfreitstrasse 20, **t** 54320, *www.cityhotel-klagenfurt.at* (*inexpensive*). A modest hotel with smallish, functional rooms (with en-suite facilities), but its central location and little extras like free Internet access make it a good bargain.

Camping
The region around Klagenfurt is popular for camping, and there are scores of campsites all around the lake. The most accessible from Klagenfurt is **Camping Strandbad**, **t** 21169, which is next to the municipal beach.

Eating Out

Klagenfurt **t** (0463) –
Klagenfurt, situated extremely close to the Italian border, boasts a wealth of Italian restaurants, of which Dolce Vita is the best.

151, Höhenweg 151, Viktring, **t** 281653 (*expensive–moderate*). This fashionable bistro is a few kilometres from the city centre, but is always packed with well-heeled locals. Located in a 350-year-old building, it serves good Austrian and international fare in a rather chichi, affluent ambience.

Savoir Vivre, Theaterplatz 1, **t** 0699 12051846 (*moderate*). If you want to have a break from Austrian cuisine, try this charming French bistro, popular with a buzzy local crowd. *Closed Sun and Mon.*

Felsenkeller, Feldkirchner Strasse 141, t 420130 (*moderate*). There are wonderful views of the lakes from the windows of this handsome old restaurant about 2km out of the city centre. Sophisticated versions of traditional Austrian recipes are featured on the menu.

Maria Loretto, Lorettoweg 54, t 24465 (*moderate*). Considered an institution, this long-established seafood restaurant boasts lovely lake views to go with its elegantly prepared fish dishes.

Dolce Vita, Heuplatz 2, t 55499 (*moderate–inexpensive*). This is not only the best Italian in town, but easily the best restaurant in town, where you can dine on superb, creative Mediterranean cuisine prepared with exquisitely fresh ingredients. In summer, there's a pretty little terrace, scented with pots of herbs.

Gasthof im Landhaushof, Landhaushof 1, t 502363 (*moderate–inexpensive*). You can dine out in the beautiful courtyard of the Landhaushof on traditional, well-prepared local specialities. There's a good-value lunch menu and the desserts are definitely worth saving room for (try the chocolate terrine).

Dermuth, Kohldorfer Strasse 52, t 21247 (*moderate–inexpensive*). An old-fashioned, sprawling tavern with several dining areas close to the forested slopes of Kreuzbergl. Tasty Austrian specialities washed down with good local wines are on offer.

Poterne, Kardinalschütt 6, t 502341 (*moderate–inexpensive*). This popular, cellar-like restaurant features a fantastic selection of wines, and serves elegant international and Austrian cuisine.

Zum Augustin, Pfarrhofgasse 2, t 513992 (*inexpensive*). A cosy *bierhaus*, where you can pull up a wooden bench and tuck into hefty portions of solid local dishes, washed down with a refreshing glass or two of beer.

Cafés and Coffee Houses

Klagenfurt t (0463) –

Café Melange, Alter Platz 7, t 56360. An institution on the Alter Platz, this has divine chocolates and cakes, which you can either take away or eat on the spot.

Café Domgassner, Domgasse 12, t 57882. This handsome, vaulted cellar bar is a good place for excellent coffee, cakes and snacks by day, and stylish cocktails and drinks at night.

Café Walter, Neuer Platz 10, t 7039394. Another classic bakery and café with a summer terrace out on the square.

Entertainment and Nightlife

Klagenfurt t (0463) –

Music, Theatre, Opera and Ballet

Stadttheater, Theaterplatz 4, t 55266, *www.stadttheater-klagenfurt.at*. This splendid Jugendstil theatre is the city's main venue for drama, classical music and opera performances.

Bars and Clubs

Most of Klagenfurt's nightlife is centred around the **Pfarrplatz**, where you will eventually find countless bars and discos, but you may have to seek them out in the little courtyards.

Café-Bar Spektakel, Pfarrplatz 17, t 04 268 3764. A cocktail bar and café serving snacks until 4am. Good music and a young, up-for-it crowd who strut around on the terrace in summer.

Scotch, Pfarrplatz 20, t 540972. This disco-bar is a classic on the Pfarrplatz bar scene: it warms up as the night wears on.

Jazzkeller Kamot, Bahnhofstrasse 9, t 56694, *www.kamot.at*. This is Klagenfurt's classic jazz venue, an atmospheric cellar with excellent live gigs, and a basic menu of hot baguettes, pizzas and the like.

Krügerl, Kardinalplatz 3, t 0650 502 5686. A trendy DJ-bar with summer terrace which is popular with a young, lively crowd.

Café Cardinal, Kardinalplatz 8, t 514797. This café is a mellower option on the Kardinalplatz, with a terrace out on the square in summer.

settlement at Virunum, before being chased out by Teutonic tribes in the 5th century AD. The area was passed from Slovenians to Bavarians before becoming an independent Duchy in 976, but the Slav influence still lingers, particularly in the southeast of the province. By the early 12th century, the region was ruled by the Spanheimers, who founded the medieval city of Klagenfurt, but it was only really put on the map after Emperor Maximilian I ordered its redevelopment as a provincial capital in 1518. Unfortunately, he didn't have the money to pay for it, and was forced to grant the city to the local Estates who ruled right up until 1848.

Much of the medieval heart of the city was destroyed by fire, but many of its crooked lanes and leaning townhouses still survive. The elegant new extension, designed by Italian Domenico dell'Aglio, was laid out according to a neat grid plan and centred on a flamboyant main square. The Renaissance mansions and palaces retain their decidedly Italian flavour, with ornate frills and flounces and charming inner courtyards full of flowers. The Turks repeatedly invaded the area during the 16th and 17th centuries, but were finally defeated in 1683.

The city flourished during the 18th century, after Graf von Self, Archbishop of Gurk, decided to move the archiepiscopal court to Klagenfurt, triggering another spate of building fever as religious orders rushed to establish convents and churches in the increasingly influential little capital. The good times came to an end with the arrival of Napoleon, who razed the city's defences before passing on.

After a brief revival of its fortunes in the 19th century, thanks to the arrival of the railways, the city was devastated by the two World Wars. Carinthia lost a swath of its land to Italy, and the region bordering on Slovenia was only retained after a plebiscite in 1920. The tourist industry, which had begun in the early 1800s, began to revive, as travellers once more came to idle by the lakeside, take the waters at a mountain spa, or simply enjoy the breathtaking scenery.

Klagenfurt remains a sleepy provincial town, where the pace of life is enjoyably slow. The alluring little courtyards are filled with boutiques and cafés, tables spill out Italian-style on to handsome squares and you'll find restaurants and bars to suit all tastes and pockets. The city's greatest asset, however, remains its proximity to the extraordinary lakes and mountains of Carinthia.

The Old City (Altstadt)

Alter Platz, and the web of crooked streets which spider off it, is now a delightful pedestrianized shopping area, but it was the core of the medieval city before its 16th-century expansion. It's crammed with ancient mansions, including the **Haus Zur Goldenen Gans**, at No.31, probably the oldest building in the city, which was sturdily built to brace the earthquakes which once shook the region. The **old town hall** (Alte Rathaus) stands at the corner with Wienergasse, an elegant palace built around 1600 and boasting a primrose-yellow triple-decker courtyard with a lacy white trim.

Further west loom the twin towers of the late 16th-century **Landhaus**, which remains the seat of the Carinthian provincial government. A graceful flight of stairs in the inner courtyard leads to the eye-popping Baroque **Great Heraldic Hall** (Grosser

Wappensaal; *open April–Oct daily 9–5; adm, combined adm with Provincial Museum available*), which is thickly covered with the coats of arms of local notables from the 17th to the 19th centuries and overlooked by Josef-Ferdinand Fermiller's dazzling *trompe l'œil* fresco depicting the Estates of Carinthia paying homage to Emperor Karl IV. Exploring the tiny passages and arcades which lead off Alter Platz and adjoining Herrengasse is one of the city's greatest charms: Klagenfurt is too small to get lost in, but it's worth chucking your map away and seeing if you can manage it all the same.

Just north of Herrengasse, **Pfarrplatz** was the site of the medieval cemetery, cleared in 1776. Tombstones belonging to the most important families were incorporated into the outer walls of the pretty church of **St Egyd**, built as a replacement for an earlier basilica destroyed during an earthquake in 1680, which contains more frescoes by local artist Fermiller.

From Alter Platz, head down **Wienergasse** (which becomes **Kramergasse**), Klagenfurt's oldest street, lined with more charming Renaissance courtyards and blooming with pretty Jugendstil façades, to **Neuer Platz**. This became the new administrative heart of the city in the early 16th century, when Klagenfurt was expanded under the orders of Emperor Maximilian I to serve as a provincial capital. At the centre of the square (surrounded by whizzing kids on skateboards) is the celebrated 16th-century statue of the **Lindwurm Dragon** (*see* box below), which describes the ancient founding myth of the city and remains its best-loved symbol. Elegant palaces and mansions still fringe the square, many with handsome arcaded courtyards spilling over with flowers. Grandest of all is the impressive Rosenburg Palace, built in 1650, and now the **town hall** (Rathaus).

Burggasse extends majestically east of the Neuer Platz, with another string of beautiful mansions set around delightful courtyards. At No.8, the **Provincial Gallery** (Landesgalerie) hosts temporary art exhibitions showcasing Carinthian artists (ask at the tourist office for a programme). In nearby **Kardinalplatz**, you can still see vestiges

The Lindwurm Dragon

The huge sculpture of the Lindwurm Dragon at the centre of the Neuer Platz recalls the founding legend of Klagenfurt. Back when the Duke of Karast ruled the land, a dark swamp spread from the shores of the Wörther See to the surrounding foothills. Eerie sounds emanated from the murk, and locals kept to the hills in fear. But when cattle and even people began to go missing the duke promised rich rewards to anyone who could kill the monster lurking in the swamp. At first, everyone refused to take up the challenge, but finally a group of labourers came up with a plan to outwit the beast. They tethered a plump bull close to the swamp and attached a hidden barb to its chain: when the hideous, scaly creature emerged from the swamp, it opened its jaws to swallow the bull, only to find itself impaled on the barb. The labourers leapt on the monster and bludgeoned it to death with their iron-studded clubs. The duke gave them the land as promised, and the village of Klagenfurt grew up on the spot where the legendary battle had taken place.

of the medieval fortifications which once surrounded the city. Further south, the 16th-century **cathedral** (Domkirche; *open daily 9–6*) was given a frilly Baroque facelift by the Jesuits, and has a small and uninspiring museum of religious art around the corner in the **Diocesan Museum** (Diözesanmuseum).

The **Provincial Museum** (Landesmuseum; *Museumsgasse 2, www.landesmuseum-ktn.at; open Tues–Sat 9–4, Sun 9–1; adm*) is the city's best museum; it offers an absorbing overview of Carinthia's history, from prehistoric pot shards and Roman mosaics (including a particularly fine one of Dionysos living it up with his pals), to the bizarre 'dragon's skull' discovered in the 14th century (really from an Ice Age rhinoceros) which served as a model for the Lindwurm Dragon. Look out for some remarkable Gothic religious art, including the sublime 15th-century altarpiece of St Veit, and a richly carved bride's chest with intricate reliefs.

Europapark

The blissfully green **Europapark** extends west of the city centre to the shores of Wörther See (*buses 10, 11 and 12 regularly make the journey from the city centre to the lakeside*). Besides the gardens and leafy paths, Europapark's main attraction is **Minimundus** (*www.minimundus.at; open daily Easter–end-April 9–5; May, June and Sept 9–6; July and Aug 9–9; adm*). You can see more than 150 scale models of the world's most emblematic buildings, from the Taj Mahal to the Vatican – along with some less obvious choices, such as the Lady Isabella waterwheel on the Isle of Man – laid out in neatly landscaped gardens. Entrance tickets also include admission to the **Planetarium**. Just beyond Minimundus is the **Reptile Zoo** (Reptilienzoo; *open daily summer 8–6; winter 9–5; closed Nov; adm*) with crocodiles and piranhas (see them being fed every Saturday at 3pm), spiders, all kinds of creepy-crawlies, tortoises and lizards. The zoo also functions as a breeding centre for Austrian snakes and other reptiles that have been threatened by increasing urbanization. Once you've seen the sights, head for the delightfully old-fashioned **city beach** (Strandbad), where you can hire a striped deckchair and soak up the sun.

Day Trips and Overnighters from Klagenfurt

Klagenfurt extends westwards to the shores of the Wörther See, Carinthia's largest and most popular lake. Beyond it lies the charming provincial town of Villach and the tranquil lake of Ossiacher See. To the north of Klagenfurt, you can journey back in time through Roman ruins, historic towns, castles and cathedrals.

The following day and overnight trips can be linked: you can add in Maria Saal and the Magdalenburg ruins to the route through historic Carinthia to make it a three-day trip, or continue west of the Wörther See to visit Villach and the Ossiacher See.

Around the Wörther See

The Wörther See, and in particular the chichi lakeside resorts of Velden and Pörtschach, has long been the preferred summer retreat for well-heeled Carinthians –

Getting There

There are two **bus** routes (with frequent summer departures, less frequent in winter and on Sundays) from Klagenfurt to Velden, which go via the resorts on the northern or southern shore. The northern-shore resorts are also served by regular **trains** from Klagenfurt Hauptbahnhof. You can hire **bikes** in the train stations and at the myriad bike-rental outlets in all the resorts.

Perhaps the most picturesque way to see the lake is to take the summer **steamer**, which plies between all the resorts: the journey from Klagenfurt to Velden takes around one-and-three-quarter hours, and costs approx €10 for a single ticket. More information is available from *www.stw.at/inhalt/schifffahrt.htm* (German only).

Tourist Information

Pörtschach: Hauptstrasse 153, **t** (04272) 2354, *www.poertschach.at*.
Velden: Villacher Strasse 19, **t** (04274) 21030, *www.velden.at*.

Eating Out

Restaurants around the Wörther See tend to be overpriced and unexceptional. The lakefront, at least along the northern shore, is crammed with restaurants, although there's little to choose between them. The best bet is to take a picnic to enjoy on the beach.

Rainer's Restaurant, Monte-Carlo-Platz 1, Pörtschach, **t** (04272) 3046 (*moderate*). An institution in Pörtschach, this is a stylish restaurant and bar where you can either dine on excellent creative international cuisine or hang out with the moneyed crowd in the bar.

Birdie, Oberndorf 70, Velden, **t** (04274) 7250 (*expensive–moderate*). After a morning out on the links, this elegant restaurant overlooking the magnificent golf course is just the place to recover.

Alte Post, Europaplatz 4, Velden, **t** (04274) 2141 (*moderate–inexpensive*). Slap bang in the heart of town, this is a good, traditional guest house serving hearty Austrian staples. There's a terrace for alfresco dining in summer.

---

with prices to match. It's hardly surprising: this is truly an idyllic spot, with the thrilling blue lake glittering against a magnificent backdrop of hazy peaks. Thermal currents ensure the temperature of the lake remains balmy all through the summer; in winter it's an entirely different story, but watching the skaters glide across the frozen lake is an equally picturesque sight. The north side of the lake, which claims to receive the most sunshine and has the best transport links, is the busiest: your first encounter is with is the lively resort of **Krumpendorf** (8km west), which has been virtually swallowed up by Klagenfurt. Krumpendorf, like all the lakeside villages, has plenty of watersports facilities, together with good beaches. Prettier and altogether more upmarket, the town of **Pörtschach**, 6km further to the west, is strung out behind a miniature peninsula, with languid bays curving off on either side of it. **Velden**, which is perfectly poised at the western end of the lake, is its largest resort – an affluent, bustling town that attracts hordes of summer visitors, who blow their holiday money at the enormous casino and dawdle on the lakefront promenade.

Returning to Klagenfurt along the southern shores of the Wörther See, the pretty little town of **Maria Wörth** is dominated by a pair of fine Gothic churches. The **Pyramidenkogel**, 7km south of Maria Wörth, is a popular tourist attraction, despite being an ugly modern tower, but its lofty hill-top location affords stunning views over the mountains and lakes. A couple of kilometres east, **Reifnitz** is another small and relatively quiet resort, popular with families.

Villach and the Ossiacher See

Villach, curled into a curve of the Drau river, is a handsome and historic town which still preserves its medieval character largely intact. At the centre of the pedestrianized old centre is the **Rathausplatz**, dominated by the 14th-century church of St Jakob and a bell tower you can climb for panoramic views. The **City Museum** (Stadtmuseum) offers an overview of the city's history, with a collection spanning everything from prehistoric artefacts to Gothic altarpieces, and the **Schillerpark**, on Peraustrasse, contains an enormous relief map of Carinthia which covers 187 square metres.

But maps and museums are not what Villach is really all about: this is a languid spa town, where you can take the (mildly radioactive) waters at **Warmbad Villach**, 3km south of the city centre, linger in the town's pretty squares and arcades or stroll along the tree-lined river bank. The town is caught between two lakes: little Faaker See 10km to the south and Ossiacher See 8km to the north. **Faaker See** has a cluster of charming little villages, which come to life on summer weekends when most of Villach abandons the town for the beach. **Ossiacher See** is considerably larger, but remains a tranquil, peaceful spot, popular with families and walkers. **Annenheim** is

Getting There

Villach is easily reached by **train** from Klagenfurt and Velden, with departures roughly every 30mins. Express trains take around 25mins, while local services take 40mins. There are frequent **bus** departures (roughly every hour), and journey times are around 40mins. Most resorts around the Ossiacher See can be reached by **boat** during the summer, or on the Villach-St Veit an der Glan rail line.

Tourist Information

Villach: Rathausplatz 1, t (04242) 2051888, *www.villach.at*. There are free guided tours of the old city every Friday at 10am between May and Oct. The useful city website has full accommodation listings.

Where to Stay and Eat

Hotel Post, Hauptplatz 26, Villach, t (04242) 26101, *www.romantik-hotel.com*. If you choose to stay in Villach, why not do it in style at this opulent 400-year-old hotel (*expensive*). Soak up some of its charm in the award-winning restaurant with a pretty summer patio, or have coffee and cakes at the traditional café.

Kaufmann & Kaufmann, Dietrichstein-gasse 5, Villach, t (04242) 25871 (*expensive–moderate*). An excellent place to push the boat out: this enchanting cellar restaurant serves sophisticated international cuisine accompanied by the finest wines, but remains resolutely unstuffy and very welcoming. In summer, you can sit out in the elegant courtyard.

Bernold, Nikolaiplatz 2, Villach, t (04242) 25442 (*inexpensive*). The best coffee and cakes in town are served in this traditional café, with an outdoor terrace in summer.

Wirt in Judendorf, Judendorfer Strasse, Judendorf, t (04242) 56525 (*inexpensive*). An old-fashioned rural *Gasthof*, in a small village on the outskirts of Villach, with local specialities served in a shady courtyard.

Urbani Wirt, Bundesstrasse 50, Bodensdorf, t (04243) 228664 (*moderate–inexpensive*). A delightful, family-run restaurant that has been going for many years and serves a good mixture of wonderfully fresh Austrian and Italian favourites. The staff are utterly charming.

Stifftsschmiede, Ossiach, t (04243) 45554, (*moderate*). For a romantic dinner, the Stifftsschmiede can't be beaten: the flower-filled gardens right on the shores of the lake and charming service make it a memorable spot. The emphasis is on seafood, usually simply prepared but deliciously fresh.

the starting point for the Kanzelbahn cable car, which connects with a chairlift to the top of **Gerlitzen**, where excellent hiking paths begin. It's a startlingly beautiful journey, with the lake dropping away as the peaks loom ever closer, which can also be made on the panoramic toll road beginning from **Bodensdorf**. **Ossiach**, dominated by an ancient abbey, is the largest of the lakeside resorts, another low-key and charming spot where it's all too easy to linger.

North of Klagenfurt: Ruins and Churches

On a hilltop 9km north of Klagenfurt, the dreamy spires of the pilgrimage church of **Maria Saal** (Domplatz; *open daily 8–4.30*) are visible for miles around. The village was ostensibly founded by St Modestus in the 8th century, and has remained a pilgrimage centre more or less ever since.

The present church dates from the 15th century when it was sturdily fortified to withstand attacks from the Turks. Inside, it contains a wealth of remarkable Gothic art, including delirious frescoes depicting the genealogy of Christ, and a pair of exquisite winged altarpieces. Over the main altar, an 18th-century statue of the Madonna remains an object of devotion, along with the tiny tomb of St Modestus. Stone reliefs and tombstones from the ancient Roman trading centre at nearby Virunum have been incorporated into the outer walls, including an odd one known as the Roman Mail Wagon – in fact, a depiction of the journey into the afterlife. Maria Saal's other attraction is the **Carinthian Open-Air Museum** (Kärntner Freilichtmuseum; *open May–mid-Oct Tues–Sun 10–6; adm*), with a collection of traditional Carinthian farms and rural buildings in extensive grounds.

Six kilometres northeast of Klagenfurt (a tiny road wiggles up from Maria Saal, past the villages of Arndof and Ottomanach), the remnants of **Magdalensburg**, the oldest Roman settlement north of the Alps, were discovered by a local farmer on a lofty peak in the 19th century. The stiff climb is rewarded with fine views in all directions of the surrounding valleys, and you can explore the Magdalensburg excavations (Ausgrabungen; *open May–mid-Oct daily 9–7; adm*), which spill in terraces down the

Getting There

Maria Saal is on the **bus** and **rail** routes from Klagenfurt north to St Veit an der Glan. There are frequent departures in both directions.

To get to Magdalensburg, it's easiest to have your own transport, but you can take one of the twice-daily **bus** services from Klagenfurt to St Veit which will drop you off close to the Roman ruins (a stiff 10min walk uphill). Be sure to check return bus times in advance.

Tourist Information

Maria Saal: Am Platzl 7, **t** (04223) 221425, *www.maria.saal.at*.

Eating Out

Maria Saal t (04223) –

Kollerwirt, Affelsdorf 3, Maria Saal, **t** 2455 (*moderate*). An atmospheric 300-year-old country house makes a fine setting for this rustic restaurant, which serves delicious regional dishes prepared with local produce. *Dinner only on weekdays. Closed Tues; also Wed in winter.*

Sever Maria Saal, Hauptplatz 3, Maria Saal, **t** 2295 (*inexpensive*). The best of several *Gasthofen* that are clustered together on the main square in Maria Saal, serving up enormous portions of excellent local Carinthian fare.

hillside. There's also a small museum where the star attraction is a copy of the *Magdalensburg Youth* (the original is in the Fine Arts Museum in Vienna – *see* p.133).

Historic Carinthia

Sleepy **St Veit an der Glan**, 25km north of Klagenfurt, never recovered its prestige once the Dukes of Carinthia decided to make Klagenfurt their new home in the early 16th century. The charming, pedestrianized old centre, huddled around the flower-filled Hauptplatz, is filled with worn testaments to its former importance, including the splendid town hall (Rathaus), a fine Gothic building with a fanciful Baroque façade. It has a wealth of traditional inns where you can linger over a long lunch.

Getting There

St Veit, Hochosterwitz and Freisach are on the main **rail** line between Klagenfurt and Vienna, with frequent departures from the Hauptbahnhof. They are all equally served by regional **buses**. Gurk and Hüttenburg, however, are served by infrequent buses (only three a day): it's wise to check bus times in advance to avoid getting stranded.

Tourist Information

St Veit an der Glan: Rathaus, Hauptplatz 1, **t** (04212) 555513. *Open summer only.*
Freisach: Hautplatz 1, **t** (04268) 4300.

Where to Stay

★★★★Fuchs Palast, Prof. Ernst Fuchs Platz 1, St Veit an der Glan 1, **t** (04212) 46600, *www.rogner.com (moderate)*. Extraordinary multicoloured hotel designed by the artist Ernst Fuchs, covered with dazzling stained glass, rainbow-coloured pillars and huge murals. Individually decorated rooms are based on astrological signs, and the amenities include indoor and outdoor pools.

Metnitzaler Hof, Hauptplatz 11, Friesach, **t** (04268) 25100 *(moderate–inexpensive)*. A 16th-century townhouse in a prime location with oodles of old-world charm, a 13th-century beer cellar and a good restaurant *(moderate)* with plenty of outdoor seating on the square.

Friesacherhof, Hauptplatz 4, Friesach, **t** (04268) 2123 *(inexpensive)*. The next best option, this is a modest, pink-painted hotel with functional rooms which are a little on the dark side. There's a good, traditional restaurant *(moderate)* and it has a perfect location on the main square.

Gasthof Kronenwirt, Gurk, **t** (04266) 8237 *(inexpensive)*. A pristine, family-run *Gasthof* right by the cathedral with bright bedrooms and a decent restaurant.

Eating Out

Pukelsheim, Erlgasse 11, St Veit an der Glan, **t** (04212) 2473 *(moderate)*. An appealing little guest house tucked down a side street, worth seeking out for its cosy restaurant. Everything is made with the freshest local ingredients – some of which are even grown in their own small kitchen garden.

La Torre, Grabenstrasse 39, St Veit an der Glan, **t** (04212) 39250 *(moderate)*. A fortified 16th-century watchtower makes an unusual setting for this elegant restaurant, where you can tuck into delicious Italian and Mediterranean specialities.

Bachler, Silberegger Strasse 1, Althofen, **t** (04262) 3835 *(expensive–moderate)*. A handsome, traditional inn surrounded by gardens in this little village about 10km south of Friesach and just off the B317, with an elegant dining area serving sumptuous local dishes and fine wines.

Craigher, Hauptplatz 3, Friesach, **t** (04268) 2295 *(inexpensive)*. You'll be dazzled by the selection at this classic *Konditorei* and café on the main square. Try Dieter Craigher's own creation, the Friesacher Pfennig, a heavenly chocolatey treat. The exquisitely wrapped chocolates make beautiful gifts.

The fairytale castle of **Hochosterwitz** (*www.burg-hochosterwitz.or.at; open daily April and Oct 9–5; May–Sept 8–6; adm*) is clamped spectacularly to a wooded crag 14km east of St Veit an der Glan and just south of the tiny village of Launsdorf. The original medieval castle was expanded and heavily fortified against the Turks in the late 16th century by Baron Khevenhüller, who added the bristling towers and no fewer than 14 gates. There are regular guided tours of the virtually unchanged interior, with its massive halls and armoury.

Friesach, 26km north of St Veit, is the oldest town in Carinthia, first mentioned in 9th-century annals. Ringed with hills that are bristling with medieval towers and fortifications, it's also the only town in Austria which is still surrounded by a moat. It's a seductive, tranquil spot, with a time-capsule medieval centre curled around the lovely Hauptplatz, and the perfect place to find a bed for the night.

Spend the morning exploring the old quarter of Friesach, or perhaps climbing up to the surrounding fortifications for breathtaking views. After lunch, return south along the B317 where a small road branches off for Strassburg and Gurk. **Strassburg** merits a brief stop for the handsome, cliff-top Renaissance castle which dominates the tiny town, but **Gurk** is the location of the finest Romanesque cathedral in Austria. A convent was established here in 1043 by a pious local aristocrat, St Gemma of Gurk, who founded several religious communities throughout Carinthia and whose tomb inside the cathedral's crypt remains an object of veneration. The original convent church was replaced by this cathedral, built between 1140 and 1220 after the area was raised to the status of a bishopric, but it languished forgotten and neglected once the episcopal court moved to Klagenfurt in the 18th century. Despite – or perhaps because of – the years of neglect, it remains an extraordinary sight: the onion domes are a Baroque addition, but the square towers, beautifully sculpted in creamy stone, and mesmerizing medieval frescoes which adorn the porches and vaulted interior have barely changed in centuries. From Gurk, return via St Veit an der Glan to Klagenfurt along the B317.

Touring from Klagenfurt

The magnificent peaks of the **Hohe Tauern National Park** and the lakeside resort of **Zell am See** (*see* 'Touring from Salzburg', p.161) are also accessible from Klagenfurt. From Villach, the A10 *autobahn* (which becomes the B106) shoots up to Obervellach, where you should follow the signs for Mallnitz and the rail-shuttle which ferries cars beneath the mountain to Bad Gastein. The journey from Klagenfurt to Bad Gastein normally takes around 1½–2 hours.

An even more spectacular route connects with the famous **Grossglockner High Alpine Road** (Grossglockner Hochalpenstrasse; *open May–Nov; toll*): take the E66 towards Lienz, and follow signs for Winklern and Heiligenblut (*see* p.162). The journey from Klagenfurt to Heiligenblut takes around two hours.

Hungary:
Travel, Practical A–Z
and Language

11

Travel

Entry Formalities

Passports and Visas

Hungary joined the EU in 2004. UK citizens need a passport valid for at least 6 months; visas are not required for UK citizens staying less than 6 months. US, Canadian and Irish citizens need a passport valid for at least 6 months; visas are not required for US, Canadian or Irish citizens staying less than 90 days. All visitors staying more than 30 days must register with the police or local government office within 48hrs of arrival.

Customs

Those arriving from another EU country do not have to declare goods imported into Austria, Hungary or the Czech Republic for personal use if they have paid duty on them in the country of origin. In theory, you can buy as much as you like, provided you can prove the purchase is for your own use. In practice, Customs will be more likely to ask questions if you buy in bulk. Travellers from the USA are allowed to take home, duty-free, goods to the value of $800, including 250 cigarettes or 50 cigars, plus one litre of alcohol.

Getting Around

By Boat

From April to September, the Hungarian shipping company Mahart PassNave runs a daily hydrofoil service up the Danube from Budapest to Vienna via Bratislava

By Car

Apart from the Hungarian tendency to overtake at absurd dangerous moments and the poor state of some minor roads, driving in Hungary is fine.

The **speed limits** are as follows: 50kph in built-up areas, 80kph on open roads, 100kph on main roads and 120kmph on motorways. They are strictly enforced, with high fines. You must have your **headlights** on even by day outside of towns. Using a mobile phone while driving is illegal, and the **ban on alcohol is 100 per cent**, with very high on-the-spot

fines. Seat belts are compulsory for driver and passengers. If you have an **accident**, you must report the news to the police. If you've moved your car a centimetre, or if you test positive for alcohol, it is curtains for your insurance claim. Third party **insurance** is compulsory and you'll probably need a **Green Card** if you are planning to take your own car.

Unleaded **petrol** is *ólommentes*, diesel is *gázolaj*. You must buy a motorway pass if you plan to use the motorways, available from petrol stations and post offices.

To **hire a car** you must be at least 21, ideally 25, and have held a licence for one year. All take major credit cards. *See* 'Budapest', p.200.

By Coach and Bus

Buses will take you where trains do not, though they cost slightly more. Buses are often the quickest way to travel between towns, and while fares are higher than on the trains they're still good value. Schedules are clearly displayed in bus stations (*autóbuszállomás* or *autóbusz pályaudvar*) in every town. Arrive early to confirm the departure bay (*kocsiállás*) and to be sure of getting a seat.

In towns and cities, transport is generally good. Buses (*busz*, pronounced 'boose' as in 'loose', not 'bus', which means 'f***' in Hungarian), trolleybuses (*trolibusz*) and trams (*villamos*) running from about 6 in the morning until around 10.30 or 11pm. Tickets are sold at tobacconists and street stands, and should be validated on board. In Budapest, there are many ticket options, whilst in some of the larger towns, it's possible to buy day passes for use on trams and buses.

By Train

Hungarian State Railways (MÁV; *www.mav. hu*) run reliable and comfortable trains, and fares are reasonable, though InterCity Express (ICE) and InterCity Rapid (ICR) trains levy a supplement. Faster trains often require a seat reservation.

Budapest is the hub of the network, and most international trains use Keleti station (District VIII); there is also Nyugati station in District VI and Déli station in District I).

For 24hr **information**, call t 461 5500 for international trains, and t 461 5400 for national services.

Practical A–Z
Crime and the Police

Police: **t** 107 or **t** 112, **tourist police** (Budapest):
V. Vigadó u. 6, **t** 438 8080

Most of the crime in Budapest is organized crime. It is generally safe to walk at night, but use common sense in outlying districts, especially District VIII. Beware pickpockets in the tourist areas, especially around crowds and on public transport.

Beware tricksters. Never change money on the streets. A common ploy is for a girl to pick up a foreign male and take him to buy her drinks. The bill is extortionate, and the man pressurized to pay. The same tactic is used in red-light venues. If anyone claiming to be the police asks to see money or a credit card, it is a scam. Demand to be taken to the police station and watch them run.

Call the police or contact the **Complaints Office**, Budapest Municipal Police HQ BRFK: XIII, Teve u. 6.

Disabled Travellers

Budapest is not geared up for disabled travellers. Wheelchair access is limited. Most sights and museums are housed in 19th-century buildings with copious steps, and most major roads can only be crossed by subway. Apart from the M1 metro line and the Airport Minibus, transport is also equally unadapted for wheelchairs.

For more information contact the **Hungarian Disabled Association**, San Marco utca 76, **t/f** 388 2388.

Electricity

The Hungarian electricity supply is 220 volts and the plugs are of the standard Continental type with two round pins. Bring an adaptor.

Embassies and Consulates

Hungarian Embassies and Consulates Abroad

UK: 35 Eaton Pl, London SW1X 8BY, **t** (020) 7235 2664, *www.huemblon.org.uk.*

USA: 3910 Shoemaker St, NW, Washington DC 20008, **t** (202) 362 6730, *www. huembwas.org.*

Canada: 299 Waverley Street, Ottawa, Ontario, K2P 0V9, **t** (613) 230 2717, **f** (613) 230 7560, *www.docuweb.ca/Hungary.*

Foreign Embassies in Budapest

Australia: XII. Királyhágó tér 8–9, **t** 457 9777, *www.australia.hu. Open Mon–Fri 9–12.*

Canada: XII. Budakeszi út 32, **t** 392 3360, **f** 392 3390. *Open Mon–Thurs 8.30–10.30 and 2–3.30.*

Ireland: V. Szabadság tér 7/9, **t** 302 9600. *Open Mon–Fri 9.30–12.30 and 2.30–4.*

New Zealand: VI. Teréz krt. 38, gr. floor 16, **t** 428 2208. *Open Mon–Fri 11–4.*

UK: V. Harmincad u. 6, **t** 266 2888, **f** 266 0907. *Open Mon–Fri 9.30–12.30 and 2.30–4.30.*

USA: V. Szabadság tér 12, **t** 475 4400, **f** 475 4764. *Open Mon–Fri 8.15–5.*

Festivals and Events

Hungary has a huge number of local festivals – ask at tourist offices for details. Wine festivals are hugely enjoyable element of the festival scene, with each wine-producing centre celebrating at some time during the year (usually May–October). In addition, the following two are marked countrywide:

March: Wreaths are laid at monuments around the country to commemorate the revolution against the Habsburgs (15th).

August: St Stephen's Day (20th). All day celebrations honouring the death of Hungary's patron saint and "founding father". The biggest jamboree of all is in Budapest with craft fairs, folk dancing and a huge fireworks display in the evening.

Health and Insurance

Ambulance: **t** 104, **fire**: **t** 105

No vaccinations are required to enter Hungary. Medicines can be obtained with prescriptions written abroad, and most common over-the-counter drugs are available. Foreign citizens are entitled to first-aid and emergency ambulance treatment free of charge if injured. EU citizens are now entitled to free treatment with a stamped E111 (available from post offices, and to be replaced by a card in December 2005), but travel insurance is still recommended.

Internet

Finding a terminal in Budapest is unlikely to be a problem, though facilities are much more scarce outside the capital – expect to pay around 500Ft/hr.

Money

Hungarian currency is the **forint** (Ft in this book, sometimes HUF elsewhere). Coins come in 1, 2, 5, 10, 20, 50 and 100Ft; notes in 200, 500, 1,000, 2,000, 5,000, 10,000 and 20,000Ft. Hungary is set to switch to the euro in 2009.

The best way to access money is using the numerous **ATMs**. Major **credit cards** are also accepted just about everywhere. Rates for exchanging cash vary wildly, the worst from hotels and tourist spots, the best from banks and some exchange offices. In the latter, always check the rate and commission that apply to you. **Traveller's cheques** are hard to change, and the rates are poor. The AEB Bank is best (there's one at Astoria). The Magyar Külkereskedelmi Bank, V. Szent István tér 11, transfers money from abroad.

There's a **24-hour exchange service** at V. Apáczai Csere János u. 1. Leftover forints can be exchanged up to 20,000Ft, more with an exchange receipt.

The rate of exchange at the time of writing was approximately £1 = 357Ft, €1 = 247Ft, $1 = 190Ft.

National Holidays

1 Jan New Year's Day
15 Mar Revolution Day.
Mar/April Easter Monday
Mar/April Whitsun
1 May Labour Day
20 Aug St Stephen's Day
23 Oct Remembrance Day
24–5 Dec Christmas (*Karácsony*)

Opening Hours

In addition to the hours given below, remember that most things close completely on public holidays.

Shops are generally open Mon–Fri 10–6 and Sat 9–1. Hours may be longer in the capital where there are also a number of 24hr stores.

In the summer months, **museums** are open Tues–Sun 10–6; in winter, 9 or 10–4 is usual, with many small museums closing throughout the winter.

Post

Post offices (*posta*) are open Mon–Fri 8–6 – small ones may close at 4 – and until 1 on Saturdays. Buy stamps (*bélyeg*) at tobacconists and remember to show your items first as rates vary. The service is basic but efficient.

Price Categories

Hotels

Prices for hotels are almost always quoted in euros (€), even when payment is expected in forints. The approximate price you should expect to pay, for a double room with bath in high season, is as follows:

luxury over €200
expensive €140–200
moderate €80–140
inexpensive less than €80

Restaurants

For a three-course meal for one with wine:

luxury over €25
expensive €18–25
moderate €10–18
inexpensive less than €10

Shopping

Apart from a thriving wine scene (it's definitely worth taking a few botles home), foodstuffs (particularly paprika, salami and goose liver, preserves and jams) are a popular choice of souvenir, though obviously check what the import limitations are in your home country before purchasing. Porcelain and traditional handicrafts such as embroidered tablecloths, houssar pots and even glove puppets are also a good buy.

Telephones

Operator, t 191; directory enquiries (domestic), t 198; directory enquiries (international), t 199.

To call abroad from Hungary, dial t 00, wait for the dialling tone, then dial the country code, area code and number.

To call Hungary from abroad, dial t 00 36. The code for Budapest is t 01, which is not necessary to dial if you're there. To dial Budapest from abroad, dial t 00 36 1 (i.e. drop the 0 from the code).

The code for long-distance calls within Hungary is t 06. You also have to dial t 06 before calling mobile phones.

Public phones are common. Some take 20, 50 or 100Ft coins, but most take cards, available from post offices, hotels, supermarkets and newsagents, costing 800Ft or 1,800Ft.

International calls are very expensive, much cheaper if using an international card (from tourist offices, Vista (see p.201), or news stands).

Time

Summer time, from early March to late October, is GMT +2hrs, Eastern Standard Time +7hrs, Pacific Standard Time +10hrs. In winter clocks go back an hour to GMT + 1hr.

Note that Hungarians represent times in a way which can be confusing to Westerners: ½8 means 7.30.

Tipping

Service in restaurants is usually 10%. Tell the waiter how much change you expect. If you say 'thank you' (köszönöm) when handing over the bill, it means you expect them to keep all the change. Give a small tip to cloak-room attendants, taxi drivers or changing room attendants at the baths. Most people leave 10 per cent where appropriate or 50Ft.

Toilets

Public toilets (WC or toalett; női or nők is women and férfi or férfiak is men) usually charge a small fee and have a concierge.

Tourist Information

Tourist information abroad is available from embassies (see above). The following websites are useful:

www.budapestinfo.hu: Budapest's official home page.

www.budapest.hu: A site maintained by the mayor's office.

www.livebudapest.com: Articles and listings.

www.timeout.com/budapest: Background information and listings.

www.budapestweek.hu: Listings.

Language

No other language that uses Latin script is as baffling as Hungarian. Normally in a European country you would expect to be able to understand a few written words – the basics, the essentials. Come to Hungary with such expectations and they are soon dashed against the harsh rocks of impossible letter combinations, absurdly long words and endless accents. The easy explanation for this is that Hungarian is one of the few languages in Europe that is not of Indo-European origin. During the course of trying to work out where the Magyars originally came from, linguistics experts found that the core vocabulary of Hungarian, the basic words that have descended through millennia, is related to languages in the Finno-Ugric family – though far too distantly for Finns and Hungarians to understand one another. This places Hungarians' origins in Western Siberia and the northern part of the Ural mountains.

The problem is compounded by the fact that the Hungarians have managed to avoid the usual fate of small countries surrounded by large predatory empires – that of having their language carefully eradicated. They love their language and are reluctant to learn anybody else's. In tourist situations like hotels and restaurants, there is usually someone who speaks some English, but in shops, museums or at the baths even rudimentary communication has to be conducted in sign language. If they do have a few words of something, it is likely to be German. Latin languages will gain no glimmer of recognition. In desperate circumstances, seek out a young person.

There's no point trying to learn to speak the language, whose grammar is as difficult as its vocabulary. What follows is a glossary of words and expressions that might make life easier for you and the Hungarians you encounter. If you do make the effort, they may find it hard to hide their amusement at your pronunciation, but they will love you for it.

Pronunciation

Hungarian pronunciation is fairly straight-forward and consistent. Letters and combinations are always pronounced in the same way; there is no nonsense with silent letters and the like. The stress pattern is regular, with the first syllable slightly emphasized and each following syllable clearly and evenly pronounced. Accents denote a longer vowel (except for é and á). Double consonants are pronounced longer.

In dictionaries and listings, words beginning with ö and ő count as separate letters, with their own listings after 'o'. **Sz** also counts as a separate consonant.

a	like *o* in hot	á	like *a* in far
e	like *e* in send	é	like *a* in day
i	like *i* in hit	í	like *ee* in feet
o	like *o* in open	ó	same but longer
ö	the sound that starts earth		
ő	like the *u* in fur	u	like *u* in put
ú	like *u* in rule	ü	like *u* in French *tu*
ű	the same but longer		
c	like *ts* in hats	s	like *sh* in cash
cs	like *ch* in touch	sz	like *s* in sit
zs	like *s* in pleasure		
j	like *y* in yes	ly	like *y* in yes
gy	like *d* at the start of dune		
ny	like *n* in new	ty	like *t* in tulip

Useful Words and Phrases

yes/no/maybe *igen/nem/talán*
please *kérem*

thank you *köszönöm*
hello (to one person) *szervusz*
hello (more than one) *szervusztok*
hello (familiar) *szia*
goodbye/bye *viszontlátásra/viszlát*
how are you? *hogy vagy (informal)/hogy van (formal)*
Do you speak English *Beszél angolul?*
I don't speak Hungarian *Nem beszélek Magyarul*
I (don't) understand *(Nem) értem*
My name is... *A nevem...*

help! *segítség!*
I'm lost *eltévedtem*
I would like a room... *Szeretnék kétágyas szoba*
How much is this? *Ez mennyibe kerül?*
Where is the...? *Hol van a...?*
How far is...? *Milyen messze van...?*
left/right/straight on *bal/jobb/egyenesen*
where *hol*
railway station *pályaudvar*
station *állomás*
platform *vágány*
departure/arrival *indulás/ érkezés*
open/closed *nyitva/zárva*
entrance/exit *bejárat/kijárat*
toilets *WC/toalett*
women *női* or *nők*
men *férfi* or *férfiak*

day *hap*
week *hét*
month *hónap*
year *év*
today *ma*
tomorrow *nap*
yesterday *tegnap*

Days of the Week

Monday *hétfő*
Tuesday *kedd*
Wednesday *szerda*
Thursday *csütörtök*
Friday *péntek*
Saturday *szombat*
Sunday *vasárnap*

Hungary: Budapest

12

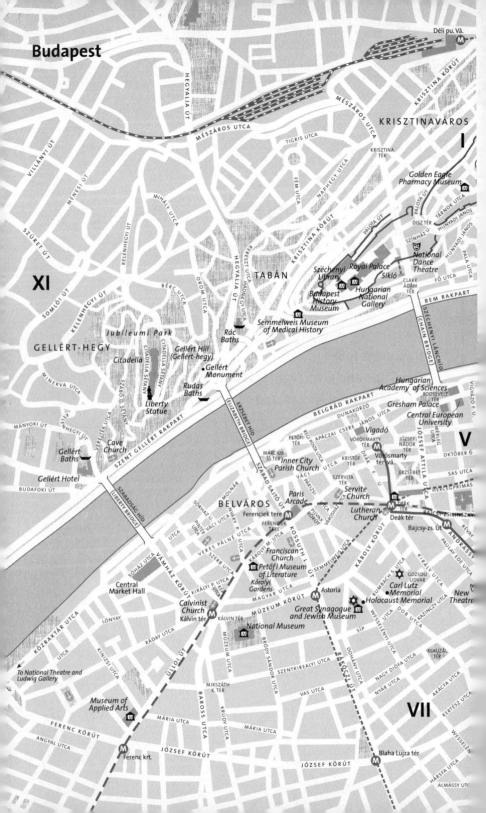

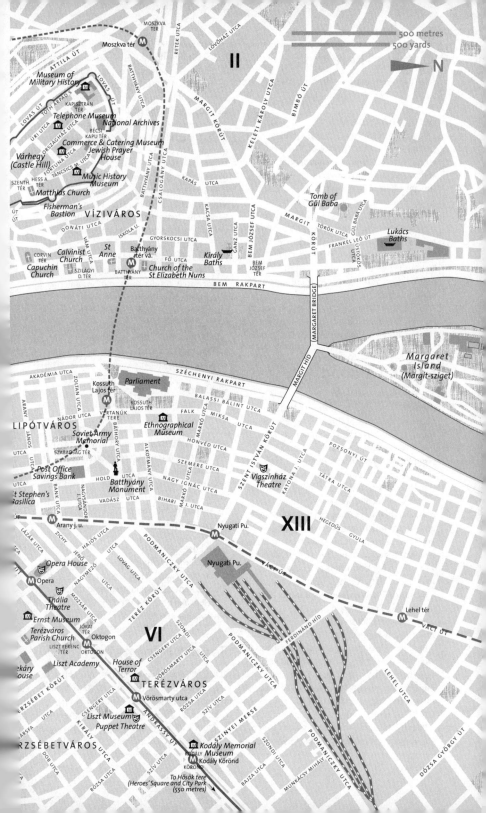

Getting There

See **Getting There**, pp.4–10, for details of airlines flying to Budapest.

Getting from the Airport

Budapest's Ferihegy Airport is 15 miles (20km) southeast of the city. LRI, the airport administration, runs a **minibus service**, bookable at its counter in Arrivals, that will take you anywhere in Budapest (2,100Ft single, 3,600Ft return). To arrange pick-up for the return, call **t** (01) 296 8555 one day in advance.

The **93 bus** runs from just outside the terminals to its terminus at the M3 metro station in Kőbanya-Kispest, taking about an hour. The last bus leaves the airport at 11.45pm. The last **metro** leaves at 11.10pm, then there's the **50É night bus** from the metro station.

To get from the airport to the centre by **taxi**, look for the board indicating fixed prices in the Arrivals area. The fare should be c. 5,000Ft.

Getting Around

The Budapest transport company **BKV**, www.BKV.hu, runs a fast, efficient and cheap network consisting of three metro lines, buses, trams, trolley-buses and local trains (HÉV). All run between about 4.30am–11.30pm. A few night buses ply the busier routes.

The same **tickets** are used for all modes of transport, one ticket good for one ride on one vehicle only: if you change metro lines, you need another ticket. They can be bought at any metro station, from some news stands, and from machines at busier bus/tram stops, which only accept change and often don't work. Buy a **book of tickets** or a **pass**. Tickets must be validated (punched) for each journey.

By metro: Trains are identified by destination rather than direction or name, Paris-style. There are three lines: yellow (M1), red (M2) and blue (M3), all connecting at Deák tér.

By tram: The most useful routes are 4 and 6, which follow the Nagykörút all round Pest, terminating at Moszkva tér in Buda. Line 2 hugs the Danube on the Pest side, and line 19 follows the Buda embankment from Batthyány tér to beyond the Gellért hotel.

By bus: Most buses are very modern. When you want to get off, press the button on the

rail next to the doors. Buses with a red square around their number are express and make fewer stops. A useful route is the 86, following the Buda embankment from Óbuda past the Gellért hotel. The 6É **night bus** follows the 4/6 tram route round the Nagykörút; 50É follows the M3 line, 78É follows the M2 line. They run every 15mins or so.

By local train: There are four suburban train (HÉV) lines. A ticket is valid as far as Óbuda.

By Boat: Ferries (**t** 369 1359, www.ship-bp.hu) run every couple of hours from May to early September between Boráros tér, at the Pest end of Petőfi Bridge, and Római part, just north of Aquincum. The last ferry stops at the Pest end of Margaret Bridge.

By Taxi: Taxis that hang around outside major hotels, tourist spots, stations and the airport often overcharge; phoning a taxi is always a safer bet. Ask how much the journey will cost before getting in. These have good reputations, and dispatchers speak English: **Fő Taxi**, **t** (01) 222 2222. **City Taxi**, **t** (01) 211 1111.

Car Hire

All the major companies are at the airport. **Avis**, V. Szervita tér 8, **t** (01) 318 4859, airport **t** (01) 296 6421, www.avis.hu. **Budget**, I. Krisztina krt 41–3, **t** (01) 214 0420, airport **t** (01) 296 8197, rentacar@budget.hu. **Hertz**, V. Apáczai Csere János u. 4 (Hotel Marriott), **t** (01) 266 4361, airport **t** (01) 296 0988, www.hertz.hu. **Dollar Thrifty**, XIII. Váci út 175, **t** (01) 237 7300, www.thrifty.hu.

Bike Hire

Bringó Hintó, XIII. Hajós Alfréd sétány 1, Margaret Island, **t** (01) 329 2073 . **Charles Rent a Bike and Accommodation**, II. Hegyalja út 23, **t** (01) 212 9196, www.charleshotel.hu.

Tourist Information

TOURINFORM, www.hungarytourism.hu, is the very helpful state-run tourist office. It can be found at: V. Vigadó u.6 (Vörösmarty tér); V. Sütő u. 2 (Deák tér), **t** (01) 317 9800; 24hr infoline **t** (01) 438 8080; I. Szentháromság tér (Castle Hill), **t** (01) 488 0475; VI. Nyugati station, **t** (01) 302 8580; VI. Liszt Ferenc tér 9–11, **t** (01) 322 4098.

Tourism Office of Budapest: V. Március 15 tér 7, **t** (01) 266 0479, **f** 266 7477, *www.budapest info.hu, info@budapestinfo.hu.*

Hungarian National Tourist Office: II. Margit körút 85, **t** (01) 355 1133, **f** 375 3819, *htbuda pest@hungarytourism.hu.*

Infotouch electronic information terminals are scattered around town. For less official advice, go to **Vista Café and Visitor Centre**, VI. Paulay Ede u. 2, **t** (01) 267 8603, *www.vista.hu.*

The **Budapest Card** currently costs 4,350Ft (2 days) or 5,450Ft (3 days). It covers unlimited use of public transport, free entry to most sights and discounts in many shops, spas, etc. Available at big metro stations, TOURINFORM offices, travel agencies and hotels.

The main **post office** is at Petőfi Sándor u. 13, *open Mon–Fri 8–8.*

Guided Tours

Boat tours: **Mahart**, **t** (01) 384 1765, *www. mahartpassnave.hu*, run up to 9 sightseeing tours daily from the dock at Vigadó tér. The *Duna Bella* combines a 1hr tour with an hour on Margaret Island. The *Danube Legend* does 1hr night cruises.

Bus tours: **Budatours**, **t** (01) 374 7070, reservations **t** (01) 353 0558, departing from the corner of Andrássy út and Bajcsy-Zsilinszky. **Cityrama** offer a whole host of different tours; pick up their booklet from Vista. **IBUSZ**, **t** (01) 485 2700, organize 'live' English tours from Erzsébet tér at 10.30 year-round and also at 3pm May–Sept.

Walking tours: **Budapest Walk** run tours from Hősök tere (M1) stop. Informative commentaries. **Budapest Walks**, **t** (01) 340 4232, the original walks company, host tours in English daily 15 April–30 Sept.

In the air: **Indicator**, **t** (01) 249 9824, organize 20min pleasure flights on request, *Mar–Nov only*. **Sup-Air Balloon Club**, **t** (01) 322 0015, can arrange balloon flights for at least two people (depending on the weather).

Internet Cafés

AMI, V. Váci u. 40, **t** (01) 267 1644. *Open 9am–midnight.*

BudapestNET, V. Kecskeméti u. 5, **t** (01) 328 0292. *Open 10–10.*

CEU Net Pont, V. Október 6. u. 14, **t** (01) 328 3506. *Open 9am–10pm.*

Festivals

6 Jan–Ash Wed: *Farsang.* Fattening up before the fasting of Lent.

Early Feb: Hungarian Film Festival.

Late Mar/early April: Budapest Spring Festival. The major annual arts event.

1 May: Labour Day. Still a big event organized by trade unions, especially in City Park.

Nearest weekend to 21 June: World Music Day.

30 June: *Budapesti Bucsú.* A celebration of the withdrawal of Soviet troops in 1991. Music, theatre and dance in squares and parks.

Early–mid-July: World Music Festival (WOMUFE). In the Budai Parkszínpad by XI. Kosztolányi Dezső tér.

Second weekend in Aug: Hungarian Grand Prix (at Hungaroring). A major event; all the hotels are full and jack up their prices.

Mid-Aug: Sziget Festival. Possibly Europe's biggest rock and pop festival, transforming Óbuda Island into a giant open-air party. *Budafest*, opera and ballet festival in the State Opera House.

20 Aug: St Stephen's Day. Rites at the Basilica, craft fair and folk dancing in Castle Hill, and procession through the streets.

Early Sept: Budapest Wine Festival.

Mid–late Sept: Budapest International Music Competition.

Late Sept–mid-Oct: Budapest Autumn Festival.

Late Sept–Oct: Budapest Music Weeks.

Shopping

Like most formerly Communist cities, Budapest has embarked on a passionate love affair with consumerism and shopping malls. The best mall is the **West End Mall** behind Nyugati station. Trawling the second-hand shops and flea markets for a quirky retro bargain can also be fun.

A staggering quantity of galleries carry works from Hungary's past, as well as showcasing the talents of today's artistic community. The many antique shops around **V. Falk Miksa utca** and the southern end of **Váci utca** will let you know what you are legally entitled to take from the country.

The best window-shopping is on **Váci utca** and its many side streets and courtyards. The north end overflows with souvenirs, folk art and Western clothes shops; the south is lined with antiques, jewellers, boutiques and cafés.

Folkart Centrum, V. Váci u. 14. The first stop for all kinds of authentic Hungarian souvenirs.

Great Market Hall, near Kálvin tér. Authentic costumes and linens: first floor.

Herend Porcelain, V. József Attila u. 7, t (01) 317 8133. Hungary's finest porcelain since 1826.

Flea Markets

Decide on a price, and start haggling at a third or half of what you're willing to pay.

Ecseri Piac, XIX. Nagykőrösi út 156 (bus 52 from Boráros tér). In a vast lot in an industrial area: follow the crowds, or get off the bus at the used-car yard and walk through it the way you came. *Mon–Sat 8–4.*

Városligeti Bolhapiac, in the Petőfi Csarnok in City Park (Széchenyi fürdő, M1). A Hungarian garage sale full of old books, records, toys and Communist relics. *Sat and Sun 7–2.*

Where to Stay

Budapest t (01) –

Breakfast-lovers will be horrified to learn that the morning meal doesn't really fit into the Hungarian scheme of things.

Buda

★★★★art'otel, I. Bem rakpart 16–19, t 487 9487, f 487 9488, *www.artotel.hu* (*luxury*). Well-located boutique hotel. The stylish, modern interior was designed down to the smallest detail by US artist D. Sultan, while the west wing consists of four renovated Baroque houses on Fő utca. *Batthyány tér (M2).*

★★★★★Budapest Hilton, I. Hess András tér 1–3, t 488 6600, f 488 6644, *www.hilton.com* (*luxury*). Luxury in the heart of the Castle district. Described by the Hilton president as the most beautiful pearl in the whole string. *Várbusz from Moszkva tér (M2).*

★★★★★Danubius Grand Hotel, XIII. Margit-sziget, t 329 2300, f 329 3923, *www. danubiusgroup.com* (*expensive*). At the north end of Margaret Island, this mansion-like building and its 19th-century period

furnishings offer the comfort and grandeur of a bygone age. You can take the waters for free in the bathing complex of the Thermal Hotel. *Bus 26 from Nyugati station.*

★★★Victoria, I. Bem Rakpart 11, t 457 8080, f 457 8088, *www.victoria.hu* (*moderate*). Simple, tastefully decorated rooms with big beds but rather small bathrooms. Buffet breakfast. Friendly English-speaking staff. *Bus 86 from Batthyány tér (M2), or walk.*

Ábel Panzió, XI. Ábel Jenő u. 9, t/f 209 2537 (*inexpensive*). A beautiful ivy-covered villa set on a quiet street away from the centre. The veranda overlooks a tree-filled garden. Highly recommended. Breakfast included. *Tram 61 from Moszkva tér (M2) or Móricz Zsigmond Körtér.*

Beatrix Panzió, II. Széher u. 3, t/f 394 3730, *www.beatrixhotel.hu* (*inexpensive*). This friendly, well-placed B&B has won awards. Good-sized rooms with decent bathrooms. Lovely front garden with terraces and a pond. Sauna, safes, and a helpful owner with good English. *Bus or tram 56 from Moszkva tér (M2), then a 200m walk.*

Helios Panzió, XII. Lidérc u. 5a, t 246 4658, *roomheli@matavnet.hu* (*inexpensive*). Classily decorated rooms, some with balconies. Excellent views. Parking, and helpful staff. *Bus 8 from Ferenciek tere (M3).*

Kulturinnov, I. Szentháromság tér 6, t 355 0122, f 375 1886 (*inexpensive*). Sixteen big, simple and clean rooms with high ceilings, housed in the neo-Gothic Hungarian Cultural Foundation building right opposite Matthias Church. Buffet breakfast included. *Várbusz from Moszkva tér (M2).*

Central Pest

★★★★★Four Seasons Hotel Gresham Palace, V. Roosevelt tér 5–6, t 268 6000, f 268 5000, *www.fourseasons.com* (*luxury*). Spacious and stylish, decked out in marble, granite and polished wood, the rooms in this newly restored historic gem adhere to its exquisite Art Nouveau mood and grandeur.

★★★★★Kempinski Hotel Corvinus, V. Erzsébet tér 7–8, t 429 3777, f 429 4777, *www. kempinski-budapest.com* (*expensive*). A Postmodern extravaganza: glass, granite and steel put together with taste and imagination. The interior is equally well executed.

Pool, sauna and fitness rooms. Its Corvinus restaurant is one of Budapest's finest.

★★★**City Panzió Mátyás**, V. Március 15 tér 8, t 338 4711, f 317 9086; **City Panzió Pilvax**, V. Pilvax köz 1–3, t 266 7660, f 317 6396; **City Panzió Ring**, V. Szent István körút 22, t 340 5450, f 340 4884. All *www.taverna.hu* and *(moderate)*. This small chain of hotels offers modern, clean, no-nonsense rooms with no real personality but handy locations. The Mátyás is best for both location and exterior.

Kálvin Ház, IX. Gönczy Pál u. 6, t 216 4365, *www.kalvinhouse.hu (moderate)*. Simple, white, huge rooms with high ceilings and wooden floors in a handsome building nicely located near the National Museum and Market Hall. TVs and tubs. Great value.

Peregrinus Elte Hotel, V. Szerb u. 3, t 266 4911, f 266 4913 *(moderate)*. Small gem of a hotel in a quiet but central location. Good-sized airy rooms with high ceilings. Good value.

Mellow Mood Central Hostel, Bécsi u.2, t 411 1310, f 411 1494, *www.mellowmoodhostel. com (inexpensive)*. A superior hostel, with small and simple but decent rooms, lockers, shared kitchens and a common room/bar. Great central location, surprisingly quiet.

Elsewhere in Pest

★★★★★**Corinthia Grand Hotel Royal**, VII. Erzsébet krt 43–9, t 479 4000, f 479 4333, *www.corinthiahotels.com (luxury)*. The views as you enter this magnificent, newly restored 1896 palace are breathtaking: an atrium courtyard crossed by a glass bridge with perspective-hugging staircases and gorgeous chandeliers. A vast labyrinth, the building features five restaurants and 414 rooms, which are plush and comfortable.

★★★★**Ambra Apartment Hotel**, VII. Kisdiófa u. 13, t/f 321 1533, *www.ambrahotel.kozep.com (moderate)*. Fully equipped, decent-sized apartments, with modern décor in pastel shades. Sauna, Jacuzzi and buffet breakfast. A great deal, just *5min walk from Opera (M1)*.

★★★**Hotel Pest**, VI. Paulay Ede u. 3, t 343 1198, f 351 9164, *hotelpest@hotelpest.hu (moderate)*. Plain outside, but a wonderful classical building inside, with a pleasant courtyard. Buffet breakfast included.

★★★**Unio Hotel**, VII. Dob u. 73, t 479 0400, f 479 0401, *www.uniohotel.hu (moderate)*. Very

spacious rooms with high ceilings, big windows and wood furnishings. Good value. *Walk from Oktogon (M1), or tram 4 or 6.*

★★★**Hotel Queen Mary**, VII. Kertész u. 34, t 413 3510, f 413 3511, *www.hotelqueenmary.hu (inexpensive)*. Smart, well-located building with simple, quiet rooms. Buffet breakfast included. Good value. *Walk from Oktogon (M1) or tram 4 or 6.*

Private Rooms

Private rooms and apartments represent a growing business in Budapest, and offer better value than hotels. Rooms often have shared bath and kitchen.

IBUSZ, V. Ferenciek tere 10, t 485 2767, f 337 1205, *accommodation@ibusz.hu*, organize rooms for €21, apartments for €40–50, will show you pictures and can be very helpful.

Vista, VI. Paulay Ede u. 2, t 26 78603, f 268 1059, *www.vista.hu*, offer a similar service.

Eating Out

Budapest t (01) –

Traditionally, culinary class barriers have not existed, so menus in the cheapest and most expensive restaurants can be identical. The food in the expensive place will normally be superior, with a big difference in the service.

In bars and some restaurants wine, juices and soft drinks are often sold by the *deci*, which is a tenth of a litre (100ml). A glass of wine usually costs twice the number on the menu, which is the cost per deci.

Buda

Arany Kaviar, I. Ostrom u. 19, t 201 6737, *www.aranykaviar.hu (expensive)*. Good portions of authentic Russian dishes, including some reasonably priced caviar, smoked salmon and beef. A good range of vodkas and wines.

Rivalda, I. Színház u. 5–9, t/f 489 0236, *www.rivalda.net (expensive)*. By the Castle Theatre, decorated with classy but over-the-top theatre regalia. There's also an expansive cobbled courtyard and live music.

Belgian Brasserie (Belga Söröző), I. Bem Rakpart 12, t 201 5082 *(moderate)*. Popular Belgian-style bar-restaurant, stylishly fitted out, with a pleasant Hungarian crowd.

A staggering range of beers. Starters include brioche, snails and frogs' legs, followed by mussels or meat dishes with a French slant. Riverside terrace. *Batthyány tér (M2), then tram 19 or walk.*

Náncsi Néni, II. Ördögárok u. 80, **t** 397 2742 (*moderate*). The most famous place in town for home-cooked Hungarian cuisine. Top marks for quality and quantity. Try the braised wild boar cutlets. Booking is essential. *Bus 56 from Moszkva tér (M2) or Children's Railway (p.219) then walk.*

Pest: City (Lipótváros)

Lou Lou, V. Vigyázó Ferenc u. 4, **t** 312 4505 (*luxury*). Two beautiful little rooms covered with small pictures. Sophisticated French-Hungarian *haute cuisine*. Attracts a well-to-do crowd. *Closed Sat lunch and Sun.*

Café Kör, V. Sas u. 17, **t** 311 0053 (*moderate*). Small, popular bistro near the Basilica, with a simple, trendy interior. The menu is small yet diverse and exciting, and the food is excellent. *Breakfast until 11.30am. Closed Sun.*

Majd Léonard, V. Balassi Balint u. 7, **t** 301 3891 *www.majdleonard.hu* (*moderate*). Decked out in a classic, old-fashioned coffee-house style. The menu is *nouvelle* Hungarian, with lots of European influences.

Kisharang Étkesde, Október 6. u. 17, **t** 269 3861 (*inexpensive*). Typical small Hungarian diner. Chequered tablecloths, the whole bit. Daily specials, tasty food, very cheap.

Lugas Étterem, V. Bajcsy-Zsilinszky 15, **t** 302 5393 (*inexpensive*). Best views of the back of the Basilica from this terrace across the main road. Laid-back and friendly, offering good portions of well-cooked Hungarian fare. There are a few veggie choices.

Pest: Belváros

Fausto's, VII. Dohány u. 5, **t** 269 6806 (*luxury*). High-quality, genuine Italian food. The pasta is home-made, the sauces exquisite. *Closed Sun. Not really Belváros, but a few minutes' walk from Astoria (M2).*

Iréne Légrádi Antique, V. Bárczy István u. 3–5, **t** 266 4993 (*luxury*). Close to Deák tér. Considered one of the best restaurants in Hungary for traditional Hungarian food. If it feels like dining in an antique shop...well, it is. Gypsy music in the evening. *Closed Sun.*

Képíró, V. Képíró u. 3, **t** 266 0430 (*luxury*). Bright assorted artistic interior: Art Nouveau stained glass, Japanese windows, Greek columns, with gentle jazz. The frequently changing menu is eclectic *haute cuisine*, such as beef tenderloin *torte* baked with sweetbreads and goat cheese. Recommended, though portions tend to be small. More affordable lunch specials.

Oroszlános Kút, Vörösmarty tér 7, **t** 429 9023 (*luxury*). The hallowed Gerbeaud institution is behind this fairly recent fine-dining venture, so it's understandably classy, and the Hungarian cuisine, with a few innovative touches, is about as good as it gets. Great outdoor seating also.

Cyrano, V. Kristóf tér 7–8, **t** 266 4747 (*expensive*). The menu, essentially French-international fusion, is one of the most daring and imaginative in town. Try the goose liver urban-style or the fresh butter-fish. Just off Váci utca, the terrace is wonderful for people-watching, while the interior is dark and cavernous.

Kárpátia, V. Ferenciek tere 7–8, **t** 317 3596 (*expensive*). An extraordinary interior, bold, busy and very medieval, the walls covered in heavy patterns, much like the Matthias Church. The food is traditional Hungarian cuisine cooked to perfection.

Pest: Around Andrássy Út

Articsóka, VI. Zichy Jenő u. 17, **t** 302 7757 (*expensive*). Light and airy, popular and lively. The menu is sophisticated Mediterranean, with some nice innovations. Vegetarian dishes include baked artichoke hearts with gorgonzola. Lots of wines and cocktails.

Fészek Művész Klub Étterem, VII. Kertész u. 36, **t** 322 6043 (*moderate*). The best of meaty Hungarian cuisine served in a leafy interior courtyard surrounded by arcades and old street-lamps, or in the expansive, sophisticated interior, with live music. Large portions at surprisingly reasonable prices. *Tram 4 or 6 or walk from Oktogon (M1).*

Karma Café, VI. Liszt Ferenc tér 11, **t** 413 6764 (*moderate*). A stunning interior that doesn't overplay the Eastern angle, with subdued lighting, plenty of brick and wood, and multiple layers. Tandoori oven specialities. Equally suitable for drinks.

Marquis de Salade, VI. Hajós u. 43, **t** 302 4086 (*moderate*). Owned by an Azerbaijani lady, and featuring chefs from many different countries. Reserve a table in the small, intimate cellar scattered with Eastern rugs.

Premier Étterem, VI. Andrássy út 101, **t** 342 1768 (*moderate*). The menu and terrace here are decent enough, but the real draw is the stunning Art Nouveau décor.

Elsewhere in Pest

Gundel, XIV. Állatkerti u. 2, **t** 321 3550 (*luxury*). Founded in 1894, Gundel is a legend: the most famous restaurant in Hungary, the highest-praised in Central Europe and among the best in the world. Of course it is expensive, and a little stiff and formal. *Hőrök tere (M1)*.

Bagolyvár (The Owl's Castle), XIV. Állatkerti u. 2, **t** 343 0217 (*moderate*). Gundel's sister restaurant is in a rustic Transylvanian building with wooden beams. The emphasis is on traditional cooking, prepared and served only by women. *Hőrök tere (M1)*.

Costes Restaurant, IX. Ráday u. 4, **t** 219 0696 (*expensive*). International fusion food involving some imaginative combinations, served in a plush, intimate environment. Lots of salads and seafood. One of several good options on this happening street.

Kádár Étkezde, VII. Klauzál tér 9, **t** 3213622 (*inexpensive*). Small, very authentic Hungarian eatery with a nice atmosphere and a great menu of well-balanced meat dishes. *Open Tues–Sat 11.30–3.30* .

Cafés and Coffee Houses

Buda

Angelika, I. Batthyány tér 7, **t** 212 3784. On the river side of St Anne's Church, this is a bastion of old-fashioned style, complete with vaulted ceilings, gilt mirrors, lamps, chandeliers, marble tables and terrace views of parliament.

Café Miró, I. Úri u. 30, **t** 375 5458. The most successfully stylish modern spot in Castle Hill, decked out to resemble a large-scale piece of art by Miró, and with a terrace offering views of Matthias Church. Good drinks, but if you're hungry, eat elsewhere.

Ruszwurm Cukrászda, I. Szentháromság tér 7. Budapest's oldest *pâtisserie*, open since 1827, its interior featuring some fine *chaises longues* and an old stove. Views of Matthias Church. Staggeringly busy. *Closed eves*.

Pest

Café Cinema, V. Semmelweis u. 2. Big café near Astoria with a low, funky ceiling and subdued lighting. Very atmospheric, alive with the chatter of a young, cheerful crowd. Good prices for coffee, cakes, juices and a fair selection of wines, liquors and cocktails.

Café Miró Grande, VI. Liszt Ferenc tér 9. The comfy armchairs, funky furnishings, aquarium and stylish long bar make this yet another satisfying spot on the square for any kind of drink. Live Latin music nightly.

Café Mirákulum, V. Hercegprímás u. 19, **t** 269 3207. Tasteful, bright café-bar with Art Nouveau prints and a laid-back atmosphere.

Café Vian, VI. Liszt Ferenc tér 9, **t** 342 8991. Big, bright, comfortable interior decorated with wonderful art, and a small, elegant terrace.

Central Kávéház, V. Károlyi Mihály u. 9. Vast old-style coffee house on Ferenciek tere with extremely high ceilings. Leather upholstery, marble tables. Reasonable prices; intimate seating upstairs. The food is good.

Gerbeaud, V. Vörösmarty tér 7, **t** 429 9000. *The* place to sit and enjoy coffee and cake at the social heart of Belváros. Sit out on the terrace to watch the crowds. The interior is replete with turn-of-the-century antique furniture and fittings. The whole affair is quite touristy, and service is rushed.

Zsolnay Kávéház, V. Váci u. 20. The nicest spot for a coffee on this busy stretch. Outside is a slightly raised terrace, inside is an old-style lounge, all wood and windows with a piano-player and fountain. Another contender for the best cakes in town.

Entertainment

The monthly *Where Budapest* magazine has excellent listings for music and English-language shows. *Budapest Program* is also very useful. Or look in one of the ticket agencies on Váci u. **Ticket Express**, **t** 303 0999, *www.tex.hu*, have 6 counters around the city, including Deák tér 19 and the Ferenciek tere

IBUSZ. Note that nearly all the theatres close for the summer (*June–Sept*).

Theatre

International Buda Stage, II. Tárogató u. 2–4, **t** 391 2500. Simultaneous translation into English during Hungarian shows. *Tram 56 from Moszkva tér (M2).*

Katona József, V. Petőfi Sándor u. 6, **t** 318 6599. Mainstream theatre. *Ferenciek tere (M3).*

Merlin International Theatre, V. Gerlóczy u. 4, **t** 317 9338. English-language performances. *Deák tér metro.*

Thália Szinház, VI. Nagymező u. 22–4, **t** 312 1280. Very attractive theatre hosting theatre (often in English), dance, musicals and foreign troupes. *Oktogon (M1).*

Vígszínház (Comedy Theatre), XIII. Szent István krt. 14, **t** 329 2340. Wonderful Baroque theatre focusing on comedy; some big musicals. *Nyugati pu. (M3).*

Classical Music and Opera

The classical scene in Budapest is booming, and audiences are well known for their enthusiasm. As well as the venues listed below, look out for events at **St Stephen's Basilica**, the **Lutheran Church**, the **Great Synagogue**, **Kiscelli Museum** and the **Old Music Academy** in the Liszt Museum. Note that most venues close for summer.

Bartók Béla Memorial House, II. Csalán u. 29, **t** 394 2100. Chamber concerts, usually on Fridays. *Bus 5 from Moszkva tér (M2).*

Hungarian State Opera House (Magyar Állami Operaház), VI. Andrássy út. 22, **t** 353 0170. Everything you could want from an opera house. Productions are lavish. *Opera (M1).*

Erkel Színház, VIII. Köztársaság tér 30, **t** 333 0540. The number two opera house, with a totally different feel. A vast, socialist building. *Blaha Lujza tér (M2).*

Vigadó, V. Vigadó u. 5, **t** 338 4721. A beautiful building and location, but terrible acoustics. *Closed July and Aug. Vörösmarty tér (M1).*

Jazz and Blues

Birdland, VI. Liszt Ferenc tér 7, **t** 413 7983. Classic interior with plain walls and B&W jazz prints. Live jazz Thurs–Sat.

New Orleans, VI. Lovag u. 5, **t** 268 0802, *www.neworleans.hu*. A comfortable,

spacious venue that has hosted some pretty big names in the jazz and blues world.

Fat Mo's, V. Nyári Pál u. 11, **t** 267 3199. Open till 2 or 4am nightly. Done up as a speakeasy, with one very long bar and B&W gangster prints.

Jazz Garden, V. Veres Pálné u. 44a, **t** 266 7364. With plastic trees and a black ceiling dotted with stars. Jazz nightly. *Open daily 6pm–1am. Kálvin tér (M3).*

Folk Music and Dance

Polished, not-so-authentic folk dancing or gypsy concert shows aimed at tourists take place more or less nightly at the **Budai Vigadó** (I. Corvin tér 8), the **Duna Palota** (V. Zrínyi u. 5) or the **Bábszinház** (VI. Andrássy u. 69). Phone **t** 317 2754 or pick up one of their leaflets.

Csángó Dance House, XII. Marczibányi tér 5a, **t** 212 5660. *Csángó* music and dancing (Wed from 8pm). On Thurs the group Muzsikás play from 8pm. *Moszkva tér (M2).*

Fonó Budai Zeneház, XI. Sztregova u. 3, **t** 206 5300, *www.fono.hu*. Alight at Fehérvári u. 108. In a former aluminium factory. Acoustic music: folk, jazz, etc. *Tram 18 from Moszkva tér (M2) or 47 from Deák tér.*

Nightlife

For the best taste of what's on offer, head to Liszt Ferenc tér or Raday utca.

A38 Ship, moored at Petőfi Bridge, Buda side, **t** 464 3940, *www.a38.hu*. One of Budapest's busiest venues, for all genres of music.

Crazy Café, VI. Jókai u. 30, **t** 302 4003. This long cellar bar has an astounding selection of beers. *Open daily noon–1am.*

Gödör Klub, V. beneath Erzsébet tér, **t** 943 5464, *www.godorklub.hu*. A stunning venue for a mixed bag of live or DJ-led sessions, from jazz to techno. *Open 4pm–2am daily.*

Leroy Café, VI. Liszt Ferenc tér 10. An extraordinary interior that has to be seen, featuring high arched stone ceilings, massive chandeliers and a spectacular bar.

Old Amsterdam, V. Királyi Pál u. 14, **t** 266 3648, open till 2am nightly. Stylish little pub with a genuinely European feel.

Old Man's Music Pub, VII. Akácfa u. 13, **t** 322 7645. Probably the most fun, popular and crowded nightspot in town. Mainly disco. *Open daily 3–3. Blaha Lujza tér (M2).*

Budapest

Wherever you are in Budapest, a point comes in the late afternoon when a magical quality of refracted light calls you to the Danube. The other cities that straddle this most celebrated of Europe's waterways have largely resisted her charms, but here she is queen, and the atmosphere she commands is one of romance. Budapest is, of course, two cities, which grew as separate entities until their union less than 130

Food and Drink

From the Mongols, the Magyars learnt the secrets of stewing meats in their own juices, the basis of *tokány* stews. The great Renaissance king Matthias is said to have imported the likes of dill, capers, figs, turkey and garlic from Italy. From Austria came *schnitzel*, meats fried in breadcrumbs (*rántott*), and the cooking of vegetables in a roux of lard and flour and/or sour cream (*fő zelék*). The most famous Hungarian flavour, **paprika**, came with the Turks, and is usually surprisingly subtle: sweet and fragrant. Along with onions, fat and smoked bacon, it forms the basis of classic stews called *pörkölt*, with cubed meat. *Paprikás* is the same thing with sour cream. These are what we know as goulash, while *gulyás* is actually a thick meat soup. As well as these dishes, a typical menu will offer a range of **meats** cooked in a variety of ways, usually with sauces containing fruit, wine or cheese. **Fish** from Hungary's many rivers and lakes is also abundant; try the hot and sour fish soup called *halászlé*. **Vegetarians** have always been ill-served here, however; breaded and fried mushrooms (*gombafejek rántva*) and cheese (*rántott sajt*) feature heavily. Salad (*saláta*) has no fixed meaning and could amount to a pile of pickled cabbage, gherkin or pepper.

Hungary's 20 **wine**-producing areas have a tradition as long and accomplished as those of France, Italy or Spain. The Hungarian wine with the greatest reputation is a natural sweet white: Tokaji Aszú, which Louis XIV called 'the wine of Kings, the King of wines'. Of the reds, the most famous, not necessarily the best, is known internationally as 'Bull's Blood' and locally as (Egri) Bikavér. Note that Hungarian sparkling wine can be every bit as good as champagne and considerably cheaper. Hungary is not historically a **beer**-drinking nation and, while the younger generation are moving in this direction, Hungarian brewers are yet to catch up. Dreher, the most common brew, is acceptable ice-cold on a sweltering day. The best bet is to look for Czech beers. The most famous national **spirit** is *pálinka*, a strong fruit brandy or *eau-de-vie*.

Coffee was introduced here by the Turks a century before it was heard of in Paris or Vienna. The burgeoning coffee culture reached its apotheosis at the turn of the 20th century, when there were between 400 and 600 cafés in Budapest. As well as a place to relax and socialize, these were forums for views to be aired and disseminated. Different groups or professions, artists, writers or businessmen, would have their own coffee shop. Cafés were such renowned bastions of free thought that the Communists closed them down, but today, all over the city, new establishments have opened with a genuine sense of style. The Central Kávéház on Ferenciek tere is a perfect example, and the coffee is probably better than ever. Finally, Budapest is famous for its *pâtisseries*, known here as *cukrászda*.

years ago, and which have maintained their own distinct characters. **Buda** is hilly and green, lorded over by the elevated Castle Hill area. Just two centuries ago, most of its inhabitants still spoke German and kept themselves apart from the expanding metropolis across the water. That flat expanse on the east bank is **Pest**, a vibrant, thoroughly modern city in all respects save for the complete lack of skyscrapers.

Almost the entire town was built at the end of the 19th century in an unparalleled period of expansion. After centuries of having to defend itself from invaders and neighbouring empires, in 1867 Hungary became part of the Austro-Hungarian Dual Monarchy, and set about transforming its newly united capital into a city that would compete with and even surpass Vienna in its grandeur. This rapid development was catalysed by the 1896 Hungarian Millennium, the 1,000th anniversary of the arrival in the Carpathian Basin of the city's Magyar founding fathers. In the four years leading up to this date, at least 3,700 buildings were completed. At 80 square miles Budapest had become the biggest city on the continent. No wonder Mark Twain had this reaction in 1899: 'Budapest was a surprise for me, really. Civilised, cosmopolitan, spacious. Young and ambitious. Can this Chicago-paced development go on forever, one wonders.' It did so long enough to benefit fully from the exciting Art Nouveau era, of which it ranks alongside Barcelona as the world's premier exponent. The progress was halted, however: by two World Wars, followed by 40 years of Communism.

Budapest is not what the visitor expects. The predominant characteristic of Hungarian architecture is an almost obsessive love of the eclectic, a mix-and-match combination of Gothic, Baroque, Renaissance, Romanesque and Art Nouveau. Lawns, parks, gardens and great playgrounds abound. The city's inhabitants are as varied as its buildings: from the start, Hungary has been a melting pot of Slavs, Serbs, Croats, Romanies, Germans, Austrians, Italians, Turks, and of course Magyars. The visitor expecting the cliché-ridden Russian-style temperament will be surprised at how Mediterranean the Hungarians seem. In fact, on a superficial level, it already feels as if 40 years of enforced Communism, with the implied atmosphere of bleak, apathetic fatalism and crippling inefficiency, never happened.

Castle Hill (Várhegy)

The black and yellow Sikló (funicular) cars glide up to Castle Hill from the Buda side of the Chain Bridge in about a minute (7.30am–10pm daily; closed every other Mon). To walk up, follow the slope to the left as you face the Sikló, then take the stairs to your right. Or take the M2 metro to Moszkva tér, then pick up the Várbusz bus from beneath the turret of the castle-like building.

First to see the strategic potential of this location was the Hungarian king Béla IV who, following the Mongol invasion of 1247, had a fortress built here. Over the centuries that followed, the castle and its royal palace were added to, destroyed, rebuilt and razed to the ground many times. As the rubble was cleared away after the last destruction in 1945, many remains dating back to the Middle Ages were found which would otherwise have been forever hidden. In the rebuilding that followed, these were left visible, and complemented by architectural styles that evoke every period of Buda's eventful history.

If you ascend by the steps, a great bronze eagle suddenly looms over you. This is the **turul-bird**, which occupies a curious place in Hungarian myth, beginning its job as national protector by raping the grandmother of the Magyar chieftan, Árpád. As the hero led his people to conquer the Carpathian Basin it flew overhead, bearing the sword of Attila the Hun. Descent from an eagle, symbol of the Creator, implied that holy blood coursed through Magyar veins.

The Royal Palace (Budavári Palota)

Nothing remains of the castle and fortifications of King Béla IV. The Angevin kings built more impressive quarters, bettered in turn by Sigismund of Luxembourg, who commissioned a large Gothic palace. Matthias Corvinus went one better, ordering a whole new set of buildings. As the palace reinvented itself as a melting pot for the new ideas on art, politics and culture, artists and scholars from all over Europe were commissioned to supply paintings, sculptures, fountains and lavish banqueting halls. Alas, the Turks were waiting in the wings to trash the place; defeating them entailed reducing Matthias' pleasure-dome to such tatters that the Habsburgs just had to build a new one. It started small under Charles III (early 18th century), grew to 203 rooms under Maria Theresia, and just kept growing through the 19th century, despite the lack of royalty. In 1945, the walls came tumbling down again. The new structure, alas, was based not on the Matthias model but on the vast Habsburg edifice completed by Hauszmann. The palace is occupied by the National Gallery (wings B, C and D), the Budapest History Museum (E) and the National Széchenyi Library (F).

Unlike many National Galleries, the **Hungarian National Gallery** (Magyar Nemzeti Galéria; *open April–Oct Tues–Sun 10–6; Nov–Mar Tues–Fri 10–4, Sat–Sun 10–6; closed Mon*) really is national. Everything is Hungarian, ranging from the Middle Ages to the present. It is a large collection but not intimidating: a couple of hours should be enough. On the **Ground Floor**, the Lapidarium displays stone objects reclaimed from the past after the 1945 destruction, but most people agree that one of the highlights is the collection of 15th- and 16th-century Gothic altarpieces and panel paintings. On the **First Floor**, among the late Gothic altarpieces, look out especially for *The Annunciation* by Master G.H. and *The Visitation* by Master M.S. In the Baroque rooms, most notable is the 1712 *Portrait of Ferenc Rákóczi* by Ádám Mányoki, which might prepare you to go back through the middle section and face the vast canvases of battle scenes that you hurried past. The most unavoidable, right at the top of the stairs, is Peter Krafft's *Zrínyi's Sortie*. These skilful, but to many unappealing, works form part of a wave of nationalism which shows itself in every aspect of the 19th century, when Hungary was sick of being ruled by the Habsburgs or anyone else. A room in wing B is devoted to the works of Mihály Munkácsy and László Paál; the former was one of the few to gain recognition in the rest of Europe. Also in wing B, look out for works by the 'father of Hungarian Impressionism', Pál Szinyei Merse. The varied collection of Károly Lotz – whose frescoes adorn the ceilings of almost every major building in town – includes the beautiful, life-size *Woman Bathing*. The **Second and Third Floors** contain the 20th-century and contemporary art collections; much of the permanent work is by The Eight, a group from the influential artists' colonies such as Nagybanya. One artist everyone agrees on is Tivador Csontváry Kosztka. He is considered self-taught, though he studied in Rome, Paris and Munich. When Picasso first saw his work he asked to be left alone with the paintings for an hour with the doors locked, then said, 'And I thought I was the only great painter of our century.'

Outside the museum is the **Matthias Fountain**. To the right, two lions guard the gate which leads into the courtyard named after them, within which are entrances to the **National Széchenyi Library** (Nemzeti Szécsenyi Könyvtár; *open Aug–June Mon 1–9pm, Tues–Sat 9am–9pm, closed July and Sun; adm*) and the **Budapest History Museum** (Budapesti Történeti Múzeum; *open Wed–Mon 10–4; closed Tues; adm*), which is definitely worth a visit, since it helps to bring Budapest's tumultuous history to life. Downstairs in the basement are exhibited the remains of the **medieval palace** that in its heyday was praised as one of the grandest in all Christendom.

North to Matthias Church and Beyond

Castle Hill's biggest asset, however, is its atmosphere. Here the past presents itself through the accumulation of details, so, as you walk north through these ancient streets, look at the huge doors; the windows with their bars and boxes; the roofs dotted with spikes, vents, chimneys or tiny windows; the wrought-iron grilles, torch-carriers, sign-holders; the pastel shades, murals, niches, sculptures, plaques.

On the far side of **Dísz tér** (Parade Square) the road splits. Tárnok utca, now sadly all dug up, leads to Matthias Church via the small **Golden Eagle Pharmacy Museum** at No.18 (*open Tues–Sun 10.30–5.30; closed Mon; adm*). This 15th-century house was the second home of Buda's oldest pharmacy. Úri utca (Lord Street), on the left, runs to the northern end of Castle Hill; the stand-out house is No.31, its almost entirely Gothic façade thought to look as it did in the late 15th century.

Dominated by the Matthias Church and Fisherman's Bastion, the broad, cobble-stoned **Szentháromság tér** is the focal point of Castle Hill, thronged by tourists. The large bronze equestrian **statue** between church and bastion represents King Stephen, justly, as a grim and powerful figure. At the end of the 10th century he unified the Magyar tribes into one nation, of which he was the first king. Born Vajk, he became Stephen (or István) when he converted to Christianity and forced his nation to do the same, a move that facilitated their integration into Europe. He is depicted here wearing the famous crown sent for his coronation by Pope Sylvester II. Nearby, a spiral staircase leads down into the **Szent Mihály Kápolna**, an atmospheric, cavernous brick and stone chapel full of modern artworks. On the square's southwest corner is the former **Buda Town Hall**, bearing a statue of Pallas Athene. Turn west for the famous **Ruszwurm Cukrászda** café, a sight to see with its lavish antique interior.

Matthias Church (Mátyás Templom; *open daily 7am–8pm; adm*) is undoubtedly one of Budapest's finest buildings. It originally resembled the northern French Gothic, before Sigismund of Luxembourg remodelled it into a hall-church in high Gothic style. Matthias made his own improvements and was married here twice. Under the Turks, the furnishings were destroyed, the walls whitewashed and the church restyled as a mosque. Back in Christian hands after the siege, it was given to the Franciscans, then the Jesuits, who decorated it in a Baroque style. When reconstruction was undertaken between 1873 and 1896, architect Frigyes Schulek was so keen to preserve its multi-layered past that he noted all the original features revealed as the walls were pulled down and built them into his new structure, including much of the wall decoration. Before going inside, have a closer look at the **Béla Tower** (front left), named after the church's original founder, which has retained many Gothic features. Above all, have a good look above the door at the **Mary Portal**, Schulek's reconstruction of one of the greatest pieces of Gothic stone carving in Hungary, depicting the *Assumption of the Virgin Mary*. Inside, every inch of wall space has been painted, not like the Sistine Chapel – there are few biblical scenes – but with repetitive patterns of a floral or geometrical nature, designed by Bertalan Székely, sometimes resembling Polynesian, Aboriginal or Native American art, and adding up almost to an Art Nouveau effect. On the north side in the **Trinity Chapel** lies the tomb of King Béla III and his wife Anne de Châtillon. A staircase leads to **St Stephen's Chapel**, containing a bust of the king, and various scenes from his life. More stairs lead to the **Royal Oratory**, exhibiting a replica of the Hungarian crown jewels and coronation thrones.

Outside the church is the **Fishermen's Bastion** (Halászbástya). In the Middle Ages there was a fish market near to this spot; the rampart was redesigned in playful style by Schulek to complement the Matthias Church. Opposite is the ugly **Hilton Hotel**. Follow the bastion to its northern end and go through the (normally open) gate that leads behind the hotel, and you will find yourself in the remains of a medieval church from 1254. This Dominican courtyard, uncovered during excavations in 1902, was incorporated by architect Béla Pinter into the hotel's design, and now provides a stage for concerts and operettas during the summer season.

Three streets run north from Szentháromság tér, roughly parallel to and east of Úri u. Furthest east is Táncsics u., which contains the **Music History Museum** at No.7 (*open April–Oct Tues–Sun 10–6; Nov–Mar Tues–Sun 10–5; closed Mon; adm*), in the grand Erdödy Palace where Beethoven stayed in 1800. The **Museum of Hungarian Commerce and Catering** on Fortuna u. (*open Wed–Fri 10–5, Sat and Sun 10–6; closed Mon and Tues; adm*) is much more interesting than you'd expect: the commerce section includes early 19th-century advertisements, antique shop fronts, a provincial grocery store and, the *pièce de résistance*, an HMV dog that taps its paws against the window. Hess András tér was named after the man who established the nation's first printing-press. His workshop is believed to have occupied the site of the Fortuna Restaurant. At No.6 is the **House of Hungarian Wines** (Magyar Borok Háza; *open June–Sept Mon–Fri 1–9, Sat and Sun 11–9; Oct–May daily 11–7*), whose extensive cellar holds some 550 different wines from Hungary's 20-odd growing regions; for a mere £5–6 you can help yourself to a selection of 60 or 70 of these.

Gellért Hill and Tabán

These two areas line the Buda embankment from the Liberty Bridge (Szabadság híd) in the south to the Chain Bridge (Széchenyi lánchíd) in the north.

As well as providing a backdrop to the Buda skyline, the 460ft dolomite cliff of **Gellért Hill** offers the best views of Pest and Castle Hill. The **Gellért Hotel** sits like a country mansion at the end of the elegant Liberty Bridge; purpose-built as a spa hotel in order to help promote Budapest as a spa town, it occupies a spot whose hot springs have been revered for their healing properties for at least seven centuries. Entrance to the **baths** is on the hotel's right flank as you face it (*t 466 6166; open 6am–7pm; adm, reduced rate after 5pm*). These mixed-sex baths offer sheer opulence, decorated throughout in ornate Art Nouveau style; rarely does life offer the opportunity to partake of so much grandeur for so little money.

Opposite the entrance to the baths, a path leads uphill (to the right) to the **Cave Church** (Sziklatemplom). Established in 1926 and based by designer Kálmán Lux on the shrine at Lourdes, the church was intended for the Pauline order of monks. It may be in a cave, but everywhere the coldness of ceiling and walls is enlivened by potted plants, stained glass and art. On the summit of Gellért Hill squats the low, bulky **Citadella**, built by the Hapsburgs as a stronghold from which to control, and today not an attraction so much as a pinnacle from which to see everything else, including that of the adjacent **Liberty Statue**, which is far too tall to take in from below.

A quarter of the way up Gellért Hill, facing Elisabeth Bridge, stands a statue of the eponymous saint (bear left on your way down from the Citadella). If you keep going down you will, of course, eventually get back to the river and the jumble of roads that carve up the area of **Tabán**. This area gets its name from the tanning workshops here during the Turkish occupation. The Turks took advantage of the waters, building two magnificent baths, the only part to survive the siege of 1686; the most atmospheric are the **Rudas Baths** (*I. Döbrentei tér 9; open Mon–Fri 6–6, Sat and Sun 6–1; adm*), built in the 16th century on a site occupied by baths since the 14th century.

The striking white **Elisabeth Bridge** which leads from the jumble of roads across to Pest was named after Emperor Franz Josef's wife. Nicknamed Sisi, she was a beautiful and tragic figure, unsuited to the straitjacket of royalty (*see* p.131). This was the only bridge destroyed in the war not rebuilt according to its original form; much older in style is the **Chain Bridge** (Széchenyi Lánchíd). Before the 1840s, Buda and Pest were by necessity separate towns because they were divided by the Danube. It was impossible to build a bridge of wood and stone over a river this wide. István Széchenyi sent to Britain for an English engineer, William Tierney Clark, and a Scottish masterbuilder, Adam Clark (no relation), and even had the iron shipped over. Today the Chain Bridge is a symbol of the city, for its beauty as much as its technological prowess.

Víziváros

The thin stretch of land north of the Chain Bridge and east of the river has been called Víziváros or 'Water Town' since the Middle Ages. While the royal court and its associated gentry enjoyed the views from the hill, people down here were mainly fishermen, craftsmen and traders. Literally meaning 'Main Street', the thoroughfare of **Fő utca** leading north from Clark Ádám tér dates back to the times of the Romans, continuing in its unrenovated form practically to Margaret Bridge and containing at least two churches that shouldn't be missed. On Szilágyi tér off Fő utca the neo-Gothic **Calvinist Church** (Református Templom; *usually closed*) was planned by Sámuel Pecz according to a design traditionally used for medieval Catholic churches. It is one of the most distinctive points of the Buda landscape and an extremely complex, impressive construction, with three shades of brick and polychromatic glazed roof tiles; note the unusual shape of the central 10-sided tower. The statue on a fountain in this square is of the church's architect Pecz dressed as a medieval master builder. The square itself is remembered for one of the more grim events of 1945: this stretch of water is one of the areas where Jews and anti-Fascists were brought to be shot. On faded Batthyány tér off Fő utca, the twin-towered parish **Church of St Anne** (Szent Anna Templom; *open only for services, Mon–Fri 6.45–9 and 4–7, Sun and hols 9–1*) is one of Budapest's most beautiful Baroque buildings.

Batthyány tér epitomizes the current nature of Vízíváros, surrounded by grand edifices gone shabby. Carrying on down Fő utca, you will get to the Turkish **Király Baths** (*II. Fő u. 84; open Tues, Thurs and Sat 9–8 for men; Mon, Wed, Fri 7–6 for women; adm*), one of Budapest's most striking and atmospheric baths, featuring a 16th-century Ottoman pool and several smaller pools beneath the original cupola. The road changes name but continues, leading eventually to the peaceful neoclassical complex of the **Lukács Baths**. A short detour off Frankel Leó u. takes you to the **Tomb of Gül Baba** (*Mecset u. 14; open April–Sept Tues–Sun 10–6; Oct 10–4*); the name of this Turkish Dervish, a member of the Sufi Bektaşi order, means 'Father of the Roses'.

The City (Lipótváros/Leopold Town) and Margaret Island

Covering the northern section of inner Pest, this is the financial, banking and business heart of the capital, containing its Parliament and cathedral. Planned in the early 19th century, it is buzzing on weekdays with people in suits talking on mobile phones, and a ghost town at weekends and in the evenings.

At the Pest end of the Chain Bridge, **Roosevelt tér** is a big grassy expanse, choked by relentless traffic. Its main draw is the **Gresham Palace**, an Art Nouveau gem designed by Zsigmond Quittner and brothers József and László Vágó in 1906, with details crafted by many of the leading artists of the day. The Four Seasons hotel group have recently completed a painstaking reconstruction that has restored its former glory, staying as close as possible to the original design. Guests pass through exact copies of the original delicate wrought-iron peacock gates into an interior that is far more overtly Art Nouveau. The lobby, inner courtyards and sweeping staircases overflow with showy details in stained-glass, wrought-iron and Zsolnay ceramic.

At the north end of the square is the neo-Renaissance **Hungarian Academy of Sciences**. The six statues on the main façade represent the Academy's original six departments: law, sciences, mathematics, philosophy, linguistics and history. On the same level are statues of six scientists: from the river, Newton, Lomonosov, Galileo, Miklós Révai (a Hungarian linguist), Descartes and Leibnitz. The statue in the middle of the square is István Széchenyi.

Sitting on Szent István tér with its back to the main road, and surrounded by buildings almost as high as itself, Budapest's cathedral, **St Stephen's Basilica** (Bazilika; *open Mon–Fri 9–5, Sat 9–1, Sun 1–5, and daily 7–7.45pm; treasury open daily 10–5; adm*), tends to creep up on you. It's hard to get a good look at it except from the front, which is easily the most attractive part anyway. Over 50 years and three architects were required to complete it, to the point that it became a standing joke. Though it is not shaped like a basilica, it received the title Basilica Minor in 1938, the 900th anniversary of the death of St Stephen, to whom it was dedicated. Strangely, it was in death that the great king provided the church with its most famous attraction: his mummified Holy Right Hand (and forearm), Hungary's most important relic. The dome is 96m high (315ft), the same as the Parliament's dome; this number alludes to the date of the legendary arrival of the Magyar tribes, AD 896. The interior, which can hold 8,500 people, is spacious; the marble walls and pillars carry mosaics, paintings and sculptures of a very high standard.

Flanked by stretches of glorious green that are home to a wide range of tree species, with a great playground at its southern end, **Szabadság tér** (Liberty Square) would almost resemble a park were it not for the intrusive fencing and frequently high police presence. Scattered throughout this almost innocuous space are objects of great nationalist and political import, and around its edges stand some huge, imposing buildings, most of them embassies or banks. But on Hold utca, behind the National Bank and now belonging to it, sits one of Budapest's real architectural highlights, the former **Post Office Savings Bank**. Ödön Lechner combined Art Nouveau with Hungarian folk art to forge a new nationalist architecture. The façade is all curves and gentle colours, simple motifs so delicate and playful that it's hard to do them justice. Note the ceramic bees climbing up the gable walls towards the hives on the roofs; these hives and the yellow majolica curlicues are the only hints from below of the extraordinary roof that is the building's finest feature. Here, multicoloured hexagonal tiles from the Zsolnay factory are ornamented with flowers, dragon tails, angel wings and Turkish turbans, a world of fairytale folk imagery. When asked who would enjoy such details, Lechner answered, 'The birds.' The best view of the roof is from the top of the Basilica with binoculars. From here it's not far to **No.3 Honvéd u.**, which has one of the nicest, most original façades you'll see: very Art Nouveau, very playful. Note the balconies, each utterly distinctive, and the use of glazed ceramics.

In Vértanuk tere (Martyrs' Square) is a **monument to Imre Nagy**. After Stalin's death in 1953, the dictator Rákosi fell from grace with Moscow. When Imre Nagy replaced him as prime minister, a period known as 'the thaw' began. The reign of terror had come to an end. When Nagy's protector in Moscow was dismissed, however, he too was removed from power and his changes reversed. Though a Communist, he had become much loved, so that, during the 1956 Uprising, the people called for him to speak. Eventually persuaded to address the crowds, he simply urged them to go home. In the end, the broader political picture sealed the country's fate, the Russians deciding they could not allow Hungary independent rule, and the Western powers agreeing not to interfere. So the Russian tanks appeared, and Nagy sought amnesty in the Yugoslavian embassy. After accepting an armistice, he was imprisoned for two years in Romania, then secretly tried in the spring of 1958 and executed on 16 June.

Kossuth Lajos tér is another square that really wants to be a park. On its southwest corner is a **statue of Attila József**, the popular working-class poet. Right in front of Parliament is a far less enjoyable **statue of Ferenc Rákóczi II**, a prince of Transylvania who led the 1703–11 struggle for independence against the Habsburgs. The neo-Renaissance palace next door was built to house the Supreme Court and Public

Prosecutor's Office. The palace is now the **Ethnographical Museum** (*open daily 10–6; adm*), worth visiting as much for the building as for its exhibitions on folk culture.

Occupying 880ft of the Danube embankment, Budapest's **Parliament** (Országház; *tours in English leave at 10, 12, 2 and 6, when Parliament is not in session*), based on the House of Commons in London, is a magnificently bold feat of virtuosity, so extravagant and pompous that the temptation is to belittle it. The ground plan is Baroque, but the façade is a fusion of neo-Gothic and neo-Renaissance. Designer Imre Steindl wanted 'to combine this splendid medieval style with national and personal features'; the Gothic harks back to better days, when Hungary was free to choose its own buildings. Inside there are 20km of stairways and 691 rooms. Much of the trimming is painted with 22 or 23 carat gold, 60kg of it; on the guided tour you will only see a fraction of what is there.

The northern chunk of Lipótváros is a paradise for lovers of big buildings. For a first-class selection, from Kossuth Lajos tér walk down Alkotmány u., turn left on to Bihari János u., then left on to Markó u. which crosses Nagy Ignac u. This last and Bihari János retain their quality up to the Nagykörút (Great Boulevard). If you feel like going this far, turn right for the beautiful **Nyugati Station** building. Constructed by the famous Eiffel company in Paris, it was the largest station in Europe until 1880. Behind it on Váci út is the postmodern **West End City Centre** shopping mall, from whose roof a moored hot air balloon called the Budapest Eye offers stupendous views. To the west the Nagykörút heads past the delightful **Vígszínház** (Comedy Theatre) to **Margaret Bridge** – with its own fantastic views, especially at night – and **Margaret Island**. Essentially one big park, Margit-sziget is greatly appreciated by Budapesters, a slice of tranquillity minutes from the city centre. Open to the public since 1869, the park's popularity with lovers generated the saying, 'Love begins and ends on Margaret Island.' Two giant hotels stand sentinel over the northern end of the island: the **Danubius Grand** is one of Budapest's classic hotels, built as a sanatorium in 1873 by Miklós Ybl. The baths to which it was attached are contained within the ugly **Thermal Hotel** next door. To the west is a **rock garden** with warm-water lily ponds.

Belváros: The Inner City

The **Kiskörút** (Little Boulevard) runs along the line of medieval Pest's walls, enclosing the city centre known as Belváros. Not much remains to identify this as the site of historic Pest: the town was razed when the Turks were driven out in 1686, and what can be seen today is mainly a result of the massive expansion at the end of the 19th century. There are a few sights, but the thing to do here is stroll.

Sitting on the Kiskörút at the junction of Pest's four inner districts and all three metro lines, **Deák tér** is undeniably the city's main hub, a busy and until quite recently rather sleazy spot. Its landmark is the squat, spireless **Lutheran Church** with its gently curving green roof. The inside is simple, and can only be seen during services or via the **museum** (*open Tues–Sun 10–6, closed Mon; adm*) next door, whose exhibits include a facsimile of Martin Luther's will and a copy of the first book printed in Hungary, a 1541 *New Testament*. The best thing on this square is the neo-Gothic **VW building** at No.3, its corner topped by a turret.

Free from traffic and lined by the terraces of cafés and restaurants, dotted with graceful iron lamp-posts and dominated by half a dozen giant trees, **Vörösmarty tér** is a focus of social activity, partly due to the hallowed institution on the north side, the **Pâtisserie Gerbeaud**. This 1861 building has been a café-confectioner's since 1870. Emil Gerbeaud bought it in 1884 and turned it into a landmark, famous as a meeting-spot as well as for its cakes. The marvellous building with turret-like corners on the square's south side is the **Bank Palace**, housing the Budapest Stock Exchange.

West from Vörösmarty tér is a small square named after the Romantic **Vigadó Concert Hall**, whose name approximates to 'making merry'. It was so badly damaged in the Second World War that reconstruction wasn't completed until 1980. Underused and neglected, with a tacky bar at ground level, it is still a beautiful building. The **Dunakorzó**, a UNESCO World Heritage site, has wonderful views of the Buda panorama, especially at night when lights dance on the water and the air is suffused with romance. In the 1900s this area was surrounded by fancy hotels, and the promenade was the place to stroll. **Petőfi tér** contains a giant Celtic tombstone, and the statue of Sandor Petőfi. More maybe than any other national hero, he stirs patriotism in the Magyar soul, thus his statue is a popular site for political demonstrations.

Petőfi tér runs into Március 15 tér and Pest's oldest building, the **Inner City Parish Church** (Belvárosi Plébániatemplom; *open daily 6.30am–9pm*). From the outside it's nothing special, yet this is Budapest's only building east of the Danube to reflect anything like the history encountered on the other side. The first occupant of this site was the 3rd-century Roman fortress Contra Aquincum, whose remains can be seen in the square beside the church. The original was razed during the Mongol invasions, though a single Romanesque arch survives in the southern tower. The 14th-century Gothic replacement provided the basis of what you see today; it is inside that the historical mish-mash, with Baroque and Renaissance features is more apparent.

Váci utca runs the length of this district and was once Pest's main road. For the last 150 years it has held Budapest's premier boutiques. The northern part has become increasingly Westernized, tacky even; the southern half, only pedestrianized in 1997, is calmer and feels less like a tourist trap. Walking north on Váci utca, before you get to Vörösmarty tér, a little square overflowing with terrace tables opens up on the right. This is **Kristóf tér**, and at its centre is a statue of a *Fisher-Girl* which apparently caused a stir due to the girl's skimpy attire. It leads into **Szervita tér**, named after the rundown 1732 Baroque **Servite Church**. The real reason for visiting this square may elude you until you look up to the west. The building known as the **Turkish Bank House** (which it used to contain) looks at ground level like any other shop. Follow it up and things get more interesting. The whole façade is covered with vast arched windows. At the top in the playfully curved gable is Miksa Róth's masterpiece, an Art Nouveau mosaic entitled *Glory to Hungary*. Angels, shepherds, and heroes such as István Széchenyi, Lajos Kossuth and Ferenc Rákóczi, pay homage to a bethroned *Patrona Hungariae* (Our Lady, Patron of Hungary).

Ferenciek tere is the main route for east–west traffic and very busy. But stand where the bridge stretches away before you and you will notice that two near-identical buildings, the **Klotild Palaces**, flank the road like mirror images, creating a gateway for the bridge. This 'gateway' is different but equally impressive coming the other way. Over the main road, the corner building smothered with gold-leaf mosaics, ironwork, busts and reliefs is the Párizsi Udvar or **Paris Arcade**.

Southern Belváros

In the calm of these narrow back streets you can catch a whiff of the past and the true spirit of the present. There is little sightseeing to be done.

Just off Kálvin tér on Múzeum krt. is the grand neoclassical edifice of the **National Museum** (Nemzeti Múzeum; *open June–Oct Tues–Sun 10–6; Nov–May Tues–Sun 10–5*). Opened in 1848, it soon played host to one of Hungarian legend's most important scenes. A huge crowd gathered on 15 March 1848 to listen to the leaders of the young revolutionaries, and heard the popular poet Sándor Petőfi recite his now famous *National Song*, marking the beginning of the revolution. Count Ferenc Széchenyi's extensive collection of manuscripts, prints, coins, coats of arms and maps was the basis of the museum's collection; today the exhibits tell the story of Hungary's history in two halves: from the foundation of the state to its reconquest from the Turks, and from the end of the Turkish wars to the 1990s. Its two great treasures are St Stephen's Sword and the Coronation Mantle, both on the first floor. In the basement is a Lapidarium with a collection of Roman remains, mainly tombstones.

East of Kálvin tér on Üllöi út is the **Museum of Applied Arts** (Iparművészeti Múzeum; *open daily 10–6*). Designed by Ödön Lechner and Gyula Pártos, it is a significant example of Lechner's blending of folk art with more eclectic elements and Art Nouveau to forge a national architecture. It features a wonderfully colourful patterned roof trimmed with yellow majolica, which also enlivens the beautiful dome. Tiles on the façade create flower and foliage patterns. Inside, all white, it resembles the Taj Mahal.

Farther round the Kiskörút to the west of Kálvin tér is the magnificent **Central Market Hall**, looking like a grand old railway station, an impression maintained inside by the height of the ceiling and the iron staircases and walkways. Next door is another notable building, the neo-Renaissance **University of Economic Sciences**; a bridge arches over its inner courtyard, commonly known as the 'Bridge of Sighs'.

Andrássy Út to City Park

Starting at one of Budapest's busiest junctions just north of Deák tér, Andrássy út runs northwest in a straight line for 2.5km, the central axis of Terézváros (Theresa Town), better known as District VI. In 2002, the street and its historic environs, conceived as a grand boulevard in the style of the Champs-Elysées and inaugurated in 1884, were granted UNESCO World Heritage status. It is worth a stroll along this most august of Budapest's boulevards just to admire the grandeur of the buildings, among them the sumptuous neo-Renaissance **State Opera House** (Állami Operaház; *guided tour 3 and 4pm daily; adm*) and the **New Theatre** (Új Színház) – a masterpiece by Béla Lajta, its extraordinay façade combining elements of Art Nouveau, modernism, even Art Deco, which it predates by some 15 years. But the main reason for coming here is the nightlife: the area around Andrássy út is easily the city's most lively quarter.

Some way up Andrássy út is **Liszt Ferenc tér**, the most happening square in town. Pedestrianized, full of trees, benches, statues and terrace tables, it feels utterly Mediterranean. At the far end of the square is the **Franz Liszt Music Academy** (Ferenc Liszt Zeneakadémia), an extraordinary Art Nouveau building with a grand interior. Where Andrássy út meets the Nagykörút is **Oktogon**. The section of Andrássy út running from here to Kodály körönd is noticably wider. The building at **No.60** has a notorious past; during the Horthy era, the ultra-right-wing regime made it their secret police headquarters, where they locked up, beat and tortured Communists. Today the building fittingly houses the new **House of Terror Museum** (*open Tues–Fri 10–6, Sat and Sun 10–8; adm*), where photos, artefacts and daunting commentaries recall the victims of those two bitter pills so hard for the Hungarians to swallow: the Holocaust, and the Communist dictatorship. **Kodály körönd**, like Oktogon, is defined by four massive buildings, but is much more sedate and elegant.

The boulevard gets even more stately as it heads towards **Heroes' Square** (Hősök tere), a site of national importance flanked by two imposing edifices, the **Millenary Monument** and a two-part semi-circular **colonnade**. To the right is the neoclassical red brick **Palace of Arts**. Inside, the largest gallery in the country (*open Tues–Sun 10–6; adm*) houses temporary exhibitions of chiefly modern art. On the north side of the square a neoclassical building with Italian-Renaissance, Romanesque and Baroque-revival influences is an appropriate building for the excellent **Museum of Fine Arts** (Szépmûvéseti Múzeum; *open Tues–Sun 10–5.30*). The European equivalent of the National Gallery, its huge collection spans all periods of art, from Egyptian to French 19th-century to Spanish Old Masters to Dutch and Italian masterpieces.

Beyond lies **City Park** (Városliget), a must for anyone with children, containing the fairytale **Vajdahunyad Castle** (*open Tues–Sun approximately 10–5; closed Mon; adm*), Budapest's **Zoo** (Állat-és Növénykert), **circus**, **amusement park** and the most family-friendly spa complex in town, the **Széchenyi Baths** (*XIV. Állatkerti körút 11; open April–Sept daily 6am–7pm; Oct–Mar Mon–Sat 6am–5pm, Sun 6am–4pm; adm*).

The Old Jewish Quarter

District VII, or Erzsébetváros, is the slice of Budapest's pie south of the Andrássy út area. The old Jewish Quarter covers the innermost part of this district. From the outset it has been a testament to anti-Semitism, its very foundation dating from the 18th century when Jews were still prohibited from living within the city walls. Ironically, there were Jews living here at least six centuries before the Magyar founding fathers arrived. When the city outgrew its walls, new laws prevented Jews from buying property. The second half of the 19th century brought a relaxing of these property laws, leading to a rapid rise in the Jewish population in this quarter. In 1867 Jews gained formal emancipation; by 1939 there were about 200,000 Jews in Budapest, many of them living here in a thriving community. A community, yes, but the area was never a ghetto until 1944, when the Nazis and Fascist Arrow Cross walled off the whole area and herded the remaining Jews inside as a prelude to deportation. Since the men had already been taken away to do forced labour, the 70,000 crammed into this small area were mainly women, children and pensioners.

Today the city's remnant of 80,000 still constitutes the largest Jewish community in Central Europe. You can get a taste of this spirit by wandering around the shabby, decaying and bullet-pocked streets, but there's little to see apart from the magnificent **Great Synagogue** on Dohány út (*open Mon–Thurs 10–5, Fri 10–3, Sun 10–2, closed Sat and at Passover; adm*), which was one of the two entrances to the ghetto of 1944. Europe's largest synagogue, and the second largest in the world after Temple Emmanuel in New York, it can hold almost 3,000 people. Built in a Romantic style in 1854–9 by Viennese architect Ludwig Förster, it incorporates many obvious Byzantine and particularly Moorish qualities. The staircase up to the **Jewish Museum** (*open April–Oct Mon–Fri 10–3, Sun 10–2, closed Sat; adm*) bears a relief of Tivadar (Theodore) Herzl, the founder of the Zionist movement, who was born and educated here.

Behind the courtyard and farther down Wesselényi utca, a garden contains Imre Varga's 1991 **Holocaust Memorial**, which channels all that pain and sorrow into the poignant form of a metallic weeping willow in the shape of an inverted menorah. The **garden** is named in honour of Raoul Wallenberg, a Swedish consul who is believed to have saved as many as 20,000 Jews by placing them in safe houses.

The other sight to see here is the amazing **Gozsdu Udvar**, a passageway linking seven courtyards between Dob u. 16 with Király u. 11. Abandoned and crumbling, this series of inelegant but enigmatic concrete squares with a dog-leg in the middle is eerie and atmospheric. Stand in the middle and look back towards the entrance and what you will see is a series of squares alternating light and shade. Run-down as it is, not much effort is required to imagine how it was at the beginning of the 20th century when this was the bustling heart of Jewish Budapest. These days the community's central focus is on Kazinczy utca, a little farther down Dob u., shortly after Hungary's only kosher *pâtisserie*, **Fröhlich Cukrászda**. If Kazinczy holds the local focus, the heart of activity is still centred on **Klauzál tér**, a block farther down Dob u. It was the heart of the 1944–5 ghetto as well, when 50,000 people were crammed into living space intended for 15,000. Nowadays, it is given over to one big playground, and the scene of so much suffering now echoes with the sound of children's laughter.

Outside the Centre

The Buda Hills

Forested countryside stretches to the west of Buda, perfect for walking and cycling. A **Cogwheel Railway** starts in the Városmajor Park, opposite the Budapest Hotel (*a couple of stops west of Moszkva tér by buses 22, 56 and 156, or trams 18 and 56; trains leave every 15mins daily 5am–11.30pm*). The terminus at Széchenyi-hegy is a short walk from the start of the **Children's Railway**. This narrow-gauge railway (760mm) covers 11.1km in about 45mins, mostly through dense woodlands. Built by youth brigades in 1948, it is run by uniformed 10–14-year-olds (*trains run Mon–Fri every hour 8–5, Sat and Sun every 30–45mins 8.45–5; Sept–May closed Mon; adm*). The terminus of the Children's Railway, **Hűvösvölgy**, is a large meadow, from where buses run back to Moszkva tér. It is also worth leaving the Children's Railway at János-hegy and following the trail across to the **Chairlift**; from here it is a short but steep walk up to the four-tiered neo-Romanesque **Erzsébet Lookout Tower**, with superb views.

Day Trips and Overnighters from Budapest

Óbuda and Aquincum

Situated on the Buda side, level with the northern tip of Margaret Island, today's suburb of Óbuda was actually the first settlement of any significance in this area. The Romans established a legionary camp and fortifications here as defence against the barbarians beyond. By the 2nd century BC a thriving civilian settlement had grown around the camp, centred on Aquincum 3km to the north. In the Middle Ages, Árpád and his successors built their royal residence here and the town flourished, but then Béla IV moved the royal seat to the more strategic location of Castle Hill. After the Turkish occupation, it enjoyed a renaissance as a market town, producer of wines and somewhat bohemian gastronomic centre.

Opposite the HÉV exit on Szentlélek tér, a splendid old white building contains the **Vasarely Museum** (*open Tues–Sun 10–5; adm*), with an exhaustive collection of Op Art by one of the fathers of the genre, Victor Vasarely. On the right, where Szentlélek and Fő squares merge, the Baroque Zichy mansion (Zichy Kúria) holds the **Kassák Museum** (*open Tues–Sun 10–4; adm*), containing works of avant-garde painting, sculpture, literature and typography. Literally meaning Main Square, **Fő tér** remains to this day the focal point of the town. With its pedestrianized cobbled streets, old buildings like the lovely **theatre** (Városháza), antique lamp-posts, and traditional restaurants that still make a living from Óbuda's *bon-vivant* reputation, it almost single-handedly retains the fragile ambience of a medieval village. At the northeast corner of the square is the strange sight of three metallic women beneath umbrellas. This is the start of Laktanya u., and the composition a prelude to Óbuda's only essential attraction, the **Imre Varga Gallery** at No.7 (*open Tues–Sun 10–6; closed Mon; adm*). Within is a substantial collection by this striking and versatile artist, who is responsible for the Holocaust Monument and the statue of Károlyi Mihály close to Parliament.

A number of **Roman ruins** pay testament to Óbuda's history. **Flórián tér**, Óbuda's largest square and an unpleasant junction of major roads, was built over the nucleus of the Roman military camp. North of Flórián tér (northwest up Vörösvári u. then right on Vihar u. as far as Meggyfa u.) is the **Hercules Villa** (*open Tues–Sun 10–5; closed Nov–14 April; adm*). A series of mosaics are preserved where they were found.

Getting There

HÉV train to Árpád híd from Batthyány tér. Bus 6 from Nyugati station, or 86 from any stop on the Buda promenade.

Eating Out

Óbuda t (01) –

Kéhli, III. Mókus u. 22, t 250 4241, *www.kehli.hu* (*expensive*). First-class, home-made food based on traditional 19th-century cuisine, served in an authentic space with a plain country feel. Their classic dish is the hotpot with marrow-bone. *Closed Mon–Fri lunch.*

Uj Sipos halászkert, Fő tér 6, t 388 8745 (*moderate*). Elegant interior resembling a country manor, and outdoor tables in a round cobbled courtyard. The menu is old-style traditional.

Gigler, III. Föld u. 50c, t 368 6078 (*inexpensive*). The cheap and cheerful option. The interior and courtyard are basic, but the food is authentic home-cooked Hungarian – tasty, plentiful and cheap. *Closed Sun eve and Mon.*

About 1km southwest of Flórián tér on a forested hilltop at Kiscelli u.108, and well worth the walk, is the **Kiscelli Museum** (*open April–Oct Tues–Sun 10–6; Nov–Mar Tues–Sun 10–4; adm*). This 1745 Baroque Trinitarian monastery contains a selection of major Hungarian artworks from about 1880 to 1990.

Roughly 3km north of Óbuda are Budapest's major Roman ruins, the former town of **Aquincum** (*HÉV to Aquincum from Óbuda's Árpád híd, or buses 34, 42 and 106; open May–Sept Tues–Sun 9–6; Oct–Nov Tues–Sun 9–5; closed Dec–April; adm*). No buildings survive, but the arrangement of the foundation walls and the underground piping give a fair idea of the scale and layout of the ancient town.

Szentendre

Situated just 20km north of Budapest, the picturesque town of Szentendre is easily the most rewarding day trip from Budapest. At the end of the 17th century, a mixture of Slav ethnic groups including Bulgarians and Dalmatians, but predominantly Greek Orthodox Serbians, arrived here, fleeing from the advancing Turks. Hard workers in trade and viniculture, they soon began building grand houses and churches with a characteristically Balkan flavour. Over two centuries later, this marvellous architecture, combined with the bucolic ambience, began to attract a stream of artists, whose numbers have swollen ever since, filling the streets with galleries and studios.

Stop to pick up a map at the TOURINFORM office, then head to the focal **Fő tér**, a picturesque cobblestoned square centred on a memorial cross and lined with restaurant terraces and private art galleries; to its north is **Blagovestenska Church** (*adm*) with a dark, atmospheric incense-scented interior and a wonderful iconostasis. Round the corner is the **Museum of Margit Kovács** (*Vastagh György u.1; open daily 10–6; adm*), which contains an extensive collection from this prolific, much-beloved ceramic artist. Heading north, **Bogdányi utca**, too quaint for its own good, is lined with restaurants, souvenir stalls and a few more worthwhile galleries, including the **Museum of Painters Anna Margit and Amos Imre** and the **Art Mill** (No.32; *adm*), a ruined sawmill exhibits works by Hungarian and international artists, as well as the local community.

The best thing to do from here is to wander the maze of cobbled streets that range over the hillside above, lined with handsome, colourful, well-preserved houses and churches. You can't miss the large and impressive terracotta-colour **Serbian Orthodox cathedral**, whose grounds also contain the **Serbian Orthodox Art Museum**.

Getting There

HÉV from Óbuda's Árpád híd or Budapest's Batthyány tér (*45mins*). **Boat** from Budapest's Vigadó tér (*summer only*). The first leaves Budapest at 9, the last leaves Szentendre 5.15.

Tourist Information

Szentendre TOURINFORM, Dumtsa Jenő u. 22, t (26) 317 965, *www.szentendre.hu*. Open *Nov–Feb Mon–Fri 9–4.30.*

Eating Out

Szentendre t (26) –
Aranysarkány, Alkotmány u.1a (*expensive*). Probably the best restaurant in town, with an interesting menu that includes sour cherry soup and trout fillets with Campari.
Labirintus Etterem, Bogdányi 10, t 317 054 (*expensive*). In the Wine Museum, with an interesting menu of Hungarian cuisine.
Chez Nicolas, Kígyó u. 10, t 311 288 (*moderate*). Good food at reasonable prices.

Getting There

Trains depart from Keleti station, 15 daily, taking 2hrs. The last intercity returns 7.10pm.

Tourist Information

Eger TOURINFORM, Dobó tér 2, t (36) 517715, www.egeronline.com.

Where to Stay

Eger t (36) –
★★★**Hotel Korona**, Tündérpart u. 5, t 313 670, www.koronahotel.hu (*inexpensive*). A large, well-equipped hotel with pool, Jacuzzi, sauna, fitness room and its own wine cellar.
★★★**Hotel Senator House**, Dobó tér 11, t 320 466, senator@ohb.hu (*inexpensive*). A handsome, comfortable 18th-century townhouse on the main square. Breakfast included.

★★★**Hotel Villa Volgy**, Tulipánkert u. 5, t 321 664, villavolgy@dpg.hu (*inexpensive*). A lovely new, big building in Szépasszonyvölgy.
★★★**Hotel Romantik**, Csíky Sándor u. 26, t 310 456, www.romantikhotel.hu (*inexpensive*). A charming little place close to the centre.

Eating Out

Eger t (36) –
Two of the best places to eat are the Hotel Korona and Hotel Senator House (*see above*).
Arany Oroszlán étterem (Golden Lion), Dobó tér 5, t 311 005 (*moderate*). Decent and central.
Imola Udvarház, Dózsa Gy. tér, t 516 180 (*moderate*). A little more fancy, but with the emphasis still on home-cooked food.
There are a number of places to eat among the wine cellars of Szépasszonyvölgy. Two of the best are **Talizmán étterem** in the lovely Tulip Garden; or **Kulacs Csárda és Borozó**.

Covering an area of 115 acres, 5km north of Szentendre, is the **Open Air Village Museum** (Szabadtéri Néprajzi Múzeum/Skanzen; *Skanzen bus from stand 7; open April–Oct Tues–Sun 9–5; closed Mon; adm, free Tues and Wed*), whose goal is to represent all the most characteristic traditional types of settlement and architecture.

Eger

Hungarians revere Eger, 128km from Budapest: during a siege in 1552, a group of some 2,000 Magyars led by Istvan Dobó kept an army of 10,000 Turks at bay here for over a month. Legends abound: apparently, Dobó opened the wine caskets so that his men would greet their attackers with red liquid dripping from their mouths. These days, the wine itself is what the town is more famous for, in particular the red blend Egri Bikavér, better known abroad as Bull's Blood. For the casual visitor, however, Eger is simply a gorgeous little town full of attractive Baroque buildings.

The **castle** itself is Eger's most obvious sight, but there hasn't been too much to see since the Habsburgs blew it up in 1702. Within its rebuilt 15th-century Gothic Palace, however, is the **Castle Museum** (*open 8–8; adm*) with exhibitions on the history of castle and city, and tours of the underground fortress (Kazamaták). The pedestrianized town centre revolves around **Dobó tér**, which contains a **Minorite Church** from 1771. Towering over nearby **Eszterházy tér** is Hungary's second biggest church, **Eger Basilica**, designed by József Hild. Opposite, the **Lyceum** contains an **astronomical museum** (*open Tues–Sun 9.30–3; closed Mon; adm*) full of 18th-century instruments, including a *camera obscura* (the 'Eye of Eger') which projects a view of the town.

A mere 25-minute walk from town is the horseshoe-shaped **Szépasszonyvölgy** or 'Valley of Beautiful Women', the perfect place to sample local wines, with dozens of small, private wine cellars. Many places are closed by evening, so arrive early.

Slovenia:
Travel, Practical A–Z and Language

13

Travel

Entry Formalities

Passports and Visas

Slovenia became a member of the European Union in 2004. Holders of EU, US, Canadian, Australian and New Zealand passports do not need a visa for stays of up to 90 days.

Customs

EU nationals over 17 can now import a limitless amount of goods, provided they are for personal use. Non-EU visitors are subject to the following cap on imports: 200 cigarettes or 50 cigars or 250g of tobacco; 1ltr spirits, 2ltr wine; 50ml perfume, 240ml eau de toilette.

Getting Around

By Bus

Slovenia's love affair with the car has been a double-edged sword for a bus network operated by local companies: the country's clean and generally comfortable buses have had their services slashed. Book ahead if you want to travel from Ljubljana to coastal or mountain destinations on Fridays or public holidays. Otherwise, tickets can be bought directly before travelling from the bus station (*avtobusna postaja*) or from the driver on boarding.

Baffling multi-coloured timetables with a colour-coordinated system of departures (*odhodi*) and arrivals (*prihodi*) abbreviate days to initial letters – Po for *Ponedeljek* (Monday), So for *Sobota* (Saturday) and throw in occasional curveballs such as SN (*Sobota, Nedelja* (Saturday, Sunday). Far easier to ask at the ticket booth.

By Car

In general, driving in Slovenia is a joy, but high car-ownership means congestion is a problem on major routes at weekends and rush hours, especially in summer.

Motorways have **speed limits** of 130kph; secondary or tertiary roads 100kph; towns and villages 50kph.

Seatbelts are compulsory for all passengers. Drivers are forbidden from using mobile phones at the wheel and dipped headlights are required during the day. Carrying a reflective breakdown warning triangle is mandatory. All drivers are expected to have to hand a **full national driving licence**. Traffic police issue on-the-spot **fines** for all driving infringements. The maximum blood alcohol limit is currently 0.05mg/100ml blood. **Penalties** for those over (or even on) the limit are severe, with fines of up to 100,000 SIT, and licences are removed from offenders.

Petrol stations (*benicinska črpalka*) dispense unleaded (*neosvinčen bencin*) fuel and diesel and are generally open from 7am to 8pm.

Car hire is a simple business – drivers generally must be over 21 (sometimes over 25) and must have held an EU or international driving licence for (usually) one year. Cheap it is not, however, ranging from 11,400 SIT (€47) a day for a modest two-door car to 28,300 SIT (€120) for a Mercedes. Local outlets are usually cheaper if you are not overly concerned with as-new cosmetics. All hire companies require drivers to present on collection of the car a passport, driving licence and credit card (sometimes two) as deposit.

By Train

Perhaps because it was pioneered by the-thorough Austrians, **Slovenske železnice** is a paragon of efficiency. Carriages are invariably clean and your *tolars* buy more kilometres on a train than on a bus. Stars of the service are express Inter-City Slovenia (ICS) trains, which journey to international neighbours such as Italy, Croatia, Austria and Germany. Then come the InterCity (IC) or EuroCity (EC) trains, which pause at fewer stations than regional trains (*regionalni vlaki*, RG). These are marginally faster than local trains (*potniški vlaki*, LP), which pause at every hamlet.

Tickets can be bought from the train station (*železniška postaja*), where yellow timetables list departures (*odhodi*) and white timetables list arrivals (*prihodi*); trains marked with an R permit free seat reservations (*rezervacije*); those with a boxed R demand one (ICS and international services) and are best purchased in advance. Timetables will also list the correct platform (*peron*) for your train. If you run late and purchase a ticket from the inspector, you'll incur a 440 SIT charge. The Tourist Weekend (*Turist vikend*) ticket concedes 30%

discounts to passengers who make return journeys on Saturdays, Sundays and holidays.

With the exception of ICS trains, all permit bicycles for an extra 630 SIT. Major stations have facilities to store luggage for up to 72hrs.

Practical A–Z

Crime and the Police

Police, t 113.

Maybe thanks to the fact that its 2 million population either lives in or retains strong ties to pastoral communities, Slovenia is safe to the point of complacency. Take precautions against petty theft in cities such as Ljubljana and Maribor (although even this is rare) by not leaving valuables unattended in public places, locking cars and hiding cameras or bags. Similarly, although street pickpockets are rare, keep your wits about you at train and bus stations. Theft from hotel rooms is unheard of.

In the unlikely event that anything is stolen, police (*policija*) are generally good-natured and courteous. Report crimes to receive an insurance claim number.

Disabled Travellers

Not Slovenia's strong point. Although awareness of disabled needs is improving, steps rather than ramps are the norm in museums and on public transport, with the exceptions of international and the most modern trains. Ask at the ticket office; larger train stations will have ramps for boarding. Similarly, only top-end hotels offer wheelchair-friendly facilities, although nearly all larger hotels provide lifts.

Your most comprehensive source of information for advice is the **Paraplegics Association of Slovenia** (Zveza Paraplegikov Republike Slovenija; Štihova 14, Ljubljana, **t** (01) 432 71 38, *www.zveza-paraplegikov.si*).

Electricity

220 volts/50 Hz, using the standard continental European plug with 2 round pins. You will need an adaptor.

Embassies and Consulates

Slovenian Embassies Abroad
UK: 10 Little College Street, London SW1 P3SJ, **t** (020) 7222 5400.
USA: 1525 New Hampshire Ave NW, Washington DC 20036, **t** (0202) 667 53 63.

Foreign Embassies in Ljubljana
UK: 4th Floor, Trg Republike 3, **t** (01) 200 39 10, *www.british-embassy.si*.
USA: Prešernova cesta 31, **t** (01) 200 55 00, *www.usembassy.si*.

Festivals and Events

February: pre-Lent carnival the **Pust**, at its most ebullient in Ptuj. Masked *kurenti*, like walking haystacks in head-to-foot sheepskins, chase out evil spirits from houses in the **Kurentovanje**, a 10-day extravaganza. More modest events in Cerkno and Cerknica.
Mid-March: the **world ski jump championships** in Planica (near Kranjska Gora).
Late June: Škofja Loka stages medieval pageant **Vererira pot** against its historic backdrop. Maribor combines popular music with high-brow culture during the riverside **Festival Lent**. In Ljubljana is the **Ana Desetnica International Festival of Street Theatre**.
July/August: **International Summer Festival**, Ljubljana, a cultural beano of classical music, theatre and dance; second billing goes to the summer festival of Primorska.
September: **Cow's Ball** in Lake Bohinj, a bacchanalian weekend celebrating the return of cows from mountain meadows.
November: **St Martin's Day** (11th), the official date when lowly grape juice becomes wine – Metilka wine village Drašiči spins out the booze-up for a week.
December: **St Nicholas Day** (6th). Christmas celebrations are rounded off with concerts.

Health and Insurance

Ambulance and **fire, t** 112.

EU citizens with a stamped E111 form (available from post offices, to be replaced by a card in Dec 2005) receive free emergency medical treatment, but be aware that the reciprocal agreement does not cover medical repatriation, private care or dental treatment. Skiers will have to pay a 'dangerous sports' supplement, as will those who intend to go whitewater rafting on the Soča river.

Town or village pharmacies (*lekarna*) proffer over-the-counter advice, usually in English, and can provide basic medicines. Embassies hold lists of fluent English-speaking doctors. These are your first port of call for sickness – a hospital (*bolnica*) is only for a genuine emergency or in case of referral.

British and US embassies recommend that those who hike in the forests in summer are vaccinated for tick-borne encephalitis. Tap water is potable everywhere.

Internet

The cyber revolution has yet to seize imaginations in a largely rural nation. Internet cafés are few and far between, even in Ljubljana. Some city tourist information centres have a lone terminal for short-term use, or try public libraries. Top hotels have ISDN connections.

Money and Banks

The official unit of currency is the Slovenian **tolar**, which divides into 100 **stolni**. Notes come in denominations of 10,000, 5,000, 1,000, 500, 200, 100, 50, 20 and 10, and brass coins are available in sums of 50, 20, 10, 5, 2 and 1. However, Slovenia plans to join the euro in 2007, a currency already accepted in motorway toll booths and many hotels, which often list prices in euros.

ATM cash dispensers (*bančni avtomat*) are ubiquitous throughout Slovenia, from city to village to (usually) motorway petrol stations; all have an English-language option. ATMs readily accept Visa credit cards, usually MasterCard/ EuroCard and American Express, and occasionally Diner's Club.

The major **credit cards** are widely accepted in towns and major tourist centres, but smaller *gostišče* (inns, guesthouses), pensions and *gostilna* (inns) may demand cash.

Travellers' cheques are the most secure means of transporting money. They can be exchanged at banks (*banka*) or at money exchanges (*menjalnica*) in post offices, tourist information centres, and hotels.

Banks are open weekdays 8.30–12.30 and 2–5, and Saturday 8.30–11/12.

Value added tax (DDV) can be reclaimed by non-EU residents (except on alcohol and tobacco) if their receipt/s on one day from the same retailer exceed 15,000 SIT. Ask sales assistants to complete a DDV-VP form or equivalent when you get the receipt, which is stamped as you leave the country, to collect refunds at Kompas offices at the border.

Approximate **exchange rates** (March 2005) are: £1 = 345 SIT; €1 = 240; $1 = 180.

National Holidays

1–2 Jan New Year
8 Feb Slovenian Culture Day (Prešeren Day)
March/April Easter Monday
27 April National Resistance Day
1–2 May International Labour Day
25 June Slovene Statehood Day
15 Aug Assumption Day
31 Oct Reformation Day
1 Nov All Saints' Day
25 Dec Christmas
26 Dec Independence Day

Opening Hours

Shops usually open weekdays 8–7, Sat 8–1, and close on Sun; however, some stores and chain supermarkets may pull up shutters on Sun morning 9–1 and in cities can extend opening hours until 5.

Access to **churches** (*cerkev*) is generally fine. Most **museums** (*muzej*) open Tues–Sun 10–6.

Post

The **Posta Slovenije**, with canary-yellow signs emblazoned with a curled bugle, sell stamps and telephone cards (*see* below), send faxes and exchange money; service is efficient, if somewhat basic. Stamps (*znamike*) are also sold over the counter at newsagents.

Post offices open weekdays 8–7, Sat 8–1, though in larger towns they may operate longer hours.

Price Categories

Hotels

Hotel prices quoted are for a double room with WC and bath or shower in peak season – July– August in most cases, but December– March in ski resorts. Not factored in is a 'tourist tax' of 200–350 SIT levied per person per night.

expensive above 33,000 SIT / €140
moderate 16,000–33,000 SIT / €65–140
inexpensive under 16,000 SIT / €65

Restaurants

Restaurant prices cover the cost of a meal for one people, with an average-priced main course and a shared bottle of house wine.

expensive over 4,250 SIT / €18
moderate 2,500–4,250 SIT / €10–18
cheap under 2,500 SIT / €10

Sports

Skiing is the most popular sport, with resorts at Vogel, above Lake Bohinge (up to 1,840m), Kranjska Gora (1,600m), Kanin, above Bovec (2,300m) and Krvavec, northeast of Kranj (1,970m). All of these are well equipped with chair lifts, cable cars, ski schools, rentals and hotels. There are also 7000km of glorious marked alpine trails for hiking.

There is a centre at Bovec from which you can practise your **kayaking**, **rafting** and **canoeing** on the unspoilt upper waters of the Soča river. **Fishing** is also popular, with good stocks of pike, grayling and trout in the Soča, Krka, Kolpa and Sava Bohinjka (near Bohinj) rivers or in the alpine lakes of Bled and Bohinj.

It is possible to hire mountain bikes and Bled and Bohinj, in Ljubljana and on the coast.

Telephones

To **call abroad from Slovenia** dial 00 then the country code (UK 44; Ireland 353; US and Canada 1; Australia 61; New Zealand 64) then dial the number, again omitting the first zero of the area code.

To **call Slovenia from abroad** dial country code 386, omit the first zero of the area code then dial the number.

Telephone boxes only accept telephone cards (*telekartica*), available from post offices and newsagent kiosks in denominations of 700, 1,000, 1,700 and 3,500 SIT. For long international calls, head for the phone booths in post offices; be warned, the bill for a leisurely chat on a hotel telephone can be huge.

Time

Slovenia is within the Central European Time zone: one hour ahead of GMT, six hours ahead of Eastern Standard Time and nine ahead of Western Standard Time.

Tipping

Although not the Communist anathema of old, tipping in Slovenia is a matter of etiquette. Because service is not usually included in the bill, as a rule of thumb round up to the nearest decimal figure in cafés and leave 10 per cent in restaurants.

Toilets

Most large shopping malls have a public toilet (*javno stranišče*), as do train stations. Men should enter Monški, women Ženske. Bar and café owners will usually let you use their facilities for free, although you should at least buy an espresso.

Tourist Information

UK: The Barns, Woodlands End, Mells, Frome, Somerset BA11 3QD, **t** (01373) 814 233, *info@slovenian-tourism.co.uk.*
USA: Slovenian Tourist Office, 2929 East Commercial Boulevard, Suite 201, Fort Lauderdale, FL 33308, **t** 0954 491 01 12, *slotouristboard@kompas.net.*

In addition, national tourism co-ordinator the Slovenia National Tourist Office is superb – its Ljubljana office (Krekov trg 10, **t** 306 45 75/76; *open June–Sept 8–9, Oct–May 8–7*) is positively bursting with Slovenia-wide information. It also operates a first-rate website, *www.slovenia-tourism.si.*

Language

The south Slavonic tongue of Slovene is one of the few Indo-European languages to retain the dual form, slipped in between singular and plural (three or more) to present scholars with another noun ending to learn. Include on the curriculum three genders and six cases for pronouns. And that's before you consider a polyglot of over 40 dialects.

Pronunciation

All 25 letters in Slovenian are pronounced, but the stress roams freely and simply has to be learned. Modified Roman consonants with a caron (ˇ) indicate 'sh', 'ch' and 'zh' phonetics, otherwise pronunciation of consonants is largely the same as English.

C is pronounced as 'ts' as in 'cats', while č is softer, spoken as the 'ch' in 'change'. D is hard unless combined as dž, as in 'j' of 'jane', and g is consistently hard as in 'gain'. J is spoken as 'y' as in 'yellow', and is far easier than it appears when combined with other consonants: nj is 'ny' as in 'canyon' or the Spanish ñ; lj is spoken as the 'li' of 'million'. R is enjoyable, trilled deliciously on the tongue. Š is pronounced as 'sh' as in 'sheet', just a mite more high-pitched than ž, which is spoken as 's' of 'leisure'. V and l are as in English unless they appear at the end of a word or before another consonant, whereupon they become the soft 'w' of 'know'; e.g. pol (half) is pronounced 'poe'.

Because phonetics change with the length of the sound, Slovenian vowels are a challenge. A and e are short, as in 'pat' and 'pet', or long when unstressed as in 'father' and 'pear'. I is pronounced either as the short 'i' of 'pit' or a longer 'ee', while o appears as the short 'o' of 'on' and the long 'or' of 'horn'. U is pronounced as 'oo' as in 'frugal'.

Useful Words and Phrases

yes/no ja/ne
hello/goodbye dober dan/ nasvidenje
please/thank you prosim/hvala
how are you?(formal) kako se imate?
how are you? (informal) kako se imaš?
fine, thanks dobra, hvala
do you speak English? govorite angleško

I (don't) understand (ne) razumijem
help! Na pomoč!
I'm lost Izgubil(a) sem/se (fem.)
Do you have a single/double room? ali imate enpostelnja/dvopostelnja sobu?
Could we have a table? Ali bi lakho dobili mizo?
Do you have vegetarian dishes? Ali imate vegeterijanski meni?
arrivals/departures prihodi/odhodi
open/closed odprto/zaprto
entrance/exit vhod/izod
where is/are kje je/so
toilet stranišče, WC (pronounced 'vay-tsay')

Days and Months

Monday ponedeljek
Tuesday torek
Wednesday sreda
Thursday četrtek
Friday petek
Saturday sobota
Sunday nedelja

January januar
February februar
March marec
April april
May maj
June junij
July julij
August avgust
September september
October oktober
November november
December december

Numbers

1 ena
2 dva
3 tri
4 štiri
5 pet
6 šest
7 sedem
8 osem
9 devet
10 deset
100 sto
1,000 tisoč

Slovenia: Ljubljana

14

Ljubljana

▲ To Museum of Modern History

Tivoli Park

Swimming Pool

TIVOLSKA CESTA

VOŠNJAKOVA ULICA

DVOŘAKOVA ULICA

Railway Station

TRG OSVOBODILNE FRONTE

Bus Station

PRAŽAKOVA ULICA

GOSPOSVETSKA CESTA

TRDINOVA ULICA

SLOVENSKA CESTA

MIKLOŠIČEVA CESTA

KOLODVORSKA ULICA

ČUFARJEVA ULICA

KOMENSKEGA ULICA

RESLJEVA CESTA

PUHARIEVA ULICA

PREŽILOVA ULICA

ŽUPANČIČEVA ULICA

ŠTEFANOVA ULICA

National Gallery

CANKARJEVA CESTA

Nebotičnik Skyscraper

TAVČARJEVA ULICA

Miklošičev Park

DALMATINOVA ULICA

Hotel Union

MIKLOŠIČEVA CESTA

MALA ULICA

Modern Gallery

TIVOLSKA CESTA

Opera House

SLOVENSKA CESTA

NAZORJEVA ULICA

Church of the Annunciation

TRUBARJEVA CESTA

TOMŠIČEVA ULICA

BEETHOVNOVA

ČOPOVA ULICA

PREŠERNOV TRG

PREŠERNOVA CESTA

Slovenian Museum of Natural History / National Museum

Parliament

ŠUBIČEVA ULICA

Ljubljanica

PETKOVŠKOVO NABREŽJE

ADAMIČ-LUNDROVO NABREŽJE

DRAGON BRIDGE

KOPITARJEVA UL.

St Nicholas' Cathedral

Vodnikov TRG

VESELOVA ULICA

VALVASORJEVA UL.

TRG REPUBLIKE

PLEČNIKOV TRG

PREŠERNOV TRG

WOLFOVA ULICA

MAČKOVA

CIRIL METODOV TRG

KREKOV TRG

ERJAVČEVA CESTA

PREŠERNOVA CESTA

Ursuline Church of the Holy Trinity

Park Zvezda

KONGRESNI TRG

HRIBARJEVO NABREŽJE

STRITARJEVA UL.

RIBJI TRG

MESTNI TRG

ZA OGRAJAMI

Town Hall

KRAGELJEVA STEZA

Ljubljana Castle

PREŠERNOVA CESTA

ERJAVČEVA CESTA

Slovene Philharmonic Hall

CANKARJEVO NABREŽJE

OLD TOWN

OSOJNA STEZA

REBER POD CERADOM

Slovenian National Theatre

IGRIŠKA ULICA

GREGORČIČEVA ULICA

University of Ljubljana

VEGOVA ULICA

DVORNI TRG

COBBLER'S BRIDGE

ČEVLJARSKA

MAČJA STEZA

GRAJSKA STEZA

RIMSKA CESTA

SLOVENSKA CESTA

GREGORČIČEVA UL.

TURJAŠKA

NOVI TRG

Slovenian Academy of Arts

STARI TRG

OSOJNA POT

AŠKERČEVA CESTA

RIMSKA CESTA

National and University Library

TRG FRANCOSKE REVOLUCIJE

SALENDROVA

City Museum

KRIŽEVNIŠKA UL.

BREG

GALLUSOVO NABREŽJE

STIŠKA

LEVŠTIKOV TRG

GORNJI TRG

ULICA NA GRAD

SODARSKA STEZA

Church of St James

RIMSKA CESTA

EMONSKA C.

Križanke Theatre

ZOISOVA CESTA

ROŽNA ULICA

St Florian's Church

MIRJE

MIRJE

KRAKOVO

KRAKOVSKA ULICA

EMONSKA ULICA

KLADEZNA ULICA

KRAKOVSKI NASIP

Ljubljanica

Gruber Palace

ROŽNA ULICA

KARLOVŠKA CESTA

GRADAŠKA

▼ To Trnovo

200 metres

20 o yards

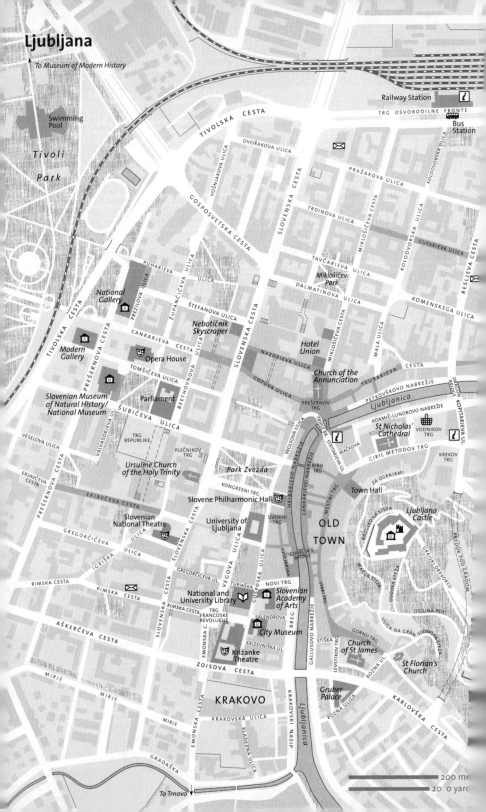

Getting There

EasyJet flies from London Stansted and Adria Airways flies from London Gatwick in 2hrs 5mins. *See* **Getting There**, pp.4–10.

Getting from the Airport

Brnik airport is 23km north of the city, linked by public **buses** which take 50mins and cost 850 SIT to shuttle to the bus station. Return to the airport is from bay 28, Mon–Fri 5.20am–8.10pm; Sat–Sun 6.10am then every odd hour from 9.10am to 7.10pm.

Private bus company Avtobusni prevozi Markun (**t** 041 670 528) takes 25mins, costs 1,000 SIT and shuttles to the bus station approx. every 1½hrs, 7.30– midnight. Its return service operates in the same intervals between 5.20am and 10.30pm. Big spenders can request an Orbita airport minibus 24 hours a day (**t** 040 887 766); it runs door to door and costs 4,100 SIT per person.

Expect to pay 8,000 SIT for a **taxi** to the bus station.

Getting Around

Public **buses** rumble along a baffling network of routes from the bus station on Trg Osvobodilne fronte (aka Trg OF), north of the centre, between 5 and 10.30pm. They cost a flat-rate 300 SIT from the driver or 200 SIT for **tokens** (*žetoni*) bought from newsagents and post offices; a **daily ticket** (*dnevana karta*) costs 900 SIT and the **Ljubljana Card** (*see* tourist information, below) buys free transport for its 72hr duration.

In truth, you'll rarely need a bus nor strong shoe leather because Ljubljana's city centre is compact and largely pedestrianized.

More useful than public transport is the tourist board's laudable **Ljubljana Bike Project** (*May–Nov*); bikes with a basket, available from central Prešernov trg, Plečnikov trg (near Trg Republike) and in front of the railway station on Trg Osvobodilne fronte, are free for tourists for the first two hours (1,000 SIT deposit), then cost 200 SIT for every extra hour. Be warned, they're popular.

If they're all taken, **Tir Bar** (in the train station) hires bikes for 2500 SIT per day.

Taxis congregate at the station and on Prešernov trg, or can be hired in advance on **t** 9700 to 9709.

Car Hire

All international players operate second bureaux at the airport.

Avis, Čufarjeva 2, **t** (01) 430 80 10; or Hotel Lev (*see* below), **t** (01) 438 32 50.

Budget, Miklošičeva 3 (Grand Hotel Union), **t** (01) 421 73 40.

Hertz, Dunajska 122, **t** (01) 530 54 38.

Ines, Mestni trg 9, **t** (01) 422 29 60.

Tourist Information

Ljubljana: Stritarjeva, before the Triple Bridge, **t** (01) 306 12 15, *www.ljubljana-tourism.si. Open daily June–Sept 8–9, Oct–May 8–7.* The main office, supplemented by a smaller office at the railway station (*Trg OF 6,* **t** *(01) 433 94 75; open daily June–Sept 8–10, Oct–May 8–7*). Both proffer advice on accommodation (hotel and private) and stock detailed city maps, informative free city guide booklets and the what's-on guide *Where to?*, plus the usual confetti of leaflets. The equally helpful **Slovenian Tourist Information Centre** (*Krekov trg 10,* **t** *306 45 75/76; www.slovenia-tourism.si; open June–Sept 8–9, Oct–May 8–7*) near the market tackles national tourism, sells tickets for city entertainments and a handful of souvenirs, and operates eight computer terminals for inveterate e-mail addicts (first 15mins free); the main tourist office also has a single terminal. All offices stock the **Ljubljana Card**; pay 3,000 SIT for free public transport or museum and gallery entry for 72hrs, plus discounts in hotels, restaurants and car hire firms.

Festivals

July–Aug: International Summer Festival (*www.festival-lj.si*), the highlight of Ljubljana's calendar: music, theatre and dance in the Križanke theatre and castle.

June: The superb **International Jazz Festival** in late June; the **Druga Godba** festival of world and alternative music early in the month.

End June–early July: Wacky street theatre during the **Ana Dsetnica** festival.

Mid-June–Sept: Cutting-edge trends of graphic art, celebrated every odd year during the prestigious **International Biennial of Graphic Arts** in the International Centre of Graphic Art and Museum of Modern Art.

December: **Christmas street fairs and events** sprawl on the river banks and fill squares.

Shopping

High street chain stores line **Čopova ulica**, but more enticing (if targeted at the tourist *tolar*) is the mish-mash of small shops in Mestni trg or independent boutiques of neighbours Stari trg and especially Gornji trg; **Rustika** (Ljubljana Castle) and **Dom** (Ciril Metodov trg 5 and Mestni trg 24) cast their net Slovenia-wide for rather kitsch souvenirs; tiny **Galerija Idrijske čipke** (Gornji trg 23) dedicates itself to delicate lacework from Idrija. An excellent range of handicrafts – Idrija lace, pottery, twee painted chests – is also available from **Skrina** (Breg 8), and **Atelje Rebeka Galerija** (Cankarjevo nabrežje 9) has home-made patchwork covers and quilts.

Best of all is the **fleamarket** which claims riverbank Cankarjevo nabrežje on Sunday mornings (*8–1*); expect the occasional antique and Communist-era relics among stalls of good old-fashioned junk. A rummage through the Pogačarjev trg section of the **daily market** on Vodnikov trg (*Mon–Fri summer 6–6, winter 6–4*) will turn up a few handicrafts stalls plus home-made olive oils and honey.

Where to Stay

Ljubljana **t** (01) –

Grand Hotel Union Executive, Miklošičeva 1, **t** 308 12 70, *www.gh-union.si* (*expensive*). You can almost smell the moustache wax in the *grande dame* of Ljubljana's hotels; beg for a room on floors 1–3, the best with balconies, to wallow in Secessionist-era proportions. The most sumptuous décor in town elegantly updates Art Nouveau. Facilities are four-star, and there's a rooftop pool.

Slon, Slovenska 34, **t** 470 11 00, *www.hotel-slon.com* (*expensive*). Apparently, Austrian Archduke Maximilian and his elephant (*slon*) lodged in an inn here to christen this four-star member of the Best Western chain. Parquet floors, homely fabrics and rugs are pleasantly old-fashioned in rooms that have more character than newer rivals.

Grand Hotel Union Garni, Miklošičeva 9, **t** 308 43 00 (*moderate*). The latest member of the GHU family is priced just the right side of expensive – for now. Colourful bedspreads add character in refurbished modern rooms.

City Hotel Turist, Dalmatinova 5, **t** 234 91 30, *www.hotelturist.si* (*moderate*). Compact but cheerful rooms in a friendly, central three-star, just east of Miklošičev Park.

Pri Mraku, Rimska 4, **t** 421 96 00, *www.daj-dam.si* (*moderate*). Comfy and modern-traditional décor in a guesthouse with a good Slovenian restaurant near Trg francoske revolucije.

Emonec, Wolfova 12, **t** 200 15 20, *www.hotel-emonec.com* (*cheap*). Not just the best cheapie – a friendly two-star newcomer (2004) with simple but stylish en suites – but also a hotel with one of the best locations in Ljubljana. The best bargain in town.

Celica, Metelkova 8, **t** 430 18 90, *www.souhostel.si* (*cheap*). The bars on the windows are the only clues that this quirky and original backpacker haven began life as a barracks' prison; reservation is essential to claim a single or two-bed room. Non-residents can tour former cells whose individual décor was created by artists (*daily at 2pm; adm*).

Eating Out

Ljubljana **t** (01) –

Chez Eric, Mestni trg 3, **t** 251 28 39 (*expensive*). Smart dining and the sort of gourmet French cuisine where smoked goose is served with chestnut purée and hints of honey or the aubergine mousse has a whiff of lavender flower sauce. *Closed Sun*.

Gostilna As, Čopova 5 (entrance on Knafljev prehod off Wolfova ulica), **t** 425 88 22 (*expensive*). An enjoyably stuffy upmarket traditionalist which prepares the finest Slovenian dishes you will eat plus superb seafood, and stocks an excellent cellar.

Reservations essential to join Ljubljana's élite for Sunday lunch.

Špajza, Gornji trg 28, t (*expensive–moderate*). Snug dining rooms furnished with homely charm, and a talented chef who prepares superb Slovenian-international crossover cuisine (try venison in wild berries or acclaimed sea food dishes such as monkfish with truffles), make this first choice for an intimate, romantic dinner.

Zlata ribica, Cankarjevo nabrežje 5–7, t 426 94 90 (*moderate*). Ljubljana's first riverside bar is now its best brasserie, laidback but stylish, with the finest terrace in town. Dishes such as grilled lamb or game in fruits-of-the-forest sauce and cheese *štrukli* plus the fish of its name (*ribica*) star on a menu which includes cheaper pastas.

Gostilna Sokol, Ciril Metodov trg 18, t 439 68 55 (*moderate*). An unassuming exterior hides a marvellous rustic-style inn which rambles over two levels and hides plenty of snug nooks. No surprise the cuisine is a taste of tradition – game goulashes, venison, wild boar and thick sausages with dumplings.

Julija, Stari trg 9, t 426 64 63 (*cheap*). Pork with feta and roast tomatoes or chicken in a basil sauce is typical of Mediterranean-influenced cooking in a café-restaurant of neo-Baroque Italian mirrors and repro *fin-de-siècle* posters. Charming for a low-key candlelit dinner or a lunch of toasted ciabatta or pasta.

Šestica, Slovenska 38, t 242 08 50 (*cheap*). This 1776 vintage inn has been modernized, but the gruff service is a taste of yesteryear and the menu of sturdy veal ragoûts, beef goulashes with dumplings and grilled sausages comes from grandma's kitchen. A bargain robust set lunch menu. *Closed Sun.*

Pri Skofu, Rečna ulica 5, t 426 45 08 (*cheap*). A cheerful Krakovo local whose Slovenian home-cooking presented bistro-style has earned it a city-wide reputation; a daily three or four-dish menu is decided by the chef's whim and the season.

Bars and Cafés

Sociable Ljubljana excels at café society: for drinks al fresco, snaffle a seat on Cankarjevo nabrežje; for old world atmosphere, take your pick on parallel Stari trg.

Planet Pločnik, Prešernov trg 1. Pricey, but an unbeatable location on the main square.

Le Petit Café, Trg francoske revolucije 4. A charmer, hugely popular with students from the nearby university library (expect to wait for a terrace seat beneath willow trees).

Vinoteka Movia, Mestni trg 1. Sample (and buy) from a wide-ranging cellar of Slovenian wines in a romantic candle-lit wine bar.

Zvezda, Wolfova 14. Décor is stylish, but the true draws to this Kongresni trg café are decadent home-made *gâteaux* and ice creams to make dieters give up.

Čajanna Hiša, Stari trg 3. A chatty and friendly teahouse with a baffling assortment of black, green and herbal infusions.

Maček, Krojaška 5. Visit – respectably late, of course – on Sunday morning to pose among the movers and shakers.

Entertainment and Nightlife

Cankarjev dom, Prešernova 10, t 241 71 00, *www.cd-cc.si*. An arts and convention space that's the city's cultural nerve centre: expect classical and pop concerts, dance, and art and photography exhibitions.

Philharmonic Hall (Slovenska filharmonija), Kongresni trg, t 241 08 00. Concerts by the Slovenian Philharmonic Orchestra and Slovenian Chamber Choir.

Slovenian National Opera and Ballet Theatre (SNG Opera in balet), Cankarjeva 11, t 241 17 40. Premier league productions of opera and ballet are staged by Slovenia's finest.

Slovenian National Theatre (SNG Drama), Erjavčeva cesta 1, t 252 14 62. Standards and challenging new works in the Austrians' Secessionist theatre.

Jazz Club Gajo, Beethovnova 8, t 425 32 06. An intimate and late-night bar which swings to trad jazz sounds: domestic and foreign acts toot and trump on Wed and Thurs.

Orto Bar, Grablovičeva 1, t 232 16 74. Raucous rock and blues in a smoky room upstairs and a louche red velvet lounge of DJs and drinkers east of the station – marvellous.

K4, Kersnikova 4, t 431 70 10. Expect everything from hip-hop to house via techno and dub in this bastion of alternative Ljubljana.

Ljubljana

This compact city makes a strong case to be crowned Europe's most convivial capital. Grand old metropolises can boast all they want about cultured minds and racy lifestyles, but the continent's easygoing younger sister has charm in abundance, whether in a Baroque old town which begs for a vintage Technicolor musical or among cafés on the willow-fringed banks of arterial river Ljubljanica.

Legend has it that Jason and his Argonauts paddled up that central waterway to found the Slovenian capital. Prosaic archaeology hails the first settlement of note as Emona in 50 BC, where 6,000 Romans pottered in a neat grid between today's Mirje and Trg Republike until blasted by Attila in AD 450. But it was Hapsburgs, not Huns, who did most to shape Ljubljana's future. The Austrians eased themselves on to the throne in 1335 and found it so comfortable that they stayed there until 1918, bar a five-year Napoleonic hiccup (1809–13). After a 1511 earthquake reduced medieval Ljubljana to rubble, the rulers peered across the Adriatic to Italy and copied its elegant Baroque styles, a rethink replayed in Viennese Secession and Art Nouveau after an 1895 quake, and it was their Vienna and Trieste rail links that filled Ljubljana's late-1800s coffers and nurtured its development as the nerve centre of a Slovene nation finding its voice.

Although the upstanding Austrians also founded a clutch of galleries and museums, Ljubljana's joys are far more human. Provincial in scale, positive in attitude as the heart of an optimistic European newcomer, lovely Ljubljana offers the city-break *par excellence*; lazy, sociable and with no must-sees of high-culture to nag the conscience. Better still, it is one that retains the feel of a secret – discover it while you can.

Prešernov Trg

There is no finer introduction to Ljubljana's engaging character than geographical heart Prešernov trg: sociable, intimate and where a ragbag of buskers toot and trump before al fresco cafés. Centre stage of the former crossroads on which medieval traders trundled to the city gate is Romantic poet France Prešeren, whose musings on love and freedom found a special place in Slovenian hearts after elevation of his tub-thumping ballad *Zdravljica* ('A Toast') to national anthem. 'God save our land and nation/And all Slovenes where'er they live... Let thunder out of heaven/Strike down and smite our wanton foe!' he thunders, then sighs: 'Our girls! Your beauty, charm and grace!/Here surely is no treasure/To equal maidens of such race.'

On the west side of the square, have a look at Art Nouveau show-off **Hauptmann House** – no surprise that its bright aqua, jade and terracotta tiles arranged in *à la mode* 1904 patterns was the whim of a paints merchant. Once isolated in a suburb, the Franciscan order's stately 1650s **Church of the Annunciation** (Cerkev Marijinega oznanenja; *open daily 8–12.30 and 3–8*) blushes on the north side of Prešernov trg as if embarrassed by its thrust into the heart of Ljubljana life. A gloomy interior is a disappointment after one of the town's grandest façades, worth a look only for its swaggering high altar (1760) by Venetian sculptor Francesco Robba.

East of the church is the Seccessionist exterior of the **Urbanc Store** (aka Centromerkur), Ljubljana's first department store, a 1903 beauty which aspires to the retail *grandes*

Food and Drink

Wherever you are in Slovenia, menus vary little. Standard **starter** (*predjedi* or *začetne*) is soup (*juha*), often thickened with noodles (*kokošja*) or in east Slovenia offered as *jota*, a beans-spuds-and-sauerkraut broth. Keep an eye out, too, for *pršut*, slivers of Karst ham like Italian *prosciutto* cured in the dry bora wind; doughy dumplings or *štruklji*, available in over 70 guises, usually cheese-filled, but sometimes as dessert; and peasants' filler *žganci*, a thick buckwheat porridge after which second courses are optional. Slovenes who huff if a main has no **meat** (*meso*) have a taste for pork (*svinjina*), which comes in a baffling variety of cuts, veal (*teletina*), beef (*govedina*) and horse (*žrebe*). Turkey (*puran*) replaces chicken (*pičanec*) as poultry of choice; lamb (*janjetina*) is a rarity. Smarter menus list rich dishes of **game** such as pheasant (*fazan*), rabbit (*zajec*) and venison (*srna*), and coastal restaurants expertly grill a net of **Adriatic fishes and seafood**, while trout (*postrvi*) reeled from the Soča river sends the nation's gourmets into ecstasies. Traditional **desserts** fill the corners: *zavitek* (strudel); *potica*, a nut, raisin and honey roll; or *gibanica*, a multi-layered pastry of walnuts, apple and poppy seeds with generous dollops of cream.

Romans sowed Slovenia's first vineyards and developed a taste for national **wines** (*vino*) best drunk young. They are not nearly as well known internationally as they deserve. Finest whites (*belo*) come from the hills of the northeast region, the Podravje – a noble Renski Rizling (Riesling) with a hint of acidity; Traminec, spicy and smooth; Šipon and Sauvignon; and a rich Beli Pinot – although medium or semi-dry Malvazija produced from over-ripe grapes is tailormade for its region's coastal fishes. Connoisseur's choice reds (*črno*) come from Primorska, the most famous being Karst tipple Teran, ruby-red with a crackle of pepper. Austro-Hungarian rulers bequeathed a taste for Pils-style **beer** (*pivo*), the best being ubiquitous national brews Laško and Zlatorog, supped by draught in little (*malo*) and large (*veliko*) measures of 0.3cl and 0.5cl. An exception to easy-sipping chilled beers is stout *temno pivo* (literally dark beer). *Špička* (schnapps) is tossed down as an aperitif and digestif. More interesting is Slovenia's drinks cabinet of **brandies**: potent plum spirit *slivovica*, aged in oak barrels; juniper brandy *brinjovec*, like dry gin; and *sadjevec*, fermented from mixed fruits. *Kava* (**coffee**) is served black in *kavarna* (cafés) unless you request milk (*mleko*), and traditional Brits will sigh in resignation at Slovenia's weak *čaj* (**tea**).

dames of Paris, Vienna and Budapest. In the Art Nouveau interior a staircase swoops up to the gallery beneath a personification of Craft.

Miklošičeva Cesta

The store is an overture for Miklošičeva cesta's Secessionist stylebook, drawn after an 1895 earthquake wiped the slate clean for experiments in a cutting-edge style. First up on the street which arrows northeast off Prešernov trg is the **Hotel Union**, still the nostalgic charmer it was when 1905 guests first gawped at the grandest dining hall in the Balkans. Two years after its doors opened, architect Josip Vancaš turned his attention to the vacant plot opposite and created a swoopy façade for the **People's Loan Bank**, at whose peak buxom belles brandish a purse and beehive, emblems of thrift and diligence. Have a peek at the contemporary stained glass inside, before you reel at the blast of colour on Ljubljana Art Nouveau showpiece the **Co-operative Bank** (1921). Enthused by studies of national architecture, architect Ivan Vurnik drafted in Viennese wife Helena to paint the traditional geometrics which bud around its windows in Slovene tricolour red, white and blue, though these are modest compared with a jaw-dropping interior which casts a jackdaw-eye around Slovenia for its stylized motifs of wheat fields, pine forests and vineyards.

Envious of parks in Prague, city father Ivan Hribar seized upon the 1895 earthquake to create **Miklošičev Park** 100m further along. Maks Fabiani's Art Nouveau flowerbeds have been lost to an uninspired X of paths, but the flanking Secessionist buildings remain as the Otto Wagner student intended. As if to celebrate the park's completion, Fabiani's first creation is his quirkiest; stylized squiggles and ceramic tile 'flower-heads' draw floral doodles on the façade of **Krisper House** (Miklošičev 20).

Architectural explorers should also seek out Art Nouveau landmark the **Nebotičnik** '**Skyscraper**' on the corner of Slovenska cesta and Štefanova ulica; it peered over every building in Central Europe when the last brick was laid in 1933. Not that everyone was enthused by it – contemporary critics fumed it was 'a punch in the eye for Baroque Ljubljana'.

Across the River Ljubljanica: the Triple Bridge, Market and Cathedral

So ubiquitous is the stamp that architect Jože Plečnik (1872–1957) left on his home town that tourist board authorities allude without hyperbole to 'Plečnik's Ljubljana'. And none of the local son's creations charm like the **Triple Bridge** (1931), which links Prešernov trg to the Old Town. Plečnik created a picture-postcard favourite when he rethought an existing stone bridge and added flanking footbridges angled to direct eyes to Ljubljana's Baroque beauties; the bridge's descending neo-Renaissance balustrades allude to Venice. Banisters like massed ranks of *Alice in Wonderland* pawns play strobing optical tricks, and there's magic in the air when lamps bathe evening strollers in a soft glow.

Abutting Plečnik's most enchanting creation is his open **Market Colonnade** (1944), a dignified sweep alongside the river, certainly, but whose main lure is its food stalls. An effervescent market (*Mon–Sat*) sprawls across Vodnikov trg and is especially bois-terous on Saturday mornings. At its shoulder, the **Dragon Bridge** bookends the riverfront colonnade with a swoopy Secessionist span across the river. Locals were so fond of Wagner pupil Jurij Zaininovich's cartoony lizards which guarded the 1901 newcomer that city councillors grudgingly adopted their nickname for a bridge intended to celebrate Emperor Franz Josef I's 40 years on the Austrian throne.

The mighty Baroque spires and dome of **St Nicholas' Cathedral** (Stolna cerkev sv. Nikolaja) blossomed above Ljubljana's roofscape in 1706 thanks to the passion for Italian Baroque espoused by the Academia Operosorum Labacensis. The intellectual think tank which exhorted architects to dress the city in the latest fashions must have thrilled at the Rome supremo Andrea Pozzo's plan to recreate the Eternal City's Il Gesù in Ljubljana, a far cry from the first Romanesque basilica built on the riverbank to honour the patron saint of fishermen. Hunt on the south façade for a *pietà* saved from the Gothic church which emerged from that 13th-century progenitor, then pass through cast iron doors and marvel at an exuberant interior that lets rip with full Catholic razzmatazz.

Even its riot of pink and cream marble trimmed with gilt pales beside fabulously frothy frescoes. Vienna commitments forced Pozzo to abandon his creation and he handed painting duties to Giulio Quaglio; the North Italian artist who nodded to Carracci and Correggio does not disappoint. His illusionist frescoes are Baroque at its flashiest and most lovable, lifting the church's lid to stage a theatrical vision of Heaven where St Nicholas undergoes his transfiguration before a rapt audience of apostles, saints and cardinal Virtues. Quaglio couldn't resist signing his masterpiece in the chancel: the artist is conspicuous by his wig among devotees who receive bread from St Nicholas. Look, too, for a ritzy Baroque pulpit, choir stalls and the swooning angels shaped by Francesco Robba's chisel on a north transept altar.

Around Mestni Trg

A cosy cat's-cradle of streets between the river and the castle, the pedestrianized **Old Town**, is Ljubljana's treat, crammed with cafés and interesting boutiques. Begin your exploration of it on handsome Mestni trg beyond the Triple Bridge. Allegories of the Slovenian rivers Sava, Ljubljanica and Krka can be seen on Robba's **Fountain Of The Three Carniola Rivers** (1751); its none-too-subtle allusions to Bernini's Piazza Navona water-feature Fontana dei Fiumi confirms the Academia operosorum Labacensis's aspirations to create a Rome of the North. No such whimsy for the stentorian **town hall** behind, which imposes itself among Baroque townhouses after its Gothic core was beefed up during a 1719 rebuild and sits in a lovely galleried courtyard (*open Mon–Fri 9–7*). Here you'll find a Baroque *Hercules*, retired after nearly 300 years atop a Stari trg fountain, and Robba's *Narcissus* absorbed by his reflection.

A side-passage nips off to **Ribji trg**, an intimate charmer named for the daily catch hawked by 1500s fishermen. An adjacent pier is the embarkation point for sprees on the Ljubljanica by tourist boat (*May–Sept, Mon–Fri 5.30, Sat–Sun 10.30, 5.30; adm*).

Few streets unite Ljubljana's charms better than adjacent riverbank promenade **Cankarjevo nabrežje**, shaded by willows and crammed with cafés. On Sunday mornings (*8–1*) a good-natured flea market sprawls along it. Potter south and you reach **Cobbler's Bridge** (Čevljarski most), another Plečnik vision (1931) which swept away a bridge where 16 shoemakers hammered nails in huts as on Florence's Ponte Vecchio.

Stari Trg and Levstikov Trg

Stari trg ('Old Square', though not really a square), appears every bit the medieval street of its origins. Keen eyes will spot quirky details and enticing window displays as you walk west to the rococo ruffles of **Schweiger Haus** at Stari trg 13 (not numbered), one of Ljubljana's grandest secular houses. Stari trg opens at its southern end as Levstikov trg. Students of the Academy of Music now practise tricky passages in the solid **Stična Manor**, which abbots treated themselves to on the square's west side. Beyond, the Jesuits' 1650 **Church of St James** (Cerkev sv. Jakoba) springs a surprise with a zingy, acid-yellow paint-job on its Baroque façade. Time a visit to coincide with

Mass (*6.30pm*) to rummage through side chapels stuffed with playful Venetian altars and a modest but lovely high altar by Francesco Robba. All chapels pale beside that of the St Francis Xavier chapel, a charming octagonal nook iced with stucco on whose altar the 'Black King' and 'White Queen' of Africa and Europe acclaim voyages of the Jesuit order founder to preach his doctrine.

Across busy Karlovška cesta is the creamy yellow **Gruber Palace**, now the Ministry of Culture national archives, which Jesuit Gabriel Gruber intended as a school of hydraulics and mechanics. Security officials will allow you to ascend one of the finest Baroque staircases you'll see, which spirals through stucco flower braids like fairy buntings to a dome with an allegorical fresco of trades, crafts and technology.

Gornji Trg to Ljubljana Castle

Gornji trg is a snapshot of Ljubljana's days before she matured into Baroque: lined with cosy medieval dwellings crowned by a single gable and separated by narrow passages for waste – household and bodily. More enticing than the architecture, perhaps, are the interesting designers and galleries that have set up shop here. After the grand airs of the Baroque lower town, 'Upper Square' relaxes as it funnels uphill to a lovely, villagey corner of the city in awe of **St Florian's Church** (Cerkev sv. Florijana). Local residents who prayed for protection while a blaze reduced much of the lower town to ashes fulfilled a vow in 1672 when they erected this homage to the protector against fire. The fact that it's inevitably locked is no hindrance because its interest is external: a Robba relief of Prague prelate St John of Nepomuk being tossed into the water on the orders of Bohemian king Wenceslas IV; and a doleful portrait of an Emona Roman beside the portal.

And so up, up, via Ulica na Grad ascending beside the church, then along paths to **Ljubljana Castle** (Ljubljanski grad; *open daily May–Sept 9–10, otherwise 10–9*), which lords it over the city from its hilltop perch; an alternative path climbs off Ciril Metodov trg opposite the market, or tourist trains pootle up from Prešernov trg (*on hour June–Sept 9–9, Oct 9–7, Nov–Mar 11–3, April–May 9–6*). History relates that Celts, Illyrians and Romans took advantage of its defensive perch; that 1144 Spanheim Carinthian dukes erected the first stone fortress to maintain a strict eye on citizens and mint coinage; and that a castle largely rebuilt after a 1511 earthquake suffered an ignominious demotion through the ranks from palace of Austrian-appointed rulers to garrison after the mid-1600s. It then hit rock-bottom in the 20th-century as a prison and shabby almshouse. You'd never know today. Despite the authoritarian, glowering looks which keep up appearances to the Old Town beneath, post-1960 renovation has modified the fortification into a cultural centre where newlyweds beam and orchestras let rip in the courtyard during concerts of the International Summer Festival. Doubtless, Plečnik would have harumphed at the bland reinvention of a monument he longed to mould into a Slovene Acropolis.

For academic minds, the fast-forward of the **Virtual Museum** (Virtualni muzej; *open daily May–Sept 9–9, Oct–April 10–6; adm*) through Ljubljana's urban and architectural development is an instructive (if humourless) reason for a visit. And even loafers should brave the didactic narrative pepped up with 3D specs, because the same ticket buys you a climb to the top of a pompous little neo-Gothic clocktower, grafted on in 1858, which provides the best views that exist over Ljubljana – a glorious 360° panorama that sweeps over a jumbled Baroque roofscape and city landmarks, such as the cathedral and Franciscan church, to the Alps that sawtooth the horizon on clear days. In your hurry up, don't overlook the Gothic **Chapel of St George**, emblazoned with cartoony heraldic crests of Carniolan governers like a child's history book.

Kongresni Trg

Taking its duties as host seriously, Ljubljana razed a Capuchin monastery to lay Kongresni trg (Congress Square) in honour of the 1821 Congress of the Holy Alliance and inadvertently created a rallying point. Slovenia celebrated the 1918 establishment of the Kingdom of Serbs, Croats and Slovenians from there; on 9 May 1945, locals gathered to cheer their liberation from the barbed wire ring with which German forces had isolated the city; and in 1999 US president Bill Clinton addressed the Slovenian people in a park dubbed Zvezda for its 'star' of paths. Most charming of its flanking buildings is the neoclassical **Slovene Philharmonic Hall** (1891), prim, neat and slightly withdrawn at the southeast corner in a display of manners as immaculate as you'd hope from the home of a royal among European orchestras – the 1701 Academia Philharmonicorum casually lists Haydn, Beethoven and Brahms among its rollcall of honorary members, and came under Mahler's baton in 1881–2. No such modesty for the neo-Renaissance braggart at its shoulder – the city governor might have splut-tered into his claret if he knew **University of Ljubljana** students would one day attend lectures in his 1902 palace.

To the west, the idiosyncratic **Ursuline Church of the Holy Trinity** (Uršulinska cerkev) is a defiantly individual member of Ljubljana's Baroque family which nods to Palladian role models on a graceful façade of stolid pillars, Gothic arches and an undulating Borromini canopy like an arrow directing eyes to heaven. An interior that's a plain Jane compared to her showy sisters in their lavish make-up only boosts the impact of the ace up the church's sleeve – a gloriously over-the-top high altar by Baroque genius Francesco Robba. Carrera marble allegories of Faith, Hope and Charity pose and pout on its grand stage, 17m high and crafted of African marble.

Novi Trg to Trg Francoske Revolucije

When the spending power of 16th-century aristocratic families muscled out fisher-men from a ramparted Middle Ages settlement, 'New Square' on the left bank of the Ljubljanica blossomed into the most prestigious address in the city. The **Slovenian Academy of Arts and Sciences** has claimed square show-off, the 1790 Lontovž (Novi trg 3), where Hapsburg rulers hammered out policy during Carniola province Diets (parliaments) – peek into a lovely courtyard if it's open. North, **Zidovska ulica** (Jewish Street) and **Zidovska steza** (Jewish Lane) recall a former ghetto in narrow medieval alleys where the Middle Ages seem just a whisper away, and south is **Breg**, now quiet after days when it rang to a polyglot of Mediterranean sailors as the city's main port until silt clotted the trade artery in the 1700s.

The brick pile studded with rough stone at the junction of Gosposka ulica and Turjaška ulica is Plečnik's most audacious work, stolid and upstanding as the **National and University Library** (Narodna in Univerzitetna Knjižnica; *open Mon–Fri 9–8, Sat 9–1*). Inside, the staircase of charcoal grey marble ascends to an upper atrium flooded with light as a metaphor for its students' transition from the 'twilight of ignorance to the light of knowledge and enlightenment'.

A block south, stretched square **Trg francoske revolucije** is punctuated by the exclamation mark of Plečnik's austere **Illyrian Monument**, a 1929 salute to Napoleon who elevated Ljubljana to capital of his Illyrian Provinces (1809–14). An 80-year-old Plečnik returned to the square in 1952, called out of retirement by city fathers to rethink a deserted monastery complex of Teutonic Order Knights of the Cross. His parting gift to his home town created the **Križanke Theatre** just east of the monument, 1,400-seater main stage of the International Summer Festival, with *sgraffito* scrawls on faux Renaissance arcades in a courtyard lit by odd lamps like Triffids.

In 2006, exhibitions in the **City Museum** (Mestni muzej; *open Tues–Sun 10–6; adm*), organized by theme, will narrate Ljubljana's tale from prehistory to the present, following painstaking renovation of the museum's building, the aristocratic palace of Auersperg counts which closes the square at the east end.

The Museum Quarter

Ljubljana helpfully gathers its dollop of high culture around the neo-Renaissance **Opera House** (1892), northwest of Prešernov trg. Cultural highbrow of the trio of galleries and museums is the **National Gallery** on Prešernova cesta (Narodna galerija; *open Tues–Sun 10–6; adm*), where premier-league Slovenian artists are treated to a palatial Hapsburg-era palace and second-division Europeans are exiled to a modern extension. To tour the Slovenians chronologically, cross the central grand hall to Gothic devotional sculptures and two star pieces: a *Standing Madonna* and a lovely 15th-century *Enthroned Madonna*. Devotional artist Valentin Metzinger, who created altar paintings in St Ursula's Church, adds characterful Baroque works in the hall whose prize is Almanach's boozy *Cardplayers I*. In an adjoining corridor are *Before the Hunt* by Juri Šubic, the first Slovene in Paris, who embraced his adopted home's bright colours and light touch with a brush; and work by Ivana Koblica, Slovenia's foremost female painter, who proves her social critique is as sharp as her technique with idyllic *Summer*, characterful *Woman Drinking Coffee* and the unflinching realism of *Woman Selling Vegetables*.

The gallery's pride and joy is its hoard of Impressionists – Ivan Grohar's speckled white-out *Škofja Loka in a Snowstorm*, Krakovo local Rihard Jakopič, teetering on Expressionism, and Matija Jama, indebted to lighter French schools. However, don't miss superb sculpture by Franz Bernecker and Ivan Kajec before you potter through Europeans in the north wing: Almanach's gamblers are much the worse for wear in *Cardplayers II* and Expressionist Alexej von Jawlensky injects cultural adrenaline beyond Baroque Venetians.

More modern tastes are catered for in the **Modern Gallery**, on Prešernova cesta 100m south (Moderna galerija; *open Tues–Sun 10–6; adm*). Here, a round-up of

Slovenian artists from 1950–2000 shifts from canvases indebted to modern art giants such as Picasso, Dalí and Bacon to playful installations of retro-kitsch by *enfants terribles* of the NSK (Neue Slowenische Kunst; New Slovenian Art).

The 1880s palace opposite houses the **Slovenian Museum of Natural History** (Prirodoslovni muzej Slovenije; *open Tues–Sun 10–6, Thurs til 8; adm*). In 2007, the collection will shift to a new home near the city zoo, and the nation's largest hoard of archaeological finds and *objets d'art* will claim the whole space as the **National Museum**. Until 2006, temporary themed exhibitions tantalise with a glimpse of the treasures stored in packing crates. Console yourself with a lovely foyer, ennobled by neo-Baroque frescoes and where porcelain girls whizz down the banisters.

Tivoli Park

Ljubljana locals can thank Austrian-appointed rulers of 1812 for Tivoli Park, their city playground; its paths relax after initial formality to idle through mature trees and criss-cross lawns. Beyond an underpass at the end of Cankarjeva cesta, Plečnik's Jakopič Promenade leads straight to temporary exhibitions at the **International Centre of Graphic Arts** (*open Wed–Sun 10–6; adm*) in the Baroque **Tivoli Castle** (Tivolski grad); visit between mid-June and September on an odd-numbered year and you're treated to the world's oldest graphic-arts beano, the International Biennial of Graphic Art.

Perhaps inspired by the Jesuits' 1713 manor, Count Leopold von Lamburger demanded his own mansion in 1720, located northwest and today the **Museum of Modern History** (Muzej novejše zgodovine; *open Tues–Sun 10–6; adm*). Its narration of Slovenia's painful birth and troubled adolescence skimps on hard details, but there are intriguing contemporary artefacts and personal mementoes.

Day Trips and Overnighters from Ljubljana

The Škocjan Caves

It speaks volumes that, in a country blessed with more than its fair share of natural splendours, the Škocjan Caves remain perhaps the most impressive. UNESCO added them to its World Heritage list in 1986, and no wonder; no matter how many cave systems you have explored, this 5,800m wonderland of natural bridges, subterranean waterfalls, arching caverns, lakes and gorges will not disappoint.

Slovene cartographers from the 16th and 17th centuries pondered the Reka river's disappearance into a gorge near the village of Škocjan before its re-emergence 40km northwest as the Timavo spring near Trieste, but true exploration of the system came late. Following in the footsteps of 1840 pioneer Ivan Svetina and, a decade later, Adolf Schmidl, who employed the expertise of Idrija miners to clamber 500m, a determined triumvirate from the German-Austrian Mountaineering Society secured a lease on the system in an effort to conquer a tricky sixth waterfall. In 1887 they reached a 14th waterfall in the Hanke Canal (*see* below).

Tours (*1½hrs, daily June–Sept on hour 10–5; April, May and Oct 10, 1, 3.30; Nov–Mar 10, 1 plus Sun 3; adm; in English*) explore 2.3km; bring jumpers and sturdy footwear.

Getting There

Trains every 1–1½hrs travel from Ljubljana direct to Divača; local trains take 1hr 40mins and cost 1,340 SIT (single), InterCity trains take 1½hrs and cost 1,660 SIT. From here a 3km footpath leads via Dolnje Ležeče to the Park Škocjanske Jamevia in the village of Matavun. Ticket office officials will confirm directions.

Tourist Information

Škocjan Caves: The cave ticket office (**t** (05) 763 28 40) sells 1:5,000 cave maps and 1:6,000 regional park map *Regijski park* Škocjanske *jame*. The Škocjan Caves Park website is *www.park-skocjanske-jame.si.*

Eating Out

Café-restaurant **Pri Jami** at the park centre rustles up basic meals and snacks, otherwise eating is in Divača.

Malovec, Kraška cesta 30a, **t** (05) 763 02 00 (*cheap*). There's *telečja krača* and *svinjska krača* (roast shin of veal and pork) for a post-walk filler, plus veal and beef steaks in mushroom and truffle sauces, served in a *gostilna* whose dining room has a whiff of old-fashioned formality.

Risnik, Kraška cesta 25, **t** (05) 763 00 08 (*cheap*). More basic fare is prepared in this no-nonsense locals' choice for a cheap feed; expect a menu of sturdy pork chops and goulashes.

A sensitive eye for lighting retains the atmosphere in the stalagmite- and stalactite-decorated Silent Cave, first cavern of a system carved by the Reka over 2 million years and enlarged by the occasional shrug of a tectonic plate. More impressive, beyond the dripstones of lovely Paradise Cavern, is the Great Hall, an understatement for the 120m by 30m cave blotched by red iron stains and furnished with a 250,000-year-old, 15m-high stalactite tower, the Giant. Nearby is the Organ, named for its stalactite pipes which thonk in pitch when rapped.

The sound of the Reka as it tumbles through rapids introduces the Murmuring Cave. For once all the clichés about jaw-dropping ring true; like a show-stopper set from *Lord of the Rings*, lights of a footpath twinkle into the distance in a cavern over 300m long and 110m high. It is, without hyperbole, astounding, nowhere more so than when seen from a vertiginous bridge which hangs 45m above a torrent that thunders along the Hanke Canal before it wriggles through 5km of caverns (off-limits to the public) to the Dead Lake, where the German-Austrian triumvirate decided to call it a day. Walk through the mighty cavern, now 276m below the surface at the deepest point, to the Bowls Hall, with bizarre limestone 'rice paddies' caused by swirling waters.

Its vaulting neighbour Schimdl Hall was home to Bronze and Iron Age settlers, who clambered down through collapsed cavern Velika Dolina (literally, big valley). From here, a funicular rises to a path towards the reception or a 2km nature trail around the valley and sidekick Mala Dolina. Follow it and you'll be rewarded with excellent views. In the hamlet of Škocjan, renovated Jurjev and J'kopin stone barns narrate respectively a chronicle of cave exploration and local ethnology (*free with cave ticket*).

Škofja Loka

History books narrate that Škofja Loka was the benevolent gift of German emperor Otto II to Freising bishops of Bavaria in AD 973. One of the nation's charmers, it is a light-hearted and colourful place, with a dollop of culture and a couple of joyfully frescoed churches within striking distance. It blossomed beneath the skirts of the bishops' '*castrum firmissimum*' of 1215, on the opposite bank from progenitor settlement Loka (today's suburb Stara Loka), and grew prosperous on wool, linen and leather. Those 14th-century traders would still recognize the single-arch **Capuchin Bridge**. Local lore relates that Bishop Leopold got in such a lather when asked to stump up the toll to cross his creation in 1381 that his horse bolted and plunged the pair into the river; perhaps that's why the Austrians, who wrested control from the bishops in 1803, added a balustrade to one of Europe's oldest bridges during 1888 renovations. The tale may also explain its statue of St John of Nepomuk, the Prague prelate tossed off the Charles Bridge by Bohemian king Wenceslas IV in 1393. The narrow stone span is christened after Capuchin monks who pondered scripture in the 17th-century church and monastery 100m west of the bus station.

Once safely across and through the Selca gateway, one of five bastions which regulated entry to a town encircled by defence walls dating from 1315, turn left through alleys faithful to a medieval street plan to reach the late-Gothic hall church of **St Jacob** (Šentjakobska cerkev). Its drab grey hulk hides a lovely three-nave interior whose stellar vaulting billows atop columns like some exotic tent; peer into the gloom to pick out anvils, keys or shears frescoed on bosses – guilds' shameless boasts of their donations to construction coffers. The arm of Ljubljana's Jože Plečnik reached as far as Škofja Loka – he created the chandeliers and baptismal font – but it is the Renaissance black marble altars flanking the choir that go straight to the head.

South is medieval square **Mestni trg**, relaxed and handsome focus of the smart upper town whose three-storey, 1500s houses boast of wealth and whose mosaic of colours has given the town its nickname 'Colourful Loka'. Square grandee is **Homan House** at the west end, a united trio of Gothic and Renaissance burgher houses daubed on the south wall with a soldier and St Christopher's legs among fishes and mermaids. Its bulk outshines the claret-red former **town hall** (Mestni trg 35), with faded Baroque frescoes, whose stolid Gothic portal leads to a Renaissance courtyard. **Martin House** closes the square and once peered over ramparts of town fortifications.

That a passageway at Mestni trg 11–13 which descends to lower square **Spodnji trg** is christened 'Hell' speaks volumes about the parallel district, once populated by poorer burghers. On a tatty square now blighted by traffic, shabby houses are reduced to two storeys, too great an extravagance for the old and less mobile in the Špital almshouse (now flats) tacked behind the humble Baroque Špital church. Škofja

Getting There and Around

Hourly **buses** from Ljubljana take 40mins to reach Škofja Loka; 670 SIT single. Velosport (Poljanska 4, **t** (04) 512 32 00) and the tourist office hire **bikes** for jaunts to Crngob and Suha.

Tourist Information

Škofja Loka: Mestni trg 7, **t** (04) 512 02 68, *www.skofjaloka.si* (open June–Sept Mon–Fri 8.30–7, Sat–Sun 8.30–12.30, 5–7.30; Oct–May Mon–Sat 8.30–7, Sun 8.30–12.30).

Eating Out

Kašca, Spodnji trg 1, **t** (04) 512 43 00 (*moderate*). Hearty fillers in an unpretentious pub-cum-wine bar in the bishops' granary. *Closed Sun.*
Homan, Mestni trg, **t** (04) 512 30 47 (*cheap*). The café in this old-timer serves pizzas and pasta, and cakes, on the best terrace in town.
Pr' Starmen, Stara Loka 22, **t** (04) 512 64 90 (*cheap*). All sorts of strange pork dishes plus veal and game are prepared in this *gostilna*. Find it by homing in on the spire of St George's, 15min walk north of the bus station.

Loka took more care over the Renaissance **granary** at its northern end – so valuable was its stock of grain collected as taxes, only the bishops' number one held door keys.

The 1511 earthquake which shook Ljubljana also necessitated a rebuild of the **bishops' castle** (Loški grad), stolid and overbearing on a hilltop. Its town history museum, the **Loka Museum** (Loški muzej; *open April–Oct Tues–Sun 9–6, Nov–Mar Sat–Sun 9–5; adm*), perks up on a second floor crammed with folksy handicrafts and costumes. More authentic still is 1755 **Nace's House** (Nacetova Hiša, in the suburb of Pustal; *open Sat plus first Sun in month 10–6 or contact Tone Polenec, t (04) 029 59 16; adm*), where you can step into the pastoral time-capsule of one of Slovenia's most treasured remnants of rural architecture.

The hamlet of **Crngob**, 4km north of Škofja Loka (map from tourist office), is renowned country-wide for a rather faded 47-part sermon of Holy Sunday dos and don'ts frescoed in 1460 on the pilgrimage **Church of the Annunciation** (Cerkev Marijinega Ozananenja). Ask for the key from the adjacent house (no.10) and you can also gawp at the razzmatazz of Slovenia's largest golden altar, a Baroque blur of nearly 100 statuettes, in an interior of painted stellar-vault cobwebs. Such is the fame of one of Slovenia's most important frescoes that it is possible to overlook those in the diminutive Gothic church of **St John the Baptist** (Cerkev sv. Janez Krstnik) in the village of Suha, 2.5km east of Škofja Loka. Don't – its presbytery (no.32 holds the key) narrates colourful 16th-century bible stories and spares no detail in its *Last Judgement*.

Lake Bled

Lake Bled is a fairytale landscape; in its absurdly picturesque locale, a Baroque church perches romantically on the islet of a lake and a picture-book medieval castle glowers on a cliff against a backcloth of alpine peaks.

Begin your exploration in the nation's oldest **castle** (Blejski grad), whose first incarnation in 1004 as a stronghold of the bishops of Brixen founded Bled. Largely rebuilt in the 16th century then renovated in Baroque, it houses a so-so **museum** (*open daily May–Oct 9–8, Nov–April 9–5; adm*), with jaw-dropping views, which evokes feudal high-living in weaponry and furniture. Don't miss its lovely **Gothic chapel** whose frescoes salute Heinrich II and wife Kunigunde, saintly donators of the estate to the bishops, before visiting the Baroque **Church of the Assumption** (Cerkev Marijinega Venbovzetja) on an islet reached by gondolas (return 2,400 SIT) or rowing boats (*see below*), with lovely Gothic frescoes. If you want to pootle on or beside the lake, the tourist agency Kompass (Ljubljanska 4) hires bikes (2,200 SIT half-day); or rent a rowing boat at the swimming area of Castle Baths (2,300 SIT/hr); or drive by horse-drawn carriage around the lake (4,500 SIT). *See also* 'Touring from Ljubljana', pp.245–6.

Getting There

Buses which depart each hour (reduced service Sun) potter north to Lake Bled in 1h 20m and cost 1,400 SIT single.

See p.245 for details on accommodation and eating out.

Tourist Information

Bled: Cesta Svobode 11, t 574 11 22. *Open Mar–Oct Mon–Sat 8–7, Sun 9–5; Nov–Feb Mon–Sat 9–5, Sun 9–2.* Advice on activities, from fishing to panoramic flights.

Touring from Ljubljana

Day 1: Blacksmiths and Beekepers

Morning: Off the A2 northbound, take the A101 exit, turn for Podbrezje then follow signposts towards Podnast to reach **Kropa**, a village renowned in Slovenia for its blacksmith skills. Admire master-forger Joža Bertoncelj's chandeliers and wrought gratings in a museum (Kovaški muzej), and pick up the work of modern artisans in the UKO workshop opposite. Then hunt out iron headstones (including Bertoncelj's) in the churchyard of Gothic Church of St Leonard (Cerkev sv. Lenarta), with lovely views of the village from its hillside perch.

Lunch: For a taste of tradition, try **Gostilna Pr' Kovač**, in Kropa, **t** (04) 533 63 20 (*moderate*), or have a pizza at **Pri Jarmu** (*cheap*).

Afternoon: Backtrack out of the village to reach **Radovljica**, whose historic square, Linhartov trg, with its colourful Gothic and Renaissance buildings, testify to the wealth of medieval merchants. The Baroque stucco Thurn Manor is home of the Museum of Apiculture (Čebelarski muzej). Renaiss-ance older sister Šivčeva House has a Gothic interior used as a gallery, and the Church of St Peter (Cerkev sv. Petar) features a Baroque altar by Ljubljana cathedral architect Angelo Pozzo. Continue north to Lake Bled.

Dinner and Sleeping: **Okarina**, Riklijeva 9, **t** (04) 574 14 58 (*expensive–moderate*) is the culinary aristocrat of Bled; its talented chef does inventive things with Slovene dishes. Or for fish, reserve a terrace table at **Ribič**, Cesta Svobode 27, **t** (04) 576 83 20 (*moderate*). **Penzion Mayer**, Želeška 7, **t** (04) 574 10 58 (*cheap*) is an alpine-style house above the lake, and its restaurant (*moderate*) is one of Bled's finest. More expensively, there's the **Grand Hotel Toplice**, Cesta svobode 12, **t** (04) 569 10 00 (*expensive*), or President Tito's former residence, **Villa Bled**, Cesta Svobode 26, **t** (04) 579 15 00 (*expensive*).

Day 2: Around Lake Bled

Morning: Bled, with its lake, church and medieval castle against the backcloth of the Alps, is Slovenia's premier tourist resort. *See* p.244 for details of excursions.

Lunch: In Bled, there's the **Park Hotel Café**, Cesta Svobode 15, **t** (04) 579 30 00 (*cheap*), with cold platters plus the usual pork and trout (and famous cream cakes) on the best terrace in town. Or in Podham, the **Gostilna Vintgar**, **t** (04) 572 52 62 (*moderate*), serves fresh trout near the walkway.

Afternoon: Pootle on or beside the lake (*see* p.244). Alternatively, drive 4km north to Podham then follow signs to the **Vintgar Gorge** (*open daily April–Oct 8–7; adm*); a 1.6km walkway clings to ravine walls above the Radovna river and twists 1.6km to the Šum Waterfall. Explorers can follow trails to the Pokljuka Luknja cave in the magnificent **Pokljuka Gorge** (Krnica, 7km west of Bled); the tourist office (Cesta svobode 11) stocks hiking maps. Return to Bled, then go west to Lake Bohinj for the night.

Dinner and Sleeping: Dining is in the hotels of the main village of Ribčev Laz, which include: the **Bellevue**, Ribčev Laz 65, **t** (04) 572 33 33 (*moderate*), where Agatha Christie stayed; the more comfortable 4-star **Jezero**, Ribčev Laz 51, **t** (04) 572 91 00 (*moderate*), with a pool; or the **Kristal**, Ribčev Laz 4a, **t** (04) 577 82 00 (*cheap*), a cheerful pension at the village entrance whose chef prepares tasty Slovene fare.

Day 3: Lake Bohinj: A Mystery Retreat?

Morning: Crowd-puller Bled preserves the allure of brooding **Lake Bohinj**; Agatha Christie dreamed up dastardly plots here, although refused to tarnish in prose a lake 'too beautiful for a murder'. Alongside natural beauty, the lake is famous for the fabulously frescoed Church of St John (Cerkev sv. Janeva Krstnika) in **Ribčev Laz**. Its Gothic narrative wanders from the decapitation of its patron to include Cain and Abel, St George and his dragon and the apostles. If it's locked, the tourist office (Ribčev Laz 48) has the key. Then stroll 1.5km east to the village of **Stara Fužina** and the Alpine Dairy Museum (Planšarski muzej). The next village, Studor, has Oplen House (Oplenova hiša), a time-capsule of peasants' lives during the industry's late-1800s heyday.

Lunch: In Stara Fužina, sample tangy soft cheeses at **Planšar** (*cheap*), or try **Mihovic** (*cheap*) for robust pork fillets and steaks on a pleasant terrace. In Srednja Vas, **Gostilna Rupa**, 3km east of Studor, **t** (04) 572 34 01 (*moderate*), serves trout from the lake.

Afternoon: Return to the lake. For a stroll, follow a footpath along the wooded tranquil north bank. Otherwise drive along the south bank to the village of **Ukanc**, where a cable car hums up to ski runs at 1,535m. Take the road away from the lake to reach the 60m plume of the **Savica waterfall** (Slap Savica). Backtrack to Bled and turn north towards Jesenice to pick up the road to **Kranjska Gora**, Slovenia's top ski resort, where Chalet Liznjek House (Liznejekova Hiša, Borovška cesta 63) is a snapshot of a traditional lifestyle that has now vanished.

Dinner and Sleeping: In Kranjska Gora, **Gostilna Cvitar**, Borovška cesta 83, t (04) 558 36 00 (*cheap*), is the locals' choice for a good-value feed. **Lipa**, Koroška cesta 14, t (04) 582 00 00 (*moderate*), is a family pension and serves steaks and game. **Miklič**, Vitranška 13, t (04) 588 16 35 (*moderate*), is another friendly family pension, with one of Kranjska Gora's finest restaurants (*expensive*).

Day 4: Into the Julian Alps

Morning: Now for the full jaw-dropping splendour of the Julian Alps. Fifty hairpin bends twist up, up and over the **Vršič Pass**. In winter, double-check conditions with Kranjska Gora locals before climbing a link-road dug in horrific conditions by 10,000 Russian prisoners of war. Park at a hostel-restaurant at 1,525m to explore footpaths in the shadow of peaks Mojstrovka (2,366m) and Prisojinik (2,547m) or continue over the 1,611m pass. Sidetrack off bend 49 to the source of the **Soča** river.

Lunch: **Tičarjev Dom na Vršiču**, the hostel at the Vršič Pass (*cheap*), has views and stolid hikers' food. In winter, when it's closed, you can eat at the **Erjavčeva Koča na Vršiču** lodge before the pass. **Kekčeva Domačija**, Trenta 76, t (05) 381 10 88 (*moderate*), is a lovely chalet near the source of the Soča river, with authentic Slovene rustic fare.

Afternoon: Continue downhill on the main road past alpine botanic garden **Alpinum Juliana** to the village of Trenta and the Triglav National Park. Follow the china-blue Soča past the **Boka waterfall**, a 106m curtain 6km south of Bovec, to lovely **Kobarid**. Hemingway's 'little white town with a campanile in a valley' (*A Farewell To Arms*) mourns the horrific trench warfare between Italy and Austria on the Soča Front in the **Kobarid Museum** (Kobariški muzej).

Dinner and Sleeping: In Kobarid, choose between **Breza**, Mučeniška ulica 17, t (05) 389 00 41 (*moderate*), with delicious home cooking; **Hvala**, Trg Svobode 1, t (05) 389 93 00 (*moderate*), Kobarid's premier hotel with a gourmet fish restaurant, Topli Val (*expensive*); or **Koltar**, Trg Svobode 11, t (05) 389 11 10 (*cheap*) – excellent value, modern accommodation and top-notch seafood (*expensive*). In Staro Selo there's **Hiša Franko**, 3km west of Kobarid, t (05) 389 41 20 (*moderate*), a classy boutique hotel with a gourmet chef.

Day 5: Mercury and Old Lace

Morning: Take a walking tour from Trg Svobode to see the Italian defences. Even reluctant walkers should stroll to the first stop, the Italian Charnel House, where lie the bones of over 7,000 soldiers. Leave Kobarid and drive east to **Tolmin**, with a regional museum (Tolminski muzej) of twee rustic furniture and serious archaeology, then drive 2km north (signposted or maps from tourist information, Petra Skalarja 4, t 05 381 00 84) to explore footpaths through the ravines of the **Tolminska Gorge** (Tolminska korita).

Lunch: In Tolmin, try **Krn**, Mestni trg 3, t (05) 388 19 11 (*moderate*), for delicious Soča trout; **Rutar**, Mestni trg 1, t (05) 380 05 00 (*moderate*), Tolmin's favourite Italian; or, in Zatolmin 2km north of Tolmar, the always busy **Zatolmin**, t (05) 388 25 33 (*moderate*).

Afternoon: Drive east to **Idrija**, famous for mercury mining and for exquisite lace. From Anthony's Main Road mine (*open Mon–Fri 10–3, Sat–Sun 10, 3, 4; adm*) descend into tunnels braced with tree trunks and which squirrel away their own chapel. For claustrophobes, there's a town museum (Mestni muzej) instead. The Lace School (Čipkarska šola) celebrates local lacemaking.

Dinner and Sleeping: In Idrija the only accommodation is **Gostišče Barbara**, Kosovelova 3, t (05) 377 11 62 (*cheap*); book ahead. Fill up on pizzas at **Pra Škafarju**, Ulica sv Barbare 9, t (05) 377 32 40 (*cheap*). For a night of antiques and lace linen, there's **Kendov dvorec**, Na griču 2, in Spodnja Idrija, t (05) 377 25 100 (*expensive*); reservation essential. Or in Razpotje, try the more modest **Fortuna**, Idršek 1a, t (05) 37 79 149 (*cheap*).

Croatia:
Travel, Practical A–Z
and Language

15

Travel

Entry Formalities

Passports and Visas

Not yet a member of the EU, Croatia nevertheless harmonizes entry regulations with the continent, so holders of full, valid EU, US, Canadian, Australian and New Zealand **passports** can enter for a period of up to 90 days without a visa. In theory, new arrivals must register with the local police, a formality handled by hotels or agencies.

Customs

Foreign travellers are exempted from **customs** duty for non-commercial goods carried as personal baggage up to the value of 30,000Kn. In addition, travellers are exempted from duty for: 200 cigarettes or 100 cigarillos or 50 cigars or 250g of tobacco; 1 litre of strong spirits; 2 litres of table wine; 2 litres of liqueurs (under 22 per cent) sparkling wine or dessert wine; 500g coffee; 50ml of perfume; 250ml of toilet water. In addition, you can only bring in and take out up to 15,000Kn.

Getting Around

By Bus

The workhorses of Croatian travel, buses (*autobusni*) nose into every corner of the country and are operated by a bewildering profusion of private companies; the most comfortable are air-conditioned **intercity express buses**. Buses on **islands** are scheduled to co-ordinate with ferry arrivals. At large city **bus stations** (*autobusni kolodvor*) **tickets** are bought before boarding from the booking hall. For local buses far less strict about timetables, simply pile on and pay the driver when boarding. The number of departures reduces at weekends.

By Car

The day trips we propose are cherry-picked to be readily accessible by public transport, but for the longer touring itineraries a car is essential. Well-maintained, three-lane **motorways** (*autocesta*) charge **tolls** for their use.

The **Croatian Automobile Club** (Hrvatski Autoklub) provides roadside breakdown assistance (**t** 987) plus up-to-date information on road conditions and ferries in English either on **t** (01) 464 08 00 or its website *www.hak.hr*.

Drivers are required to hold a full, valid licence and if driving their own vehicles must also keep to hand documents of registration and a certificate of third-party insurance (including a Green Card). **Speed limits** (generally ignored) are 130kph on motorways, 80kph outside built-up areas and 50kph in towns. The word for petrol (unleaded) is *bezolovni*. No alcohol is permitted in the bloodstream .

Car hire is expensive: expect to pay around €65 per day for a two-door manual runaround, and a blanching €190 per day for a four-door estate with air-conditioning. All hire companies require drivers to be over 21 (sometimes older) and to have held an EU or international driving licence for (usually) one year.

By Ferry

Ferries are cheap (at least for foot passengers). Roll-on, roll-off ferries ply short hops on busy **mainland–island** routes, but most jaunts will be on scheduled ferries that link islands to each other and to hub ports like Dubrovnik (Elafiti islands, Mljet). National ferry company **Jadrolinija** claims most routes, bolstered by a clutch of private companies, especially in summer. Whatever the company, **tickets** are bought before boarding from a company office or booth near the quay, or, for ports which are little more than a quay, from kiosks, approx 30mins before departure. Expect to pay around 10–30Kn for a foot passenger and between 60–200Kn for a car according to journey distance and vehicle size. Buy tickets in advance wherever possible and even then expect to have to arrive up to 2hrs before the departure time if you are driving

By Train

National operator **Croatian Railways** (Hrvatske Željeznice) hopes an upgrade of track to accommodate go-fast trains will woo back customers from faster buses: by summer 2005 trains will blast from Zagreb to Split in 4hrs 40mins. Until then trains (*vlakov*, singular *vlak*), though clean and smooth, are slower than buses but around 10 per cent cheaper. Timetable information is published in English on Croatian Railways' website, *www.hznet.hr*.

Practical A–Z

Crime and the Police

Police, t 92

Maybe because of the newly independent nation's eagerness to show off its charms, Croatia is a tourist's delight. Foreigners are welcomed, hotel room theft unheard of and violent crime is a genuine shock. Although the petty crime rife on the other side of the Adriatic has not crossed the water, you should still exercise the usual precautions. Police are courteous and helpful, businesslike without being effusive.

Disabled Travellers

Disabled toilet facilities are provided in most major bus and train stations, which are generally wheelchair-friendly, and ramps are on the increase in cities. In Zagreb, the **Zagreb Electric Tram Company** (ZET/Zagrebački Električni Tramvaj, **t** (01) 66 00 443; *www.zet.hr*) provides a free vehicle for disabled visitors plus one passenger. Elsewhere, those in wheelchairs will struggle – access to public buildings is limited and public transport is not accessible without help from a usually sympathetic population. Ferries provide no ramps and you will have to rely on a steward or crew member. Similarly only high-end or modern hotels offer either disabled rooms or a lift. For country-wide information, consult Zagreb-based advice organization the **Association of Organisations of Disabled People in Croatia** (Savez Organizacija Invalida Hrvatske; **t** (01) 48 29 394).

Electricity

Mains voltage is 220V, 50Hz. British and Irish appliances require a standard two-prong, round-pin adaptor; North American appliances require a transformer.

Embassies and Consulates

Croatian Embassies Abroad

UK: 21 Conway Street, London W1P 5HL, **t** (020) 7387 2022.

USA: 2343 Massachusetts Avenue NW, Washington DC, 20008-2853, **t** (202) 588 5899.

Canada: 229 Chapel Street, Ottawa, Ontario K1N 7Y6, **t** (613) 562 7820.

Foreign Embassies in Zagreb

UK: I Lučića 4, 10000 Zagreb, **t** (01) 66 09 100; *www.britishembassy.gov.uk/croatia.*

USA: Thomasa Jeffersona 2, 10010 Zagreb, **t** (01) 66 12 200; *www.usembassy.hr.*

Canada: Prilaz Gjure Deželića 4, 10000 Zagreb, **t** (01) 48 11 200.

Festivals and Events

Few national folk events unite the nation. Instead, as well as each town's impressive spread for the day of its patron, staunch Roman Catholic Croatia uses its bewildering number of saints as excuses to host slap-up celebrations.

February/March: The year's major event is **Karneval** (carnival), a **pre-Lent** indulgence of costumed parades usually on **Shrove Tuesday** or the preceding weekend. An event in Samobor lures half of Zagreb; and cultured Dubrovnik holds a stylish bash.

March/April: Holy Week before **Easter** is an important ecclesiastical beano on the Adriatic.

July–August: July and August herald a cultural jamboree. Classical, folk and pop concerts and theatre is staged in almost every town on the Adriatic; the most prestigious is Dubrovnik's **Summer Festival**, which transforms historic courtyards and squares into beautiful venues for international acts. Not to be outdone, capital Zagreb hosts its own summer festival plus a varied programme of summer music events, but is more famous for the nation's premier folk-fest the **International Folk Festival** over the last or penultimate weekend in July. **Assumption** (15 August) is a popular religious festival.

Health and Insurance

Ambulance (*bolesnička kola*), **t** 94

Croatia's reciprocal arrangement with the EU provides the continent's citizens with free consultation and emergency care on the presentation of a passport or stamped **E111** (available from post offices, soon to be replaced by a card). Non-EU residents may enjoy the same deal (check with government before departure), otherwise private **medical insurance** is a sensible precaution. Standards of public health are high, tap water is drinkable everywhere and the most common complaint is sunburn.

Medicines for minor illnesses plus first aid advice can be sourced at **pharmacies** (*ljekarna*). More serious complaints are treated at a doctor's surgery, best found through tourist information or a hotel concierge; for emergencies and pressing health problems outside consultancy hours, visit a hospital (*bolnica*). Adequate English is spoken by many doctors, especially younger graduates.

Internet

Whether in dedicated cafés, tourist agency rooms crammed with computers or simply a bar with a terminal in a corner, you will have little problem going online on the Adriatic coast – expect to pay around 20–30Kn/hr.

Money and Banks

Until Croatia resolves its dithering over the euro, the official unit of currency is the **kuna**. Notes come in denominations of 5, 10, 20, 50, 100, 200 and 500Kn, and coins come in 1, 2 and 5Kn sums. Each kuna divides into 100 **lipa**, available as pocket-filling 1, 2, 5, 10, 20 and 50 lipa coins.

Currency cannot be bought in advance at home and must be exchanged or withdrawn on arrival. In addition, you can only take 2,000Kn out of the country. **Travellers cheques** (in dollars, pounds or euros) can be exchanged in almost all banks and exchange bureaux for about 1–2% commission. Otherwise, **ATM cash dispensers** are ubiquitous on the Croatian coast and in major inland cities as well as motorway petrol stations.

Banks are usually open Mon–Fri 8–5 and Sat 8–12 or 1, except on the coast where some follow shop hours.

Current **exchange rates** (March 2005) are: £1 = 10.8Kn; $1 = 5.6Kn; €1 = 7.5Kn.

National Holidays

1 Jan New Year's Day
6 Jan Epiphany
March/April Easter Sunday-Monday
1 May Labour Day
Early-mid June Corpus Christi
22 June Anti-Fascist Resistance Day
25 June Statehood Day
5 Aug National Thanksgiving Day
15 Aug Assumption
8 Oct Independence Day
1 Nov All Saints' Day
25–26 Dec Christmas

Opening Hours

Normal business hours for **shops** are 8–7 or 8 on weekdays and 8–2 or 3 on Saturdays. Most shops shut for a 12–4pm siesta in summer, then operate later evening hours, some until 10pm in tourist locales.

Museums in cities such as Zagreb or Split operate strict hours, but elsewhere times are unpredictable; don't be surprised if a place is closed. Many museums close during winter.

Churches usually operate set opening hours, typically with a 12–4 pause. Tiny ones in small towns and villages usually only open for mass.

Post

You can buy **stamps** (*marke*, singular *marka*) at *pošta* of the **HPT Hravtska**, announced by a yellow spiral with a stripy triangle on its tail, but far easier is to purchase them from newsagents and tobacco kiosks, then pop postcards into canary-yellow post boxes.

Post office standard hours are Mon–Fri 7–7, Sat 8–1 or 2, but village and island offices usually open only Mon–Fri 7–2. At some post offices, you can also buy telephone cards (*see* below) and make international calls, and change travellers' cheques and money.

Price Categories

Hotels

Hotel prices are quoted for the price of a double room with WC and bath or shower in

July–August peak season. Not factored in is a 'tourist tax' levied per person per night.

expensive over 1,000Kn / over €135
moderate 500–1,000Kn / €65–135
inexpensive under 500Kn / €65

Restaurants

Restaurants are quoted as the cost of a meal for one person, with an average-priced main course and a shared bottle of house wine.

expensive over 160Kn / over €23
moderate 110–160Kn / €15–23
cheap under 110Kn / €15

Sports

Croatians enjoy a range of sports. Football (*nogomet*), basketball (*košarka*), handball (*rukomet*), volleyball (*odbojka*) and water polo (*vaterpolo*) are all popular spectator sports.

Telephones

Local directory enquiries, **t** 988; **international directory enquiries, t** 902; **Croatian Angels** (state-operated tourist info, mid-Mar–mid-Oct), **t** 062 999 999.

To **call abroad from Croatia**, dial 00 then the country code (UK 44; Ireland 353; USA and Canada 1; Australia 61; New Zealand 64) then dial the number, again omitting the first zero of the area code.

To **call Croatia from abroad**, dial the country code 385, omit the first zero of the area code, then dial the number.

Telephone boxes only accept magnetic-strip **telephone cards** (*telekarta*) which are sold by post offices and newsagent kiosks in credit units (*impulsa*) of 25, 50, 100, 200 and 500. Rates are 5 per cent lower from 4–10pm, and Sunday is deemed off-peak (50 per cent off). For international calls head to phone booths of post offices.

Croatia employs GSM 900/1800 standard for its **mobile phone network**, compatible with Europe and US tri-band phones, but not with the North American GSM 1900/900.

Time

Croatia is within the Central European Time zone: one hour ahead of GMT, six hours ahead of Eastern Standard Time and nine ahead of Western Standard Time. Clocks go forward one hour on the last Sunday in March, back one hour on the last Sunday of October.

Tipping

Tips which are not included in the price of drinks or food are only expected for meals. As a rule of thumb, 10 per cent is standard practice. Taxi drivers will not expect a tip, but will obviously appreciate the sentiment.

Toilets

Public toilets are clean and hygienic, but few and far between. Train and bus stations have maintained public facilities (*zahodi* or *WC*) which charge *c.* 2Kn. Men should enter **Muški**, women **Ženski**. Bar and café owners will usually let you use their facilities.

Tourist Information

Croatian National Tourist Board, Iblerov trg 10/4, 10000 Zagreb, **t** (01) 4699 333; *www.croatia.hr*.

Useful sites for pre-visit searches include: colourful Croatian National Tourist Board site *www.croatia.hr*, country portal and online magazine *www.croatica.net* and coastal tourism site *www.adriatica.net*; regional tourism sites *www.dalmacija.net*, *www.istria.com* and *www.tzzz.hr* (Zagreb region); Croatian Ministry of Foreign Affairs site *www.mvp.hr*, with links to national embassies; and *www.hr*, an excellent directory with a neural network of Croatian connections organized by theme.

Croatian Tourist Offices Abroad

UK: 2 The Lanchesters, 162–4 Fulham Palace Road, London W6 9ER, **t** (020) 8563 7979.
USA: 350 Fifth Avenue, Suite 4003, 10118 New York, **t** 800 829 4416/**t** (212) 279 8672/8674.

Language

Even for confident linguists *au fait* with Indo-European languages rooted in Latin, Greek or Germanic, Slavonic-based Croatian is fiendishly complex. Most Croatians speak another language – hotel staff and young Croats speak excellent English, the older generation prefers German, especially inland, and Italian is widely spoken on the Adriatic coast – and locals will not huff if you baulk at wrestling with their national tongue.

Pronunciation

Every letter is pronounced, and most are spoken as English except for below. As a rule of thumb, the stress falls on the first syllable, and never on the last. Pre-trip tuition can be found on website *www.visit-croatia.co.uk*.

C is pronounced as 'ts' as in 'cats', č is spoken as 'ch' as in 'church' and ć is softer, like the 'ch' of 'cheese'. Đ/đ is spoken as the 'j' of 'jam' and very occasionally is written as 'dj'.

G is always hard, as in 'get'. J is spoken as 'y' as in 'yacht' and looks a tongue-twister when combined with other consonants, but is straightforward: nj is said as 'ny' as in 'canyon', like the Spanish ñ; lj as the 'li' of 'million'.

Rs are marvellous, rolled on the tongue and functioning as a vowel when placed between two consonants such as in 'Hrvatska' (Croatia). Š is pronounced as the 'sh' of 'sheet', similar to ž, spoken as the 's' of 'leisure'.

Vowel sounds are short: a as in 'cat'; e as in 'met'; i is as the 'ee' of 'feet'; o as in 'dog'; and u as in 'oo' of 'hoot'.

Useful Words and Phrases

yes/no *da/ne*
hello *dobar dan/zdravo*
goodbye *dovidjenja*
please/thank you *molim/hvala*
how are you?(formal/informal) *kako ste?/si?*
fine, thanks *dobra, hvala*
do you speak English? *govorite li engleski?*
I (don't) understand *(ne) razumijem*
Do you have a single/double/room? *Imate li jednokrevetu/dvokrevetnu sobu?*
how much is it? *koliko košta?*

I am vegetarian *Ja sam vegeterijanac/ vegeterijanka (fem.)*
I am lost (m/f) *izgubio/izgubila sam se*
toilet *zahodi/ WC (pronounced 'vay-tsay')*
ladies/gents *ženski/muški*

when is the next train/bus/boat for... *kada polazi slijedeći vlak/autobus/trajekt za...*
when does it arrive? *u koliko sati stiže?*
arrivals/departures *dolazak/odlazak*
entrance/exit *ulaz/izlaz*
day/week/month *dan/tjedan/mjesec*
today/yesterday/tomorrow *danas/jučer/sutra*

Days and Months

Monday *ponedjeljak*
Tuesday *utorak*
Wednesday *srijeda*
Thursday *četvrtak*
Friday *petak*
Saturday *subota*
Sunday *nedjelja*

January *siječanj*
February *veljača*
March *ožujak*
April *travanj*
May *svibanj*
June *lipanj*
July *srpanj*
August *kolovoz*
September *rujan*
October *listopad*
November *studeni*
December *prosinac*

Numbers

1 *jedan*
2 *dva*
3 *tri*
4 *četiri*
5 *pet*
6 *šest*
7 *sedam*
8 *osam*
9 *devet*
10 *deset*
100 *sto*
1,000 *tisuća*

Croatia: Zagreb and Dubrovnik

16

Zagreb

Few cities express their multiple personalities as readily as Zagreb. Side by side in Croatia's contradictory capital are an easygoing Baroque kernel and a dollop of grandiose Mitteleuropa built on a human scale; walk 500m from the bucolic chatter of a farmers' market on Dolac and the air rings to the city-slicker gossip of a stylish (and dedicated) café society in Preradovićev trg and Bogovićeva.

Perhaps we should blame the schizophrenia on the Hapsburgs, because it was the 19th-century Austrians who truly expanded Zagreb's horizons beyond the upper town kernel. Although a power-player by the 1700s, the city which made its debut as bishopric Kaptol, then merged with Hungarian garrison neighbour Gradec in the mid-1500s, firmed its grip on the national reins after the parliamentary capital of Varaždin (see p.269) to the north went up in smoke in 1776. The Sabor (parliament) shifted south and Zagreb, swelled by success, let go its feisty adolescence and settled into maturity. As nationalist sentiment grew in the mid-1800s and Zagreb intellectuals furiously penned prose and poetry to fire Slavic pride, Zagreb's Austrian rulers dreamed up onto the plain below the old city all the grand architecture and tree-lined boulevards requisite for a Central European power. The paint is peeling, exhaust fumes can choke you, but you can almost smell the pomade in the Austrians' parks flanked by stiff stalwart buildings, or in the foyers of their public showpieces. The cultural elevation which accompanied the architecture has also bequeathed some of Croatia's finest galleries and museums.

Trg Bana Jelačića and Dolac

A fountain gushes from the Manduševac spring now buried beneath the flagstones of **Trg bana Jelačića**, Zagreb's spiritual heart, set between the nostalgic upper town (Gornji grad) and grand lower town (Donji grad). The square, conceived in 1641 as a marketplace for an upper city where space was at a premium, was paved by 1765, then fringed with cutting-edge Viennese Secession show-offs a century later to create Zagreb's equivalent of Times Square; in this main theatre for public revels, trams on seven routes rumble backstage, locals rendezvous beneath a clock tower in the wings, and at centre stage national hero Ban Josip Jelačić charges into History.

Not that the history of the Croatian favourite is a tale of glory. Hoping to appease flickers of nationalist sentiment fanned by European revolution, the Viennese masters elevated the popular garrison commander Jelačić to *ban* (viceroy) in 1848, and the nation's new leader marched on anti-Hapsburg forces in Hungary, hoping to curry favour for Croatian independence. But his good turn for the Hapsburgs was forgotten, his demands brushed aside, though the Austrians still felt able to unveil Viennese sculptor Antun Fernkorn's wonderfully pompous bronze in the capital's heart in 1866, just seven years after Jelačić died. Nearly a century later, Josep Broz Tito was suspicious of a figure he viewed as a rabble-rouser, and in 1947 the newly declared Yugoslav president demanded the statue be removed from a square he had rechristened Trg Republike. Croatians weren't so quick to forget their glorious failure, however. Amid a crescendo of calls for Croatian independence from Yugoslavia, President Franjo

Zagreb

200 metres
200 yards

N

Zagreb City Museum

KAPTOL

RIBNJAK

Natural History Museum

DEMETROVA

Meštrović Studio

St Mark

KAPTOL

Ribnjak

Ban's Palace

MARKOV TRG

Sabor

KAMENITA

Stone Gate

Croatian History Museum

MATOSEVA

CIRILOMETODSKA

JESUITSKI TRG

GRADEC

Museum of Naïve Art

Lotrščak Tower

KATARININ TRG

Museum of Modern Art

St Catherine

KRVAVI MOST

SKALINSKA

Cathedral

VLAŠKA

funicular

STROSSMAYEROVO ŠETALIŠTE

RADIĆEVA

DOLAC

Dolac

POD ZIDOM

Archbishop's Palace

VLAŠKA

MESNIČKA

ILICA

ILICA

Gavella

FRANKOPANSKA

GUNDULIĆEVA

Serbian Orthodox Church

PRERADOVIĆEV TRG

TRG BANA JELAČIĆA

JURIŠIĆEVA

TESLINA

Archaeological Museum

ZRINJEVAC

GAJEVA

PETRINJSKA

PALMOTIĆEVA

MASARYKOVA

DONJI GRAD

TRG MARŠALA TITA

Croatian National Theatre

PRERADOVIĆEVA

Zrinjevac

Museum of Arts and Crafts

KLAIĆEVA

HEBRANGOVA

Modern Gallery

Strossmayer Gallery of Old Masters

STROSSMAYEROV TRG

BOŠKOVIĆEVA

ROOSEVELTOV TRG

Ethnographic Museum

TRG BRAĆE MAŽURANIĆ

Mimara

SAVSKA CESTA

ZERJAVIĆEVA

GAJEVA

PETRINJSKA

PALMOTIĆEVA

MARULIĆEV TRG

GUNDULIĆEVA

Art Pavilion

TOMISLAVOV TRG

Library

MIHANOVIĆEVA

BRANIMIROVA

Esplanade Hotel

GRGUROVA

Station

Botanical Gardens

...hnical ...seum

SAVSKA CESTA

To Vatroslav Linsinki Concert Hall

Tudman pulled off a public relations coup when he opened the packing crates in 1991 and restored the statue to a square returned to its former title.

Keep your eyes high to spot a corner relief of figures with muscles like polished walnut by Croatia's finest 20th-century sculptor Ivan Mestrović as you walk north to **Dolac**. Moments from the grand airs of its main stage, Zagreb suddenly bursts out with a farmers' market that sprawls good-natured chaos across a piazza ringed by cafés and cheap-eat restaurants; fruit and vegetables, olives and nuts are piled on stalls, women in aprons hawk home-made cheeses wrapped in soggy cloths, and on a second tier stallholders tout chunky wooden toys, lacy tablecloths and embroidery.

Addresses

Be aware that inconsistency between maps and street signs is the rule not the exception in Zagreb, whose casual disregard for a standard between colloquial names (on maps and postal addresses) and official names (on street signs) demands intuition from visitors; for example, eastern park Strossmayerov trg is interpreted on the ground as Trg Josipa Jurja Strossmayera, north–south street Gajeva is rendered on street signs as Ulica Ljudevita Gaja, and Trg Nikole Šubića Zrinskog becomes, bewilderingly, Zrinjevac. Good luck.

Getting There

See **Getting There**, pp.4–10.

Getting from the Airport

A Croatia Airlines **bus** shuttles from Pleso International airport 17km southeast of the city to the bus station (25Kn) every 30mins between 5.30am and 7.30pm and at other times to co-ordinate with flights (bus information, **t** (01) 61 57 992). The bus station is southeast of the city centre on Držićeva, a long 15min walk west of the train station; you can take tram 6 to Trg bana Jelačić.

Expect to pay 150–200Kn for a **taxi**.

Getting Around

The compact upper town (Gornji grad) doesn't demand top-grade shoe leather, but for rainy days and tired legs back to hotels catch **ZET trams** between 4am and 11.45pm; in theory **night trams** take over in the wee hours, in practice walking can be faster than waiting and night trams represent a new route map to grapple with, as the tourist information city maps feature only a day route map.

A single **ticket** bought from the driver costs 8Kn, from post offices and ZET kiosks located at major stops and termini 6.5Kn; and a **one-day ticket** which lasts till 4am is 18Kn. All tickets must be validated in ticket cancellers on boarding: inspectors have heard all the excuses and simply issue on-the-spot 150Kn fines; while baffled foreigners may receive a little leeway, they may also have their passport number taken to ensure a fine is paid

within 8 days (after which it rises to 200Kn) or simply be marched to a police station via an ATM. Buy a **Zagreb Card** (60Kn, *see* below) and you won't reach into your pocket for 72hrs. Most trams trundle through transport hub Trg bana Jelačića, just below the old town, and location of the tourist office.

Fleets of **taxis** gather outside the bus and train stations and at central ranks at the north end of Gajeva, just south of Trg bana Jelačića, and by the National Theatre on Trg Maršala Tita. In theory, they charge a flat fee of 25Kn, plus 7Kn/km. Advance bookings can be made with **Taxi 970**, **t** (01) 66 82 505.

Car Hire

All the major players operate in the airport.
Hertz, Vukotinovićeva 4, **t** (01) 48 46 777.
Budget, Kneza Borne 2 (in hotel Sheraton), **t** (01) 45 54 943.
Europcar, Pierottijeva 5, **t** (01) 48 28 383.
Jameks90, Vlaška 58, **t** (01) 46 17 495.

Tourist Information

Zagreb: The helpful central tourist information office is on Trg bana Jelačića, **t** (01) 48 14 051/052/054, *www.zagreb-touristinfo.hr* (*open Mon–Fri 9–9, Sat 9–6, Sun 9–2*), and a smaller office is at Zrinjevac 14, **t** (01) 49 21 645 (*open Mon, Wed and Fri 9–5, Tues and Thurs 9–6*). Both provide excellent free city maps, can book hotels and entertainment tickets and sell the **Zagreb Card** (60Kn; also from most hotels), a three-day pass for public transport plus 50 per cent discounts on museum entry and 10–20 per cent reductions in selected shops and on car hire.

Guided Tours

The larger central tourist office operates a unashamedly touristy stroll around the sights led by a costumed guide for 95Kn, half-price with a Zagreb Card.

Festivals

Zagreb enjoys itself in summer. Trg bana Jelačića is centre stage of the **Folklore Festival** (*Međunarodna smotra folklora, www.msf.hr*), a five-day jamboree over the last or penultimate weekend in July, when Croatian folk groups, plus a few international acts, twirl and toot in colourful costume.

More highbrow music and dance are provided by: the **Contemporary Dance Week** in the first week of June; the **Summer Festival** which woos international stars of classical music between mid-July and mid-August; and the **Zagreb Biennial**, which celebrates contemporary classical music every odd-numbered year.

Shopping

Central high street **Ilica** lays out a window display of independents and chain stores in *fin-de-siècle* shop-fronts. Funky fashion boutiques plus the occasional antiques shop and gallery line **Radićeva**, which extends north off **Trg bana Jelačića**. For example, **Galerija Bil Ani**, Radićeva 37, pioneered in Croatia the Lilliputian ceramic models of streets and buildings of Zagreb, Dalmatia and Istria.

For more fashions, explore smart boutiques in yesteryear grand arcade the **Oktagon** off Ilica, or go to **Croata**, Kaptol 13, and pick up a silk tie from the country of its birth: inspired by the neckwear of a crack Croat regiment he inspected in 1635, fashion-conscious French king Louis XIV knotted bright silk handkerchiefs '*à la Hrvat* (Croat)', cravats caught on and the rest is history.

Foodies should sample Dalmatian *pršut* (prosciutto ham), sold by the slice (or leg), and browse a wonderland of tasty treats – fiery *raikija*, olive oils, sheep's cheeses from island Pag – at **Pršut Galerija**, Vlaška 7, and **Devin**, Hebrangova 23. **Zigante Tartufi**, Rotonda Centar, Jurišićeva 19, offers more of the same plus mysterious herbal liqueurs said to be aphrodisiac, but its heart is in Istrian truffles, which come fresh, sliced, minced and preserved in olive oil.

The finest Croatian wines are available from exclusive *vinothek* **Bornstein**, Kaptol 19; grasiner, kraviner and chardonnay plonks of local vineyards come straight from the barrel at a cellar *vinarija* opposite (Kaptol 14) – bring an empty water bottle if you want to take some home.

Zagreb's whimsical souvenir pictured on every tourist board brochure is the *licitarsko srce*, a gingerbread love heart laced with icing

frills – pick up yours at the Trg bana Jelačića tourist office and you'll realize the tough treat is intended as a decorative love token, not a snack. The tourist office also retails *paprenjak*, gingerbread pastries made with honey, walnuts and pepper and munched by Renaissance locals.

Markets

A daily market on **Dolac** (*7–3*) hides folksy traditional fabrics, wicker baskets and charming, naïve wooden toys beyond its fruit and veg, and a Sunday antique and flea market (*8–2*) on **Britanski trg**, off Ilica, is all tatty, cheerful fun. Early birds can even pick up a bargain.

Where to Stay

Zagreb **t** (01) –

Put this on the expense account, because Zagreb accommodation is not cheap. Budget hotels are in short supply and their few rooms are snapped up quickly in peak season. Hotels cluster south of the centre around the train station and unless you pay top rate are generally uninspiring, business-orientated ones.

Regent Esplanade, Mihanovićeva 1, **t** 45 66 666, *www.regenthotels.com* (*expensive*). A lengthy refurbishment has done nothing to dilute the glamour of this Zagreb *grande dame*, fashioned to serve the Orient Express and with a marble lobby fit for an Agatha Christie whodunnit. Luxurious rooms (deluxe are worth the extra money) maintain the nostalgia: fabrics are delicious shades of plum and moss, and rich chocolate woods are lit with hints of gilt. Croatian-Mediterranean fusion food in restaurant Zinfandals is first-class and Zagreb locals say the *štrukli* of its bistro is the best in town. The connoisseur's choice.

Palace, Strossmayerov trg 10, **t** 48 14 611, *www.palace.hr* (*expensive*). You half expect to smell moustache wax in the oldest hotel in Central Europe, created from a central 1891 palace. Its lobby is reassuringly stuffy thanks to vintage walnut panelling, brass fittings and leather chairs. Elegant rooms were modernized in 2003 to boast four-star facilities and marble bathrooms.

Sheraton, Kneza Borne 2, t 45 53 535, *www. sheraton.com* (*expensive*). Five-star facilities in a hotel that's everything you expect of the American chain; it's pricey – almost two-thirds more than the Regent Esplanade, with cheaper rates online – but reliable.

Arcotel Allegra, Branimirova 29, t 46 96 000, *www.arcotel.at/allegra* (*expensive*). Streamlined minimalist design relaxes with the colourful fabrics of a hotel targeted at slick business suits who like high-tech toys – all the rooms boast vast TVs, DVD and CD players and ISDN lines for inveterate e-mail addicts.

Dubrovnik, Gajeva 1, t 48 18 499/446, *www. hotel-dubrovnik.htnet.hr* (*moderate*) The best of the mid-range hotels, with an unbeatable location in the thick of Zagreb's buzzy café scene. Its plush four-star rooms, with tubs for a post-sightseeing soak, are far more elegant than an unsightly shopping mall-style exterior suggests.

Central, Branimirova 3, t 48 41 122, *www. hotel-central.hr* (*moderate*). Unspectacular but competitively priced businessman's choice 50m east of the train station.

Jadran, Vlaška 50, t 45 53 777 (*moderate*) Clean and modern(ish) en suite rooms have satellite TV in a dated three-star worth considering for its central position 400m east of the cathedral.

Pansion Jägerhorn, Ilica 14, t 48 33 877, *www. hotel-pansion-jaegerhorn.hr* (*moderate*). Perhaps overpriced for the minimal facilities of its 13 chirpy rooms, but its location, two minutes' walk from the central square, is excellent.

Ilica, Ilica 102, t 37 77 522, *www.hotel-ilica.hr* (*inexpensive*). Chintzy glamour in en suite rooms where there's no room to swing a suitcase. Location is good, however, and the price – just 1Kn the right side of moderate (for now) – a bargain. Reserve ahead, then confirm and reconfirm all rooms, especially if you might be arriving later in the day.

Sliško, Supilova 13, t 61 94 210, *www.slisko.hr* (*inexpensive*). Spotless en suite rooms with simple furnishings, TV and air-conditioning in a friendly cheapie located in a quiet residential street two minutes from the bus station.

Eating Out

Zagreb t (01) –

Baltazar, Nova Ves 4, t 46 66 999 (*expensive*). High-end traditional dining from a Zagreb culinary king: the eponymous rustic tavern prepares a superb stuffed rump steak and a menu of perfectly grilled meats; and **Gašpar** is a classy fish restaurant furnished with antiques and palms. You may have to wait for a table in its wine bar christened – what else? – **Melkior**. *Closed Sun.*

Okrugljak, Mlinovi 28 (tram to Mihaljevac), t 46 74 112 (*expensive*). A star-studded clientele make the trek north for the acclaimed spit-roast lamb, choice dish on an upmarket menu of traditional dishes elevated with modern nuances. The rustic dining room is elegant, the wine list sensational. Reserve at weekends.

Paviljon, Tomislava trg 22, t 48 13 066 (*expensive*). Execs tuck into steak with truffles and gorgonzola and sea bass tinted with saffron and basil on a bed of fried rocket over high-powered business lunches in the ground floor of the 19th-century Arts Pavilion. *Closed Sun.*

Pod Gričkim Topem, Zakamarijeve stube 5, t 48 33 607 (*expensive–moderate*). Folksy charm – a cosy wood-panelled dining room and friendly, attentive service – meets top-notch Croatian cuisine of fresh fish and succulent slivers of beef at the top of the funicular; reserve a terrace table for a panorama which sweeps over Zagreb. Worth every kuna. *Closed Sun eve.*

Dubravkin put, Dubravkin Put 2, t 48 34 970 (*expensive–moderate*). A stylish and award-winning restaurant where fish is expertly grilled or flavoured with saffron or scampi sauces and seafood is exquisite; try Dalmatian favourite *jastog na buzara* (lobster in garlic, tomatoes and white wine).

Dida, Petrova 176, t 23 35 661 (*moderate*). A tiny piece of the Dalmatian coast wafted inland to Zagreb, 100m west of park Maksimir. Rustic charm abounds in a snug stone dining room of chunky beams and rustic knick-knacks, there is all sorts of interesting fish and seafood to explore, and its owners are liable to burst into song mid-evening. A gem. Book at weekends.

Maškin i Lota, A Hebranga 11a, t 48 18 273 (*moderate*). Just smart enough to feel like dinner, but without any of the formalities, serving turkey or veal stuffed with *pršut* (prosciutto ham) and sheep's cheese, or tasty Dalmatian fish, in a candlelit cellar.

Stari Fijaker, Mesnička 6, t 48 33 829 (*moderate*). A taste of tradition continental Croatia-style – thick winter-warmer soups plus meat-feast plates of beef, pork, veal and venison – in an enjoyably old-fashioned dining of traditional tablecloths ruled by waiters in black and whites.

Vinodol, Teslina 10, t 48 11 427 (*moderate*). Spit-roast lamb and *peka* dishes are the choice in this reliable restaurant one block south of Trg bana Jelačića, with a candlelit courtyard for summer evenings.

Kereumph, Kaptol 3, t 48 19 000 (*cheap*). Lunching professionals and rustic market-goers alike salute the no-nonsense inland Croatian cuisine at this small restaurant whose lunch menu is a bargain. You'll need to move fast to claim a terrace table with a grandstand view over the Dolac market (*see* p.257).

Leonardo, Skalinska 6, t 48 73 005 (*cheap*). Pastas in cream and truffle sauces, pizzas and good-value meats on a terrace adjacent to the crafts stalls of the Dolac market. Service can be slow when busy.

Boban, Gajeva 9, t 48 11 549 (*cheap*). Ever-popular cellar restaurant whose Italian dishes come in portions to make dieters weep; the resolute can deliberate over a large menu of salads.

Cafés and Bars

Zagreb takes its café society seriously and loses entire weekends to gossiping over a *kava* in café-bars of Bogovićeva and Preradovićev trg. Bar-hopping venue of choice is Tkalčićeva, northwest of Trg bana Jelačića.

Bulldog – Belgian Beer Café, Bogovićeva 6. Ever-busy café thronged at weekends and with a frequently boisterous bar inside at the centre of Bogovićeva.

Gradska kavana, Trg bana Jelačića 10. Reassuringly old-fashioned café where silver-hairs enjoy grandstand views of Zagreb's Times Square.

Charlie Brown's, Bogovićeva 1. Come rain, sun or snow, movers and shakers exchange politics and pose at the doyenne of Bogovićeva cafés.

K&K, Jurišićeva 3. A cosy bohemian retreat just off the main square, crammed with photos of prints of old and new Zagreb.

Kazališna Kavana, Trg maršala Tita. Zagreb's arty set once debated in this Viennese-style old-timer opposite the theatre.

Hemingway, Tuškanac 1. Dress to impress in this slick 'n' stylish cocktail bar favoured by Zagreb's fashion-conscious.

Kaptolska klet, Kaptol 5. A refined take on the beer hall, with stucco and heavy beams and a menu (*cheap*) of robust local fare.

Entertainment and Nightlife

Zagreb t (01) –

The visitors' cultural bible is monthly pamphlet *Events & Performances*, available free from the tourist office.

Croatian National Theatre (Hrvatsko Narodno Kazalište), Trg Maršala Tita 15, t 48 28 532. The Hapsburgs' neoclassical *grande dame* is the prestigious venue for classical theatre, ballet and opera from Croatian big names plus international visitors.

Gavella, Frankopanska 8, t 48 48 552. Excellently staged and less stuffy theatre staged alongside visiting productions, occasionally in English.

Vatroslav Linsinski Concert Hall (Koncertana dvorana Vatroslav Linsinski), Trg Stjepana Radića 4, t 61 21 166/167/168. Orchestral extravaganzas in the main auditorium, home to the Zagreb Philharmonic, ensembles and jazz in the small hall.

Croatian Music Institute (Hrvatski glazbeni zavod), Gunduliceva 6, t 48 30 822. Chamber music recitals and virtuoso soloists.

BP Club, Nikole Tesle 7, t 48 14 444. A cosy, intimate jazz bar-club which swings on gig nights, but is also a treat for a smart evening drink.

Sax, Palmotićeva 22, t 48 72 836. Blues, swing and occasional rock acts play to an enthusiastic crowd every night.

The Upper Town (Gornji Grad): Kaptol and Gradec

Kaptol

The rustic sentimentality evaporates in stately Kaptol, northeast of Dolac. Zagreb made its 1094 debut as a bishopric of Hungarian king Ladislas on the hill named for Middle Ages canons of the cathedral chapter – Kaptol is a corruption of *Capitulum* – and the main street, still claimed by Catholic institutions, has an air of quiet formality thanks to a parade of Baroque erected after a fire reduced earlier buildings to ashes. Showpiece residences include Nos.9 and 28, and, at the south end, the 1730s **Archbishop's Palace**. The residence of Bishop Juraj Branjug rings the neo-Gothic **cathedral** (Katedrale Marijina Uznesenja) which follows to the letter Gothic's guiding principle of guiding eyes to heaven with two filigree spires that punctuate Zagreb's skyline like exclamation marks. Viennese architects Friedrich von Schmidt and Hermann Bollé sketched the 105m-high steeples to crown a cathedral rebuilt after an 1880 earthquake reduced to rubble the Gothic original, itself a replacement for a Romanesque church levelled by marauding Mongols in 1242.

Scraps of medieval fresco in the south aisle, nearby Renaissance choir stalls inlaid with cartoony saints and plait motifs handed down from medieval style books (incorporated today on the bands of policemen's caps), and a Baroque pulpit like a pagoda, survive in a lofty interior whose scale reveals the Austrians' aspirations for their Central European acquisition. Look, too, at the rear of the south aisle for the Ten Commandments on a 1941 tablet that celebrates 1,300 years of Croatian Christianity in an alien-loooking Glagolitic script scratched by 12th-century monks – and also in the north aisle for Archbishop Alojzije Stepinac, who kneels before Christ, ecstatic and awed, in a Mestrović relief which marks his tomb. In 1988 Pope John Paul II beatified the Croatian church leader, whose criticism of oppression under Tito's newly empowered partisans earned him 16 years' hard labour until ill health forced the regime to shift him grudgingly from a Stepinac prison to house arrest in Krasic in December 1951. His effigy reclines in a glass sarcophagus behind the altar. Far more cheerful are Fernkorn's gilded *Virgin and Child*, who swoon on a pillar before the cathedral.

Outside, walk around the former **ramparts** which abut Vlaška. A section of 15th-century **defence wall** that ringed a cathedral then on Christianity's ramparts as Europe's most easterly church borders Ribnjak to the northeast.

From Tkalčićeva into Gradec

When 1898 engineers filled a stream, Potok (brook) became **Tkalčićeva** and pickled an absurdly pretty street of 18th- and 19th-century houses to give camera shutter fingers cramp, with lovingly restored town houses once owned by workers in a street of textile mills. Today this is prime bar-hopping territory, and on warm summer evenings there is almost no space to stroll. Off the south end of Tkalčićeva, **Blood Bridge** (Krvavi most) recalls the vicious border wars between chalk-and-cheese city founders Kaptol and Gradec (*see* below). Bloody skirmishes were commonplace as the sacred and secular rivals wrestled to be chief regional power player – in fits of pique, Middle Ages Kaptol frequently excommunicated its mercantile neighbour – and it took the newly elevated Hapsburg king Ferdinand to knock together heads in 1527. The bitter enemies put to the sword by 13th-century Mongols agreed a sulky truce in the face of a new common enemy, ambitious Turks.

The street links Tkalčićeva to parallel **Radićeva**; at its northern end is the **stone gate** (Kamenita vrata). The sole survivor of a quartet of town wall gateways where guards kept a sharp eye on incoming traders has found its second wind as a shrine for a 16th-century statue of the Virgin, found without a singe among the ashes of a gate destroyed by a 1731 blaze, and who now quietly works miracles from a niche.

Beyond is **Gradec**, a genteel district of Baroque alleys and squares that barely recalls its roots as the Hungarian garrison town King Béla IV of Hungary rebuilt after the 1240s Mongol rout, then fattened up into to a royal free town. You can also enter its cosy pocket of lanes via a funicular off Ilica (*see* below). Just beyond the stone gate is Croatia's second-oldest **pharmacy** on the corner of Kamenita – Dante's grandson Niccolò Alighieri once dispensed cures from this mid-1300s chemist's shop.

Markov Trg

The physical and symbolic heart of Gradec, Markov trg seems far too charming to be Croatia's political power base. While other parliament buildings aspire to induce awe, the **Sabor** on the east flank reveals itself as a modest palace (1910); from its balcony, Croatia declared emancipation from Austro-Hungarian rule on 1 December 1918, and behind its stately neoclassical façade politicians ratified the 25 June 1991 split from the Socialist Yugoslav republic. Retaliation came on 7 October 1991, when Yugoslav jets dropped bombs on the **Ban's Palace** (Banski dvori) opposite, where political strategists now stride past armed police into the government administrative and reception building fashioned from two Baroque palaces for Hapsburg-appointed Croatian viceroys. The Yugoslav republic's clumsy attempt to assert authority – and, say some observers, to assassinate Croatian president Franjo Tuđman – only prompted Croatia to sever all links with Belgrade, but then, the square has always been a venue for expressions of political might. Here in 1573 peasant revolutionary 'king' Matija Gubec was crowned with a band of white-hot iron before he was quartered; local lore claims the stone head which gazes mournfully from the corner of Čirilometodska on the south side of Markov trg is his portrait.

For all the square's elegant Baroque buildings, none stands a chance beside the explosion of colour on centrepiece **St Mark's Church** (Crkva svete Marka). City tourist board and travel photographers alike probably whisper a votive prayer to the Austrians who unwittingly created a Zagreb icon when they patterned ceramic roof tiles into two coats of arms: a united shield of the Kingdom of Croatia (red and white check), Dalmatia (three lions) and Slavonia (a marten); and the city of Zagreb. Their shot of cultural adrenaline, injected during rigorous renovation in the 1880s, was just the latest in a history of home improvements which also added an awkward Baroque tower to the 13th-century parish church christened after St Mark's Day fairs in Gradec's main square; a snapshot of the Gothic original remains on a south portal crowded with biblical bigwigs. Inside, gloomy Croat kings strike a pose among biblical personalities in muscular 1930s frescos by painter Jozo Kljakovic, and the ever-present Mestrović pens powerful lines for a *Crucifixion* and *Pietà* bronzes.

Around Katarinin Trg

Canvases fizz with character in the quirky **Museum of Naïve Art** (Hrvatski muzej navine umjetnosti; *open Tues–Fri 10–6, Sat–Sun 10–1; closed Mon; adm*) south on Čirilometodska. Enthused by Rousseau-esque concepts of 'primitive' integrity, Professor Krsto Hegedušić seized upon self-taught daubers in the Slavonian village of Hlebine and moulded their raw talent into the 'Hlebine School', writing the first chapter of a style demeaned as 'peasant' then 'primitive' art until Croatian politicians proposed the more flattering 'naïve' in 1994. Although not the cerebral fare of expressionism or surrealism, despite the museum's protests, there is still much to admire in glass-on-oil works by Ivan Generalić, as vivid and fizzy as cartoon cell acetates. The Hegedušić *protégé*'s bucolic scenes of fairytale whimsy are far more charming than second-generation superstar Ivan Večenaj – thick globs of blood and tortured trees in *Evangelists on Calvary* are the stuff of which Grimm nightmares are made. Look, too, for works by Ivan Lacković Croata, a star among later Hlebine painters.

Čirilometodska opens into **Katarinin trg**, guarded on the south by the **Lotršćak Tower** (Kula Lotršćak; *open Tues–Sun 11–8; adm*), a relic of 13th-century defences named for the 'Robber's' bell which rang to warn locals of city closing time. Zagreb locals have set their watches by the cannon, which has blasted above rooftops at midday sharp, since 1876 – be warned, it's loud. Miss it, and the tower still offers temporary art exhibitions and superlative views over Donji grad from its turret, just topping those spread below hillside promenade **Strossmayerovo šetalište**, where weekend lovers moon beneath a canopy of chestnut trees. In front of the tower is the terminus of Zagreb's **funicular** from Ilica (*every 10mins 6.30am–9pm; 3kn*); its dinky carriages first huffed up by steam in 1871.

The **Museum of Modern Art** (Muzej suvremene umjetnosti; *open Tues–Sat 11–7, Sun 10–1; adm*) tracks trends of home and international artists on the north side of Katarinin trg, and, on the east, St Catherine feigns surprise like a starlet at the fuss in her honour on **St Catherine's Church** (Crkva svete Katarine). Jesuits looked to Rome's Il Gesù when they sketched a new church (1620) whose outward public decorum drops no hint of the bewitching interior; walls are iced with sugar-sweet pink and white stucco in intimation of spiritual ecstasy through decorative excess in Zagreb's Baroque treasure. Concerts of classical music here score high on the tingle factor. Almost overpowered by the candy walls, frescoes of Catherine with the pagan philosophers she dared to out-debate play witty *trompe l'œil* tricks behind the main altar; his war of words lost, furious Emperor Maxentius answered the patron saint's impudence by torturing her on the spiked wheel she holds outside.

After nearly two centuries of being press-ganged into military service until 1945, Baroque **Jesuit monastery** the Klovićevi dvori on adjacent Jezuitski trg is enjoying its freedom as a **gallery** (*open Tues–Sun 10–8; closed Mon; adm*) for international blockbusters and a lovely courtyard venue for concerts of the Zagreb Summer Festival.

North of Markov Trg

One block west of Gradec's central square, on Matoševa, the ritzy Baroque Rauch mansion is a suitably grand setting for questions of Croatian history posed by temporary exhibitions in the **Croatian History Museum** (Hrvastski povijesni muzej; *open Mon–Fri 10–5, Sat–Sun 10–1; adm*). Doyenne of Gradec museums, however, is the **Mestrović Studio** (Altelje Mestrović; *Mletačka 8; open Tues–Fri 9–2, Sat 10–6; closed Sun and Mon; adm*). Flushed by the success of the first one-man show in the Victoria and Albert Museum in London, Croatia's finest modern sculptor treated himself to the Mletačka town house in which he crafted 20 years of bronzes – including the bronze Indians in Chicago's Grand Central Park – until persecution by Ustaše fascists forced him into exile in America in 1942. Even models of more swaggering public works relax in the house, which preserves Mestrović's dusky frescoes and furniture. The sculptor who shaped swaggering Croat icons such as bishop Grgur Ninski in Split, on show in miniature as a study, also reveals unexpected tenderness in a lovely bronze of his second wife Olga breastfeeding their son Tvrtko. It's a treat – not something which can always be said of the stuffed mammals and geology displays in the **Croatian Natural History Museum** (Hrvatski prirodoslovni muzej; *open Tues–Fri 10–5, Sat–Sun 10–1; closed Mon; adm*) a block north on Demetrova.

Last up in this cultural quarter, squirrelled away in the back streets, is the **Zagreb City Museum** (Muzej grada Zagreba; Opatička 20; *open Tues–Fri 10–6, Sat–Sun 10–1; adm*), which chronicles local history from days when Zagreb was a twinkle in the eye of 7th-century BC settlers to modern triumph in the Homeland War, in the 17th-century Convent of the Poor Clares. Rejoice – for once, captions that describe artworks and weapons, costumes and city models are also provided in English.

The Lower Town (Donji Grad)

After the *rubato* of winding alleys in the upper town, Donji grad beats strict four-four time in a grid of streets drawn by late-19th-century Hapsburgs, one element in their aspiration to elevate Zagreb into the sort of cultured duchess who could hold her own among European grandees, a sort of metropolitan *My Fair Lady*. The pencil of urban architect Milan Lenuci didn't stray far from the ruler, but he softened his formal plan with a U of leafy squares dubbed, inevitably, Lenuci's Green Horseshoe.

From Trg Bana Jelačića to Zrinjevac

The Romans would have approved of the architect's grid, and the east–west road which marched past their *municipium*, laid waste by AD 600 Slavs, blazed a trail now followed by **Ilica**, Zagreb's longest street and shopping parade. Dive south as it blasts west from Trg bana Jelačića and you reach **Preradovićev trg**, christened in honour of romantic poet Petar Preradović at its centre but nicknamed Cvijetni trg (flower square). A few lonely florists' stalls recall the now-banished market in a square abuzz with the gossip of a dedicated café society. On the north side is the **Serbian Orthodox Church**, its congregation seriously depleted by recent history, its interior scented by incense and full of shimmering icons steeped in mystery.

Lenuci confesses his hankering after the elegant parks of European *grandes dames* in his first green creation, **Zrinjevac**, two or three blocks to the southeast. *Fin-de-siècle* strollers who took the air and doffed hats probably marvelled at the reinvention of a cattle fairground into a handsome park (1872) where you can almost hear the swish of Sunday-best silk skirts or click of ebony walking canes. Structure in late-19th-century Zagreb's favourite promenade comes from busts of Croatian luminaries, a wrought iron bandstand and a bizarre fountain like a stack of gyroscopes, a whim of a Hermann Bollé, freed from the architectural straitjacket of the neo-Gothic cathedral. A daffodil-yellow paint-job highlights the **Archaeological Museum** (Arheološki muzej; *Trg Nicole Subića Zrinjskog 19; open Tues–Fri 10–5, Sat–Sun 10–1; closed Mon; adm*) among the late-1800s stalwarts on the park's west flank. Despite impressive national artefacts which start at prehistory and peter out at invasion by medieval Tartars, the crowds clog the two rooms of Egyptian mummies, one prized for the world's longest script of Etruscan text, inked on bands that cocooned the body. The star exhibit is far more modest: so highly does Croatia treasure the *Vučedol Dove*, a tubby bird-shaped vessel crafted by Bronze Age settlers near Vukovar, Slavonia, that it is celebrated on the 20Kn note. Rest in a courtyard café that leads a double life as a Roman lapidarium.

Strossmayer Trg and Tomislavov Trg

Bishop Juraj Strossmayer found time between denouncing papal infallibility and promoting Croatian nationalism (he argued that its tinder box of resentments was preferable to foreign rule) to found the brick pile Academy of Science and Art in 1884; Mestrović portrays the benefactor behind his creation, his head crowned by hair tufts like Mercurial wings. Later acquisitions have expanded the bishop's private gallery to 120 canvases and turned it into the **Strossmayer Gallery of Old Masters** (Strossmayerova galerija starih majstora; *open Tues 10–1 and 5–7, Wed–Sun 10–1; closed Mon; adm*), whose star players are Venetians such as Tintoretto, Bellini and Carpaccio. Brueghel and van Dyck fly the flag for the Flemish, and El Greco adds a dainty *Mary Magdalene*. Security guards will permit you to ponder for free the *Baška tablet* (*c.*1100) in the foyer; Croatia's most celebrated slab, etched with bizarre liturgical script Glagolitic, was discovered on the island of Krk. Zig-zag west and the **Modern Gallery** (Moderna galerija; *open Tues–Sat 10–6, Sun 10–1; adm*) on the corner of Hebrangova may have flung open doors after protracted renovation to showcase the cream of Croatian art from 1850–1950 in 16 rooms. If not, try the **Art Pavilion** (Umjetnički paviljon; *open Mon–Sat 11–7, Sun 10–1; adm*). One of the pioneers among European prefab buildings, it now hosts passing exhibitions. You can't miss it – it's yellow.

South is the manicured lawn of **Tomislavov trg**, named in salute to the first king of the fledgling Croatian state. The 10th-century ruler brandishes his sceptre south-wards at the neoclassical train station, which was briefly in Europe's spotlight when royalty, diplomats and the bourgeoisie en route to Istanbul disembarked from the Orient Express. Those high rollers bedded down in the **Hotel Regent Esplanade** (*see* p.257) moments west of the station, whose luxurious Art Deco foyer remains the 'triumph of architecture and crafts' it was lauded as when doors opened in April 1923. Appropriately, the hotel's first registered guest was a Herr Glück (Mr Luck).

Botanical Gardens, Technical Museum and Ethnographic Museum

For an intermission in the lower town's symphony of high culture, flee to the **Botanical Gardens** (Botansički vrt; *Mihanovićeva; open Tues, Wed and Fri–Sun 9–7,*

Mon and Thurs 9–2.30). The base section of Lenuci's horticultural horseshoe (*see* p.263) is a lovely place to amble along paths which meander through naturalistic gardens, or laze by pea-green ponds speckled with waterlilies. State archives now fill the former **university library** opposite, an architectural hotch-potch with window stripes and stern owls shouldering globes, that toys with Viennese Secession. **Marulićev trg**, behind, honours Split Renaissance poet Marko Marulić, who penned the first epic in Croatian, *Judita.*

Never mind official opening hours, the **Technical Museum** (Teknički muzej; *open Tues–Fri 9–5, Sat–Sun 9–1; closed Mon; adm*), on Savska a sidetrack to the southwest, is all about timing. Plan carefully and you can explore historic fire engines, central Europe's oldest driving machines and a hall crammed with the usual modes of transport – automobiles, aeroplanes, a dinky submarine swiped from careless Italians in 1942 – before you join tours which: burrow into a 300m mine shaft (*Tues–Fri 3, Sat–Sun 11; adm*); conduct electricity experiments in a mock-up study of Nikola Tesla (*Tues–Fri 3.30, Sat–Sun 11.30; adm*), the Serbian inventor who pioneered alternating current (Tesla coils still power many radio sets) and whose dark mutterings about being able to split the Earth like an apple or a ray capable of obliterating a 10,000-strong squadron at 250 miles made him a favourite with sensationalist editors; or star-gaze in a planetarium (*Tues–Fri 4, Sat–Sun 12; adm*). A dry section on geology is highly missable if you're pushed for time.

North, the penultimate building block of Lenuci's green horseshoe Trg braće Mažuranić is home to the **Ethnographic Museum** (Etnografski muzej; *open Tues–Thurs 10–6, Fri–Sun 10–1; closed Mon; adm*), with African sculptures and sleepy Buddhas brought home as holiday souvenirs of late-1800s explorers, but best visited for displays which rummage into Croatia's own corners: lace like spider webs from the island of Pag; Sunday-best folk costumes which celebrate the country's cultural mishmash; and ritzy Slavonian scarves threaded with gold.

Mimara Museum, Art and Crafts Museum and Trg Maršala Tita

If the small fleet of school group coaches on Rooseveltov trg don't give the game away, the imposing neo-Renaissance building declares the **Mimara** (*open Tues, Wed, Fri and Sat 10–5, Thurs 10–7, Sun 10–2; adm*) to be the heavyweight of Zagreb (and Croatian) museums, stuffed with the private treasures amassed by Ante Topić Mimara. Possibly. Intrigue and plot still surround not only the art collector's identity – some claim the Dalmatian peasant-farmer's son adopted 'Mimara' as a *nom de plume* while studying under Italian portrait painter Antonio Mancini, others that Mirko Maratović stole the identity of First World War battlefield victim Ante Topić, then tagged on Mimara as a sly nod to his own name – but also how the shadowy art collector acquired such a rich, century-spanning collection. 'The master swindler of Yugoslavia,' hiss critics, alluding to allegations that Mimara used a post-war ruse of Yugoslav repatriation to swipe art snatched by the Nazi élite. Other art detectives list forgery alongside theft on Mimara's crime sheet. Either way, the flamboyant collector donated his hoard to the nation and was paid royally by a government convinced it had struck a bargain for a 3,600-strong *œuvre* of canvases and *objets d'art* it valued at a billion dollars. In 1987, the ribbon was snipped, champagne corks flew and the Zagreb Louvre opened its doors, only for critics to denounce as fakes many of its Michelangelos, Rembrandts and Botticellis. Croatian authorities are reluctantly addressing the claims, and many canvases have been downgraded to 'School of...' to be on the safe side. Of course, the museum holds no truck with such slanders, and sets aside a top-floor homage to its benefactor, who smiles from his death mask, and whatever the truth, there's an astonishing range of art and objects here. Those disputed artworks are on the second floor; big-name canvases which span from almond-eyed Byzantine icons to French Impressionists such as Renoir and Manet.

There are no authenticity problems in the **Museum of Arts and Crafts** (Muzej za umjetnost i obrit; *open Tues–Sat 10–7, Sun 10–2; closed Mon; adm*) a block north. Its stylistic tour through the decorative arts begins in the 1400s with stolid Gothic furniture, then perks up in rooms crammed with frothy Renaissance objects. Don't miss a Mary altar from the village of Remetinec in a room of devotional sculpture – statuettes of the willowy Virgin are a press release of her good deeds; building cathedrals, protecting lambs, etc. – before you inspect heavy historicism inspired by Austria and Italy above. Arts and Crafts furniture and elegant Tiffany lamps, plus a gallery of Sixties poster art, provide light relief. Worth a peek in their own right are the atrium and staircase of the museum's ritzy neo-Renaissance palace, a vision of the ever-industrious Hermann Bollé. The museum flanks the west side of **Trg maršala Tita**, western tip of Lenuci's horseshoe, and a square with a swaggering centrepiece, the **Croatian National Theatre**. Viennese architects sketched its columns and cupolas in 1894, then knocked up the neo-Baroque pile at lightning speed to impress Emperor Franz Josef, who cut the ribbons at the 1895 opening. Overlooked but more enchanting before it is Mestrović's sculpture *Well of Life* (1905) – it's no surprise that its luxurious eroticism came from the imagination of a 22-year-old student.

Outside the Centre

Maksimir Park

3km east of the centre; trams 12 and 7 (to Dubrava), 11 and 12 (to Dubec) from Trg bana Jelačića.

Ask about the easiest escape from summer crowds and most locals will point you to Maksimir Park. Zagreb archbishop Maksimilijan Vrhovac is honoured with his name on the map for seeding a modest French-style garden in 1784 to create the first public promenade in southeast Europe, but the real debt of gratitude is owed to his successor. Enamoured by naturalistic English-style gardens, archbishop Jurjaj Haulik incorporated an existing oak wood and expanded the 18-hectare progenitor into today's 316-hectare expanse of meadows, woods and lakes perfect for a lazy Sunday stroll. If there are better places for a summer picnic, Zagreb is keeping them secret.

An avenue of trees channels arrow-straight alleys past Croatia's largest **zoo** (*open daily 9–5; adm*) and adjacent 19th-century whimsy the **Echo Pavilion** towards romantic belvedere building the **Vivikovac** (1843), now a café with a view – expect to wait for a table at weekends. A contemporary **Swiss chalet** nestles among woods nearby, but the real escapist treats – thicker woods, less-populated meadows – are revealed to those who indulge the more meandering paths north of the belvedere.

Mirogoj Cemetery

2km northeast of the centre; bus 106 from the cathedral or tram 14 east (to Mihaljevac) from Trg bana Jelačića, then 10min walk from Gupčeva zvijezda (stop four).

So beautiful is one of Europe's finest cemeteries, goes the quip, that its occupants fare better than some of the living. Hermann Bollé would be quietly thrilled. The industrious architect who designed much of Zagreb's Hapsburg-era cityscape turned his attentions to a burial ground for the expanding city in 1876 and created a fortress-like necropolis whose walls are crowned with cupolas and pierced by a gateway which tempers sombre stolidity with grace. Don't be put off – Mirogoj's leafy park cocooned in hush is a serene spot to hunt out mixed-denomination tombs; Communist partisans honoured with five-pointed stars lie beside Orthodox Jews named in Cyrillic, and Muslim headstones like obelisks lie next to Christian. Ponderous family mausolea beneath evocative colonnades on either side of the entrance draw a late-19th-century stylebook of funerary sculpture carved by some of Croatia's finest: Ivan Rendić's 1872 mourner in billowing skirts, who lays a flower on the simple sarcophagus of Slavophile poet Petar Preradović (he of the central square); or the stooped Jewish patriarchs that Robert Franges Mihanović shaped for the Mayer family vault. Famous deceased include Stjepan Radić, Croatian Peasant Party founder whose demands for national independence were silenced by an assassin's bullet in the Belgrade parliament, and Croatia's first non-aristocrat *ban* (viceroy), Ivan Mazuranic. And then there's Franjo Tuđman; church bells tolled countrywide and jets flew over Mirogoj in December 1999 when Croatia's first president was entombed in a black granite crypt on the doorstep of the Christ the King Church.

Day Trips from Zagreb

Mount Medvednica

Nature-loving 19th-century strollers knew what they were talking about when they extolled jaunts on 'Bear Mountain', because 'Zagrebačka gora' (Zagreb's Mountain) is now treasured as a city playground. On summer Sundays, an army of Zagreb silver-hairs don walking boots to tramp thickly wooded slopes while families idle in meadows over a picnic, and in winter skiers swish down slopes (ski hire available at Sljeme summit). Be warned: the nature park is busiest at weekends.

For once, the journey itself (*see* 'Getting There') to the uplands just free of Zagreb's northern suburbs (easily combined with a visit to Mirogoj cemetery) is part of the attraction, because the **cable car** (*daily 8–8; 10Kn single, return 17Kn*), which glides 4km up to Sljeme, the giant of the range of hills which border Zagreb, also offers the best views there are over its urban sprawl. Keen walkers can also reach the 1,035m summit on a footpath from the lower cable car terminus (*approx 2hrs*). A TV tower spikes the

Getting There

Tram 14 from Trg bana Jelačića terminates at Mihaljevac, where tram 15 begins for the four-stop hop to Dolje. A subway and woodland path leads to the **cable car** (signposted Žičara) for the ascent to Sljeme. A **footpath** from Zagreb street Dubravkin put (northwest of Gornji grad) also ambles north through wooded suburbs to Medvedgrad (*c.* 1hr 40mins).

Tourist Information

Bliznec bb, Zagreb, **t** (01) 45 86 317; *open Mon–Fri 8–4*. Zagreb tourist offices also stock free maps which mark footpaths and mountain bike trails through the park.

Eating Out

Okrugljak, Mlinovi 28 (left fork just before Mihaljevac terminus), **t** (01) 46 74 112 (*expensive*). A member of Zagreb's culinary élite; *see* p.268, and book at weekends.

Šestinski Lagvić, Šestinska cesta bb, **t** (01) 46 74 417 (*moderate*). North Croatian specialities served on a wonderful terrace or dining room which oozes bucolic charm in a restaurant downhill from the Medvedgrad fortress.

Zlatni Medved, Sljeme; no tel (*cheap*). A busy and cheerful Alpine-style chalet at the summit which rustles up no-nonsense fillers: bean soup grah, sturdy pork cutlets and thick stews.

summit despite the best efforts of the Yugoslavian People's Army in 1991, and an adjacent belvedere provides a sensational panorama north over the Zagorje – a fairytale carpet of villages and forest which on gin-clear days stretches to the Slovenian Alps.

Turn right from the cable car's upper terminus and cross a steep meadow and the boxy **Shrine of Our Lady of Sljeme** (Sljemenska kapelina; *open Tues, Thurs, Sat, Sun 11–3*) displays Byzantine, Romanesque and Gothic – an academic's 1932 salute to a millennium of Croatian Christianity. **Fortress Medvedgrad** (*open daily 7–10; adm free*) provides different views over Zagreb and a goal for exploration 5km southwest of Sljeme. To save a return to Sljeme, a road threads downhill to suburb Šestine, from where bus 102 trundles back to Zagreb centre.

Samobor

Though just 22km west of her big sister, this intimate town snuggled among wooded slopes hums with a provincial prosperity that's a world away in atmosphere; in the central square alone, old-fashioned grocers display tins in exact rows and the Gradna brook chuckles contentedly in a corner.

The earliest relic of the settlement saluted as a royal free market town in a 1242 charter is 13th-century castle **Stari grad** (literally, 'old town'), isolated on a western spur – more on this later. The heart of the town which blossomed beneath, alongside the Gradna, is **Trg kralja Tomislava**, lined by the smart Baroque townhouses – plus one Art Nouveau newcomer topped by blasé angels – which replaced a townscape reduced to ashes by fire in 1797. If you want to sample local delicacy *Samoborske kremšnite*, a thick slab of custard which quivers between flaky pastry, this is the place to do it. For intellectual nourishment there's the **Samobor Museum** (Samoborski muzej; *open Tues–Fri 9–3, Sat–Sun 9–1; closed Mon; adm*) west of the square. This streamside villa was formerly the home of composer Ferdinand Livadićev, and musty displays of town documents, hunting weapons and gloomy local dignitaries perk up (slightly) in period rooms where the advocate of Slavic independence and promoter of the national tongue composed the 1883 rallying cry 'Croatia Has Not Yet Fallen'.

Getting There

Buses from Zagreb main bus station every 20–30min take 40mins and cost 23Kn single.

Tourist Information

Samobor: Trg kralja Tomislava 5, **t** (01) 33 60 050, *www.samobor.com*. Open Mon–Fri 8–7, Sat 9–7, Sun 10–7.

Festivals

Sedate Samobor is anything but during Carnival (*Samoborksi fašnik*), held since 1827 on the weekend before Shrove Tuesday.

Eating Out

Samobor sausages (*češjovke*), acclaimed by connoisseurs, are best munched with local mustard then washed down with *bermet*, an aromatic, slightly bitter local tipple whose wine-based recipe is guarded by a family firm. Develop a taste for it and you can buy a bottle (plus jars of mustard) from a factory outlet at Stražnička 1a (off Trg kralja Tomislava).

Pri Staroj Vuri, Giznik 2, **t** (01) 33 50 548 (*expensive–moderate*). A charming dining room cluttered with the 'old clocks' of its name sets the tone for a traditional menu. Fat smoked sausages are served with sauerkraut, baked pork comes in a spicy red wine sauce and local trout is laced with Riesling wine and garlic.

Samoborska Pivnica, Šmedhenova 3, **t** (01) 33 61 623 (*moderate*). Every cut of a pig is fried, smoked and grilled in this old-fashioned cellar restaurant with a platter of sausages.

U Prolazu, Trg krala Tomislava 6 (*cheap*). Terrace tables to people-watch and Samobor's best *Samoborske kremšnite* on the showpiece square.

Look, too, for a large model of 1764 Samobor as a cosy village before the blaze, barely recognizable were it not for the Baroque parish church of **St Anastasia** (Crkva svete Anastazije) whose pastel yellow hulk still lords it over the east end of Trg kralja Tomislava. Amble beside it up street **Svete Ane** and a path just beyond the cemetery picks through woods towards the diminutive 16th-century chapel of **St Anne** (Kapela svete Ana). Stations of the cross count down the ascent to a sister chapel of **St George** (Kapela svete Jurjan), beyond which a path threads through the trees to Stari grad. Or does in theory. To guarantee you are not left pathless and stranded above a castle mailed in ivy and whose shell (*no access*) is crumbling into a romantic ruin after abandonment by 18th-century feudal counts, instead take the gravel path which potters along the hillside west of St Anne's.

Varaždin

*You can visit Varaždin by car, but it is also accessible by public transport: hourly buses (54Kn) from the main bus station journey northeast in 1hr 40mins (tourist office at Vana Padovca 3, **t** (042) 210 987, www. varazdin.hr).*

The old parliamentary capital of Varaždin, razed to the ground by fire in 1776 and gloriously rebuilt, is Croatia's most perfectly preserved Baroque townscape, a spacious charmer shaded duck-egg blue, cream and saffron. Music-lovers should not hesitate to visit in September, when international orchestras visit during three-week classical music beano Varaždin Baroque Evenings. For more on the sights of Varaždin, plus suggestions on how to spend a day here, or where to sleep if you wish to stay overnight, *see* 'Touring from Zagreb', 'Day 5', p.271.

Touring from Zagreb

Day 1: Miracles and Beginnings

Morning: Head north towards Varaždin on the A4, but take the Popovec exit and turn left at Soblinec for **Marija Bistrica**, Croatia's most venerable pilgrimage site. A divine beam of light revealed a black Madonna lost in the parish church after it was hidden from Turks in 1545, then on 15 July 1684 a mystical women in blue beseeched the priest to liberate the statue bricked into a niche – restored to the altar the next day, the Madonna cured a noblewoman's daughter.

Lunch: In Marija Bistrica, try **Dioniz**, Trg Pape Ivanan Paval II, **t** (049) 469 103 (*cheap*), in the central square. For more substantial fare there's **Mladost**, Zagrebačka 9, **t** (049) 469 099 (*cheap*), a bistro on the Zagreb road serving grilled pork chops, squid and fish. **Loljzekova hiža**, 6km west of Marija Bistrica, signposted off Gusakovec road, **t** (049) 469 325 (*cheap*), is a rustic charmer with a menu of home-cooking and a peaceful setting.

Afternoon: Drive west through Donja Stubica until, just beyond the motorway, you turn north to spa town **Krapinske Toplice**; four outdoor pools in a park are ideal for a dip on hot days. Refreshed, continue north to pick up signs to **Krapina**, 17km northeast. In 1899, Dragutin Gorjanović Kramberger unearthed the 30,000-year-old bones and tools of Krapina Man in a cave north of the town. The world's richest Neanderthal finds were snaffled by Zagreb, but Krapina has a museum of fossils and early skulls.

Dinner and Sleeping: In Krapinske Toplice, **Aquae Vivae**, Antuna Mihanovića 2, **t** (049) 202 202 (*inexpensive*) is bland but comfortable – a modern three-star hotel with a pool and spa treatments. In Krapina, try **Pod Starim krovovima**, Trg Ljudevita Gaja 15, **t** (049) 370 536 (*inexpensive*), a friendly central *pension* with modest but cheerful en suite rooms; locals tuck into strange cuts of pig in its restaurant. **Pizzeria Picikato**, Magistratska 2 (*cheap*), serves pizzas and pastas in a courtyard. In Bežanec, Croatia's only five-star manor house hotel, **Dvorac Bežanec**, Valentinovo bb, Pregrada (13km north of Krapinske Toplice), **t** (049) 376 800 (*moderate*), is carved from the Count of Keglević's 17th-century home.

Day 2: Over the Border to Slovenia

Morning: Return to Krapinske Toplice, follow signs to Pregrada and at the junction shimmy left (to Zagreb), then right (Tuheljske Toplice) to reach **Kumrovec**, birthplace of Josip Broz Tito in 1892; see the Old Village Museum, then follow a stream which chuckles through Croatia's largest open-air museum, full of immaculate cottages which spin idealized tales of late-1800s lifestyles.

Lunch: Hearty Zagorje cooking is prepared in country portions in Kumrovec's best restaurant, **Stara Vura**, Josipa Broza 13, **t** (049) 553 137 (*cheap*), 100m right of the entrance. **Kod starog**, Josipa Broza 24, no tel (*cheap*) offers light bites for a summer's day opposite Tito's house. Or try **Zagorsko Klet**, Staro selo, no tel (*cheap*), where home-made cakes, doughy *štrukli*, cheese and wine are served in the cellar of a buffed-up 1887 farmhouse.

Afternoon: Go west just into Slovenia, head north to Podčertrek, then enjoy a lovely drive to the **Olimje Monastery**. Temptation comes from the goodies on sale in a *chocolateria* east of the monastery.

Dinner and Sleeping: In Olimje, **Amon**, Olimje 24, **t** (00 386) (0)3 818 2480 (*moderate*) is a haven of upmarket rusticity near the monastery – reservation essential. Its regional acclaim is as a winery of Smarje-Virstajn tipples. **Haler**, Olimje 6, **t** (00 386) (0)3 812 1200 (*inexpensive*) is a friendly hotel with pine furniture and cheerful modern fabrics in simple but homely en suite rooms, and a reliable menu of pork and trout.

Day 3: A Brace of Castles

Morning: Take the Miljarla border crossing back into Croatia, then potter east towards Desinić. You'll spot **Veliki Tabor** (*open daily 10–5; adm*) before you see the signposts because the Zagorje's mightiest castle hunkers down on a hilltop above the village.

Lunch: Desinić has just one address for lunch, **Grešna gornica**, Taborgradska 3, **t** (049) 343 001 (*cheap*), east of the castle signposted off main road, but it's a charmer.

Afternoon: Allow an hour to wriggle east through hills to **Trakošćan**: in Pregrada turn off the Zagreb road to reach Putkovec and at Đurmanec head north as if for Slovenian town Maribor, then follow signposts. The set-square-perfect castellations of the region's most visited castle (*open summer 9–6; winter 9–4; adm*) betray its origins as the conscious antiquarianism of 19th-century count Juraj Drašković. The living quarters are furnished with wistful portraits of locals by Croatia's first trained female painter, Julijana Erdödy Drašković. For picture-postcard views of the castle, scull a rowing boat across the count's ornamental lake or walk a 5km circuit through woods.

Dinner and Sleeping: In Trakošćan, **Coning**, Trakošćan 5, t (042) 796 495 (*inexpensive*) is a comfy if characterless two-star of the Coning chain, bang opposite the castle. Its restaurant is a carnivore's heaven. Or blast north on the Slovenia road (B9/E59) to locate historic Ptuj. Here, spacious proportions reflect the 1870 vintage of the super-central hotel **Mitra**, Prešernova 6, t (00 386) (0)2 787 74 55 (*inexpensive*). Eat at classy fish restaurant **Ribič**, Dravska 9, t (00 386) (0)2 749 06 35 (*moderate*).

Day 4: Back into Slovenia: Putj

Morning: Begin your exploration of pretty Ptuj's two millennia of architectural hand-me-downs at central square **Mestni trg**, with a neo-Gothic town hall. South on Krempljeva ulica is the **Minorite monastery** (*adm free, by appt*). Book a time to see its Baroque summer refectory with thick stucco icing and frescoes of saints Peter and Paul. Northeast on Slovenski trg is the marble **Orpheus Monument**, carved for a 2nd-century Roman mayor, but used as a Middle Ages pillory. Here, too, you'll find **St George's Church**, a Romanesque gem stuffed with exquisite Gothic and Baroque altars.

Lunch: Tuck into huge pizzas and bowls of pasta within **Cafe Europa** on Mestni trg (*cheap*). A block north, **Perutnina Ptuj (PP)**, Novi trg 2, t (00 386) (0)2 749 06 22 (*cheap*), offers no-nonsense pub-grub in a tavern.

Afternoon: A bug-eyed 1400s mask at No.1 and Ptuj's oldest house (No.4) inaugurate arterial traders' street **Prešernova**. Go west to the Dominican monastery, home to the **Archaeological Museum** with its rambling celebration of Ptuj's Celtic and Roman roots. Both founded settlements on the hilltop now claimed by the castle, once a stern 12th-century stronghold, now a Baroque dandy; as the **regional museum** (*open daily 9–5; adm*).

Dinner: **Amadeus**, Prešernova 36, t (00 386) (0)2 771 70 51 (*cheap*), is a cheerful rustic with a large menu of tasty Slovene standards.

Sleeping: Hapsburg-era beauty Varaždin is 34km east of Ptuj; the B228 heads over the border and continues direct to the town. **Pansion Maltar**, Prešernova 1, t (042) 311 100 (*inexpensive*) has good-value modest rooms. The three-star favourite, **Turist**, Aleja kralja Zvonimira 1, t (042) 395 394 (*moderate–inexpensive*), is 100m west. For dinner, try **Zlatna Guska**, J Habdelića 4, t (042) 213 393 (*moderate*), in a barrel-vaulted cellar.

Day 5: Varaždin

Morning: Greatness nipped in the bud characterizes Varaždin. The wealthy merchant town lost its brief status as parliamentary capital after a 1776 fire. But atrophy made this Croatia's most perfectly preserved Baroque town, at its grandest around main square **Trg kralja Tomislava**. Just east is the **cathedral**, with a glorious altar on which saints preach from niches like fairground showmen. More Baroque show-offs put on the Ritz west on Franjevački trg – hub of 1700s high-life the **Patačić Palace** still swaggers despite demotion as a bank, and the Herzer Palace west is now home to the **Entomology Museum** (*open Tues–Fri 10–5, Sat–Sun 10–1; adm*).

Lunch: **Dominico**, Trg slobode 7, t (042) 212 017 (*cheap*) offers 15 styles of pizza beside the park. **Kavana Korzo**, Trg Kralja Tomir 2, t (042) 320 914 (*cheap*) is auntie's favourite café.

Afternoon: Pause at the Baroque **Ursuline church** as you thread north to the **castle**; its **museum** (*open May–Sept Tues–Sun 10–6; Oct–April Tues–Fri 10–5, Sat–Sun 10–1; adm*) rambles through local history and interior décor styles. Then stroll west on Hallerova aleja: town cemetery overseer Hermann Heller rejcted lugubriousness and strove for 'a park of the living' in 1905.

Dinner and Sleeping: A traditional dining room of starched white tablecloths and antique dressers sets the tone for a good-value menu of continental Croatian fare at **Grenadir**, Kranjčevićeva 12, t (042) 211 131 (*cheap*). **Park**, J Habdelića 6, t (042) 211 499 (*moderate–cheap*) is another timewarp. You can return directly to Zagreb in the morning on the motorway south.

Food and Drink

The Venetians may have retreated back across the Adriatic, and the Austrian Hapsburgs slunk north inland, but both former rulers left behind a little piece of themselves in Croatia's contradictory cuisines. Cuisine on the coast is typically Mediterranean – super-fresh and simple. Excellent first courses are *pršut*, similar to Italian prosciutto, and *Pakši sir* (Pag cheese), a tangy, hard sheep's cheese from island Pag. Both are pricey but worth it. *Salata od hobotnice* may also come as a starter, although this salad of octopus, potatoes and onion soaked with olive oil and a tang of vinegar is also delicious as a light lunch, as is a list of appetisers bequeathed by the Venetians: pastas and simple but tasty risottos. The Adriatic catch of the day is brought fresh from the boat and priced by weight and category: gourmets' choice is *bijela riba* (white fish), such as John Dory, mullet and gilthead bream. Pick from a platter brought to the table and your fish is grilled (*na žaru*) over wood and splashed with olive oil, or baked (*pećnici*). For a cheap eat, there's traditional fish stew brodet, served in the pan and best eaten with bread. The classic fishy side dish is *blitva*, a filling medley of Swiss chard, potatoes and garlic. For a break from charcoal-grilled steaks, *kotlet* (pork chops) and *miješano meso* (mixed meats), seek out the Dalmatia speciality *pašticada*, a rich dish of beef slow-cooked in wine, or *janjetina*, spit-roast lamb. And throughout Dalmatia menus include dishes cooked under a *peka*: octopus, lamb and veal (*teletina*) is covered with a metal lid then heaped with charcoals. Desserts are simple: creamy *torta* (gâteaux) or *palacinke* (pancakes) with chocolate (*sa čokoladom*) or jam (*sa marmeladom*), plus *sladoled* (ice cream) or seasonal fruit. Around Dubrovnik, keep an eye open for *rozata*, a local crème caramel. Tastes are similar north in Istria, although a region enthralled by neighbour Italy has stronger Latin accents. More than anything, Istria is truffle (*tartufi*) country.

Continental Croatians on the Hungarian and Slovenian borders prefer robust dishes. The classic Zagorje starter is *štrukli*, a dumpling filled with curd cheese. Less filling is bean soup *grah*, often with hunks of sausage. For main courses Zagreb locals make a special trip to Samobor to eat *češnjovka* (garlic sausages), and Slavonia indulges its passion for paprika in *salami kulen*. Slavonias also pour the paprika into freshwater fish stew *fiš paprikaš*, but this is an exception in an inland area with a taste for farmyard favourites: pork in a baffling variety of cuts, and *gulaš*, duck (*patka*), *zagrebački odrezak* (Zagreb Schnitzel, actually cordon bleu and fried in breadcrumbs), and Zagreb and Zagorje institution turkey (*purica*) ubiquitously served with *mlinci*, thin baked noodles, as *purica z mlincima*.

It is no surprise that **wine** (*vino*) is a part of everyday life in a country which basks in over 2,400 hours of sunshine on an average year; 70 per cent of the country's 620 wines are Quality standard. Connoisseur's choice red wine (*crno vino*) is Dingač, luxurious and velvety; it just outranks rich Postup. Faced with greater temperature extremes, continental Croatia prefers hardy white grapes. Croatia also turns its grape harvest into *rakija* or *loza*, a potent *eau de vie* tossed off as an aperitif with a salute of '*Živjeli!*' (cheers). The Austro-Hungarian rulers who nurtured Croatia's taste for **beer** (*pivo*) instilled a taste for pale lagers, some with a hint of sweetness and all served chilled. Zagreb's local brew is Tomislav, darker and rich in malt.

Dubrovnik

Byron acclaimed it the Pearl of the Adriatic and George Bernard Shaw sighed that 'those who seek paradise on Earth should come to Dubrovnik'. August crowds can make it more purgatory than paradise, but Dubrovnik remains a stunner – a Canaletto cityscape of Baroque mansions and churches painted in cool stone and clear light as if caught in a back-eddy of modernity's riptide. For all the praise lavished on the city inked on to UNESCO 's World Heritage list way back in 1978, the sentiment Croatia's *belle* truly prizes is that on her buses – *Libertas*; it's no accident that St Blaise, city icon of independence, salutes citizens in every niche.

Dubrovnik has good reason to eulogize. Its status as an independent city-state guaranteed fat profits and high living almost as soon as the trader on Balkan and Mediterranean land and sea routes set up its stall in the 12th century. And while other towns on Croatia's seaboard laboured under the Venetian yoke, the Ragusan Republic developed as a world power through good sea legs – with one of the world's largest fleets – and a sweet tongue: the canny diplomat maintained relations with Balkan and Ottoman empires when other Christians states let cannonballs do the talking. During a Renaissance golden age, the queen of the Adriatic held court to the region's brightest stars and became a dynamo of literature, art and architecture. Even if the latter was largely reduced to rubble by a 1667 earthquake, its Baroque replacement makes up for in elegance what it lacks in Renaissance fizz.

That refined cityscape lures still, huddled tight within iconic city walls that articulate Dubrovnik's defiance better than any words and which have thwarted all invaders bar Napoleon Bonaparte – and even that all-conquering dictator was forced to besiege rather than storm the republic that he dissolved in 1808. And it seems only proper that it was the Serbian shelling of this independent city which truly alerted Europe to Croatia's struggle for freedom.

The Pile Gate, City Walls and Lovrijenac Fortress

Enter Dubrovnik's old town (the city sprawls wide to east – Ploče – and west – the Lapad and Babin kuk peninsulas – but this is the city's heart), like the majority of visitors throughout its history, through the western **Pile Gate** (Gradska vrata Pile). From 1537 guards kept a sharp eye on trade passing through the republic's principal gateway atop a new outer bastion where, framed in a niche, **St Blaise** (*see* box, over-leaf) cradles a model of the Renaissance city. During the republican era, the wooden drawbridge to the Pile Gate was hoisted each night with considerable pomp in a cere-mony which delivered city keys to the Ragusan rector. Today it spans a dry moat whose garden offers respite from crowds.

Pass through the Pile Gate's original Gothic inner gateway – this St Blaise is by Croat 20th-century giant Ivan Meštrović – to reach one of a trio of access points to the **city walls** (Gradske zidine; *open summer daily 8.30–6.30, winter 9–4; adm*) which offer the finest introduction to Dubrovnik there is (*access also in Svetog Dominika near the Ploče Gate, and by the Aquarium*). Although sections of Dubrovnik's defining feature date back to the 10th century, the stone girdle finally hugged the city tight four centuries

St Blaise, Patron Saint

Four centuries after his AD 316 martyrdom under Roman emperor Diocletian, the Armenian bishop-saint Blaise tipped off a dreaming cathedral priest that a fleet of Venetian galleons anchored off Lokrum (*see* p.284) under the pretence of replenishing water barrels was actually poised to attack. Or so goes the tale to explain the saint's 10th-century adoption as Dubrovnik patron (more prosaically explained by the arrival of his relics) – and a republic never slow to trumpet its freedom after 150 years' rule by arch-rival Venice (until 1358) hailed its hero in sculpture and painting throughout the city. Nor is such votive salute simply ancient history. In 1991, despairing of half-hearted peace negotiations in The Hague, a band of Dubrovnik refugees invoked the saint as humanitarian aid mission the 'St Blaise Foundation' and attempted to brazen their way through a Yugoslav naval siege of their city on a passenger ferry. Among their number was Croatian president Stipe Mesić, who warmed to his heroics under the protection of global publicity and declaimed, 'You can shoot if you want to, but remember Europe is listening.' It was, too; the Montenegrin army and Yugoslav navy slunk off, embarrassed by the PR disaster of shells casually lobbed into one of the world's most perfectly preserved citadels.

later, then was bolstered at lightning pace after shockwaves of panic rippled north from the bombshell of Constantinople's fall to rampaging Ottomans in 1453.

Florentine architectural supremo Michelozzo di Bartolomeo Michelozzi took no chances. Sections of the fortifications power 25m high and are a no-nonsense 6m thick on vulnerable inland flanks, protected by the front-guard of a deep moat and scarp wall to thwart siege cannons; seaward walls are a modest 3m thick. Michelozzi also erected or strengthened fortresses which stand watch at each corner of the city. Clockwise from the Pile Gate entry, they are: the mighty **Minčeta Tower**, whose crenellated battlements and central tower are saluted as an icon of unconquered Dubrovnik; the **Revelin Fortress** adjacent to the southeast Ploče Gate; **St John's Fortress**, a powerful gun emplacement which has kept watch over the port since the 1350s; and the **Bokar Bastion**, which guards sea approaches.

Whatever the defences' warlike conception, the reason to march their 2km circuit today is for peaceful picture-postcard views over bell-towers, spires and a terracotta roofscape like patchwork. Partly because of its UNESCO status, partly due to pride, Dubrovnik was so precious about repairs to a historic kernel two-thirds destroyed by 20th-century Serbian shells – maps at the city gates pinpoint direct hits and minor scars – that it scoured Europe to match the *kupe kanalice* tiles shaped over medieval thighs. Those sourced from French and Slovenian factories are a shock of orange beside the soft tones of the weathered originals, but there's magic in the air when late-afternoon sunshine rakes low and ripens the palette of orange and saffron, ochre and cream, especially from the Minčeta Tower.

For a jaw-dropping perspective of the city huddled like a model town, puff uphill to the main road above (shame about the traffic). For an alternative view closer to hand, ascend the **Lovrijenac Fortress** (Tvrđava Lovrijenac; *open daily 8.30–6.30; same ticket as city walls*), which hunkers down on a knuckle of rock opposite the Bokar bastion.

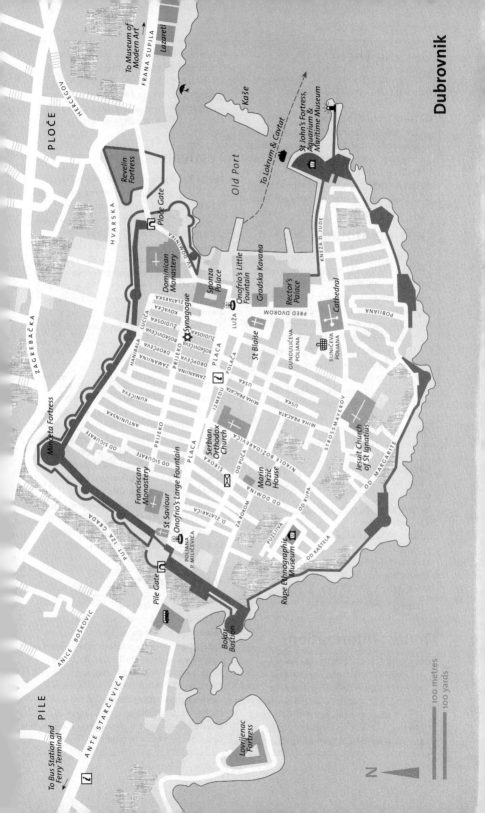

Dubrovnik

PLOČE

HERCEGOVAČKA

To Museum of
Modern Art

Lazareti

FRANA SUPILA

Revelin
Fortress

HVARSKA

Ploče Gate

OD DOMINIKA

Kaše

Old Port

To Lokrum & Cavtat

St John's Fortress,
Aquarium &
Maritime Museum

ZAGREBAČKA

Dominican
Monastery

ZLATARSKA

Sponza
Palace

Onofrio's Little
Fountain

Gradska Kavana

KNEZA D. JUDE

Synagogue

ŽUDIOSKA

Luža

Rector's
Palace

Cathedral

Minčeta Fortress

LUCIĆA

BOŠKOVIĆEVA

DROPČEVA

ŽUDIOSKA

KOVAČKA

KUNIĆEVA

ŽAMANJINA

PRIJEKO

PLACA

POLAČA

St Blaise

PRED DVOROM

POBIJANA

HANIBALA

BOŠKOVIĆEVA

DROPČEVA

ŽAMANJINA

PLACA

BUNIĆEVA
POLJANA

ANTUNINSKA

OD SIGURATE

PRIJEKO

IZMEĐU

POLAČA

USKA

GUNDULIĆEVA
POLJANA

OD SIGURATE

Franciscan
Monastery

PLACA

Serbian
Orthodox
Church

MIHA PRACATA

USKA

STROSS-MAYEROV

St Saviour

Onofrio's Large Fountain

ŠIROKA

MIHA PRACATA

Jesuit Church
of St Ignatius

POLJANA
P. MILIČEVIĆA

OD PULA

NIKOLE BOŽIDAREVIĆA

OD MARGARITE

Pile Gate

D. ZLATARIĆA

Marin
Držić
House

ZA ROKOM

OD DOMINA

OD RUPA

PUT IZA GRADA

PUŽLJIVA

Rupe Ethnographic
Museum

OD KAŠTELA

ANICE BOŠKOVIĆ

Bokar
Bastion

PILE

ANTE STARČEVIĆA

To Bus Station
and Ferry Terminal

Lovrijenac
Fortress

N

100 metres
100 yards

Getting There

You can reach Dubrovnik by air, or by ferry from Italy, *see* **Getting There**, pp.4–10.

Getting from the Airport

Croatia Airlines **transfer buses** (30Kn) scheduled around its flights drop off passengers at the Pile Gate, and pick them up from the main bus station on Put Republik 2hrs before flight departure. Expect to pay 200Kn for a **taxi**. *See* below for transport from the **ferry** terminal.

Getting Around

Libertas **buses** 4, 5 and 7 operate circuits from the Pile Gate to hotels on the western peninsulas between 6am and 2am at a fixed price of 10kn – have the exact money ready – or you can buy a 7kn ticket from a Libertas counter at the Pile Gate, newsagents or hotel receptions. Buses 1a, 3 and 7 shuttle between the ferry terminal and the Pile Gate via the principal bus station at Put Republike 7, north-west of the old town.

Taxis wait night and day at a rank outside the Pile Gate or can be called on **t** 970.

Forget **driving**: parking near the old town is near-impossible in summer and expensive year-round. Use a car only for touring.

Car Hire

International players also operate desks at the airport.

Hertz, Frana Supila 9, **t** (020) 425 000, *www.hertz.com*.

Europcar, Kardinala Stepinca 32, **t** (020) 437 179, *www.europcar.com*.

Avis, Vladimira Nazora 9, **t** (020) 422 043, *www.avis.com*.

Mack, Frana Supila 3, **t** (020) 423 747, *www.rentacar-croatia.com*.

Tourist Information

Dubrovnik: Placa, **t** (020) 321 561, *www.tzdubrovnik.hr*, near the Franciscan monastery; *open daily 8–10*; and Ante Starčevića 7, **t** (020) 427 591/426 253, near the Pile Gate bus station; *open 8–8*. Both stock city maps, timetables for Jadrolinija ferries, the usual confetti of brochures and excellent free booklet *Dubrovnik*, a mine of information which contains central and Lapad/Babin kuk peninsula maps, bus routes, ferry timetables, current museum opening times, what's-on listings and a directory of restaurants and services.

Festivals

Feb: **St Blaise's Day** on 3rd fills the old town with religious pomp and is closely followed by three days of **Carnival**, whose good-humoured lunacy of costumed parades and merriment ends on Whit Sunday.

Early July–Aug: Highlight of the Dubrovnik calendar is internationally acclaimed cultural beano the **Summer Festival** (*www.dubrovnik-festival.hr*). This feast of classical music and theatre takes full advantage of Dubrovnik's stage-set squares, courtyards and castles for its venues.

Shopping

Placa's mansions are stuffed with touristy shops, boutiques, bookshops and smart jewellers, but don't expect any bargains. Nor are there many in parallel **Od Puča**, although it offers a more intriguing mish-mash of leather work, jewellers and galleries. More quirky souvenirs are to be found in **Art Studio I Hajdarhodžić**, Zlatarska 1, which has 15 years' practice of crafting clay fishing boats.

Foodies should peruse the olive oils, wines and liqueurs and good things sold in **Franja**, Od Puča 9, and gallery-delicatessen **Dubrovačka Kuća**, Sv. Dominika 4.

Where to Stay

Dubrovnik **t** (020) –

Bar two exceptions in the old town where reservation is essential and a spanking new Hilton, most of the beds are in pricey hotels 10mins' walk east of the Ploče Gate, or mid-range package offerings 2–4km west on the Lapad and Babin kuk peninsulas. Dubrovnik's fame means bargains are thin on the ground; budget accommodation comes largely from private rooms and in high season you are likely to be met by a crack team of silver-haired touts; triple-check the location of rooms before agreeing.

Pucić Palace, Od Puča 1, Old Town, **t** 326 200, *www.thepucicpalace.com* (*expensive*). Rooms in this five-star boutique hotel carved out of an old town aristocrat's mansion are on the snug side, but benefit from 18th-century high ceilings and quietly flamboyant décor – a mix of modern, antique and opulent fabrics – and the location is unbeatable.

Hilton Imperial Dubrovnik, Marijana Blazica 2, Old Town, **t** 416 553, *www.hilton.com* (*expensive*). A £14m renovation has buffed up two 19th-century palaces to create this 2005 newcomer to Dubrovnik's luxury hotel scene, moments from the Pile Gate and as classy as you'd expect of a five-star member of the international old-hand.

Grand Villa Argentina and **Villa Osrula**, Frana Supila 14, Ploče, **t** 440 555, *www.hoteli-argentina.hr* (*expensive*). Deluxe if rather heavy style meets five-star mod cons and service in a plush traditionalist 10 minutes' walk east from the Ploče Gate; incorporated Villa Orsula retains a whiff of 1930s nostalgia in its rooms of dark woods. Both share a concrete 'beach' and outdoor pool.

Villa Dubrovnik, Vlaha Bukovca 6, Ploče, **t** 422 933, *www.villa-dubrovnik.hr* (*expensive*). Ten minutes further east is this tranquil and friendly retreat snuggled in pines, a bright modernist building flooded with light and arty tastes. Simple rooms are stylish – beg for 101–107 or 222–225 to wake up to glorious views of the old town – and a hotel ferry pootles guests into the centre.

Dubrovnik Palace, Masarykov put 2, Lapad, **t** 430 000, *www.dubrovnikpalace.hr* (*expensive*). Boutique style on a package hotel scale in a five-star Lapad peninsula newcomer. The decorative tones are delicious – cream, chocolate and *café au lait* – every room has sea views from its balcony and there are all sorts of pools, bars and restaurants to tempt you.

Stari Grad, Od Sigurate 4, Old Town, **t** 321 373, *www.hotelstarigrad.com* (*moderate*). A little pricey considering the adequate but unspectacular furnishings on offer in eight three-star rooms, but the only medium-range hotel within the old town walls, smuggled up a side street off Placa.

Neptun, Kardinala Stepinca 31, Babin kuk, **t** 440 100, *www.hotel-neptun.hr* (*moderate*). Flowery fabrics and blond wood in simple, modern rooms of two blocks set among the unspoilt scrub on the Babin kuk peninsula west of the old town. The sea views are knockout, especially those to the Elafiti islands from rooms 211–14, 311–14 and 411–14. Distance from the peninsula restaurants may be a problem without transport.

Kompas, Šetalište kralja Zvonimira 56, Lapad, **t** 435 777, *www.hotel-kompas.hr* (*moderate*). A little bland in taste, but a comfortable and friendly three-star, well-located above the Sumratin beach.

Zagreb, Šetalište kralja Zvonimira 27, Lapad, **t** 436 500 (*inexpensive*). Pleasant small hotel among leafy palms a few minutes' walk from the beach, with 1924 proportions but décor that benefits from a 2005 modernization. Adjacent sister hotel Sumratin (same tel, cheap) offers more of the same if its 22 rooms are full.

Ohran, Od Tabakarije 1, nr Old Town, **t** 414 183 (*inexpensive*). Overlook the fact that the 11 rooms (although spotless and en suite) are basic, and concentrate instead on the location, hidden away in a quiet cove beneath the old town Lovrijenac Fortress. A bargain, and one with a good restaurant to boot.

Private Rooms

A little more expensive are private rooms offered by private tourist agencies.

Atlas, Brsalje 17, near the Pile Cate, **t** 442 574/565, *www.atlas-croatia.com*. Friendly.

Globtour, Prijeko 12, Old Town, **t** 321 599.

Generalturist, Frana Supila 9, near the Ploče Gate, **t** 432 974, *www.generalturist.com*.

Dubrovnik Turist, Put Republike 7, by the main bus station, **t** 356 969, *www.dubrovnik turist.hr*.

Eating Out

Dubrovnik **t** (020) –

You'll never be short of a new restaurant in Dubrovnik. Restaurant alley is Prijeko, although it's an uninspiring affair of tourist-orientated offerings. For eats on the go, 24-hour bakery **Tanti Gusti** (Između Polača 11) bakes filled croissants for breakfast and

Buffet Škola (Antuninska bb) rustles up delicious sandwiches prepared with thick home-made bread and local ingredients.

Lokunda Peskarija, Ribarnica bb (beside the old port), **t** 324 750 (*cheap*). The locals' choice for an early morning gossip over coffee, or mussels or risottos of seafood or cuttlefish, served in saucepans and washed down with a chirpy local plonk. Unpretentious and excellent – expect to wait for a seat.

Dubrovački kantun, Boškovićeva 5, **t** 331 911 (*cheap*). A taste of tradition in a bistro-café that prepares chunky sandwiches and Dalmatian *tapas*, much of it vegetarian and all using the freshest local ingredients. Anchovies are delicious, there's tangy sheep's cheese from Pag soused in olive oil and smoky *pršut* ham is ever-reliable.

Buffet Kamenice, Gunulićeva poljana 8; no tel (*cheap*). You'll queue for a table in this good-value, brisk favourite of locals and tourists alike in intimate Gunulićeva poljana. Mussels are fat and come piled high; *mala riba pržena* (whitebait) and octopus salad make a tasty light bite.

Rozarij, Prijeko 2 (*moderate*). A little pricey, but by far the most atmospheric restaurant of the glut on Prijeko, with a menu of fresh fish and candlelit tables snuggled against the tiny church of St Nicholas.

Marco Polo, Lučarica 6, **t** 323 719 (*moderate*). There's a chef's special *riblja plitica* (fish platter) for a two-person blow-out plus reliable fallback appetisers such as *rizoto od morskih plodova* (seafood risotto) and *crni rižot* (squid ink risotto) in a 10-table charmer squirrelled away down a side alley behind St Blaise's church.

Proto, Široka 1, **t** 323 234 (*expensive*). A semi-smart 1886 old-timer just off Placa, with consistently high-quality cooking: chef's favourite recipes come from grandma's cookbook, but he also prepares a delicate langoustine dish in saffron sauce.

Domino, Od Domina 6, **t** 323 103 (*moderate*). Carnivore heaven in a restaurant which prepares speciality steaks in a polyglot of styles and offers a good-value four-course menu. Dining is on the terrace or in a stone house in winter.

Levant, N&M Pucića 15, **t** 435 352 (*moderate*). A romantic gem on the Baban kuk peninsula (on the road to Hotel Neptun) with lovely views across the bay which are magic at dusk and friendly service. The inventive menu ranges from traditionals like fish stew *brodet* and an ink-blackened salad of cuttlefish and olives from Elafiti island Šipan, to modern creations such as fish carpaccio and rocket leaves fried with mozzarella.

Atlas Club Nautica, Braslje 3, **t** 442 526 (*expensive*) The formal address for visiting dignitaries (Pope John Paul II came in 2003), expense account lunches and evening blow-outs offers views of the city walls and Lovrijenac to accompany exquisite seafood and a house-special lobster.

Cafés and Bars

Buža, Od Margarite. Hunt for a sign which announces 'Cold drinks' to find this locals' secret outside the walls, whose tables shaded by palm leaves gaze out to Lokrum.

Gradska kavana, Luža. Cakes and coffee brought by waiters in black and white in the silver-haired *grande dame* of Dubrovnik cafés located in the former arsenal and with terraces over Luža square and the old port.

Hard Jazz Café Trubadour, Bunićeva Poljana. The best place to sample the buzz of a Dubrovnik summer evening – wicker chairs sprawl across the square and a stylish clientele sip a cocktail to live jazz.

Libertina, Zlatarska. A locals' favourite, cluttered with junky knick-knacks and where service is refreshingly gruff; an antidote to high-season posing.

Entertainment

Monthly booklet *Dubrovnik* (free from tourist information) is a what's-on bible which lists everything from concerts of the Dubrovnik Symphony Orchestra to football matches. Treats are candlelit classical concerts staged in churches, the Dominican Monastery cloisters and the atrium of the Rector's Palace, intimate and atmospheric. More chirpy are the twice weekly showcases of Croatian traditional songs and dance folk group Lindo stages in the Lazareti (*see* p.284; in 2005, Tues and Fri at 9.30pm).

City fathers demanded walls 12 metres thick for the castle in order to guard western sea approaches – except for those walls facing inland, whose 60cm wafer provided no protection. Enter the stripped shell of the late 15th-century fortress and you can understand why its fame today is not as a scourge of sea galleons but as the setting for 'Elsinore' during Summer Festival productions of *Hamlet*.

Along Placa

The cameras come out again for **Placa** (aka Stradun) just inside the Pile Gate. So handsome is Dubrovnik's showpiece street that you'd never guess its origins as a swampy channel filled in in the 11th century to unite islet Laus – where the city made its 7th-century debut as Ragusa, founded by Greco-Roman refugees from Epidaurum (*see* p.285) – with the mainland Slavic town christened after holm-oak woods (*dubrava*). The devastating 1667 earthquake which allowed city fathers to rethink their map also allowed them to take in hand Placa's jumble of Gothic palaces and impose a Baroque dress parade. For all the authoritarian bent of its conception, there's no denying Placa's good looks; a handsome stretch of green-shuttered mansions in delicious shades of honey and clotted cream, an occasional touching blush of pink, on a street whose limestone cobbles have been buffed to a sheen by millions of pairs of feet.

The 1667 earthquake which razed Placa also did for **Onofrio's Large Fountain** (Velika Onofrijeva fontana) just inside the Pile Gate; the 16 masks that spout water on a bare dome today barely hint at the heavily ornamented Renaissance beauty of the original, designed in 1438 by architect Onofrio della Cava. More recent destruction is visible as shrapnel scars which pock the Renaissance trefoil façade of the diminutive **St Saviour's Church** (Crkva sv. Spasa) opposite, a rum deal for a church which survived the 1667 quake in better shape than its sisters and was itself erected as a thank you for the city's survival of a 1520 earthquake. The spartan Gothic interior now serves as a temporary exhibition space and concert venue.

The 1667 earthquake also destroyed a **Franciscan Monastery** (Franjevački samostan) far more ritzy than the present hulk if a surviving late-Gothic portal is any evidence; local sons the Petrović brothers carved its late-Gothic *Pietà* flanked by St Jerome (in a penitent's hairshirt) and St John. Don't linger in the barn-like interior stuffed with so-so Baroque altars; devote your time instead to the delightful late-Romanesque **cloister** (*open daily 9–6; adm*), accessible from a passageway adjacent to tourists trying out the traditional test of balance atop a stone beside the west portal – not as easy as it looks. Craftsmen in 1360 gave free rein to their imaginations on capitals that crown the cloister's double colonnade of pillars with a menagerie of dragons, dogs and griffins. It's best appreciated around midday, when the tour groups bustle off for lunch and the garden of fruit trees and palms returns to serenity, then you can explore at leisure the curate's egg of ecclesiastical goodies in the **treasury** (*same ticket and hours*). More charming than its Byzantine icons, votive jewellery and bizarre gold and silver reliquaries of saints' feet and St Ursula's head are the china jars and painted shelves which once graced Europe's oldest apothecary, still doling out medicines beside the cloister as it has done since 1317.

North of Placa, steep staircases crammed with pot plants clamber uphill and beg you to explore; residential alleys beyond **Prijeko** allow a glimpse behind the scenes of Dubrovnik's stage-set looks. At the east end of Placa's shimmering river of cobbles, **Žudioska** (Jews' Street) was named for the ghetto established by Jews hounded from Spain in 1492 and 1514–15 exiles from southern Italy. With an open mind derived from its coastal trading traditions, the republic presented the community with a medieval town house, which explains why Europe's second-oldest **synagogue** (Sinagoga; *open summer daily 10–8; winter Mon–Fri 10–1; adm*), a lovely Baroque nook where 19th-century brass lamps and candelabras are suspended from a ceiling framed by Stars of David, is on the second floor rather than in the conventional basement. Not that Dubrovnik embraced its newcomers entirely without reservation – the Ragusan Republic demanded that Jews wash in a separate fountain rather than share those of Christians. A small **museum** chronicles the Jewish community, today 30-strong.

Luža Square

Café society idles and tour groups clog the ensemble of attractions in Luža Square, still centre stage of Dubrovnik life as it was during the medieval republic. Here the 3 February procession of the Feast of St Blaise climaxes with the full authority of Catholic pomp, and poetry recited at the event inaugurates the Summer Festival's arts extravaganza (*see* 'Festivals'). Centrepiece of the handsome piazza is **Orlando's Column** (Orlandov stup). The 1418 lectern for public declarations and shaming post for chained miscreants flew the white banner of *Libertas* from its flagpole until Napoleon lowered it after French troops stomped into a city weakened by siege in 1806. The events of 1990 prompted the city council to restore the flag as a morale-booster. The column is named after its Gothic effigy of Orlando (aka Roland). A tale claims that the chivalric knight slew a 9th-century Saracen pirate named Spucente near Lokrum to lift a 15-month siege of Dubrovnik – overlooking the fact that the nephew of Frankish king Charlemagne and hero of medieval French epic *Chanson de Roland* actually died in AD 778. It is more probable that the favourite of North European cities was imported by Sigismund, 15th-century ruler of Hungary, Bohemia and much of modern Croatia. And whatever the truth, respect was hardly uppermost in the minds of the market traders who measured out 51.2cm lengths of cloth on their hero's forearm.

He stands opposite the splendid **Sponza Palace** (Sponza-Povijesni arhiv; 1522; *often open Mon–Fri 9–2 but times vary by exhibition; adm free*), whose Renaissance colonnade and refined Venetian-Gothic windows by architect Paskoje Miličević, frothily ornamented by renowned Korčula sculptor-brothers the Andrijićs, offer a tantalising glimpse of elegant Dubrovnik before the 1667 destruction. The city archives are stored in upper floors where intellectuals once debated and the republic minted its own currency. But downstairs, enter its galleried courtyard, now quiet after years when it rang to the polyglot babble of merchants in the customs house. Here you can hear summer concerts and visit the ground floor exhibitions – don't miss the moving 'Memorial Room of Dubrovnik Defenders' at the rear.

Local favourite 'green men' clang the hour in the 31m **bell tower** (Gradski zvonik) at the palace's left shoulder, rebuilt in 1929 to 15th-century plans after the building's drunken tilt became too woozy to ignore. From here you can sidetrack through an arch to the Dominican Monastery (*see* p.283) or pass the moustachioed guard on the massive Baroque portal of the **House of the Main Guard** to **Onofrio's Little Fountain** (Mala Onofrijeva fontana); pigeons bathe in the light-hearted sister to its big relative at the other end of Placa, and its cherubs are by Milanese sculptor Pietro di Martino.

The backdrop to Luža's ensemble piece is **St Blaise's Church** (Crkva svetog Vlaha); at the peak the city's patron (*see* p.274) waves a cheery salute between Faith and Hope. Small wonder those two Virtues were chosen, because the elegant Baroque church rose over the square in 1715 as a replacement for a Gothic number battered in 1667, then reduced to rubble by a 1706 fire. Inside, upstaged by angels and *putti*, a silver statue of the saint clutches the inevitable city model on the high altar, removed only when it is paraded solemnly on St Blaise's Day as a miraculous survivor of the blaze.

The Rector's Palace

Follow the limestone cobbles that flow from Luža past *grande dame* of Dubrovnik cafés **Gradska kavana**, located in the former city arsenal, to the **Rector's Palace** (Knežev dvor), state headquarters of the Ragusan Republic and temporary home of the local son elevated to preside over council meetings for a month. For all the high talk of republican egalitarianism, the ruling aristocracy kept a firm grip on power and the incumbent was little more than a ceremonial puppet – during his tenure, the symbol of sovereignty, aged 50-plus, lived apart from his family and was only permitted to leave his glorified prison on state business.

But what a prison. Gunpowder explosions (the palace originally led a double life as an arsenal), fire and earthquake, which necessitated over 230 years of home improvements, have fashioned a stylistic encyclopaedia of Gothic and Renaissance from the drawing boards of a *Who's Who* of Adriatic architects: Naples' Onofrio; Michelozzi, putting fortifications work on hold; and Korčula's Petar Andrijić. If the city fathers hoped for public showiness, they must have been delighted with Michelozzi's Renaissance *loggia*, even if the conservative custodians frowned at most of his plans as too racy and the architect harrumphed back to Florence. Do hunt among his frothy capitals for Asclepius in his pharmacy – a vainglorious attempt to appropriate the classical authority of a Greek demigod physician linked with Epidaurum (today's Cavtat, *see* pp.285–6) – before you enter its elegant Renaissance atrium, prize venue for classical music concerts. For want of an heir, powerful ship owner and merchant Miho Pracat from Lopud (*see* pp.286–7) bequeathed his fortune to the city and is honoured in a 1638 bust at the rear of the courtyard.

Musty displays of coins, official seals, documents and weaponry are in the ground floor former courtroom and prison cells, then the **city museum** (Gradski muzej; *open summer daily 9–6; winter daily 9–2; adm*) perks up in first-floor state rooms, reached via a Baroque staircase that sweeps up to the assembly hall. Councillor nobles pout shamelessly on the walls of period rooms whose *objets d'art* and costumes such as the rector's red damask toga fast-forward through decorative styles and hint at Ragusan glory snuffed out by Napoleonic dissolution. Informative the rooms are not, however; a museum guide is a must if you want to do anything but skim.

The Cathedral and St John's Fortress

Making an emphatic full-stop to **Pred Dvorom** is the powerful **cathedral** (Katedrala), crowned by a surprisingly dainty cupola. An ex-pat intellectual, enthused by the churches of his Eternal City adopted home, recommended Andrea Buffalini of Urbino to draw its Roman Baroque, which rose over the ruins of a Romanesque church destroyed in 1667. Fiction – or at least local legend – claims the progenitor was funded by Richard the Lionheart in thanks for his life after shipwreck near Lokrum after an 1192 Crusade. Fact – or at least early foundations – retorts that a church has existed at the location on former islet Laus since the 7th century.

The star artwork in a bleached but stately interior is a gloomy *Assumption of the Virgin* polyptych above the altar, attributed to Venetian master Titian. Inevitably, St Blaise and his model put in an appearance on the left-hand panel, although this time with good reason because bits of the saint are venerated in the **treasury** (Riznica; *open Mon–Sat 8–5.30, Sun 11–5.30; adm*), a wonder of the Adriatic before the 1667 earthquake, which the republic safeguarded by entrusting its different keys to the archbishop, cathedral rector and state secretary. Among body parts crammed into Byzantine gold reliquaries and displayed on gloriously cluttered shelves like a holy junk shop are the saint's right and left hands; his throat, in a bizarre 11th-century monstrance like a foot; and, the treasury's prize, his head, encased in a jewel-encrusted Byzantine crown. Overlooked among such star pieces is a 16th-century silver casket – apparently crafted to treasure baby Jesus's nappies.

Narrow **Kneza Damjana Jude**, opposite the main portal of the cathedral, burrows past tatty side-streets stuffed with once-splendid Renaissance nobles' mansions, now living in reduced circumstances, towards stolid port guardian the **St John's Fortress** (Tvrđava sv. Ivana). Its refurbished ground floor houses a 27-tank **Aquarium** (Akvarij; *open summer daily 9–8; winter Mon–Sat 9–1; adm*). Also in the fortress, rooms where cannons once thundered above now salute the maritime prowess which elevated Dubrovnik to world power-player as the **Maritime Museum** (Pomorski muzej; *open summer daily 9–6; winter Tues–Sun 9–1; adm*). Exquisite models of tubby traders and an intriguing snapshot of everyday life afforded by cargo salvaged from a 1600s trader are a highlight of the museum's bosun's locker of nautical knick-knacks.

Around Gundulićeva Poljana

For all her wardrobe of architectural ballgowns, Dubrovnik is just as charming in her everyday dress, worn in Gundulićeva poljana, home to a morning **market** (*Mon–Sat*) whose stallholders also hawk Hvar lavender, fat cheeses and, decanted into old water bottles, home-made wines and *rakija*, a spirit laced with herbs which locals swear is medicinal. The drama queen who poses in the centre is Ivan Gundulić (1589–1638). Such is the acclaim afforded the Ragusan poet's epic *Osman* – a eulogy to Polish routs of the Turks saluted in relief beneath Ivan Rendić's 1892 statue – that he is afforded a place on the 50Kn note.

Climb a 1738 staircase that alludes to Rome's Spanish Steps off the square's south side to stand before the **Jesuit Church of St Ignatius** (Jezuitska crkva i samostan), quiet above the market's chatter and modelled on Rome's imposing Il Gesù. As if to

compensate for the restraint shown in other churches, Dubrovnik's 1729 prize of
Baroque lets rip the razzmatazz; the roof is a frothy gush of pinks, side-chapels whirl
with *trompe l'œil* knobbles and drapes painted in rich hues, and in a richly frescoed
sanctuary Jesuit founder St Ignatius proffers his religious credo before a quartet of
comely *belles*, the four continents on which the order spread the word. Less cultural
but just as enjoyable is a Lourdes grotto by the entrance, whose glorious dollop of
kitsch has filled a north aisle chapel since 1885.

Od Puča and Around

Halfway along Od puča, the street parallel to Placa which is crammed with interesting jewellery boutiques and galleries, is the **Serbian Orthodox Church** (Srpska
pravoslavna crkva), spacious and dignified with a painted panelled ceiling, and a few
doors away at Od puča 8 is the **Orthodox Church Museum** (Muzej pravoslavne crkve;
open Mon–Sat 9–2; adm) of religious icons. More culture is five minutes' walk away at
Široka 7. Croatia's Shakespeare, Marin Držić (1508–67), would probably have knocked
over his inkpot in shock were he to see the interior of his former home. Gutted as
Marin Držić House (Kuča Marina Držica; *open summer daily 9–6; winter Mon–Sat 9–2;
adm*), the museum displays meagre everyday relics from Držić's era and a mock-up of
his cell-like bedroom. Far better is its 40-minute audiovisual presentation (*available in
English*) which explores the Ragusan society he lampooned in comedies such as Croat
favourite *Dundo Maroje* (*Uncle Dundo*). On Od Rupe the **Rupe Ethnographic Museum**
(Etnografski muzej Rupe; *open daily 9–6; adm*) houses three floors of homespun
tradition – costumes, from simple smocks to embroidered Sunday best and rural
handicrafts – let down by dull displays and a lack of labels. As much of an exhibit is
the museum's Renaissance building itself; storage bins dug from the rock bed visible
through holes (*rupe*) in the ground floor confess its origins as the granary of a city
twitchy about sieges and wholly reliant on imported grain.

The Old Port and Dominican Monastery

Suddenly intimate after the grand airs of Placa, **Sv. Dominika** east of the Sponza
Palace twists past the **old port**, where fishing boats not traders' barques nod at moor-
ings, ferries thrum to Lokrum (*see* p.284) and Cavtat (*see* pp.285–6), and tourist boat
captains tout sprees to admire the city walls as merchant sailors knew them. Coffee-
drinkers in café **Gradska kavana** now laze before the three arches through which
state-owned galleons were hauled from the port to be refitted in the city arsenal; not
a city to take chances, Dubrovnik bricked them up while new ships were in build.

Beyond on Sv. Dominika, the **Dominican Monastery** (Dominikanski samostan;
open as museum, see below) presses hard against the city walls following its conception as a fortress to protect a chink in Dubrovnik's stone armour. Chipping in funds,
the Ragusan government exhorted citizens to put other projects on hold until the
14th-century edifice stood for 'the preservation, protection and safety of the city of
Dubrovnik'. Fearing for this city on the outer ramparts of Christendom, Pope Benedict
XI issued a 1304 papal bull 'inviting' church members to dig deep into their coffers.
Ascend a **staircase** whose classy balustrade is marred by concrete filler – the

vandalism of monks desperate to spare brothers the temptation of churchgoing ladies' shapely ankles – to reach a beautiful **cloister** whose restrained Gothic and Renaissance triforas beat time around a garden of palms and orange trees. Its hushed haven, a world away from Dubrovnik's summer hubbub, comes from the drawing board of Rector's Palace architect Michelozzi, and is a cerebral overture to a hoard of devotional art treasures stored in the city's richest **museum** (*open summer daily 9–6; winter daily 9–5; adm*). A trio of Renaissance works by Nikola Božidarević, finest artist of the city's golden age, steals the show: his humanist *Virgin and Child* altarpiece seems wafted from the other side of the Adriatic; a lower panel of an *Annunciation* played out to a rapt audience of cherubs features the anchored vessel of the Lopud captain who commissioned it; and, in a lovely *Madonna and Child* steeped in Byzantine mystery, St Blaise holds out for inspection a model of 16th-century pre-'quake Dubrovnik. In the same room is a polyptych by Lovro Dobričević: first Dominican Order martyr St Peter suffers the cutlass and sword of pirates to witness the baptism of Christ. Star piece among works by Baroque foreigners is a Titian altarpiece of *Mary Magdalene and St Blaise* in an adjacent room.

The **church** itself is a let-down after such magnificence, worth a look only for a *Miracle of St Dominic* altarpiece by late-19th-century Cavtat artist Vlaho Bukovac.

Through the Ploče Gate

As eastern counterpart to the the Pile Gate, the 15th-century **Ploče Gate** signs off the old town with its own drawbridge and statuette of Dubrovnik's bearded patron, and beyond is the 1540s **Revelin Fortress**. Beyond the walls, modernity returns with a jolt, broken only by the **Lazareti** 200m away – artists' studios and the performance space of folk group Linđo now occupy the 16th-century brick sheds on the Turkey trade route where all foreign travellers sat out 40 days' quarantine. If you can find towel space in summer, shingle beach **Banje** is an enticing spot for a dip, otherwise continue uphill to the **Museum of Modern Art** (Umjetnička galerija; *open Tues–Sun 10–7; adm*). Vlaho Bukovac's formal portraiture, which dabbles with Impressionism, wins plaudits among the gallery of 20th-century Croatian artists; more enjoyable are blasts of noisy colour in local landscapes by Marko Rešica or *Lapad*, a dainty but delectable work by Antun Masle. The gallery's ground floor hosts temporary exhibitions.

Lokrum

Ferries every 30mins from old port, summer daily 9–6; 15mins, 35Kn return.

Covered in a thick fuzz of pine tantalizingly close offshore, Lokrum is the perfect escape when Dubrovnik's summer crowds induce claustrophobia, a 72-hectare idyll unofficially dubbed 'Magic Island'. Benedictine monks founded an abbey and monastery here in 1023. Their order dissolved by Napoleon, the monks are said to have laid a curse on anyone who claimed their sanctuary for anything so frivolous as pleasure, and superstitious locals swear it cursed Archduke Maximilian Ferdinand von Hapsburg: he purchased Lokrum as an idyllic retreat in 1859, only to be executed as emperor of Mexico by soldiers in 1867. In the three halcyon years before Maximilian travelled to Mexico to accept his poisoned chalice, he rethought the monastery as a pleasure palace, imported peacocks and dug a **botanic garden** in which to ponder verses of poet Heinrich Heine. Only his garden remains open to the public, somewhat neglected at the side of his mansion; more enticing is the monks' semi-ruined **cloister**, going nicely to seed with agave, palms and cacti. Explore Maximilian's paths, which idle around a drowsy island cocooned in hush, and you'll discover **Fort Royal**, a star-shaped gun battery built by Napoleon as an 1806 stronghold.

Trsteno

Tell the driver and any bus travelling north – the 12 to Brsečinem, 15 to Ston, 21 to Orebić and those to Split – will stop in Trsteno. Average journey time is 45mins, the cost 12Kn each way. Open daily May–Oct 7–7; Nov–April 8–3; adm.

Gazing over his clifftop estate in 1494, Dubrovnik nobleman Ivan Marinov Gučetić-Gozze realised the site's potential for a fashionable summer retreat and seeded one of the finest landscaped parks in Croatia. Visit in spring to see his relic of Renaissance sophistication, lovingly tended and expanded by future generations of the aristocratic dynasty until seized by a nation enthused by Communism and presented to the public in 1948 as the **Trsteno Arboretum**, exploding with colour and promise. Idle among its 63 acres of aromatic greenery or gaze out to the Elafiti islands in summer and you'll wonder how 16th-century humanist Nioklai Vitov Gučetić ever roused himself sufficiently to jot down his philosophical musings.

Day Trips and Overnighters from Dubrovnik

Cavtat

After heady days as medieval sidekick to the Dubrovnik republic, charming Cavtat spends her dotage as a gentle lady of leisure. Yes, there's a whiff of aristocracy on a seafront promenade of Baroque stone mansions – Dubrovnik's Placa in miniature – but the real seduction of this village snuggled in a pine-fringed harbour is as the lazy resort which lured in-the-know Austro-Hungarians in the early 1900s.

Ironically, it's Dubrovnik which owes Cavtat a debt. Slavic and Avar tribes ripped through 7th-century **Epidaurum**, founded by Greeks from island Vis then Romanized as Civitas Vetus in 228 BC, and evacuees fled north to start afresh on the town that became Dubrovnik. After Dubrovnik looked inward during a collective tightening of belts in the 18th century, Cavtat shrugged and turned to fishing instead.

During its halcyon years, a Dubrovnik-appointed governor lorded it over Cavtat from the Renaissance **Rector's Palace**, a grand opening statement to the old town and host to its finest museum, the **Baltazar Bogišic Collection** (Zbirka Baltazara Bogišića; *open Mon–Sat 9.30–1; adm*). Treasured books and early European prints of the Cavtat-born promoter of Slavic culture claim most space, although the 19th-century lawyer reveals his cultured mind and jackdaw enthusiasms in *objets d'art* cherry-picked from France and Italy. His personal treasures are upstaged by the vivacious *Carnival in Cavtat*, whose depiction of the town's finest – Bogišic included – kicking up their heels in fancy dress is by local son Vlaho Bukovac. Three more Bukovacs plus a gallery

Getting There

Hourly **bus 10** from Dubrovnik takes 40mins to trundle 22km south to Cavtat and costs 12Kn. Alternatively, private companies operate summer-only **ferries** (45mins, 40Kn single, 60Kn return) from the old port (Gradska luka), and there's a Nova International ferry (25min, 50Kn single).

Tourist Information

Cavtat: Tiha 3 (200m from the bus station), t (020) 479 025, *www.tzcavtat-konavle.hr.*

Eating Out

Leut, Trumbićev Put 11, **t** (020) 479 050 (*moderate*). Passing celebrities salute the privacy of its terrace, but the main reason to visit this family restaurant near the Rector's Palace is for the catch of the day or a house special cold platter of *pršut* ham, cheese, octopus salad and mussels.

Galija, Vuličevićeva 1, **t** (020) 478 566 (*moderate*). The locals' choice for a slap-up near the monastery church serves consistently excellent fresh fish, perfectly grilled or in rich olive sauces, plus sea urchin caviar.

of glitzy Italian devotional works hang in the **Pinakoteka-Galerija** (*open summer Mon–Sat 10–1; winter by appointment, tel on door; adm*) of parish church **St Nicholas**, at the shoulder of the Rector's Palace. Far better, however, is the career-spanning *œuvre* of the 19th-century father of Croatian art on show in his restored **birthplace** (Kuća Bukovan; *open May–Nov Tues–Sat 9–1 and 4–8, Sun 4–8; Dec–April Tues–Sun 10–5; closed Mon; adm*), located in side street Bukovčeva. Bukovac also painted the Cavtat harbour scene that spans the chancel in the Franciscan monastery church of **Our Lady of the Snow** (Samostan snježne gospe) which signs off the seafront promenade. A path around the peninsula leads you to Cavtat's most enticing coves for a dip. Pebble **beaches** are a 10-minute stroll around the bay before package hotels.

Crowning glory of the town **cemetery** at the peak of the hill above is the **Račić mausoleum** (*open daily 10–12, summer also Mon–Sat 5–7; adm*), a dream of creamy white stone from Brač, beautifully sited over the coastline. Croatia's finest modern sculptor Ivan Meštrović designed the Cavtat shipowners' 1912 tomb to honour a parting request of rumoured sweetheart Maria Račić.

The Elafiti Islands

'Those islets lovelier than gardens,' sighed 16th-century Dubrovnik bishop Lodovico Beccadelli of the enchanting Elafiti islands just off the coast of Dubrovnik to the northwest. His comment echoes through the centuries because the three inhabited 'deer islands' – a corruption of the Greek *elafos* – are minor paradises where tourism is acknowledged only with a casual shrug and cars are outlawed.

Just 3km from Dubrovnik, little **Koločep** is a speck just 2.35km² that gathers its 150 residents in drowsy hamlets **Donje Čelo**, the port on the northwest coast, and **Gornje Čelo** on the southeast. Little more than clusters of stone houses and a parish church huddled in verdant bays (the best beach is at Donje Čelo), the pair are linked by a footpath which idles through pines.

Home to 76 families, middle island **Lopud** has hosted tourists for nearly a century, but then it was always the most outgoing of the trio. In 1457 the 2km by 4.5km island was elevated to regional headquarters, a nod of gratitude perhaps for its tradition of local seamen who drip-fed wealth into the Ragusan Republic as prosperous merchants and commanded Dubrovnik fleets as admirals. An 80-strong fleet which called Lopud its home port also swelled the coffers of ship-owners, who erected the stone mansions which crumble on the bay of its eponymous village-port.

As you enter the bay, keep an eye open for a trio of **Gothic windows** which recall the Rector's Palace of Lopud's golden age, then start your tour at the 15th-century parish **church of the Franciscan monastery**; the guardian of the harbour's northern entrance was fortified into a refuge from Turks a century after it was built in 1483.

Crests on the lintels of harbourfront mansions salute the merchant owners, none more successful than Miho Pracat (1522–1607). A nook-like **chapel** just beyond the tourist office is that of the shipping magnate celebrated in bronze in Dubrovnik's Rector's Palace (*see* p.281).

Past a small **museum of local history and traditional skills** (*adm*), which opens according to whim on the central square, a signposted path ascends inland past the shell of **St John the Baptist's Church** (Sv. Ivan Kristitelj) to the ruins of **Fort Kaštio** (Trđava Kaštio). Its battlements command the sweeping views over neighbouring islands and sea approaches which made it a prize fortification during Lopud's merchant heyday. Energetic strollers can continue on a 12km circuit of the island via the signposted **Pjšačka staza** (trekking way); everyone else should wind downhill past tiny Romanesque chapel of **St Nicholas the Greek** (Sv. Nikola grčki), almost lost among olive groves, to **Šunj**, a pine-fringed notch in the coast whose sand beach backed by a beach restaurant and snack bar is the stuff that escapist dreams are made of.

Šipan may be the largest of the Elafitis, but it's by far the least developed – come here to enter a timewarp. Ferries thrum into principal settlement **Šipanska Luka**, a palm-fringed bay at the end of a deep inlet where the occasional summer manor of a 15th-century aristocratic family hints at former glories; one Dubrovnik dynasty, the Sorkočevićs, fronted theirs with a leonine balcony. A scrap of sandy **beach** is a short walk from the centre. In enjoyably tatty fishing village **Suđurađ**, at the opposite end of Šipan, smaller Renaissance villas huddle in awe of a pair of 16th-century towers that stood guard over the palace of an Dubrovnik noble and, nearby, the **Church-fort of the Holy Spirit**, village refuge during Turkish raids. Between the two villages is **Šipansko Polje**, a lovely valley of olive groves and vineyards.

Getting There

From Dubrovnik port, Jadrolinija **ferries** skip along the islands year-round: ferries to Koločep take 25mins (22Kn single); to Lopud 50mins (22Kn single); and to Šipanska Luka on Šipan 1hr 15mins (28Kn single). Marginally faster are the summer-only Nova International ferries which fill holes in the Jadrolinija timetable and cost 40Kn. For those in a hurry, Dubrovnik tourist agencies such as Atlas organize rushed one-day trips around the trio: expect to pay 200Kn per person.

Eating Out

Obala, Obal I Kuljevan 18, Lopud, **t** (020) 759 108 (*moderate*). Stylish dining on the seafront, with waiters in black and whites and jazzy Muzak providing a soundtrack to a lunch of catch of the day or excellent salads.

Barbara, Od Šunja 2, Lopud, **t** (020) 759 087 (*moderate*). On the footpath to Šunj from Lopud, this has a vine-covered terrace.

Domaca Prirodna Hrana, Od Šunja 19, Lopud; no tel (*moderate*). An evening-only treat just uphill from the Barbara, with a changing menu prepared from fresh ingredients.

Mljet

Timetables may swear the island of Mljet is just 1½hrs from Dubrovnik, but the distance in atmosphere to the Adriatic's greenest island is centuries. Explore this 32km sliver of an island clad in Aleppo pines and vineyards and you'll discover a Mediterranean idyll where tourism is a sideshow to traditional obsessions of fishing, wine and olive oil. It doesn't stretch the imagination too far to believe this is indeed Homer's Ogyia, the 'wave-washed island' of 'wood in abundant growth – alder and aspen and fragrant cypress' where the love-sick Calypso, nurturing dreams of marriage, held Odysseus captive for seven years. Hotel Odisej in the resort town of Pomena organizes summer sprees to south coast cove Uvala Jama, supposedly the 'arching caverns' where she whispered sweet nothings into the Greek hero's ear.

At **Polače**, buses squeeze through an arch of the 4th-century palace (*palača*) which christened the village. Overlooked nearby is the shell of a century-older Christian **basilica**, inspired perhaps by St Paul, who is said to have preached in Mljet after shipwreck enforced a three-month pause in his Adriatic voyage.

Officially, the hamlet strung out along a perfect natural harbour is within the **Mljet National Park** (*adm mid-June–mid-Sept 65kn, mid-Sept–mid-June 45Kn; tickets from kiosks at Pomena and Polače*), but the main draws of the protected area on Mljet's western third are little and large lakes **Mala jezero** and **Veliko jezero**, reached via a well-signed path (*approx 1hr*). Even summer tour groups cannot mar idyllic tidal lakes fringed by aromatic pines and knitted together by the **Mali most** (Little Bridge), where you can hire bicycles, canoes and rowing boats (*20Kn/hour, 100Kn/day*) or laze on a scrap of 'beach'. Explorers can truly escape the crowds by climbing island peak **Montokuc** southeast of Veliko jezero. The island high point for most tourists, however, is a jaunt on hourly ferries from Mali most and Pristanište (*price included in park ticket*) to romantic **St Mary's Islet** (Otočić svete Marije). Circle the **monastery** whose 12th-century core is rebuilt in Renaissance style, then peer into the gloom of its **church**, with turquoise pillars and ruby scrolls of Renaissance and Baroque altars.

Getting There and Around

Year-round Jadrolinija **car ferries** chug to Mljet port Sobra in 1hr 50mins, where a connecting bus travels to Polače and Pomena. However, its afternoon departure necessitates an overnight stay. In summer only, day trippers can catch Nova International's high-speed morning catamaran to Polače (*daily May–Sept; 1hr 30mins; 90Kn return*). A limited **bus** service prevents true exploration: hire one of the handful of **cars** or a **scooter** or **mountain bike** from agencies in Polače and Pomena.

Tourist Information

Polače (opposite ferry dock): **t** (020) 744 086.
Babino Polje: t (020) 745 125. *Open as above.*

Where to Stay and Eat

Hotel Odisej, Pomena, **t** (020) 744 062, *www. hotelodisej.hr* (*moderate*). Mljet's only hotel features 150 simple but spotless three-star rooms. *Closed Nov to mid-April.*

Pension Pomena, Pomena 14, **t** (020) 744 075 (*inexpensive*). If that's full, try this cheap and cheerful restaurant-*pension* next-door, which offers 10 rooms.

Mali raj, Babine Kuće 3, **t** (020) 744 067 (*moderate*). House special lobster comes super-fresh from the tank, and kid goat cooked in a *peka* is washed down with local wines and brandy.

Galija, Pomena bb, **t** (020) 744 029 (*expensive–moderate*). Smartest of the harbourfront *pension*-restaurants opposite Hotel Odisej.

Serbia:

Travel, Practical A–Z and Language

17

Travel

Entry Formalities

Visas and Passports

Visas are not required by citizens of the UK, Ireland, Canada, the USA, Australia or New Zealand for stays of up to 90 days. Passports should be undamaged and valid for the duration of your visit.

Customs

On arrival, you will need to declare details of your personal luggage – articles for personal use (including an allowance of a litre of strong alcoholic drink, a litre of wine, 200 cigarettes or equivalent in tobacco products, and personal medicines) up to €100 equivalent in value are exempt from any duty. There is no restriction on the amount of foreign money you can take into the country (you should declare this and get a receipt allowing you to take it out again), and you can take in up to 120,000 dinars in 1,000-dinar notes or smaller denominations.

Getting Around

By Bus

Several bus companies operate in Serbia, mercifully using the same stations. Some are better than others, but on the whole the bus system is faster and easier, and only a little more expensive, than the railway, with more frequent departures and fewer delays. For many destinations, bus is the only choice.

In larger towns, tickets are bought from station kiosks; on minor routes from the driver or conductor, who can be extremely surly.

By Car

AMSS (Automobile and Motorists Association of Serbia) has workshops and tow-away services along all main roads; for help on the road, **t** 987.

The problem with driving in Serbia is not so much other drivers – though you are advised to drive defensively and to avoid confrontation with other drivers – who can be as crazy as elsewhere, but the roads. These are frequently in appalling condition, and signposts are virtually unheard of.

Speed limits are 40–60kph in towns, 60–80kph on country roads and 80–120kph on highways.

You must have a valid international driver's licence to drive legally. If you are taking your car, you must have vehicle registration/ownership documents and a locally valid insurance policy. European green card vehicle insurance is valid. Driving is on the right-hand side of the road.

You are required, by law, to wear a seatbelt. The consumption of alcohol before or during driving is absolutely forbidden and there are heavy fines. All transportation accidents which result in personal injury, death or material damage must be reported to the police Persons younger than 12 years must not ride in the seat next to the driver.

A number of car-hire companies operate from the airport and in Belgrade (see p.298).

By Train

The trains are operated by Jugoslovenske Železnice (JŽ), **t** 629 400, www.yurail.co.yu. They are relatively cheap, but tend to be unnecessarily slow. Delays and tardiness are all too common. It's best to stick to express (ekspresni) and rapid (poslovni) trains, which only operate on the main routes, and don't require prior reservation. Positively avoid the slow (putnicki) trains.

Most ticket clerks will have enough English to help you, but it usually helps to have your destination and train time written down.

Practical A–Z

Crime and the Police

Police, t 92

Corruption, the black market, and organized crime are endemic in Serbia. There is also a tangible, widespread sense of desperation, no doubt the cost of war. For all that, visitors are far less likely to be victims of serious crime here than in their own countries. Even the streets of Belgrade at night feel surprisingly safe. Pickpocketing is the most obvious danger, especially in crowded central areas. Keep valuables well out of the way, beneath clothing, or in the hotel safe.

Mugging is less of a concern, but walking alone at night in poorly lit or unpeopled areas like parks, especially for lone females, should always be avoided. Car theft is also a concern, with foreign cars particularly targeted.

The police keep an unexpectedly low profile, but are not above fishing for large pocketable fines if the possibility arises. If fined, ask for a receipt. If arrested, wait to speak to someone in English, and notify your consulate.

Disabled Travellers

There are no facilities for disabled travellers, and most Serbian towns, especially Belgrade, are a nightmare for wheelchair users.

Electricity

The current in Serbia is 220v AC, using round two-pin plugs. Bring an adaptor. For 110v appliances, you'll need a transformer.

Embassies and Consulates

Serbian Embassies Abroad

UK: 28 Belgrave Square, London, SW1X 8QB, t (020) 7235 9049, f (020) 7235 7092, *www.yugoslavembassy.org.uk*.
USA: 2134 Kalorama Road, N.W. Washington D.C. 20008, t (202) 332 0333, f 332 3933, *www.yuembusa.org*.
Canada: 17 Blackburn Avenue, Ottawa, Ontario, K1N 8A2, t (13) 233 6289, f 233 7850, *www.yuemb.ca*.

Foreign Embassies in Belgrade

UK: Resavska 46, t (11) 645 055.
USA: Kneza Miloša 50, t (11) 361 9344.
Canada: Kneza Miloša 75, t (11) 306 3000.

Festivals and Events

Early Jan: Street of the Open Heart (Ulica otvorenog srca), Belgrade.
Late Mar–April: International Musical Youth Competition, Belgrade.
April: Ascension, with giant processions passing through Belgrade.

Early–mid-May: International Children's Theatre Festival, Sobotica.
Mid-May: Agricultural Fair, Novi Sad.
Late July–early Aug: International Tourist Regatta on the Danube, taking place at various locations.
Early Aug: Waterpolo Tournament, Belgrade.

Health and Emergencies

Ambulance, t 94; fire, t 93; pharmacies and clinics, t 9821
No inoculations are required to enter Serbia. Embassies advise visitors to have their tetanus, hepatitis A, diptheria and typhoid shots up to date, but in practice the danger is minimal.

For minor ailments, go to a pharmacy (*apoteka*). Hospitals (*bolnica*) are reserved for serious cases. In case of emergency, treatment and ambulance service are free, though medicine must be paid for. Remember to take any specific medication, which may not be available locally.

Serbia's doctors are competent, but have to cope with old equipment, poor funding and bad wages, and their treatment of patients is not necessarily as gentle as in Western countries. A lengthy hospital stay is not likely to be a pleasant experience, so consider heading home instead.

There are 24hr pharmacies in Belgrade at: Srpskih vladara 9, t (11) 324 0533; Nemanjina 2, t (11) 643170; Glavna 34, Zemun, t (11) 618 582. There's also a Health Clinic at Paterova 2, t (11) 361 8444, and a 24hr dentist (*zubar*) at Oblićev venac 30, t (11) 635 236.

Internet

Internet cafés are much harder to find in Serbia than almost anywhere else in Europe. If desperate, you could try local libraries. In Belgrade, two of the handier places are at Vuka Karadžića 12 and Svetogorska 18.

Money

Serbia's currency is the **dinar**, divided into 100 **para**. Coins: 50 para, 1, 2, 5, 10 and 20 dinars. Notes: 5, 10, 20, 50, 100, 200, 500, 1,000 and 5,000 dinars.

The best way to travel is with a bank card, using **ATMs**, which are copious in Belgrade and Novi Sad, but not elsewhere. If heading off the beaten track for any length of time, be sure to have a good stock of cash. Exchange offices are everywhere, and offer the best rates, but be wary of scams, and double-check rates and commission first. **Traveller's cheques** are hard to change anywhere, even in some banks, who usually charge a hefty commission for the service. Delta Banka is the best (there's a branch on Knez Mihailova). As a minimum commission is charged per transaction, change all the cheques you will need at once rather than one by one.

Bank hours are generally Mon–Fri 9–4, Sat 8–3. Never change money on the street.

The current **rates of exchange** are US$1 = 62.07 dinars, €1 = 80.45, £1 = 116.21.

National Holidays

1 Jan New Year's Day
7 Jan Orthodox Christmas
14 Jan Orthodox New Year
15 Feb Serbian Statehood Day
Late Mar–April Easter
1 May Labour Day
9 May Victory Day
26 Nov Republic Day

Opening Hours

Most **shops** (*prodavnica*) in Serbia open their doors from 8 or 9am to 8pm on weekdays, close at 3pm on Saturdays, and remain closed throughout the day on Sundays. Those in malls are open every day.

Most **churches** (*crkva*) and **monasteries** are open from dawn till dusk.

Hours kept by **museums** (*muzej*) vary, but the majority are open Tues–Sun 10–5, with some closing around 2pm on Sundays and maybe also Saturdays.

Post

Mail can take 7–10 days to reach Britain, and 2–3 weeks to reach Canada and the USA, unless sent express or airmail, which is twice as fast.

Most post offices are open Mon–Fri 8–7, Sat 8–3.

Parcels are cheap to send, but you must take items into the post office and have a customs declaration filled out before they are wrapped and weighed.

Price Categories

Hotels

You'll find that prices for hotels are almost always quoted in euros (€), even when the payment is expected in local currency, dinars. The approximate price you should expect to pay, for a double room with bath in high season, is as follows:

luxury over €160
expensive €100–160
moderate €60–100
inexpensive less than €60

Restaurants

For a three-course meal for one with wine:

luxury over €20
expensive €15–20
moderate €8–14
inexpensive less than €8

Shopping

Serbia has many of the high-street retailers commonly seen in the West, and fashion is clearly a major concern for the population. For all that, visitors will find the shopping scene rather disappointing. Unfortunately, there is not enough support for artisans to make the craft industry boom, although with luck, this may change as the tourist industry continues to develop. **Folk arts** do exist, however: costumes, textiles, wooden toys and ceramics are distinctive and cheap.

Those who have a love of **ethnic painting** should consider undertaking an organized trip to Kovačica (*see* **Belgrade**, 'Tourist Information', p.298), which is renowned for its tradition of 'naive painting'.

Given the exceptional wealth of religious art in the country, the most inspiring souvenir to take home with you is an **icon**.

Sports and Activities

The cold winters are particularly conducive to good **skiing**, although it is fair to say that standards may be a little more basic than those in Western European countries. This should not, however, spoil your enjoyment of the sport. The season lasts from December to March and one of the best centres is Kopaonik. Durmitor National Park also has great skiing, as well as good opportunities for **hiking**.

You can also practise your **white-water rafting** skills on the Tara River in Durmitor National Park.

Serbians are also unexpectedly enthusiastic about **basketball**. They are currently world champions, a situation which could continue with a home advantage at the next World Championship, due to be held in Belgrade in 2005.

Telephones

International operator, t 901; **domestic information, t** 988
Online phone book: *www.telekom.yu.*

To **call abroad from Serbia**, dial 00 then the country code (UK 44; Ireland 353; US and Canada 1; Australia 61; New Zealand 64) then dial the number, again omitting the first zero of the area code.

To **call Serbia from abroad**, dial the following international access codes, followed by the local area code. From the UK and Europe **t** 00381; from USA and Canada **t** 011381.

The area code for Belgrade is (0) 11; you need to drop the first zero from the city code before dialling the main number.

Phone cards can be bought at post offices (after a long queue), whose own phone booths are cheap, and keep longer hours than the postal section.

Time

Serbia is within the Central European Time zone: one hour ahead of GMT (two hours in summer), six hours ahead of Eastern Standard Time and nine ahead of Western Standard Time.

Tipping

Just like elsewhere, restaurant waiters expect a 10% tip, though this should always reflect quality of service. Check, however, that service has not already been included in the bill. It is customary to round up the fare for taxi drivers.

Toilets

Public toilets in Serbia are scarce indeed. Where they do exist, in train and bus stations, there is usually a small fee for their use. This does not guarantee the toilet's cleanliness. As you get out into rural areas, toilets can get truly horrible.

Tourist Information

There are no Serbian tourist board offices abroad, though information can be sought from the embassies (*see* p.291).

The most useful websites are *www.serbia-tourism.org* and *www.tob.co.yu*.

Tourist offices sell poor but adequate maps of Belgrade. The locally published *Belgrade Tourist Guide* is cheap and has some very useful maps, including bus, trolleybus and tram routes.

Language

Serbo-Croat is a South Slavonic language along with Bulgarian and Slovenian. Two alphabets are widely used, Latin and Cyrillic. In practice, shop signs, menus and most other useful everyday items are in Latin script, while street names are almost always in Cyrillic. *See* p.318 for this alphabet.

Pronunciation

Serbian has a phonetic alphabet: one letter for one sound, which is always the same regardless of which letters proceed or follow it. Pronunciation is as in English except in the following cases:
  a as *a* in 'art'
  e as *e* in 'end'

i as *ee* in 'feet'
o as *o* in 'dog'
u as *u* in 'flu'
c as *ts* in 'cats'
č as *ch* in 'much'
ć is similar but softer
đ as *deu* in 'deuce'
dž as *j* in 'jug'
j as *y* in 'yes'
š as *sh* in 'shell'
˘ as *si* in 'vision'.

Useful Words and Phrases

yes/no *da/ne*
hello *zdravo*
please *molim vas*
thank you *hvala*
goodbye *do viđenja*
excuse me *izvinite*
I'm very sorry *veoma mi je žao*
I beg your pardon? *Molim?*
My name is... *Ime mi je*
How are you? *Kako ste?*
I don't understand *Ne razumem*
Do you speak English? *Govorite li engleski?*
Please repeat it slowly *Molim vas, ponovite polako*
gentlemen *muški*
ladies *ženski*

I am vegetarian *Ja sam vegetarijanac/ vegetarijanka (fem.)*
I don't eat meat *Ne jedem meso*
menu *jelovnik*
exchange office *menjaćnica*

I want to go to... *Želeo bih da odem u...?*
How much is it? *Koliko košta sve to?*
When does the bus/train for ... leave?
  Kada polazi autobus/voz za...?
station *stanica*
where is...? *gde je...?*
arrival/departure *dolazak/polazak*
left/ right *levo//desno*
entrance/ exit *ulaz/ izlaz*
open/ closed *otvoreno/zatvoreno*

today *danas*
yesterday *juče*
tomorrow *sutra*
day *dan*

week *sedmica*
month *mesec*
late *kasno*
early *rano*

Days and Months

Monday *ponedeljak*
Tuesday *utorak*
Wednesday *sreda*
Thursday *četvrtak*
Friday *petak*
Saturday *subota*
Sunday *nedelja*

January *Januar*
February *Februar*
March *Mart*
April *April*
May *Maj*
June *Juni*
July *Juli*
August *Avgust*
September *Septembar*
October *Oktobar*
November *Novembar*
December *Decembar*

Numbers

1 *jedan*
2 *dva*
3 *tri*
4 *četiri*
5 *pet*
6 *šest*
7 *sedam*
8 *osam*
9 *devet*
10 *deset*
100 *sto*
1,000 *hiljadu*

Serbia: Belgrade

Belgrade (БЕОГРАД)

The Balkan peninsula is a natural crossroads, a watershed between East and West. The Roman Empire was divided here, and every crusader, merchant and warring or migrating tribe since has been obliged to pass through. The resultant combination of extreme desirability and unparalleled ethnic diversity led Churchill to describe this as 'the cockpit of Europe'. Strategically situated at the junction of two major rivers, with fertile plains on one side, ore-rich mountains on the other, and a flat vantage point atop a steep hill, Belgrade has always been a particularly coveted prize, fought over continuously, by Celts, Romans, Huns, Slavs, Avars, Byzantines, Magyars, Crusaders, Bulgarians, Turks, Serbs and Austrians. Invaded more than any other city in the world, it has been levelled to the ground over 40 times, and given countless names. Many were translations of the 8th- to 9th-century Slav settlement Belgrade, meaning 'White City', inspired by the ruins of a Roman/early Byzantine fortress. Others, such as

Food and Drink

Most meals start with a salad (*salata*), such as *shopska*: tomato, paprika and aged hard cheese. The most common **soups** (*supa*, or *čorba*/broth) are chicken (*kokošja*), pea (*graška*) and potato (*krompira*). **Starters** (*predelo*) also include various salamis and patés, cheese (*sir*), tastiest when from goat (*kozji*) or sheep (*ovčji*), stuffed peppers (*punjeni paprika*) and cabbage rolls stuffed with minced beef (*sarma*). These can be more interesting than the main courses, which are predominantly **meat** dishes (*jela od mesa*), and usually chicken (*pile* or *kokošja*) or pork (*svinjetina*), though beef (*govedina*), lamb (*jagnjetina*), turkey (*ćurka*) and veal (*teleći*) are often available, and some restaurants offer goose (*guska*) and game like deer (*jelen*), rabbit (*kunić*) and boar (*vepar*). Meat is most commonly grilled (*na žaru*) or barbecued (*na roštiliju*), but may also be baked (*pečen*), fried (*pržen*) or served as a schnitzel (*na bečki način*). **Fish** (*riba*) is often trout (*pastrmka*). Hungarian-style stews (*paprikaš*) and ragouts (*ragu*) can be very tasty. **Side dishes** are generally ordered separately, including potatoes (*krompir*), vegetables (*povrće*) and rice (*pirinač*). You will usually be asked how many slices of bread (*hleb*) you want. There's little for **vegetarians**, but look out for tasty dishes made with aubergine (*plavi patlidžan*). **National specialities** include *ćevapčići*, heavily spiced, roasted and ground meat, served with onion in a roll; *pite gibanice*, a 'pie' made from paper-thin layers of hand-made dough, layered with a cheese-egg sauce; and the rare, elaborate and delicious *svadbarsk kupuš*, literally 'wedding cabbage'. Don't miss *kajmak*, a rich dairy product akin to clotted cream. **Dessert** (*poslastice*) usully amounts to pancakes (*palačinke*), ice cream (*sladoled*), pie (*pita*) or cake (*torta*), and is best ordered in a pâtisserie (*poslastičarnice*). Serbs love their takeaway food. Although many of the savoury pastries sold on the street are too greasy to be enjoyable, the slices of pizza are usually excellent.

Serbian **wine** (*vino*) is not up to much, nor is the domestic **beer** (*pivo*), though imports are readily available. The **coffee** (*kafa*), however, is usually excellent. If you want it with milk, order a *bela kafa*.

Getting There

See **Getting There**, pp.4–10.

Getting from the Airport

Belgrade's Surčin Airport, t (011) 601 424, www.airport-belgrade.co.yu, is 20km west of the centre. JAT **shuttle bus**, t (011) 675 583 (cost 120 dinars), leaves from Arrivals on the hour, 7am to 10pm, with stops at the train station and Hotel Slavija, returning on the hour from 5am to 9pm.

Getting Around

GSP, t (011) 629 019, www.gsp.co.yu, operate a cheap and surprisingly efficient network of **buses**, **trolleybuses** and **trams**. Their website features a useful map of routes worth copying before arrival. Tickets, valid for one trip on any vehicle, cost 30 dinars (45 dinars for zones 1 and 2, which should not affect visitors), and are available from news kiosks. Certain night buses operate from midnight to 4am (tickets cost 50/70 dinars). Routes to more distant destinations are often express, including the useful 704 and 706 services to Zemun from Zeleni Venac. Most of Belgrade's other sights can be seen on **foot**. The neoclassical **train station**, t (011) 629 400, is on Savski Square, less than 1km southwest of Terazije, with the **bus station**, t (011) 636 299, next door, and the Lasta bus station next to that at Železnička 4, t (011) 488 1364, www.lasta.co.yu.

Taxi drivers are generally honest, except those at the airport, but check that their meters are running, and order cabs by phone where possible: **Beotaxi**, t (011) 970, or **Naxi Taxi**, t (011) 157 668.

Car Hire

Hertz, Nikole Pašica Square 1, t (011) 334 6179, reservation@hertz.co.yu; airport, t (011) 228 6017. From €40 per day.

Eminence, Sava Centar, t (011) 397 266, www.eminence.co.yu. From €30 per day.
Star Car, Hotel Metropol, Bulevar Kralja Alexandra, t (011) 323 7045, www.starcar.co.yu. From €20 per day.

Tourist Information

Belgrade: The **Tourist Organization of Belgrade** (TOB) has its main office in the underground passage where Knez Mihailova meets Terazije, t (011) 635 622, www.tob.co.yu. Open Mon–Fri 9–8, Sat 9–4. Other offices are: Knez Mihailova 18, t (011) 629 992 (open Mon–Fri 9–8, Sat 9–6, Sun 11–5); airport, t (011) 601 555 (open daily 9–8); train station, t (011) 361 2732 (open Mon–Fri 9–8, Sat 9–5); Zmaj Jovina 14, Zemun, t (011) 192 094. They organize the following tours: 'Town Centre on Foot' (2hrs); 'Belgrade Fortress on Foot' (2hrs); 'Old Zemun' (3hrs); 'Belgrade by Boat' (3hrs); 'Belgrade by Bus' (90mins, 10am Sun from Nikole Pašica Square 12); 'Churches and Monasteries by Bus' (4hrs). Ask also about their longer excursions, including the archaeological site of Vinča (11am Sat from Nikole Pašica Square 12), a wine tour of Sremski Karlovci and Fruška Gora (see p.311) and a visit to the village of Kovačica, renowned for its tradition of 'naïve painting'.

Festivals

Late Feb–early Mar: 'Fest', Film Festival.
Mid-April: International Regatta.
Late April: Belgrade Marathon.
Mid-May: International Wine Festival.
Mid-June: Tour de Serbie Cycling Race.
July: Echo contemporary music festival, Lido Beach, Veliko Batno Ostrvo Island.
July and Aug: BELEF festival. Theatre, music and fine arts.
Early Aug: International Basketball Tournament.

'Gates of Death', 'Home of Everlasting Night', 'House of Battle and Glory', 'Walls of Christianity' and 'House of Holy War' are more revealing. Medieval Belgrade's most prosperous period began in 1397, when Despot Stefan Lazarevic named it capital of a Serbian kingdom. Little more than a century later, however, the country fell into Ottoman hands, where it remained for over 300 years. A second golden age followed

Late Aug: Beerfest.
Sept: BITEF international film festival.
Mid-Sept: European Heritage Days.
Early–mid-Oct: Bemus Music Festival.
Mid-Oct: Vinofest.

Shopping

Most locals do their window-shopping on Knez Mihailova, which also has the most useful shopping centres: **New Millennium** at No.19–21; and **City Passage** on Oblićev Venac, **t** (011) 303 1234. The main daily **market** is Zeleni Venac, on and around Brankova, selling just about everything at very low prices. This is the place for food specialities like dried meats and cheeses.

The best things to buy in Belgrade are unique craftworks, made by hand using traditional techniques and natural materials, often brought in from the surrounding villages. These are best found at the Saturday **Bezistan Open Market**, on Čika Ljubina Street in summer; in winter it moves to Nušićeva, the alley next to Kasina Hotel on Terazije. Old ladies sell their embroidery in the parks. For a good range of contemporary textiles go to **Artefakt**, **t** (011) 334 5979, www.wtwn.org.yu, an NGO cooperative for underprivileged women.

For souvenirs, try the **Ethnographic Museum**, or **Singidunum** at Knez Mihailova 42, **t** (011) 185 323. Gorgeous but expensive **icons** can be bought at **Petar Bilić's Icon Workshop**, Braničevska 5, **t** (011) 244 6508.

Where to Stay

Belgrade t (011) –

★★★★★Hotel Aleksandar Palas, Kralja Petra I 13, **t** 330 5300, **f** 305 334, www.aleksandarpalas. com (luxury). An upmarket boutique hotel with nine impeccable suites: spacious, tastefully decorated and beautifully furnished with painstaking attention to detail. The best in town by a long shot. Showers only, though, and fewer facilities than the price would suggest.

Le Petit Piaf, Skadarska 34, **t** 303 5252, **f** 303 5353, office@petitpiaf.com (luxury). Smallish but chic; modern rooms and suites with showers. It's overpriced, but in a very desirable location.

★★★★Hotel Moskva, Balkanska 1, **t** 268 6255, **f** 268 8389, www.hotelmoskva.co.yu (expensive). Fair-sized rooms whose hardwood floors, big windows and fake period furniture manage to hold on to a feel of old-world opulence... just (see p.305).

★★★★Hotel Palace, Topličin Venac 23, **t** 185 585, **f** 184 458 (moderate). Reasonable if variable rooms, not especially tasteful. Those on the south side are bigger and brighter. Great location, with a panorama restaurant.

★★★Hotel Park, Njegoševa 4, **t** 323 4723, **f** 323 3029 (moderate). Totally renovated in 2004, the Park's rooms and lobby are quite small, but refreshingly bright, modern and upbeat.

★★★★Hotel Skala, Bežanijska 3, Zemun, **t/f** 196 605 (moderate). Recently renovated old warren of a building set around a tiled atrium courtyard. Rooms are bright, spacious and modern, with bags of character.

★★★Hotel Balkan, Prizrenska 2, **t** 268 7466, **f** 286 7581 (inexpensive). A typical example of a faded, state-run hotel. Almost as cheap as it gets, and the location is excellent.

★★★Hotel Royal, Kralja Petra I 56, **t** 626 426, **f** 626 459 (inexpensive). The rooms here are small and pretty faded, but decent and brighter than some, so it's relatively good value, and the location is great. The lobby is colourful and always pleasantly bustling.

★★Hotel Taš, Beogradska 71, **t** 324 3507, **f** 323 8027 (inexpensive). Bright and pleasant, with hardwood floors, the rooms and spacious apartments (moderate) here are the best value in town. Situated on the top floor of a sports centre, with a vast swimming pool and views of St Mark's from the roof.

the Second World War, when Marshal Tito brilliantly forged a union of non-aligned countries as an alternative to the Cold War superpowers. Shortly after his death, a certain Slobodan Milošević came to power, opening a chapter that ended in 1999 with the latest round of bombardment, this time at the hands of NATO. History, fascinating but almost too long and complex to bother with, is everywhere, but very

Eating Out

Belgrade t (011) –

The bohemian area of Skadarlija, centred on the street of Skadarska, is famous for its restaurants and bars. All of them aim at a similar atmosphere of *bon-vivant* hedonistic revelry, with stylishly rustic, historic interiors and live gypsy music. The food is traditional Serbian of the highest calibre. The most often recommended (all *moderate*) are **Dva Jelena** at No.32, **t** 323 4885, **Ima Dana** at No.38, **t** 323 4422, and **Tri Šešira** at No.29, **t** 324 7501.

Kalemegdanska Terasa, northeast side of fortress, above the zoo, **t** 328 3011 (*expensive*). A huge space with a tacky, fake classical interior and two vast terraces overlooking the park. Live music nightly, accompanied by the sound of howling wolves. The usual menu, tarted up and over-priced. Also a café in the handsome castle tower next door.

Restoran Madera, Bulevar Kralja Alexandra 43, **t** 323 1332 (*expensive*). Eatery of choice for Belgrade's wealthy, with fancier versions of the usual dishes. Inside is large and sophisticated, outside is a gorgeous circular terrace overlooking Tašmajdan Park and St Mark's.

Čarda Stara Koliba, at the tip of Ušće Park where the rivers converge (*moderate*). Floating thatched log house in the ultimate location, low on the water with views across to the fortress, and reached by a boardwalk through the trees. Seafood only.

Dorian Gray, Kralja Petra 87, **t** 634 151 (*moderate*). Trendy and popular bar-restaurant with a chic Art Nouveau interior, subdued lighting, a nice balcony and a patio. The refined international menu features many salads, seafood, game and risottos.

Que Pasa?, Kralja Petra I 13 at the Hotel Aleksandar Palas, **t** 328 4764 (*moderate*). Serb versions of Latin American food served in a hip, sophisticated space with red leather seats, movie-set lighting and live music nightly. Also one of the nicest terraces in town. *Open till 2am.*

Saran, Kej Oslobođenja 53, **t** 618 235 (*moderate*). Most highly recommended of many fine fish restaurants on the Danube embankment in Zemun.

Srpska Kafana, Svetagorska 25, **t** 324 7197 (*moderate*). Modern, colourful, trendy version of a traditional, rustic eatery. Popular with artists. Serbian food at good prices.

Tribeca, Kralja Petra I 20, **t** 110 2677 (*moderate*). One of the only interesting menus in town, embracing European fusion cuisine. The mix'n'match interior is trying way too hard, but the patio deck is in a prime spot. *Open till 2am, and just as good for a late drink.*

Vuk, Vuka Karadžića 12, **t** 629 671 (*moderate*). An extensive menu of well-prepared, typical Serbian food. The interior is classic, with a great patio on a traffic-free street. Very central and popular.

Aeroklub, Uzun Mirkova 4, **t** 626 077 (*moderate*). Upmarket Central European food and Serbian specialities at surprisingly reasonable prices given the setting: a private club's very formal dining room, decked out with antiques and period furniture.

Dijalog, Sava embankment, Ušče Park, near the Modern Art Gallery, **t** 311 4847 (*moderate*). Elelgant dining on a striking red boat with views to the Fortress. Menu in Serbian only, mostly seafood, steaks and salads.

Na Dnu Mora, Dobračina 30, **t** 625 869 (*moderate*). Delightful brick and column cellar, with intimate spaces, a marine-inspired décor and a great atmosphere. Serbian menu only, mostly seafood. It's popular with locals.

Kafe Restoran Mali Kalemegdan, U Veliki Kalemegdan Br. 2, **t** 631 999 (*inexpensive*). Less pretentious than the park's other restaurant, with a standard, reasonably priced menu, and a terrace stretching along the fortress walls, romantic at night.

little actually remains to see. Comparisons with an iceberg contain a poetic truth that is scant compensation for today's visitor, confronted with a polluted, overpopulated, confusing city. Surprisingly, what most redeems modern Belgrade is its climate, sidewalk cafés and moored-barge bar-restaurant scene.

Cafés and Coffee Houses

Belgraders love their cafés, and their city has a great climate for sitting at the terraces that occupy whole streets. The prime example, Obilićev Venac, has something for everyone, including the sumptuous **Café Restaurant Opera** at No.30, and the genuinely stylish **Kafé Simbol** at No.27. Also worthy of mention are **Rezime Centar Caffe**, 41 Kralja Petra I, a very comfortable coffee house with leather armchairs and classic décor in a gorgeous building, and **Greenet Café**, 4 Nušićeva (the alley next to Kasina Hotel on Terazije), a nice spot away from the traffic, and favoured by those who take their coffee seriously (also at Bulevar Kralja Alexandra 74 near St Mark's). Many cafés could just as easily be called bars or restaurants, so see 'Eating Out' and 'Bars and Nightlife' as well.

Entertainment

Belgrade t (011) –
The best place for information, tickets and books is Kulturni Centar Beograda, Knez Mihailova, t 262 1469, www.kcb.org.yu.

Theatre, Ballet, Opera and Music
National Theatre (Narodno Pozorište), Francuska 3, t 620 946, www.narodno pozoriste.co.yu. The main venue for theatre, opera and ballet.
Beogradska Filharmonija, Studentski Square 11, t 630 744, www.bgf.co.yu. This is the main venue for classical concerts.
Jugoslovensko Dramsko Pozorište, Kralja Milana 50, t 306 1957, www.jdp.co.yu. Serious drama housed in an exceptional post-modern building (see p.302).
BITEF Teatar, Mira Trailoviç Square 1, t 322 0608, www.bitef.co.yu. More alternative theatre, performed in a striking, rather sinister brick church.

Cinemas
Tuckwood Cinema, Kneza Miloša 7, t 322 6517. The first multiplex, and still the best.
Palace Šumadija Cinema, Turgenjeva 5, t 555 465. The other best central venue for first-run films.

Bars and Nightlife

Belgrade t (011) –
Bar-hopping is one of Belgrade's most enticing activities. The most novel locales are strips of moored barges on the Sava alongside Ušće Park, or better still, on the Danube in Zemun (see p.307). At the latter, check out the ultra-stylish **Amfora**, near Hotel Yugoslavia, t 351 154. A lively spot on bustling Skadarska is **Guli** at No.13, t 323 7204. Strahinjića Bana from Kralja Petra south to Skadarska is a strip of café-bars favoured by the city's young and trendy, and nicknamed 'Silicon Valley'. The very attractive **Kandahar** at No.48 has an Eastern theme, with silks, satins and soft lights; even its terrace resembles a desert tent. **Insomnia** nearby is deliberately louche, with tiger and leopard-skin cushions, cosy seating, tinted glass, and dark lace curtains round the patio. Many of the café-bars on Obilćev Venac stay open till late, including **Ulaz** at No.20, t 328 1636, and **OK No** at No.28, t 629 072. The open-air bar-club upstairs from Kalemegdanska Terasa in the Fortress, t 328 400, has an unbeatable location, and stays open till 4am. **Ben Akiba Cocktail Club**, Nušićeva 8, 1st Floor, t 323 7775, is a prime example of a Belgrade curiosity: a bar that's literally someone's living room. For good beer, go to the **Kasina**, Terazije 25, t 323 5574, Serbia's first micro-brewery. The dark brew, a rare commodity, is particularly good, and the terrace is perfect for people-watching.
There are two good jazz clubs: **Plato**, at Vasina 19, t 635 010, and **Café del Mar**, at Rajiçeva 12, t 185 653.

Old Belgrade

Linking the focal hub of Terazije with the strolling grounds of Belgrade Fortress, **Knez Mihailova** is the city's pedestrian-only, continuously buzzing main drag. Its southern end throngs with café terraces and ugly, functional modern buildings, but suddenly the emphasis shifts, and graceful 19th-century façades abound, with the odd modern interloper, like the successful Delta Bank building at No.30. **Delijska Fountain** at this junction is the most prominent of many that grace the city. The busy **Little Market** (Pjaceta), with its book market and café terraces, leads east past the reconstructed remains of a Roman bath that line the wall of the Romantic red-trimmed **Captain Miša Building** on the corner of Studentski Square. The northern half of Knez Mihailova contains most of Belgrade's oldest buildings, mainly from the 1860s–70s, including the School of Fine Arts at No.53–5, and the **Town Library** (Biblioteka grada Beograda) at No.56, whose cellar contains a 'Roman Hall', with remnants of two towers that flanked an ancient Roman gate. None is as exciting as a trio of fabulous Art Nouveau buildings on Kralja Petra. At No.16 is the 1907 Robni Magazin, very modern for its time, and still fresh today. Those at Nos.39 and 41 are awash with elaborate details, while the post-modern Zepter building across the road benefits from the sheer contrast.

Close by is the excellent **Ethnography Museum** (Etnografski muzej; *t (011) 328 1888; open Tues–Sat 10–5, Sun 9–2; adm*), which groups this ethnically diverse region into four zones – Central-Balkan, Pannonian, Dinaric and Coastal – according to broad natural, economic, historical and cultural similarities. Much is made of assemblies, ethnic gatherings which traditionally presented a chance to discuss state, political and church matters; and to meet family and friends, choose marriage partners, exchange goods and news, and dance the 'kolo'. As such, these were the true wells of folk art. Extensive exhibitions of costumes, textiles, house interiors and tools are tremendously interesting, with thorough commentaries in English, finished off with some fine models of traditional buildings. The **Gallery of Frescoes** nearby on Cara Uroša houses numerous copies of 11th- to 14th-century Serbian frescoes. When Byzantium fell in the 13th century, Serbia, with its own church and political life, and an already highly developed culture, became the only legitimate heir to the art of the entire Christian East, making this a very significant collection.

Halfway down Knez Mihailova, Vuka Karadžia leads west to the **Museum of Applied Arts** at No.18 (*open Tues–Sat 10–5, Sun 10–2; adm*), with varied temporary exhibitions and a permanent exhibition of mostly furniture. The core of Belgrade's 'Old Quarter' huddles around the **Orthodox Cathedral of St Michael** (Saborna crkva) on Kneza S. Markovića. Built in 1840 with late Baroque and classical elements, the church's plain brick exterior conceals an exuberant gold-lavished interior covered in biblical paintings, with an over-the-top iconostasis. The mosaics on its façade echo the one above the arched doorway of the plain, dome-capped **Patriarchate** (Patrijarsija) opposite, which contains the **Museum of the Serbian Church** (Muzej Srpske pravoslavne crkve; *t (011) 328 2596; open Mon–Fri 8–3, Sat 9–12, Sun 11–1; adm*). The nearby **Palace of Princess Ljubica** (Konak Knjeginje Ljubice) contains the **Belgrade City Museum** (*t (011) 638 744; open Tues–Fri 10–5, Sat–Sun 9–4; adm*). Displays of furniture and ornaments from Belgrade homes of the 19th century mirror the country's divided soul: some rooms are Turkish-Balkan, others Vienna-influenced Middle European. The vaulted basement, worth seeing, houses temporary exhibitions. Nearby on Pariska, the **Austrian** and **French Embassies** are interesting buildings. The latter has a strikingly modern, curved, white façade topped with three figures representing Liberté, Egalité and Fraternité.

Belgrade Fortress (Beogradska Tvrđava) and Kalemegdan

This strategically advantaged site has been fought over, destroyed, occupied and rebuilt so many times, by so many different nations, that what remains is a mish-mash, most of it buried. It was the hated Turks who gave the fortress its current shape in the 1740s, although theirs was probably just a simplified version of former incarnations. The TOB-published *Tourist Guide* will talk you through the tumultuous history, but few of the buildings it discusses remain to be seen. For all that, Kalemegdan is the nicest place to be in Belgrade, a 130-acre (52ha) park topped with evocative ruins and vista-rich ramparts.

Walking from Knez Mihailova, you'll pass busts of poets and politicians, the focal 'Struggle' fountain and the Monument of Gratitude to France. Beyond Karađorđe Gate to the left is the **Military Museum** (Vojni muzej; *t (011) 334 3441; open Tues–Sun 10–5; adm*), the bastions and trenches all around littered with cannons, tanks and artillery. A small 1835 classical building to the right contains the **Gallery of the Natural History Museum**, a small collection of animal, plant and mineral life. Through the massive, iron-plated wooden doors of the Inner Stambol Gate is the distinctive white octagonal **Sahat Tower**, erected by the Turks in Baroque style. Alongside the Sahat Gate, the **Museum of Belgrade Fortress** (*t (011) 631 766; open Tues–Sun 10–5; adm*) consists of models, a castle plan from 1688, a thorough chronology, tools, weapons and Roman statues.

Beyond the tower is the Upper City. The small octagonal structure at the centre of its wide-open green space holds a **mausoleum** dedicated to the Turkish dignitary Damad Ali-pasha. To its left, a large Balkan-style military building houses the **Belgrade Landmarks Preservation Bureau**. This western tip of the ramparts is the best for views. Nearby is the 200ft deep so-called **Roman Well**, probably dug by the Austrians in the 18th century. The adjacent bronze sculpture atop a lofty Doric column represents **The Victor** (Pobednik), a popular symbol of Belgrade. Symbolically, he holds a sword in one hand and a dove in the other. Behind him, on the site of the castle built in the 15th century by the first Serbian ruler, Despot Stefan Lazarević, is a **bronze model** of that very castle, whose structure took years of archaeological research to ascertain. The inscription repeats his words, 'I found the most beautiful spot ever, the great town of Belgrade.'

At the Upper City's northeast corner are the 15th-century **Despot Gate** and **Dizdar Tower**, once the medieval citadel's main entrance, now its best-preserved remnant. Telescopes in the tower's **observatory** are open to the public on Friday and Saturday nights. The nearby 15th-century **Zindan Gate** consists of an arched gate flanked by two round towers once used as dungeons, leading to a drawbridge. Beyond Despot Gate is the **Rose Church** (Bogorodičina crkva Ružica), a gunpowder warehouse converted into a church in 1867 by the addition of a bell tower and cross. Its two bells, and the relief icons above the entrance, were cast from Turkish cannons. The bronze statues flanking the entrance represent a medieval knight and a soldier from the First World War. Below is another pretty church, the **Chapel of St Petka**, built over a miraculous spring. The octagonal **Jakšić Tower** that guards the intersection of the two northern bulwarks is a likeable structure that now contains a café.

A slope beside St Petka leads down to the once-fortified Lower City, now an expansive riverside park. To the southwest is a 300-year-old *amam* (Turkish bath), now used as a **Planetarium**, images of the night sky projected on to its gently curving cupola. Beyond are the arched remains of the 15th-century Gothic **archbishop's lodgings**. Castlewards, beyond Defterdar Gate, is a fountain built in honour of Turkish grand vizier Mehmed-pasha Sokollu. Northwards is the imposing **Charles VI Gate**, whose inside entrance bears the oldest surviving Serbian coat of arms. Past the stone-and-brick **Cannon Factory** is the octagonal **Nebojša Tower**, the largest and best preserved here. Erected in 1460, it later became an infamous dungeon, in which Greek poet Riga of Fera and Archbishop Methodius were imprisoned and executed. Wandering clockwise past the sports centre and the horrendous zoo, you'll eventually rejoin Pariska via the **Cvijeta Zuzorić Art Pavilion**, which hosts spring and autumn exhibitions as well as one-off retrospectives. The 'Awakening' fountain outside was sculpted in the 1920s, blown to pieces, then put back together in the 1980s.

Republic Square and Skadarlija

Republic Square was once Belgrade's prime junction, and location of the Stambol Gate, medieval Belgrade's biggest, most solid, most beautiful gate, but infamous as the site where St Avakum martyred himself in 1814 by refusing to accept Islam and save his own life. Destroyed in 1862 by order of Prince Mihailo as a symbol of Belgrade's final freedom from the Turks, much of its stone went into the foundation of the elegant neo-Renaissance **National Theatre** (Narodno pozorište) built later that year. A statue of the Prince, created by Florentine sculptor Enrico Pazzi in 1882, stands on the site of the old gate. Names of the cities regained from the Turks during his reign are engraved on the base, while the bas-relief on the pedestal's sides shows him receiving the keys to Belgrade Fortress. On the square's north side is the 1913 **National Museum** (Narodni muzej; *t (011) 433 886; open Tues–Sat 10–5, Sun 10–2; adm, Sun free*), a huge construction that contains a massive permanent collection of international art, including some big names, almost none of which is currently on display.

Striking northeast from here is **Skadarska** street, heart of **Skadarlija**, a Bohemian quarter that blossomed around a brewery at the end of the 19th century; it enjoyed a renaissance in 1966, when the old cobblestoned street was relaid, the traffic diverted, and the numerous old café-restaurants renovated and re-opened. Though the atmosphere is slightly phony, this is still a great, bustling place to eat top-notch traditional Serbian food, listen to gypsy violins, drink and get merry. A few tucked-away courtyards even preserve a more authentic vibe. Interesting sculptures include a bronze portrayal of writer and painter Đura Jakšić whose house, now a gallery, is at No.34, and 'Monument to the Travelling Actor'. At Skadarska's eastern end is an interesting Arab-style public fountain, or *sebilj*. From here, **Strahinjića Bana** heading north is also lined with café-restaurants, though of a more modern variety.

Nearby on Cara Dušana is **St Alexander Nevski Church** (Crkva svetog Alexsandra Nevskog), a small, beautifully proportioned gem from 1929. Featuring latticework reminiscent of Celtic designs, rosettes and numerous arches, its elaborate but unpretentious ornamentation possesses a wonderful sense of flow. Above the main door is a perfectly executed Christ mosaic. The interior is dark and in disrepair, yet strangely powerful, especially the cavernous cupola.

Terazije

Named after the Turkish word for the water-towers it once contained, modern Belgrade's most important hub is dominated by the giant but irresistible **Hotel Moskva** (1906). Built in neo-Realist style with Art Nouveau elements, its most striking feature is the use of green ceramica on the roof and façade ornamentation. A central relief entitled 'The Glorification of Russia' represents the Motherland's economic and naval power. The **Terazije Fountain** beside it, a favourite meeting place, was built to honour Prince Miloš. MO, his initials, and 1860, the year he returned to power, are engraved on all sides. To the west off Brankova, Belgrade's main daily market, **Zeleni Venac**, spills out into surrounding alleys and subways. Terazije has some great buildings, such as the 1912 Smederevska Bank at No.39, an outstanding example of Art Nouveau. The 1885 neo-Baroque house opposite at No.34 was the temporary palace of the Kingdom of Serbia in 1918 when the unification of Serbs, Croats and Slovenes was pronounced. At No.40 is a faded but interesting building: designed by and for a photographer, the relief above the central window portrays two cupids operating a large, salon camera. At No.2 Kralja Milana is the area's best and oldest structure. Built for Belgrade's mayor in 1871, the rich ornamentation of its façade was inspired by the stylized interweaving of the Morava School. Above the solid, medieval gate-style doors is the coat of arms of the Kingdom of Serbia. Almost opposite is the Italian Renaissance-style **Old Palace** (or City Hall, Skupština grada Beograda; 1882), and, a little further on, the very similar **New Palace** (or Presidential Palace, 1918). Both are contained within **Palace Park** (or Pionirski Park), which occupies a big chunk of the parallel Bulevar Kralja Alexandra, and holds some rare trees and various sculptures.

Bulevar Kralja Alexandra and St Mark's Church

Formerly called Marx and Engels Square, Nikole Pašića Square is dominated at its northern end by a monstrous curved edifice exemplary of Communist tastes and, sure enough, built in 1952 as the **Labour Unions Centre**. The undulating building to its east houses the **Museum of Yugoslav History** (*open Tues–Sun 12–8*). Apart from a letter from Churchill to Tito congratulating him on the liberation of Belgrade, there's literally nothing to see. Running south, traffic-choked Bulevar Kralja Alexandra is lined with monumental and significant buildings. Opposite Palace Park, the neoclassical **Federal Parliament Building** (Zgrada Skupštine SRJ; 1907–36) has witnessed some major events, including the first conference of the leaders of non-aligned countries, and the protests in October 2000 when an enraged populace stormed the building and forced Slobodan Milošević to resign. Behind is the more friendly **Old Telephone Building**, a fine example of Serbian-Byzantine style, with an unusual ribcage tower, and lively, red-chequered ornamentation. The similar **Museum of Postal Services** behind it (PTT Muzej; *t (011) 321 0325; open Tues–Sun 9–5*) is also worth a look. Back on the boulevard, the **PTT Beograd** building is another monolithic Communist-style structure, though it was built in 1938.

Just beyond is **Tašmajdan Park**, built over a cemetery and centuries-old quarry (*tašmajdan* in Turkish). Beautifully illuminated at night, **St Mark's Church** (Crkva svetog Marka) is an extraordinary, typically Byzantine building, a copy of the famous 14th-century Gracanica Church in Kosovo. A near-excess of shapes cascades down from an octagonal dome, but it's the masonry that makes the composition exceptional: giant blocks of grey sandstone alternate with thinner layers of red sandstone, both vertically and horizontally, throughout the whole building, to playful, highly dramatic effect. The beguilingly simple interior with its blank walls and uncluttered iconostasis draws attention to the giant chandelier – apparently one of the biggest in the world – and the building's awesome structure, its roof supported by four massive red marble pillars. An elaborate copper sarcophagus decorated with anthropomorphic scenes contains the relics of Czar Dušan (1308–55). Next door, and dwarfed by St Mark's, is the cute **Holy Trinity Church** (Crkva svete Trojice; 1924).

Close to the southern end of the park is the **Nikola Tesla Museum** (Muzej Nikole Tesle; *Krunska 51, t (011) 626 630; open Tues–Fri 10–6, Sat–Sun 10–1; adm; ring bell*). Though his name is mysteriously unknown in the West, this Serbian visionary worked out how to generate, transform and transmit over large distances the AC power we use today. With original newspapers and extensive commentaries in English, and working examples of many ingenious models, this is a very educational experience.

St Sava Cathedral

South of the busy Slavija Circle, St Sava Cathedral (Spomen-hram svetog Save) is hands down the most impressive sight in Belgrade, and well worth the short trip from the centre (take trolleybus no.19, 21, 22 or 29 from Terazije). The church's namesake was quite the Renaissance man: an aristocrat who renounced his wealth to become a monk and monastery builder, he became a national hero through the skilful application of international diplomacy, and was rewarded with Serbia's first archbishopric. His church and legal writings formed the basis of the Serbian legal system, while his 'Biography of Saint Simeon' marked the beginning of Serbian medieval literature. After his death in 1235, he became a cult figure whose very bones were believed to possess magical healing properties. Following the Serbian Uprising, the Turks punished the country by burning those bones on the spot where today's church was later constructed.

Work began in 1935, was interrupted in 1941, and only recommenced in 1985. The 400-ton cupola is visible from miles around and crowned with a 40ft, four-ton gold-leaf cross. The church's complex but elegant, typically Balkan structure cascades down via a series of squares, towers, arches and semi-domes to four identical entrances. From above, the effect would resemble a mandala. The surface is white marble with very little space given to windows. Sadly, the interior is currently still under construction. Next door is the tiny **Old Chapel of St Sava** (Crkva svetog save), its interior entirely covered by superb frescoes that for once are brand new, thus affording a rare opportunity to see how these older churches and monasteries once looked. Outside is a fearsome statue of the saint himself. By the main road, on the very spot where he camped in 1806 prior to conquering the Fortress, a statue portrays Karađorđe (see 'Oplenac', below), after whom this small park is named.

Ušće Park and Zemun

The expanse of green opposite Belgrade Fortress at the confluence of the Danube and Sava Rivers is Ušće Park, a charmless place which contains the **Museum of Contemporary Art** (Muzej savremene umetnosti; *t (011) 311 5713; open Wed–Mon 10–6; adm, Wed free*). Half the year this ugly building hosts temporary exhibitions, the other half selections are presented from its extensive collection of modern Yugoslavian artists. A number of barges converted into floating café-restaurants line the Sava river here, with more between the two bridges.

The best stretch of such barges, however, is in **Zemun**. Technically part of the city, Zemun has little in common with Belgrade, and actually belonged to the Austro-Hungarians until as recently as 1918. The atmosphere here is calmer, the pollution less oppressive, the buildings older and more consistently attractive. It's close enough to consider as a place to stay, and may be the place for dinner. The road from Belgrade (take express bus no.704 or 706 from Zeleni Venac on Brankova, and go just two or three stops) passes the fearsome bulk of the Hotel Yugoslavia, then turns into Zemun's main drag, **Glavna**. Due east is the Danube, whose busy, well-paved promenade is lined with all kinds of bars and restaurants right back to the Hotel Yugoslavia, most of them set in moored barges. This is Zemun's principal draw, but it's worth a wander around town, most of whose sights are churches. Head northeast, through the street **market**, into the maze of Zemun's old quarter, and find the Baroque **Church of the Transfer of St Nikola's Relics** (Nikolajevska crkva). Within its dark and decaying interior is a vast and exquisite engraved iconostasis from 1762, holding 71 icons. Up on the hill behind, surrounded by crumbling walls that are all that remains of the medieval **Gardoš Fortress**, is the fantastical **Milenijumski monument**, erected (like four others) by the Hungarians in 1896 to celebrate their Millennium, marking the southeastern limit of their territory. Neither castle, church nor power-station, it has elements of all three.

Day Trips and Overnighters from Belgrade

Oplenac (ОПЛЕНАЦ)

The First Serbian Uprising of 1804 began when the inhabitants of **Topola** (ТОПОЛА) set fire to the Turkish taverns in their town. Their leader was the phenomenally tall (almost 7ft), famously dark and passably handsome Đorđe Petrović, nicknamed **Karađorđe**, Black George. A small, tight-knit group of Topola men remained the core and inspiration of Serbian resistance through five years of fighting against tremendous odds, and Karađorđe himself became the leader of a country that was free for the first time in 285 years. Thereafter, his ancestors periodically assumed the Serbian throne as one of two competing royal families. In 1903, his grandson, King Petar I, selected a site on the top of Oplenac Hill in Topola for the construction of a church dedicated to St George. War intervened and he died before it was completed, but his son, King Alexander II, saw the task through.

From the outside, **St George's Church** is a typical Byzantine construction, smallish and built from plain white marble, bearing a mosaic of St George, and the Karađorđević family crest. Nothing prepares you for the mind-blowing interior. Following the king's decision that the interior be decorated with a mosaic depicting the most beautiful medieval Serbian frescoes, five artists spent years researching, copying and designing. A total of 725 compositions, gleaned from 60 medieval churches and monasteries and comprising 1,500 figures, cover every square inch of space with mosaic: 3,500 square yards of it, made up of 40 million pieces, of 15,000 different shades. In the narthex are scenes from St George's life, including *Victory*, which covers the whole north wall above the crypt entrance. In the southern apse, above the base, is the **Gallery of Serbian Medieval Rulers**, in which each is depicted with his main memorial. Above this are scenes from the life of Christ. In the *naos*, on the columns holding the main dome, are depictions of St Simeon, and 24 compositions from the life of St Sava. Below the dome, in the corners of the four main columns, are the four evangelists; within the dome are the prophets who foresaw Christ's coming. In the *calotte*, 90ft above the temple floor, is a superb, 30ft-wide image of Christ. In the altar are frescoes of the *Apostles*, the *Last Supper* and the *Road to Golgotha*. In the altar niche is a 16ft high figure of Mary at prayer, and the *Secret of the Holy Communion*. In the northern apse is the *Wedding at Canaan*, and a collection of medieval Serbian warriors. Above the choir are compositions of the *Ascent of the Virgin Mary*, and the *Descent of the Holy Ghost*. At the entrance to the crypt are the Archangels Michael and Gabriel. On the lower side of the arches behind the small domes of the altar and southern apses are medallions bearing images of Serbian saints and sages. The only uncopied composition, but executed according to fresco traditions, is the picture of King Petar I over the entire southern wall of the narthex. In his left hand he holds a model of this memorial church. By the right, he is being led by St George to the Virgin Mary, who is awaiting him with Christ on the throne.

Complementing this astonishing anthology of medieval Serbian art is a patterned floor of coloured polished marble; a 3,300lb candelabra hanging from the main dome, which contains an upside-down crown, symbol of the lost Serbian empire at the battle of Kosovo in 1389; and two white sarcophagi of smooth, unembellished marble, containing King Petar I in the northern choir, Karađorđe in the southern. Down in the crypt, much of whose vaulted ceilings are covered with snowdrop-like mosaic patterns, are 19 other members of the Karađorđević dynasty from five generations, in tombstones made of onyx.

Opposite the church, **King Petar's House** (*t (034) 3481 1280; open Tues–Sun 9–5; adm*), a refectory where the king lived while overseeing construction until 1915, contains a museum whose changing exhibits are always connected with the Karađorđević royal family. More interesting is the **Karađorđev Konak Museum**, to the left at the bottom of the hill at Kraljice Marije 2 (*open Tues–Sun 9–5; adm*). In the 'palace' Karađorđe had built for himself, all that remains of the town's fortifications are artefacts about his

Getting There

Buses to Topola leave Belgrade roughly hourly, taking about 75mins. From there, it's a 15min walk uphill, following signs first to the town centre, then to Oplenac.

Tourist Information

Topola: Kneginje Zorke br. 13, **t** (034) 811 172, *www.topola.com, www.sotoplola.org.yu. Open daily 10–6.* There is also a small **info booth** opposite Karađorđev Konak Museum at the bottom of Kraljice Marije. They have a

supply of town maps and can give you directions.

Eating Out

Topola t (034) –
Hotel Oplenac, on Oplenac Hill close to the Church, **t 811 430 (*moderate*). The best place to eat is in the smaller restaurant of this hotel. Décor and food are somewhat rustic.

The options in town are pretty limited. **MS kod Nola**, at Vožda Karađorđa 48, **t** 812 614, and **Breza**, Krajiškikih Brigada 25, **t** 812 393 (both *moderate*) are about as good as it gets.

life and the Serbian Uprising he led. Highlights include his gun; his bronze cannon, missing the right handle, out of which King Petar I made his crown; an original letter he wrote to Napoleon in 1809; and a powerful painting of his head being chopped off with an axe. Yes, he was assassinated in 1817, upon the order of his godfather, Prince Miloš Obrenović, whose inclination towards diplomacy over warfare ultimately gained a lasting freedom for Serbia, and is usually given as the reason behind the murder. Next door is the attractive little **Church of Our Lady**, also built by Karađorđe, which contains a particularly elaborate engraved wooden iconostasis, as well as some of the finest frescoes of their time. Outside on a black marble plinth is a statue of the man himself.

Novi Sad (НОВИ САД)

Novi Sad is Serbia's second biggest town, and capital of Vojvodina, a land of low-lying fertile plains that provides much of the country's wheat and corn. Occupied by the Turks for much less time than the rest of the country, this was a popular refuge for Serbs fleeing from the south. Hapsburg empress Maria Theresia encouraged people from all over Europe to settle here, converting swamps into rich agricultural land. So much was it touted as a promised land (Novi Sad means New Garden – i.e. of Eden), that people brought all their money, making the town rich enough in 1748 to buy the status of free royal town, the first in Serbia. Development proceeded at an accelerated pace following the 18th-century Habsburg construction of the mighty Petrovaradin Fortress, which looms over the town from its hill-top across the Danube. Until the Trianon Treaty of 1918, Novi Sad remained a part of Hungary, after which it was an autonomous province until the Serbs annexed it in 1990. Not surprisingly, then, the atmosphere here is markedly different from Belgrade, a mere 80km to the south: more relaxed, more intact, and in many ways more modern.

Known as the Gibraltar on the Danube, the strategic value of lofty Petrovaradin Hill was first seen by the Romans; their Cusum Fortress was destroyed by Attila the Hun in the 5th century. A second fortress built by Hungarian King Béla IV in the 13th century was destroyed by Suleimon the Magnificent. Between 1687 and 1691 the site

Getting There and Around

There are two **trains** daily, the first leaving at 8am, and two trains back, the last leaving at 8.43pm. **Buses** leave every half-hour or so. Both take about 90mins. Both stations are 1.5km northeast of Novi Sad centre. Take any local bus south on Bulevar Oslobođenja and ask for the post office. Rail station, **t** (021) 443 200. Bus station, **t** (021) 444 021. **SOS Taxi, t** (021) 480 400, **Dunav Taxi, t** (021) 451 111.

To hire a **car**, try **Avis**, Balzakova 29, **t** (021) 469 655, or **DTD Tours**, Bulevar Mihajla Pupina 25, **t** (021) 457 205.

Tourist Information

Novi Sad: Bulevar Mihajla Pupina 9, **t** (021) 421 811, *www.novisadtourism.com*, Open Mon–Fri 9–8, Sat 9–2.

Festivals

Mid-April: Musical Festivities.
End May–early June: Sterija Theatre Festival.
Early July: Exit Festival, four days of modern music on 20 different stages within the fortress walls, attracting 260,000 visitors.
Early Sept: European Film Festival.
Sept: Street Musicians' Festival.
Late Nov: Jazz Festival.

Where to Stay

Novi Sad t (021) –
Hotel Zenit, Zmaj Jovina 8, **t** 621 444, **f** 621 327, *www.hotelzenit.co.yu* (*moderate*). Small, central hotel whose 15 rooms are large, modern and newly decorated in warm shades. Some have their own patios. Easily the best choice.
Hotel Vojvodina, Slobode Square 2, **t** 622 122, **f** 615 445 (*inexpensive*). Another big, old, faded hotel left over from Communist days. Rooms are clean and simple, with showers.
Pension Rimski, Jovana Cvijica 26, **t** 443 237 (*inexpensive*). A friendly, low-key B&B on a quiet street, 10mins' walk from the centre, handy for the stations. Simple but decent rooms. Breakfast included.

Eating Out

Novi Sad t (021) –
Fontana, Nikole Pašića 27, **t** 621 779 (*expensive*). Upmarket Serbian dishes served either in an elegant interior room or in a pretty enclosed courtyard.
Plava Frajla (Blue Lady), Sutjeska 2, by the Sports Centre, 500 yards from the centre, **t** 613 675 (*moderate*). Grilled meats and other Serb staples. Playful interior with chairs stuck to the ceiling, and a big deck. Very popular with locals.
Pomodoro Rosso, Nikole Pašića 14 (*moderate*). Serb classics in a colourful interior. Central and popular.
Restoran Kod Lipe, Miletićeva 7, **t** 615 259 (*moderate*). Standard fare plus some fish served in a simple, slightly rustic setting. Cheap daily specials.
Tyrdava Restaurant, within the fortress walls (*moderate*). Standard menu, but it has a fantastic terrace with views over the city.

changed hands several times, until the Holy Alliance built the current **Petrovaradin Fortress** and its massive walls. Designed by Sebastian Vauban, the leading military architect of his day, construction continued from 1692 to the 1780s amid perpetual war. Made of 30 million bricks, and covering 286 acres (112ha), with five subterranean levels, it is the world's second biggest fortress after Verdun, with 12,000 holes for rifles and room for 25,000 soldiers and 400 cannon. Its effect was almost immediate. On 5 August 1716, the most celebrated battle on Serbian soil took place here when the Austrians, led by Eugène de Savoy, defeated a much more numerous Turk army, helped by a legendary midsummer snowfall. The Turks never came back.

Today the castle and its walls remain intact, though one of the buildings was dynamited by Tito to clear a car park when the Heads of Non-Aligned countries met here. The **Military Museum** (*open Tues–Sun 9–5; adm*) documents the fortress's prowess and history. Highlights include a set of stone tools that suggest the site's occupation by Neanderthals 70,000 years ago; a fine 5th-century nine-soldier dugout carved from a single giant oak; and a cannonball so big it required a 230ft cannon to fire it. Tours also take in the first subterranean level.

Across the river on Dunavaska the **Museum of Vojvodina** (*t (021) 420 566; open Tues–Fri 9–7, Sat–Sun 9–2; adm*) exhaustively documents the region's long history with many artefacts from all eras, plus reasonable explanations. Look out for the red-haired fertility goddess from *c.* 5000 BC, and two rare Roman ceremonial gold helmets bearing the names of craftsmen and warriors. Try to get the enthusiastic guide to show you round. A separate building deals with the two world wars, and hosts temporary exhibitions. The pedestrianized zone starts here and leads into Novi Sad's focal street, **Zmaj Jovina**. The pseudo-maverick **Serbian Orthodox Bishop's Palace** (1901) and adjacent **Orthodox Church** have more style than the neo-Gothic **Catholic Church**, a stark, spartan building with an equally understated interior. **Slobode Square** is the town's centre, surrounded by handsome, well-preserved 19th-century Baroque buildings, such as the **town hall**. Further west is the **Church of Holy Mother's Assumption**, whose small, dark interior contains a valuable (but gaudy) Baroque iconostasis and a famous Italo-Cretan icon of the Holy Mother. On Jevrejska is an interesting **Synagogue** (1906), built in classical style with Art Nouveau leanings.

Around Galerija Square, just south of Bulevar Mihajla Pupina, are three worthwhile and greatly varied art galleries. The **Paul Beljanski Gallery** at No.2 (*t (021) 528 185; open Tues 1–9, Wed–Sun 10–6; adm, Thurs free*) has an excellent collection of Serbian 19th-century paintings, mostly postimpressionist with clear European influences. The **Matice Srpska Gallery** (*Proleterskih Brigada Square 1, t (021) 524 155; open Tues and Thurs–Sat 10–6, Wed 12–8; adm, Wed free*) has local paintings and graphics from the 17th century to today, with some copies of frescoes. The **Rajko Mamuzic Gallery of Fine Arts** (*Bace Crajnħa 1, t (021) 520 467, www.galerijamamuzic.org.yu; open Tues–Sun 10–6; adm*) presents high-calibre, theatrical works by modern Serbian artists.

Sremski Karlovci (СРЕМСКИ КАРЛОВСКИ) and Fruška Gora (ФРУСКА ГОРА)

During the Turkish occupation, the sleepy village of Sremski Karlovci became the spiritual and cultural centre of the Serbian people, and still occupies a special place in the nation's heart. Today it is a quintessential Serbian village that benefits greatly from a particularly scenic location at one end of the Fruška Gora valley, and is renowned for its wine. A number of impressive historical buildings are crammed into this small area, scattered among the picturesque houses. Best among them are the twin-towered **Upper Orthodox Cathedral**, the **Bishop's Palace**, the **Karlovci Grammar School**, the **Patriarch's Palace** and the white **Lower Orthodox Church**. Away from the centre is the small, round **Chapel of Peace**, famous as the site where the Peace Treaty of 1699 was signed with the Turks. For the first time in world diplomacy, a round table was used so that all might feel equal, and the building's four doors allowed all parties to enter simultaneously.

Getting There

Local **buses** run regularly from Novi Sad (16mins) and Belgrade (75mins) to Sremski Karlovci. There is no public transport to Fruška Gora, nor is there anywhere to eat.

Cars and **taxis** can be rented in Novi Sad, but those keen to go it alone will find the roads confusing, in appalling condition and almost entirely devoid of signposts.

Tourist Information

No local map of monasteries exists, and the whole area is clearly unprepared for tourism. Sadly, the easiest thing by far is to go with a tour company: try **Magelan Travel Agency**, Zmaj Jovina 23, Novi Sad, t/f (021) 472 2028, *www.magelancorp.co.yu*, who arrange tours of five monasteries, plus walking and cycling tours; or **Five Star Travel**, Studenski Square 10, Belgrade, t (011) 616 619, *fivestar@tehnicom. net*. In summer, the **Tourist Organization of Belgrade** runs wine tours to Fruška Gora and Sremski Karlovci, and a historic Romantic Train to the latter.

Festivals

Early–mid-Jan: Karlovci Christmas Festivities.
Late Sept–Oct: Grape-picking.
Late Dec–Jan: Fine Arts Salon.

Where to Stay and Eat

**Hotel Boem, Branka Radićevića 5, t (021) 881 038, *www.hotelboem.com* (*inexpensive*). This is the best place to sleep and eat in Sremski Karlovci.

Sremski Karlovci is the starting point for tours of **Fruška Gora**, famed for its beauty (especially in spring), diverse flora and fauna, wine-making and monasteries. With 17 of these in just 20km, it is often compared to Mount Athos, and ranks as the Serbs' holiest site after Kosovo. Built mostly by members of the royal family, these monasteries once dominated the country's spiritual, cultural and political life. The closest and most important is **Krušedol**, built in Moravian-Byzantine style in 1509–12 by Serbian king Đorđe Branković. Its church, shaped like a three-leafed clover with an octagonal cupola, contains the mausoleum of the Branković royal family, as well as the body of patriarch Arsenije III Čarnojević, who led the great Serbian migration during late 17th-century Turkish invasions. In 1716 it was totally destroyed and many of the skeletons burnt. Reconstruction began five years later, after which it became the Bishop's Palace and seat of the Serbian Orthodox Church. The interior is extremely atmospheric, with frescoes covering every square inch of the walls and ceilings. The pillars in the inner sanctum feature some fairly well-preserved original paintings from 1543–45, only discovered in 1963. The valuable iconostasis, topped with an elaborate cross, consists of three groups, including a particularly important 16th-century Deisian group in Italo-Cretan style. Of the woodcarvings, the *Great Crucifixion* and the *Undreaming Eye* of 1653 are simple but very strong. The Baroque throne icons are also very fine. Uniquely, frescoes also cover the outside walls, including the powerful *Day of Judgement*.

Of Fruška Gora's other monasteries, the **Velika Remata** is probably most worthwhile, featuring a stunning fresco of St Dimitri, four precious icons donated by Russian nobles, and a handsome Baroque bell tower. The **Mala Remata Monastery** is generally regarded as the most architecturally interesting.

Bulgaria:
Travel, Practical A–Z
and Language

19

Travel

Entry Formalities

Passports and Visas

Citizens of the UK, Ireland, Canada, the USA, Australia and New Zealand can visit Bulgaria without a visa for only up to 30 days within a six-month period. Citizens of other EU countries can stay without a visa for up to 90 days. All visitors must register as a foreigner within 48 hours of arrival. This should be done for you by your hotel; if not, you will need to take your passport, your host and their ID to the local police station. Keep your registration slip with you throughout your stay; it will be surrendered upon leaving the country.

Customs

If you arrive with more than 8,000 Bulgarian leva or the equivalent in foreign currency or traveller's cheques, you must declare it, or your entire funds could be confiscated later. It's also advisable to declare all valuables upon arrival in order to avoid difficulties when leaving. Regulations are subject to change, so check before you travel. On departure travellers are exempted from duty for: 200 cigarettes or 100 cigarillos or 50 cigars or 250g tobacco; 1 litre of strong spirits; 2 litres table wine; 2 litres liqueurs, sparkling wine or dessert wine; 500g coffee; 50ml perfume; 250ml toilet water.

Getting Around

By Bus

It's often easier and faster, if not necessary, to travel by bus. Run by private companies, these can be comfortable and fairly new, but journeys still take much longer than they should. When catching a bus that started its journey elsewhere, tickets are often only sold when the bus arrives. In rural areas, tickets are often bought from the driver.

By Car

Road assistance, t 146; traffic police, t 665 060
Bulgarian drivers are not as dangerous as in certain other countries, but still tend to drive too fast. All journeys take much longer than they should, owing to poor roads. Signposts are inadequate, and often in Cyrillic.

You can drive on your own national driving licence, and must have **third-party insurance** and a **green or blue card** (these can be bought on arrival). If using your own car, you will receive a special visa tag on arrival, and you must carry this and the **registration document** with you at all times.

Speed limits are 60kph in built-up areas, 80kph on the open road and 120kph on highways). Motorists are legally required to report accidents, and there are spot fines for minor transgressions. The word for petrol is *benzin*; petrol stations (*benzinostatsiya*), though sometimes hard to find, are generally located every 40km or so on main roads and motorways.

Driving with any alcohol in your blood is prohibited and the punishments are harsh: a heavy fine or even imprisonment.

Car hire can be arranged in Sofia (*see* p.322), but it may be cheaper to book before you go. You could also hire a car with a driver through one of the hire firms.

By Train

Trains operated by **Bulgarian State Railways** (BDZh), t 931 1111, *www.bdz.bg*, are relatively cheap, but can be extremely slow, and delays are common. Intercity and Express trains only operate on the main routes, and must be reserved. They can be very busy in summer and on weekends, so book ahead. Most stations have a left luggage office. In smaller stations, timetables may be scribbled on a piece of paper, and are usually in Cyrillic.

Practical A–Z

Crime and the Police

Police, t 166; 24hr police hotline (in English; Sofia only), t 988 5239
For the most part, Bulgaria is far safer than Western countries, but petty crime in Sofia is rife, especially pickpocketing in crowded central places and the stations. Sadly, the presence of a large, desperately poor Roma (gypsy) population is a big part of the problem. Keep valuables well out of the way, beneath clothing, or in the hotel safe. Mugging and even rape are also on the increase here, so take care at night, when poorly lit areas

should be avoided. Car theft is endemic, with foreign cars particularly targeted. Be vigilant on trains, and try not to fall asleep unless in a sleeper. The police are not above fishing for large pocketable fines. If fined, ask for a receipt. If arrested, wait to speak to someone in English, and notify your consulate (see below). By law, everyone is expected to carry ID at all times.

Disabled Travellers

Sofia's pavements are almost totally inaccessible for wheelchair users, and streets in more rural towns are often cobbled.

Electricity

The current in Bulgaria is 220V AC, using round two-pin plugs. Bring an adaptor. For 110V appliances, you'll need a transformer.

Embassies and Consulates

Bulgarian Embassies Abroad

UK: 186–8 Queen's Gate, London, SW7 5HL, t (020) 7584 9400, *www.bulgarianembassy. org.uk*.

USA: 1621 22nd St NW, Washington DC 20008, t (202) 387 0174, *www.bulgaria-embassy.org*; 121 East 62nd St, New York, NY 10021, t (212) 935 4646, *www.bulconsul.org*.

Canada: 325 Stewart St, Ottawa, Ontario, K1N 6K5, t (613) 789 3215, *mailmn@storm.ca*.

Foreign Embassies in Sofia

UK: Moskovska 9, t 933 9222, *www.british-embassy.bg*.

USA: Saborna 1, t 937 5100, *www.usembassy.bg*.

Canada: Assen Zlatarov 11, t 943 3704.

Festivals and Events

March–April: *Note that Easter is celebrated a week later in the Orthodox calendar.* On **Palm Sunday** (*Tsvetnitsa* or *Varbnitsa*), Bulgarians hang willow branches in their homes in preparation for the **Easter** services on Thursday and Saturday nights. Candles are lit by the congregation at midnight on

Easter Saturday to symbolize the Resurrection, and with these, they walk around the church three times. Painted eggs are then knocked together and eaten.

August: The **Feast of the Assumption of the Virgin** (*Golyama Bogoroditsa*; 15th, New style calendar; 29th, Old style calendar) is celebrated with services at churches dedicated to the Virgin and with processions of icons. The **Birthday of St John of Rila** (18th) at the Rila Monastery also attracts large crowds. The **Koprivshtitsa Folklore Festival** is a huge gathering of traditional musicians and singers and is a distinctively Bulgarian event. It is held every five years (the next is due in 2005), although a smaller version occurs annually.

September: The pilgrimage to Krâstova – a shrine on a mountain-top and Bulgaria's chief pilgrimage site – on the eve of **Krâstovden** (14th) is an event marked by many Bulgarians.

October: **Feast day of St John of Rila** (19th) at the Rila Monastery.

December: The celebrations for **Christmas** (*koleda*) are family-orientated and normally take place on the 25th, though according to the Old calendar, the festival falls on **January 6th/7th**.

Health and Emergencies

Ambulance, t 150; 24hr pharmacies, t 178

No inoculations are required to enter Bulgaria. There is rabies in Bulgaria, and though reported cases of rabies in the capital are few, seek medical assistance if bitten.

For minor ailments, go to a pharmacy (*apteka*) or health centre (*poliklinika*). In case of emergency, treatment and ambulance services are free, but medicine must be paid for. Take any specific medication with you, as it may not be available locally.

Doctors are competent, but have to cope with old equipment, poor funding and bad wages, and their treatment of patients is not necessarily as gentle as in Western countries. A lengthy hospital stay is unlikely to be a pleasant experience, so go home, if possible.

Medical/travel insurance is therefore highly recommended.

Internet

Internet cafés are common in Bulgarian cities, though rural areas may be devoid of Internet access. Try the libraries.

Money

Bulgaria's currency is the **lev**, plural **leva** (BGN), made up of 100 stotinki. Notes: 1, 2, 5, 10, 20, 50, 100 and 200 leva. Coins: 1, 2, 5, 10, 20 and 50 stotinki, and 1 lev.

The best way to travel in Bulgaria is with a bank card, using **ATMs**, which are frequent in all major towns. If heading off the beaten track for any length of time, be sure to have a good stock of cash. **Exchange offices** have the best rates, but be wary of scams, and double-check rates and commission first. **Traveller's cheques** are hard to change anywhere. Only certain banks will touch them; Bulbank is the best bet.

Bank hours are generally Mon–Fri 9–4. Never change money on the street.

The rate of exchange at the time of writing was approximately £1 = 2.80 leva, €1 = 1.95, $1 = 1.50. The lev is tied to the euro.

National Holidays

1 Jan New Year's Day
3 Mar Liberation Day
9–12 April Orthodox Easter
1 May Labour Day
24 May Day of the Cyrillic Alphabet
6 Sep Union Day
22 Sep Bulgarian Independence Day
24–25 Dec Christmas
31 Dec New Year's Eve

Opening Hours

Shops are generally open 9–6 or 10–7 weekdays, close at 2pm on Saturdays, and remain closed on Sundays.

Churches in Sofia stay open during daylight hours, but elsewhere they may be closed outside service times. If so, the hour before the morning liturgy (8 or 9am) and evening mass (5 or 6pm) is the best time. **Monasteries** are usually open from dawn till dusk.

Museums are generally open Tues–Sun 8–5.30, though in rural areas they're likely to close 12–2pm.

Post

Most post offices are open 8.30–5.30 Mon–Sat. Mail can take 7–10 days to reach Britain and 2–3 weeks to reach the USA, unless sent express or airmail. Parcels are cheap, but you must take items into the post office and have a customs declaration filled out before they are wrapped and weighed.

Price Categories

Hotels

Prices for hotels are almost always quoted in euros (€), even when payment is expected in leva. The approximate price you should expect to pay, for a double room with bath in high season, is as follows:

luxury over €160
expensive €100–160
moderate €60–100
inexpensive less than €60

Restaurants

For a three-course meal for one with wine:

luxury over €20
expensive €15–20
moderate €8–14
inexpensive less than €8

Shopping

Bulgaria has a rich tradition of **folk arts**, including costumes, rugs, textiles and wooden toys. There is also a very long history of **icon-painting**. Readily available throughout the country, and often bright to the point of garishness, with oodles of gold leaf, these make the ultimate souvenir.

Bulgarian **wine** is also very good and cheap, so taking some home is almost essential.

Sports

Football is the nation's favourite spectator sport. Professional teams in the big towns play on Saturday or Sunday afternoons. Bulgaria's relatively cheap **ski** resorts, such as Borovets or the less commercial Bansko, are receiving more visitors every year.

Hiking is a very popular activity, with many trails and huts in the mountains. The Pirin Range is the most wild and scenic in Bulgaria, with many high peaks and deep valleys, and over 200 glacial lakes. The Rila Range features the highest peak in the Balkans, and also offers spectacular alpine scenery. The town of Maliovitsa is the main starting point, with hikes to many destinations, including Rila Monastery and on to the Seven Rila Lakes. The Rhodopes are lower, but if anything more beautiful. The elongated Balkan Range, or Stara planina, is less dramatic, but offers plenty of hiking opportunities, especially around Karlovo. For more info, speak to the people at Zig-zag (*see* p.322), or SunShine tours in Sofia, Shipchenski prohod 47, **t** 971 3628, *sunshine@techno-link.com*, both of whom can also give advice regarding **climbing**, and **mountain-biking**, for which there is much untapped potential here. The best biking areas in this guide are Bansko, Gabrovo, Troyan and Tryavna. For advice on **caving**, contact the Bulgarian Federation of Speliologists, **t/f** (02) 987 8812. **Birdwatching** is popular, especially in the Rhodopes or the Danube's flood plain, with some 400 species resident in spring or passing through in autumn. Contact the Bulgarian Society for the Protection of Birds, **t** (02) 722 640, *bspb_hq@mb.bia-bg.com*.

Telephones

There are three types of **pay phone** in operation. The increasingly rare coin phones use 0.50-leva tokens, available from news stands. Blue phones (*Mobika*) and Orange phones (*Bulfon*), take different cards ranging from 4 to 25 leva, available at certain shops, news stands and post offices. In some towns, only one type of phone exists if the company has a monopoly. **Telephone offices** exist in post offices, and can be open 24hrs. There are no peak and off-peak rates in Bulgaria.

Phone codes for rural areas may be different if you're calling from within the region than if you're calling long distance. Often the first 0 is

substituted for 99. To **dial abroad from Bulgaria**, use the international code, followed by the local area code minus the first 0. The **international operator** is **t** 0123.

To **call Bulgaria from abroad**, use the following international access codes, followed by the local area code (e.g. Sofia **t** 02), but dropping the initial 0: from the UK and Europe **t** 00 359; from the USA and Canada **t** 011 359.

Time

Bulgaria is two hours ahead of GMT (three hours in summer).

Tipping

Tipping is expected in restaurants, generally 10 per cent, or the nearest round number. Never leave a tip if it is unmerited, and check the bill to see if it has already been added. Taxi drivers expect you to round up the fare.

Toilets

Public toilets are found in train and bus stations and in many large parks. Most charge 20–50 stotinki, though this does not ensure their cleanliness. *Mazhe* means Gentlemen, and *zheni* or *dami* means Ladies.

Many toilets get blocked if paper is flushed down them, so use the wastepaper basket.

Tourist Information

There are no Bulgaria Tourist Board offices in the UK, the USA or Canada, but information can be sought from the embassies. The following websites are good sources: *www.travel-bulgaria.com* is the best all-round tourism site; *www.infotour.org* has general tourist and hotel info; *www.sofiacityguide. com* and *www.plovdivcityguide.com* are up-to-date online guides to the big cities; *www.sofiaecho.com* is the best source for current events; *www.hotelsbulgaria.com* is the best of the accommodation sites.

Language

Bulgarian is a South Slavonic language, along with Serbo-Croat and Slovenian. Some knowledge of English is common in Sofia, but scarce in more rural areas. While Bulgaria uses both the Latin and Cyrillic alphabets, almost all street signs and many road signs are only in Cyrillic, making life difficult for outsiders. Note also that Bulgarians usually shake their head for 'yes' and nod for 'no' – but not always!

The Cyrillic Alphabet

А а   a as in 'cat'
Б б   b as in 'bed'
В в   v as in 'vet'
Г г   g as in 'goat'
Д д   d as in 'dog'
Е е   e as in 'egg'
Ж ж   zh as s in 'leisure'
З з   z as in 'zoo'
И и   i as in 'fit' (or 'fee' when at the end of a word)
Й й   y as in 'yes'
К к   k as in 'kite'
Л л   l as in 'last'
М м   m as in 'man'
Н н   n as in 'no'
О о   o as in 'hot'
П п   p as in 'pet'
Р р   r as in 'red'
С с   s as in 'set'
Т т   t as in 'top'
У у   u as in 'rule'
Ф ф   f as in 'fast'
Х х   h as ch in 'Bach'
Ц ц   ts as in 'hits'
Ч ч   ch as in 'much'
Ш ш   sh as in 'wish'
Щ щ   sht as 'shed' in 'wished'
Ъ ъ   u as in 'hut'
Ь ь   softens the preceding consonant
Ю ю   yu as in 'you'
Я я   ya as in 'yard'

Useful Words and Phrases

yes/no *da/ne*
please/thank you *molya/blagodarya*
hello/goodbye *dobar den/ dovizhdane*
how are you? *kak ste?*

I don't understand *ne vi razbiram*
Do you speak English? *Govorite li Angliski?*
Help! *Pomosht!*

today *dnes*
yesterday *vechera*
tomorrow *autre*
where is...? *kude e...?*
entrance/exit *vhod/izhod*
How much is...? *Kolko stroova...?*
Do you have a single/double room? *Imate li staya s edno leglo/dve legla?*
I am vegetarian. *.Az sam vegetarianets/ vegetarianka (fem.)*

Days and Months

Monday *ponedelnik*
Tuesday *vtornik*
Wednesday *sryada*
Thursday *chetvurtuk*
Friday *petuk*
Saturday *subota*
Sunday *nedelya*

January *Yanuari*
February *Fevruari*
March *Mart*
April *April*
May *Mai*
June *Juni*
July *Juli*
August *Avgust*
September *Septemvri*
October *Oktomvri*
November *Noemvri*
December *Dekemvri*

Numbers

1 *edin/edna/edno*
2 *dve/dva*
3 *tri*
4 *chetiri*
5 *pet*
6 *shest*
7 *sedem*
8 *osem*
9 *devet*
10 *deset*
100 *sto*
1,000 *hilyada*

Bulgaria: Sofia

Sofia (СОФИЯ)

Strategically located on the road between Constantinople and Belgrade, the Thracian city of Serdica, renamed Sofia after a church in the 14th century, was made regional capital by the Romans, and even considered by Constantine as a possible capital of Byzantium. A fleeting sense of national identity was forged in the 8th century when Bulgar leader Han Asparouh defeated the Byzantines to create the First Bulgarian Empire, but this was all but erased by five centuries of Ottoman rule that only ended with the intervention of Russian forces in 1878. For the last century of occupation, armed uprisings were accompanied by a renewed grasping at cultural identity, known as the National Revival. To see the wonderful rustic buildings this inspired, head out of Sofia to almost any of the other towns mentioned later. Sofia was chosen as capital of the new independent state thanks not to its prominence,

Food and Drink

The best thing about Bulgarian cooking, especially in rural areas, is the freshness of the ingredients, which are usually organic or free-range. Bulgarians often start their meal with a **salad**, like *shopska salata*: chopped tomatoes, cucumber, peppers, onion and sheep's cheese. *Snezhanka* is chopped cucumber with garlic in yoghurt. Favourite **hot starters** include *parzheni chushki* or *chushki byurek*, a pepper stuffed with cheese and herbs and fried in breadcrumbs; *sirene po shopski*, white cheese baked in a clay pot with an egg and a pepper on top; *lukanka* and *pasturma*, spicy salamis. **Soups** (*chorba*) include *bob* (bean), *pileshka* (chicken) and *shkembe* (tripe).

Most **main courses** are chicken- or pork-based, though lamb is usually available, and many restaurants offer game. Grilled meats (*na skara*) are ubiquitous, as are chops (*parzhola* or *kotlet*) and fillets (*file* or *kare*). *Gyuvetch* and *kavama* are popular stews baked in clay pots and akin to Hungarian goulash. Fish (*riba*) tends to be trout (*pasturva*), fried or grilled. Other popular traditional dishes are *sarmi* (stuffed cabbage leaves) and *imam bayaldi* (stuffed aubergine). **Dessert** usually means *palachinka* (pancakes), though pastry shops also serve *baklava* and chocolate cake (*garash torta*). Yoghurt, rumoured to have originated here, is a national speciality, and very good. *Ayran*, a slightly salty and watered-down yoghurt, is a popular drink. Restaurants tend to open 11–11, less in rural areas. Particularly outside Sofia, head to a *mehana* (taverna) or *han* (inn) for traditional food in a down-to-earth setting.

Bulgaria has become one of the world's leading exporters of **wine**, particularly full-bodied reds such as Cabernet, Melnik, Gamza and Mavrud. These can be very good even when cheap. The best of the whites is Traminer Han Krum. The most common varieties of domestic **beer** – Zagorka, Kamenitza and Astika – are all uninspiring lagers, but imported brands are widely available. Local **spirits**, strong and cheap, include *mastika* (similar to ouzo) and *rakiya*, a fruit brandy best made from plums (*slivova*) or apricots (*kaisieva*). In bars these are sold by the gram, with 50g (*pedeset grama*) equivalent to a double shot. Bulgarian **coffee** can be very good, especially where *kafe espresso* and *kapuchino* are available, or very bad when just *neskafe*. Cheaper still is *turska* (Turkish coffee), which is an acquired taste.

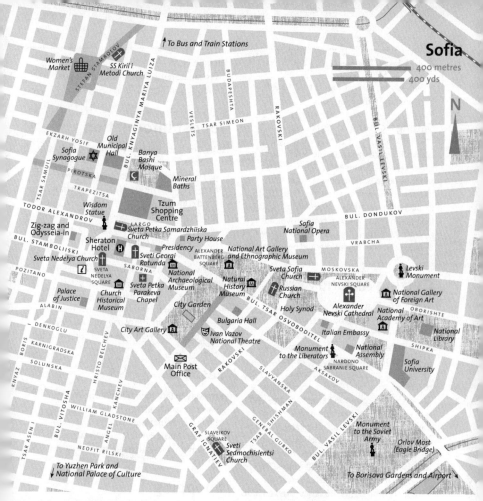

400 metres
400 yds

To Bus and Train Stations

Women's Market

SS Kiril i Metodi Church

STEFAN STAMBOLOV

BUDAPESHTA

RAKOVSKI

BUL. VASIL LEVSKI

TSAR SIMEON

VESLETS

BUL. KNYAGINYA MARIYA LUIZA

EKZARH YOSIF

Old Municipal Hall

Sofia Synagogue

Banya Bashi Mosque

PIROTSKA

TSAR SAMUIL

TRAPEZITSA

Mineral Baths

Tzum Shopping Centre

Sofia National Opera

BUL. DONDUKOV

VRABCHA

TODOR ALEXANDROV

Wisdom Statue

Zig-zag and Odysseia-in

LARGO

Sveta Petka Samardzhiiska Church

Party House

BUL. STAMBOLIISKI

Sheraton Hotel

Presidency

ALEXANDER BATTENBERG SQUARE

National Art Gallery and Ethnographic Museum

Sveta Sofia Church

MOSKOVSKA

Levski Monument

Sveta Nedelya Church

Sveti Georgi Rotunda

ALEXANDER NEVSKI SQUARE

National Gallery of Foreign Art

POZITANO

SABORNA

SVETA NEDELYA SQUARE

National Archaeological Museum

Natural History Museum

Russian Church

Palace of Justice

Church Historical Museum

Sveta Petka Parakeva Chapel

City Garden

BUL. TSAR OSVOBODITEL

Holy Synod

Alexander Nevski Cathedral

National Academy of Art

OBORISHTE

ALABIN

DENKOGLU

BORIS

KARNIGRADSKA

HRISTO BELCHEV

City Art Gallery

Bulgaria Hall

Ivan Vazov National Theatre

Monument to the Liberators

National Assembly

SHIPKA

National Library

KNYAZ

SOLUNSKA

KANCHEV

Main Post Office

RAKOVSKI

SLAVYANSKA

NARODNO SABRANIE SQUARE

AKSAKOV

Sofia University

BUL. VITOSHA

WILLIAM GLADSTONE

ANGEL

TSAR ASEN I

NEOFIT RILSKI

GRAF IGNATIEV

SLAVEIKOV SQUARE

Sveti Sedmochislentsi Church

TSAR SHISHMAN

GENERAL GURKO

BUL. VASIL LEVSKI

Monument to the Soviet Army

Orlov Most (Eagle Bridge)

To Yuzhen Park and National Palace of Culture

To Borisova Gardens and Airport

but to its location on a wide plain fringed by mountains: defensible, yet with room to expand. Rapid development indeed ensued, but Bulgaria's aspirations were disappointed, and soon the country shouldered a new yoke, that of Communism. A handful of buildings remain to document its long history, but the overwhelming proliferation of impressive yet monolithic edifices crammed into Sofia's compact centre speaks most loudly of the cold-war era. Straddling a cultural divide, Bulgaria is a proud, scenically beautiful but economically poor country, again seeking its own true character. The result, in Sofia, is a strangely likeable and atmospheric city.

Sveta Nedelya Square and Around

Sofia's most important hub, known until recently as Lenin Square, was also Serdica's main crossroads. Occupying a paved island on a spot that has housed a succession of churches since the Middle Ages, the eponymous **Sveta Nedelya Church** is a typical Byzantine construction made of grey-brown volcanic rock, with a large central cupola and a marble-floored interior whose walls are covered with modern frescoes. On the square's south side, a mustard-coloured building with a colourful frieze houses the

Getting There

There are no budget flights to Sofia yet (*see* **Getting There**, pp.4–10).

Getting from the Airport

Sofia Airport, **t** (02) 211 1213, *www.sofia-airport.bg*, is 10km east of the centre. **Bus 84** runs every 15–20mins to Sofia University. **Minibus** no.30 is more unpredictable, but handily terminates at the Largo. The bus stop is 100m right of Arrivals. A small kiosk sells bus tickets. On the minibus, pay the driver. Both operate 7am–11pm. Taxis will try to charge €20 or more, but the real fare should be about €6.

Getting Around

SKGT, **t** (02) 987 7187, *www.skgt-bg.com*, operate a network of **buses, trams and trolleybuses** that is cheap and generally efficient. Most services run from roughly 5.30am to 11pm. Single trip tickets (0.50 leva), available at news stands and sometimes from the driver, must be stamped when boarding. Inspectors are common. Large baggage requires its own ticket. One-day (2 leva) and 5-day (9 leva) passes are also available. There is a single **metro** line, but it's utterly useless to visitors. Privately run **minibuses** (*marshrutki*) cover some useful but difficult routes. They're faster than buses, and good value at 1 lev. ASofia's central sights are best visited on **foot**.

Taxis are reasonably inexpensive, but prone to rip off foreigners. Stick to **OK Supertaxi**, **t** (02) 973 2121, or **Yes Taxi**, **t** 91919, book by phone where possible (have your hotel call) and ensure the meter is working. Rates per km are 0.30–0.56 leva, depending on the time.

Car Hire

Ina Em, 89 SS Kiril i Methodi 89, **t** (02) 831 7992, *www.inarent.com*. From €10 a day.
Tany, **t** (02) 963 0797, **f** 963 2588; airport **t** (02) 937 3329, **f** 937 3328, *www.tany.bg*.
Rentacars Driver, **t** (02) 868 4848, *www. rentacarsdriver.dir.bg*. From €35 a day for a car and driver.
Hertz, bul. Vasil Levski 47, **t** (02) 980 0461, airport **t** (02) 959 217.

Bicycle Hire

Bikes can be rented at Zig-zag (*see* 'Tourist Information' below).

Tourist Information

Sofia: The **National Information and Publicity Centre** is at Sveta Nedelya Square 1, **t** (02) 987 9778, *www.bulgariatravel.org* (*open Mon–Fri 9–5*). The weekly *Sofia Echo* has good cultural listings. *Sofia Inside and Out*, published four times a year, has plenty of useful info. The private agency **Zig-zag**, and its sister agency **Odysseia-in**, both at bul. Stamboliiski 20, **t** (02) 980 5102, **f** 980 3200, *www.zigzagbg.com*, are more useful for some queries, but they charge a 5-leva consultation fee unless you buy something. They're good for outdoor pursuits, rent equipment, run lots of day trips (*see* p.331), and organize a walking tour of Sofia for €36.

Festivals

Late May to late June: Sofia Music Weeks. International classical music.
Mid-Nov: International Jazz Festival.
Early Dec: Music Evenings. The cream of Bulgarian classical musicians.

Shopping

Vitosha boulevard is the best street for window shopping and major fashion outlets. **Tsar Shishman** street, behind the Radisson hotel, is good for smaller, privately owned stores with a bit more character.

Sofia has a lot of fine art galleries, selling locally produced contemporary work of a high standard. **Art Alley** at William Gladstone 51a, **t** (02) 986 7363, carries a lot of interesting modern paintings and sculptures. **Testa Gallery**, Tsar Shishman 8, **t** (02) 981 8363, and **Astry Gallery**, Tsar Samuil 34, also have good selections of contemporary Bulgarian art.

For folk arts, try **Zekman Gallery** at Rakovski 88, a small store with a big selection of traditional Bulgarian costumes, rugs, textiles, souvenirs and antiques. **Traditzia**, bul. Vasil Levski 36, **t** (02) 981 7765, *www.traditzia.bg*, sells Bulgarian handicrafts made by socially excluded artisans.

For icons, go to **Noé Art Gallery**, Vrabcha 12a, **t** (02) 980 6941, or for a larger selection head to the **market** on Alexander Nevski Square, where you'll also find a quite bewildering collection of Second World War memorabilia, musical instruments, Communist leftovers, junk and antiques.

There are many stores with broad selections of Bulgarian wine, one of the handiest being at Angel Kanchev 19.

Where to Stay

Sofia **t** (02) –

★★★★★Sheraton Sofia Hotel Balkan, Sveta Nedelya 5, **t** 981 6541, **f** 980 6464, *www.luxurycollection.com/sofia* (*luxury*). The Sheraton's grandiose lobby with its giant chandelier is impressive indeed, as is the gallery of superb modern Bulgarian art. Rooms are nicely furnished, but small. Facilities include a health club and sauna, and breakfast is included.

★★★★★Grand Hotel Sofia, General Gurko 1, **t** 811 0811, **f** 811 0801, *www.grandhotelsofia.bg* (*luxury*). A genuinely luxurious, brand new hotel, solidly furnished with huge slabs of marble and wood, original art and lots of greenery. Spacious, tasteful red or green rooms come with big windows and huge, well-equipped bathrooms. Facilities include a health club and sauna, and breakfast is included.

★★★★Radisson SAS Grand Hotel, Narodno Sabranie Square 4, **t** 933 4334, **f** 933 4335, *www.radissonsas.com* (*luxury*). A modern, recently renovated building that enjoys the best location in town. Rooms are bright and comfortable with giant windows and bathrooms. Ask for views of the Parliament and cathedral. Excellent facilities include a fitness room, sauna and solarium, and breakfast is included.

★★★★Hotel Crystal Palace, Shipka 14, **t** 948 9488, **f** 948 9490, *www.crystalpalace-sofia.com* (*luxury*). Housed in a beautifully modified historic building full of antiques and classical décor, the rooms are equally comfortable and stylish, with big windows

and beds. Some have balconies and views. Extras include parking, a jacuzzi, large fitness room, sauna and a quiet location near the University. No breakfast included, though.

Kashtata s chasovnika (The Clockhouse), Moskovska 15, **t** 987 5656 (*expensive–moderate*). Three very spacious suites in a lovely historic house on Sofia's nicest street, immaculately kitted out with elegant furniture, huge beds and hardwood floors – does it get any better than this? There's also a restaurant; *see* 'Eating Out'.

★★★★Light Hotel, Veslets 37, **t** 917 9090, **f** 917 9010, *www.hotellight.com* (*moderate*). The Light's lobby and rooms are bright and modern, the facilities reasonable and the staff young and helpful. The only problem is a poor location.

★★★Hotel Niky, Neofit Rilski 16, **t** 952 0110, **f** 951 6091, *www.hotels-bg.com/niky* (*moderate*). This pleasant building on a central, quiet street contains mostly smallish suites that are modern, new and nicely decorated. They also have a few great-value doubles (*inexpensive*).

★★★Sveta Sofia, Pirotska 18, **t** 981 2634, **f** 983 1723, *www.svetasofia-alexanders.com* (*inexpensive*). A gorgeous historic building on Sofia's only pedestrianized street. The rooms and apartments (*moderate*) are bright and pleasant. Those on the first and second floors are bigger, with high ceilings. The very helpful manager speaks perfect English. Facilities include sauna and jacuzzi. Breakfast is included.

★★★Hotel Baldjieva, Tsar Asen I 23, **t/f** 987 2914, *www.baldjievahotel.com* (*inexpensive*). Eight freshly painted rooms and apartments with old-fashioned furnishings. Not a bad bet at this price, with a little garden at the back, and a decent, quiet location. The apartments have balconies and tubs.

Hotel Maia, Trapezitsa 4, **t** 989 4611 (*inexpensive*). The rooms here are old-fashioned, but do have some character, and the location and price are hard to beat.

Red Star Hostel, Angel Kanchev 6, **t** 986 3341, *internethostel@yahoo.co.uk*; also **Internet Hostel**, Alabin 50a (*both inexpensive*). As well as dorms, these two well-located hostels have between them five large, nicely decorated double rooms. Good value, with very helpful owners. Shared baths and kitchen. Breakfast is included.

Private Apartments and Rooms

Private rooms in Sofia represent a good-value alternative. The helpful lady at **Markela Agency**, Ekzarh Yosif 35, office 103, **t** 980 4925, *www.markela.hit.bg*, has photos of rooms that can be rented for about €19, and apartments with kitchen, TV and lounge for around €30. Variable, they can be very nice, and all are in or near the centre.

Zig-zag (*see* 'Tourist Information') also deal with rooms and apartments (*inexpensive*) around the centre, and will also show you pictures. Or you can take a chance and arrange everything by Internet before leaving home.

Eating Out

Sofia **t** (02) –

Da Vidi, Han Asparuh 36, **t** 980 6746 (*luxury*). Essentially European fusion, this restaurant has hands down the most interesting, experimental menu in town. Try the salmon with anchovies and capers. Self-consciously chic, with white brick walls, black and white pictures and dried roses strung below the ceiling, the décor is an acquired taste. Extensive wine list.

Kashtata s chasovnika (The Clockhouse), Moskovska 15, **t** 987 5656 (*expensive*). An exquisitely elegant restaurant. The food is high-class Bulgarian with European influences, featuring a lot of game such as wild boar, stuffed quail with pistachio and mushrooms, deer with blackcurrant. Also fish, steaks, lots of salads, and some tasty starters like prosciutto and caviar. It's also a hotel; *see* 'Where to Stay'.

Beyond the Alley, Behind the Cupboard, Budapeshta 31, **t** 983 5545 (*expensive*). Decked out with elegant period furnishings, the interior here resembles a drawing room, while the tiled courtyard terrace is surrounded by trees and vines. The imaginative, European-inspired menu features lots of game as well as fish, duck, goat's cheese, baked aubergine, foie gras and great salads. Heartily recommended.

Rotisserie Nationale, Neofit Rilski 40a, **t** 980 1717 (*expensive*). Part of the prestigious French chain founded in 1248, the quality of food served in this atmospheric cellar is guaranteed, though service and presentation verge on the pretentious. Seasonal game dishes are a speciality. Bizarrely decorated with icons and the top half of a bronze trombone player, **Café-Bar Calvados** upstairs stays open till 2am.

Before and After, Hristo Belchev 12 (*moderate*). A gorgeous, parlour-like room set around a fountain in a stand-out Art Deco building. The menu is disappointingly standard, however.

Krim, Slavyanska 17, **t** 981 0666 (*moderate*). One of the only survivors from the Communist era, which says a lot. A 19th-century mansion containing several small rooms whose plush furnishings and wood panelling resemble a Victorian parlour. Famously large portions of high-class Bulgarian cuisine, plus caviar, lots of fish and some Japanese dishes. Reasonable daily menus and an attractive garden terrace.

Mahaloto (The Pendulum), bul. Vasil Levski 47, **t** 617 972 (*moderate*). Grilled meats and other favourites with some more modern, eclectic touches, and lots of good starters. The cavernous, brick cellar is nicely unpolished, and there's outdoor seating in the back.

Revue, Graf Ignatiev 11a, **t** 980 2548 (*moderate*). The Revue's fake courtyard setting, with lamp-posts and plastic vegetation, is off-putting, but the food is consciously fresh and healthy, and recommended by those who know. There are pastas, grills, lots of fish and salads, and some nice starters.

Dani's, Angel Kanchev 18a, **t** 987 4548 (*inexpensive*). A stylish bistro serving expensive but generously sized gourmet soups and sandwiches, using the freshest ingredients and some imagination. *Open 12–10 only.*

Divaka, William Gladstone 54, **t** 989 9543, and 6 Septemvri 41a, **t** 986 6971 (*inexpensive*). Standard but well-prepared Bulgarian food, including breakfast, and a good range of wines and beers. Surprisingly reasonable prices, and staggeringly popular. The Gladstone venue is more classy, with a plant-filled atrium, a pleasant patio and intimate spaces up and down. The other is more plain and laid-back, with atmospheric seating downstairs.

Pri Yafata, Solunska 28/Tsar Asen I, t 980 1727 (*inexpensive*). Done out like a rustic but upmarket village eatery with colourful textiles and cartwheel chandeliers, and one of the best places for authentic Bulgarian home cooking. Lots of game, such as rabbit in a jug, and a long list of national wines. Live folkloric music and entertainment.

Trops-kashta, Saborna 11 and Graf Ignatiev 12 (*inexpensive*). Top-notch self-service Bulgarian food at very reasonable prices. Fast, tasty and incredibly popular.

Cafés and Coffee Houses

Café Colours, Graf Ignatiev 4. Ever-so-trendy, spacious café with soft lighting, pastel décor and comfortable armchairs, where Sofia's young and beautiful come to watch fashion shows on a giant screen.

Café Boutique Mara, Tsar Asen I 53. The bright interior with its pretty lighting and hanging stars, and the cheerful, colourful garden courtyard, are both lovely, relaxing spaces for a drink.

Club Lavazza, bul. Vitosha 13. Beautiful, classic café-pâtisserie, all wood, tiles and original paintings. Its two floors are always packed. A small, classy restaurant in the back serves authentic Italian cuisine.

Laguna, Hristo Belchev 13. A riotously colourful space full of shapely pillars and bizarre art.

Luciano Viennese Café, Moskovska/Rakovski. A fancy turn-of-the-20th-century coffee house close to the cathedral, all dark wood, chandeliers and black and white prints.

Wiener Konditerei, Orlov Most. A large, bright and gleaming Viennese-style coffee-house with huge windows. Great coffee and cakes.

Entertainment

Sofia t (02) –

Music, Opera and Ballet

Sofia's main entertainment venue is the enormous **National Palace of Culture** (NDK) in Yuzhen Park, t 916 2368. Its many halls host all types of music from classical to avant-garde, plus film festivals, art exhibitions and fashion shows. **Bulgaria Hall** at Aksakov 1, t 987 7656, is the other main venue for classical music, and home to the Sofia Philharmonic Orchestra. It has excellent acoustics. Another fine venue is **St Sofia Hall** at Alexander Battenberg Square 1, home to the New Symphony Orchestra. Bulgaria is internationally renowned for the excellence of its opera. The main venue, also for ballet, is the **Sofia National Opera** at Vrabcha 1/Rakovski, t 981 1549.

Cinemas

Mokva, Alabin 52, t 987 3178.
Arena Multiscreen, bul. Tsaritsa Ioanna 8, t 920 9999.
Multiplex, NDK subway, t 951 5101.

Nightlife

Sofia t (02) –

Backstage, bul. Vasil Levski 100, t 946 1377. Varied live music nightly. *Open till 5am.*

Black Label Whisky Bar, bul. Tsar Osvoboditel 9, in the Military Club, t 987 8664. Dark and exclusive. *Open till 5am.*

By the Way, Rakovsky 166. Painfully trendy bar renowned for its cocktails. *Open late.*

Club 703, Tsar Shishman 24. An intimate spot with dark red walls, soft lighting and a big wooden bar.

Kamepuha Cocktail Bar. Pleasantly dark and low-key bar tucked away in a courtyard just north of the Graf Ignatiev/Rakovski junction.

Selfish, William Gladstone 40. Dark, cavernous brick interior with some nice Art Nouveau stained glass, and a sophisticated clientele.

Swinging Hall, bul. Dragan Tsankov 8, t 963 0696. The best spot for contemporary music, with two live acts nightly, usually jazz and rock. *Open till 4am.*

Tobaandco, Moskovska 6, behind the National Art Gallery, t 989 4696. A single long curving French window reveals this beautiful bar's enticing interior: romantic lighting, leather armchairs, a long, well-stocked bar and a smart clientele. Outside is a terrace on a cobbled courtyard in a quiet leafy park. *Open till late, with frequent DJs after 10pm.*

Church Historical Museum (*open Mon–Fri 9–12 and 2–5; adm*), with a limited collection of icons, robes and assorted religious artefacts. Nearby, beneath a bank on Saborna, is the subterranean chapel of **Sveta Petka Parakeva**, a bright and busy little space, with a fine carved iconostasis and bags of character.

Heading south past the mighty 1928 **Palace of Justice**, its neo-Egyptian façade guarded by cast-iron lions, is Sofia's main shopping street, **Vitosha** boulevard, lined with designer stores. The triangle it makes with **Graf Ignatiev** and **Patriarh Eftimy** boulevard is also Sofia's most rewarding district for restaurants, bars and cafés. The only real sight in this zone is the church of **Sveti Sedmochislentsi**, a small, stone, Balkan-style structure with red-brick stripes, an oversized dome and an unusually broad gold iconostasis. There's a daily **produce market** alongside on Ignatiev, and a daily **book market** to the north on Slaveikov Square, where two bronze Bulgarian writers sit on a bronze park bench. Ignatiev leads south to Borisova Gardens (*see* below), while Vitosha heads to the large and mostly unattractive **Yuzhen Park**, site of the colossal **National Palace of Culture** (NDK), Sofia's primary entertainment complex.

North of Sveta Nedelya Square, the elongated plaza of the **Largo** heads east, surrounded by monumental buildings. To its north is the mammoth, formerly state-owned **Tzum** shopping centre. West of this busy crossroads, on a spot occupied by a giant statue of Lenin until it was demolished in 1990, is a tall female figure representing Wisdom. She has a distinctly Egyptian appearance, with an owl on her left arm and a laurel wreath on her right hand. On the Largo's south side is the hulking **Sheraton Hotel,** whose lobby contains the finest collection of modern Bulgarian art in town. Hidden in its courtyard is Sofia's oldest church, the 4th-century **Rotunda of Sveti Georgi** (*open summer 8–6 ; winter variable*). Within its red-brick exterior are some very old frescoes, and behind are some scattered Roman remains. Poking out from the plaza within the Largo's underpass is the brick and stone 14th-century church of **Sveta Petka Samardzhiiska**. Three layers of frescoes from the 15th, 17th and 19th centuries cover its walls, but sadly they're difficult to see.

Ugly Knyaginya Mariya Luiza boulevard heads north of the Largo towards the stations, passing a nicely harmonized quartet of buildings, then nothing worth seeing. **Banya Bashi Mosque** is a brick and stone structure built in 1576, with one large dome and a single, elegant minaret. Beyond a tiled square set around a fountain is the white triple-domed **mineral baths** building, with rich ceramic decoration on its façade and roofline influenced by medieval Bulgarian folk art. It's currently surrounded by an ugly iron fence covered in uglier billboards. Nearby is a public fountain where locals fill their plastic bottles with mineral water. Opposite the mosque is the **Old Municipal Hall** (Halite; *open daily 7am–midnight*), an ornate indoor market topped by a clock tower, renovated in 2000. Behind this is the 1909 **Sofia Synagogue** (*open Mon–Fri 9–5, Sat 9–1; ring bell*), whose façade – attractive enough but neglected – conceals a newly restored interior that features a brass chandelier weighing over 4,400lbs and a ceiling reminiscent of a blue sky dotted with stars, framed by Art Nouveau style friezes.

Adjacent **Pirotska**, cobbled, pedestrianized and dotted with cast-iron lamp-posts, is the most pleasant and safe example of a 'real' Sofia shopping street. It joins Stefan Stambolov at the southern end of the **Women's Market** (Zhenski pazar), an intense, cheap, bustling affair, where peasants from the surrounding countryside come to sell their wares. The market's north end skirts the attractive 1897 **SS Kiril i Metodi** church, whose interior contains some fine, complex wooden carving on the iconostasis and pulpit, and some interesting paintings and frescoes.

Towards Alexander Nevski Cathedral

Starting with the Largo, one long, wide boulevard heads east past most of Sofia's key sights. Its opening gambit is the hulking white corner building known as the **Party House**, built in the 1950s for the Communist Party's Central Committee. The red star was removed from its roof in 1990 after an angry mob torched the building, but the Communist party itself was only kicked out in 1992. In front, a subway contains remains of the **Istochna Porta**, the eastern gate of Roman Serdica. The amazing structure to the south, built in 1494 as the Big Mosque (Buyuk Djami), now houses the **National Archaeological Museum** (*t (02) 988 2406; open Tues–Sun 10–6; adm*). Its nine massive white domes are even more impressive from the inside, supported by huge arched columns. Unless you're a real aficionado, the impressive, well-labelled collection here renders a trip to the distant National History Museum redundant. The best stuff is on the ground floor: Thracian helmets, carvings and vessels; Greek statues and votive tablets; the famous 6th-century BC Stela of Anaxander; superb 8th- to 10th-century gold jewellery; four stone relief plates from the 10th–11th centuries; a collection of finely carved Macedonian grave stelae; and a collection of 2nd- to 3rd-century AD Roman chariot ornaments. The highlight upstairs is a collection of finely crafted 16th- to 18th-century Ottoman jewellery.

To the west is the **Presidency**, guarded around the clock by soldiers in silly costumes who change on the hour. Across Alexander Battenberg Square is a grand Ottoman palace with a yellow neoclassical facelift, containing the **National Art Gallery** (*t (02) 980 0093; open Tues–Sat 10.30–6.30; adm*). The collection of Bulgarian paintings within is deeply disappointing, and all labelling is in Cyrillic. Across the hall is the **Ethnographic Museum** (*t (02) 987 4191; open Tues–Sun 10–6; adm*). Its exhibitions change yearly, but invariably involve a large display of folk costumes and textiles from Bulgaria's varied ethnic regions, as well as models of traditional dwellings.

Opposite is the lovely **City Garden**, a series of wide paths through trees and flower beds, surrounded by more limestone megaliths, and the terracotta red **Ivan Vazov National Theatre**. Built in Baroque style in 1907, its roof is topped by a giant sculpted chariot, while the tympanum contains a bas-relief of Apollo with the muses of art. The **City Art Gallery** (*open Tues–Sat 10–6, Sun 11–5*), built as city casino in 1908, now hosts temporary exhibitions of contemporary Bulgarian art and occasional concerts. The streets behind the theatre, lined with government ministry buildings, are well worth exploring, especially around the lively **Rakovski** street.

The boulevard continues east to the small but perfectly formed **Russian Church** (1912–14). White with gold trim on the rooflines and a wide multi-coloured frieze, it has five golden domes, a bright green tiled spire, a cute little bell tower and vivid yellow ceramic ornamentation. Note the majolica icon of St Nicholas above the main entrance. The interior is small and atmospheric, smelling of incense and beeswax, with very fine frescoes, especially in the dome behind the delicate carved iconostasis, and a gorgeous, ornate chandelier. This need not be missed by taking instead the leafy **Moskovska** street that runs behind the Art Gallery, a nicer way to approach the scenic climax to come. On one side is a statue-dotted park, on the other a series of interesting, mostly dated buildings, including an understated Art Deco affair at No.7, and the elegant post-modern British Embassy.

Alexander Nevski Cathedral and Around

The square around Alexander Nevski Cathedral (*see below*), undeniably Sofia's *pièce de résistance*, hosts an excellent daily **Flea Market**, a treasure chest of icons, war memorabilia, antiques, souvenirs and junk. On its north side is the triple-naved, red-brick church of **Sveta Sofia** (*open summer 7–7; winter 7–6*), after which the city was named. Originally built in the 5th or 6th century on the site of four even older churches, it has suffered many wars and earthquakes (the last one in 1858), and was significantly rebuilt in 1930. While the floor plan, a regular cross with a dome at the intersection, is typically Byzantine, the round arches are Romanesque, thus combining elements of East and West. The irregular layers of plain brickwork give some indication of the church's age, and come as a relief after so many frescoes elsewhere. There are plans for restoration and exhibition of the archaeological level beneath the church. Round the back, an engraved boulder marks the grave of popular writer Ivan Vazov, while beside the church's southern wall is the **Tomb of the Unknown Soldier**.

Across the square, the beige building with a bright ceramic frieze is the Bulgarian Orthodox Church's **Holy Synod**. Finished in 1910, its ornamentation nicely combines Byzantine and Art Nouveau styles.

Begun in 1882, and only completed 30 years later, the ambitious five-naved **Alexander Nevski Cathedral** is the largest basilica on the Balkan Peninsula and a supreme example of Byzantine-Muscovite style. Designed by Russian architect Pomerantsev, it is dedicated to the 200,000 Russian soldiers who died during the 1877–8 War of Liberation, and named after the patron saint Tsar Alexander II. The exterior is dominated by two golden domes – one massive cupola at its centre and a smaller one atop the front tower – that shimmer with 18lb of gold leaf donated by the Soviet Union in 1960, and gleam magnificently in sunlight. Cascading down from these is a complex, typically Balkan structure of arches, squares and semi-domes. Dotted around the white façade are multiple mosaics, including a portrait of Alexander Nevski above the entrance. The interior is gloomy, despite numerous candelabras, yet impresses by its sheer size. A giant, white-bearded God covers the central cupola, the Last Supper is above the altar, and a warning Day of Judgement is at the door. The unusual white marble iconostasis is Russian, with the Slavic patron saints, Cyril and Methodius on its right, and on the left Bulgaria's patron saint Boris I, who introduced Christianity into the country. The church's excellent acoustics and celebrated choir can be appreciated on Saturdays at the 6pm service.

Entered from outside, the **crypt** contains the first-class **Museum of Medieval Bulgarian Art** (*open Wed–Mon 10–6; adm*). Originating all over Bulgaria, most icons here are from the 18th and 19th centuries, with a few medieval examples such as the

14th-century processional icon of Poganovo and a wooden bas-relief of Sts George and Dimitar from Sozopol. Replica icons are also on sale.

The boulevard, now named Tsar Osvoboditel, 'Liberator', in reference to Alexander II, passes the gorgeous **Italian Embassy** before widening into an attractive, flagstoned, semi-circular plaza whose central Monument to the Liberators focuses on the Tsar himself. This is Narodno Sabranie Square, named after the plain, cream-coloured **National Assembly** building of 1884 on its north side. All roads lead east to Vasil Levski boulevard, named after the 19th-century freedom-fighter whose dull obelisk monument stands at the junction with Moskovska.

Tucked behind the cathedral is the **National Gallery of Foreign Art** (*t (02) 980 7262, www.ngfa.icb.bg; open Wed–Mon 11–6.30; adm, Sun free*), all of whose collections are superb, extensive and entirely labelled in English. On the ground floor are Indian sculptures and miniatures, Christian sculptures from Goa, Japanese prints, wooden sculptures and masks from Africa, and Buddhist sculptures from Burma. Upstairs is a fine collection of 19th–20th-century European art including a Courbet landscape, J.-F. Millet's beautiful pencil drawing *Young Woman*, five sculptures and a watercolour by Rodin, and a Delacroix. Less inspiring works from the 17th–19th centuries follow, with contemporary art on the second floor. In the basement (and not always open), a collection of Thracian gravestones from the necropolis that once occupied Nevski Square is arranged around a rebuilt mortuary chapel from late Roman times.

Behind the cathedral, Vasil Levski is dominated by imperious limestone buildings, including the neoclassical **National Library** (1939–52) and the Baroque **University** building (1934) with its massive, gently curving façade. Shipka and Oborishte streets, heading east, are worth exploring. The handsome terracotta building opposite the library is the 1906 **National Art Academy**. A powerful, rough-hewn modern sculpture in the small adjacent park depicts literary and church activist Kliment Ohridski, after whom the university is named. Tsar Osvoboditel continues past the enormous **Monument to the Soviet Army**, now a favourite with skateboarders, to **Eagle Bridge** (Orlov Most), named after its four impressive bronze eagles. Beyond here is Sofia's largest park, **Borisova Gardens**, which does get better the further into it you go.

The National History Museum and Boyana Church

To reach the **National History Museum** (*t (02) 955 4280; open 9.30–6; adm*), take trolleybus no.2 from the university to its terminus, cross the highway and follow the path straight ahead. Whether it merits the effort depends on whether the collection of gold Thracian vessels from Panagyurishte is resident in Hall 2, or on loan elsewhere. The rest of the collection has its moments. Hall 2 contains some Thracian and Greek artefacts, including many finely preserved black and red vessels from the 4th century BC and a large bronze funeral mask. Hall 3 is dedicated to medieval pieces like frescoes, icons and bas-reliefs, but almost everything of interest is a copy. The church's struggle to keep Bulgarian art alive during Turkish occupation is dealt with in Hall 4, where artefacts are complemented by pictures and photos dealing with National Revival architects. Upstairs, Hall 5 is a muddled jumble of early 20th-century artefacts, ending at a room full of ceramics and explanations of Greek and Thracian history, apparently a work in progress. On the whole, it's a bewildering and potentially disappointing experience.

Buses continue from the trolleybus terminal to **Boyana (БОЯНА) Church**. Despite the fact that it has been on UNESCO's World Heritage list since 1979, there are no signs whatsoever to the church. Look for terraced walls to the left, follow these up through a park and keep climbing, bearing roughly left. Better still, take a taxi. The simple brick and stone church, mostly built between the 11th and 13th centuries, is home to a set of frescoes of exceptional significance. Painted in 1259 by an artist known simply as the Master of Boyana, the 240 extremely realistic portraits in the *Life of Christ* series were produced at a time when stylization was expected in religious art, predating Italian Renaissance master Giotto, who is generally considered the first to inject life and compassion into Western art. For example, the food on the Bulgarian checked tablecloth set for the *Last Supper* is typical peasant food: radishes, bread and garlic, and those eating it are dressed in medieval Bulgarian garb. Also notable is the first ever depiction of medieval holy man St Ivan Rilski. Perhaps the finest portraits, however, are of patrons Desislava and Sebastocrator Kaloyan, depicted holding the church, and the haloed king and queen, Konstantin Asen and Irina. To protect the fragile and priceless frescoes, visitors are only admitted in small groups, and only allowed 10 minutes inside. The adjacent **museum**, however, contains replicas of the frescoes, as well as an English video about the church's history.

Mount Vitosha (ВИТОША)

Just 7km from Sofia, and a constant presence looming over the city, the awesome granite massif of Mount Vitosha is renowned as much for its flora and fauna (more than 3,000 different plants grow on its forested slopes) as for its views, fresh air, hiking and skiing. Most **hiking** trails radiate out from the focal Shtastlivetsa Hotel in the recreation centre of **Aleko (АЛЕКО)**. The ascent of Vitosha's highest peak, **Cherni Vrah** (7,510ft), is 3.2km (1½hrs) from here, or just 30mins from the top of the Romanski chairlift; but the 7.8km (3hr) hike from **Zlatnite Mostove** on the western slopes is more varied and satisfying. This is also the place to see the remarkable 'Stone River', an eerie valley full of giant boulders. **Skiing** from December to mid-March is pretty low-key, though equipment rental and instruction are available at the small resort of Aleko. You can get to Aleko by chairlift from **Dragalevtsi (ДРАГАЛЕВЦИ)**, or by gondola from **Simeonovo (СИМЕОНОВО)**. These are unattractive village-suburbs, though the pretty **Dragalevtsi Monastery**, reached by a path from the lift station, is worth a look, mostly for its 1345 church with very well-preserved frescoes from 1476.

To reach all these places, take tram no.9 or no.12 to their terminus at Hladilnika. Go through a small bazaar, turn left and proceed for 300yds. The following buses leave every 30mins or so: no.66 to Aleko; no.64 to Dragalevtsi village; no.93 to Dragalevtsi chairlift when it's running; no.98 to Dragalevtsi village and Simeonovo village; and no.122 to Simeonovo gondola when it's running. The ski lifts can only be relied upon at weekends. Ask at the tourist office to be sure, and for the more complicated directions to Zlatni Mostove. For more advanced hiking and recreational options, talk to the Zig-zag travel agency (*see* p.322), who also rent equipment.

Day Trips and Overnighters from Sofia

Note that Zig-zag (see 'Tourist Information', p.322) arrange day trips to Rila Monastery (€90), Koprivshtitsa (€90), Plovdiv and Bachkovo Monastery (€98), Seven Rila Lakes (€85), Sofia Holy Mountain (includes Boyana Church and three monasteries; €75) and Mount Vitosha (€65). All prices are for two or three people, including everything but food and entry fees.

Rila (РИЛСКИ) Monastery

Bulgaria's most famous monastery and UNESCO heritage monument was named after the country's top, 9th-century holy man, Ivan Rilski (St John of Rila), who chose this quiet spot for his hermitage. The first of many periods of construction began in 1335, but today's buildings mostly post-date the fire of 1833. Lofty walls, designed to withstand Turkish attacks, appear stern and impenetrable from outside, but the interior is colourful and photogenic. Ranged around a picturesque flagstoned courtyard, the monastery's four-floored wings are a honeycomb of arches and balconies, striped in red, white and black. Pride of place goes to the National Revival-style **Virgin Mary Church**, whose five domes, colourful wavy cornices, rustic red brickwork and ground-floor arcades make a glorious composition, beautifully framed by the mountain setting. The rich exterior wall paintings in the gallery are fascinating for their obsession with the apocalyptic and grotesque. Decoration of the interior took 23 years to complete. There's some greatly detailed and varied wood carving on the canopies, thrones and wonderful, broad iconostasis. Mixing rural scenes with classic Orthodox images, the bright murals are in exceptional condition. Hidden in a wooden box behind a curtain before the iconostasis, a silver case contains the left

Getting There

The easiest option is to take one of the organized day trips that are offered by **Zig-zag** (€90 for 2–3 people; *see* details above) or by **Balkantourist**, bul. Vitosha 1, t 980 2324, *www.balkantourist-bg.com.*

By **bus**, it is only just possible as a day trip. Take a bus from Sofia's Ovcha Kupel station to Dupnitsa (every 30mins; journey time 1½hrs), then one of the two daily buses to Rila Monastery (journey time 1hr).

Festivals

15 Aug: Golyama Bogoroditsa. Parade of icons.
18 Aug: Birthday of St John of Rila.
19 Oct: Feast day of St John of Rila.

Where to Stay and Eat

A few hotels and restaurants are clustered beyond the East Gate. For novelty value, sleep in the **monastery's basic cells** (*inexpensive*); the gates close at 8pm and the lodgings office is in the southeast of the courtyard.

Tsareh Vrah Hotel, just beyond Rila (*see* below), t (07054) 2280, *tzarev@infonet. techno-link.com* (*moderate*). Attractive and comfortable, with a good restaurant.

Rilets, t (07054) 2106 (*inexpensive*). To reach this reasonable hotel, with sweeping views, walk up the road for 15mins, cross the bridge and turn right. Decent restaurant.

Drushliavitsa, near the East Gate (*moderate*). Restaurant with a lovely streamside terrace, where you can eat freshly caught trout.

Rila (*moderate*). This restaurant nearby has a broader menu of Bulgarian dishes.

hand of St John of Rila, while a wooden drawer halfway down the nave holds a fine 12th-century Byzantine icon of the Virgin.

The very attractive, single-turreted **Hrelyo's Tower** next door, built as a defensive tower in 1335, is the only building preserved from old times. On its upper floor is a chapel, richly ornamented with wall paintings. The **treasury** (*open daily 8–5; adm*) beneath the modern east wing houses many worthwhile icons and artefacts, including the original monastery church door. Its bizarre highlight is a 14-inch wooden cross whose 140 tableaux contain over 1,500 tiny human figures, some just millimetres high. It was carved in the 1790s with a needle by a monk who lost his sight as a result. In the basement of the northern wing, full of giant cauldrons, is the dark and dirty old **kitchen**. Surprisingly, this is actually a massive tower in the form of a pyramid, with ten rows of arcs over an octagonal base, passing through all the floors and ending above the roof with a dome.

A number of **hikes** provide an excuse to commune with the gorgeous setting, including a 2hr return walk to the **cave** where St John of Rila passed his last 20 years. Next to the cave is the **Chapel of St John of Rila**, with the chapel of his nephew, St Luke, passed along the way.

Koprivshtitsa (КОПРИВШТИЦА)

Occupying a scenic valley in the Central Highlands (Sredna Gora), Koprivshtitsa is remembered as headquarters of the **April Rising** against Turkish occupation in 1876. Greatly outnumbered, the rebels used guerrilla tactics, hiding out in the mountains in small armed groups, sustained by local supporters, awaiting the word to mobilize. This came earlier than planned, following the betrayal and attempted arrest of leader Todor Kableshkov, and the whole attempt ended in disaster. Only public outrage at atrocities committed by the Ottomans in reprisal led the Russians to declare war, almost a year later. The rebellion would not have happened without the renaissance in Bulgarian cultural identity known as the **National Revival**, a movement that began with education and the written word, and spread to all aspects of life, including a rediscovery of vernacular architecture.

In 1876, **Koprivshtitsa** was a wealthy trading town of 12,000. This number has dropped by 80 per cent, resulting in a living relic whose streets are lined with over 380 examples of National Revival architecture. Mostly built between 1842 and 1870, these half-timbered houses tend to have high stone and timber walls, their upper storeys jutting out, and façades painted in bright shades, with lots of windows, colourful friezes, red-tile roofs and undulating yoke-like rooflines. The interiors feature carved ceilings and furniture, cosy niches and vividly coloured rugs. Slender wooden columns flank their doorways, large wooden gates conceal hidden gardens; outside, winding cobbled lanes dotted with carved stone fountains and troughs lead to picturesque stone bridges over mountain streams.

Although the whole town is worth seeing, six of the most elaborate houses are open to the public (*open Tues–Sun 9.30–5.30*), the finest being **Oslekov** and **Lyutov Houses**. A combined ticket for all six, and a map, is available at the Museums Administration Centre (*see* box), which can also line up an English-speaking guide.

Getting There

There are six daily **trains** from Sofia, taking 1½–2½hrs. These are met by **buses** that ferry passengers to the town, 12km to the south. To make this a day trip, it is better to take an organized tour with an agency like Zig-zag (*see* 'Tourist Information', p.322).

Tourist Information

Information, maps and tickets are available from the **Museums Administration Centre** at 20th April Square 6, **t** (07184) 2191.

Festivals

The **Koprivshtitsa National Music Festival**, a huge affair just outside town, takes place every five years in mid-August, including August 2005. Otherwise, a smaller **regional music festival** happens on the same date.

Where to Stay

Koprivshtitsa **t** (07184) –

Family Hotel Kalina, Liuben Karavelov 35, **t** 2032 (*inexpensive*). This attractive, centrally located house is surrounded by a beautiful garden. Their restaurant is also to be recommended.

Rai, Dyado Liben 8, **t** 2637 (*inexpensive*). A little removed from the centre, but consequently more quiet in the busy summer months, this small hotel has two fine, spacious rooms with balconies, and a well-equipped apartment, all offering fantastic views.

Tryanova Kashta, Gerenilo 5, opposite Oslekov House, **t** 2250 (*inexpensive*). A fine National Revival house centred round a lovely courtyard, with gorgeous, traditionally furnished rooms, and a tavern downstairs.

Eating Out

Koprivshtitsa **t** (07184) –

Lomeva Kashta, bul. Hadzhi Nencho Palaveev, just north of the main square (*moderate*). Large portions of traditional Bulgarian food served in a colourful rustic house, or outside in the courtyard.

Dyado Liben Inn, across the river from the main square (*moderate*). An even lovelier house with equally good traditional meals and a pleasant courtyard.

Dalmatinets Hotel, Benkovski 62, **t** 2904 (*moderate*). More of the same, but in a cosy modern environment.

The inscription on the **Apriltsi Mausoleum** outside reads, 'Let us guard the national freedom for which the heroes of the 1876 uprising fell.' Way south on the east bank, the **Benkovski House** is typical of the early 19th-century buildings that preceded National Revival. From the stairs behind it, where an equestrian statue of hero-tailor Georgi Benkovski stands, a spectacular view opens out of the valley and the surrounding mountains.

Plovdiv (ПЛОВДИВ)

Bulgaria's second biggest city (population 370,000) is in many ways a more interesting and sophisticated destination than the capital. Originally a Thracian settlement, it thrived during Roman times, was plundered by the Huns in AD 447, slumbered through most of the Middle Ages, awakened under Ottoman rule, and developed into a wealthy merchant town in the 19th century. Plovdiv's burgeoning middle classes were enthusiastic supporters of the National Revival movement, filling their huge, timber-frame mansions with traditional art and furnishings. Today the old and new quarters sit very comfortably together, crowded with showcase houses, art galleries and archaeological remains from several eras.

Getting There

Trains and buses both leave roughly hourly from Sofia, taking 2–2½hrs. Train and bus stations are south of central Plovdiv. It's a 15min walk up Ivan Vazov, or three stops on buses nos.2 or 102 to Tsentralen Square.

Tourist Information

For some reason, Plovdiv has no tourist office. Seek information from the larger hotels, who should have the latest copy of the *Plovdiv Visitor's Guide*, or try *www. plovdivcityguide.com.*

Festivals

Early Jan: Winter Festival of Symphony Music, presided over by the Plovdiv Philharmonic.
June: Festival of Chamber Music, featuring international musicians (in odd-numbered years only).
Aug: Trakiisko Lyato (Thracian Summer). Pop and classical music, plus international folk dancing, in the Roman theatre.

Where to Stay

Plovdiv t (032) –
★★★★Novotel, Zlatyu Boyadzhiev 2, t 652 505, f 551 979, *reservation@novotelpdv.bg* (*expensive*). Plovdiv's most upmarket hotel, with facilities including two pools, tennis courts, sauna and fitness room. Situated north of the river within easy walking distance of Dzhumaya Square. Rooms are comfortable if not huge.
★★★Hotel Bulgaria, Patriarh Evtimii 13, t 633 599, f 633 403, *www.hotelbulgaria.net* (*expensive*). One of the most comfortable options in town, with good facilities and a handy location close to Knyaz Alexander I.

Hotel Hebros, Konstantin Stoilov 51, t 260 180, f 260 252, *www.hebros-hotel.com* (*moderate*). A beautiful National Revival house close to Balabanov House, whose six comfortable, newly renovated rooms are beautifully kitted out with period furniture. There are also a few spacious apartments. Sauna and Jacuzzi.
Hotel Central, Konstantin Stoilov 4, t/f 622 348, *hotel_central@abv.bg* (*inexpensive*). Five fairly spacious, well-equipped rooms with snazzy, modern décor and a great location just off Dzhumaya Square.
Old Town B&B, Kniaz Tseretelev 24, t 265 679 (*inexpensive*). Two pleasant, slightly rustic wood rooms decorated in pastel shades. Great location close to the Roman theatre.
Turisticheski Dom, Petko Slaveykov 5, t 633 211 (*inexpensive*). A lovely National Revival building situated on a quiet street close to Lamartine House, offering simple but clean and attractive doubles and dorms. There's a nice little café downstairs.

Eating Out

Plovdiv t (032) –
Apoloniya, Vasil Kanchev 1, t 632 699 (*expensive*). Choose between several small, intimate rooms in this National Revival house, or the large and lovely courtyard , for some of the best Bulgarian food in town.
Ritora, Tsar Ivailo (*expensive*). Upmarket Bulgarian cuisine in a historical house near the Roman theatre.
Philipopol, Stamat Matanov 56b (*moderate*). Situated close to the Balabanov House, this National Revival building centred around a courtyard is another favourite for fine traditional Bulgarian food.
Alafrangite, Kiril Nektariev 17, t 269 595 (*moderate*). A classic Old Town *mehana* in a historic house with carved ceilings and a vine-covered courtyard.

Old and new Plovdiv meet at the bustling **Dzhumaya Square**, whose market stalls and cafés are arranged around the remains of a massive **Roman stadium**. The square is named after the striking **Friday Mosque** (Dzhumaya dzhamiya), whose expansive domes and diamond-patterned minaret are rumoured to date back to the 14th century. To the northeast, the narrow streets of the old bazaar quarter butt up against the modern, pedestrianized thoroughfare of Raiko Daskalov. This leads beneath a footbridge to the

Maritsa river, and two more Ottoman remains: the red-brick **Imaret dzhamiya mosque** (1444) on Han Krubat street, and the Turkish baths on Hebros Square. A decaying building on nearby Saedinenie Square contains the **Historical** and **Archaeological Museums** (*both open Mon–Fri 9–5.30; adm*). The former contains artefacts and photos concerning the Liberation; the latter has a more interesting and varied collection, including some fine Roman and Thracian pieces, and an exhibition about pagan mystery cults. South of Dzhumaya Square, Plovdiv's main street, the pedestrianized Knyaz Alexander I, leads to the dull main Tsentralen Square, dotted with remains of a Roman forum. On the way, at No.15, is the **City Art Gallery**.

Saborna street leads east from Dzhumaya Square into Plovdiv's exceptional **Old Quarter**, a jumbled maze of picturesque cobblestoned streets lined with invigorating architecture. Almost immediately to the right, steps lead to **Danov House** (*open Mon–Fri 9–12 and 1.30–6; adm*), and beyond to a viewpoint over the substantial remains of a large 2nd-century AD **Roman amphitheatre**, still used for concerts and plays. Follow the road round to reach the impressive **Lamartine House** (*open Sun–Tues 9–12; adm*), whose small exhibition concerning the French poet provides an excuse to view the interior. Continue along scenic Kiril Nektariev, past the magnificent blue house at No.15, and you may emerge by Georgiadi House (*see* below).

Just past Danov House on Saborna, the church of **Sveta Bogoroditsa** contains some impressive frescoes and icons. Further on, the **State Gallery of Fine Arts** (*open Mon–Sat 9–5.30; adm, Tues free*) houses a good collection of 19th- and 20th-century Bulgarian paintings. The nearby **Apteka Hipokrat** (*open daily 9–5*) is a pharmacy museum decked out with 19th-century furnishings. Next is **Zlatyu Boyadzhiev House**, a gallery dedicated to a 20th-century painter whose romantic portrayals of peasant life gained him great popularity with the Party and people alike. Just beyond, the **Museum of Icons** (*open Mon–Sat 9–5.30*) is full of regional works from the 15th and 16th centuries. Next door, the church of **SS Konstantin and Elena** has a gloriously vivid interior centred on a masterful gilt iconostasis.

Here is a crossroads. Turn left for the burgundy **Balabanov House** (*open daily 9–5.15, winter until noon*), which houses an impressive model of Old Plovdiv, and temporary exhibitions of modern art. The exceptional pale blue **Hindlian House** downhill contains an array of antique furniture and ornaments. Note the paintings of cities such as Venice and St Petersburg in the niches upstairs. Head north from the crossroads for the photogenic **Kuyumdzhioglu House**, its striking Baroque façade richly ornamented with folk motifs and a classic undulating yoke-like roofline. Its equally delightful interior now houses the **Ethnographic Museum** (*open 9–12 and 2–5; closed Mon and Fri; adm*), with displays of folk costumes and jewellery, as well as European *objets d'art*. Beyond are the neglected but interesting ruins of **Nebet Tepe Citadel**, occupying a hill-top that has been fortified since the 5th century BC. East of the crossroads, through the oft-destroyed **Fortress Gate** (Hisar Kapiya), is the large and structurally outstanding **Georgiadi House** (*open Mon–Sat 9–12 and 2–5*), which now contains the **Museum of National Liberation**. Next door, the **Nedkovich House** (*open Mon–Fri 9–2 and 1–6.30*) exhibits 19th-century furniture in a sumptuous *salon* with a finely carved wood ceiling.

Touring from Sofia

Day 1: Getting Rila

Morning: Follow highway 1, then highway 79, south to the signposted minor road that leads east to **Rila (РИЛСКИ) Monastery**, a folksy confection of arches and balconies set around a picturesque cobbled courtyard, with a stunning mountain backdrop. The National Revival church, a rare blend of architectural features, is richly decorated inside and out, while the turreted Hrelyo's Tower is a rare survivor from 1335.

Lunch: Behind the monastery, **Drushliavitsa** (*moderate*) has a lovely terrace beside a stream, where you can eat freshly caught trout dishes. Nearby, **Rila** (*moderate*) has a broad menu of Bulgarian dishes, while **Tsareh Vrah Hotel** (*moderate*) offers slightly more upmarket fare.

Afternoon: Continue south on highway 79. About 7km south of Sandanski, follow signs east to **Melnik (МЕЛНИК)**, which is a tiny, quaint town squeezed into a narrow gorge, flanked by sandstone cliffs eroded into weird shapes and points. National Revival houses abound here, most with wine cellars, restaurants, terraces and balconies. A big wine-making area, it's packed and lively during the summer months.

Dinner and Sleeping: There is no shortage of traditional taverns in Melnik, all offering typical menus with lots of grilled meat and local wines. The rustic **Mehana Loznichite**, t (07437) 283 (*inexpensive*), is where many locals choose to eat; otherwise all of the following hotels have great restaurants. The new and very beautiful **St Nicola Hotel and Wine Cellar** (*moderate*) is the best choice all round. Nearby **Despot Slav**, t (07437) 248 (*inexpensive*), is also new, and extremely stylish. The **Lumparova Kashta** (*inexpensive*) stands out for its hilltop setting and the great views this affords.

Day 2: Bansko's Guest

Morning: Before leaving, drive 7km further east to the sleepy **Rozhen (РОЖЕН)** village, whose quaintness is more authentic than Melnik's, and climb up to the 12th-century monastery. Follow minor roads via Melnik,

Lozenitsa, Harsovo and Katounsi to the mellow little town of **Gotse Delchev (ГОЦЕ ДЕЛЧЕВ)**. Here you can take a diversion to the south, switchbacking up past orchards and vineyards, to the atmospheric village of **Delchevo (ДЕЛЧЕВО)**, its rustic houses arranged round the mountain like an amphitheatre, with wonderful panoramas of the valley.

Lunch: The best place to eat in Gotse Delchev is the **Malamovata Kashta Hotel**, Hristo Botev 25, t (0751) 29135 (*moderate*). If you want to sit outside and watch the world go by, head for **Gradina**, T. Panitsa (*inexpensive*), which is just off the main square.

Afternoon: Follow highway 19 north to **Bansko (БАНСКО)**. This low-key ski town nestles beneath the highest peaks in the Pirin range, a quite spectacular location. Set respectively around the attractive Vazrazhdane and Nikola Vaptsarov squares, Bansko's old and new quarters meld seamlessly, with plenty of pedestrianized streets adding to the joy of wandering past stately National Revival stone houses.

Dinner and Sleeping: Bansko has no shortage of places to eat, most of them typical *mehanas* serving traditional food, many also hosting live Macedonian folk music. Probably the best choice is **Dyado Pene Hotel**, Bujnov, t (07443) 5071 (*moderate*), where large servings of home-cooked food are dished up in a bright, rustic interior or in the lovely courtyard. **Dvata Smarcha**, Velyan Ognev 2, t (07443) 2632 (*inexpensive*), is a lively hotel with a gorgeous garden terrace sheltered by two big spruce trees.

Day 3: Plovdiv

Morning: Head north to Razlog, then east on highway 84 to the attractive spa town of **Velingrad (ВЕЛИНГРАД)**. North of the centre is the area of Kamenitsa, with the most appealing baths.

Lunch: In Velingrad, the restaurant at **Kamena Hotel**, Edelvais 4, t (0359) 28538 (*expensive–moderate*), is a rather upmarket affair. Or eat at **Omar**, bul. Saedinenie 500 (*inexpensive*), where a fine terrace is ranged around a swimming pool.

Afternoon: Continue east on highway 84 to **Plovdiv (ПЛОВДИВ)**, Bulgaria's second city, and possibly its most interesting. The old town's picturesque cobbled alleys are overflowing with National Revival mansions, art galleries, museums, ruins and a particularly fine Roman amphitheatre (*see* p.335). If time allows, you can take a 30km diversion south on highway 86 to visit **Bachkovo (БАЧКОВСКИ) Monastery**, Bulgaria's second most important monastery, and another UNESCO World Heritage site.

Dinner and Sleeping: Close to the Balabanov House in Plovdiv's old town, **Philipopol**, Stamat Matanov 56b (*moderate*) is regarded as one of the town's best locations for traditional Bulgarian food, and is housed in a gorgeous National Revival building centred round a courtyard. **Ritora**, Tsar Ivailo (*expensive–moderate*), occupies an equally fine historic house near the Roman theatre, and is recommended for upmarket Bulgarian cuisine. There's also a reasonably good choice of accommodation; *see* p.334.

Day 4: Thracian Tombs and Bulgarian Heritage

Morning: Take highway 64 north to **Karlovo** (КАРЛОВО), whose atmospheric Old Quarter, centred on the striking Church of Sveta Bogoroditsa, is worth a wander. Take highway 6 east to **Kazanlak** (КАЗАНЛЬК), capital of the Valley of Roses but now more famous for its Thracian tombs. A replica of the most impressive tomb from the 4th–3rd centuries BC is open to visitors, featuring some impressive paintings. Tours of other tombs can be arranged through the Iskra Museum (*t (0431) 26055; adm*), with three days' notice.

Lunch: Kazanlak has limited choices, with the **Hotel Kazanlak** on the main Sevtopolis square, **t** (0431) 27210 (*moderate*), offering the best food in a good location. Or there's **Kashtata** (*inexpensive*), heading north out of town on bul. Osvobozhdenie, serving traditional Bulgarian food, with a garden.

Afternoon: Take highway 85 north past the spectacular golden domes of the Shipka Memorial Church over the dramatic **Shipka Pass**, site of the Russo-Turkish War's most famous episode. On a clear day, consider climbing the 500 steps to the Freedom Monument for an awesome panorama. Before reaching Gabrovo, look for signs to **Etara (ЕТЪР)**. This impossibly quaint village, with its picturesque riverside location, was artificially created, using genuine and recreated National Revival houses, to serve as a museum complex where the traditional crafts for which Gabrovo is famous could be preserved. Real artisans practise their skills, and the results are for sale. Continue to Gabrovo and follow signs east to **Tryavna (ТРЯВНА)**, a real-life town whose Old Quarter, focused on the outstanding Kapetan Dyado Nikola Square and the incredibly well-preserved Slaveykov street, is probably the most perfect in Bulgaria.

Dinner and Sleeping: Close to Tryavna's gorgeous main square, **Maestorat**, Kaleto 7 (*inexpensive*), is the best of many restaurants occupying historic houses and serving first-class home-cooked Bulgarian specialities. Restaurant **Starata Losa**, Slaveykov 27 (*inexpensive*), has a standard menu, but its patio occupies a prime spot in the heart of the Old Quarter. **Hotel Triavnenski Kat**, on the main square at Angel Kanchev 8, **t** (0677) 2033 (*inexpensive*), has spacious, very attractive traditional rooms with lots of wood. Its restaurant, in a very large, rustic courtyard, is also recommended. A little removed from the centre, on a steep hill, **Ralitza Hotel**, Kaleto, **t** (0677) 2219 (*inexpensive*), compensates with wonderful views of the town below. It's also the most comfortable in town, with good facilities and a nice restaurant terrace.

Day 5: Veliko Turnovo

Morning: Backtrack to Gabrovo and head north on highway 5, looking for signs east to **Bozhentsi**, yet another museum-village, with over 100 listed buildings. Continue north on highway 5, and follow signs east to **Dryanovo (ДРЯНОВСКИ) Monastery**, whose gorge setting is half the appeal. Or skip both, and go straight to **Veliko Tarnovo (ВЕЛИКО ТЪРНОВО)**, which certainly merits a whole day.

Lunch: In Veliko Tarnovo, the central street, Stefan Stambolov, has many restaurants whose verandahs hang out over the gorge of the Yantra Valley. Of these, **Starata**

Mehana (*moderate*) is recommended for its tasty traditional food. Close to the road into town, **Lovna Sreshta**, Todor Balina 16 (*moderate*), supplements the usual menu with lots of game dishes, and has a garden.

Afternoon: Capital of Bulgaria's Second Kingdom (1185–1396), scene of three uprisings and the site where the country's first constitution was drawn up in 1879, Veliko Tarnovo is perhaps most famous for its location. Its picturesque houses cling to the steep slopes of the Yantra river valley, surrounded by hills and chasms. The thing to do is wander, particularly through the narrow lanes of old **Varosh Quarter** above the **bazaar**, and over the stone causeway to the remains of the hill-top **Tsaravets Fortress**. The selection of arts and crafts on sale here is possibly the finest to be found anywhere in Bulgaria.

Dinner and Sleeping: Down some steps near the Konstantin and Elena Church on Stefan Stambolov, **Belite Brezi** (*moderate*) is recommended for its food and terrace, and often has live music. Even more likely to entertain with music and dancing is the lively, down-to-earth **Mehana Mecha Dupka**, Rakovski (*inexpensive*), where ample portions of traditional dishes are served up in an atmospheric cellar. In the heart of the action is the trendy **La Belle Epoque** café-restaurant, Stefan Stambolov (*inexpensive*). The town also has some far more enticing café-bars than either Sofia or Plovdiv. ★★★★**Hotel Premier**, Sava Penev 1, **t** (62) 615 555, **f** 603 850, *www.hotelpremier@ablv.bg* (*expensive*), is the plushest place in town to stay, and has some great valley views. **Deyan**, Yanaki Donchev 22, **t** (062) 30532 (*inexpensive*), has shared bathrooms only, but its location on a quiet cobbled street in the old Varosh Quarter is pretty hard to beat.

Day 6: To Koprivshtitsa

Morning: Head west on highway 772, then south on highway 35 to **Troyan** (ТРОЯН), whose monastery, Bulgaria's third biggest, is famous for its collection of colourful and often sinister frescoes by Bulgaria's supreme exponent of the art, Zahari Zograf. His brother painted the icons in the outstanding carved iconostasis.

Lunch: In Troyan, the **Starata Kashta**, General Kartsov (*moderate*), 10mins south of the main square, is the best bet for Bulgarian food, with a nice courtyard. Housed in a National Revival building opposite the tourist office on Vasil Levski, **Nunki Hotel** (*moderate*) offers reliable home cooking in a rustic ambience.

Afternoon: Continue south over the Troyan Pass, then go west on highway 6 for some 35km before turning south to **Koprivshtitsa** (КОПРИВЩИЦА). Famed as the headquarters of the April Rising in 1876, this living relic contains over 380 National Revival houses. Mostly built between 1842 and 1870, these half-timbered houses tend to have high stone and timber walls, their upper storeys jutting out, and façades painted in bright shades, with lots of windows, colourful friezes, red-tile roofs, and undulating yoke-like rooflines. The interiors feature carved ceilings and furniture, cosy niches and vividly coloured rugs. Slender wooden columns flank their doorways, large wooden gates conceal hidden gardens; outside, winding cobbled lanes dotted with carved stone fountains and troughs, lead to picturesque stone bridges over mountain streams. Six house-museums are open to the public (*see* 'Day Trips and Overnighters from Sofia', pp.332–3, for further information about this town).

Dinner and Sleeping: In Koprivshtitsa, **Lomeva Kashta**, just north of the main square on bul. Hadzhi Nencho Palaveev (*moderate*), serves large portions of traditional Bulgarian food in a colourful rustic house with a courtyard. Across the river, **Dyado Liben Inn** (*moderate*) is an even lovelier house with equally good traditional meals and a pleasant courtyard. The nicest place to stay is **Tryanova Kashta**, opposite Oslekov House, Gerenilo 5, **t** (0718) 2250 (*inexpensive*). This historic house has beautiful, traditionally furnished rooms, as well as a delightful porch area overlooking the courtyard. There's also a handy tavern downstairs. Further removed from the centre of the town is the quiet **Rai**, Dyado Liben 8, **t** (0718) 2637 (*inexpensive*), where two fine, spacious rooms with balconies, and a well-equipped apartment, all offer fantastic views.

Index

Main page references are in **bold**. Page references to maps are in *italics*.